The Laurel and the Ivy

The Laurel and the Ivy

THE STORY OF CHARLES STEWART PARNELL
AND IRISH NATIONALISM

Robert Kee

HAMISH HAMILTON · LONDON

HAMISH HAMILTON LTD

Published by the Penguin Group
Penguin Books Ltd, 27 Wrights Lane, London w8 5tz, England
Penguin Books USA Inc., 375 Hudson Street, New York, New York 10014, USA
Penguin Books Australia Ltd, Ringwood, Victoria, Australia
Penguin Books Canada Ltd, 10 Alcorn Avenue, Toronto, Ontario, Canada m4v 3b2
Penguin Books (NZ) Ltd, 182–190 Wairau Road, Auckland 10, New Zealand

Penguin Books Ltd, Registered Offices: Harmondsworth, Middlesex, England

First published 1993
3 5 7 9 10 8 6 4 2

Filmset in 11/13 pt Monotype Bembo
Typeset by Datix International Limited, Bungay, Suffolk
Printed in England by Clays Ltd, St Ives plc

A CIP catalogue record for this book is available from the British Library

ISBN 0–241–12858–7

Contents

Acknowledgements

My thanks are due to many people for help and encouragement, personal and professional, over the long period of gestation of this book. I list them here in something like chronological order: Oonagh Oranmore, the late A. J. P. Taylor, Cynthia Kee, the late Mark Boxer, the late Professor F. S. L. Lyons, Raymond Carr, Alistair Horne, Jeremy Isaacs, Robin Denniston, George Weidenfeld, Jacqueline Korn, the Rev. J. F. Maunsell, the late Sir Jocelyn Lucas, Deborah Devonshire, Ged Martin, Christopher Sinclair-Stevenson, Kate Trevelyan, Paul Bew, the late Terence Kilmartin, Joanna Kilmartin, Ludovic Kennedy, Tom McGurk, Roy Foster, Ruth Dudley Edwards, Noel Kissane, Frank Callanan, Peggie Trevelyan, Mrs John Barry Ryan, my daughter and son-in-law Georgie and Jean-Pierre Martel, Frances Partridge, Anne Chisholm, and my daughter Sarah and my son Alexander. I also thank for their consistent courtesy and skill over a number of years the staffs of the London Library and the British Library Reading Room, and particularly those of the Newspaper Library at Colindale, on whose distinctive energy and goodwill I have long been dependent. I am grateful too for exemplary occasional assistance from the staffs of the National Library of Ireland and the New York Public Library, and from the Librarians of the University of Chicago and the University of Virginia.

I owe a particularly heavy debt of gratitude for patience to the Trustees of the Alistair Horne Research Fellowship of St Antony's College, Oxford; to my expert typist and friend Judy Mooney, and to my expert typist and friend Topsy Levan; to my dextrous indexer, Douglas Matthews; to my incomparable agent and friend Gill Coleridge; to Bob Davenport, for his skills, courtesy and sensibility as copy-editor; at Hamish Hamilton, to Keith Taylor for like qualities, and to Andrew Franklin, without whose tolerance, understanding, enthusiasm and hard-headed realism this book would never have appeared at all.

Preface

The story of Charles Stewart Parnell is also a chapter, perhaps the most crucial one, in the story of modern Irish nationalism. What happened in the seventeen and a half years of his political life determined much of the way Irish nationalism was to go in the twentieth century, and how it became whatever exactly it can now be said to be.

A British Liberal Prime Minister, Gladstone, thought Parnell the most remarkable man he had ever met; another, Asquith, that he was one of the three or four men of the century. The Liberal statesman Haldane said he was the strongest man the House of Commons had seen in a hundred and fifty years. But Parnell has now virtually vanished from intelligent view in all but name.

This book is for anyone who may know the name of Parnell and even that of 'Kitty' O'Shea (without knowing that those who knew her never called her that) and may want to know more of the historical context in which they figured. It is not a comprehensive study of that context, for I have focused here on the man in relation to it. But I hope that the treatment of those phases of his life on which I have concentrated will be thought to be adequately based on sources and that some of the detail and even argument here will be new to those familiar with the story.

Many biographies of Parnell have made their appearance since his premature death in October 1891, the first of them, and one of the most useful, in 1898 – though a sister who survived him deplored it. The most recent major work, published in 1977 by the late Professor F. S. L. Lyons, is in general unlikely to be superseded as a fine comprehensive analysis of Parnell's career; an invaluable scholarly examination of Parnell's family background by Roy Foster had appeared the year before. But the academic framework within which these last two important works are cast may discourage some who know only the legend of Parnell's name from finding out more about him. It is for them that I have hoped here to provide a selective narrative.

I have not annotated the text, but an account of sources appears chapter by chapter at the end of the book.

Oh roses for the flush of youth,
        And laurel for the perfect prime;
But pluck an ivy leaf for me
        Grown old before my time.

Christina Rossetti, 'Song'

I cannot tell you how much I think about him, and what
an interest I take in everything concerning him. A marvellous man, a terrible fall.

W. E. Gladstone, December 1895

Parnell was a man full of smallness and dishonour, without
ideals or originality . . . Charlatan, charlatan!

Frank Hugh O'Donnell, 1914

During our acquaintance he often puzzled me greatly: as I
look back upon it, I am puzzled still.

Alfred Robbins, 1925

Part I: 1891, 1846–1880

BRIGHTON, GLASNEVIN, AVONDALE, CAMBRIDGE,
DUBLIN, USA, CO. MEATH, WESTMINSTER, CONNAUGHT,
USA, WESTMINSTER

Chapter 1

Anyone who on Friday 9 October 1891 happened to be passing the last house on the western end of the front at Brighton, 10 Walsingham Terrace, would at almost any time of that day have seen a small crowd outside staring up at the windows and wondering in which room it was that the famous man had died.

Personal curiosity about this man had long been a feature of the interest he commanded as a politician, both in England and Ireland. For much of the past decade he had dominated the political limelight, but he had kept much of his personality in shadow, even from his parliamentary colleagues. His mother and the brothers and sisters who now survived him had earlier known him better than most, but perhaps the only person who had ever known him really well was the wife in whose arms he had died three days before in the large first-floor front room of this Brighton house by the sea.

They had been married just over three months. She was described as prostrate with grief, but that was not the only reason why she did not accompany his corpse when it left on the beginning of its long journey the following day. If it had been a matter for her, she would have preferred him to be buried in Brighton. But the death of such a man could not be only a matter for her.

The coffin was a handsome one of polished oak, of medieval shape with a cross on the lid and substantial brass fittings. A brass plate bore the inscription:

CHARLES STEWART PARNELL
BORN 27TH JUNE 1846
DIED 6TH OCTOBER 1891

Some of his colleagues had seen the face in death. One of them, fourteen years before, in his secret Irish republican revolutionary days, had looked Parnell over in the interests of that cause and had then said of him, astutely, 'I am not quite sure if he knows where he is going.' Now the old revolutionary, in these days a respectable Member of the British House of Commons, when interviewed in Brighton's Grand Hotel simply said of him that he looked very peaceful and to be sleeping rather than dead.

Rain was falling heavily on the morning of Saturday 10 October as the coffin, almost hidden by wreaths, moved off from the house on an open-sided funeral carriage drawn by four black horses. Mourning-carriages containing several Irish Members of the House of Commons followed, watched by about a hundred people standing soaked on the pavement, and by others from the shelter of carriages parked in the road. As the cortège proceeded at walking pace through the Brighton streets to the railway station it attracted a similar detached attention but on no great scale. Brighton, though it had played a part, had never seemed exactly central to Parnell's career.

At the station, where some two hundred people were waiting, hats were raised and the coffin was put into a van at the rear of the 1.45 to Victoria. But arrangements had been made for this van and the special coach of mourners to be slipped off at Croydon and, after a wait of one and a half hours, taken on to Willesden. There, many Irish from the population of north-west London came to pay their last respects.

There was no time to remove the coffin from the van. Instead, the lid of the wooden packing-case in which it was travelling was taken off and the public were allowed to pass through the van in single file, stepping out on to the platform on the other side. Among them was one English Member of Parliament.

An hour later the train moved off again and after an eight-hour journey arrived at Holyhead for the Irish boat. The coffin was wheeled along on a trolley to the lower deck, where a space was cordoned off for it in the centre of the smoking saloon. A black cloth was drawn round it over which was draped a large green flag. The twenty-eight wreaths which had come up in cases with it were now piled in front. One bore the legend 'Died fighting for Ireland'. Another, 'In fond memory of one of Ireland's greatest chieftains, who was martyred in the struggle for her independence'. There had in fact been an early rumour of suicide, but it was soon rightly dismissed. The death certificate actually specified five days of rheumatic fever, an excessively high temperature and heart failure, but modern medical opinion thinks it most likely that he suffered from coronary heart disease and that after a period of exceptional strain he died of a heart attack. But, stretching a metaphorical point or two, the wreaths' dramatic assertions were not without some truth.

The shock caused by the news of his wholly unexpected death travelled round the world. The London *Times*, recently his arch-enemy, wrote that his death had removed from the political stage 'one of the most remarkable figures of the century', a view echoed by papers as far apart as the *New York Post* and the *Berliner Tageblatt*. In New York his death overshadowed all other news in the press, while in hotels, clubs and saloons Parnell and his life were the one general topic of conversation. In the fourth ward of the city, with its large immigrant Irish population, pictures of him were to be found outside buildings, draped in black. Other pictures in mourning-frames appeared in the windows of many shops and bars. The correspondent of the Irish *Freeman's Journal* in London wrote that there too the news 'utterly dwarfed into insignificance all other topics of current interest'. But it was in Dublin itself that the greatest obituary tribute awaited.

Dublin had long raised public funerals to the level of a political art form. Parnell's was to transcend politics altogether, even though the political climate there had seldom been more bitter and much of the bitterness up to the moment of his death had been directed against Parnell himself. This was to be the most stirring, solemn occasion in the Irish capital since the funeral of another very different but equally great Irish leader, Daniel O'Connell, nearly half a century before.

At Kingstown harbour, where great crowds had once welcomed Parnell with wild enthusiasm as he arrived from England, there was a great crowd once more but they stood sombre and silent in the rain and wore black crêpe armbands tied with a green ribbon. Most of the sounds were those of the boat, the *Ireland*, manoeuvring, and of the gale which had given it a rough passage across the Irish Sea and continued to lash the waves and the harbour wall. The coffin was brought ashore quickly and put aboard the waiting train, but there was a slight delay while the mail was transferred too.

It was 7.30 a.m. when the train steamed in to Dublin's Westland Row station. Again there was a crowd on the platform with black bands on their left arms tied with green ribbon. The hearse too was ready there, and when the large deal case in which the coffin had been travelling was removed, people on the platform broke it up and took fragments of the wood as relics.

The coffin itself was placed on the hearse and, piled high with wreaths, moved out followed by carriages of the accompanying mourners into the streets of Dublin. The rain was coming down hard, and such a strong wind was blowing that the crowds already massed on the pavements struggled to keep up their umbrellas. A drenched contingent of at least a thousand members of the Gaelic Athletic Association, a strongly nationalist body devoted to the pursuit of Irish instead of British sports, and infiltrated by the old secret society, the Irish Republican Brotherhood, waited with hurley sticks tied with black crêpe and green ribbon to escort the procession on its well-planned way. Accompanied by outriders and followed by lines of men walking six abreast between the crowds on the pavements, it was soon to assume enormous proportions.

One of the thirty-three brass bands that were to march that day in punctuation of the procession's densely winding progress struck up 'The Dead March' from Handel's oratorio *Saul*. The cortège moved forward to the first of a number of ceremonial halts at selected sites on the way to the cemetery. These had been chosen with an eye to their historical significance, as witness to the continuity of an Irish national sentiment which, after long-continuing rule from England, history itself had left in painfully fragmented form.

The touch of theatre was not inappropriate. Parnell had appeared on the political stage as an unknown, seventeen years before, with apparently little qualification for a role there other than the wish to have something to do. What he had in fact done was to give the fragmented national tradition the most effective and coherent political shape it had ever assumed.

The first halt, only for a minute or so, was at the fine eighteenth-century building in College Green which housed the Bank of Ireland. A hundred years before, this had been the last home of an Irish parliament, an institution which, under the British Crown and subordinate to control from London, had existed since medieval times. It had been in this building in 1782 that the Anglican Protestants of Ireland, a relatively small minority of the total population, thinking of themselves as 'Patriots', had grandiloquently asserted their legislative freedom from Westminster, proclaiming themselves guardians of an independent Irish nationhood under a Crown shared with Britain.

Most of these men's families had then lived in Ireland for at least a hundred years, some very much longer. Like the American colonists of the same era, they had attached a new national identity to their wish to run their own affairs free from British interference. What compromised their rhetoric was the fact that they only incidentally included in their civic thoughts the great majority of the people of Ireland, the Catholics, who, though much less disadvantaged than previously, were still not even allowed the franchise until 1793, let alone any Member of the parliament.

An ideological attempt on the part of a small group, mainly Protestant, North and South, inspired by the French Revolution to change this anomalous state of affairs had led to a conspiracy of 'United Irishmen' intending to unite Protestant, Catholic and Dissenter and to separate Ireland from Britain altogether. In the event their revolution had degenerated into little more than a primitive, mainly Catholic rebellion in 1798, and it was after the shock of this that the 'Patriot' parliament had allowed itself to be merged into a parliamentary Union with Westminster in 1800. But across the distance of time 'the old House on College Green' had acquired the status of a symbol for later popular aspirations.

As the hearse bearing Parnell's coffin came to a halt before the building on this day in October 1891, time had long blurred memories of the Protestant nationalist parliament's anomalous character. Nostalgia for 'the old House on College Green' had been absorbed into a political nationalist tradition which Catholics themselves had by now appropriated. Parnell himself provided an apposite link. His own great-grandfather had been one of 'the old House''s prominent members. Now Parnell, also a Protestant, had made the return of an Irish parliament to Dublin a serious possibility again in an age when the Catholic majority of the Irish people would have control of it. Symbolically uniting strands in Irish identity which reached much further back than the eighteenth century, he, though a Protestant, would go on to be buried in the great Catholic cemetery of Glasnevin.

But there were other stops first. The next was at St Michan's Church, where the first half of the funeral service was held, to be completed later at the graveside. In this church were the remains of two Protestant brothers named Sheares. These Sheares brothers, disillusioned with the exclusively Protestant parliamentary politics of the end of the eighteenth century and inspired by the republicanism of France, had been part of that small middle- and upper-class group of 'United Irishmen' who had hoped to rally the Catholic peasantry behind the rebellion for all Irish interests in 1798 which had been so chaotically ill-starred, degenerating largely into crude sectarian violence. Like so many of those they had hoped to help lead, the Sheares brothers had been executed. Parnell had never specifically advocated open rebellion. But after almost a hundred years a mystic ambivalence between violent and constitutional nationalism had been allowed to settle into Irish political rhetoric. It was something which could be left harmlessly unresolved, it seemed, and he had seldom gone out of his way positively to discourage such an approach.

From St Michan's Church the procession moved on to the City Hall.

There the coffin lay in state amid icons of the nationalist legend in the vast sombre interior. Light from the dark day outside hardly penetrated through a central opening in the gilded roof. Heavy black hangings draped the place from ceiling to floor, relieved only by a broad white banner spreading across the hall from pillar to pillar and carrying what purported to be the last words of the dying 'Chief', as Parnell had long been known and was so described on posters outside. 'Give my love to my colleagues and the Irish people,' ran the words.

That the message itself had been manufactured along with the banner seems probable. His wife, many years later, affirmed that Parnell had been incapable of anything so affected and that his last words had in fact been 'Kiss me, sweet Wifie, and I will try to sleep a little.' In the political context of this event, such words would have been unsuitable for display. Parnell himself – with an eye, like the funeral organizers, to the political main chance – might have forgiven the misattribution, if such it was.

His coffin, which was railed in to allow passers-by to stream past, rested appropriately before the central, black-shrouded statue of Daniel O'Connell, 'the Liberator' who had first effectively politicized the Catholic people of Ireland over fifty years before. This he had done first in a successful campaign for Catholic Emancipation, giving them the right to have Catholic representatives in Parliament, and then in an unsuccessful one for a Repeal of the parliamentary Union. Now at O'Connell's feet lay the body of the man who had succeeded in bringing one of the two great British political parties of the day to agree to repeal that Union and give Home Rule to Ireland, though still under the British Crown.

Close by hung flags from the days of the Protestant parliament which had come from Parnell's own Irish home in Co. Wicklow. They had been the property of his great-grandfather, Chancellor of the Exchequer in that assembly, though a rather less single-mindedly independent 'Patriot' than legend liked to maintain. But this was no day for subjecting Irish national legend to scrutiny. In any case the statue of Henry Grattan, a more correctly classifiable 'Patriot' of that period, was at hand to confirm the support of all good men from the past for the 'nationalist' party whatever it might turn out to be.

Wreaths were piled high in front of the catafalque on which the coffin stood, prominent among them that from Parnell's wife. Three and a half months earlier she had been Katharine O'Shea – Mrs O'Shea – divorced at the end of 1890 from one of Parnell's former Members of Parliament. The wreath was of white lilies on a background of laurel leaves. On a card she had written: 'My own true love; best, truest friend, my husband. From his broken-hearted wife.'

There were wreaths too of roses and lilies in the names of her three daughters. These were marked: 'To my dear mother's husband, from Nora', 'From little Clare' and 'From little Katie'. In the case of the last two the form of address concealed part of the truth. Although they would not then have known it, and few if any of those present would have known it either, it was their father who was dead.

Many of the public wreaths reiterated the theme of martyrdom, with phrases such as 'To the soldier dead for Ireland, with bitter regret that a misguided section of his countrymen . . . allowed him in an evil hour to be hounded to the grave.' These echoed the many unanimous resolutions of regret passed by public bodies throughout Ireland. The Navan Town Commissioners believed that 'those who in their infinite malice and tiger-like thirst for his blood hounded him on to his death sent a poniard into the heart of Erin'. Some tributes in their fulsomeness, giving a sharp definition to that aspiration for Ireland which he had usually been careful to leave undefined, struck a stirring prophetic note. The faithful in Rathmines declared, 'He has sown the seed of freedom, and under his motto of independence, it will grow and ripen and in the near future Ireland will owe to him the benefit she will reap.'

The most striking floral display in the City Hall was a vast Celtic cross of arum and eucharis lilies, white chrysanthemums and ferns mounted on an ebony frame and placed beside the statue of O'Connell, a tribute from Parnell's parliamentary supporters. In a special position of honour among the wreaths was a simple ivy leaf sent by a woman from Cork.

The crush in the hall was very great as, for over three hours, some thirty thousand people, hurried along by officials, filed past in a continually moving queue, several deep, so that those on the outside were hardly able to see more than the great floral cross. A number of people fainted. Members of the Dublin Fire Brigade in polished helmets stood guard and maintained order.

When, at some time after one o'clock, the coffin was brought out of the hall so that the procession could reassemble, the weather had started to clear. The day which had begun so stormily was to end in an afternoon of bright sunshine. The moment the first pallbearers emerged, every man outside uncovered his head and an observer looking down on the scene found the sudden startling transformation of the previously dark mass of the crowd into a sea of white upturned faces a weird and affecting experience.

It took half an hour to arrange the wreaths around the coffin on the hearse. There were so many that the coffin could hardly be seen at all as the cortège set off again. Members of Parliament walked on each side, again escorted by men carrying hurley sticks. There followed the mourning-carriages, in the first of which sat Parnell's younger brother Henry, his married sister Emily Dickinson, her niece Miss Dickinson, and, according to one source, another young girl, a Miss Maud Gonne, who had dined in his company on his last visit to Ireland just over a week before. In one of the carriages close behind rode three men who had spent much of their lives conspiring in the long apparently moribund cause of an Irish Republic: James Stephens, over thirty years before founder of the Irish Republican Brotherhood (known as 'Fenians') but long since replaced in its arcane councils by other men; John O'Leary, a literary figure who had missed the Fenian Rising of 1867 by being in prison but after years of subsequent exile was still on police files as titular head of the Brotherhood's Supreme Council; and P. N. Fitzgerald, thought to be representative of that Council in the province of Munster. The organization of the funeral had been partly the Council's work. Parnell's horse, saddled and with his boots reversed in the stirrups, was there too. Some doubted that it was actually his horse, but emotional associations rather than strictly accurate connections with the past were what mattered that day.

The civic dignity of the occasion was completed by the Dublin City Marshal riding in full uniform at the head of a further line of carriages which contained the Lord Mayor, the High Sheriff and other dignitaries. After them there stretched into the distance the seemingly unending lines of followers on foot, representatives of trade groups, clubs and societies of many sorts, walking usually six abreast.

Here in Dublin for this afternoon it was almost as if the bitterness which for the past ten months had attached to the name of Parnell had never been. Only two significant groups of people were absent: priests and those Irish Members of Parliament who in fact constituted the majority of the nationalist parliamentary party which Parnell had made so effective but which had split from him ten months before in consequence of his long liaison with Mrs O'Shea. One Member from the minority of that party which had continued to support Parnell, asked by a newspaper reporter before the funeral whether he thought that Members who had opposed Parnell would be attending, replied that he thought it would be 'a very risky thing to do'. An Irish crowd, he said, was apt to be very hasty, and their presence on such an occasion might lead to scandalous scenes. In the event the crowds everywhere behaved with a dignity and discipline which much impressed observers used to scenes of less decorum in great public Dublin funerals of the past.

The only colour in the spectacle apart from that of the wreaths and the green armbands came from the white armlets of the marshalling stewards, from the occasional glint of brass on the musical instruments of the bands and from green flags hanging from crowded windows along the route. Women on the pavements keened and clapped their hands as the coffin passed. There were sobs and muttered prayers for the dead. All men doffed their hats. At least one estimate of the total numbers present was as high as two hundred thousand. It took an hour and three-quarters for the whole procession to pass a given point and, as the route to Glasnevin had been planned in the shape of a three-mile loop, at one stage it almost caught up with itself.

Two more symbolic halts were made on the way. The first was at the spot where a former United Irishman, Robert Emmet, had been executed in 1803 after trying to lead a republican rebellion through the Dublin streets, a small, pathetic postscript to the tumultuous events of 1798. Like them it had entered a national myth in which failure had almost become an adequate substitute for successful reality. That such myth was alive, the funeral made clear enough. What was being mourned that day was the loss of the best chance of successful reality that popular nationalist Ireland had had within its grasp for centuries.

The last halt before the end of the journey was at another house in the same street. Here another Protestant United Irishman, the radical aristocrat Lord Edward Fitzgerald, had been arrested in 1798, receiving in the process a wound which was to prove mortal. In manner at least there had been something of the aristocrat about Parnell. He too was now on his way to join Fitzgerald and other national heroes in mythical status. The south-east wind had quite blown the clouds away. He proceeded to Glasnevin under the clear blue skies of a fading day.

Thousands had been waiting at the cemetery for hours – some, earlier, in the pouring rain. A grassy plot in which paupers had once been buried – famine victims, some thought – had been chosen as the site for the tomb. It was not far from O'Connell's.

The coffin was first placed on a platform outside the cemetery while the crowds were let in. There was a rush for the graveside. People were lifted off their feet, clothes were torn, hats lost, women shrieked, some fainted. The Dublin *Freeman's Journal* wrote next day of the whole funeral, 'No greater upheaval of emotion had ever been witnessed in Ireland.'

Irish Members of Parliament were among the pallbearers. The second half of the funeral service was read. The wreath from Mrs Parnell went first into the grave. Many of the crowd dropped in flowers. The moon was up before all was over.

One of those near the grave had been the young girl, Maud Gonne, who according to one newspaper had travelled with the family in the first of the mourning-carriages. She was herself mourning the loss of a three-year-old daughter who had died only a few days before. She was a friend of the young poet W. B. Yeats, whom she told that evening in a state of some emotion that as Parnell was being buried a shooting star had suddenly appeared in the sky. The story of this portent, its significance undefined, went into legend. No other eyewitness of the burial at Glasnevin seems to have mentioned this, but it is an indisputable fact, recorded by the Dunsink Observatory, that at 6.30 p.m. that Sunday evening a remarkably brilliant bluish-white meteor 'much larger and brighter than Jupiter' was seen falling for four seconds in several parts of Ireland, 'lighting up the sky like a flash of lightning'.

After scenes which the London *Times* said had never been more remarkable in a public demonstration, and which the *Irish Times*, equally an opponent of Parnell, said would prove ineffaceable from the minds of all, young or old, who witnessed them, the day ended and Parnell was left alone in the moonshine.

A void was left in the affairs of national Ireland to be filled effectively only many years later by quite other men.

Two days after the funeral a great storm played havoc with the wreaths around the grave. Almost all were blown away, and the magnificent Celtic cross was completely destroyed. And although a group of faithful ladies were soon at hand to tidy the place up, it was not until 1940 that a boulder of granite from his home county of Wicklow was placed upon the grassy site of the tomb. It bore, and still bears, a single word: Parnell.

Chapter 2

Who was he? Where had he come from? And how had he managed in so relatively few years not only to transform the nature of Ireland's political relationship with England but to assume such a powerful place in the imagination of the Irish people that for many years after his death there were those who refused to believe that he was really dead? Well into the next century there were said to be some in rural Ireland to whom he would appear in dreams to offer comfort and reassurance about the future. In the imaginations too of Yeats, Joyce and other Irish writers he was to assume mythological significance. To identify the reality is not an easy task. Something about him remains elusive to the end.

It was not until Parnell was getting on for thirty that he came to public notice at all, emerging quite suddenly from a respectable well-to-do 'Anglo-Irish' background in Co. Wicklow, within the conventions of which he had appeared to fit without trouble. Outside it he caused trouble almost at once.

Throughout his life he was to maintain a small, though not unfriendly, distance between himself and most of the people with whom he came into contact, though all testified to a gentle charm alongside a quiet pride which only occasionally, and usually only in public life, broke into impatience or curtness. A myth about him arose even in his lifetime. It was assisted by the fact that, while the new technology of wireless telegraphy made his speeches available in the press within a day of their delivery, relatively few of those whom his speeches moved and inspired ever actually saw him or even a picture of him. The distant, enigmatic quality which was undoubtedly part of his personality became enshrined within public perception. He left few papers and no diaries. Reminiscences of him are in most cases those of people aware that they were dealing with a myth in the making. Even the memoirs of his own family, often written long after his death, must be partly discounted for the inaccuracies of solemn hindsight. In general, impressions of him have to be sought obliquely, by glimpses incidental to the grand political narrative, or by sidelong appraisal of his public utterances, often between the lines.

The only direct insight into his feelings is contained in nearly a hundred of his intimate letters which the woman who became his wife in the last year of his life published along with her own memoirs, nearly a quarter of a century after the sad Brighton scene. A certain mystery attaches even to this publication, casting occasional doubt on aspects of the story as she tells it, and on the selection though not the authenticity of the letters.

There is even today some difficulty about how his name should be pronounced. His widow was to write of 'that horrible emphasis on the 'nell which is so prevalent'. This suggests that he cannot have liked it either. That it was often so pronounced is clear from the rhythms of a number of popular ballads of the day.

> It was the tyrant Gladstone
> And he said unto himself:
> I never will be aisy
> Till Parnell is on the shelf.

And again:

> When famine o'er our suffering land
> Its wings of foe extended . . .
> What hero brave
> Stood forth to save
> And keep us bright and early?
> Why, need I tell?
> It was Parnell,
> Our own beloved Charlie.

James Joyce too, in verses reflecting the doggerel of the time, suggests the same pronunciation:

> They had their way: they laid him low.
> But Erin list, his spirit may
> Rise, like the phoenix from the flames,
> When breaks the dawning of the day,
> The day that brings us Freedom's reign.
> And on that day may Erin well
> Pledge in the cup she lifts to Joy
> One grief – the memory of Parnell.

Yeats, on the other hand, clearly favoured stress on the first syllable in his last poem on Parnell, entitled 'Come Gather Round Me Parnellites', which ended:

> . . . Parnell loved his country
> And Parnell loved his lass.

In the end, as with much about Parnell, one has to make up one's mind for oneself.

He was born, seventh child and third son of an American mother and a well-to-do Protestant Irish landlord, into an Ireland on the threshold of an experience which left a deep trauma on its history.

On the very day of his birth, on 27 June 1846, there appeared in the Dublin *Freeman's Journal* the headline 'DISEASE IN THE NEW POTATO CROP'. A report beneath it from Co. Mayo ran, 'all descriptions of crops are coming forward rapidly but we are sorry to have to add that the disease has made its appearance in the new potatoes'.

On that day the population of Ireland stood at over 8 million, about half that of the rest of the United Kingdom of which it was then all constitutionally a part. The Famine which afflicted most of Ireland between 1845 and 1849, accompanied by emigration which continued heavily over the next two years, reduced the Irish population by a quarter. About a million people died; another million emigrated, mainly to the United States and Canada. In the week in 1848 in which the little 'Charley' Parnell had celebrated his second birthday in the comfort of the family estate at Avondale in Co. Wicklow, nearly one-eighth of the entire Irish population were on outdoor relief or in workhouses where they had been dying in hundreds.

The Ireland in which he began to grow up, however, had about it the stability and quietude of exhaustion. Shortly before the Famine, a Government Commission had reported that over one-third of all the smallholdings in Ireland must be assumed unable to support the families who lived on them after they had paid the rent. The shortfall was made up by earnings from migrant labour in England and Scotland. The Famine in fact reduced the total number of holdings by something not far short of that very figure which the Commission had said could not support its occupiers. A landlord travelling through West Cork in the summer of 1849 had been painfully struck by the number of farms he saw lying waste and untenanted, with their cabins derelict and in ruins, and by the large parties of emigrants frequently to be met with on their way to the ports. But before long all this was being regarded as the calm after the storm. An experienced and not inhumane land-agent was able to say by 1852 that the 'thinning' of the population by the Famine meant that things were 'getting straight'. And when, in September 1855, the foundation-stone of the Carlisle Tower was laid at Lismore Castle in Co. Waterford, its inscription recorded not only the visit of the Lord Lieutenant after whom the tower was named but also 'the dawn of happy days which has at length appeared to illumine the prospects of Ireland'.

Wicklow was in any case one of the most prosperous counties in Ireland. Even before the Famine, significantly more of its farms had been over ten acres in size than under five; in Ireland as a whole the pattern was the reverse. Wicklow was therefore less affected by the Famine than most other counties: it had had a much smaller percentage of its population on outdoor relief or in workhouses than the national average.

There was thus no particularly strong local impact from the Famine to make an impression on Parnell as a little boy. His father, grandson of the famous 'Patriot parliament' politician through whom the Avondale estate had come into the family, was a master of foxhounds who seems to have continued hunting at least through the immediate aftermath of the Famine. Parnell's American mother continued to give the excellent dinner parties for which she was then renowned.

Mrs Parnell seems, however, to have felt at least a sentimentalized concern for the sufferings of the peasantry. In the year of 'Charley's' birth she had written a poem, 'The Irish Exile', with a verse which ran:

> Dear home of my soul, dear Erin, farewell,
> My fond heart now beats to thy sorrowing knell.
> Thy glory is fled and thy spirit lies low,
> And deep the despair where hope once shed a glow.

Her eighth child, Fanny, born in 1848, of whom Charley became particularly fond, was to become by her early teens a poetess writing very much in this vein.

Parnell's father, John Henry Parnell, had been travelling in the United States in 1834 with another Irish landlord, his cousin Lord Powerscourt, when he met the girl he was to marry the following year: Delia Stewart, the eighteen-year-old daughter of a famous American naval hero, Commodore Charles Stewart, who was himself the son of an Ulster emigrant in the previous century, and the stepson of a member of George

Washington's bodyguard. The Commodore himself had among other naval exploits captured two British ships off the coast of Portugal at the end of the war of 1812, and had been voted a gold medal by Congress for his gallantry. His wife, Charles Parnell's grandmother, could, through her family name Tudor, claim kinship with England's monarchs, but her father had fought as an American in the War of Independence. Thus when in 1835 John Henry Parnell brought Delia to live on his estate at Avondale in Co. Wicklow, which, as the guidebook put it, his 'consummate taste' was in the process of rendering 'one of the most elegant and interesting seats in the kingdom', she came without any necessary ties of loyalty to British Government.

On the other hand it would be wrong to think that she arrived with any predisposition to oppose it. The Commodore, her father, had shown no animosity towards his wartime British foes, chivalrously entertaining after the battle the captains of the two ships he had taken. In any case he was not the formative influence on his daughter's upbringing, for he brusquely abandoned her mother when Delia was only nine and never saw his wife again, living happily for many years with a married woman whom he came to refer to as his wife instead. Delia was then brought up by her mother and grandmother, both of whom were fond of England, where they had lived happily for a time, and their hopes for Delia's social success on her way to a good marriage did not exclude the fashionable European worlds of Paris and London. The young Anglo-Irish landlord John Parnell, whose hand she accepted in Boston when she was only nineteen, may not have been quite the splendid match they had envisaged for her, but, as her grandmother wrote to another daughter, he was connected with 'the nobility of Ireland' and was just the sort of man 'to settle quietly down at Avondale with Delia and to encircle her with all his relations'.

Avondale was situated near the small town of Rathdrum in what was sometimes referred to as 'the garden of Ireland'. A short walk away, in the Vale of Avoca where two rivers joined, was a scene immortalized by the poet Tom Moore in the lines:

> There is not in the wide world a valley so sweet
> As that vale in whose bosom the bright waters meet.

The house had been built in 1777 on a modest scale but had some proportionate charm of its period, with a central hall above which was a gallery in which a band played at dances, a fine library, a billiard-table, and a great bow-window looking on to the beautiful Wicklow countryside. Here the Parnells lived the conventional life of the Irish Protestant gentry of their day, with outdoor recreation provided by the usual gentlemanly sports: hunting, shooting and fishing and, in summer, cricket played on an excellent pitch within the grounds. And in this house at almost regular two-yearly intervals Delia Parnell gave birth to a child, nine of them in the same room.

Understandably, perhaps, she was later to content herself with only occasional visits to Avondale. The son whom she named after her famous father was to inherit it. He too was to spend much time away. But it was with Avondale that he formed the second most important bond of his life.

The extent to which his American mother exercised an influence on the son she named after her American patriot father inevitably became a source of speculation after the son's political career had taken the shape it did. Much imaginative insight was indeed let loose on Parnell's early years after his dramatically sudden death. A woman who had known his great-aunt, for instance, recollected how this great-aunt had complained in his childhood of 'mischief brewing at Avondale' from Delia with her 'hatred of England' educating her nephew 'like a little Hannibal to hate it too'. But there was some confusion in the recollection, for Parnell was not a 'nephew' but a great-nephew of the woman quoted and anyway no more than three years old at the time. Delia Parnell herself, shocked by her son's death, talked to an interviewer of 'English dominion' and suggested that to dislike the English was a logical consequence of her son's ancestry. But while, after her own death, Parnell's brother John described her as having been 'a burning enthusiast in the cause of Irish liberty, and possessed of an inveterate hatred of England', rhetoric of a fairly empty sort seems to have been at work in the language of memory. He quoted her at the same time as admiring Queen Victoria, if not her ministers, and disliking extremists.

That any early rhetoric of Delia Parnell must have stayed well within the acceptable bounds of convention is suggested by the pattern of her own social life after her husband died suddenly in 1859. During the 1860s she fairly regularly attended dances, dinner parties and other receptions at Dublin Castle – centre of the Irish administration – as well as British regimental functions in the city, and she took care to have her daughters presented at court in London. In the summer of 1862 she was to be found at the Viceregal Lodge in three successive weeks. Contemporary portraits of her reveal a handsome woman of firm character who is likely to have instilled into her son pride in the battle honours of the grandfather whose name he had been given and who was to live on until Parnell himself was twenty-three. But that his mother can have played no effective part in indoctrinating him in an anti-British, or indeed any recognizable political attitude at all, is made plain by the fact that, as he himself later admitted, even in early manhood he was 'not very interested in politics'. There is no documented instance until he was twenty-two of him showing any real interest in politics at all other than in an incident proudly recalled by his mother in later life of his precocious discussion at the age of eight with the passengers of the Rathdrum coach about the Crimean War. When twenty-two he canvassed in Wicklow for an aristocratic relative standing as a Liberal candidate, but this seems to have been more of a social than a political act. By his own account – and all the available evidence supports it – he hardly turned his mind to political affairs again at all for the next four years, and did not seriously think about entering politics until he was twenty-seven. It is worth noting too that Fanny Parnell later in life complained strongly of the stultifying Tory atmosphere in which she had been brought up.

That there was, however, something about Delia Parnell's effect on the family which her husband disliked is suggested by a clause in the will which he drew up shortly before his death in 1859. In his lifetime he was said to have 'tabooed' politics at Avondale. By 1859 husband and wife had been living apart a good deal. Something more than matrimonial antipathy may have lain behind the clause which he now inserted. '. . . I absolutely forbid', he wrote, 'any interference on the part of my wife or any of her relatives with the management of my children or property.' But this may have reflected concern for her financial competence as much as for her political views.

Certainly, her readiness not to let politics interfere with social conformity was later demonstrated clearly enough not only by her attendances at Dublin Castle but also by the respectable Saturday-afternoon musical, literary and dramatic gatherings in her own home at which she sought to encourage original Irish talent. The likelihood is that what Parnell principally inherited from his American mother was a freedom of spirit to go his own way as he wanted; it would have blended with that other sense of detachment inherited from the Protestant Patriot tradition of his great-grandfather, Sir John Parnell, Chancellor of the Exchequer in the Patriot parliament, whose portrait hung in the hall at Avondale with the faded banners of those legendary patriotic days. Closer still to Charley in time and in spirit was his grandfather, William Parnell, who had become a Union MP, but one with a deep, radical concern for the well-being of Irish Catholics untypical in his day of members of his class.

There was one further independent influence which may also have permeated the young Parnell's upbringing at some level of consciousness. A tradition of purifying evangelicalism, present anyway in the Protestant Church of Ireland, was particularly strong in Co. Wicklow. Parnell's maternal uncle actually went so far as to convert to the austere sect of Plymouth Brethren which had been founded by a Co. Wicklow curate. And one of his early teachers was a Dissenter.

What Parnell was like in childhood is difficult now to distinguish from what people looking back afterwards felt he ought to have been like. He was at the time of his death still such an enigmatic figure to the general public that every scrap of information that could be collected about his early years seemed fascinating. There is even today an absence of contemporary documentation about his boyhood. The material available is largely anecdotal, mostly remembered much later by his elder brother John, his elder sister Emily, his mother, and one or two other contemporaries.

Innocuous details such as that he rode a rocking-horse, was good at marbles, was fond of dogs and fishing, and collected birds' eggs may well be believed. Certain stories, such as his fondness for the children's game of 'follow-my-leader' in which he always wanted to be leader, or the story of his nurse saying, 'Master Charley is born to rule', whether true or not, are suspect. Others, particularly those recounted by his mother, who was a vigorous woman in her early and mid seventies when she first wrote them down, with sight so good that she still did not need to wear glasses, may well be substantially true and provide genuine evidence of characteristics displayed in later life.

One of the first such stories she told was about a nursery game played with lead soldiers against his younger sister Fanny, in which casualties were to be inflicted by rolling a spiked ball across a floor, but in which he had taken care to stick his own soldiers to the floor with glue. That he could be belligerently protective of, as well as competitive with, his sisters appears from his mother's account of his behaviour to his younger sister Anna at times when she and a nurse wished to punish her. To thwart the nurse on one occasion he put Anna on a table, pushed it into a corner of the room, and stood in front of it with a big stick. To his mother, about to punish her on another occasion, he cried out, 'Oh mother, she'll die, she'll die!' until she changed her mind.

That he showed at least a normally sensitive child's concern for the poor emerges from her story of a ragged poor boy seen without shoes as they drove one day along a cold road near Rathdrum and of her son's wish to take him home and dress him in his own clothes. She also said that he used to get angry with his father for not feasting the tenantry when they came to pay their rents on rent day, and his sister Emily confirmed that 'as a little boy he showed consideration for all things helpless and weak whether human beings or animals'.

His brother John, who described him in childhood as slender and small for his age, with dark brown hair, pale complexion and very dark brown and very piercing eyes, said that he was wiry, bright, playful and fond of mechanics. An interest in science, which was to remain with him all his life, seems demonstrated by early plans for a perpetual-motion machine which his mother at any rate regarded as likely to give rise to an explosion. His natural curiosity is also said to have made him try to make bullets by dropping hot lead from the roof of Avondale to the earth below. To do this he carried an iron pot of burning coals up two flights of stairs and two ladders to the coping before being brought down by an exasperated family servant. Whatever the truth of such reminiscences, when his brother said that he 'liked fighting for fighting's sake' the statement may be accepted as accurate, for there were to be two pieces of documented contemporary evidence before his entry into public life to confirm an easy combativeness in Parnell's nature.

His mother later took pride in having made her son translate Caesar and Virgil and in having given him a facility for writing and speaking English. In fact his facility in writing was never conspicuous and in speaking was patently self-acquired. She summed him up as having been in childhood 'remarkable for his wit, his poetical fancies, his sprightliness and his enterprise'. Her words may at least indicate a side to his nature of which the public was not always aware. But certain indisputable facts clearly played some part in developing what his brother John described as 'the complexities of his strange and baffling character'.

In 1853, at the age of six, he was sent away to boarding-school in England, partly to separate him from John, who had a stammer which he was beginning to imitate. An education outside Ireland was normal for gentry of the class of the Parnells. John himself was sent to Paris for a time, where Mrs Parnell's brother had a fine apartment at 122 Champs-Élysées and where the Parnell daughters were all educated. In Charley's case the inevitable shock of separation from mother and family at such an age must have been made more traumatic by the fact that the school in Yeovil, Somerset, to which he was sent was a girls' school in which he was the only boy pupil. But the headmistress became very fond of him and described him forty years later, as if the memory of him as a child were still vivid to her, as 'quick, interesting to teach, very affectionate to those he loved (a few), reserved to others; therefore not a great favourite with his companions'. He went back to Avondale for the holidays. After returning to school from the summer holiday of 1854 he fell seriously ill with typhoid and was nursed by his headmistress 'for six weeks, night and day, to an entire recovery'.

In 1855 the Parnells' eldest son, Hayes, died after a hunting accident and Charley was brought back from Somerset to Avondale for a time, to be taught by a governess and a tutor. He was then again sent back to a boarding-school in England (at Kirk Langley, in Derbyshire) where he told his brother he was happy, enjoying the games.

Then in the summer of 1859 came a shock. His father died suddenly in the Shelbourne Hotel, Dublin, where he had gone hoping to play in a cricket match. Mrs Parnell and some of her daughters were in Paris at the time, where another daughter was now living after marriage to a wealthy American. Charley, then just thirteen, seems to have been the only member of his immediate family at the funeral.

His father's will contained some terse clauses apart from that which forbade Mrs Parnell any hand in the management of her children. Another ran, 'I make no provision for my wife, she being amply provided for from other sources.' (Her American brother living in Paris, like her new son-in-law, was a man of considerable wealth. She was later to inherit a fortune from her father, though not to keep it.) Another clause of her husband's will ran, 'I make no provision for my daughter, Emily ... who has grievously offended me.' (She had maintained a persistent association with an army officer named Dickinson during the recent London season and was eventually to contract a disastrous marriage with him.) Finally, in a gesture which suggests disappointment with his elder son John, afflicted as he was with his stammer, 'I make my son Charles heir-at-law to all intents and purposes.' The smaller family estate in Armagh was left to John, who was however known also to be heir to a considerable fortune from his uncle, Sir Ralph Howard. But Avondale went to Charley. Sir Ralph Howard, with whom Emily had been staying at his house in Belgrave Square in London, was made executor of the will, and the children were made wards of the Court of Chancery.

The Avondale estate, together with some other estates in Co. Kildare which Charley now inherited from his father, brought in rents of about £2,000 a year (some £90,000 a year in late-twentieth-century real terms). Though the estate was later to become heavily encumbered with mortgages, the family, further supported by Mrs Parnell's own private income, was for the present in no financial difficulties.

Mrs Parnell did not want to live at Avondale, but since the children, as wards in Chancery, could not be taken outside the jurisdiction of the court, she could not go back to Paris or America, either of which she might have preferred to Ireland. She therefore rented a house, 'Khyber Pass', at the small seaside town of Dalkey, about eight miles from Dublin. Thereafter the Parnell household long continued to reside in rented houses: at Dalkey for a year, then at Kingstown – where her mother, the American naval hero's deserted wife, came to stay and died one day in a chair after lunch, much distressing Charley – and then for some years more at 14 Upper Temple Street, Dublin. Avondale was let to an engineer of the Dublin, Wicklow and Wexford Railway, then being completed. Such political conversation as took place in the family in these years seems to have centred more on the American Civil War than on British domestic issues. The Parnells identified with the Union cause, thus distancing themselves here from a British Government whose sympathies were in the main with the South.

The Parnells kept the use of the Avondale dower house, 'Casino', where John and Charley, educated for a time by private tutors, came to play in cricket matches on the Avondale ground. In general their leisure seems to have been spent in the normal outdoor activities of boys in their early and mid teens – swimming, boating and fishing at Dalkey and Kingstown – while Charley, according to his brother, 'shot many a rabbit' even from indoors.

Eventually his mother again sent him to England, this time on the advice of her friend Lady Londonderry, to be prepared for Cambridge at a crammer run by a clergyman at Chipping Norton in Oxfordshire. Years later a contemporary there recalled him as having been interested only in cricket and mathematics, at both of which he was good. He also recalled that Parnell's brother John, who had come with him to Chipping Norton, had been popular, 'but we did not like Charles. He was arrogant and aggressive, and he tried to sit on us and we tried to sit on him.'

He went back to Ireland for the holidays, and in the summer played a good deal of cricket on what was now his own ground at Avondale (though the house remained let) and elsewhere. He played in four different matches in the three weeks between 15 July and 5 August 1863 and seems to have been a fair all-rounder at the game. At Avondale on Friday 17 July, going in first for the home team – which included his

brother John – he scored eight runs and six runs (not by the standards of
the time such low scores as they might seem) and took six of his
opponents' wickets when put on to bowl. 'C. Parnell played well,'
commented the *Wicklow News-Letter*. On 4 August, playing again at
Avondale for South Wicklow against the town of Bray, he made fourteen
runs in an innings which was favourably commented on by the local
paper and contained 'a splendid hit to leg for six'. His bowling was
described as 'superior', and the fielding of the whole South Wicklow side
was considered 'worthy of special mention'.

It was while at the crammer in Chipping Norton that, according to
John Parnell, Charley, then sixteen, developed a sentimental affection for
a local girl with whom he used to go for country walks. At the time his
brother was writing – about 1905 – it was Parnell's reputation as a lover
that dominated popular thought about him, and it can be assumed that a
publisher would have wanted John Parnell to strive to remember any
early romances in his brother's life. On the other hand, John Parnell's
book, though often inaccurate in detail, is a fairly sober affair. It can
probably be accepted at least that Charley at the age of sixteen was not
without some normal interest in girls.

His fondness for cricket continued to be displayed each summer in
Ireland. There was a story told of him long afterwards that he had been so
keen to extract the maximum advantage from the strict rules of the game
that he had sometimes insisted on claiming a wicket if one of the
opposing batsmen took too long to come out to the pitch. The obvious
analogy here with a later meticulous ruthlessness in politics makes the
story suspect. But it is as likely to have been true of Parnell as of anyone
in the history of the game and may account for a curious item in the score
of a match between Rathdrum and Arklow in the summer of 1864.
Parnell was there credited with the stumping of two batsmen, though no
bowler's name is given in the score, as it should have been if Parnell had
been the wicket-keeper (the only player a scorer would normally describe
as 'stumping'). The fact that he was a 'superior' bowler and indeed
opened the bowling for Wicklow at least once that summer makes it
unlikely that he would also have played as wicket-keeper.

An innings by him of twenty-five out of a total team score of thirty-
nine was the high spot of his 1864 season, made at Avondale before a
large number of spectators on his eighteenth birthday, 27 June. Eventually
bowled by 'a daisy-clipper' – a ball that ran low along the pitch – he was
described as having played 'in splendid style'.

In all these games in which Parnell played regularly each summer, his companions were drawn from the same élite section of Irish society as himself: other gentlemen landowners or officers of the army. It was a time when the social life of the Irish gentry remained very much centred in Ireland. Seaside towns outside Dublin, like Bray and Malahide, and resorts like Killarney in the South, or Bundoran in the West, still regularly drew the gentry for their holidays, and the fashionable comings and goings to different high-class hotels in such places were respectfully chronicled by the press. Parnell himself had as yet given no sign whatever of deviation from the conventional pattern of respectability to which he had been born. In March 1865, at the age of eighteen, he was gazetted Lieutenant in the Wicklow Militia, his county territorial unit which consisted of half a dozen officers and some five hundred men called up each year for a few weeks' training. His fellow-officers were his landed Wicklow neighbours. The following month his brother John also received his commission as Lieutenant in that county's militia.

The late summer of 1865, the last before he went up to Cambridge, saw Parnell again playing a great deal of cricket in Ireland. In one period of nine days that September he was playing on no less than seven. In a particularly disastrous match in which he turned out for Dublin City, the entire side were out for nine in the first innings, with Parnell (going in first wicket down, and therefore possibly Captain) bowled for nought. The *Dublin Evening Mail* commented that 'too much eagerness for hot play was evinced by the City members, and they did not observe the cool and superior manner' in which they were bowled to.

Within a week the newspapers had more startling matters to report. A widespread conspiracy to shatter the comfortable world of the Irish gentry for ever and create by force of arms an independent sovereign Irish republic had been unearthed by the Government.

Chapter 3

When, in the 1790s, inspired by the new French Republic, idealists in Ireland calling themselves 'United Irishmen' had tried to create a modern nationalism for the island and to separate it from Britain, they had set themselves an extremely ambitious task. Nationalism is the political projection of a sense of identity. There were then three distinct identities settled in Ireland. These were detectable by religion: Catholic, Anglican Protestant, and Presbyterian and other dissident Protestants known as Dissenters. To unite the three was the United Irishmen's aim, but the net effect of their rebellion in 1798 was in fact to consolidate the distinction between all Protestants and Catholics, and to ensure that British power in Ireland was strengthened and not removed.

Power in Ireland, insofar as it did not lie with the British Government, lay with that minority Protestant Anglo-Irish 'Ascendancy' which had its own nationalist aspirations similar to those of the recently successful American colonists, and exclusive of the majority of the population. There were few idealists among them ready quickly to bridge that gap. The deterioration of the United Irishmen's rebellion into little more than a sectarian peasants' revolt had led this Ascendancy to accept that their safest interests in future lay in parliamentary Union with Britain. Their Ascendancy in Ireland was thus preserved; their independent power was subsumed in that of Westminster.

As for the Catholic majority, their identity had hardly in modern times been successfully harnessed to political effect. They covered a wide social and economic range, but they all had some share in an ancient Gaelic identity which had been enriched by Christianity and had then proved capable of absorbing to a remarkable extent Viking, Norman and early English settlers. But internal dissensions and Elizabethan conquest had broken the political character of this identity. Subsequent attempts to rally it politically had been under the banner of English kings losing civil wars of their own – Charles I and James II. The identity itself had survived strongly, preserved in the patina of pre-Reformation Catholicism, in language and in the isolation of civil disadvantage. But, by definition, in that disadvantage it had no power.

It was Daniel O'Connell, Catholic lawyer and landlord, who first organized the Irish national identity of the majority of the population for political effect. This he had done, within the Union, first by campaigning for and eventually winning in 1829 that Catholic Emancipation which enabled Catholics to be Members of Parliament, and then by organizing them even more successfully in the 1840s in his campaign, which was itself to be a failure, for Repeal of the Union.

The social tidal wave of the Famine swept O'Connell's Repeal movement away, making all Irish politics temporarily a side-issue, but it left behind the indelible fact that O'Connell had been able to organize the Irish masses for political potential. His popular title, 'the Liberator', though of no literal validity, was in this sense well earned.

Some of O'Connell's young intellectual supporters, known as 'Young Ireland', constructed upon his achievement an intellectual ideology of Irish nationalism which combined the United Irishmen's theories with the romantic European nationalist thinking of the mid-century. But in this they were less in tune with the Irish masses than was O'Connell himself.

As he well knew, the multitudes who flocked to his 'monster meetings' were instinctively motivated by feelings more complex than the simple call for 'the Repeal'. A folk memory persisted from the Gaelic past in which a social and cultural, if not in any modern sense a political, 'nation' had been taken for granted. Within this rested traditional echoes of resentment about past confiscation of land by 'the stranger' together with insecurity for a population much of which lived as tenants-at-will of owners of the land which gave them life. A Government inquiry in the 1820s, years before the Famine, heard evidence of a prevailing 'predisposition to discontent' among the rural population attributed to 'recollections of ancient times . . . kept alive in the minds of the people'. Such feelings, partly inarticulate and partly economic in the simplest sense, were not easy to adapt to the sophisticated aspirations of the modern age. It was the concerns of life on the land which were at the heart of the strongest feelings about Irish life.

The land system of Ireland, before the great changes in which Parnell was to play a crucial part, was a more intricate affair than historical legend and those with a political interest in perpetuating it often allowed. Middlemen between landlords and tenants, strained relations between tenant farmers and labourers, and above all crude and uneconomic farming render the frequent oversimplification of its problems into a matter of rack-renting landlords and simple peasantry an unhistorical cliché. However, the cliché itself – widely current at the time – was to play a not insignificant part in history.

Rents were generally not excessive, though some were, while others turned out to be unpayable in times of bad harvests or adverse economic factors and particularly when both appeared together. In any case, it was in the interest of all who paid rent – and they were the majority of the people in Ireland – to agitate for as little payment of rent as possible. Similarly, although the prevailing system by the 1840s of tenantry-at-will undoubtedly made tenants subject to capricious eviction, and although evictions for no other reason than that the landlord wanted the land did take place, modern research shows that actual ejections, as opposed to the issuing of notices of eviction, took place less frequently than has often been supposed. Those evicted were often readmitted as 'caretakers'. But many cruel evictions did take place, and, again, it was in the interest of those even theoretically at the mercy of capricious eviction to remove such a permanently unpleasant source of insecurity and to agitate for a change in the system.

Such agitation was increasingly formulated within the concept of 'tenant right', a claim sporadically recognized as of some validity by landlords in some parts of Ireland, particularly in Ulster, whence such recognition had come to be known as 'the Ulster custom'. The claim implied a code of relationship between landlord and tenant which acknowledged some fundamental interest in the property for the tenant as well as the landlord and sought ultimately to cover the so-called 'three Fs': fair rent, fixity of tenure and the freedom for an outgoing tenant to sell his interest in his holding to an incoming tenant.

O'Connell's Repeal movement had drawn much of its popular strength from the belief that an Irish parliament would magically transform the land system. To the vast audiences O'Connell enchanted at public meetings, he consistently suggested that this would be the great effect of Repeal: to enable an Irish parliament to do justice to the Irish people on the land. But any such immediate prospect disappeared with the Famine.

A last-minute ineffectual attempt by Young Ireland to raise a nationalist rebellion in the south of Ireland in 1848 had ended in a pathetic disturbance to be known as the battle of the Widow McCormack's cabbage garden. Thereafter, for the time being the Famine created almost as shocking an emptiness in politics as it did on the land among the tumbled homesteads. 'For the first time these many years,' declared an Irish newspaper in August 1848, 'this country is without any political association. There is no rallying point ... A more prostrate condition no country was ever in ...'

Only slowly did new rallying-points emerge. In tune with the chastened mood of the country after its shock, the political reawakening when it came was at first moderate and restrained. A 'tenant right' movement – the Tenant League – was founded in 1850, and for a time a small group of Irish Members in the House of Commons pledged themselves to act together for this independently of English party affiliations. But it soon succumbed to the political pressures of a Westminster Parliament in which the interests of the Irish tenant farmer seemed by no means the most urgent. In any case, a tranquillizing element in the situation was the comforting early impression that the Famine, for all its harshness, had, with the subsequent emigration, most successfully relieved the strain on the land system; and this impression was even strengthened by the impact of a series of good harvests and high prices between 1853 and 1858.

For a time a number of Irish tenant farmers felt relatively prosperous – which, in Irish terms, meant that, though a larger proportion of what they cultivated than they would have liked still went to pay the rent, they could feel reasonably sure that they could pay it and stay relatively secure in their tenure of the land. Officially listed agrarian outrages – a good indicator of conditions on the land, since they included the sending of the threatening notices by which the long-established agrarian secret societies maintained some protective hold on the countryside – fell from 1,362 in 1850 to 255 by 1855, a figure around which they settled for over a decade. In that year a knowledgeable observer of the Irish scene could write that as a result of the Famine the old land system of Ireland had been remoulded 'into a hopeful system' and that 'the rude shocks of famine' had 'preluded the emancipation of the soil and the regeneration of Irish agriculture'.

But already by the early 1860s three bad harvests in a row had made it clear to anyone concerned with land conditions in Ireland that nothing had changed fundamentally and that talk of a new 'hopeful system' and 'emancipation of the soil' was optimistically astray. The commentator who had used those phrases looked back at them from the end of the 1860s and found them embarrassing, conceding that 'Time, unhappily, has not fulfilled the brightest hopes which, in common with most other persons, I formed of the future prospects of Ireland in 1854–5.' No dramatic deterioration was to occur for many years, but an awareness that there was a land problem which was still unsolved formed part of any realistic appraisal of political conditions in Ireland. And the underlying discontent generated by the bad harvests of the early 1860s contributed wide latent sympathy at least, though limited active support, for a new political movement on nationalistic lines that had sprung from the ashes of Young Ireland. This was the conspiracy of which, in the summer of 1865, news came to disturb – however slightly – the Ascendancy world of the young Charley Parnell and his cricketing companions.

The new movement was very different from O'Connell's and was embodied in a political secret society (a type of organization he abhorred) to be known as the Irish Republican Brotherhood (IRB), formally founded in Dublin in 1858. Its members were known popularly by the name given to the Brotherhood in America, after a legendary Gaelic warrior band, as 'Fenians'.

The Fenian movement constituted the first full-blooded expression of serious political nationalism since O'Connell's time, but of a different order. Its founders were men of a consciously radical disposition. Some had been junior participants in Young Ireland's half-hearted and abortive attempt to raise the peasantry in 1848. They were determined now to be more effective, and they defined the Irish 'cause' in sharply uncompromising political terms, taking as their aims those which the Protestant radical Wolfe Tone had proclaimed for the United Irishmen of the 1790s: total separation from Britain and a national republican independence to be achieved by physical force. They had also found new models as well as old, having spent some time in Paris after 1848, where they had acquired a knowledge of the secret European revolutionary societies which then flourished there. They had absorbed something of the democratic radicalism of these societies as well as of their arcane procedures. Secret societies were in themselves no novelty in Ireland, but, with the principal exception of the United Irishmen, their pattern had been primarily agrarian rather than political, though in some instances with strong national undertones. By the oath of the new secret Brotherhood, its members swore loyalty to an 'Irish Republic now virtually established'.

The new movement had two important sources of strength. The first was the mass of Irish emigrants in America, filled with bitterness for what had happened to them in their own country under British government during the Famine and now, living as citizens of a separate country, able to canalize their feelings into hatred of Britain. Their political potential in terms of cash and manpower was enormous, and a sizeable proportion of that manpower had in the course of the American Civil War of 1861–5 received military training in modern warfare.

The movement's other source of strength, at least at first, lay in the personality of its then leader in Ireland, a Protestant and former railway engineer named James Stephens. Stephens was an egotistical but energetic man who was for some years the movement's dominating figure on both sides of the Atlantic. In a series of tours through Ireland during which he seems to have persuaded at least some members of the secret agrarian societies to subscribe to his own political ends, he had by 1865, by his own reckoning, some eighty-five thousand men effectively organized in Ireland, drilling and even running their own primitive munition factories, in preparation for an eventual rebellion to be carried out with American Fenian support.

The authorities in Ireland knew something of what was going on through their detectives and informers, but on the whole they knew only enough to make them apprehensive of what they might not know. The situation was confused for them by the fact that Stephens had initiated in Ireland an open public side to the movement in support of the American Fenian Brotherhood, and in 1863 had launched a weekly newspaper, the *Irish People*, to extol American Fenian ideas and propagate the theory of a Wolfe-Tone-like concept of Irish nationality, while not itself openly advocating insurrection.

By 1863 this invisible Fenian 'threat' had in fact already begun seriously to disturb the post-Famine tranquillity of Irish public life. It had even penetrated to the social world of the Viceregal Lodge in which Mrs Parnell figured. At a daytime reception which she attended there on 27 June 1863 (her son Charley's seventeenth birthday) with three of her daughters, Emily, Sophia and Fanny, and some seven hundred other people, the Earl of Carlisle – the Viceroy and Lord Lieutenant – while commenting in his diary that 'all did well', also remarked that Lord Shannon was 'uneasy about drilling in his neighbourhood'.

How disturbed Mrs Parnell and her daughter Fanny in particular might have been by such information, had they heard it, must be uncertain, though in view of the family's fairly steady association with the viceregal court it seems unlikely that they would have approved the violent overthrow of all it stood for. However, it also seems that, for the fourteen-year-old Fanny Parnell at least, some romantic sympathy with those concerned for 'Erin's' plight could be compatible with such social activity. In the following year, 1864, within a period of four months she contributed four poems to the *Irish People*, under the pseudonym 'Aleria'.

The *Irish People*, run by leading members of Stephens's secret organization, was a plausible 'front' product, an elegant, well-printed paper, edited by a man of some literary taste, John O'Leary, who over a quarter of a century later was, together with Stephens, to sit in a forward carriage at Parnell's funeral. In many ways the paper looked more like a literary weekly than a political journal, containing regular contributions of original poetry, literary reviews and an intelligent correspondence section. Nevertheless, even as romantic fantasy, there is no mistaking the belligerent radicalism in Fanny Parnell's adolescent poems of this period. One, entitled 'Massada', scene of the heroic Jewish mountain stand against the Romans, ended

> God hath seen and God hath heard you,
> God will soon arrive to save.

It carried an obvious analogy with a beleaguered Ireland. Another, entitled 'The Poor Man to his Country', for all its awkwardness made no concessions to analogy at all. Its last stanza ran:

> O brethren, prove the mettle of your work by noble deeds;
> Far better he who in the patriot's strife untimely bleeds,
> Than he who spends a long inglorious life in heaping gold,
> With heart that unto Erin's sacred cause is false and cold;
> Not such are we – oh we would scorn to fly from poverty!
> All suffering would we gladly, boldly face for liberty;
> Yea, and the poor man's hand on Erin's brow shall place the Crown,
> When 'neath the poor man's sword usurping might in the dust lay down.

What Fanny's brother Charley, who was particularly fond of her, might have made of such a poem is not known. She herself had been at the Viceregal Lodge for a reception only a few months before its appearance. And it was a few months afterwards, in 1865, that Charley was gazetted Lieutenant in the Wicklow Militia.

Had the identity behind the pseudonym 'Aleria' become known, it must have caused him embarrassment among his fellow-officers as well as among those landed gentry and regular officers with whom he played cricket more enthusiastically than ever during the summer of 1865. He may have been personally relieved to hear, the day after his last match of that season on 16 September 1865 at Navan (in which he scored two and eight run out and made a catch in the opposing team's second innings), that the Government had struck at the conspiracy during the night, arresting its leaders on the staff of the *Irish People* and suppressing the paper itself. While Fanny attended at least one of the Fenian trials that followed, at which the prisoners, including O'Leary, were sentenced to long terms of imprisonment, Charley himself, a few weeks later, went up to Cambridge as an undergraduate of Magdalene College, where he was to remain on the books for four years.

Many years later, when he was deep in politics, and had a certain interest in saying such things, Parnell said that he had watched the Fenian events of 1865 and subsequent years 'with some interest and attention'. But it was on the same occasion that he also admitted he had paid no close attention to politics until 1872, by which time the Fenian conspiracy in its original form had totally collapsed. It was certainly his brother John's distinct later recollection that in fact the Fenians made no particularly favourable impression on 'Charley' at the time. Moreover, while more Fenian trials were in progress during the following January, 1866, on the 30th of that month Parnell attended the Viceroy's first levee of the year at Dublin Castle and was 'honoured with invitations' to two grand balls at the lodge of the Chief Secretary for Ireland in February 1866.

Searches for Fenian arms were then proceeding almost daily. No one living in Ireland at the time can have been unaware of the Fenians; with their American connection, they constituted a threat long after the arrest of most of the original leaders and the eventual replacement of Stephens as Chief Organizer, by an American colonel named Thomas J. Kelly. Throughout 1866 American ex-soldiers of the Civil War continued to arrive in Ireland for an anticipated rising; they were said to be easily recognizable from their square-toed boots and felt hats. It was some of these, in fact, who were responsible for focusing the young Parnell's particular attention on Fenianism in that year, even if nothing else had done.

Numbers of these footloose American soldiers of fortune were being arrested by the Government and held without trial under the suspension of habeas corpus in Ireland. As an American, Mrs Parnell, who was living with her family at 14 Upper Temple Street, Dublin, concerned herself for the welfare of her imprisoned fellow-countrymen, particularly three men, Captains O'Boyle, Murphy and O'Doherty. Her work on these men's behalf seems to have led her to see some Fenians who were still at large and were active in the conspiracy, though it also seems that she cannot have realized exactly who they were and that they passed off their interest as being, like hers, philanthropic. The arrival of visitors at 14 Upper Temple Street, some of them presumably American, had aroused suspicions in Dublin, and 'highly respectable persons' reported to the Superintendent of the Dublin Metropolitan Police's 'G' (detective)

Division that Mrs Parnell was 'active in aiding the Fenian conspirators'.

Unfortunately for her, a chemist's shop only a few doors away, at 3 Upper Temple Street, was being used by the Fenians as a meeting-place. One of the chemists there, a leading Dublin Fenian, had been busy seducing members of the military from their loyalty with the Irish Republican oath, and distributing arms. When, on 3 December 1866, the police went to 3 Upper Temple Street and arrested him, they found a letter from Mrs Parnell in his pocket. His assistant in the chemist's was also arrested and in a statement said that they had 'a patient' at 14 Upper Temple Street. The police jumped to extravagant conclusions and began to think they might find one of the Fenian 'centres' for all Ireland for whom they were looking, a man named Duffy, in Mrs Parnell's house.

In fact the assistant's remark seems to have been quite innocent, for he was later discharged by the police as uninvolved in the Fenian affair. He was almost certainly referring to Mrs Parnell herself as the patient, for we know she was 'indisposed' that week. On top of the report about Mrs Parnell from 'highly respectable persons', however, this was enough to spur the police to immediate action. The Superintendent of 'G' Division determined to 'clear up all suspicions', and had Mrs Parnell's house searched on the morning of 6 December 1866.

Mrs Parnell was in her bedroom 'indisposed' and three of her daughters were at breakfast when the police arrived. Their visit must have come as something of a shock to her, for one of her daughters had after all been dining at the Viceregal Lodge only just over a fortnight before. The whole house was now searched, and Mrs Parnell was asked to leave her room for that purpose, while the Misses Parnell were not allowed back into their own rooms except in the presence of policemen. Mrs Parnell explained her interest in the Fenian prisoners, and copies of letters relating to this, though not very numerous, were removed by the police to be 'read over at leisure'. According to the Superintendent, 'the search was made as quietly as was practicable and Mrs Parnell did not appear to feel much annoyed, but on the contrary was quite calm and cool and seemed to understand the expediency of searching all suspected places under existing circumstances'.

Three weeks later the Superintendent received an unpleasant surprise. The Chief Secretary, Lord Naas, asked him for a report on the incident, having received a sharply worded complaint direct from Mrs Parnell. A large body of police, she maintained, had arrived at the house, taken complete possession of it, and placed everyone under arrest. Her and her daughters' private letters were read and many were taken away, though she added tartly to the Chief Secretary, 'the police having acted as the instruments of others had the good feeling to apologize before leaving'. She described the incident as an outrage and an insult to her family, and requested that her papers be restored. The Chief Secretary seems to have considered the complaint as a matter of some urgency, for he dealt with it on Christmas Day itself.

The Superintendent, in a self-justificatory memo, explained the reasons for the search and drew attention to Mrs Parnell's rather milder attitude at the time. The letters can have contained nothing suspicious, for they were now returned to her with great regret for 'the necessity which recent circumstances have imposed on the police authorities of making searches in private residences'.

Moreover, the suspicions must have been dismissed for all time, since – and this is probably evidence that no hard feelings survived on either side – Mrs Parnell was back at a Viceregal entertainment when a great ball was given in Dublin Castle on 7 March 1867. The date is particularly significant, for only two nights before an abortive though momentarily alarming Fenian rising had at last broken out in the mountains round Dublin and in other parts of Ireland. It was quickly brought under control.

The only real mystery in the affair may be found in the three-week delay which occurred between the search and the complaint, and Mrs Parnell's sharpening of attitude in the interval. Perhaps it is not over-fanciful to suggest that Charley Parnell, at Magdalene, Cambridge, when the raid occurred, but having returned for the Christmas vacation, became indignant at hearing what had happened and persuaded his mother to protest. Some years later he told a colleague, with some poetic licence, that the first time he ever thought seriously of politics was when he heard of the search and of how the police had insisted on penetrating even his mother's bedroom. If he had been there, he said – and his eyes 'lit up with fire' as he said it – he would have shot the policeman. Whether or not he inspired the complaint to the Chief Secretary, it is revealing that what he later chose to regard as an early political motivation should have sprung from pride rather than from any political consideration. In fact, according to his brother John, his dislike for the Fenian sympathizers with whom his mother had been in contact was as strong as his resentment of the police, and he had on more than one occasion literally kicked them out of the house. The abortive rising itself in March 1867 seems not to have affected him at all.

The shooting of a policeman by an Irishman later in 1867, in the course of a rescue from a prison van in Manchester, was a Fenian event that obviously registered in his mind at the time as it did in that of most other Irishmen. And it is clear from something he was to say nearly ten years later that he came to share the conviction of a great many Irishmen that the Fenians subsequently hanged for the shooting had been executed for their Irish political affiliations rather than for the deed itself, which was an accident. But there is no sign that the incident helped to form within him any coherent political thought at the time, and his brother John categorically denied that the Fenian movement 'in any sense' had an influential effect on him.

Parnell's lack of serious interest in politics at this age might even seem remarkable were it not typical of the young Protestant Irish squirearchy of which he was still representative. In the field of respectable national politics, a lead was being given by a body under Catholic leadership, the Irish National League, which had inherited the objective of O'Connell's movement for Repeal and for the creation of an Irish parliament under the Crown. But it lacked the dynamism and mass support of O'Connell's movement and lingered on perfunctorily, a Catholic middle-class affair, backed by priests, of weekly meetings and educated speechifying in public halls, largely confined to Dublin. Fenianism had attracted some popular support among the poorer classes in towns as well as in the countryside, but on nothing like the scale of O'Connell's movement. Its attempt at rebellion had been a total failure. But it had inevitably raised the general political temperature, incidentally reanimating long-voiced demands for the disestablishment of the Protestant Church and for some legalized measure of tenant right. It had even by his own later admission converted the leader of the English Liberal Party, Gladstone, to a belief that such measures were necessary to do 'justice' to Ireland. There is no sign, however, that any of this excited serious political interest in Charley Parnell during the four years he was at Cambridge, between 1865 and 1869.

Chapter 4

In later life Parnell spoke little about his time at Cambridge and, on at least one occasion when he did so, said that he had thought a good deal more about cricket than about his studies there. In fact he does not appear even to have played a great deal of cricket. He did not get a freshman's trial, and he played only occasionally for Magdalene and not at all in any university team. All of which only confirms the impression that his four years' attendance at the university was an experience he went through more for convention's sake and from a lack of compulsion to do anything else, than with any particular purpose or enthusiasm. Certainly a contemporary of his at Magdalene, though writing forty years later, seems to have classed him as one of the 'three or four genuine loafers' in the college in his time – 'men, that is to say, who were keen about nothing'. Certainly he took no advantage of the facilities for political involvement there. During his very first term there was a debate at the Union on the proposal to disestablish the Irish Church, and it turned out to be the best-attended debate of the term, but Parnell never became a member of the Union.

Magdalene at this time was one of the smallest colleges in Cambridge, with only sixty-six undergraduates, of whom forty-eight resided in college and the rest in lodgings in the city. Parnell had rooms on the ground floor of the right-hand cloister in the Pepysian buildings (now part of the library). Some nervous tension in his psychological make-up is suggested by his mother's warning to the college that he still occasionally walked in his sleep as he had done since childhood. A college servant was instructed to sleep in an adjoining servant's room as a precaution, but, finding the man there on his first night, Parnell brusquely sent him away.

Besides being a small college, Magdalene had a reputation for being smart, high Tory and one of the wildest and most laxly disciplined in the university. Perhaps because its academic admission standards were not exacting, it attracted a number of what a snobbish contemporary later referred to as 'sons of monied parvenus from the North of England' who 'tried to liken themselves to country gentlemen and succeeded in looking like stable boys'. Parnell, with almost five thousand acres in Co. Wicklow and his lineage in the Irish gentry traceable directly back for two hundred years, could not conceivably have been taken for one of these; yet it is significant that it was among these sons of social outsiders at Magdalene that he found some of his friends. In the 1860s there was still a sense in which an Irish gentleman, proud enough at home, could find himself isolated among English gentry and made to feel at least different if not inferior. Far apart as Parnell's family background may have placed him from the mainstream of Irish identity in Ireland, he was early aware that, where England was concerned, his identity was Irish.

In spite of what he himself said about his neglect of studies at Cambridge, there is some evidence of his having done some work. Although marked 'absent' from his college midsummer examinations at the end of his first year, he did succeed in passing, at the beginning of his second year, his 'Little Go' examination in the category 'First Class' – no particular feat, perhaps, since 362 Cambridge undergraduates out of a total of 503 taking it did the same. The examination included a paper in Latin and Greek, and a little more Euclid than usual that year. Writing thirty years later, a contemporary of his at Cambridge said that Parnell had had 'a considerable aptitude for mathematics' and that one of his tutors had described how, when given the ordinary solution of a problem, he 'would generally set about to find whether it could not be solved equally well by some other method'.

In general, very little is known of Parnell's four years at Magdalene, and lack of material has led to some inventive filling of the gaps. His sister Emily, writing forty years afterwards, told a story of his Cambridge days which some later biographers rashly accepted at face value. Parnell, she said, 'one of the most enthusiastic oarsmen on the river, spending nearly all his spare time in flannels', fell in love with a farmer's daughter called Daisy whom he had often seen picking fruit in an orchard as he rowed past; he seduced her, made her pregnant, and then abandoned her. The girl committed suicide by throwing herself into the river. Parnell, so the story ended, came along the river-bank just as her corpse was being dragged out of the water, and appeared as a witness at the inquest.

The fact that Parnell rowed neither for the university nor for his college – indeed was exceptional in refusing to participate in the college boat – suggests that Emily must have made some mistake here. But that does not necessarily wholly invalidate the story, and it understandably troubled his later admirers. One of these, the Irish Nationalist MP Henry Harrison, who, as a very young man knew Parnell in his last years and indeed was one of those to view him in his coffin in Brighton, later wrote a book to vindicate him on more than one charge, including that of causing this girl's death. He found from coroners' records not only that no girl called Daisy had been drowned in Cambridgeshire while Parnell was at Cambridge, but that no girl called Daisy had been the subject of any inquest at all while he was there. Moreover, in view of a confused statement by Emily to the effect that the incident, which according to her took place in Parnell's second year, was also the reason for his leaving the university (where in fact he stayed four years), Harrison took the trouble to ascertain that no inquest on any drowned girl of any name had taken place in Cambridgeshire during Parnell's last eleven months there. Oddly, he does not seem to have realized that this would be irrelevant if the incident had in fact taken place in Parnell's second year. Emily said she had circumstantial evidence to confirm the story. She remembered how, late one night when she had been staying at Avondale, Parnell had woken from a nightmare moaning about a girl called 'Daisy', having even thought he had seen the figure of 'Daisy' standing at the foot of his bed.

The impression left by Emily's book is that, though there was probably some substance in most of its facts, these were distorted not only by the long interval between occurrence and recording but also by the efforts of some ghost-writer to make the book as vivid as possible in the light of Parnell's final notoriety. We know from his mother's warning to the Magdalene authorities that Parnell suffered from sleepwalking; he may well have had some such nightmare as Emily described when she was staying at Avondale. It may be odd that R. Barry O'Brien, Parnell's first biographer, who consulted Emily personally some ten years before the publication of her book, made no reference to the story, but then he omitted much embarrassing detail that was undoubted fact from Parnell's later life as well. Emily afterwards claimed that she had had the story both from their mother and from Sir Ralph Howard, joint guardian of the children, and that because of it Sir Ralph had cut Charley out of his will. In fact his will had been drawn up long before Parnell went to Cambridge. More useful evidence is provided by the behaviour of Parnell's younger brother, Henry, on publication of Emily's book.

If the story of the seduction and its tragic consequence had been true, it is unlikely that Henry would not have heard something of it before, for he was already eighteen in the year his brother came down from Cambridge. Yet clearly he had heard nothing about it at all, for on publication of Emily's book he immediately wrote to the authorities at Magdalene College to seek enlightenment, and he even suggested that the story might have arisen from a confusion of his brother's name with that of one E. K. Purnell, who had been a contemporary of his brother's at Magdalene. Since E. K. Purnell – by then a master at Wellington School and writer of the official history of Magdalene – was more highly thought-of by a Tory college than C. S. Parnell, the suggestion was not well received. But Henry Parnell's total mystification (and he mentions that of other members of the family too) is a sizeable addition to the weight of suggestion that the story was substantially untrue. John Parnell, the brother closest to Charles, made no mention of the story at all when he published his own book many years even after Emily's. This could of course be taken as an inference either way. But very convincing evidence against the story can be found in the statement of a Senior Fellow of Magdalene in residence at the time Parnell was there. Though apparently unfavourable to certain aspects of Parnell's career, he wrote that he could 'positively declare that no story or report to his discredit such as is alleged, ever reached my ears, while had there been such a rumour I must have heard of it'. And he added that there was nothing against Parnell's character.

Was there no substance in the story at all? For all Henry Harrison's diligent researches, he did neglect one tangential piece of evidence. There was a girl of sixteen who was found drowned in Parnell's second year at Cambridge. Her name was Annie Smith, and the verdict on her was that she had committed suicide after accidentally setting fire with her night-candle to the curtains of the inn at Grantchester where she worked as a servant. No undergraduate attended the inquest. It is not wholly impossible that the twenty-year-old Parnell may have known her or even have formed some affection for her and been upset by her death. To have got a two-syllable girl's name wrong would have been by no means the only slip in his sister's book. If, however, the real-life Annie was the fanciful Daisy, there is one more fact that is relevant, and it alters the whole nature of the story as it affects Parnell. For the post-mortem on Annie Smith revealed that she was not pregnant.

At the end of his second year at Cambridge Parnell reached the age of twenty-one and entered his full inheritance as owner of Avondale. The local *Wicklow News-Letter*, describing the birthday celebrations there – the bonfires, the merry-making and the frequent and hearty expression of wishes for the health and happiness of the young squire – wrote, 'Mr Parnell is a young gentleman of no ordinary talent and capacity, and we hope ere long to see him assume that position in his native County to which his own talents and station as well as his ancestral antecedents so fully entitle him.'

Nothing could then have seemed more improbable than the manner in which this prophecy was one day to be fulfilled. In all the paper's conventional tribute, one note alone suggests something of what was later to seem so much part of the character of the man: his elusiveness. For, from these festivities celebrating his coming-of-age, he was 'unavoidably absent . . . his presence being required for important legal business in the Court of Chancery'. He made amends three weeks later with a cricket match held at Avondale on Saturday 20 July 1867, of which the newspapers merely recorded that it was to be between 'Mr Parnell's XI' and 'Mr Crossdale's XI' and was to start at 11.00 a.m.

This is almost certainly the July cricket match 'shortly after he came of age' beginning at 11.00 a.m. described in vivid and almost sensational detail in his sister Emily's book. According to her there was a large house party to which she acted as hostess, composed of officers and pretty women, and the champagne flowed freely to the accompaniment of music by day and by night. The match, which had been scheduled to last three days, virtually disintegrated on the second and third days in favour of general revelry and pastoral flirtation under a cloudless sky. The young man whose coming-of-age was being celebrated spent some time in the company of a 'Miss May P –', for whom his pet name was 'Mouse', but, though her father hoped she would marry him, 'Charles could never be brought quite to the point, and May afterwards married a lord.' Retrospective romantic colouring probably figures in Emily's description of the event, but in general it may be a reasonably authentic evocation of the lifestyle of the Irish gentry to which Parnell succeeded on his majority.

Not incompatible with this was his first dilettante excursion into political activity in the following year, 1868, when, during the general election, he absented himself from Cambridge for part of the term to canvass for his Whig kinsman and fellow landowner the Hon. H. W. Fitzwilliam, who was standing as a Liberal for one of the two seats in Co. Wicklow. Fitzwilliam was duly elected. Another kinsman was elected as a Conservative.

Fitzwilliam was the great-grandson of a famous Viceroy of the end of the eighteenth century who had early favoured Catholic Emancipation. In his election address he was vague and well-meaning in the conventional tradition of Irish Whiggery. He favoured 'measures conducive to the improvement of the country, the development of its resources and the welfare of its people'. On the now dominating issue of the disestablishment of the Irish Protestant Church he was in favour of 'religious equality for all' and thought that the Church funds released by disestablishment should be devoted to Irish objectives. On the land question he went out of his way in gentlemanly fashion not to offend. He maintained that where confidence between landlord and tenant existed there was little necessity for legislation, but 'unhappily such is not always the case, and some measure I hope may be devised to enforce on all landlords principles of liberality and fair dealing towards tenants . . . Apart from this and some other questions on which unfortunately differences of opinion may be honestly entertained, there are many subjects of general interest on which all parties may happily agree . . .'

To these innocuous doctrines, Parnell at the age of twenty-two was happy to subscribe.

From his last term at Cambridge, in the summer of 1869, there is one fully documented incident which, because it gives a vivid personal glimpse of the natural aggressiveness which his brother John maintained had been one of his characteristics from childhood, is worth recounting in detail.

By the time it happened, Parnell had, it seems, already earned a reputation for some combativeness of spirit at Magdalene. He told his brother how on one occasion five undergraduates had come to break up his room, but he had succeeded in throwing them all out. A contemporary years later described how, in some town-and-gown fracas after the college gates had been closed, Parnell's tutor had been going out to investigate when Parnell came up to him saying, 'Sir, do let me go out to protect you.' This is only retrospective hearsay, though possibly true enough. Of the incident which occurred in his last summer term there is no doubt. It led to his being sent down for the rest of the term by the Magdalene authorities, and he chose never to return.

Between ten o'clock and half past ten on the evening of Saturday 1 May 1869 a manure merchant from Harston, just outside Cambridge, was walking with his manservant along Station Road, Cambridge, towards the station when he saw a tall man, dressed like a gentleman, recumbent in the pathway with another gentleman leaning over him. The man on the ground was Charles Stewart Parnell, and the man beside him was his friend Robert Bentley, another Magdalene undergraduate, from Bawtry in Nottinghamshire. The manure merchant, whose name was Hamilton, turned to Bentley and asked, reasonably enough, 'What's the matter with this 'ere cove?' Bentley replied forcefully that they didn't want any help from him and told him to mind his 'own damned business'.

The truth was that Parnell with Bentley and two other friends had taken a cab to the station refreshment rooms an hour or so before and had spent some time consuming champagne, sherry and biscuits. Parnell was the worse for drink, though the police constable who testified to this said he was not in a sufficiently bad state to justify an arrest. Bentley and Parnell were simply waiting while their other friends fetched a cab.

Taking affront at Bentley's brusque rejection of his offer of help, Hamilton, the manure merchant, then said that it wasn't usual to insult people when they offered help. According to Parnell in court, what he actually said was that he did not expect 'such bloody impertinence'. Parnell from the ground then asked him what he meant by insulting his friend, to which the merchant replied, 'Your friend has been impertinent and I won't have any from you.' Whereupon Parnell jumped up and, after a short scuffle, knocked Hamilton down with a blow on the mouth which cut his lip and nose. Later in court Hamilton also claimed that he had been struck another blow on the collar-bone which disabled his arm for three days, and that Parnell had kicked him severely on the inside of his right knee. His clothes, including a jacket which cost him five guineas, were stained with blood, he said, and his trousers, which had cost him thirty shillings, were torn in the struggle.

Parnell denied that he had kicked Hamilton, though a surgeon who examined the knee some days later said that a kick was most probably the cause of its injury, and Hamilton's servant testified that he had seen Parnell kick his master twice while on the ground. According to Parnell, after he had floored Hamilton, the servant retaliated by knocking him down, striking him twice in the right eye. Parnell then turned his attention to the servant, who said he was sent sprawling right across the road. Parnell commented laconically in court, 'As soon as I got him down I picked him up again.'

Hamilton and his man, followed by Parnell and Bentley, then went to make a formal complaint at the police station. The constable who took Parnell's name said that Parnell had offered him money to forget all about it, and many years later, when telling the story of this affray to a political colleague, Parnell confirmed that he had tried to bribe the man but had unfortunately offered him a halfpenny in mistake for a sovereign. However, no criminal charge was made against Parnell.

Hamilton had claimed from him the cost of his damaged clothing (£6. 15s. 0d.) and civil damages of twenty-five guineas for assault, which would be given to a local hospital. But, although an attempt was made to reach an amicable settlement, Parnell, thinking the claim inordinately high, had allowed the matter to be brought to court.

Although in Parnell's version of the affair he had received a severe blow from Hamilton on the left eye and had been struck twice on the right eye by Hamilton's servant, he was physically none the worse for the encounter. Two days later, batting for Magdalene on Parker's Piece in a cricket match against Trinity Hall, he made his college's second highest score – nineteen – before being run out. Three days after that he went over to Ireland, thus incidentally revealing his cavalier attitude to attendance at the university in term time. He returned to Cambridge only for the court hearing, which took place on 21 May before a jury.

Feeling ran high in the case. The court was crowded, and Parnell was accompanied by numbers of his friends. His solicitor did not try to make out that he was blameless but said that the sum demanded for damages was extortionate; five shillings, he maintained, would cover the blood-stained clothing which had been produced in court. The Judge in his summing-up read Parnell and his friends a small lecture. It was a most unfortunate thing, he said, that these young gentlemen should hire a fly to go to the station for the sole purpose of taking wine; he did not say there was any 'moral turpitude' in the act, but he did say that had they not committed this indiscretion they would have escaped this unfortunate occurrence. He told the jury that in his view evidence for the plaintiff commanded more respect than did that for the defendant. After a short consultation, the jury found for Hamilton, with twenty guineas damages against Parnell.

Five days later a college meeting was held at Magdalene and it was decided that Parnell should be sent down for the rest of the term. There were only two weeks of the term left, so it was not a particularly drastic punishment. But he never came back to Cambridge and did not take his degree.

Before the summer was out he was involved in another fracas, this time in a hotel at Glendalough in Co. Wicklow close to his own home, Avondale.

There on the evening of Tuesday 27 July an English couple, a Mr and Mrs Coleman, were entertaining guests, including a number of ladies, in two rooms off which there led a small conservatory. On the same evening Parnell with his brother-in-law Captain Dickinson, the undesirable military man whom his elder sister Emily had finally married, and who had a fondness for drink on which the marriage was eventually to founder, were in two rooms upstairs. They knew about the party in progress below them, for Captain Dickinson on arriving at the hotel had wandered into those rooms with his hat on and had been informed that they were private. However, on hearing the sound of a piano from below, Parnell and Dickinson sent for the proprietor of the hotel, a Mr Jordan, and asked him to introduce them to the people downstairs so that they could have a dance. The proprietor demurred, saying that he didn't know the English couple himself and thought it wrong for Parnell and Dickinson to go in without an introduction.

Disregarding this, Parnell and Dickinson went downstairs into the small conservatory adjoining the room where the ladies were. The Englishman, Mr Coleman, and a friend of his named Dwyer remonstrated with them, saying the rooms and the conservatory were hired privately for the evening. A row broke out, as a result of which Parnell and Dickinson refused to leave but ordered brandy and cigars which were brought to them in the conservatory. Meanwhile they deposited their hats and coats in the adjoining sitting-room. Coleman and Dwyer then drew down the blinds between the sitting-room and the conservatory, though one of these unfortunately did not quite reach to the bottom of the window. According to Coleman and Dwyer, Parnell and Dickinson then seated themselves on the steps leading from the conservatory to the sitting-room and gave much annoyance to the party inside by peeping in from under the blind.

The proprietor lost patience and sent for the police. None of the constabulary was to be found in the barracks. Threats were uttered; Parnell was called 'no gentleman' and, though it is not clear who actually struck the first blow, a fight broke out. It was some time before the gentlemen could be separated.

It seems clear from a bald statement of the facts that, whatever the strict rights and wrongs of the case, Parnell and his brother-in-law had taken up a fairly provocative attitude. But this time Parnell was more fortunate than at Cambridge. For the court in which the case of *Ralph Jordan* v. *Charles S. Parnell* came up for hearing on 2 September 1869 was the Petty Sessions in his own local town of Rathdrum, and the two magistrates were Wicklow landowners who were friends of his. They declared that the fact of anyone refusing merely to leave the room of a hotel was not an offence within the meaning of the Act of Parliament and dismissed the case. Dwyer, they considered, had been to blame for starting the fight, and they fined him five shillings with costs – the low figure of the fine making it impossible for him to appeal, though he asked for it to be raised to forty shillings so that he could do so.

The story seems to epitomize a certain aimlessness in the young Parnell's life now that he had given up even the nominal purpose of studying for a university degree and was falling back, at twenty-three, on the not particularly demanding role of landlord to his five thousand Wicklow acres. Five days later he was playing cricket for 22 of Wicklow against the English club I Zingari, but he was disappointingly bowled for nought. Certainly he concerned himself capably enough with the business of his estate, introducing sawmills to cut the timber there in an effort to increase his income, which, though a comfortable one, had at this stage to provide for his mother and his unmarried sisters. And he had a natural position of distinction within the county to give him status. On 27 November 1869, the second anniversary of the execution of the 'Manchester Martyrs', he was returned with two others to be High Sheriff of Wicklow for 1870. He had already been nominated to the Wicklow Grand Jury while still at Cambridge, and of course for some years he had held a commission in the Militia. At least he could settle down within the conventional pattern of his class. But even here he does not seem to have found it easy to commit himself.

His gardener, Thomas Gaffney, won prizes for him with his broad beans and other vegetables, asters, carnations, dahlias, pansies and hollyhocks at the Rathdrum Horticultural Society's annual show; and when a local worthy died the young Parnell was on the committee to present his family with a testimonial, subscribing a rather higher than average sum of five pounds. But he did not become active in the management of the Rathdrum Poor Law Union as his father had done. Above all, on the land question, which had been much aired in Wicklow and elsewhere during 1869, he seems to have had nothing to contribute. Just as he had made no effort to attend an important debate on the subject at the Cambridge Union during his last term at the university, so he did not now join in the considerable local correspondence about it which took place in the *Wicklow News-Letter* of that year. When on 27 December 1869 a meeting of two thousand Wicklow ratepayers was summoned to discuss the land question in the town of Wicklow, he was not present and showed no awareness of it, though the Irish politician Isaac Butt thought it right to send a letter of apology for non-attendance. Parnell did, however, attend Rathdrum Steeplechases, held at Dundrum on 2 May 1870, where he was a steward of the course with, among others, his relative the Earl of Wicklow, his millionaire American brother-in-law Livingston Thomson (married to his sister Delia) and the Liberal Member of Parliament for the County whom he had helped to elect, his relative the Hon. H. W. Fitzwilliam. But he does not seem to have been a fanatical racegoer either, for he did not attend the races at Punchestown a fortnight before or the Baldoyle summer meeting a fortnight later.

Similarly, though both his brother John and his sister Emily describe him as having been fond of hunting, and though Wicklow presented some excellent hunting country, Parnell does not appear in 1870 in any lists of those who turned out either with the Wicklow Harriers or with other famous packs in Kildare and Meath, though the name of Livingston Thomson figures more than once. It is possible that an earlier medical diagnosis of heart disease, which his sister says was to prove erroneous but which had stopped him from hunting at one time, still restrained him, though he was to hunt enthusiastically at least once in later years. But even in his attitude to his favourite game of cricket he seems to have been less committed than usual in 1870, for the Wicklow Cricket Club was one of the few of the hundred or so cricket clubs in Ireland to be still without a Secretary at the beginning of the season in April. He played the game rather less often that summer. He made twenty-four batting for South Wicklow against North Wicklow on 26 July, but did not turn out for the Wicklow team when they played the Dublin club, the Phoenix, on 7 August.

There was, however, a good reason why his attention in this period should have been distracted. He had fallen in love.

Mrs Parnell had by now given up her house in Upper Temple Street, Dublin, and had moved to Paris to live with her brother in his apartment at 122 Champs-Élysées and to be nearer her married daughter Delia, whose house was in the Bois de Boulogne. Visits to Paris now became a regular feature of the young Parnell's life. He stayed with his uncle in the Champs-Élysées and seems to have lived a full social life there, even attending balls at the British Embassy. It was on one of these visits that he was introduced to and formed a strong and serious affection for a pretty and vivacious fair-haired American girl, a Miss Woods from Newport, Rhode Island. Between sporadic returns to Avondale to look after his estates, his preoccupation with her dominated his life during 1870.

Parnell was always a good-looking man. One who knew him in his twenties described him as tall, slim and handsome 'with the figure and face of a Greek statue'. His frame was slight, and his eyes were brown 'with a strange inscrutability of expression'. He had a long and rather large nose which was nevertheless straight and well-chiselled. His mouth was small and finely carved, but easily mobile with pride, passion or scorn. He had a fine, white, lofty forehead. He spoke with the English accent common to many of the Irish landed class.

The beautiful Miss Woods, whom Parnell met at his uncle's apartment, was a wealthy heiress. This can have been no disadvantage, but he seems genuinely to have fallen in love with her, and his feelings appear to have been reciprocated. They met often in the social life of Paris and became, in John Parnell's words, 'almost inseparable'. They were regarded as being engaged. When her parents, who do not seem to have been as enthusiastic about Parnell as their daughter, took her on a fashionable visit to Rome in October, Parnell could not follow her at first but had to return to Avondale on business. He did, however, go to see her in Rome a little later, and the mutual attraction seems to have been maintained. He also visited her again in Paris that winter, after another business visit to Avondale. But it was while he was again back at Avondale in the spring of 1871 that he suddenly received a short letter from her saying that she and her mother were returning to Rhode Island. It made no reference to any engagement.

He rushed to Paris to find that they had left for America. Perhaps to give himself greater freedom of movement, he had, the previous December, resigned his commission as a Lieutenant in the Wicklow Militia (his place was taken by Lord Powerscourt). Now, having obtained some advice from his American uncle in the Champs-Élysées about prospective investment opportunities in the United States, he made these the excuse for a journey there in 1871 to pin down the girl he thought of as his fiancée.

He found her in her home at Newport. She and her family received him in friendly enough fashion, but he was soon disillusioned about the engagement. The girl made it clear that she did not intend to marry him. In a state of great dejection he sent a telegram to his brother John, who a few years before had successfully set himself up as a peach farmer in the state of Alabama, telling him that he was coming to see him. He passed the rest of 1871 in the United States, spending some of the time with his brother and the rest on visits around the country in pursuit of investment opportunities, showing particular interest in coal and iron mines.

During this year Parnell seems to have shown no interest in politics whatever. But then, as his brother said, recalling the visit some twenty years later, 'you could never very easily find out what he was thinking about. If something turned up to draw him, then he would talk; and I was often surprised to find on these occasions that he knew of things of which he never spoke before.' One sentiment that seems to have lodged in his mind, and may well have originated in his Cambridge days when he made friends with undergraduate 'outsiders' from the English provinces, was a conviction that the Irish were despised as Irish. And in this he was thinking of himself, an Anglo-Irish Protestant, as Irish in an eighteenth-century sense. Visiting a state governor in America one day with his brother John, he said afterwards, 'You see that fellow despises us because we are Irish. But the Irish can make themselves felt everywhere if they are self-reliant and stick to each other. Just think of that fellow, where he has come from, and yet he despises the Irish!'

On another occasion during these months, his natural pugnacity seems to have shown itself again when his brother took him to see a fellow Irishman for whom he was building a house. The man made a complaint which John himself described in his later account of the incident as reasonable. 'Charley, however, went quietly over to the man and said, "I tell you what it is, the house is a good deal too good for you."' Coats were off in a flash and the two were only just prevented from flying at each other, but a reconciliation was effected over lunch, where it was decided that Irishmen ought to stick together.

At the same time, in a land of so many poor Irish immigrants Parnell maintained a certain haughtiness. 'For God's sake, John . . .' he said one day to his brother when they were about to visit a Southern colonel, the coal-mining pioneer of Birmingham, Alabama, then little more than a collection of wooden houses, 'for God's sake don't tell him we are from Ireland, as they've never seen a real Irish gentleman, and wouldn't know one if they did.'

The tenderness in Parnell's nature, to which both his mother and his sister testified, revealed itself again after he and his brother had been in a serious railway accident in Georgia. Parnell himself was unhurt, but his brother was disabled for several weeks afterwards. 'No one', said his brother, 'could have been a better nurse than Charley; he was thoughtful, patient, and gentle as a woman.'

The two brothers returned to Ireland together at the end of the year, sailing from New York on the SS *City of Antwerp* on New Year's Day, 1872. Parnell did not speak much of Miss Woods again, though he was to tell his future wife about her. And once he said to a colleague, suddenly and rather sadly, 'You know I was jilted,' as if it explained something about him.

Chapter 5

While Parnell had been away, striking political changes had been taking place at home in Ireland.

The disturbing phenomenon of Fenianism had already prompted the great English statesman who became Prime Minister in 1868, William Ewart Gladstone, to try to remove what he saw as the prime causes of Irish discontent. He had carried through Parliament two important measures designed to do just this: in 1869, an Act which disestablished the Protestant minority's Church as the official Church of the country; and, in 1870, a Land Act designed to help the tenant farmer. For the first time since the Union, a British Government seemed seriously concerned to make the Union work in compliance with the wishes of the Irish people. The key political question now was whether the Irish people would consider that the Government's compliance went far enough.

The disestablishment of the Irish Protestant Church was naturally universally welcomed by the Catholic majority in the country. The Catholic hierarchy regarded Gladstone's declared new policy of 'justice to Ireland' with general indulgence, anticipating with some optimism the concession of separate denominational public education and the foundation at last of a Catholic university, which were now their two principal political concerns. They were thus not, in principle, unfavourably disposed towards a Union parliament. This predisposition in Gladstone's favour was a factor of political importance, for the Church still provided virtually the only nationally organized leadership for the popular masses of Ireland.

However, Gladstone's 1870 Land Act affected a question more directly relevant to the day-to-day needs of the masses than the disestablishment of the Protestant Church, and was far less well received.

It dealt with one, and only one, of the proclaimed inequitable aspects of the Irish land system. It decreed that henceforth a landlord evicting a tenant for any reason other than non-payment of rent must pay to that tenant a sum of money in compensation for the improvements the tenant had carried out during his period of tenancy. In this way Gladstone sincerely hoped to put an end by law to capricious evictions which he understood to be the crux of the Irish land problem. Unfortunately he had not understood the full nature of that problem, as all who sympathized with the tenant were quick to point out.

He had not grasped that the Irish tenant's principal desire was not for compensation for eviction but for avoidance of thought of eviction altogether. The Act did not guarantee him freedom from eviction, however regularly he paid the rent. Certainly Gladstone hoped that the need for the landlord to pay compensation would act as a disincentive to eviction, but he had failed to realize that the sense of competition for land was still a vital psychological factor in Irish society and that a landlord could theoretically recoup whatever he had to pay out in compensation to an outgoing tenant by raising the rent to an incoming one. Compensation could thus be seen as only a very minor disincentive to eviction.

Moreover the Act specifically excluded from right to compensation any tenant evicted for non-payment of rent unless the tenant should take the landlord to court and succeed in getting the rent pronounced 'exorbitant'. Quite apart from the poor man's natural disinclination to take a rich man to court, this left out of account the fact that, although rents were not in general 'exorbitant', the fear ever since the Famine was of rents which might leave the tenant with no margin of subsistence in times of bad harvests. A new, more businesslike type of landlord – nearly always Irish – had emerged after the Famine. Such men had bought up bankrupt estates amounting to about a quarter of the entire land of Ireland; they were proving themselves more purposeful than their predecessors in exacting economic profitability from their property.

In addition to the disappointments of the Land Act, there was another source of disillusionment for those in Ireland initially inclined to place their trust in a new approach on the part of an English Prime Minister. This lay in Gladstone's refusal to release from English prisons a number of Fenians still held under long sentences, among them John O'Leary of the *Irish People*.

It was in a way remarkable that, as early as 1869, Gladstone's Government had in fact shown sufficient clemency to release as many as forty-nine out of eighty of these prisoners. They had, after all, been convicted in one form or another of rebellion against the Queen, and at least one of those released had originally been sentenced to be hung, drawn and quartered. In Ireland, however, all these Fenians were widely regarded not as traitors but merely as misguided men who had tried to achieve for Ireland that improvement in general conditions which many who

abhorred their extremism agreed was necessary. An Amnesty Association,
run by a Fenian named John Nolan but supported by many respectable
men of moderate views, conducted a vociferous and popular campaign
for their release. An indication of the strength of feeling in Ireland on this
score alone can be gauged from the result of a by-election which took
place late in 1869 in Tipperary, when one of the best-known of such
Fenian prisoners, O'Donovan Rossa, then in Chatham prison, was duly
elected against an Irish Liberal supporter of Gladstone. Rossa was of
course disqualified from taking his seat. The election incidentally revealed
a significant popular ability to act independently of Church leadership
when feeling ran high enough, for the Church had backed the Liberal.

Out of these two main, and at first uncoordinated, strands of dissatisfaction with Gladstone's new policy – embodied in the Amnesty Association
and the Tenant League – a new political movement now came about.
This took up the old rhetorical national call from Repeal days: that only
from a domestic Irish parliament could be expected legislation which
would prove adequate and acceptable to Ireland. Soon to be known as the
Home Rule movement, its inauguration was primarily the achievement
of one man. This was an Irish barrister named Isaac Butt, a former
Member of Parliament who, though a Protestant and a man who had
begun political life as a Conservative, had defended in court with great
verve and style the rebels both of 1848 and 1865–7. He was closely
involved in both the tenant-right movement and the amnesty campaign.
It was Butt's respectability from a Conservative point of view that was
important for the movement's inaugural phase, which took a curious
form.

What was to be virtually the last flash of the old independent Protestant
nationalism of the past made its appearance in early support of the new
movement. Protestant Conservatives, resenting betrayal by Gladstone
over Church disestablishment and seeing themselves forced back on their
own resources in Ireland, for a time joined with militant supporters of
tenant right and the amnesty campaign to demand an Irish parliament.
Twenty-eight of the sixty-one members of the first committee of what
was at first called the Home Government Association, founded in May
1870, were in fact such Protestant Conservatives.

However, except as an indication of the sort of independence of mind
which the Protestant gentry could still demonstrate politically, this was a
phenomenon that was to prove of little relevance. Conservative
enthusiasm for Home Rule fell away sharply as it became clear from by-
elections that it was Home Rule as a means to tenant right that com-

manded popular appeal, and that it was the Fenians who provided many of the movement's activists. Butt himself, aware of where real political strength lay in Ireland, was unashamedly stressing the advantages which Home Rule would mean for tenant right, together with specifically Catholic issues such as denominational education and a Catholic university. He was himself elected for Limerick in September 1871, by which time Home Rulers had won four and lost three by-elections since the Home Government Association's formation. In general, the more radical their candidate, the more successful.

A few months later a by-election in Co. Kerry revealed more clearly still the direction in which the new political wind seemed to be blowing. A young Protestant landowner, Rowland Ponsonby Blennerhassett, only just down from Oxford, stood for Home Rule with the backing of many Catholic and Protestant nationalists and succeeded in defeating his Catholic opponent, a nominee of the great local Catholic family the Kenmares, who represented the Gladstonian Liberal interest. Some distinguished nationally minded men supported the Liberal. So did the Catholic hierarchy in the form of the Bishop of Kerry. But many of the lower clergy, it was said, supported Blennerhassett, the Home Rule candidate, and his victory showed clearly a growing identification of popular feeling with the Home Rule idea rather than with Liberalism.

The result of this Kerry by-election had been announced on 9 February 1872, a month after Parnell had landed back in Ireland from America with his brother. It was a recent public event to catch his attention. It is difficult not to think that the example of young Blennerhassett, whose Irish background was similar to his own and who, like himself, was a man of no political experience or skill but who had now acquired for himself the dignity and status of a Member of Parliament, might have struck him as one worth considering in relation to his own future – all the more so, perhaps, since one of the reasons why Miss Woods was said to have rejected him was his lack of consequence in the world. Seven months later Parliament introduced the secret ballot for elections, and according to Parnell's own later testimony it was this Act and its implications for the future which first seriously drew him to politics. Meanwhile he lived at Avondale, looking after his sawmills and otherwise quietly contemplating the relatively unchallenging life of a Wicklow country gentleman.

His knowledge of Irish history at this time was not very great. As a youth at Avondale he had heard a horrifying tale from a gatekeeper who claimed as a child to have witnessed, after the rebellion of 1798, a man being flogged at a cart-tail down the road to Rathdrum by strokes of the cat-o'-nine-tails applied not to his back but to his belly. And the Avondale shooting-lodge itself, Aughavannah, had been built as a military barracks from which to deal with the roving bands who for some time after the suppression of that rebellion had operated in the Wicklow Hills. But such events had long been shrouded in the mists of legend, and even as legend were less a part of the everyday life of a young landlord with five thousand acres than of that of some other Irishmen. The young Parnell's reading, such as it was, seems to have been about horses or science – he particularly enjoyed an account of a brave polar exploration conducted in the interests of science.

One of the very few chapters of Irish history he does seem to have read at this time was concerned with a relatively dull and uneventful episode: that of the attempt to form an independent Irish party to fight for tenant right at Westminster in the early 1850s. This had foundered on a lack of coherent resolution; its members were seduced into joining the two great English parties. Now, however, after the introduction of the secret ballot and in the atmosphere created by Butt's new movement, such a precedent offered some interest to a proud and restless young man whose prospects otherwise seemed aimless, and who might be disposed to contemplate a future in politics in something of a scientific spirit.

Early in 1873 Gladstone finally produced an Education Bill. In trying precariously to please both his English Nonconformist Liberal supporters and the Irish Catholic hierarchy, he deeply disappointed the Catholic hierarchy. The Bill left a proposed new Catholic university unendowed and the sacred principle of separate denominational education in Ireland flouted. The Church which had so patiently looked with indulgence on Gladstone's unrolling policy of 'justice to Ireland' now rushed in the opposite direction.

'It is time to proclaim', declared one bishop in his 1873 Lenten pastoral, 'that we have had enough of legislation from a Parliament ... that confessedly loathes our religion and ourselves because of our religion.' And the hierarchy in a body called for 'most energetic opposition' to the Education Bill from the country's parliamentary representatives.

The nucleus of firm Home Rulers in the Home Government Association seized the opportunity to woo the Church towards Home Rule. At the same time, they set about a much-needed reorganization of the Association. After a four-day conference held in Dublin in November 1873, it was replaced by a new body, founded under Butt's leadership, to be known as the Irish Home Rule League. This was dedicated to the establishment of a domestic or federal Irish parliament, under the Crown, with a claim to control Irish affairs only. Two months later, before the new Home Rule League had had time to organize its national machinery effectively, came the surprise news that a general election was to be held in February 1874.

According to John Parnell, if his brother's pursuit of the beautiful Miss Woods had been successful, or if he had liked America better on his long visit, he would never have involved himself in politics at all. He would have stayed in America and, busying himself with his investments, would have become a wealthy but unremembered mining magnate. However, for two years now – 1872 and 1873 – he had stayed at Avondale with John, grouse-shooting, arranging coursing matches, looking after the sawmills and the turf production on his estates, acting as steward at local race-meetings with the aristocracy and other gentry, paying visits to London – where his former guardian Sir Ralph Howard died, leaving a substantial sum to John Parnell – and to Paris – where his uncle died, leaving a fortune to his mother. One morning at breakfast in 1873, John had suggested to him that he should continue the old family tradition of an interest in public affairs and go into Parliament. Knocking the top off a boiled egg, Parnell revealed rather to his brother's surprise that he had been giving such matters a certain amount of thought. He was, he said, in favour of the tenants and Home Rule, but wanted to see a little more of the mettle of the men who were running the new movement first. In the end he suggested that John, as head of the family, should go into Parliament. He left it at that.

As his brother later commented, 'Charley kept his own counsel even as a boy'; it was always quite difficult to know what he was thinking, or even if he was thinking at all. A family servant at Avondale said of him that as a boy he would never do anything at once, 'and when he grew up it was just the same. I would sometimes ask him to make some alterations about the place. "I will think of that, Jim," he would say, and I would think he would forget all I said; but he would come back, maybe in two days' time and say, "I have considered it all," and would do what I asked, or not, just as he liked.'

Late in January 1874, when the writs had just been issued for the general election in Wicklow, and only a short time after Charles Stewart Parnell had again been gazetted High Sheriff of the county, he did persuade his brother John to stand there in the Home Rule interest.

Very many years later John gave two contradictory accounts of how this decision came about after a dinner party, stressing in each case that

Charles had in fact wished to stand himself and had tried to get relieved of his post as High Sheriff of Wicklow – which debarred him from standing in that county – but that the Lord Lieutenant had refused to release him. Contemporary evidence simply states that on the same evening as the writs for the Wicklow election were issued (27 January 1874) John Parnell went to consult Sir John Gray, proprietor of the Liberal-nationalist newspaper the *Freeman's Journal*, and a recent convert to the cause of Home Rule, 'as to the propriety of coming forward'.

Gray seems to have approved. But it turned out that two Home Rule candidates were already in the field for the two Wicklow seats, standing against the incumbent Tory and the incumbent Liberal. John Parnell decided not to proceed with the idea. Then on Saturday evening, 31 January, it was announced that one of these 'Home Rulers' had retired, leaving only a Mr O'Byrne to represent the new cause. Somewhere in Charles's mind a decision was taken: John must stand. Nomination day was on Wednesday 4 February; the poll was on the following Saturday, the 7th. On Monday the 2nd, John Parnell came forward at the end of a meeting of the Co. Wicklow Farmers' Club and Tenants' Defence Association in the town of Wicklow to offer himself as a candidate.

The farmers had already just adopted another candidate (named Archer) to run with O'Byrne. But it was John Parnell who received the nomination on 4 February in the formal presence of the High Sheriff – his brother Charles, who had helped him write his election address. This stressed the ancestral link with Sir John Parnell of the eighteenth century's Patriot parliament and declared for 'Repeal of the Union under its new name of Home Rule'. It also demanded the legalization of the Ulster custom of tenant right for the whole country – 'which is practically Fixity of Tenure' – and came down in favour of denominational education, both university and primary. 'Also,' it concluded, 'owing to the great tranquillity of the country, I think it would now be a graceful act to extend the clemency of the Crown to the remaining political prisoners.'

It was also his brother the High Sheriff who, with his assistants, started counting the poll on the Monday of the following week and declared the result at 1.00 p.m. as follows:

O'Byrne	(Home Ruler)	1,511
Dick	(Conservative)	1,146
Fitzwilliam	(Liberal)	927
Parnell	(Home Ruler)	553

The High Sheriff had been the driving force behind his brother's candidature. He had not been disheartened by the result. Three weeks later Charles Stewart Parnell and his brother-in-law Captain Dickinson had their names put forward for membership at a meeting of the Home Rule League in Dublin. Their sponsor, one of the few original Conservatives who were still prominent in the movement, Professor Galbraith of Trinity College, said of the two gentlemen he was proposing that 'one of them', he hoped, 'before long would have an opportunity afforded him of enrolling himself among the gallant band of Home Rule members – he meant Mr Parnell High Sheriff of Wicklow [*Cheers*]'. Galbraith's proposal was accepted, and so on 2 March 1874 Parnell became a member of the Home Rule League.

'We have got a splendid recruit,' said Butt to a colleague in Dublin, 'an historic name, young Parnell of Wicklow; and unless I am mistaken the Saxon will find him an ugly customer.'

Other political figures who met Parnell that month were less impressed. 'I was struck', said one subsequently, 'by what I thought his extraordinary political ignorance and incapacity. He knew nothing and I thought he would never do anything.'

Such political capacity as he could muster was almost immediately put to the test, for within five days of his becoming a member of the Home Rule League he was signing his own first election address from Avondale. He had been adopted as the Home Rule candidate for a by-election in what had hitherto been the safe Tory seat of Co. Dublin. The vacancy had been caused by the rule of the time which compelled a Member of Parliament accepting office under the Crown to seek re-election – in this case a Colonel Taylor, who had been made Chancellor of the Duchy of Lancaster in the new ministry of Disraeli.

The council of the Home Rule League had had a few doubts about Parnell's reliability as a genuine Home Rule candidate, on account of his class background. But a venerable former Young Irelander of 1848, now MP for Co. Meath, John Martin, had said that he would trust any of the Parnells if they gave their word; and, after taking a look at him along with the rest of the Home Rule League's council, A. M. Sullivan, the editor of the *Nation*, spoke out enthusiastically for Parnell at a meeting of the Home Rule League in the Rotunda, Dublin, on Tuesday 10 March 1874. He proposed that 'we hail with great satisfaction the unfurling of the Home Rule banner, in the county of Dublin, by a gentleman so eminently entitled to command the popular confidence as Charles Stewart Parnell'. He went on to declaim, 'A new race of men have sprung up, and in the County of Dublin to-day the old historic names . . . are once more rising to view. If we have nothing else to point to for all our faith and all our sacrifices in the national cause, we are repaired when we see the names of these men once more coming back to the ranks of the people. [*Cheers.*]'

At this moment, as if on cue, Parnell came into the room and took his seat on the platform amidst enthusiastic cheering; Sullivan commented that 'literally as well as figuratively his friend Mr Parnell had come there'. Continuing, he appealed to everyone present to act as a canvasser in the coming campaign, and to 'constitute himself . . . an Irish Volunteer like one of those which Mr Parnell's ancestor led in 1782'. And he wished that Parnell himself would bring out that banner of his ancestor's Volunteer Corps which hung in the hall at Avondale. 'Torn and tattered and dust-covered that banner might be, but it symbolized one of the most glorious periods of Irish history and it represented a cause that was imperishable and unconquerable. All the power of the British Empire had failed to destroy the principle that had caused that banner to be unfurled.'

The self-centred nationalism of the old Protestant Ascendancy might be remote from and only confusedly and romantically related to the diverse aspirations of Catholic Ireland in the 1870s, but such rhetoric was in fact as serviceable as any in giving coherence to a historical cause difficult to define more precisely than by saying it was Irish and a national one. It can have occurred to no one there, except possibly at some level himself, that the young Wicklow squire on the platform was ever likely to provide more than a happy personification of this traditional rhetorical design. That he was before long to build a realistic Irish political power which after his death would successfully challenge that of the British Empire is something only historical perspective discerns. Yet any twenty-year-old bystander at that meeting who would reach the age of sixty-eight was to witness what to the great majority of the Irish people was then realistically unthinkable: the creation of an independent Irish state.

Butt himself seconded the resolution in support of Parnell, which was carried unanimously. A little later Parnell himself rose to express his thanks.

In writing of this moment some years later, Sullivan said,

To our dismay he broke down utterly. He faltered, he paused, he went on, got confused, and, pale with intense but subdued nervous anxiety caused everyone to feel deep sympathy with him. The audience saw it all, and cheered him kindly and heartily; but many on the platform shook their heads, sagely prophesying that if he ever got to Westminster, no matter how long he stayed there, he would be either a silent Member or be known as 'single-speech Parnell'.

One of those on the platform was the Fenian John O'Connor Power, who also later said, 'we all listened to him with intense pain while he was on his legs, and felt immediately relieved when he sat down'.

The *Freeman's Journal* of the day was more merciful. It merely recorded that Parnell was received with loud applause, that he said the warmth of his reception gave him the greatest possible gratification, and that it made him believe that next week in the polling-booths the men of the county of Dublin would be true to the cause, and return the popular Home Rule candidate at the head of the poll.

His election address was very similar to that which he had helped write for his brother in the Wicklow election. It put Home Rule and his loyalty to the principles of the Home Rule League first. Then came denominational religious education; security of tenure and such an extension of the Ulster custom to the rest of Ireland as would secure to the tenant 'continuous occupation and fair rents'; an amnesty for all Irish political prisoners without distinction; and, finally, equality of treatment for Irish civil servants with English civil servants. He wound up, 'If I appear before you as an untried man, my name and my family are not unknown in the history of Irish politics.' And he made reference both to his great-grandfather Sir John Parnell, the former Chancellor of the Exchequer, and to his relative Sir Henry Parnell, who 'rendered in the British Parliament services to the cause of Catholic Emancipation and of Ireland which the Irish people have not forgotten.' He added, 'If you elect me, I will endeavour, and I think I can promise, that no act of mine will ever discredit the name which has been associated with these recollections.'

Parnell's address was immediately criticized by Colonel Taylor's supporters as being too long. Their own candidate's address ran to only a few lines saying that he appealed with confidence to his old friends. In general the Tories treated Parnell in the campaign with a mixture of resentment and amused contempt. He was 'an adventurer', a stranger, with no property in the county of Dublin, 'half a Yankee'. Colonel Taylor himself said that he had known Parnell's father at Eton and felt sure the son would not be standing in opposition to him now if the father were still alive. He referred to his opponent as 'Charles Stuart', a 'pretender' in the county, and said that the section of Parnell's address which dealt with tenant right looked like little short of confiscation – the transference of the land from the owner to the occupier.

At another meeting, Taylor said he did not have the pleasure of knowing Parnell (whereat a voice called out, 'Who does?') but his opponent had men behind him who would stick at nothing. They had, for instance, been round the constituency pulling down Taylor's placards to try to give the impression he wasn't standing after all. Another Conservative speaker said that if they gave Parnell their confidence he would 'lead them into the mysteries of disguised Fenians'.

The next day the two candidates came face to face at the nomination proceedings and shook hands. Colonel Taylor looked Parnell over, and at an election meeting later that day said he thought his audience would like to know, as almost no one had ever seen his opponent, that 'he didn't look a bit like a winner'.

But Parnell was doing what was expected of him, attending meetings in the constituency and forcing himself to speak, however painful it might be to himself and to others. His often abstracted, rather stumbling manner of political speaking – low-toned, and without any great wealth of vocabulary or ideas – was later, at first, to cause his colleagues in the House of Commons embarrassment. But this very awkwardness was eventually to become something like a rhetorical device, concentrating attention on the forcefulness of what he had to say. Now, the day after he had so distressed his backers at the Dublin meeting, he launched out at least at greater length to about two hundred people in a Temperance Hall at Kingstown where Butt was once again on the platform.

Parnell's handsome personal appearance seems to have made a good initial impression; he was greeted with 'loud and prolonged applause'. But, although he was by no means tongue-tied, his speech was rather flat and mechanical – the performance of a man doing his best to adapt himself to an unfamiliar *métier*. He concentrated on Home Rule as being, as the *Dublin Evening Mail* quoted him,

a question embracing and embodying every other; for when they obtained it they would then have the power to make their own laws upon every matter. They really however in this did not ask so very much. It was only what every country had and what Ireland was entitled to as any other. The name of the Irish people had been distinguished by its men in every country all over the world and nowhere more so than in the United States where they had helped so largely to form the immense numbers that had left these shores and made America what it was. So soon as they got Home Rule they would help produce similar results and similar prosperity here.

A less successful meeting was held in the open air at Terenure three days later. In spite of the fact that an ample platform had been constructed and a large supply of free seats had been provided so that the candidate could be heard on the points in his election address, the meeting had to be abandoned half an hour after it was due to start 'owing to the absence of an audience'. The absence of the candidate may have had something to do with it too, for, in spite of the fact that he had been billed as the attraction, it had to be announced to such audience as there was that he was 'busy with his candidature elsewhere'. In fact one of the journalists who was there maintained later that he had seen Parnell in a jaunting-car behind the boundary hedge of the field, apparently unable to face the meeting and making his getaway.

He did manage to put in an appearance at a meeting in Rathmines two days before polling. An obviously prearranged question was put to him by John Nolan of the Amnesty Association about the desirability of releasing the remaining Fenian prisoners. Gladstone had made a further release of Fenian prisoners in 1871, including the leaders, on condition that they did not return to Ireland. They had sailed to America. But several smaller fry, about whose exact numbers there was some un-certainty, remained in jail.

Once again it did not seem to come naturally to the young Parnell to rise to the occasion. His answer had a slightly lame, even perfunctory, ring about it. He said he thought the remainder of the political prisoners would soon be released, 'as there did not seem to be any gain by detaining them much longer'. This was hardly a crusading reply, but it proved adequate and he thereupon received a public pledge of the Amnesty Association's – and thus the Fenians' – support. As evidence of the breadth of the common 'national' front behind him in the campaign, the pledge was seconded by the former Young Irelander John Martin.

On the whole, Parnell's performance at this first election seems to have been much what his backers expected of him. The impression left is of a graceful figurehead being put forward by more hard-headed political men who were making the most of the past associations of his famous name. He himself was personable, and that was enough. 'We thought him a nice gentlemanly fellow who would be an ornament but no use,' said one nationalist later. Recognizing the need to fill in the background about him for the public, a loyal supporter wrote to the *Freeman's Journal* that he was 'generous in his dealings with his tenantry' and that 'he may be counted amongst the truest and most disinterested of patriots – the finest fellow that breathes'.

The Co. Dublin Tenants' Defence Association had hailed the candidacy of this 'young man of great promise and illustrious descent', as Professor Galbraith described him, 'with the greatest pleasure'. But some unpleasant insinuations had been put about by his opponents to the effect that the Parnell family were in fact not always altogether generous in their dealings with their tenantry. These were occasioned by a dispute between the tenants and the agent on his younger brother Henry's estates. Parnell, reacting sharply to attack, as he was always to do, immediately wrote to the *Freeman's Journal* explaining that he had been in no way, directly or indirectly, connected with the dispute, 'nor could I in any way control or influence the matter'. He privately thought his chances 'slender' enough from the start, and found they 'vanished entirely' in the face of apathy in getting voters to the polls and of Tory landlord 'intimidation'.

When the result of the poll in this safe Tory seat was announced at Kilmainham on 19 March 1874, it was found – not surprisingly – that Colonel Taylor, who had held the seat for thirty-three years, had won it again. The voting was

Taylor   2,183
Parnell 1,235

Seventy-five per cent of the electorate had voted, and the Home Ruler's performance was no worse and even slightly better than that of the Liberal who had last contested the seat in 1869 but who had not bothered to contest it this time. Considering that there were many Liberals in that constituency who were not yet Home Rulers and who probably did not vote, Parnell's reduction of the former majority by forty-two may be seen as a marginally successful achievement.

Excessive Home Rule hopes had, however, been raised and the result was a disappointment to some, though no one suggested that it reflected discredit on the candidate. He himself had attended the count for most of the morning but had slipped away when the result began to look certain. This led to a slight awkwardness, for he was not there to thank the Sheriff, the Returning Officer, as he should have been, on the announcement of the result. He wrote to the newspapers immediately to explain that this was only because he had been wrongly told that the result would be announced at 2.00 p.m. when in fact it was announced at 1.30. He had returned to Kilmainham on time at 2.00 p.m. but found the proceedings over. This trait of implying that he at least was beyond reproach, in a situation in which admittedly reproach was in the air, was to become characteristic.

The election had cost him personally over £1,000 – a considerable sum by the standards of the time and nearer £45,000 in today's terms. One of the servants at Avondale recounted many years later the mood in which Parnell returned to the house on the day of his defeat: 'looking so handsome and grand and devil-may-care'. 'Well, boys,' he recalled him as saying – or perhaps just words to that effect – 'I am beaten but they are not done with me yet.' And the driver of the cab which had brought him home told the servants afterwards that Parnell had talked all the way about fighting again and smashing them all, and that he had looked 'wild and fierce'.

A young Home Rule Member of Parliament, Frank Hugh O'Donnell, who at the general election had been elected for Galway – though he was soon to be unseated after an election petition – also met the young Parnell at this moment. Writing of the meeting many years later, when he had long been critical of Parnell and his policies, O'Donnell was still able to say that he had then 'liked him at once'. Parnell, whom O'Donnell described at the time as 'slight and slightly nervous, anxious to please while modestly firm in his own opinions', had congratulated him on his better political fortune. At first sight he had reminded O'Donnell of his 'very beautiful sister, Fanny', whom O'Donnell had met in Paris, where she was thought of as 'the young American beauty' and was 'always the centre of enthusiastic worshippers of her loveliness and wit'. 'Her brother Charles', continued O'Donnell, 'had just her way of looking with a peculiar wondering glance which was not wonder at all, but critical observation.' Both brother and sister were 'most intelligent', though on public affairs O'Donnell, like others who had met Parnell at this time, recalled him as having been 'phenomenally ignorant'. He had about him an acute family pride, and O'Donnell summed him up as being like a 'grand seigneur manqué'.

But a role was awaiting him.

Chapter 6

The Home Rule 'Party' which had entered the House of Commons after the general election of February 1874 was hardly a party at all in any coherent sense of the word. Fifty-nine of those Irish MPs elected had put 'Home Rule' in their addresses, but even the meaning of the phrase 'Home Rule' was not always precisely agreed among the Members. It was generally assumed to mean a restoration in some form of self-government to Ireland, and with that a due acknowledgement of national pride, but the way in which this was to work in detail had not been closely defined. Isaac Butt, the leader, had outlined a federal type of arrangement by which the Irish parliament should have control of Irish domestic affairs but should leave to the Westminster parliament everything affecting the Crown, including foreign relations, the question of peace or war, and the right to levy taxes in the general interest. It was this 'federal' relationship, with many constitutional questions of detail still to be worked out, which had been adopted in a resolution at the Home Rule Conference just before the general election.

More than one Member of Parliament present at the Conference had pleaded that even this represented already a too rigid commitment to detail, and the resolution did not carry any pledge that its terms should be binding on future Home Rule Members. Several months later one Home Rule Member was able to tell his constituents blandly that he looked forward to seeing in detail exactly what Home Rule was going to mean. In terms of tactics too, the party was very loosely constructed. An attempt at the Home Rule Conference to get future Home Rule Members of Parliament to act together in an organized body on all questions in the House of Commons had been indignantly rejected by a large majority, including Butt himself, as an intolerable infringement of the rights of an individual Member. In fact the only obligations imposed on future Home Rule Members by the Conference had been to vote for an annual Home Rule motion, whatever precisely that might consist of, and to give an account of their parliamentary stewardship to their constituents at the end of each session.

The truth was that the Home Rule banner now embraced a very wide expanse of opinion from all parts of the contemporary Irish 'national' spectrum. At one end there were the Fenians, members of the Irish Republican Brotherhood who, while not abandoning their ultimate goal of total republican separation from Britain, had secretly agreed temporarily to drop their dogma of physical force and to give Butt and the Home Rule movement support for a trial period, probably of three years. Three members of the IRB had been elected to Parliament in the election of 1874: Joseph Ronayne for Cork, J. G. (Joe) Biggar for Cavan and John O'Connor Power for Mayo. Then there were men who, while commending 'Home Rule' in their election addresses, had righteous reservations about anything so moderate as mere federalism and clung with doctrinaire obstinacy to the old orthodox O'Connellite formula of total Repeal of the Union, retaining only the constitutional connection with the Crown.

Of the bulk of the party there was a hard core and a soft core. The hard core consisted of enthusiastic, rhetorical, constitutional nationalists, like A. M. Sullivan, the barrister-editor of the weekly the *Nation*, who had been calling for a restoration of 'the old House on College Green' in general terms for over a decade. These now arrayed their enthusiasm and rhetoric behind Butt and the new movement. The soft core consisted of former Members of Parliament who had jumped on the popular Home Rule bandwagon at the 1874 election and whose dedication to the cause was half-hearted at best. Within three years, one of them who, in accordance with his right under the movement's rules to support whoever he liked in Parliament on all matters save that of Home Rule, usually sat on the Conservative Government benches, was writing of the 'shibboleth' of Home Rule which he had had to accept as the alternative to retirement for ever from public life. 'And many of my colleagues', he added, 'feel the same.'

Even before the new Parliament met, the Home Rule Members' lack of strong cohesion had been sadly manifested. Four of the fifty-nine who had put Home Rule in their election addresses failed to join the party at all. This left a nominal roll of fifty-five. But the effective strength, in terms of attendance both in the House of Commons and at the party's own meetings at its offices in King Street, Westminster, quickly sank to between twenty and thirty. When at the very opening of the parliamentary session Butt proposed an amendment to the Queen's Speech calling for an investigation into the Irish people's dissatisfaction with their government, he was actually opposed on the issue by a member of his

own party, Lord Robert Montagu. And when the moment for the
party's major political début arrived, on the occasion of Butt's first Home
Rule motion on 30 June 1874, the meeting at which the terms of the
motion were drafted was attended by only thirty-two members.

Yet, in the context of the time, what was significant was not the
shortcomings of the party so much as the fact that there was some such
party at all. There had been nothing like an Irish party in the House of
Commons for fifteen years, and even then it had been focused primarily
on the issue of tenant right. Now tenant right and other issues were being
sought within a loftier framework altogether – that of the complex,
imprecise ideal loosely known as 'Irish nationality'. Home Rule had not
yet attained anything like the dimension of O'Connell's movement for
Repeal of the Union, but it was the first positive theoretically national
movement since that time. What seemed immediately exciting was its
potential. Ireland waited to see what Butt and his colleagues would do
with it. It was the excitement of anticipation rather than the disappointments which made an impact.

Thus, when the first Home Rule motion in the Commons – simply a
motion for the House to resolve itself into a committee to consider the
present parliamentary relations between England and Ireland – was lost
by 458 votes to 61, the mood in Dublin was not despondent. 'The result
was a foregone conclusion but it does not exclude the hope of a more
satisfactory issue at no distant date,' wrote the *Freeman's Journal* on 3 July
1874. The next day the paper decided that the Irish had 'good reason to
be satisfied with the great debate', reiterating that 'the wall of
misunderstanding cannot be removed in an hour'.

Butt had made a very conciliatory speech, deploring separatism and
insisting that his plan involved no change in the constitution of the House
of Commons, simply a wish to 'relegate' some of its functions – namely
its Irish business – to another assembly. The English press reported the
debate with harsh realism. 'The speeches of his [Butt's] supporters', wrote
the *Daily Telegraph*, 'had not the ring of reliability which we expect in
the harangues of men who hope to win. They know that they might as
well climb the moon as hope for the creation of a Parliament which . . .
would paralyse the right arm of Great Britain by its hostility to the
Imperial Parliament and which might have to be extinguished at the price
of civil war.'

In Ireland, a country which in politics had long had to put up with the
shadow for the substance, expectation was as important as reality. One
who, in even stronger terms than the *Freeman's Journal*, saw no reason to

be downcast at the result of this first Home Rule vote was the young High Sheriff of Wicklow with the historic name, who for all his political gaucheness had put up such a passable showing as a Home Ruler at the Dublin by-election in March.

Already by the summer of 1874 Parnell was indicating that his sortie into the political field would be something more than the move of a dilettante. He had meant it when he had told his servants at Avondale that he would fight again. He had kept in touch with the men who ran the Home Rule League, and they continued to be pleased by his association with them. When on Saturday 11 July 1874 the first meeting of the Home Rule League after the Home Rule debate was held in a packed hall in Dublin, in the presence of Butt and other MPs, it was Charles Stewart Parnell who was asked to take the chair. He did so to loud cheering, and in opening the proceedings he declared that it was the moment 'to show the world that though beaten they were not vanquished'. Here a voice from the audience called out, 'And never will be.'

Parnell went on to draw an analogy between the present set-back and the far greater disappointments which the Protestant patriot Henry Grattan had had to put up with before winning nominal legislative independence for the old Irish parliament in 1782. He reminded his audience too of how long it had taken to win Catholic Emancipation. 'Let the 11th July', he concluded, 'see the beginning of gigantic exertions for Home Rule by every Irishman who respects himself and loves his country.' He sat down to applause, and thanks were voted to him at the end of the meeting.

He was now a member of the Council of the Home Rule League and in August and again in October he attended meetings at its offices at 29 Sackville Street. At the meeting in October he met a man with whom he was later to be connected in dramatic circumstances. This was one of the founders of the Amnesty Association, a member of the Home Rule League and also of the secret Irish Republican Brotherhood, the owner of a prosperous Dublin baking business named Patrick Egan. Parnell saw a good deal of Egan about this time, and, though he afterwards insisted that Egan never spoke to him about the IRB or told him anything about it, it was by that later date in his interest to play down former revolutionary associations. Even then, he conceded that he 'may have heard from others' at the time that Egan had been a Fenian. In fact, in keeping with the IRB's decision to cooperate with Butt, in addition to the three Fenian Members of Parliament there were several other members of the secret society who in their undercover roles were closely associated with the Home Rule League's activities, and it would have been a routine matter for anyone connected with the League to come into contact with them. At a Home Rule meeting in November which Parnell did not attend, two other men with whom he was later connected in dramatic events with Egan were present: Thomas Brennan and Patrick Sheridan, both undercover members of the Irish Republican Brotherhood.

In those days parliamentary sessions ended in August, and Parliament did not normally meet again until the following February. The autumn of 1874 was spent, politically, in Ireland in a not unoptimistic stocktaking of the Home Rule Party's prospects. But impatience at the lack of progress was being expressed in some quarters. It was countered in a speech to his constituents by the then undercover IRB Member of Parliament for Mayo, John O'Connor Power. Such impatience was, he thought, 'unreasonable'. Both Catholic Emancipation and the Reform Bill, he reminded his audience, had taken years of agitation. 'Whenever', he went on, 'I am asked how long it will take to carry Home Rule I answer: that depends entirely upon the amount of pluck and energy we are prepared to expend on the movement . . . If we bend to our task with a will and work like earnest men, the time will not be distant when the portals of that classic edifice in College Green will be thrown open to receive the elected Members of an Irish Parliament.' When, the next day, a Home Rule meeting at Cork, presided over by another IRB Member of Parliament, Joe Ronayne, was interrupted by recently released Fenian prisoners with cries against the Whiggish character of the Home Rule movement, they were put firmly in their place by Ronayne himself. The IRB was still prepared to stand by its compact with Butt to let him have his chance.

As for Parnell himself, the sense of purpose with which he had by now decided to make for himself a political career, strengthened by the pride and combativeness of his natural character and the independence of mind that was his American and Irish Protestant inheritance, led him to see things much as O'Connor Power did. Pluck, energy and determination were what were needed by the cause he had adopted, and he seems to have relished the prospect of displaying such qualities on its behalf.

The ideological content of his thought at this time is hard to assess. Certainly his lack of real interest in politics up to the later part of 1873 suggests that ideology was not his prime motivation. But he was the sort of man who, having decided to pursue a way of life, would do so single-mindedly and in whom the acquisition of strong feelings would be an automatic result of the pursuit. Certainly events were soon to show that those radical elements in the new national movement which in one sense might have seemed inimical to his conservative social background made a natural psychological appeal to him.

In the meantime, what was impressive was the extent to which he was making up for lost time by doing his political homework. The cause of tenant right was an integral part of the cause of Home Rule – in fact it could still be said to concentrate political energies much more directly than the cloudier appeal of those 'national aspirations' which embraced it – and on 21 January 1875 a well-attended 'Land Conference' took place in Dublin, of which the *Freeman's Journal* said that 'a gathering more important, respectable and representative' had seldom been seen in the Irish capital. Chosen – doubtless primarily for his asset still as a young figurehead – to second a resolution which the *Freeman's Journal* regarded as the most important of all was Charles Stewart Parnell. The resolution was to the effect that Gladstone's Land Act of 1870 had been 'insufficient to remedy the admitted evils of the system of Irish land tenure and that no measure can be just or satisfactory to the people of Ireland which does not give the tenant security of tenure, protection against capricious or arbitrary eviction and also against arbitrary increases of rents, acknowledgement of the tenant's property in the value created by his improvements, and the free and unrestricted right of sale of his interest in his holding'.

In speaking to this resolution, Parnell emphasized that he had a double interest: both as a landlord who wanted the tenant to have an inducement to improve his land and as a tenant farmer himself (though it is not clear to what tenancy he was referring). The remark was greeted with applause. He went on to make two quite radical points, one on the social and the other on a purely nationalist level. In the first he concentrated on what was popularly seen as the heart of the Irish land problem: the question of rents. He pointed out that even the Ulster custom was weak in the protection it gave to the tenant in the matter of rents, and he called for a subcommittee which would see that 'rack-rented tenants might have their rents fairly reduced when they were obviously in need'. Second, while appreciating the Ulster custom, he reminded his audience that originally in other parts of Ireland there had been a far older Gaelic basis of tenure which 'in its original and ancient integrity, many centuries back, gave equal claims to the tenant with those enjoyed by the North at a comparatively modern date'. This is in fact a questionable selective view of the working of the Gaelic social system, but was always much in vogue among nationalists.

The next day he attended a large public Home Rule meeting in Dublin at which Butt took the chair, and in the following month he himself took the chair at an afternoon meeting of the Home Rule League's Council.

Meanwhile, for all his claim to be a tenant farmer, his private circumstances were unmistakably those of a well-to-do landed proprietor. He seems to have been living most of the time at Avondale, though he did not figure particularly prominently in local affairs. He was on the Wicklow Grand Jury, as appropriate to someone in his position, and also a magistrate, though he rarely sat on the bench at this time. Although a member of the parish Board of Guardians, he attended only one of their meetings in the twelve months to 24 April 1875. His family seem sometimes to have stayed with him at Avondale, for his youngest sister, Theodosia, now twenty, performed at a concert in Rathdrum in September 1874, playing 'Home They Brought her Warrior Dead' as a piano solo. He may have visited his mother and sisters in Paris for Christmas.

The anomaly between his social background and his growing political activity was well evidenced in March 1875. On 13 March he was announced as a steward of the Co. Wicklow steeplechases to be run at Rathdrum at the end of April. Among his fellow stewards were to be the Marquess of Drogheda, the Marquess of Waterford, the Earl of Wicklow (his kinsman) and the Earl of Clonmel. By contrast, only eight days earlier he had written to the *Freeman's Journal* a public letter of support for the candidacy at a by-election in Tipperary of a man, still technically an undischarged felon, whose name was a symbol of implacable republican hatred for any form of British rule at all in Ireland.

This was John Mitchel, an Ulster Presbyterian who, as a Young Irelander, had been moved to bitter desperation by the Famine and had at that time openly, though ineffectually, incited the Irish people to revolt, in his newspaper the *United Irishman*. After sentence in 1848 to fourteen years for treason-felony, Mitchel had escaped from his convict exile in Australia in 1850 and had lived ever since in the United States. He had remained unchanged in his fanatical beliefs about Ireland, though wary and sceptical of the personalities who dominated the Fenian movement in the 1860s. With intelligent tolerance, the British Government had let him visit Ireland unmolested in the summer of 1874. He had been accompanied by an American-Irish nationalist of extreme views, a Dr William Carroll of Philadelphia. Observers noted that, though Mitchel was now white-haired, asthmatic and looked older than his fifty-nine years, his eye had 'lost none of its old fire'. He had stayed with Ronayne, the IRB Member of Parliament for Cork, and on his eventual return to the USA he was to write an interesting report on the state of Ireland as he had found it after more than a quarter of a century.

The country people, he said, were now better housed, better clad and much better educated, almost all the young being able to read and write. A calm and settled resolution seemed to have taken the place of the former noisy and demonstrative patriotism that had expressed itself chiefly in threats and boasts – 'no patriot needs to tell them that he is going to lead them in three months to fight the British Army with their naked hands'. At the same time Mitchel found Home Rule too mild a political objective, though he respected some of the men behind the movement. His conclusion was that 'the force, the power now existing in Ireland is that which is designated by the three mystic letters, "I.R.B."'

This was the 'courageous and honourable man' whom Parnell, writing from Avondale, urged the public to support as a matter of 'the utmost importance' and to whose election committee he sent a personal contribution of twenty-five pounds.

The by-election was taking place in exceptional circumstances, for Mitchel had already successfully contested Tipperary the month before but had been disqualified as an undischarged felon. His disqualification was seen as a spiteful and insulting manœuvre on the part of the Government and rallied Irish national feeling even more strongly for him the second time. The Home Rule movement, which had been rather equivocal towards him at the first by-election, for fear of disapproval by the Catholic Church, now gave him its support. Even so, Parnell's intervention was strikingly personal, for he was at the same time one of five honorary secretaries to a testimonial fund then being raised on behalf of his own moderate leader, Isaac Butt.

At the second by-election Mitchel was again elected but again disqualified, and, already ill, died suddenly within the week. His death had immediate practical consequences for Parnell. He had already been sounding out advanced nationalists about the possibility of taking Mitchel's place in Tipperary when, on the way to Mitchel's funeral, another elderly former Young Irelander of national distinction, John Martin, Member of Parliament for Meath, also died. This created a vacancy in the parliamentary representation in that county. Parnell came forward with alacrity to offer himself for that seat.

The very day after Martin's death, Parnell was among four possible candidates being 'confidently spoken of' as a successor. But two of the others had hitherto been nationally more prominent than he, and the other had the advantage of being a local solicitor. Of the two prominent candidates, one was the Lord Mayor of Dublin and the other Sir Charles Gavan Duffy, a leader of the Young Ireland group and editor in

O'Connell's time of the *Nation*, the paper which in the 1840s had first most forcefully and coherently propounded a nineteenth-century romantic creed for Irish nationality. Duffy, unsuccessfully prosecuted in 1848, had since made a respectable political career for himself in Australia and had even been knighted. Now, with the encouragement of some local Meath clergy, he offered to stand as a nationalist for the county, though making clear that he was still a doctrinaire believer in outright Repeal of the Union rather than federal Home Rule.

But the Home Rule League wanted its own candidate. Duffy gracefully backed out. The Lord Mayor made no showing, but the local solicitor, John Thomas Hinds, was determined to stand as a Home Ruler and as such received the support of the local newspaper, the *Meath Herald*. The paper, trusting 'that a stranger would not be imported into the county', saw 'absolutely no reason whatever that a Meath man should not represent Meath'. However, it was the stranger, Charles Stewart Parnell, who was first off the mark with his adoption address, which he published from Avondale on 2 April 1875, three days after returning from John Martin's funeral.

The address was immaculately clear on all the necessary points. 'Upon the great question of Home Rule,' it ran, 'I will by all means seek the restoration to Ireland of our Domestic Parliament, upon the basis of . . . the principles of the Irish Home Rule League of whose Council I am an active member.' He would 'act independently alike of all English parties'.

His next point – a judicious one, in view of the importance of Catholic Church support – was an assertion of the principle of religious education, 'of affording to every parent the opportunity of obtaining for his child an education combined with that religious teaching of which his conscience approves'.

This was followed by an equally clear statement in favour of tenant right. He would support the extension of the Ulster custom to the rest of Ireland, with the object of securing to the tenant 'continuous occupation at fair rents'.

He also called for 'a complete and unconditional Amnesty' for all prisoners suffering for taking part in Irish political movements.

As before, he reminded voters of his ancestor 'Sir John Parnell, in the old Irish Parliament', and of his relative, Sir Henry Parnell, 'who rendered in the British Parliament services to the cause of Catholic Emancipation and of Ireland which the Irish people have not forgotten'. He again wound up with the words with which he had concluded his address to the electors of Dublin the year before: 'If you adopt me, I will endeavour, and I think I can promise, that no act of mine will ever discredit the name which has been associated with these recollections.'

But he had not yet been adopted. His rival Hinds's address covered the same political points but in a few words only, and with a total lack of personal style. Only in the phrase 'Home Rule at Least' did he imply that he might be standing for something more than Parnell's mere domestic parliament.

The *Meath Herald* continued to call upon Parnell to withdraw. But he had the advantage not only of a famous name but of political experience the previous year. The resources of the Home Rule League were put behind him, and by Sunday 11 April he was emerging clearly as the popular candidate. On the evening of that day he went to Kells and received an unexpectedly large ovation from the crowd. After addressing them he was carried on their shoulders to his carriage accompanied by enthusiastic cheering and the strains of a brass band playing national airs. He and his party were then able to drive only a short way before the crowd removed the horse from the traces and drew the vehicle themselves. There was a final chorus of 'God Save Ireland!', the song written to the tune of 'Tramp, Tramp, Tramp, the Boys are Marching' to enshrine the cry of Fenian prisoners condemned to death for the Manchester shooting in 1867. 'Kells', wrote the *Nation* afterwards, 'lit the fire and the whole county quickly caught flame.'

The next day, Monday 12 April, a great county rally held at Navan came out unanimously in favour of Parnell as the official Home Rule candidate. A procession with bands and banners marched through the town from the railway station, with Parnell himself, a 'slight, handsome, delicate-looking figure', accompanied by a party of political dignitaries who had come up on the morning train from Dublin. His great-grand-father's time-worn Volunteer flags from Avondale were carried before him. At a big open-air meeting at which more than thirty priests sat on the platform, one of them contrasted the inadequate political enthusiasm of Mr Hinds in the past with 'Mr Parnell . . . to whose lineage they could look with pride, whose honesty and goodness shone from his very face'. Ireland, he declared, was growing young again.

Another speaker reminded the crowd that, though in Parnell they were advocating the cause of a landlord, he was a landlord who, like his father before him, had never evicted a tenant or changed the rent roll of his estate. This, the speaker claimed, was more than could be said of the great majority of landed proprietors in Ireland.

Parnell was adopted with acclamation, and came forward to immense cheering to thank the crowd. His speech revealed a noticeable improvement in political grasp since the electioneering of the year before. He concentrated at once on the issue that appealed primarily to the electors of a great farming county like Meath – that of the relationship between landlord and tenant – and he spoke in clear, radical terms.

He attacked Gladstone's Land Act of 1870, saying that it had not given the slightest protection to the tenantry over three-quarters of Ireland. Speaking as a landlord, he declared that the tenant as well as the landlord had property in the land, and that a Bill was required to define the tenant's interest and to protect it. In and out of Parliament, he said, he would support 'fixity of tenure and fair rents'.

On Home Rule he said, with questionable hyperbole, that 'since I first could think I had the principles of that movement ever fixed in my heart, for I always believed that the day would come when the voice of the people in this country would rule her affairs and make her laws and that was what I understand by Home Rule. [Applause.] . . . England should remember the example set by her American colonies, and bear in mind that if she refuse to Ireland what her people demand as a right, the day would come when Ireland would have her opportunity in England's weaknesses . . . [*Applause.*]' This seemed to be suggesting that something rather more than a mere domestic parliament could one day be the final goal.

That England's difficulty was Ireland's opportunity was a favourite IRB slogan. The adroit blurring of eighteenth-century 'patriot' nationalism and mid-nineteenth-century Fenian talk into a rhetorical whole was his first public hint of something he was to keep in reserve in his mind for the rest of his life: a refusal in the last resort to commit himself to a limit to Irish nationalism. Such hidden imprecision was to become part of his strength.

According to the *Freeman's Journal*, the proceedings were throughout 'of the most enthusiastic and unanimous character'. A leader in that paper on the eve of the poll endorsed his candidacy with enthusiasm. 'Mr Parnell . . .' it declared, 'is no convert of yesterday, but a tried, proved and faithful servant of Ireland, and we are confident that his parliamentary career will be as honourable and useful as that of his two ancestors who in the old times upheld the Irish cause in our own and the Imperial Parliaments'.

It was already becoming difficult to remember that he had entered politics as something of a dilettante.

Intensive canvassing of the county by Parnell and his friends followed the Navan meeting, and other meetings were held in many towns and villages. A most useful tribute to him by the local Catholic parish priest of his home town of Rathdrum had already been circulated, praising his 'unimpeachable' dealings with his tenantry and stating that the rents on his estate were 'in all cases moderate, and in many instances very low'. It concluded, 'I believe Charles to be a man of great pluck, considerable promise, and of the strictest propriety of conduct.'

By now the candidate apparently felt sufficiently confident to take time off from canvassing to appear in the stands at Rathdrum steeplechases as a steward, with his fellow Wicklow landed proprietors, on Saturday 17 April. There was a large and fashionable attendance from Dublin. What can have been the conversation in the stands that afternoon about the young squire of Avondale, former High Sheriff of the county, and his eccentric departure into the new radical politics of which his fellow stewards and kinsmen must have disapproved almost to a man? Did they comment on it to him? Did they ask him what he thought he was doing? Or joke about it or protest about it behind his back? Or were they just too embarrassed to let themselves talk about it with him there? All we know for certain is the result of the Meath election, which was declared at Trim in the middle of the afternoon of Monday 19 April:

Parnell	(Home Rule)	1,771
Naper	(Conservative)	902
Hinds	(Home Rule)	138

Parnell's majority of 869 was larger than John Martin's had been. 'The young Irish patriot', declared the *Freeman's Journal*, 'is at the head of the poll,' and it went on to state that Parnell had 'no spots on his record' and that he was 'an Irishman – Irish bred, Irish born, "racy of the soil", knowing its history, devoted to its interests'.

In Meath itself, delight at the result was unbounded. In Navan, sprigs of laurel and green boughs were fastened on the fronts of houses. In Kells, Althy, Slane and other places, bands came out and played national airs in the streets, while bonfires were lit all over the county. Parnell himself was kept busy. Immediately after the declaration of the poll he addressed a large crowd outside his own committee rooms at Trim, and later, after a hospitable welcome from the local clergy, a crowd of some five to six thousand people in the streets of Navan. An enormous bonfire of tar-barrels, casks and boxes was lit in front of the priest's house where he was entertained, and on leaving for his hotel he was hoisted on to the shoulders of the crowd, carried round the bonfire, and made to give another short address from the top of a barrel before finally retiring.

'So ended the Meath election of 1875,' concluded the *Nation* of 24 April, 'an election which was of the utmost consequence to the National cause . . .'

No one could then have guessed how prophetic the words would prove.

Chapter 7

Three days later, on the evening of Thursday 22 April 22 1875, Parnell, at the age of twenty-eight, entered the House of Commons for the first time. The slight, tall, fair-bearded figure was greeted with loud cheers from the other Irish Members.

There is a generally accepted view, partly suggested later by Parnell himself and officially promulgated by his first biographer and followed by all others, that he played very little part in parliamentary proceedings for his first two years in the House. But this gives a quite misleading impression of his early political career and distorts the picture of its steady development.

It was in fact clear from the start that he intended to enter the game wholeheartedly. He made his maiden speech within four days of taking his seat, and he had spoken in one form or another thirteen more times before the session ended three and a half months later. By the end of 1875 he had noticeably advanced himself in Ireland as an active though junior member of the new national movement.

The day on which he entered the House of Commons was a historic one. The passage through the House of Commons of what were often generally referred to as 'Coercion Bills', giving special powers to the forces of law and order in Ireland, had been a feature of British legislation for much of the period of the Union. These Coercion Bills varied in severity depending on the prevailing agrarian conditions there. The milder versions, which did not involve for instance the suspension of habeas corpus but perhaps merely an extension of the normal right of police search or restrictions on the holding of arms, often took the form of a re-enactment of existing measures. In the session of 1874 one of the Home Rule Party's more successful forays had been against just such an Expiring Laws Continuance Bill. The Irish had managed to get the period for which special restrictions were to be re-enacted reduced from one year to three months. The parliamentary battle had then been marked by some particularly obstructive tactics on the part of Butt's Home Rulers. Constant amendments or motions for adjournment had delayed the Bill's passage. Some members of the party, in particular J. G. Biggar, a Belfast pork butcher who was MP for Cavan and, at that time, a secret member of the Supreme Council of the Irish Republican Brotherhood, had even pursued such tactics to lengths of which Butt himself finally disapproved.

Before Parnell's arrival, the session of 1875 had already seen renewed scenes of obstruction carried out against a Peace Preservation (Ireland) Bill. This reimposed special restrictions on certain parts of Ireland to deal with the dangers of agrarian crime – particularly in the central regions, where there had been a recurrence of agrarian secret society or 'Ribbon' activity at the beginning of the 1870s.

Obstruction, in itself, was not new as a tactic on the parliamentary scene. It had been used at times by English parliamentary minorities, most recently by the Conservatives themselves against the Liberals during Gladstone's last administration. Its possible use as a tactical measure had been openly considered by the Home Rule Conference, when Butt himself had said that 'extreme cases might justify a policy of obstruction', though he had given a warning against its excessive use.

In the session of 1874, Butt had on one occasion threatened Disraeli, the Prime Minister, that the Irish would 'resolutely obstruct his measures' – only reasserting the need to consider the 'dignity of the House' when Biggar, in Butt's opinion, went too far. In the session of 1875 it was Butt himself who again at first used the obstructive devices of amendments and motions for adjournment to some effect against the Peace Preservation (Ireland) Bill, until Biggar once again got out of hand. Whereas Butt regarded obstruction as a useful occasional device to force a compromise, Biggar saw it as a tactic for parliamentary sabotage.

Biggar's most dramatic development of the tactic took place on the very day of Parnell's arrival in the Chamber. He had been asked by Butt to 'slow up' the passage of the Coercion Bill, and, on inquiring how long he was to slow it up for, had been told 'a pretty good while'. Biggar spoke, in fact, for nearly four hours in a performance which was to become one of the most famous in the history of the House of Commons.

His main contention was that a new Coercion Act was quite unnecessary, for there was no 'Ribbonism' or agrarian crime about; unnecessarily, therefore, 'the whole country would be left entirely at the mercy of one man', the Chief Secretary for Ireland, who would have 'dictatorial powers'. In addition, he said, 'powers were to be given to magistrates which were liable to continual abuse'. Biggar then proceeded to read long extracts from the Report and Evidence of the Westmeath Commission of 1871 on agrarian crime, from Irish newspapers, and from statements and resolutions of various public bodies and meetings, in a manner which, according to Hansard, made it impossible to follow the application. 'The general purport', commented Hansard drily, 'appeared to be to denounce the necessity for any exceptional legislation in regard to Ireland.' Biggar himself was not without humour, accusing the Government at one point of 'wasting the time of the House with this measure'.

The Times said that Biggar spoke in a tone so indistinct that it was impossible to tell in the Reporters' Gallery whether the words which reached there were his own or quoted extracts. And after an attempt to 'count out' the almost empty House had been frustrated by a sudden influx of Irish Members, the Speaker himself complained of Biggar's inaudibility and of a manner which by then, according to Hansard, was totally unintelligible. The Speaker pointed out that it was a rule of the House that Members, when speaking, should address the chair. Biggar said that his non-observance of this rule was partly because he found it difficult to make his voice heard after speaking so long and partly because his position in the House made it inconvenient for him to read his extracts directly towards the chair. He would, however, with permission, take a more favourable position. He then moved down with his papers and a glass of water to a point above the gangway on the Opposition benches, which had long been without a single occupant, and for another ten minutes or so proceeded to read more extracts from there. Then, being as he said 'unwilling to detain the House at further length', he sat down.

It was an instructive performance for that day's new Member for Meath – a man with his own leanings towards belligerence. Four days later, in a continuation of the debate on the same Bill, Parnell's maiden speech carried a clear uncompromising note of its own. An Ulsterman, the Member for Derry, in the course of a speech, had said that what really mattered for England was to give the Irish farmer security of tenure through a Land Bill and that, as a result of this, 'Ireland instead of being a source of weakness would be a source of strength to England.' Parnell went quite far out of his way to deliver a formal challenge to this and to raise, on an idealistic level, the whole patriotic principle of Irish nationality. He said he did not believe that the Irish tenant farmers, even those living in the Black North, were so locked up in self-interest as to be inclined to give up the interest of their country to serve that of their class. When the proper time came, he continued, perhaps it would be found that he was as true a friend to the tenant farmer as even the Member for Derry, and, he added, he said this knowing full well the importance of securing the tenant farmer in his holding, but knowing too that in the neglect of the

principles of self-government lay the root of all Irish trouble. He concluded with a reference to a statement by a former Chancellor of the
Exchequer to the effect that Ireland was a geographical fragment. 'Ireland',
he said, 'is not a geographical fragment. She is a nation.'

It was an impressive public début on the national political scene, but
the speech attracted little public attention, though it was accorded a
report in *The Times* without the concluding paragraph, and the *Nation*
described it as 'admirable'. Perhaps the manner was less striking than the
content: the speech was described by Parnell's first biographer as 'spoken
in a thin voice and with manifest nervousness' and delivered 'spasmodically'.

He spoke three more times on the Peace Preservation (Ireland) Bill
within the next ten days, calling the whole Bill 'tyrannical' on one
occasion and speaking on another for an amendment which sought to
exclude Meath from the working of the Act on the grounds that 'the
Chief Secretary had not shown that any such [Ribbon] conspiracy [as in
1871] now existed'. Finally, on 6 May, in opposing a clause which gave
the Lord Lieutenant power to imprison any man suspected of being a
member of a Ribbon society, he summed up the objection to all such
legislation with the simple question 'How is the Lord Lieutenant to know
whether the suspicions are well-founded?'

On less sure ground he repeated that he was firmly convinced that no
Ribbonism existed in Westmeath either.

Altogether there were thirty-four divisions on the Coercion Bill after
Parnell entered Parliament in that session, and he voted against the
Government in thirty-three of them. The Bill passed its third reading on
11 May. Four days later, on Saturday 15 May, he returned to Avondale
for the first time since his election for Meath.

The townspeople of Rathdrum and the tenants on his estate turned out
at the railway station and on the roads leading to Avondale to greet him
with bands and banners. He was escorted through triumphal arches and
with much waving of boughs and banners and tremendous cheering to
Avondale itself, where he and two priests made speeches. Then 'the
people, after cheering till they made the old place ring as of old, and
having drunk Mr Parnell's health with three times three, quietly
separated'.

The long rail–boat–rail journey between London and Avondale and
back again was now to become part of the pattern of his life. He made it
several times that summer of 1875. Early in June he was back again in
London, where he had taken lodgings in 16 Keppel Street, off Gower

Street, in what was then a pleasantly 'Bohemian' quarter of London, favoured by artists and literary men. The houses in Keppel Street, though old and unfashionable by the standards of the time, had a certain dignity, and they contained spacious and handsome apartments which were relatively cheap. A neighbour of Parnell's, who now came to know him well, was Justin McCarthy, an Irish writer and journalist, then a political leader-writer for the *Daily News*. Parnell used to collect McCarthy from his house in Gower Street in the early afternoons before going on with him to the House of Commons. He made himself a favourite with McCarthy's wife and especially her two young children, showing an unaffected interest in all their activities. Looking back later, McCarthy remembered him in those days as 'a handsome man, still quite young with a singularly sweet and winning smile'.

During his first few weeks in Parliament, Parnell is said to have once approached a colleague and asked him where he got the material with which to ask a question of a Minister in the House. The colleague had replied with a smile, 'Why, from the newspapers, from our constituents, from many sources!' 'Ah,' Parnell had said, 'I must try and ask a question myself some day.'

His first venture in this direction was not a particularly successful one; on the other hand, like his maiden speech, it revealed political truculence and an immediate, exclusively Irish-orientated approach that was to be a consistent feature of his behaviour in the House of Commons. Even later in his political life Parnell admitted to extreme nervousness when he had to ask a question in the House from the notice paper, and he came to avoid doing so as far as possible. He found it almost intolerable, he said, to have to wait until his turn came. He didn't mind standing up and putting, on the spur of the moment, some question which had just occurred to his mind; but it gave him a nervous horror to have to sit, perhaps for half an hour, waiting in silence for his turn to be called to put a question printed on the notice paper.

This happened to him for the first time on 10 June 1875. On being called, he asked the Secretary of State for War to lay upon the table of the House recent correspondence between the parish priest of Navan and the commanding officer of the Meath Militia. This concerned the former's request that the men should be allowed to attend divine service on two days (other than Sundays) in May on which, by the rules of the Catholic Church, they were bound to attend. He also asked if Queen's Regulations in any way prohibited commanding officers from allowing their men to attend mass. Trivial and time-wasting as such matters may have appeared to the House of Commons, they were well calculated to appeal to the 'national' emotions of Catholic Ireland.

The Secretary of State for War, Gathorne Hardy, replied that the only correspondence on the subject was one letter from the priest in question to the commanding officer in which the priest had indeed made such a request, with which the commanding officer had not complied. No Queen's Regulations prevented a commanding officer from allowing his men to attend mass, but he was only bound to order them to attend such Church parades as were customary in the service. On other occasions he would give every facility for their attendance, provided this did not interfere with the proper discharge of their military duties.

A routine questioner might have been satisfied with this answer, but Parnell was back on the subject a few days later. He began rather surprisingly by asking if the letter to which he had referred in his previous question was still in existence. If not, he wanted to know when it had ceased to exist. He also asked if there were not in fact another letter from the priest to the commanding officer of the Meath Militia asking for the men to attend mass on one of the days mentioned. Was it not a fact that the Tipperary and Westmeath Militias had this facility of attending mass on Catholic Church holidays other than Sundays? Could not the command-ing officer of the Meath Militia be directed to grant it to his men too?

Gathorne Hardy first indignantly rejected the suggestion that he had somehow done away with the first letter. The truth was, he said, that he was holding it in his hand at that moment. He conceded that he had also had another letter from the priest but said that was on another subject, being a request for the alteration of the times of mass on certain Sundays. In answer to the last part of the question, he really could not expect the War Office to spend its valuable time going into details of when every militia regiment did or did not allow its men to attend divine service.

Again, this might have been thought to put an end to the matter. But Parnell had brought his fighting instincts to the House of Commons. He asked the Secretary of State if this meant that he declined to take the matter further. Gathorne Hardy merely replied that the facilities for attending divine service were ample and he did not intend to increase them. The War Office would see to it that they were not interfered with.

Parnell was still not satisfied. He did not, he said, intend to make any imputation against the Right Honourable Gentleman, but at the same time he must say that the Right Honourable Gentleman by his answer . . . Here the Speaker cut him off, saying that he was only in order if he made a personal statement respecting himself.

Three days later Parnell was back yet again on the same subject, with a slight variation of detail. Was not the confinement to barracks of the Meath Militia during the hours of one of the non-Sunday masses in question, and their engagement in parades during the hours of another, contrary to the War Office position that Catholics should have facilities to attend mass when requested to do so by their clergy?

Gathorne Hardy showed some patience. He replied that the granting of facilities to attend divine service applied not only to Catholics but to all denominations. The men of the Meath Militia had not been confined to barracks. The parade had been a normal routine one. Only one man had asked permission to attend divine service, which had been granted; and the man had fallen out and gone.

And there, at last, Parnell had to leave it.

In all this, by the standards of the House of Commons, he had been made to look rather silly. He had perhaps been gauche in his handling of the matter. But what he had made clear was that he was not particularly interested in whether or not he looked silly or gauche in the House of Commons.

On 8 July he again jarred on the mood of the House, when in a debate on the remaining Fenian prisoners he cited the case of Daniel Reddin, now released, who during his imprisonment had been subjected to particular ill-treatment. According to Parnell – who had presumably received his information from the Amnesty Association – Reddin had become paralysed as a consequence of the generally severe conditions of prison life, whereupon 'the prison officials acting upon the assumption that he was malingering, applied strong electric batteries to him twice a day and thrust sharp instruments into the muscles of his legs'.

At this point a burst of laughter revealed the extent to which Parnell had failed to catch the sympathy of the House. 'It is no laughing matter,' he declared, probably making things worse, 'I am only stating facts . . .'

When Sir Michael Hicks Beach, the Chief Secretary for Ireland, got up to reply he said it was not the matter of such statements which caused laughter, 'although the manner of some Hon. Gentlemen opposite was calculated to cause a smile'. He said that it had seemed to him from Butt's face as if even he had for a moment seen something rather funny about the proceedings. Butt, however, then declared slightly ambiguously that 'if his countenance had betrayed a laugh, then his countenance was false'.

Again Parnell, while appearing slightly ridiculous to the House, had demonstrated indifference as to whether he appeared ridiculous or not.

Later in the month, on 27 July, he took part in a sudden storm which blew up in the House over the discussion of Irish business. Butt had intended to move another Home Rule motion before the end of the session, but the Government suddenly announced that it was appropriating for its own business those two nights a week normally allocated to private member's bills. The motion proposing this procedure was put down for discussion on the evening of 27 July, but the Government, in a piece of legitimate parliamentary sharp practice, suddenly brought it forward in the early afternoon instead, when there were few Irish Members present. Parnell was one of them and valiantly supported the more experienced A. M. Sullivan in a protest against the proposed removal of Irish time. There were many Irish Members, said Parnell, who believed that the House of Commons could never effectually legislate for Ireland, and they were being deprived of the opportunity of making their case. He appealed to the Government at least to let the matter stand over until all the Irish Members who wished to speak could be present. But the Government was adamant. Parnell acted as teller in the subsequent division. The Irish lost by an overwhelming majority, but his intervention was noticed by the Irish newspapers.

Four days later he made a strong speech on the vote of funds for the national education system in Ireland. He swept aside the relevance of figures for literacy and school attendance which the Chief Secretary had produced as evidence of the system's success and concentrated on the nationalist principle. If, he said, the people of England or Scotland had a system of education forced on them of which they disapproved, they would protest against the principle as much as the Irish did. The people of Ireland as ratepayers should not be made to pay for a system which Ireland did not want. If England wanted to enforce a system of education on Ireland to which the people objected, then the English should pay for it themselves. His intervention showed a growth of self-assurance.

Nevertheless, on 2 August he once again earned a certain contempt from Hicks Beach, the Chief Secretary. Parnell had put to him a question which at least emphasized the industry with which he was prepared to pursue the interests of Catholic Ireland. Was it true, he asked, that the board of superintendence at Trim jail had recently refused a request for new vestments 'and other requisites' for divine service, although the old ones were more than twenty years old and had been condemned by the Bishop? Would the Chief Secretary see that those prison boards which were at present nominated by Grand Juries had more democratic representation in future? Hicks Beach replied that he did not know whether such a request had been recently refused nor whether the vestments had been condemned by the Bishop. Requests had been refused in the past because it was not the practice in most of the jails of Ireland to provide such vestments and requisites for any denomination. 'With reference to the second part of the question which appears to have no connection with the first', he said he could promise nothing but would consider the matter.

Unaffected by the snub, Parnell a few minutes later asked the Home Secretary for an inquiry into the sentencing of a military prisoner named O'Brien, who, it was suggested, had been given life imprisonment rather than ten years because of something he had shouted from the dock after being found guilty. The Home Secretary replied coldly that he had communicated with the Judge Advocate General and there was no record of any such incident ever having taken place, nor could such a thing possibly have taken place.

For all his nervousness, Parnell was breaking himself into the habit of asking questions. The next day he asked another, this time of the Solicitor-General, about an Irishman who, he said, in a London court case had been treated with some jocularity and sarcasm by the Master of the Rolls just because he was Irish. The lofty reply was that in any event the man had been held to have no case.

Finally, after journeying to Dublin to attend the celebrations there for the hundredth anniversary of Daniel O'Connell's birth, Parnell came back to London for the last three days of the session. Indefatigably, he moved for a return of those Irish jails 'where vestments and other requisites for Divine Service *were* supplied to chaplains of different denominations by the authorities'. This motion was agreed to.

At this stage it would have been easy for anyone, particularly an Englishman, to dismiss Parnell as a figure of some eccentricity but of little consequence to the parliamentary scene. Many doubtless did so. But at least one English observer found that there was something about Parnell's personality which jarred awkwardly for all the wish to dismiss him. The correspondent of the weekly the *World*, later, as Sir Henry Lucy, the author of celebrated diaries covering parliaments of the period, was already exasperated by Parnell in a manner which suggested underlying unease.

In his later published diaries Lucy omitted all his earliest parliamentary references to Parnell, presumably because he thought that in the light of subsequent events they did his political judgement little credit. But in fact his first comments reveal awareness of a disturbing force at work, even though they fail to gauge its true dimension. After Parnell's question about the prison treatment of the Fenian Reddin, Lucy had written sourly of 'that fresh and convincing argument for Home Rule, Mr Parnell, who combines in his person all the unlovable qualities of an Irish Member with the absolute absence of their attractiveness'. And during the ensuing recess he referred more than once to Parnell and 'the nonsensical stuff' he talked, coupling him with both Biggar and Ronayne as an example of all that was most deplorable in the Irish party. What Lucy and other English observers did not recognize was that by making himself deplorable in English eyes a Home Rule politician might become a force to be reckoned with in Ireland. This in the long run could become a force to be reckoned with in England.

Chapter 8

In the summer of 1875 it was not only at Westminster that Parnell was following with characteristic aggressiveness the career he had chosen rather as an afterthought. In Ireland, the celebrations of the centenary of Daniel O'Connell's birth had given rise to a drama in which Parnell was soon involved. In keeping with the traditionally disparate character of the Irish national movement, the event quickly revealed bitter internal dissensions. Parnell made instinctively for the radical side.

The organizing committee for the celebrations was largely under the control of the Lord Mayor of Dublin, Peter Paul MacSwiney, a former liberal nationalist who was not a Home Ruler. With some support from the priesthood, he now sought to use O'Connell's name for a demonstration of old-fashioned Catholic sectarian solidarity – the safe provincial political ticket on which his own career had so far prospered. To outmanoeuvre the more ambitious Home Rulers who hoped to capture the popular appeal of O'Connell's name for their own cause, MacSwiney formed an anti-Home-Rule nationalist alliance with a man who opposed Home Rule from another angle, the doctrinaire Repealer, once Young Irelander, P. J. Smyth. Smyth held the federalist Home Rule movement to be a sacrilegious betrayal of the old full-blooded O'Connellite Repeal faith.

The main opposition to this alliance came, on behalf of the Home Rule movement, from the Fenian-dominated Amnesty Association. The Association correctly diagnosed in P. J. Smyth more plain conservatism than true enthusiasm for Repeal, and announced brusquely to the Centenary Committee that, whatever other arrangements might have been made, the Association itself would be taking part in the organized procession through the streets of Dublin on the day in question, 6 August.

The Amnesty Association was unlikely to approve of any orator chosen for the great occasion by such a committee. In fact the Centenary Committee had chosen Lord O'Hagan, an old supporter of O'Connell who in later years had sufficiently compromised on Repeal to become Solicitor-General in an administration of Gladstone's. Even after O'Hagan had decided to let a convenient family illness prevent him from delivering his address himself and had asked the Lord Mayor to read it for him, the omens were not good. The Amnesty men were determined to make the occasion as relevant to the political present as to the past and to use it to carry out a strong demonstration on behalf of the forty-four Fenian prisoners still said to be held in Australian or British jails. With this extreme wing of the Home Rule movement, Parnell aligned himself.

He was already close to the Amnesty Association. His questions about Daniel Reddin in the House had shown this. On Sunday 1 August the Association held a large and successful demonstration in London, in Hyde Park, where he made a short speech which was cheered, saying that 'the Irish political prisoners had drawn the sword not to strike against the liberties of Englishmen, but to defend the liberties of Ireland'.

At a meeting of the Association in Dublin two days later, at which Patrick Egan was present, letters were read out from O'Connor Power and four other MPs, among them Parnell, 'intimating their intention of following the Amnesty banner in the O'Connell centenary procession'. The Amnesty Association had also been one of the three organizations to which Parnell had subscribed money for the purposes of the celebrations, though he sent nothing to MacSwiney's committee itself.

On the great day of the centenary, 6 August, the procession exceeded all expectations by the vastness of its numbers. Trouble started when the Amnesty men, with black banners and a great black flag on their carriage, tried to join the procession at a point just in front of the Dublin coal porters' contingent – men who in the old days had been the traditional bodyguard of O'Connell and who were now headed by P. J. Smyth himself, mounted on a horse. A fracas took place, in the course of which, either on Smyth's orders, as some maintained, or by spontaneous initiative on the part of the coal porters, the traces of the Amnesty carriage were cut, leaving it stationary while the horses walked on by themselves and were lost in the throng.

Parnell's first biographer reported him as being present at this moment and among those who then linked themselves with ropes to the Amnesty carriage and dragged it through the procession to the platform near Carlisle Bridge from which the speeches were to be delivered. Subsequent biographers have repeated this. In fact Parnell stated clearly later that year that he was not there when the traces of the Amnesty car were cut; he had been accidentally prevented from taking part in the procession as he had meant to do. He was, however, present later, he said, near the platform which he did eventually mount.

The Lord Mayor, whose own gilt coach had brought up the rear of the extremely long procession, had finally made his way into a densely thronged Sackville Street. But he found that the platform from which he was to deliver Lord O'Hagan's address had already been surrounded by noisy members of the Amnesty contingent. Their great black flag had been placed prominently close by, and black banners were waving which not only bore the inscription 'Still in Chains' but were festooned with real chains which clanked at intervals in macabre fashion. The Amnesty men had already been leading the crowd for an hour or so, to the music of successive bands, in choruses such as 'God Save Ireland'.

The Lord Mayor's reception from the crowd was enthusiastic enough on arrival, but the moment he mounted the platform, which was largely occupied by Catholic priests, a harsh rattle of chains broke out as the Amnesty banners were waved, and when he began to read Lord O'Hagan's address he was interrupted by shouts, groans, whoops and whistles and an overall demand for 'Butt! Butt!' – the Home Rule leader. Little of the address could be delivered, which was perhaps as well for the Lord Mayor, for not only was it excessively long but, while paying an effusive tribute to O'Connell as a Catholic leader, it managed never once even to mention the word 'Repeal'. The Lord Mayor soon abandoned the platform to Butt and other Home Rule speakers, including O'Connor Power, and it must have been at this juncture that Parnell too mounted the platform, though he himself did not speak.

A further scene took place towards the end of a great celebration banquet that evening, when the Lord Mayor tried to call on the old Repealer and foremost nationalist opponent of Home Rule, Sir Charles Gavan Duffy. He was shouted down with cries of 'Butt!' The Lord Mayor abruptly left the chair and, after some altercation, in the course of which Butt reproved him for abandoning the banquet, the gas lighting was turned down and the celebration ended in a scene of indecorous confusion.

Parnell had not been at the banquet but had dined that evening peacefully at a Dublin hotel. He had earlier attended a special meeting of the Council of the Amnesty Association, at which it was decided that P. J. Smyth, still technically a member, should be summoned to account for his behaviour in ordering the traces of the Amnesty car to be cut during the procession. On a motion of Patrick Egan, he took the chair for a short time so that thanks could be voted to the main Chairman, O'Connor Power.

Four days later he was himself the main Chairman at a very well-attended meeting of the Association at which a letter was read from Smyth categorically denying that he had ordered the traces to be cut. Evidence that he had done so was heard from Frank Hugh O'Donnell and John Barry, Secretary of the Home Rule Confederation of Great Britain.

Parnell said it was a very unpleasant duty to have to meet for such proceedings. He paid tribute to Smyth for his part in Irish politics in the distant past, and remarked that he himself had been inclined to make excuses for him, at least on the grounds of sincerity, for his deviation since the election of 1874 'from the proper course he should follow' – i.e. Home Rule. However, he had completely changed his mind about him in the past three weeks, for he 'saw that gentleman, with the eyes of the country upon him, join a clique'. And he touched adroitly on the total contradiction of Smyth, who opposed Home Rule from an orthodox out-and-out Repealer point of view for being too mild, forming an alliance with certain clerics and the Lord Mayor who opposed it for being too radical.

Finally, on a resolution of Egan's, seconded by Thomas Brennan, and put to the meeting after further reference to the 'painful' nature of the occasion by Parnell, Smyth was told his reply was unsatisfactory and that he must either resign or be expelled from the Amnesty Association. A vote of thanks to Parnell was passed by acclamation for 'his dignified and impartial conduct as President of the meeting'.

It had been a busy political day for him, for earlier, at a special meeting of the O'Connell Centenary Committee, he had seconded a resolution proposing that Lord O'Hagan's address should not be printed at the public expense because of its very serious omission of any mention of Repeal. Next day he was back in London on the penultimate day of the parliamentary session to put in his motion for a return of those Irish jails at which vestments were provided by the authorities.

For this period, though we have detail enough of his political activities, we know almost nothing about Parnell's private life in Ireland and very little, beyond the glimpse given by Justin McCarthy, of his life in London. There, it can be assumed, his way of life was solitary, even lonely. He would dine out alone – being spotted once at least in his early years in Parliament in a restaurant in the Strand – or, on the spur of the moment, would persuade a colleague to go with him to a music-hall. In Ireland he was obviously much at Avondale, where at least he had personal roots. But what prevented him from taking part in the first stage of the O'Connell procession in Dublin; why he was having a peaceful dinner at a Dublin hotel instead of attending the disrupted banquet and whether or not he was alone there; what thoughts, what hopes or doubts were in his mind about his new way of life – these things we are never likely to know.

Publicly he had now been a Member of Parliament for four months, and in that time he had done much to build a position for himself on the political scene. It was clear that he did not intend to be a cipher, like other gentlemen Home Rulers. By no means a leading member of the party, he was already not an insignificant one.

But in what sort of shape was the Home Rule Party itself? In its second year in Parliament, 1875, it had failed to bring any Home Rule motion before the House at all.

At a large public Home Rule League meeting in Dublin on 14 September, which Parnell attended with a seat on the platform, some speakers quoted their opponents as saying that Home Rule as a movement was already dead. The suggestion was strongly rejected. Butt himself tended to evade parliamentary reality by looking ahead: 'Let the nation give eighty Members at the next General Election,' he said, 'and the day is not far distant when there will be a Parliament in College Green . . . The time is come for action, to arouse the Irish people into action . . . The power of the people's representatives in Parliament . . . will depend on the consciousness of the English Parliament that we are not speaking with our own voices but have at our back the voice of the Irish nation.'

The *Freeman's Journal*, further refuting assertions by Whig and Tory that Home Rule was dead, said it was confident that the meeting inaugurated 'a vigorous autumn campaign on behalf of Home Rule.'

The new young Member for Meath, who at this meeting too had the honour of being moved to the chair for the vote of thanks to the Chairman, himself figured in a large Home Rule demonstration in Wexford at the beginning of October. This was held on an emotive national site, at the foot of Vinegar Hill, the scene of the final defeat of the Wexford peasant rebellion in 1798. Butt, A. M. Sullivan, the local Member, Sir George Bowyer, and the young Fenian Thomas Brennan were all present to address the crowd of some ten thousand, who were rewarded after a soaking wet morning with a bright afternoon. Members of a 'Working Men's Home Rule Society' were there too, wearing a white satin badge trimmed with black and bearing the word 'Amnesty' on their right arms.

Parnell was introduced as a man 'whose great-grandfather had refused the bribe of a peerage . . . to vote for the Union'. He responded to the special associations of Vinegar Hill by showing at once his instinct for the way the Irish nation liked to hear itself speak.

'Surely, surely,' he cried, 'when I look around me I may say with the pale-faced martyr, Emmet, in the dock, that if it is permitted to the spirits of the departed just to behold and mingle in what passes here below, there are looking down upon this scene, with blessings from the realms above, the spirits of the brave and true men who died for Ireland on yonder hill, not to forget the men who are still suffering imprisonment for political offences. I urgently ask the men of Wexford not to rest until every man of the fifty men in chains should be liberated.'

This was the traditional stuff of Irish populist appeal. The unusual thing was to hear a Protestant landlord voicing it. He was greeted with immense cheering. He concluded that whether it was for education, Home Rule, or Amnesty, England must yield if Irishmen were determined on it. He was given a final cheer.

The following day, 4 October, he attended the annual banquet of the Wexford Home Rule Association with two hundred other gentlemen, while ladies were accommodated in the gallery. The room was decorated with flags and flowers and such slogans as 'Ireland for the Irish' and 'Our Own Again', while at the top of it there was an Irish harp and crown.

When the Chairman proposed among other toasts that of 'Prosperity to Ireland and a speedy Restoration of our National Parliament', he coupled it with the names of Butt, 'the beloved leader of our Home Rule Party – and also his lieutenant gentlemen, Mr A. M. Sullivan and Mr Parnell, the worthy successor of Mr John Martin in the representation of Meath'. This was greeted with loud cheers, and the toast was drunk with enthusiasm.

Parnell himself responded to the toast 'and in the course of an extremely forcible address urged upon the people, firmness, determination and union'.

An eyewitness who sat by the door at this banquet remarked of Parnell, 'What a fine pleasant countenance! He is a noble young fellow, and is destined yet to do great things for Ireland. With what a noble vehemence he utters his sentences. He is "surely one of the coming men . . ."' And he concluded, 'there is fire in that young man'.

Parnell seems to have made an equally good public impression when two days later, on the evening of 8 October, he addressed a large crowd of his own constituents in a hall at Navan. The *Nation* described his speech as 'capital' and as having been enthusiastically received. In fact it reads as a fairly routine survey of the salient political topics of the day: the land question – with a renewed demand for fixity of tenure and fair rents – religious-based education, and the general wider and vaguer national aspiration for Home Rule.

On the latter point Parnell showed himself well aware of doubts arising about the party's effectiveness. He said that, though many people might think he and his colleagues were not working because the results were not yet to be seen, they would become known at the right time. 'We are working hard,' he added, 'though we may be working silently.'

Paying a polite compliment to the absent senior Member for Meath, Nicholas Ennis, Parnell described him as 'an honest and true man'. 'But,' a voice from the audience called out, 'you are as good as two of him yourself.'

The last speaker of the day, a priest, having referred, perhaps with excessive zeal, to Parnell's 'burning eloquence', associated him particularly with the issue of religious education and called out to the audience, 'Tell me, is not the cause of education safe in his hands?' To which the answer came at once: 'It is! It is!' And when he asked again, 'Tell me, how many Lord Mayors would you take in his stead?' a voice replied, 'We wouldn't take a hank of them.'

However, the Lord Mayor of Dublin, Peter Paul MacSwiney, taking advantage of the Home Rule Party's barren practical record after two annual sessions of Parliament, had been making some attempt at a political comeback after his noisy rebuffs on the day of the O'Connell centenary celebrations. Under the conservative Catholic slogan 'Faith and Fatherland', he was continuing, still in alliance with P. J. Smyth, to try to gather to himself the general body of nationalist opinion by playing up the distinction between Home Rule, with its federal compromise, and out-and-out old-fashioned Repeal. His movement was not in itself of great significance except insofar as it showed the extent to which Home Rule was still in 1875 very far from dominating 'nationalist' thought.

Attacks on Home Rule from the unofficial Fenian 'left' had also begun the month before, though the Irish Republican Brotherhood itself was still proving loyal to its compact to give the movement a trial. At a Home Rule meeting in his own constituency of Limerick in September, Butt had had to face quite a strong demand from a section of the audience for a resolution committing the party to one final demand for Home Rule in the next session. The implication was – since the proposal came from a well-known Fenian – that if the demand were unsuccessful Ireland would then turn to other means, involving at the very least the party's withdrawal from Westminster. Butt succeeded in rejecting such a commitment, but only after an embarrassing and noisy scene in which the proposer of the resolution withdrew angrily from the hall. The party's Chief Whip, Richard Shaughnessy, had to go so far as to concede that what had been proposed might indeed one day prove correct policy, citing the Hungarian withdrawal from the imperial parliament of Austria as an analogy.

But it was the attack from the 'right' wing, combining the Lord Mayor's conservative clericalism with traditionally stirring rhetorical overtones of the old Repeal movement, which seemed to present the more formidable intellectual challenge. It concentrated on the obscurity of the federalist compromise which Home Rule seemed to involve. How 'national' really would a parliament be which had only limited control over its own affairs under Westminster's sovereignty, with the limitations not yet precisely determined? It was a reasonable question.

Even the useful defence put up for Home Rule by the old O'Connell supporter and Repealer W. J. O'Neill Daunt – to the effect that Home Rule was the only possible objective attainable *at present*, but that it was always a possible precursor to eventual full Repeal – displayed the weakness of the Home Rule movement's lack of definition. For if, as a genuinely puzzled correspondent wrote to the *Freeman's Journal*, ultimate Repeal still remained the goal, 'are English Ministers so short-sighted as not to foresee that in that event Home Rule would be only a stepping-stone to Repeal?'

It was to such dissension that Parnell boldly turned when he addressed a further group of his constituents at Nobber in Lower Meath on Saturday 16 October.

The meeting was an afternoon one, and some three thousand people welcomed their 'popular Member', as the *Freeman's Journal* called him, with resounding cheers. He immediately proposed a resolution that 'we declare our continued and unalterable adhesion to the cause of Home Rule . . . and our abhorrence of any attempt, come from what quarter it may, to sow the seeds of dissension or division in the national ranks'.

His speech, which was much cheered and applauded throughout, is valuable in conveying that at this point he was still genuinely optimistic about the possibilities for Butt's party in Parliament. People might think, he said, that as they had seen the Home Rule Party repulsed in the House of Commons night after night it had been badly beaten and had done nothing. He would assure them it was not so, and he told them that in all sincerity; and God forbid he should tell them a lie.

There were great cheers and cries of 'You never told us a lie.'

He went on, 'In the House of Commons the Irish party are daily gaining ground.' What was necessary, he added, was for the party's Members to be able to feel they had the Irish people at their back – a statement which was followed by more cheers and cries of 'You will always have them at your back.'

When he confronted the dispute between the old Repealers and the new Home Rulers, he did so with a magnificent dismissal of its substance. His words were characteristic of what was always to be his flexible approach to any definition of Irish nationalism. They also indicated a subtler appreciation of some of the details of Irish history than that with which he has been credited at this time.

'Much', he declared, 'has been said of the difference between Home Rule and Repeal. Well, I could never see the difference. It is a fact that to obtain Home Rule we must first repeal the Union. Nobody doubts that. We have also heard much of the Constitution of 1782. Well, there were some very good points in the Constitution of 1782 but there were some very bad ones too ... The strings were then pulled by the English Government and they will still continue the same system. Any difference which exists is between Home Rule and the Constitution of 1782, which latter is to be amended in whatever respects it disregards the rights of the Irish people. As for any difference between Repeal and Home Rule, I have been looking through a mental microscope but I can find none between them. If any difference exists it is merely one in name and no more.'

Whether or not this did successfully dismiss the issue was immaterial: he was making clear that, difference or not, it was of no significance to him.

Similarly the ease with which he all along glossed over the real question of how, for all the 'hard' and even 'silent' work in Parliament, the present Home Rule Party was ever to 'gain ground' revealed not weakness in argument but confidence of vision. It was impossible at this stage to say how the fight for 'the national question' in which he had chosen to involve himself would develop. What mattered was that he had entered the fight. What exactly was to be won could be defined as the fight proceeded. He had already publicly shown himself unhampered by theoretical limitation on the nature of final victory. Whether any sort of victory at all was likely to be won by a Home Rule Party of its present nature under the leadership of the amiable Butt was a matter about which he probably had doubts. But he was already enough of a pragmatist in politics to know that it was too early to express them.

Chapter 9

October 1875 was a busy political month for Parnell. Even though Parliament was in recess for the winter, nationalist politics of a sort continued in Ireland. He attended with Butt (they were the only two MPs present) a meeting of the Dublin Tenant Farmers' Association on 18 October at which, after a very long speech by Butt, he made a short speech on request. He expressed a firm belief that the tenant farmers of Ireland would ultimately get a settlement of the land question on the only possible basis: the principle of fixity of tenure at fair rents. But he also expressed a doubt about their getting it from the present Parliament.

Towards the end of the same week he attended a big Home Rule meeting held by the MP for Galway at Tuam, where he proposed a resolution on behalf of the Fenian political prisoners, saying that 'sound policy, humanity, justice and constitutional law all imperatively demanded their release'.

The next day he appeared at another meeting in the same constituency and was welcomed as part of 'an important delegation from the Home Rule League and as one of the most active and patriotic members of the League'. He spoke to a resolution about the need to avoid dissension in the movement and according to the *Galway Vindicator* made a 'spirited' speech which was received with loud cheers.

He then seems to have had a rest from public life for about three weeks, presumably at Avondale, whence he subscribed the rather higher than average sum of three pounds to a fund for the erection of a statue to the eighteenth-century Protestant patriot Henry Grattan.

In the second week of November 1875 he again became involved in a fracas within the O'Connell Centenary Committee. The row centred on a technical point raised by A. M. Sullivan over the passing of the Committee's final accounts for the celebration. But behind it lay all the emotional rivalry that had arisen from the political dispute between the Lord Mayor and the Home Rule movement in preceding months. And behind that lay the inert disorder of Irish national thinking in that day.

Sullivan was prepared to agree the main accounts for the celebration, even including a slightly controversial provision of £300 (£1,400 today) for a portrait of the Lord Mayor by his own secretary. But he insisted that one item, for printing a record of the celebrations, should be held over while inquiry was made into how exactly the contract for the printing had been allotted. It was the sort of squalid, trivial, internal row into which Irish national energies were so easily diverted – a reflection of apparently permanent frustration on the wider political scene.

Parnell at once became Sullivan's ally. When the Secretary of the Committee, a Lord Mayor's man, tried to obscure the real issue by saying how important it was that the record of the celebrations should be printed, for it contained material from American newspapers and indeed newspapers all over the world which people at home had not had an opportunity of seeing, Parnell interrupted brusquely: 'I must protest, my Lord Mayor, against the time of this meeting being wasted by the Hon. Secretary making a speech about newspapers and America and different other things – speaking about America and matters that don't really concern us here at all.'

When a further attempt to obscure the issue was made by suggesting that what Sullivan really wanted to get at in the accounts was the allocation of a sum for a portrait of the Lord Mayor, Parnell again intervened and denied this strongly. 'Ever since I was that high,' he said in passing, lowering his hand to the table in an appropriate gesture, 'I have entertained the most profound respect for your Lordship.'

But as Sullivan continued to press for an inquiry into the printing contract the Lord Mayor grew more and more indignant, finally declaring that such a motion was a vote of censure against himself and refusing to remain in the chair while it was put. He walked out of the room, shouting and gesticulating at Sullivan in a scene of 'indescribable confusion'.

Sullivan called out, 'I now move the Hon. [sic] Charles Stewart Parnell to the Chair.'

In spite of a protest from one spectator ('Oh no, not in the Lord Mayor's house!'), Parnell lost no time in taking possession of the vacated seat.

When the Secretary tried to remove the committee's books and papers, Parnell peremptorily placed his hand on top of them and forbade him to do so, saying that he was Chairman of the meeting now. He called for a show of hands to regulate his position, and received the approval of a large majority. He then put Sullivan's original motion that a subcommittee should inquire into the placing of the printing contract, and this too was carried.

Meanwhile the Secretary, taking advantage of Parnell's preoccupation, and shouting that he would send for the police if necessary, made off out of the room with the books and papers.

Parnell was then instructed by the remnant of the meeting to notify the Lord Mayor and other members of the Centenary Committee of the passing of the motion and to request them not to go ahead with the printing contract. He sent the necessary letter to the Lord Mayor from Avondale the next day.

He received a sharp reply from the Lord Mayor's secretary, the portrait-painter. He was told that he could not even be recognized as a member of the O'Connell Centenary Committee, to whose fund he had never subscribed. Far less, therefore, could the Lord Mayor recognize 'your pretension to be chairman of a meeting of that Committee'. P. J. Smyth, whom Parnell had also notified of developments the day before, was even ruder, simply writing to the *Freeman's Journal* that he had been 'amused' by the receipt of a letter from a 'person who, over the name of Charles Stewart Parnell, attempts to usurp the title of "Chairman" of the O'Connell Centenary Committee'.

Parnell sent a spirited reply to the Lord Mayor. Irish Members of Parliament who had wished to cooperate in the centenary were *ipso facto* members of the Committee. He *had* subscribed to the celebrations. Finally he took up a gratuitous passage in the secretary's letter which expressed regret that 'the bearer of an honoured name should have allied himself with the disturbers of the O'Connell Celebration, both on the day of the procession (August 6th) and at the banquet in the evening.'

Accident, Parnell said, had in fact prevented his taking part in the procession itself; he had not mounted the speaking platform until after the Lord Mayor had left it. With a sly dig at the turning-down of the lighting in the confusion at the end of the official banquet, he concluded by saying that he was in fact then 'enjoying a peaceful dinner and a plentiful supply of gas at an hotel'. Thus it had been 'physically impossible for me to disturb either the procession or the banquet'.

He seems to have ignored P. J. Smyth's insult, but a correspondent in the *Freeman's Journal* spoke out on his behalf. Smyth, he said, was publicly reviled for his 'political recreancy', but the county of Meath had 'yet to learn to regret having given her suffrages to the young and popular Mr Parnell'.

The matter was resolved in a final stormy scene at a public meeting of the Centenary Committee on 23 November. An immediate dispute broke out as to whether or not a report of the earlier proceedings after Parnell had taken the chair should be officially incorporated in the minutes. One of the Lord Mayor's supporters said that he had more respect and regard for Parnell than for many of those who had dragged him into the affair. Whereupon Parnell interposed indignantly, 'I entirely object to that statement. I was not "dragged".'

The real argument centred on whether or not Parnell was a member of the Committee. He admitted that he had not in fact subscribed to the Central Committee's fund but pointed out that there had been many other ways of contributing financially to the centenary celebrations – for instance to the Meath Bakers' contingent, the Drogheda Band and the Amnesty Association. He hoped the Lord Mayor was not trying to deny the part such contingents from outside the capital had played in making the procession a success.

On the question of his right to be a member of the Committee he displayed further forensic skill. Members of Parliament were indeed *ex officio* honorary members of the Committee, provided they had replied positively to a circular sent them in March that year. Parnell said he was an MP but had never received such a circular. An official of the Committee said one had been sent him, but he had not replied.

'A circular', asked Parnell, 'informing me that, as a Member of Parliament, if I cooperated with the Committee I should be an honorary member of the Committee?'

'Yes.'

'A few days subsequent to the passing of a resolution to that effect?'

'Yes.'

'Well,' replied Parnell, 'I was not a Member of Parliament for a month after that.'

When it was recalled that such circulars had also been sent to distinguished county gentlemen and the Secretary said he distinctly recollected one being sent to Parnell at Avondale, Parnell said he left it to the meeting to consider what sort of recollection the Secretary had.

Eventually, however, he and Sullivan lost the day. A new attempt was made to refer back the business of the printing contract for reconsideration, and this time the Lord Mayor remained at his post as Chairman. He refused to allow their votes. Even if their votes had been allowed, they would in fact have lost by a majority of one.

The *Freeman's Journal* tried to draw a veil over the whole embarrassing scene. 'Let us most earnestly trust', it wrote, 'that from this day out the world will have heard the last of the O'Connell Centenary Committee.' And it prayed 'that the wretched story may be buried out of sight in the

Sea of Forgetfulness and obliterated from the record of our nation. The
dignity of Ireland has already been too grievously wounded.'

It is difficult not to form the impression that Parnell had rather enjoyed
himself, and that his political appetite was being continually whetted by
such activity. At the same time, the experience may have confirmed in his
mind a growing impression that the dignity of Ireland was becoming a
sadly hollow concept when those who professed concern for it could
bicker among themselves like that, and that the fight for it would have to
be conducted very much more tenaciously and at a very much higher
level from now on.

The following week he made a belligerent speech at a meeting of the
Home Rule League in Dublin. The Chief Secretary for Ireland Sir
Michael Hicks Beach (known as 'Black Michael' on account of his beard)
had been in Belfast at a meeting of 'the Conservative working classes',
pouring scorn on Home Rule and calling upon them to show 'determined
and consistent resolve to resist to the uttermost what you believe will be
destructive to the institutions of the United Kingdom'. He had reminded
them of the old Fenian saying that England's difficulty was Ireland's
opportunity and had inverted it, expressing his confidence that, were
England to find herself in any foreign difficulty, the opportunity his
audience would take would be to rally Irish valour on England's behalf.

Parnell now jeered at Hicks Beach for having to run off to Belfast for
an audience, being unable to find one in Dublin that would listen to him
'abusing seven-eighths of the people of this country'. As for what Hicks
Beach had said about England's difficulty, Parnell said it seemed to show
'a great weakness' somewhere when he could only appeal to such a small
section of the Irish people for support. He hoped 'the day would soon
come when England would see her mistake and recognize the people of
this country as a self-governing people who would insist on their right to
self-government and who would have it. He did not care when or how it
was to be, but he was convinced that whether by peaceful solution, by the
pressure of circumstances, or by other measures which he was not there to
enlarge upon, the day would come when the Irish people would be self-
governing . . . Until then let not England go to war with any foreign
nation . . . England had to look to herself, for hers was a power that
would want supporting if Irish grievances were not redressed.'

The speech, one of several at the meeting, interwove moderation and
extremism in masterly fashion. Though applauded, it may, by its hints of
'other measures' than peaceful ones, have troubled some of the more
moderate members of the Home Rule League.

The party as a whole was already looking to its tactics for the next session of Parliament, due to reopen in February 1876. A meeting was arranged to consider these early in January. Parnell appears to have spent Christmas out of the country, possibly with his mother and sisters in France, for he returned to Ireland via England on 31 December. However, even on the way back he had combined business with pleasure by attending a meeting of the Home Rule Confederation of Great Britain with Butt at Liverpool on 30 December.

The conference of Home Rule Members of Parliament took place in Morrison's Hotel, Dublin, on 4 January, and was attended by thirty-one of them – only just over half the total number. It lasted from 12 noon until 5.00 p.m. and, although it was a private meeting, the *Freeman's Journal* reported, with inside knowledge, that there had been unanimous approval for a course of action which would include the introduction of Bills on the land question and on education, and of a resolution on Home Rule to go forward immediately after Easter.

Recent dissensions and anxieties were easily forgotten in excitement at the prospect. The *Nation* even went so far as to state, 'The national movement has now grown to such strength that one of the evils most necessary to be guarded against is over-confidence.'

The year 1876, the third in which Home Rulers had sat as a party in Parliament, was to be a crucial one in determining both the party's own fortunes and those of its increasingly active young recruit, the Member for Co. Meath.

Chapter 10

Those who, earlier, had expected Parnell to prove a mere graceful political ornament, a gentleman dilettante whom the Home Rulers could display in the framework of his social standing and his famous forebears, must already have noticed that he was turning out differently. He continued to be very active.

The day after taking part in the party's policy-making decisions for the new session of 1876, he was at a meeting of the Home Rule League in Dublin described as 'one of the most crowded and enthusiastic ever held'. The next day he was one of the fourteen MPs on the platform when the statue to Henry Grattan to which he had subscribed was unveiled at College Green. He was present at the large banquet which the Home Rule Party gave in the Antient Concert Rooms afterwards.

There were plenty of nationalists in Ireland whose nationalism was virtually confined to this sort of nostalgic look back at 'the old House on College Green'. But that Parnell himself was not in this category he emphasized eleven days later, when, at another meeting of the Home Rule League, he delivered a hint of a rebuke to the party leadership in the previous session of Parliament.

'The Irish people', he said, 'have always shown themselves in earnest in this matter of Home Rule, and by continuing to do so I have no doubt they will get it. It is also of importance that Irish Members should show themselves in earnest and anxious to keep the cause of Home Rule preeminent, and to be obtained first and above everything. Last session the question was not brought forward at all – there were many reasons for that – but this session we have been promised it will be brought forward at an early period. By doing this we shall be enabled to show the country that the Members are determined to press the question and, backed up by the Irish people, I am confident our efforts will succeed.'

His speech was punctuated by applause, and when A. M. Sullivan spoke later in the meeting of his pleasure at seeing on the platform 'the chivalrous and patriotic Member for Meath' the remark was greeted with cheers.

In the political circumstances of the day it could, however, reasonably be asked, even of Parnell, whether talk of Irish Members bringing forward Home Rule in earnest in the House of Commons was not itself as rhetorical as other traditional Irish national talk. How could a party whose total nominal strength was under sixty hope to get its way against a majority of well over five hundred Members of both English political parties? No one entertained a serious hope of converting in the foreseeable future more than a very small handful of English politicians – independent-minded radicals – to the Home Rule cause. English critics of the Home Rulers seemed to have had some justification when they described the group as 'the feeblest and hollowest organization that ever pretended to the name of a political party'.

There were virtually three courses of action open to anyone meaning business about Home Rule at that time. None remotely guaranteed success, but each was at least an alternative to the stalemate of the House of Commons. One course was to disrupt the proceedings of the House of Commons by obstruction along the lines of Biggar's earlier examples to a point at which Parliament's normal business simply could not proceed. At such a point, conceivably, some political bargain might become feasible. An alternative was for the entire Home Rule Party (or as many of its members as could be persuaded to do so) to withdraw from the House of Commons *en bloc* and set up its own parliamentary body in Ireland. This action had been periodically recommended ever since the early days of O'Connell's Repeal movement in the 1840s. It had seemed to many Irishmen to acquire a certain plausibility from the action of the Hungarian deputies in withdrawing from the Austrian imperial parliament. This was the action to which the Irish Republican Brotherhood, having temporarily shelved military action after the fiasco of the Fenian rising, had hoped for a period to persuade the party. Finally there was a third course of action to which the second might indeed prove a prelude, namely that physical-force insurrection which, though temporarily shelved, was indeed still the purest form of IRB doctrine.

In the realities of the time, none of these courses of action seemed very practicable – the last not at all. Obstruction was the most plausible, but suffered as a party tactic from the disadvantage that the leader of the party, Butt, and many of its members were strongly opposed to it in any extreme form, though in extremes alone lay its ultimate sanction.

Given what we now know about Parnell's later political characteristics, he is unlikely to have looked at any specific course of action too closely at this point, but rather would have kept an open mind on the possibility of

any course proving useful. The element of unpredictability in politics is
one with which every serious politician must reckon. And, however
improbable, the prospect of the eventual conversion of one of the two
great English political parties to the Home Rule cause did at least remain
theoretically there. In 1876, however, it seemed so remote from the realm
of practical politics as hardly to be a matter for consideration.

Writing of times that now seemed over, the *Daily Telegraph* at the
beginning of the new session commented that there had been a period
'when in England itself an Irish contingent taking advantage of English
party feeling would have done the State much harm . . . These days are to
a great extent past.'

Additional substance was given to this feeling in this year by the
apparently permanent retirement from the leadership of the Liberal Party
of the one English statesman whose principles had been seriously engaged
on behalf of Ireland, William Ewart Gladstone. Disclaiming any intention
of again taking a leading part in the history of his country, he was, he
said, 'too old to again advance into the forefront of the battle'. His place
as Liberal leader was taken by the stolid Whig figure of Lord Hartington.

In these circumstances, obstruction was the policy which made the
greatest appeal to activists in the Home Rule movement. Activists,
represented primarily by that undercover Fenian element which had
agreed to cooperate with Butt in 1873, were now proving restless. The
last of the years for which such cooperation had been agreed had arrived.
The Home Rule Confederation of Great Britain, representing immigrant
Irishmen in Britain and always largely under Fenian control, repeated its
support for parliamentary obstruction.

The Queen's Speech which opened the session of 1876 said not a single
word about Ireland. This helped sharpen the Home Rulers' attack. Parnell
himself was one of the four Irish Members who spoke critically of the
Speech on 8 February, tacitly emphasizing his sympathy with the more
advanced elements among nationalists by another plea for the release of
the remaining political prisoners. But he did so in almost conciliatory
vein. The Government, he said, could do nothing which would give as
much satisfaction to Irishmen, and he went on in words which Fenians
might have found a little odd to say on behalf of the military prisoners:
'They were not even ring-leaders, but brave soldiers and sailors who had
fought well for England.' The conciliatory note, if such were intended,
was largely wasted, for by the time he spoke there was only a very thin
attendance in the House.

Nevertheless he remained remarkably active in the first month of the new session, earning a special commendation from the *Nation*, even by the end of the first week, for being prominent in 'obstructing the course of legislation' by questions or notices of motions.

By the end of the month he had intervened in the House on eight occasions, which was more often than either Biggar or Butt. His questions ranged over such widely differing subjects as: what the Government would do about the possible danger to shipping of the sunken naval vessel HMS *Vanguard* off the Irish coast; whether Meath could be exempted from the renewed Coercion Act; why a subadar of the 25th Bombay Infantry had been dismissed; the extent to which the Bombay native army was supplied with breach-loading rifles; and the fate of the American citizen Edward O'Meagher Condon, condemned to death but reprieved to life imprisonment for his part in the killing of a Manchester police sergeant during the rescue of Fenian leaders from a prison van there in 1867. Asking whether Condon was now in Spike Island prison and whether he was handcuffed or chained in his cell during any periods of the day, and how long for, he was told curtly that Condon had never been on Spike Island and that he had never been chained or handcuffed. But the *Freeman's Journal* commented on 'the admirable and dignified manner' in which Parnell had put his questions. The material for the Indian questions had been given him by Frank Hugh O'Donnell, the young nationalist who had been unseated after an election petition at Galway in 1874 and who, while hoping to return to the House of Commons, was working in Fleet Street for the *Morning Post*. He was at the same time the London correspondent of the *Bombay Gazette*.

The programme of Irish Bills and motions agreed on by the Home Rule Party was unfolded with disciplined regularity. Of the total of eighty-five Private Member's Bills for the session, forty – or almost half – were Irish, and the parliamentary correspondent of the *World* noted that Butt's strategy was brought to bear with a success that had 'non-plussed Parliament'. The success was relative, however, for the Bills were regularly defeated. Bills for Grand Jury reform and for reform of the Irish franchise for municipal elections, a motion to bring the Irish borough franchise into line with the English for parliamentary elections and a Bill to benefit Irish fisheries had all been defeated before the Easter recess of 1876.

A disturbing note was the unsatisfactory turnout of Home Rule Members in the divisions. The Irish did receive some support from English Liberals and radicals, but the Government victories could have been made much narrower if the Home Rule vote itself had been mustered in full strength. The *Freeman's Journal*, acting 'with regret and under a strong sense of duty', pilloried by name in its leader columns fifteen Home Rulers in particular who had been repeatedly absent from divisions without the excuse of illness, remarking with reason that it was 'very bad encouragement to those English members who, in division after division, are now supporting the cause of Ireland, to find that cause deserted by so large a proportion of men returned specially to promote it'. A few days later Butt wrote to all Home Rule Members about such criticism, but merely stated in characteristically gentlemanly terms that he was sure they would forgive him for earnestly requesting their presence at the next division.

Parnell's own parliamentary record contrasted strongly with that of the other young Protestant landlord, Rowland Blennerhassett – the Member for Co. Kerry – to whose engagement in politics Parnell's had, at first, seemed similar. Blennerhassett was now one of the fifteen Members pilloried for inattendance in the columns of the *Freeman's Journal*; Parnell's voting record was impeccable. Parnell made no major speeches in the Irish debates but was increasingly using the House's rules of procedure to interfere with the House's business. The *Nation* singled him out in this respect as early as the middle of February 1876.

On one occasion he even used the obstructive technique of 'espying strangers' to the benefit of the Government itself, getting it out of an embarrassing personal wrangle in which two of its own supporters had landed it. He was developing a sort of gift for incongruity as part of his natural political equipment. He had the power to baffle. This might at times seem to stem less from design than from gaucheness and a curiously locked-in sense of self-confidence, but the power to baffle confers a useful advantage in any arena. As he slowly became professional in politics, he learned to exploit this power to increasing political effect.

In March 1876, in the traditional role of an aggrieved Irish Member, he took part in an obstructive manœuvre which he stuck to even after such an experienced parliamentary hand as A. M. Sullivan had decided that enough was enough.

The occasion arose from a protest by Sullivan himself that there were only two Irish Members on the committee of twenty-one which decided on the hearing of Private Member's Bills. Neither was a Home Ruler. He proposed that the committee should be increased to twenty-three by adding two Home Rulers. The Government refused. Sullivan said he would challenge by a division the nomination of every single Member proposed for the committee. A remarkable demonstration of concerted Irish obstruction then followed.

It was about two o'clock in the morning and there were fewer than a hundred Members in the House, of whom thirteen were Home Rulers. After the first name had been challenged and the small band of Irish had been defeated, it was suggested to them by the Government that, having made their protest, they should abandon the tactic. But Parnell rose and said that they had deliberately adopted this course and would stick to it. After the division on the next name had been just as inevitably defeated, Captain Nolan, the Home Rule Member for Galway, moved the adjournment of the House. But this motion too was of course lost. Parnell again rose to say that they intended to persist. He moved the rejection of the next name on the list. At the tenth division, Sullivan told the House that he was advising his friends not to divide any further.

The next two names for the committee happened to be the two Irishmen who were not Home Rulers. They were not challenged. But when the next English name came up it was challenged, alone at first, by Major Purcell O'Gorman, the popular Member for Waterford. He eventually found a seconder in Captain Nolan, who, though he had apparently previously agreed to Sullivan's decision, remembered that he had also given his word to act as seconder to O'Gorman. Sullivan, anxious not to show dissension among the Irish, actually voted again in this division, but then left the Chamber for the night.

The remaining band of Home Rulers, now down to six including Parnell, proceeded to challenge all the other names on the list – ineffectually, of course, but they succeeded in keeping the House up to 4.15 a.m. They were elated by their achievement, and the *Freeman's Journal*'s parliamentary correspondent singled out Parnell and four colleagues by name for their 'indomitable perseverance'. The next day the House was full of talk of the affair, in the Lobby, the Reading Room and the Dining Room, though the English newspapers gave no prominence to it.

The incident was the cause of a public exchange of letters between Sullivan and Parnell later in the week, in the course of which Parnell drew attention to the fact that English and Scottish Members had continually stated in the course of the debate that Ireland was no more specially entitled to representation on these committees than Lancashire or London. 'In other words,' he concluded, 'it is part of an organized attempt to blot out the name of Ireland as a country from the map of Europe, to consider her a county of England, to make our people forget their inheritance and succumb to the demon of centralization, which sooner or later must recoil upon the originators and prove their own destruction if persevered in.'

Chapter 11

Parnell began to specialize in far-fetched opportunities to score aggressive Irish nationalist points. On 21 March 1876 there was a long debate on the seizure of the British steamship *Talisman* by the Peruvian Government and the imprisonment for over a year of eighteen British subjects in the crew. Parnell eventually rose to say he was surprised at the Government making such a fuss about the matter, 'considering that last year they pushed through a House a Bill depriving Her Majesty's subjects in Ireland . . . [*Cries of 'Oh!' 'Oh!'*] . . . depriving Her Majesty's subjects in Ireland . . . [*Cries of 'Order!'*] . . . depriving Her Majesty's subjects of the right of trial in certain counties in Ireland'. By the time he had got to the end of this sentence there was such a hubbub, accompanied by cries of 'Question', that Parnell declared that as the House would not listen to him he begged to move the adjournment of the debate and sat down.

Captain Nolan protested that Parnell, who was the first Irish Member to speak in a four-hour debate, had not been allowed to be on his feet for more than two and a half minutes. But Butt recommended Parnell to drop his motion for adjournment, saying that he himself would have to vote against it if he did not. Parnell agreed to do so, but showed he was still not fully master of the rules of the House by going on to address Butt in person. 'I need not assure him', he said, 'that there is no one in the House whose opinion I value more highly. I do not in the slightest degree . . .'

Here the Speaker reminded him that he could not now make another speech on the motion. Paradoxically, since the hour was late anyway, the Government then agreed to the adjournment without a division. W. E. Forster, the Liberal Member for Bradford, added patronizingly that 'the Hon. Member for Meath had rather got us out of a difficulty'.

The parliamentary correspondent of the *World*, Sir Henry Lucy, again sought to ridicule Parnell, saying that the acceptance of his motion for the adjournment had made him 'a laughing stock'. For him, Parnell was now '. . . the least lovable of all the Irish Members'. He had, Lucy wrote, 'no redeeming qualities unless we regard it as an advantage to have in the

House a man who unites in his own person all the childish unreasonableness, all the ill-regulated suspicion, and all the astounding credulity of the Irish peasant'.

This last term was a curious one to apply to a Cambridge-educated landlord with nearly five thousand acres. But at least it showed that, where they noticed Parnell at all, the English were unable to make sense of him. This did him no harm in Ireland.

He had been back to Avondale at least once during these first two months of the 1876 session. On 20 March he was sworn on to the Grand Jury at the Wicklow Spring Assizes. And, though back at Westminster the next day for his intervention on the Peruvian Government's seizure of the *Talisman,* he returned to Ireland for the Easter recess. On Easter Monday, 17 April, he attended an Easter vestry of Rathdrum parish church as a synodsman, and on 22 April he was honoured by being given the chair for the first time at a meeting of the Home Rule League in Dublin. At this meeting, Butt, after stressing some immediate advantages to be had from short-term collaboration with certain Liberals in the House, delivered the by now rather stale message that 'with patience and endurance he was convinced that many years could not elapse before their efforts were crowned with success – before they had a native parliament sitting in their capital encouraging native industry and enterprise, protecting the rights and liberties of all classes of the people, and rendering Ireland what she should be – a great, glorious and free nation'.

That this sort of approach with its talk of 'many years' was unlikely to be acceptable much longer to the extreme nationalists who had originally given the Home Rule movement their support had been made clear to Butt only a very few days before in a most personal manner. A handful of Fenians had tried to break up a procession in his honour in his own constituency of Limerick. The attempt had been a complete failure, but in a letter to him beforehand they had written, 'Most of the people here have lost all faith, if they ever had any, in the movement, and the number of defeats sustained by the Home Rule Members in the House for the last three sessions should convince every unprejudiced mind that constitutional agitation is useless.'

Parnell himself took a few more days off before returning to Westminster, attending as a steward in the stands at the Co. Wicklow steeplechases held at Rathdrum on Saturday 29 April. It was an afternoon of piercing wind and continuous rain, and his fellow stewards in the stands once again included his kinsman the Earl of Wicklow and other landed aristocrats. Again it is tempting to wonder what, apart from horses, they talked about.

Back in London at the beginning of May 1876, he continued to develop his role in the House of Commons. On 4 May he spoke in a debate which had no connection with Ireland and in which, unusually, he refrained from dragging in any Irish reference. His speech, however, is of interest in disclosing already that genuinely radical quality in his temperament which, allied to his aggressiveness, was before long to give the Irish people new political power.

The issue was Samuel Plimsoll's Merchant Shipping Bill. Picking up an allegation of Plimsoll's that the Navy was selling off to the Merchant Navy old naval food stores which had deteriorated, he said it was monstrous that an ordinary tradesman selling food unfit for human consumption should be prosecuted while he 'supposed a right honourable Gentleman [i.e. a Government Minister] would hardly be sent to prison for such an act'. He was told by the Committee Chairman to stick to the point.

This was another instance of what was becoming Parnell's own special effect in the House: that of making the House apprehensive and uncertain of what he might be up to next.

The next day he was back again at serious obstruction, with Biggar, on the Cattle Diseases (Ireland) Bill, moving unsuccessfully to suspend debate and report progress 'on account of the lateness of the hour'. He resorted to the same device again on 22 May, on a Committee of Ways and Means sitting after 1.15 a.m. He objected, in concert with Nolan and Biggar, to business being run through 'in this hurry-scurry way'. Earlier that evening he had returned to the cause of the remaining Fenian prisoners. His name had been sixth of 138 signatures of Members of Parliament on a petition for their release recently presented to Disraeli by O'Connor Power. When Disraeli said he did not intend to release any of them, O'Connor Power moved the adjournment of the House.

There were in fact now only fifteen Fenian prisoners left in custody. The rest had either served their time, escaped or been already amnestied. Nine of the fifteen – former soldiers – were in penal settlements in Australia, where Disraeli made out that their lot was not a particularly hard one. Of the six in Britain, two had been convicted of murder after the Manchester rescue of 1867. Another was a one-armed Fenian named Michael Davitt, who had been sentenced in 1870 to fifteen years for trying to run arms to the IRB from Lancashire. The other three were former soldiers who had taken an active part in the Fenian rising. That these in particular, in being spared execution, had enjoyed some measure of clemency by the standards of the time was not an argument to which any sort of Irish nationalist was inclined to listen.

All the prisoners except for Michael Davitt were now in their tenth year of confinement in the rigorous conditions of mid-nineteenth-century convict prisons. One at least, a Sergeant McCarthy, was known to be suffering from heart disease. Some of the intense bitterness felt in Ireland at the refusal to release them was expressed in the debate by Biggar in a remarkably savage attack on Disraeli. It was not, he said, surprising that England did not feel sufficiently secure to release the men when the command of the army was held 'by a German prince [the Duke of Cambridge] and we find a Prime Minister . . . alien in race and probably religion to the English people'.

Parnell, after stating that he believed the American Edward O'Meagher Condon 'perfectly innocent of the crime of killing Sergeant Brett at Manchester', and recommending mercy for Sergeant McCarthy on the grounds that he had fought well as a soldier for England in other parts of the world than Ireland, spoke of Davitt. The reason he had been sentenced to fifteen years while another man charged with a similar offence but since released had been given only seven was, Parnell suggested, that Davitt was an Irishman and the other an Englishman. He did not know, he said, how much effect Davitt's being an Irishman might have had with the Judge.

There were cries of 'No! No!'

Parnell went on. It was, he said, very hard to be superior to prejudices on all occasions. He had little doubt that it was Davitt's being an Irishman, at a time when the Manchester rescue and the explosion at Clerkenwell prison had created a great deal of strong feeling in middle- and upper-class minds, that had determined the heaviness of his sentence. The Government remained unaffected by the reproach. None of the prisoners was released. Davitt was before long to be playing a crucial role in Parnell's political career.

This speech marked the beginning of a fortnight in which Parnell was more active than ever before. One of the rules of the House of Commons was that opposed business could not be taken after 12.30 a.m. Later that week when Sir Michael Hicks Beach said he hoped that he might take the second reading of the Juries Procedure (Ireland) Bill, Parnell got up and said, 'No! It is ten minutes past two!', and by opposing it with some of his colleagues he succeeded in getting it postponed.

The sight of Parnell rising to his feet was already recognized as a portent by the House, if not as yet a very serious one. When at 12.15 a.m. on Monday 29 May, after considerable debate in committee on the Commons Preservation Bill, clause 2 was finally ready to be added to it,

Parnell arose amid ironical cheers and groans to move that the Chairman should report progress. He said that notwithstanding the result of the last division and 'recollecting that two hours of the valuable time of the House had been wasted the other night . . . [*Cries of "Oh! Oh!"*]' He said, 'Yes, two hours of time had been wasted the other night . . . [*Renewed cries of "Oh!"*]' He said 'wasted . . . [*Laughter and loud cries of "Oh!"*]' He moved that 'the Chairman report progress and ask to sit again.' His motion was then negatived without a division and the clause was carried.

Parnell was unabashed. A few minutes later he was involved in another confused scene on the same subject in the course of which he was so loudly interrupted that an English Liberal Member said that the conduct of the House was that which might be expected not from an assembly of gentlemen but from an assembly of coal porters, and the Chairman himself felt compelled to draw attention to Parnell's right to be heard. Eventually the House decided it had had enough and adjourned at one o'clock in the morning of 30 May.

He was back disturbing Government business the same afternoon. Altogether on 30 May 1876 he spoke on four separate occasions, at one moment delaying proceedings by speaking after the Government spokesman had already wound up a debate on the electoral system in order actually to make clear his support of the Government motion because in this instance at least, he said, there was no distinction drawn between one part of the country and another.

Or rather, that is what the Hansard reporter understood him to say – it was difficult to make out his exact words because of the loud cries of 'Division!' with which members attempted to drown them. But the correspondent of the *Freeman's Journal* seems to have picked up more through the 'great tumult' with which Parnell was received. 'As no Irishman has spoken a lot,' it reported him as saying, 'I wish to say a few words. Many Irishmen feel that they cannot obtain equal rights' (great uproar). 'If there were any doubt, this debate settles it' (noises). 'I have no more to say' (great cheering). 'You are not yet out of the wood,' he went on (uproar and laughter). The report concluded that 'he wound up by saying something about Honest John Martin and Royal Meath, but the sentence was unintelligible during the uproar'. Later on the same evening, in what the *Freeman's Journal* headed 'Another Scene', he was again howled down, trying to make himself heard while seconding a motion for the adjournment against cries and counter-cries of 'Sit down!', 'Go on!', 'Order!', and 'Speak up!'

This fortnight's burst of parliamentary activity by Parnell induced in

Henry Lucy something of a frenzy. 'Something really must be done about Mr Parnell,' he wrote at the beginning of June 1876. He quoted a *Times* leader which, he said, in referring to some 'incoherent observations' Parnell had made in the Fenian debate, had suggested that Parnell 'was not all there'. He went on:

Whether Heaven has blessed Mr Parnell with a full measure of intelligence, or whether in the composition of his mind something material was omitted are speculations interesting in themselves but out of place in this department of a journal . . . I repeat that something really must be done about Mr Parnell . . . about Mr Parnell there is not the faintest glimmer of humour. He is always at a white heat of rage, and makes with savage earnestness fancifully ridiculous statements, such as you may hear from your partner in the quadrille, if you ever have the good fortune to be a guest at the annual ball at Colney Hatch [a well-known mental asylum].

But the sophisticated view of the parliamentary correspondent of the *World* was less perceptive of the Irish political scene than was the primitive instinct of the young Member for Co. Meath. 'It is Ireland', concluded Lucy, 'that Mr Parnell wounds now almost nightly, in the face of mankind, and no one who is capable of cherishing affection and admiration for a country that has done so much to leaven the world with genius, wit and social charm can look on without sorrow and resentment.' This was a political misjudgement of a traditional English sort. It failed to appreciate the heartening effect of English disapproval on most popular Irish opinion. To regard the Irish primarily as simply good company was a luxury the English would not be able to afford much longer.

It is true that in some polite nationalist quarters in Ireland Parnell's behaviour was causing a flicker of disquiet. The *Freeman's Journal*, organ of respectable middle-class constitutional Home Rule nationalism, noted a recent 'unfortunate tendency to make scenes and to stir that forbearance and easy-going temper for which the House is celebrated'. After saying piously that it was not going to name names, it continued, 'We must say that within the last month or six weeks there have been movements and squabbles which have had but one effect – that of weakening the great and daily increasing strength of the Irish Party.' But a few days later in another context the paper was happy to name Parnell as 'that resolute gentleman'. There was no sign that either its approval or disapproval meant anything at all to him.

He returned to Westminster some days after the end of the Whitsun recess and was soon intervening in debate again with small concern for the parliamentary susceptibilities of the *Freeman's Journal* or anyone else. On a motion for a select committee to inquire into Royal Irish Constabulary pensions, on 28 June, he seized the opportunity to put a straightforward nationalist argument, saying he hoped the time would come when good and true Irishmen, as these men were, would not be employed by the Government in hunting down their fellow countrymen.

Two days later Butt's long-awaited Home Rule motion – only the second since the party's successes in the election of 1874 – was heard in the House of Commons. This time the motion was merely one for a select committee to inquire into the Irish demand for a restoration of the Irish parliament – a formula which, it was hoped, would secure a larger vote of sympathetic English Members than two years before.

Butt went out of his way to placate English feeling, stressing the Home Rule demand as evidence that Irishmen did not want separation and arguing that the continued presence of some Irish MPs at Westminster – which that demand then envisaged – was a desirable demonstration of concern for Ireland's part in the Empire. He quoted with approval what *The Times* had said two years before when it had called on Disraeli to see 'how far he could gratify the spirit of nationality without danger to the Empire'.

This in effect was a reasonable definition of Home Rule as most Irishmen of the time understood it. But there was clearly ambiguity in any such demand from representatives of a 'nation' which at other times expressed its aspirations in more forthright terms. This was a weakness in the Home Rule case on which many hostile speakers touched. Perhaps the most effective speech of all in this sense was made by the renegade foundation member of the Home Rule Party, P. J. Smyth. In nominally proclaiming the doctrinal purity of total Repeal of the Union, he was cheered to the echo by Unionist Members because in doing so he decried Home Rule as 'weak and obscure'. He quoted the Archbishop of Tuam John MacHale's reference to Home Rule as 'a very ambiguous phrase' and John Mitchel's out-and-out definition of it as 'foreign rule'. Even a man now theoretically supporting the Home Rule Party, O'Connell's old supporter O'Neill Daunt, had referred to it as 'half a loaf'.

In his reply to the debate, Hicks Beach made the most of the ambiguity. He asked Members not to be misled by suggestions that Home Rule was not a threat to the Union. 'Some time ago last autumn,' he said, 'the Hon. Member for Meath made a speech in which he said that Home Rule and Repeal meant the same thing . . .'

Parnell rose to his feet. 'What I said', he explained, 'was that Home Rule would necessarily entail Repeal of the Union.'

Hicks Beach merely pointed out that Butt in fact repudiated any wish to repeal the Union, to which Butt himself added an embarrassing 'Hear! Hear!'

Parnell was to get his own back on Hicks Beach within the hour.

Earlier in the debate O'Connor Power had declared, 'If Ireland had a Parliament entrusted with the management of its own affairs, my belief is that we should never again hear of a Coercion Bill or of political prisoners, because the people of Ireland would not then think of revolution.'

Hicks Beach, either deliberately or through genuine misunderstanding, twisted the sense of this. 'Of all the extraordinary illusions concerned with the subject,' he said, 'the most strange to me appears the idea that Home Rule could have the effect of liberating the Fenian prisoners, the Manchester murderers.' It seems likely that some of the cries of 'No! No!' from the Irish benches with which this comment was greeted were intended reasonably as a denial of Hicks Beach's interpretation of what O'Connor Power had said. But the Chief Secretary countered such denial with the remark 'I regret that there is any Honourable Member in this House who will apologize for murder.'

Parnell again rose. 'The Right Honourable Member', he said, 'looked at me so directly when he said he regretted that any Member should apologize for murder, that I wish to say as publicly and directly as I can that I do not believe, and I shall never believe, that any murder was committed at Manchester.'

He was echoing a sentiment that had been expressed in similar terms before in the House, and by other Irishmen elsewhere, but the pugnacity with which he seized the opportunity to do so was typical of the parliamentary character he had now developed.

Parnell's first biographer, R. Barry O'Brien, writing some twenty years later, was informed by a veteran Fenian that it had been this remark of Parnell's which had first attracted the IRB's attention to him. O'Brien unfortunately incorporated into this blurred recollection his own inaccurate comment that 'up to the end of 1876 Parnell continued undistinguished and almost unnoticed . . . not yet drawn out of the ruck'. This view has been widely accepted, and subsequent biographers have recorded that it was with his 'Manchester murder' intervention that Parnell for the first time seriously caught the attention of the public. The record of his political activity in the years 1875–6 shows this to be incorrect. Moreover, curiously, the 'Manchester murder' intervention, unlike his parliamentary activity earlier in the session, attracted no public attention at all at the time.

Finally, what gave a particularly Parnell-like twist to the whole incident, both as enshrined in historical legend and in the reality of the time, is that three months earlier in the House of Commons, when speaking on behalf of those imprisoned after the events at Manchester, he had had no scruple about twice referring to the shooting there as 'murder'.

Chapter 12

Butt's second attempt to get a motion to consider Home Rule through the House of Commons was lost, as was to be expected, by an enormous majority (291 to 61). The failure confronted nationalist opinion in Ireland more awkwardly than ever before with the reality of what seemed its impotence in Parliament. It was true that, for all the majority, there were in fact 167 fewer votes cast against the motion than in 1874 and that one eyewitness of the debate reckoned that, of those Members who had not voted, two-thirds had abstained on principle. But the chances of ever getting enough English Members actually behind such a motion in order to carry it through still seemed hopelessly remote.

The optimism in the face of set-back which had been easy enough to come by in the fresh dawn of 1874 was already becoming a laboured act of faith. There was increasing restlessness at the grass roots of the movement, however much the *Freeman's Journal* might argue that Ireland must be patient and that 'a childish petulance at every delay' itself argued incapacity for self-government. Several of the Home Rule Members now received telegrams or letters from their constituencies calling on them to propose the withdrawal of Home Rulers from Westminster in a body. And the extreme nationalist weekly the *Irishman*, using a phrase that was soon to become famous in a slightly different context, called for 'a new departure' along these lines. The *Nation* probably best summed up the mood of determined Home Rulers:

The defeat affords full justification for a much stronger line of action than any ... hitherto adopted ... Home Rulers should consider whether the time has not come when it is advisable to do something more than merely travel slowly again over the ground which has been so lately trodden ... The business of English legislation is now very much at the mercy of the Irish Members ... they can block it, and stop it, and turn it into a mass of inextricable confusion if they choose.

A few days later the North London branch of the Home Rule

Confederation of Great Britain passed a resolution urging that 'the vigorous and somewhat obstructive tactics adopted by Mr Parnell, Mr Biggar, Mr O'Connor Power, Dr Ward and Captain Nolan' should be taken up by the other members.

There was only just over a month of the 1876 parliamentary session left, and Parnell did not trouble to play much part in it. His own feelings of frustration made themselves felt in a speech outside Parliament when, on 4 July 1876, a group of advanced nationalists held a large public evening meeting at Harold's Cross, Dublin, to adopt an address of congratulation to the American President on the hundredth anniversary of American Independence.

Parnell had arrived in Ireland that day straight from Westminster, and, as darkness fell, he drove in a wagonette with, among others, the Fenian Patrick Egan, through vast crowds waving green flags and the Stars and Stripes to a platform where an enormous Stars and Stripes had been unfurled.

Egan spoke first. He talked of the United States – 'that great Republic to which Irishmen were banished with a vengeance' – shaking off the hated yoke of England, and of the thousands upon thousands in Ireland 'whose hearts beat for the day when their banished kindred and descendants will be coming back with a vengeance'.

Parnell moved the main address. This referred to America's enjoyment of a hundred years of freedom and Ireland's seven centuries of oppression.

'The spirit which has proscribed and oppressed every nation on the face of the earth with which [England] has come into contact lives to-day as strong as ever,' he said. And then, in a reference to England's involvement in the European crisis which was then developing between Turkey and Russia in the Balkans, he went on, 'It is said that there are 50,000 Irishmen in the British Army. Just now when the war cloud is bursting in the East, when England gives token of a design to back up Mahomedanism [*Hisses*], to back up the Crescent against the Cross, I hope that no Irishman will so far forget his own self-respect and his religion [*Applause*], I hope no Irishman will so far forget his country as to aid England in her nefarious attempt [*Applause*].'

This seemed a thinly veiled invitation to Irishmen in the British Army to disregard their oath of loyalty to the Queen, and an attempt was made to raise the matter in the House of Commons. The Conservative Member for Peterborough, B. H. Whalley, gave notice of a question to ascertain from Parnell whether this report of the words he used was correct. Parnell returned to London specially to confront the attack, but, to

Whalley's indignation, the question was never called. An interview then took place between him and Parnell in which, in the best traditions of the House of Commons, Whalley actually apologized to Parnell for the personal inconvenience involved in bringing him over. Parnell placidly told him not to distress himself, adding that he might like to know that the report of the speech was 'very accurate and reported to a nicety what he wished to convey to those he addressed'.

Just before returning to Ireland he attended an important party meeting in London at which a unanimous resolution was passed, intended to dispel some of the developing criticism of Butt. The resolution declared 'our unalterable confidence in our distinguished leader . . . our admiration for his unrivalled wisdom and tact'. As one who clearly considered tact of peripheral importance in the conduct of Irish affairs in the House of Commons, Parnell may have had reservations about the wording, but in the absence of any other leadership he was probably content to confirm such coherence in the movement as there was. Though Butt had disappointed advanced nationalists, it had to be said that in little over three years he had begun to transform Irish nationalist prospects by at least creating any sort of Irish party at all.

At the Home Rule Convention in Dublin that August, the annual report commented optimistically that the organization had created 'a third party in the state' eschewing both Liberals and Conservatives and had control of enough electors in Britain 'to decide the fate of a Ministry'. But one of the resolutions urged 'a much more determined attitude in the House of Commons'. Another expressed 'every confidence in our great leader, Isaac Butt'. Unresolved ambiguity about Butt and his style of leadership cannot, at this stage, have been any more of a problem for Parnell than unresolved ambiguity about the nature of the final national objective itself.

As a Home Ruler, he theoretically subscribed to a limited federal demand for an Irish parliament with domestic powers only. Yet he had more than once in public indulged in thoughts which implied something much more whole-heartedly and emotionally nationalist. At Wexford in 1875 he had not hesitated to invoke the cause of the rebels of 1798. This very summer of 1876, at Harold's Cross, so far from being content with a domestic parliament only, he had seemed to incite the Irish soldiers of the British Army not to fight for the Crown in time of war. So where exactly did he stand? Only ten years before he had been happy to kick extreme nationalists out through his mother's front door.

Much later, when experience had given him a practical consciousness of strategy, he was to define his own simply in terms of an attitude to the British Government: 'They will do what we can make them do,' he said. Given the personal nature of his commitment to Irish politics, the identification of his own self-esteem with that of the majority of the people of Ireland, he needed no other principle. His sensitive pride, his temperamental belligerence and his inherited self-confidence in detaching himself from things English had all been placed at the service of the Irish people.

For the present, the still vague field of Home Rule politics provided at least room for manœuvre. For the fight into which his nature had led him, options could remain open. 'We must make matters disagreeable for those English fellows,' he was heard to say about this time – 'as disagreeable as we can.'

In Ireland that summer he attended for a time to his local duties as squire of Avondale. He was sworn on to the Wicklow Grand Jury on the morning of 18 July, and it sat on the 20th and 21st. A case of bigamy, one of larceny and one of firing at a magistrate were up for trial, but the Judge told the Grand Jury that the county appeared to be in a most satisfactory state.

He was at a meeting of the Rathdrum Poor Law Guardians on 1 August and again on 15 August, discussing such local matters as the election of poor-rate collectors, adulteration of the workhouse milk, drainage works for the village of Kilfedder and the source of an offensive smell (originally from the premises of a manufacturer of manure) in a street in Wicklow town. He was one of two magistrates sitting at Rathdrum on 17 August when he declared of a man named Byrne prosecuted for the already detected adulteration of the workhouse milk that he was 'quite sure it was not put in with Mr Byrne's knowledge but there can be no doubt that there was some water in the milk when it was delivered at the workhouse'. He inflicted the minimum penalty, a fine of £2. 10s.

He had been dutifully attending Home Rule meetings in Dublin too, taking the chair at one on 24 July, again in the company of Patrick Egan, and suggesting, presumably with reference to criticism of Butt, that 'personal matters should be avoided'. But he almost certainly derived more direct political stimulus from the two-day Convention in Dublin of the Home Rule Confederation of Great Britain, which he attended as a delegate on 21 and 22 August.

This organization, which now had quite sizeable branches with their own Home Rule halls in most large towns of England and Scotland, had

Butt as its nominal President, but it was largely the creation of Fenians or former Fenians who still provided most of its activists. Its new Hon. Secretary was an activist of less dogmatic outlook – that Frank Hugh O'Donnell who had been helping Parnell with advice and research for his parliamentary questions from the offices of the *Morning Post*. O'Donnell was an egotistical but energetic man who, while he had no time for the chimera of military rebellion, was a strong advocate of obstruction.

The Confederation claimed to represent 150,000 Irish electors in England, Scotland and Wales and to be able to throw their electoral weight on to the side of whichever of the two great parties would do most for the Irish nationalist cause. On the eve of the Dublin Convention, the Confederation had by-election victories to celebrate at Burnley and Manchester, where it had backed Liberal candidates who had given individual pledges of support for Home Rule. It confidently claimed that there were at least thirty-five other English boroughs in which the Irish vote had as much influence as in these two.

At the Dublin meeting a resolution was passed to the effect that it was 'expedient for the Irish Members to adopt a much more determined attitude in the House of Commons on all matters in which Ireland is concerned'. Butt was again elected President of the Confederation, but there were only two other MPs among the five Vice-Presidents – Biggar and Parnell. Parnell himself had had a vivid reminder of the nature of Fenian discontent with Butt when, at a meeting of the Home Rule League on the first evening of the Confederation's Convention, a man known to be on the Supreme Council of the IRB had pushed his way on to the platform and delivered an unscheduled speech calling for the principles of Wolfe Tone, Robert Emmet and the Fenian exile Jeremiah O'Donovan Rossa. In the subsequent fracas, Parnell had been forced backwards by the surge of the crowd.

Another scene, at the Convention's concluding banquet for two hundred, at which Parnell sat at the head table, three seats to the left of Butt, was more comic, though it too had its political undertones. One of the diners recognized a Dublin Castle detective named Scully trying to pass himself off as one of the waiters, and the man was dragged up in front of Butt 'with a very stupid air, looking foolishly about' and asked if he had a ticket. He admitted he had none and grudgingly conceded his identity. He was then thrown out ('very rapidly removed by a number of persons, after experiencing considerable inconvenience'). The Chief Secretary for Ireland later virtually apologized for the intrusion, explaining that the detective had exceeded his authority. Butt must have been quite grateful for even this amount of evidence that something with which he was connected could still be held to warrant police supervision.

The ambiguity which was always to be a valuable asset for Irish nationalism brought its own pitfalls. O'Connor Power and Biggar, who were still simultaneously members of the Supreme Council of the IRB and Home Rule MPs, had a nasty shock on a Sunday in September. They had gone over together to Manchester for a lecture which O'Connor Power was to deliver to nationalists there on 'Irish Wit and Humour'. He was peremptorily asked at the start if he believed in the principles of Tone and Emmet where Home Rule for Ireland was concerned. Trying to make himself heard above shouts and hisses, he merely said that he had come to lecture on 'Irish Wit and Humour' and not on Home Rule. Whereupon the meeting broke up in violent disorder with chairs and sticks wielded vigorously, while Biggar, who had been presiding, sustained a scalp wound from which he bled profusely.

O'Connor Power himself, when addressing his constituents at Castlebar a week later, took some trouble to spell out more carefully his wish to be many things to many men where nationalism was concerned. Though criticizing Butt's timidity, he said he had no desire to weaken his influence. However, he intended 'to remain in the future as in the past, an uncompromising advocate of Irish nationalism, one who thought his country called upon him for the very last sacrifice'. He would, he said, be a coward and poltroon if he was not ready to bare his breast to shield her from the shafts of her enemies. The cheers which greeted this effusion were not diminished by the simultaneous statement that he had 'no faith whatever in people ready at any moment to die for Ireland'.

Such gyrations of view typified the predicament of the extreme nationalists of the day. From the very beginning of his own venture into politics, Parnell had always been careful to give the extremists due recognition. They supplied valuable activists like O'Connor Power, Biggar and Egan for the general political scene, but such activists often found themselves at loggerheads with their theoretical superiors in the IRB – men more concerned to preserve the doctrinal purity of revolutionary theory than to countenance any alternative action. One such was the President of the IRB's Supreme Council, Charles Kickham, a half-blind, half-deaf novelist of talent, who conducted much of his conversation in deaf-and-dumb language, and who, cruelly, could thus be seen as a symbol of the IRB's detachment from the real political world. Total separation from Britain, to be achieved by military rebellion, was the bedrock of the purists' ideology; any other means was seen as a compromise on the purity of the ideological end. Their difficulty was that military rebellion had to be regarded for the foreseeable future as a totally unfeasible proposition. The problem: how to prevent nationalistic doctrine from seeming unfeasible too. The agreement to work through Parliament and the Home Rule movement had been one attempt to do this; but it was beginning to seem an increasingly inadequate solution, and Kickham was to withdraw the IRB's official support for it at the end of 1876 when the three-year trial period was over.

On the other hand, no satisfactory alternative seemed to offer itself. Thus for extreme nationalists, for many Home Rulers and for those whose position was blurred somewhere between the two it was a period in which rhetoric underlined optimism or impatience, according to temperament, and was substituted for precise political thought.

That September Parnell went for the second time in his life to his mother's country, the United States. Those Dublin Fenians who had sponsored the meeting at Harold's Cross had chosen him and O'Connor Power to present their centennial address of congratulation to President Grant in person. He crossed the Atlantic – a nine-day journey – a fortnight ahead of O'Connor Power, to spend some time with his mother, his sister Fanny and his brother John, who were all then in New York.

O'Connor Power doubled his mission with that of IRB envoy to the undercover American-Irish secret society the Clan na Gael, the most plausible of the various extreme Irish nationalist émigré groups in the USA. Clan na Gael was run by an exiled Fenian, John Devoy, now a journalist on the *New York Herald*, working closely with the Philadelphia doctor William Carroll, who had visited Ireland with John Mitchel at the time of the by-election in 1875. As a child Carroll had emigrated with his parents from Donegal before the Famine. He had been a surgeon-major in the Union armies during the Civil War.

There seems no reason to think that Parnell knew of his colleague O'Connor Power's secret mission. If he did, he showed little interest in it, remaining in bed uncontactable when Carroll called on them both at their Philadelphia Hotel. Parnell's interest in Philadelphia at the time centred on the Machinery Hall of the city's Centennial Exhibition, where he saw stonecutting machinery which struck him as suitable for his quarries at Avondale. He was also taken with a model bridge, the roof of which gave him an idea for the design of a cattle-shed.

Carroll, though doubtless attentive to such news as O'Connor Power brought of the moribund IRB in Ireland, was little interested in the

presentation of the centennial address to President Grant, being preoccupied with revolutionary plans of his own. In the land of the free,
backed by large sums of money contributed by embittered Irish emigrants,
these could be made to assume a certain plausibility. Carroll's and
Devoy's own concern at the time was to try to take advantage of the
opportunity presented by England's current difficulty with Russia in the
Balkans. Both men were in touch with the Russian Ambassador to the
USA. Carroll was toying with the idea of raising a force of some ten
thousand men in the USA to be infiltrated into Ireland, possibly in
detachments of 'friends coming to see their relatives'. Intelligent men like
Carroll and Devoy, contemplating such projects from the vantage point
of their American status, found no difficulty in seeing themselves as more
relevant to Ireland's national destiny than were men from the apparently
sterile world of Irish home politics.

Meanwhile Parnell's and O'Connor Power's own immediate enterprise
was taking on a near-farcical character of its own.

In New York on 2 October, three days after Power's arrival, they sent
a note to President Grant asking him when it would be convenient for
him to receive the congratulatory address they had brought from the Irish
people. They waited for a reply for over a week. None came.

The approach was, of course, quite unofficial. Wondering whether it
might not have been simply kept from the President altogether, they took
advantage of Grant's presence in New York on 11 October to solicit a
personal interview with him. He received them cordially. They learned
that this was indeed the first he had heard of their mission. He asked them
to come to Washington and present themselves at the White House the
following week.

They went to Washington, where they were told that before seeing the
President again they must first submit a copy of the address to the State
Department. Compliantly they went with a copy from their hotel, the
Arlington House, to see the Under-Secretary of State, John Cadwallader.
Cadwallader told them that, happy as he would be to help such a friendly
mission, protocol prescribed that addresses from people of a foreign
country should be presented through that country's Ambassador to the
United States. In this case, of course, that meant the British Ambassador.

Oddly, Parnell and Power agreed to this, though there was to be a
dispute about the terms on which they had done so. Cadwallader
maintained that they had 'concurred in the wisdom of the rule'. Parnell
and Power, in language which suggests the hand of Parnell, maintained
that they had merely 'concurred in [Cadwallader's] declared resolution to

act . . . in accordance with [his] sense of duty . . . without venturing to concur in the wisdom of the rule'.

From this point onwards the two Irishmen can hardly have seriously thought that they would be able to complete their mission. It was improbable that the British Ambassador would approve phrases in the address such as that which declared that, while America had enjoyed a hundred years of freedom, Ireland had 'borne seven centuries of oppression'.

But diplomatic fencing continued for a time. On 19 October Parnell and Power were informed by Cadwallader that, pleased as the Ambassador, Sir Edward Thornton, would be to present them personally to the President, and happy as he would have been to convey any congratulations to the President on the centenary, he could not present the address because he had received no instructions. Again Parnell's hand can be detected in the reply. 'Deeply sensible' as the two Irishmen were of Cadwallader's and Thornton's kindness, for which they tended their 'warmest thanks', they said there was actually no need for them simply to be presented to the President since they had already met him in New York. Thornton apparently had raised no objection to the address itself, so they could not see why its presentation 'without the aid which he is absolutely unable to give should appear discourteous to him'.

Cadwallader replied curtly. They were wrong, he said, to think that Thornton did not object to the language of the address: it was on this that he based his refusal to take part in the proceedings. This put it beyond his power to do anything further. However, he expressed appreciation of their kindly remarks. That was the end of the matter. This last letter was dated 23 October.

At some point in his stay, Parnell managed to visit not only the Philadelphia Exhibition but a coalmine in Virginia in which he had once made an investment. He reported to his brother John that he did not think much of its prospects. For the last three nights of October he was back at the Fifth Avenue Hotel, where his family and indeed President Grant himself sometimes stayed, and, having arranged for O'Connor Power to present an address from the Irish people to Congress instead of to the President, he sailed back across the Atlantic on 1 November. Beyond referring to Grant at one stage in conversation with his brother John as 'a vulgar old dog', he did not seem particularly resentful about what had happened.

Indeed, the rebuff had done him no harm at all in activist circles in Ireland. When the exchange of letters was published in the press, there was some amusement in London. Even in moderate circles in Dublin there was some suggestion that the matter had been handled rather clumsily. But there was righteous indignation among extreme nationalists, and approval for his stand against this insult to the Irish people.

He landed at Liverpool from the steamship *Scythia* on 11 November, and, instead of going straight on to Ireland as he had originally intended, stayed on to speak at a meeting of the Liverpool Home Rule Association which was being held to celebrate two recent municipal election successes in the city.

He was given a rousing welcome by the audience, and cheered over and over again as he rose to speak. With characteristic self-assurance, he began by saying that he had almost forgotten about Irish politics in the two months he had been away. But he at once showed himself in touch with the sensitive nerve of the contemporary Irish political scene.

Many years later one of the Fenians present on this occasion described the 'bad, halting delivery' of the speech Parnell made that day, and reported that he seemed constantly stuck for a word, as if he would break down at any moment. 'It was horribly awkward for the people listening to him,' this eyewitness said. 'But, oddly enough, it never seemed awkward to him.' He described how those on the platform would helpfully suggest a word to Parnell from time to time, but he always rejected it. 'There he would stand, with clenched fists which he shook nervously till the word he wanted came . . . And what we talked of afterwards was that Parnell's word was always the right word, and expressed exactly the idea in his head; our word was simply a makeshift for which he did not even thank us.'

But, however wooden in style, Parnell tackled at once the thorny question of the exact degree of Irish nationality which Home Rule could be said to embrace. The Home Rulers' position in Ireland was, he admitted, peculiar. Some said that they went too far in the Home Rule agitation; others that they did not go far enough. 'We have been told', he said, 'that we have lowered the national flag, that the Home Rule cause is not the cause of "Ireland a nation" and that we would degrade our country into the position of a province. There is no reason why Ireland under Home Rule will not be a nation in every sense and for every purpose that it is right that she should be a nation.'

Such attribution of indefinable flexibility to the concept of Home Rule skilfully begged the question of what a nation actually was. But lest his audience should too long ponder such rhetorical sleight of hand, he went on to describe a review of the New York Militia he had seen recently while in the USA. It was a force solely answerable to that city, and he implied that just such a militia would one day be Ireland's, to look after her interests 'without wishing to do harm to the integrity of the English Empire, or to do harm to those we would then call our English brothers. It is a foolish want of confidence that prevents Englishmen and the English Government from trusting Ireland. They know that Ireland is determined to be an armed nation and they fear to see her so.'

He ended with a reference to his rebuff in America, stressing that it was not the American people who had rejected the address but only the President, who had so far forgotten his position as the leader of a great nation as to take orders from a British Ambassador. 'No imputation should rest on the people of America,' he said. And he concluded, perhaps rather lamely, 'America I love, reverence and respect, and look for a great future for that country.'

Whatever the Fenian eyewitness may have thought of such a peroration, the audience showed no sign of disappointment. The vote of thanks was carried with loud and enthusiastic applause.

So, by the end of 1876, Parnell had established himself as a figure of considerable promise for those advanced nationalists who, for all their occasional misgivings, were prepared to disregard Charles Kickham's authority and to hope to realize their goal from within the framework of the Home Rule movement. Before much more than half the following year was out, his capacity for hard work, his restless energy and that self-confident disdain with which he had always enjoyed treating enemies were to bring him a position of significance within the movement from which he would eventually shake the structure of British politics to its foundations.

Chapter 13

The figure of Parnell presents one of history's most striking instances of an individual's power to shape forces already independently at work into a series of events different from what they might otherwise have been.

Looking back from over a hundred years later it is easy to see Parnell at the beginning of 1877 ready to assume such a role in the history of Ireland. He can seem from now on primarily a factor in the unfolding historical process: a factor first and a human being second. The real emphasis was of course the other way round: it was his individual human characteristics which made him the factor. Indeed his private life was soon to become an integral and finally decisive factor in events. The year 1877 therefore provides a useful time at which to consider as much as one can at this stage the human being about to become inseparable from history.

His physical appearance at the time is not a problem. There are black-and-white photographs. Everyone agrees that he was good-looking, and his brother John has left a conventional description of him in his first years in politics: 'striking ... tall and thin ... erect though without stiffness ... hair a darkish brown, or auburn ... rather long behind, curling slightly upwards to the back of his neck'. His pale but quite healthy complexion 'contrasted vividly with his hair, and accentuated the brilliancy of his dark grey eyes with their steady ... far away look ... long features and firm lips curving slightly downwards gave him a slightly melancholy appearance which was lively at times and at all events philosophical'. He had his own sense of humour, and was fond of making dry, pointed jokes about men and events.

Much of his personal character can already be inferred from his public and private performance to date – from his attitude to the Cambridge manure merchant and the English couple in the Rathdrum hotel, as well as from his sometimes quite humorous handling of situations such as that concerning the Dublin Lord Mayor and General Grant's protocol department in Washington, and from his own obstructive behaviour in the House of Commons.

An ability to dissemble usefully without the appearance of guile was already manifest in his public speeches. He could make the most extravagant appeal to the emotions of national myth without seeming to prejudice in any way a palpable, even cold, preoccupation with reality. That he could evoke personal loyalty from an audience in addition to the awe they felt for his name and status had often been made clear. In the House of Commons the complexity of his personality had successfully bewildered experienced observers like Henry Lucy. He had seemed to many Members slightly absurd, but he had proved his stamina and capacity for hard work in long night sittings and in the care he was prepared to devote to research for his questions, helped as he was at times with these by Frank Hugh O'Donnell to whose rooms at Serjeant's Inn he travelled from Keppel Street by bus or London's (then) only underground railway.

The charm and delicacy which Justin McCarthy found in his nature when the 'handsome . . . tall and stately figure . . . with . . . a singularly sweet and winning smile' came to know his family in 1875 is confirmed from other sources and in his brother John's account of how he had helped nurse him so devotedly after the American rail accident in 1871. Even Frank Hugh O'Donnell, writing with distortion and some bitterness in retrospect many years later, had to admit that he had liked Parnell at once on first meeting him in 1875 and had remarked on his modesty and anxiety to please as well as on his intelligence, his good looks and that 'peculiar wondering glance that was not wonder at all but critical observation'.

In the years of his historical fame Parnell was to acquire a reputation for being distant and aloof, but, while there were to be practical reasons for this, McCarthy, looking back some twenty years after their first meeting, insisted that he had never found anything 'ungenial or uncompanionable about him'. He was, McCarthy said, fond of his intimate friends and was to enjoy giving small dinner parties in the House of Commons or in restaurants, at which he was always a considerate and charming host, though himself not particularly interested in food or, by now, drink. O'Donnell is slightly at variance with McCarthy on this, saying that Parnell at this time was partial to the odd bottle of burgundy, but at least this can be taken as a further sign of companionability.

The former Fenian John Barry, also looking back some twenty years to his memories of Parnell, said he could not go so far as to call him exactly genial or sociable but said he was 'pleasant, certainly' and he had an undoubted sense of humour, though you never could tell what would amuse him. Leaving the House of Commons one evening in April 1877

they had gone, on Parnell's suggestion, to see a walking-match at the
Agricultural Hall, Islington, between a Cork man, Dan O'Leary, and an
American named Weston. The Cork man had won, and when to Parnell's
disgust the German band concluded the evening by playing 'God Save
the Queen' Parnell had taken great pleasure in bribing them to follow it
with the tune of 'God Save Ireland', to the bewilderment and annoyance
of many in the audience.

A fellow MP who worked with him on obstruction also described him
as more pleasant than genial or sociable, and added that he always had a
charm of manner which made him a most agreeable companion.

Both McCarthy and O'Donnell say the lodgings he had taken in
Keppel Street were cheap, but McCarthy insists that, while Bohemian
rather than fashionable, there was nothing squalid about such accommodation and he described the apartments in the houses there as 'spacious and
handsome'. O'Donnell, on the other hand, writes of Parnell's 'disgust at
the stuffy two rooms' and that to have to live in such furnished apartments
'plainly stung his pride'. Both witnesses were probably accurate up to a
point. O'Donnell was concerned to attribute much of the force of
Parnell's nationalism to a sense of outlawry from his class – 'a malcontent
patrician, inspired by pride of race and difficult circumstances' – and there
was some substance in this assessment, though by no means to the
exclusive extent O'Donnell assumed. McCarthy just saw that the rooms
had their own dignity.

This, then, was the thirty-year-old Parnell who, within five days of the
opening of the Parliament of 1877, made his first characteristic intervention
of the new session. By moving the adjournment of the House, he tried to
prevent the second reading of a widely approved Bill to eliminate certain
electoral anomalies. It was a warning to the House that it could expect no
slackening of Irish obstruction. Even when the radically minded Liberal
Sir Charles Dilke pleaded with him to withdraw his motion, Parnell
persisted, as if to demonstrate his disregard of Butt's argument that
excessive obstruction antagonized Ireland's best English friends. His
motion for the adjournment mustered only six votes.

But the next day he showed that in addition to his role as obstructionist
he was maturing as a politician. His position on the land question hitherto
had been that he was a supporter of 'tenant right' with its traditional
demand for the 'three Fs': fair rent, fixity of tenure (provided that the
rent was paid) and freedom for the tenant to sell his improvements to the
property on leaving it. Now, on 14 February 1877, he moved the second
reading of a Bill to amend certain provisions in the 1869 Irish Church

Act. This Act, while disestablishing the Protestant Church in Ireland, had made it possible for the State to help tenants of former Church lands become owners of the property they occupied, on certain terms. Parnell wished to amend these terms to make them more favourable. The enacted terms were that the tenant should pay a quarter of the purchase price in cash and the remainder in half-yearly instalments for thirty-two years, with interest on the outstanding amount at 4 per cent. Parnell's proposal was that no immediate cash payment should be required but that the whole of the purchase price should be paid in instalments over fifty-two years, with interest at 4.9 per cent on the outstanding amount – annual mortgage payments which would have amounted to little more than the rent the tenants were already paying. Over half of the 8,432 tenants of Church lands at the time of the 1869 Act had already become absolute proprietors of their holdings under the existing terms. The likelihood was that the terms proposed by Parnell would prove attractive to the rest.

The Bill's second reading was in fact voted to be 'put off for six months', leaving Parnell and his supporters (who included Butt) in a respectable minority – of 110 to 150. But what was of importance was the indication that he had been turning his mind seriously to the land question. It has sometimes been suggested that he was late to do this, being hustled into it by events. But this short Commons debate of February 1877 shows at least that he had already seen to the heart of the matter. He had outlined what, after great social convulsions still just beyond the political horizon, was to be the land question's eventual solution: the conversion of a landlord–tenant relationship into one of peasant proprietorship by means of State-financed mortgages on easy terms, after the State had bought out the landlords.

The Government's objections to Parnell's proposal were based on what it regarded as the excessive financial cost to the State. But he was thinking about social forces which might have political impact. 'There is no doubt', he said, 'that the agricultural tenants are almost universally anxious to purchase their farms, and would do so if they had the means.'

Land was soon to determine the most decisive phase of his political career.

For most of 1877 there seemed little public awareness of any impending land crisis. But a leading article in the *Freeman's Journal* as early as January that year had drawn attention to some hint of trouble to come. Prophetically it began, 'The economic condition of Ireland at this moment is a precarious one, and this day twelve months it is at least possible that it may be a desperate one . . .'

More than 80 per cent of Irish agriculture was now concerned with the cattle trade, upon which therefore, as the paper pointed out, a great proportion of the Irish population was more or less directly dependent. 'A means has been discovered', it reported, 'of importing fresh American beef in good condition and at a cheap rate . . .'

The means was ship-board refrigeration, and although the imports from Texas, Mexico and Canada, which had begun on a very small scale over a year before and had developed in the past four months, were still comparatively low, they were increasing all the time. Selling at a lower price than English or Irish beef, they were already affecting markets. One Manchester businessman warned, 'Ere long it is expected that a large fleet of Atlantic steamers are to be fitted up with cool larders.'

It was to be a combination of man-made and natural causes that eventually produced the crisis. Few could as yet see it coming. Irish agricultural output had reached an all-time peak in 1876, though 1877 was to witness the first of three wet summers and bad harvests in a row. But for the time being it was the parliamentary scene which continued to command attention in England, Ireland and the columns of the *Freeman's Journal*.

Despite the fact that a great deal of Irish business had to be shelved as a result of unsuccessful balloting for Private Member's Bills, the *Freeman's Journal* noted that 'Mr Parnell and Mr Biggar seem determined to come to the front' and that the topics on which Parnell was prepared to fight were almost as multifarious as Biggar's.

Certain things stand out in any survey of Parnell's activity throughout this session. There is a continuing growth of self-assurance derived from the clear though usually unspoken nationalist theme underlying all his obstruction, namely that the resulting inconveniences for the House of Commons just showed how necessary was a separate legislature for Ireland. Complementary to this, a dry humour is often at work – the humour of a man happy enough to let others notice that his eye is in fact on something quite other than the matter immediately in hand. At the same time, on some of the major topics which were to provide him, Biggar and a few other Home Rule Members with their opportunities for obstruction, he revealed often a natural moral passion about the matter in hand – whether conditions in prison or flogging in the Navy. Passion was always to be a natural part of his political strength. It was a quality almost conscientiously absent from the manner in which Isaac Butt mainly saw fit to conduct affairs in the House of Commons. A clash between Parnell and his still widely respected leader thus became increasingly and quite rapidly inevitable.

On 26 February 1877 just after midnight, Parnell was opposing motions to report progress which, if agreed to, would have allowed the Government to introduce other opposed business before the hour of 12.30 a.m. (Beyond 12.30 a.m. business in the House to which notice of opposition had previously been given could not, by the Government's own rules, be introduced.) Parnell recommended that the House should simply go on with its present discussion on supplementary votes for the Civil Service until 12.30, 'when they could get home to bed'. He objected, he said, to the Government trying to hurry on with business like this. It was just this sort of procedure that had led to 'the lamentable scenes of last session – scenes which did not tend to raise the House in the eyes of the country . . . sooner or later Parliament will break down, unless the business of the separate nationalities is handed over to home Legislatures.'

To exploit the chance the 12.30 rule gave them to delay legislation, Biggar and Parnell had registered their opposition to sixteen Government Bills. As the session proceeded, they were execrated by the British press. The *Daily News* protested that their action was without precedent in the history of British legislation. But, as the *Nation* replied from Dublin, 'Let *The Times*, the *Pall Mall Gazette*, the *Daily News* and *Express* rant . . . This means nothing to them [Biggar and Parnell] . . . they know that their constituents and the people of Ireland generally approve of their conduct.'

However, many in the party – including Butt himself – were becoming increasingly critical of these two. After obstruction on the Navy Estimates on the night of 19 March, the party met the next day at King Street, Westminster, with neither Biggar nor Parnell present. The Member for Sligo, Edward King-Harman, complained strongly of Parnell's and Biggar's behaviour. Parnell's opposition, he said, had been 'a sham and a pretence'. Butt tried to make a non-committal statement, but his embarrassment was clear. He did not know what Parnell's and Biggar's motives were, he said; they had not explained their object to anyone. While he did not approve of obstruction, he thought it could not be concluded that this was in fact their object.

Parnell's growing confidence was shown by the sharp letter to King-Harman he immediately sent to the *Freeman's Journal*. 'I cannot suppose', he wrote, 'that you could have attacked an Irish Member – much less a member of the Irish party of which you are a member – in his absence.' He wanted to know if King-Harman had been correctly reported.

No public reply from King-Harman was immediately forthcoming, but Parnell was off again only a few days later with a major piece of obstruction on the Prisons Bill, detailing at great length, in discussion of an amendment about prison rules, particulars of the case of Daniel Reddin which he had raised the year before. He was reading from a number of affidavits alleging ill-treatment of Reddin when another Member, a Scottish admiral, rose to ask whether this was in order. The Chairman of the committee of the House had to concede that it was, but said he did not think Parnell ought to go into all the details of the case. Parnell replied that he could not very well do that as there were thirty-five affidavits in all, but he would just refer to the salient points. He then went back to the affidavits.

Pulled up again and told that what he was doing was more suitable for a separate motion than for a continuing debate on the amendment in question, he replied that the House could not stamp too strongly on the Bill its determination that all prisoners, whether tried or untried, should be treated in a humane manner, and he said he would therefore go on to read 'a few more affidavits'.

During Irish efforts later the same evening to bring discussion to a halt by motions to 'report progress' or that 'the Chairman do now leave the chair', he said at one point that it was all very well for another Member who had already spoken to advise going on, but he himself had not had a chance yet to do so on the subject and wanted to do so, and yet felt very tired 'and quite unequal to speaking now'. A little later, on another motion to report progress, he said, 'It is entirely impossible for me or anyone else to go into the subject at this hour . . . What I shall have to say tomorrow really will not take up as much time as has been wasted tonight.'

This and two other similar motions, one of which he proposed himself, were lost with only four Members voting in favour and more than 130 against each time. The House eventually adjourned exhausted at 3.15 a.m.

The extent to which in some quarters, even in nationalist Ireland, some hesitation was being felt about the obstructive methods Parnell and Biggar were employing was emphasized by the *Freeman's Journal*. As the House went into the Easter recess, the *Freeman's* wrote that, while on the whole approving, it was 'not prepared to give a full assent to the doctrine of obstruction, and on more than one occasion last session we thought fit to suggest the two Members erred and seriously erred, in irritating the House by a mischievous course of conduct.'

But the radical weekly paper the *Nation* backed the two up: 'What in the name of Heaven is "the business of the House" to us that we should have regard to it? . . . what claim has the House of Commons on the goodwill of Irishmen?'

The long, twelve-hour journey of those days from Dublin to London, the quite different world in which Irish Members found themselves more or less agreeably at home once they got there, the flatteringly dignified atmosphere of the Palace of Westminster itself, all served to give Members a remoteness, in spite of themselves, from the political mood of the country they had come to represent. And yet it was to these men alone that the political mood in Ireland had to look for a lead. National feeling there, diffuse and uncoordinated as it had been for so long, particularly since the death of O'Connell thirty years before, was still really without a convincing lead, even though a party committed to 'Home Rule' was in being.

Butt, for all the respect in which he was held in Ireland for his past legal services to arrested Fenians and his achievement in at least formulating Home Rule, was a leader only inasmuch as he was attuned to the House of Commons. It was Parnell's political strength – demonstrated throughout his parliamentary career to date – that, like very few other Irish Members, he carried a political mood for Ireland wherever he was.

At this point, no question arose of Butt's replacement, except conceivably somewhere deep in the mind of Parnell. Least of all, given the mood of the official Home Rule Party, did the question arise in its parliamentary offices in King Street, Westminster. When, earlier in the year, Butt's need to earn money by practising at the bar had raised the possibility of his withdrawal from politics, Mitchell Henry, an English-born Irish landlord who represented Co. Galway as a Home Ruler had written, 'Who is there amongst our ranks that would for a single week supply the place of Mr Butt? To ask the question is to answer it. In the contemplation of such an event I see before me a picture of dejection, weakness, speedy disorganization, national disgrace . . .' A financial tribute to Butt to help obliterate the appalling vista was already under way.

When the House of Commons reassembled on 5 April 1877, Parnell came forward at once and proposed an amendment to the Prisons Bill by which all 'political' prisoners (those convicted of treason-felony, sedition or seditious libel) would be placed in a less rigorous category of treatment than that for ordinary criminals. In doing so he cited at length, from several volumes of Hansard, instances of ill-treatment of Irish prisoners in the past. He was interrupted seven times by the Chairman of the committee in which the House was then sitting to be told that he was out of

order. Arguing persistently against such rulings, he eventually agreed to
alter course in his speech, though not before saying at one point that the
Chairman's ruling was 'thoroughly wrong' – an expression which he
immediately had to withdraw.

Henry Lucy, who by now was developing some respect for Parnell,
gives a vivid picture of his parliamentary demeanour in the course of this
speech. He describes how, after acquiescing in one reproof from the
Chairman with a polite 'Quite so', and expressing the greatest solicitude to
save the time and patience of his audience, Parnell continued implacably
on his way:

Having turned over a great many pages of one book, glanced into another, and
explored a considerable collection of manuscripts on the seat behind him, Mr
Parnell proceeds with his remarks which consist of a strange mixture of dogmatic
assertion and plaintive argument. For in the height of his greatest triumphs, when
the House lies prostrate at his mere persistence, Mr Parnell with the modesty of
true greatness, invariably bears himself as an injured man bravely confronting an
obnoxious tyrant. His studied deliberation is something fearful . . . His observations proceed in a series of short jerks with a long and tantalizing pause after each
brief sentence. Should the slightest sign of weariness, or the least indication of
pent-up feeling escape unguardedly from some overcharged bosom, Mr Parnell
merely balances himself on his feet with still more regard to an imaginary
plumb-line, drops his clenched hands lower down on either side, so that they
hang in the direction of his knees like two weights intended to assist in preserving
the perpendicular with undeviating exactitude, and silently gnashing his teeth,
while he glares fixedly in the direction of the supposed intruder, waits until all
shall have again become still. Then to the increasing admiration of the attendant
and admiring Mr Biggar, he resumes, evincing a greater aversion to speed than
ever . . . So long as he stops the way, the State machine cannot move an inch;
and there is nothing to be done but to endure unto the bitter end.

But this time he was cheered by a number of English Members sitting
near him, including the radicals, Joseph Chamberlain and Charles Dilke.
And Butt, speaking in measured tones, supported Parnell's amendment.
On Parnell's saying that he was prepared to strike 'treason-felony' out of
his amendment because in fact 'the number of persons liable to be
confined for that offence were so few', the rest of it was passed.

'A most creditable achievement for Mr Parnell,' commented the *Freeman's Journal*. Its parliamentary correspondent noted that Parnell had had
a couple of hunters brought over from Ireland. This, Parnell had explained

to him, was because he expected to have a number of late sittings in Parliament and 'a spin on horseback each morning will help to sustain him in the expected demands on his physical capacity'.

They were demands which he was making on himself. On the night of his success on the Prisons Bill he was by no means finished after the successful passing of his amendment. One of those clauses in the Bill which had been passed before Easter had ensured that untried prisoners were to be treated differently in prison from those already convicted. Parnell had then wanted to include within the untried category all persons arrested under suspension of habeas corpus, an event experienced more commonly in Ireland than England. The Government had opposed him on the grounds that such cases were in fact already covered by certain rules, and though he had persisted with a motion it was lost by 67 to 150 – some English radicals being with him. Then, on the night of 5 April, he showed dogged persistence by bringing in another motion to the same effect.

The Chairman of the committee considering the bill argued that the clause about untried prisoners recently passed actually covered habeas-corpus prisoners by implication. Parnell said he wanted to remove any legal doubts by a new clause specifically including them. Butt himself then appealed to Parnell to drop the matter, saying he agreed with the Chairman and indeed the Home Secretary that such persons were already covered. The awkward circumstances of his supporting the Government against one of his own Members did not seem to strike him. Parnell withdrew on the understanding that Butt's interpretation was correct, but a little later the same evening he was involved in another clash with Butt which presaged a wider opening of the division between them in coming weeks. The manner in which Butt allowed this to happen itself showed how far he had lost his way as an Irish leader in the sense in which the Irish people needed one.

At about 12.20 a.m. a stage had been reached in the discussion of the Civil Service Estimates when the Government wanted to suspend the proceedings by reporting progress in order to permit the reading of the Public Health (Ireland) Bill before the cut-off hour of 12.30. Parnell said openly enough that he wished to 'prevent' that second reading at a time when the Bill could not be properly discussed owing to the lateness of the hour and the presence in the House of so few Irish Members. He raised a laugh by saying that he was quite willing to have the House divided into two halves, one sitting by day and the other night, and that he was quite willing to take his share with each portion, but under the present arrangement he really did not see how the House was to get through the business.

Butt then rose and said that, while he agreed that Bills likely to cause dispute should not be discussed at a late hour, the Bill which his Honourable Friend 'wished to obstruct' was simply a Bill for consolidating the sanitary laws in Ireland and it was the universal opinion of those who administered those laws that it should be passed. He thought that anyone who prevented sanitary legislation would not find his conduct approved of by the people of Ireland.

Parnell replied 'out of deference' to Butt that he would not press his opposition to the Government motion, but ended with a restatement of his general objection to the way in which Irish business was transacted.

When the Chief Secretary for Ireland, Sir Michael Hicks Beach, rose to say that Parnell had by his motion attempted to obstruct the measure, Parnell scored a quick pedantic point by reminding him that he had not in fact made any motion at all, merely opposed the Government one. Hicks Beach admitted he should have said 'by his speech on the Motion for reporting progress', but, having reiterated the Government's position, concluded that he would leave the House to judge Parnell's conduct. Butt then made the extraordinary mistake of following Hicks Beach with his own criticism of Parnell. He protested against 'a good Bill like this being stopped from passing simply because it came on at that hour'. Parnell replied that he had *not* prevented its second reading, merely its second reading at that hour. He went on to ask why, if the Bill was such a very good one and no time was necessary for its discussion, it could not have been brought on at an early hour in the evening.

All this had taken the House beyond 12.30, when, being opposed, the Bill could no longer be brought up that sitting.

The extent to which Butt misjudged the approval or disapproval of the people of Ireland can be gauged from the accolade with which even the *Freeman's Journal* greeted Parnell that weekend. 'Every Irishman', it wrote, 'whose sense of self-respect has not been obliterated by the infatuation of party spirit will gladly recognize the admirable and business-like manner in which Mr Parnell has worked out his successes on the Prisons Bill.'

The paper reminded its readers that it had itself been opposed to obstruction in the past at times, but went on:

For a man who has made serious mistakes in this direction, Mr Parnell has shown wonderful temper in retrieving his reputation and in gaining ground which at one time, and quite recently, seemed beyond the reach of an Irish Member . . . Mr Parnell deserves credit as having been the Irish Member who first dared the dogged opposition of the House and compelled it to listen to a case for which it had no sympathy.

An ambivalence in the *Freeman*'s attitude to Parnell's performance was to reappear periodically throughout the summer. It was as if 'respectable' nationalist Ireland found itself succumbing only rather reluctantly, and against its better judgement, to a force for change which it nevertheless recognized as necessary. The paper's present tribute to Parnell, for instance, could not help implying criticism of Butt, but shrank from expressing it.

On 12 April the Mutiny Bill came up for discussion in committee in the House. It was to provide a turning-point in the political relations between Parnell and Butt. Parnell had already intervened on different clauses of the Bill a number of times in a humanitarian vein, trying without success to deprive courts martial of the right to impose penal servitude in certain cases, and again to have the term of solitary confinement for certain others reduced from seven days to three. On this latter point Gathorne Hardy, the Secretary of State for War, tried to put down Parnell by saying that solitary confinement for such offences could anyway only be awarded in time of war. But it was Parnell who won the point, asking, 'And on board ship it can be done?' Gathorne Hardy had to admit that this was so. Parnell's amendment was lost by 233 to 35.

He then tried to remove a clause which enabled deserters to be arrested without a warrant. This too he lost.

When clause 55 of the Bill was reached, Biggar got up and proposed that the debate should now be suspended by a motion to report progress. There were, he said, another fifty-five clauses to go, and they could not be properly discussed so late at night. Parnell supported him, saying the business was merely formal anyway up to clause 93 and thus could well be postponed.

Gathorne Hardy insisted he was going to take the clauses up to 93.

Parnell protested it was 1.15 a.m. and too late to go on. Anyway, he suddenly added, with a brazenness typical of the political character he was developing, as to those 'unopposed clauses' which he had previously said were merely formal, he had in fact himself a number of amendments to propose, though 'circumstances had prevented him from putting them on the paper'.

Gathorne Hardy replied with force that Parnell had been in daily attendance on the House and yet here he was now saying that 'circumstances' had prevented him from putting down his amendments.

Hansard, trying to report the ensuing argument, could only record that 'after some time' Butt (who had not been in the House before but had been sent for in desperation) rose to deliver a sharp rebuke to his Member for Meath. He thought, he said, that Parnell should at least have waited until they came to one of the clauses he wished to amend. 'He regretted that the time of the House should have been wasted in this miserable and wretched discussion . . . It was a course of obstruction – and one against which he must enter his protest. He was not responsible for the Member for Meath and could not control him. He had, however, a duty to discharge to the great nation of Ireland, and he thought he should discharge it best when he said he disapproved entirely of the conduct of the Member for Meath.'

Parnell could not help saying pointedly that Butt had not in fact been there to hear him put his case. Then a Government supporter got up to express 'on behalf of several Hon. Members his acknowledgements to the Hon. and Learned Member (Mr Butt) for his manly protest.'

After what Hansard again could only describe as 'a long time', Biggar's motion to report progress was withdrawn. No more was heard of Parnell's proposed amendments. Clauses 56 to 93 were agreed to, and the House adjourned at 3.00 a.m. For all the delay he had managed to cause, it could seem like a defeat for him.

But in another arena altogether, that 'great nation of Ireland' to which Butt had so complacently felt himself able to appeal, the event had a different look.

Parnell himself merely wrote Butt a letter the next day, saying that, though he had on this occasion finally yielded his judgement to his leader's opinion, he would in future claim for himself that full individual liberty of action which was the agreed prerogative of members of the party on imperial and English matters. He would, he said, continue to follow his leadership on Irish affairs.

But a distinct crack in that leadership had now appeared.

Chapter 14

The scene with Butt on the Mutiny Bill immediately triggered the ambivalence of the *Freeman's Journal*. It accused Parnell of 'mere wantonness and folly' in his behaviour, saying that he had lost his temper, and that he should have had his amendments on the later clauses ready. Though no one doubted his sincerity, the paper wrote, it now lay with him 'to prove his wisdom by resuming that line of humble loyalty which bound him to his leader'.

The comment revealed a curiously late failure to appreciate the sort of person Parnell was. Far from showing humility, Parnell replied with a column-length letter in the paper reproving both it and Butt himself for their criticisms. 'England', he wrote, 'respects nothing but power,' and he added that such power was within the reach of the party if only it would exhibit that attention to business, method and energy which could secure it. The implied criticism of Butt was clear.

In a similar way to that in which, three years before, it had somehow not been his fault that he had turned up at the wrong time for the declaration of his first electoral poll, so now he claimed that the only reason he had not been able to put his amendments on the order-paper was that he had had to be in Salford supporting the Liberal candidate in the by-election there, who was in favour of Irish Home Rule. It was always to be important for Parnell to show that he was, in his own eyes, in the right.

His activity in the House of Commons was, if anything, stimulated by Butt's attack. In the days immediately following he intervened in the House frequently, delaying proceedings either with his own amendments or in support of those of other Irish Members on the Marine Mutiny Bill and the Mutiny Bill, both of which would have been passed normally with little more than routine discussion. In both instances the general tactical principle of obstruction was at work, but it worked at the same time to promote humanitarian changes for which Parnell clearly felt a genuine personal concern. He expressed this forcibly in these days a number of times, and occasionally with humour.

How, for instance at one point, he asked the First Lord of the Admiralty, who was duty-bound to endure these long late-night sessions and with whom he was disputing the severity of certain punishments for certain offences, how would the Right Honourable Gentleman like it if on those occasions when he unfortunately fell asleep at his post he incurred the penalties of penal servitude, death or imprisonment?

Except on active service, the Army had given up flogging by this date, but when O'Connor Power introduced an amendment to the Marine Mutiny Bill to reduce the full number of lashes still generally permitted in the Navy from fifty to twenty-five, Government supporters urged that since fifty lashes was still permissible for civil criminals and had had 'a wholesome effect' on garrotters, the same number should be retained for serious offences in the Navy. Parnell intervened to say that 'it would be time enough to discuss the amount of flogging for garrotters and wife-beaters when that subject occupied their attention'. He himself denied that even a garrotter ought to be flogged, and he hoped 'that the Right Honourable Gentleman would yield to the dictates of humanity, and consent to this inhuman and disgusting punishment being altogether removed from the Statute Book'.

Altogether he spoke in the Commons thirteen times in one evening on various clauses of the Marine Mutiny Bill.

On 19 April when the Army Mutiny Bill again came up for discussion the Government itself proposed an amendment similar to that which Parnell had previously attempted, limiting the duration of solitary confine-ment at least in some cases to seven days at a time at intervals of at least fourteen days. He also managed to get the Government to agree to examine in committee his proposal for the representation of the accused at courts martial by counsel. Both changes were agreeable humanitarian by-products of his central purpose. The London correspondent of the *Free-man's Journal*, noting that Parnell was 'popular with his colleagues in the House', remarked that his intervention on flogging in the Navy had made such an impression that it was 'held by all to have sealed the doom of the barbarous practice'.

Two days later Butt wrote Parnell a strong letter, which he published, criticizing him for 'aimless and objectless obstruction'. Besides taking up time which might be used for discussion of Irish grievances 'in some form or another', such a policy exposed the party to the taunt of being unfit to administer the forms of representative government and ended in 'discredit-ing and damaging every movement we make'.

Parnell did not even bother to reply for a month, but he showed his contempt for the argument and his disregard of Butt's authority in a speech the very next day, when he took the chair at a lecture on Irish poetry in a London hotel. He used the opportunity to speak plainly about what he was doing in the House. He said he did not know what they could do to stop him obstructing, other than get rid of the Irish Members altogether. In the long run the best thing would indeed be 'to leave the Irish Members at home in peace and quietness'. And he complained that if there were only as many as ten such obstructive Members they could 'put a stop to a style in which matters are at present conducted'.

The same week the annual Home Rule motion came up in the House of Commons. This was in the form of a proposal that a select committee should '... inquire into and report upon the nature, the extent, and grounds of the demand made by a large proportion of the Irish people for the restoration to Ireland of an Irish Parliament with power to control the internal affairs of that country'.

The almost apologetic manner with which this was presented by William Shaw, the Member for Co. Cork, epitomized the ineffectualness of the party as a vehicle for the expression of Irish nationalism. He said he brought the question forward 'with very great reluctance', arising from the fact that Butt had already brought it forward more than once in previous years, and that 'at present the question is very unpopular'. Strangely, to substantiate this point he quoted a passage from *The Times* which declared that the demand for Home Rule lay 'beyond the reach of practical discussion'. The utmost that the House of Commons could do for its advocates, said the paper, was 'to listen to them with patience and courtesy once a year'.

The 1877 version of the Home Rule performance was notable chiefly for an intervention by Gladstone in which he strongly objected to a suggestion that he had lent special support to the Liberal candidate in the recent Salford by-election as a result of the latter's declaration in favour of Home Rule. Parnell himself made no speech at all. He merely intervened in the debate once to protest that his words about obstruction at the poetry lecture, to which derogatory attention had been drawn by a Member, had been misquoted by the *Daily Telegraph*.

To ask why he did not speak leaves one of those gaps which frequently confront an attempt to keep Parnell's personality in view through his political career. Was it because he did not want to associate himself too openly with such a half-hearted approach to the nationalist issue? Certainly the party's official aspiration as duly expressed by Butt was a feeble thing compared with the sort of rhetoric to which Parnell had long shown himself temperamentally akin. They wanted, said Butt, 'an Irish Parliament to determine all questions relating to the internal affairs of Ireland, leaving to the Imperial Parliament . . . everything relating to questions of peace or the foreign relations of the country'. Late in his speech Butt even left it open as to whether Ireland should have charge of its own post office. Though Parnell, as a member of the party, officially subscribed to this formula for 'Home Rule' it was a far cry from the call of the popular song that 'Ireland, once a province, be a Nation Once Again.'

However, for him to have broken ranks in the House on such a central issue as Home Rule would at this stage have appeared unacceptably disloyal even in Ireland. Virtual silence meant nothing one way or the other unless anyone wished so to interpret it. At least he went into the division lobby dutifully enough among the sixty-seven Members who wished to 'inquire into and report upon the nature, the extent and grounds of the demands made by a large proportion of the Irish people', whereas 410 did not.

The *Freeman's Journal* actually commented that these figures represented an advance on the results of the year before ('small, it is true, but an advance'). That such a result could be seen as cause for satisfaction gives some idea of the vacuum in which words then had to do duty for deeds in Irish nationalism.

But that a strong sense of Irish individuality – cultural, economic and personal – waited to be given dynamism was now part of the instinct of the Member for Meath. How it was to happen was still unclear. Given the strength of the instinct, this may not have seemed immediately important. Parliamentary obstruction, and its implied disregard for the status quo accepted by Butt, at least proclaimed attack in a new form. And he and the very few Irish Members who were prepared to join with him in this attack persisted with it vigorously for the rest of the 1877 session.

Parnell continued to use obstruction positively to try to humanize prison regulations and the practice of discipline in the Navy and Army. The length of time prisoners could be kept in irons, the nature of the tests to be applied to prisoners accused of malingering, the rights of prisoners to have their complaints brought to the notice of Parliament were all matters on which he intervened throughout the summer, adding to the time-consuming business of the Government's legislative burden but at the same time now and again successfully changing legislation for the better.

He steadfastly maintained his support of the six remaining Fenian convicts (three of them soldiers) and their right to be regarded as political prisoners, singling out particularly the one-armed civilian Michael Davitt, convicted of helping to smuggle arms into Ireland from Lancashire.

He was not beyond allowing himself occasional flights of conventional oratory, one of which went some way to substantiate his mother's claim to have educated him in the classics – or at least in classical cliché. Returning in June to the theme of political status for Fenian prisoners, he chided an English Member who 'Hecuba-like bewailed the evils of the past and then Cassandra-like prophesied dire events for the future'.

The vigour with which he and a few others were prepared to use the forms of the House to disrupt its proceedings showed no sign of abating. In a discussion of the Army Estimates at the beginning of July he was happy to remind a complaining Government Minister of the principle on which they were acting. Irish questions, he said, were treated 'in a half contemptuous way' in the House, and it was only by determined action that the representatives of Ireland could force upon the House the conviction that Irish questions were entitled to be respectfully considered. Only after eighteen separate motions to try to suspend proceedings on the Army Estimates had been lost, with no more than five Members voting for them, did the sole remaining occupant of the Treasury bench give up and, after warning Members that the probable result of the course they were pursuing would be a change in the rules of debate, allow the House to adjourn at a quarter to seven on the morning of 3 July.

The most dramatic display of obstructive technique in the history of Parliament took place over a series of days late in July, when the House went into committee after the second reading of a Bill to bring about confederation of the different colonies in South Africa, including the previously independent Boer republic of the Transvaal. Parnell's first intervention immediately related the business to Ireland. Opposing the Bill, he said he wanted to explain how it was that he who identified himself with a federal State for Ireland was against the confederation of the colonies in South Africa. The difference, he said, was that, whereas Ireland *wanted* a federal State, the colonists of South Africa did not: it was being sought by the imperial Government in its own interests. This, he suggested, was typical of England: 'History showed that England always neglected the interests of her colonies. She annexed Fiji for example, then introduced the measles, and then taxed the people to pay the expense of the annexation.'

In a further contrived allusion to Home Rule, he pointed out that, whereas one of the specific arguments against this had always been that in the event of 'the restoration to Ireland of its native Parliament' it would be impossible to define which powers should belong to it and which to the imperial parliament, here in the South Africa Bill the Government 'did define those matters and appeared to find no difficulty about it'.

Parnell was at once joined in opposition to the Bill by O'Donnell (returned at a by-election in 1877) and Biggar, and then, on the first unsuccessful vote to try to change its course, by a few other Irish Members and the two prominent English radicals, Joseph Chamberlain and Charles Dilke. The tone of the proceedings on this first day (24 July) was well captured by Hansard, which, while allotting only two columns to a speech of one hour and twenty-five minutes by O'Donnell, described it as taking place 'amid great inattention and confusion, arising from continued cries of Order! and Question! the interruption of several counts, and the distraction arising from the assembling and dispersion of Members on each occasion'.

Parnell himself provided a short individual coda when, on the South Africa Bill's being postponed to the next day, he twice appeared in a minority of one, supported by two tellers, in efforts to obstruct discussion of a quite different Bill, the County Officers and County Courts (Ireland) Bill, which in fact he had already said would greatly benefit the people of Ireland. When a Member, Sir William Harcourt, drew attention to this anomaly and said that the Irish people ought to know just who was obstructing such a Bill, Parnell conceded that he had formerly said the Bill 'was one of great importance to the Irish people' but said that he had not wanted the two tellers who were trying to get the Chairman to leave the chair to have no one to tell, and that, anyway, when Harcourt 'set himself up as instructor to the Irish people, he was attempting to instruct people who did not ask for his advice'.

When the South Africa Bill came up again next morning (25 July) Parnell was again soon on his feet, protesting at the words of a Member who said that the forms of the House were being abused for the purpose of delaying the progress of the Bill. 'The limits of forbearance', Parnell said, 'have been passed in regard to the language which Hon. Members opposite have thought proper to address to me and to those who act with me.'

When a few minutes later the accusation against him and his friends was repeated, he began his speech on the Bill itself by complaining of 'the persistent interruptions with which I have been met by certain Hon. Members while I have been attempting to discharge my duties and of the intimidation to which many of the Members of this House resort'.

The Chairman of the committee said it was not in order for Members to be accused of intimidation. Parnell replied, without strict regard for the truth, that he had been speaking of intimidation in the English press, and the Chairman let him get away with this. But when Parnell concluded with the statement that, as an Irishman, coming from a country which had experienced to the fullest extent the consequences of English cruelty and tyranny, he felt 'a special satisfaction in preventing and thwarting the intentions of the Government in respect of this Bill' he seemed at last to be in serious trouble. The Chancellor of the Exchequer himself, Sir Stafford Northcote, rose to move that after such an unrepentant admission of obstruction the Member for Meath should be suspended for two days.

Parnell was ordered to retire while the House discussed the matter. Lucy described how Parnell bowed to the Speaker 'with lowly magnanimity and marched stiffly out of the House, leaving the assembly to draw what inferences they pleased from the inflexible rigidity of his back'. He withdrew to the Gallery to look down on the ensuing debate.

In the course of this it was pointed out to Northcote – and not only by Irish Members – that Parnell had been talking about satisfaction in thwarting the intentions of the *Government*, not those of the House, and that there was nothing democratically wrong with that. It was Northcote who was made to seem to be at fault, though he cloaked his retreat with a remark about it being not just the words Parnell used which he had been getting at, but the whole pattern of his recent behaviour – with which new rules soon to be introduced would deal. A pale Parnell was allowed to return to the Chamber, led by Biggar, who had a mischievous twinkle in his eye. Parnell immediately began a new speech saying that, before he had been interrupted 'by circumstances to which I shall not further allude', he had been reminding the House that as an Irishman, whose country had experienced even worse treatment than that which the Government proposed to mete out to the South African colonies, he had 'a special interest in endeavouring to thwart the objects of the Government in reference to those colonies'.

He clashed with the Chairman several times again before the day was out. At one point, disregarding frequent interruptions and calls to order, he said he knew he had to exercise caution because he did not know when Northcote might 'start up, and with tones and words of indignation move that my words be taken down and submitted to the sure and speedy vengeance of the House'. Told that such language was out of order, he said he had 'only wished to express his timidity in discussing the Bill' and proceeded, as Hansard put it, 'at great length' to argue that the Dutch Boers hated English rule.

Hansard was reduced to this sort of summary a number of times in the course of the proceedings, later simply reporting that 'Mr Parnell continued to address the House for some time', before the House finally adjourned relatively early at 5.55 p.m.

Two days later the Government announced its new rules for debate. First, any Member judged twice out of order by the Speaker or Chairman of Committee could be suspended for the rest of that debate. Second, on a point being debated, no Member could in future move more than one motion to report progress or that the Speaker or Chairman leave the chair, or speak more than once to such motions.

But there was still nothing to stop Members making speeches of whatever length they chose, and Parnell again took advantage of this, saying that 'as the House has taken a great deal of trouble on my account I think I ought to requite it by a few observations'. He said he was not going to oppose either rule, though he thought they were 'unconstitutional in the highest degree', being intended to muzzle him.

On Monday 30 July the South Africa Bill came up again in committee and Parnell was again soon at work, moving four different amendments and intervening sixteen times. Not unexpectedly, while engaging seriously with the technical details of the Bill, he once more took the chance to remind the House why it particularly concerned him. This time, typically, he actually managed to turn his previous argument about federation on its head. 'We had already', he said, 'in the case of Ireland an example of federalism in which union was forced upon the weaker by the stronger party, and it was necessary to guard against such a result under this Bill.'

The full drama took place on Tuesday 31 July, and extended continuously into much of the day after that. The pages of Hansard give invaluable glimpses of Parnell's style and character at a moment in his life for which there is otherwise relatively little first-hand documentation.

O'Donnell began soon after 5.15 p.m. with a motion to report progress, which Parnell supported. He was almost immediately involved in a long delaying wrangle with the Chairman and other Members over what it was and was not in order for him to discuss about the Bill on a motion to report progress. One Member charitably put the inconvenience down to Parnell's and others' 'want of experience' as 'novices', and Parnell, straight-faced, thanked him for his 'courtesy and good nature'. At another point, finding the Chairman's attitude to him on the whole more tolerant than that of his fellow Members, Parnell was able to express to him his 'obligation for . . . continued protection . . . afforded him in the face of persistent interruptions'. Such interruptions of course did much of Parnell's and Biggar's work for them. Episodic extracts from Hansard reveal something of the prevailing confusion:

After further remarks from Mr O'Donnell, Mr Parnell again rose to speak but his attempt – for the Hon. Member had now addressed the House many times on this question – being put down by overwhelming cries for a division . . .

Mr Parnell rose (amid continued cries) to point out . . .

The dissatisfaction now prevailing throughout the House was so great that the Hon. Member, unable to gain attention from his usual seat, advanced to the Table, from which position he again put the Question . . .

Mr Parnell again addressed the Committee at considerable length, but his speech was received with continued cries of remonstrance and dissatisfaction and calls for a Division . . .

That vote – taken 'at length', as Hansard put it – went 134 to 2, with Parnell and Biggar acting as tellers.

As the night proceeded, Parnell, Biggar and O'Donnell between them moved amendment after amendment to different clauses of the Bill, with periodic assistance from about five other Irish Members and the occasional English radical. Voting was repeatedly in the order of well over 100 (over 200 on one motion) to between 2 and 5 (depending on how many were resting) with two tellers.

Parnell, whose objective was to delay the Bill for as long as possible but not necessarily to keep the House up all night, at one point asked the Government how long it intended to go on. He said he himself was quite prepared to go on as long as necessary, but he thought they should stop for the night at about 4.00 a.m. It could in fact be said, and one Liberal Member so complained, that it was the Government which was keeping the House up, being determined to press the committee hearing through to a conclusion. There was a strong rumour in the lobbies that it was prepared to go on until 8.00 a.m. or even 6.00 p.m. and was bringing in reserves for the purpose. This, however, as Parnell was to point out some time after 7.00 a.m., was something which could be done by both sides, with the mail-boat already bringing fresh Members from Ireland and with Biggar in London, as he said, by then 'peacefully asleep' though soon to return 'like a giant refreshed'.

Butt had left long before then, having made his short contribution in the small hours. He had had no censure for the Government, only for those who were obstructing.

When a Member had quoted against Parnell a public speech of his made a fortnight before, about the need for a policy which 'must not be one of conciliation but of retaliation', O'Donnell had risen to Parnell's defence and had asked what was wrong with that? He said he spoke for the advanced party in Ireland and repeated that if they could not have 'conciliation' they would indeed have 'retaliation'.

Butt had angrily intervened to say of O'Donnell, 'He has no right to use on his lips the name of the Irish party; he has no right to speak for the Irish party in the House.'

O'Donnell, amid what Hansard described as 'loud cries of dissatisfaction', pointed out that he had claimed to speak only for 'the most advanced or, if you please, the most disaffected portion of the Irish Party'. Whereupon Butt specifically repudiated him, saying that he would be false to his country if he did not do so. He sadly illustrated his waning powers as well as his grasp of Irish nationalist realities when he added, 'If I thought he represented the Irish Party and the Irish Party represented my country – but it does not – I would retire from Irish politics as a vulgar brawl, in which no man could take part with advantage or honour to himself.' The Commons greeted his words with loud cheers, which received no echo from the Irish people whom he so confusedly claimed to represent.

Later, even Parnell began to show momentary signs of tiring, and found himself moving an amendment about which he could say no more than, after a pause, 'I candidly confess I cannot explain.' But he battled on, intervening repeatedly, and voting or telling in division after division in which the minority was five.

At one point he calmly turned the charge of 'obstruction' against the Government itself: 'How can simple Irish Members like myself do their duty if they are met with the course of conduct which the Government and their supporters at both sides of the House have adopted?'

After taking part in fifteen divisions altogether in the course of the night, he withdrew for a short rest at about 8.00 a.m. But he was back again in his place just after noon, proposing – against ironical cheers and loud cries of 'No!' – that, because O'Donnell was by now 'physically unable to proceed with the numerous amendments which stood in his name', the Government should proceed with other business.

When, just after 2.00 p.m., the South Africa Bill was at last sent to be printed, he switched his attention at once to the debate on a Supreme

Court of Judicature (Ireland) Bill which followed, remarking that 'the day was still young'. But he was afraid that after all that had happened the House was scarcely in a proper frame of mind to deliberate the Bill. Not that this would make much difference, he added, because he had noticed that, whenever Irish Bills were discussed, Members absented themselves until the Whips brought them back in to tell them how to vote. 'Baseless claptrap!' cried the old Whig Member of the Irish party, The O'Donoghue, maintaining that, like most of Parnell's statements about the conduct of business in the House, this was 'perfectly inaccurate'. In spite of a protest from Parnell, the Chairman decided that 'baseless claptrap' was not unparliamentary language.

The House finally rose that evening at a quarter past six, having been in continuous sitting for twenty-six and a quarter hours. The South Africa Bill, harried to the last by Parnell, O'Donnell and Biggar, went through to its third reading on 4 August.

Parnell's final achievement of the 1877 session took place on a different matter on 4 August, when the Chief Secretary, Hicks Beach, agreed to accept into the Prisons (Ireland) Bill eight new clauses proposed by Parnell for the benefit of prisoners. For all the execration to which he had been subjected for his obstructive technique, Parnell had by now won a certain wary respect from the House. The parliamentary correspondent of the *Freeman's Journal* noted that, in the acceptance of these Prison Bill clauses, Parnell could not have been more graciously received 'had Mr Parnell been leader of Her Majesty's Opposition'.

He made one last intervention on 10 August. This was to ensure that the Government's measures to prevent possible inroads of the Colorado beetle should be fully protective of Irish potatoes. He seems to have stayed in London over the weekend, for he was among the hundred or so Members still present on 15 August when Parliament was finally prorogued for the year. Understandably perhaps, he was looking 'pale and worn'.

He went back to Ireland to reap his reward.

Chapter 15

If one looks at the years 1877–9 without reference to what is now known of Parnell's future, it is easy to see many doubts attaching to that future. What, for instance, in terms of political goal, was obstruction actually achieving? Given the disapproval within his own party of his and his few colleagues' behaviour in the House, was he at all likely ever to succeed Butt as leader? How, even if Butt's gradualist approach to Home Rule were to be superseded, was progress towards Home Rule to be envisaged in a House of Commons implacably uninterested in it? How far was 'Home Rule' in any case an adequate formulation of the Irish people's national feeling? And, as always, who in any case were meant by 'the Irish people'? What was to be done about the awkward fact that such 'national feeling' did not embrace a considerable section of the Irish population, particularly in the North? These were all uncertain questions of the day (though the last, curiously, was little confronted), and trying to answer them was part of the reality of that time.

Only Parnell's personal bearing has an assured look. Whatever the uncertainties of the political future, he had now most clearly fixed for himself a place within it. This was what mattered to him. He was, as he was shortly to say of himself, 'a young man and could wait',

The search for some clear direction for his definite and often restless personality was over. A need for self-fulfilment had been unappeased by cricketing prowess, by four conventional years in the semi-alien environment of Cambridge, and by the undemanding social life of the Anglo-Irish Protestant gentry to which with Avondale he was heir. He had experienced a major disappointment in love, but for which he might have settled for a very different life in America. Now at last, in politics, he had found a satisfactory life for himself, to which his aggressive temperament and instinctive hauteur were well suited.

By the late summer of 1877 the amateurishness with which he had entered the field was already largely a thing of the past. He was never to be totally free of political awkwardness, but he had by now succeeded in turning it into something of a professional asset. His personal commitment to a professional stance in politics was total. Ironically, that commitment would in time become something of a burden to him. Now it was the force which gave him being.

For all the respect in which Butt was still held by many Home Rulers, his lack of effective handling of the party aroused increasing contempt among advanced Irish nationalists. Even moderate nationalists reflected a growing sense of the likelihood of change. The *Freeman's Journal* reported a news-agency telegram to the effect that Butt was thinking of resigning by applying for the Chiltern Hundreds so that he could put his leadership to the test in an election in his own constituency of Limerick. The paper's leader summing up the parliamentary session used a phrase already current and soon to become historic. The student of the time, it wrote, could not but discern that 'a new departure' had been reached in relations between England and Ireland. But it deplored a rally now planned in support of the obstructionist policy as likely to widen the breach in the party.

The rally took place on the evening of 21 August, when the Rotunda Rooms in Dublin were filled to capacity by some four thousand people. Large numbers were kept out after the doors were shut. Parnell and Biggar arrived just after eight o'clock to deafening cheers, and when Parnell's turn came to speak the great crowd rose to its feet cheering and waving hats and handkerchiefs for nearly ten minutes. In London he had just published a well-balanced defence of himself in a letter to *The Times*, stressing the constructive aspect of obstruction. But now he could let himself go. 'I care nothing for this English Parliament and its outcries,' he said. 'I care nothing for its existence, if that existence is to continue a source of tyranny and destruction to my country.'

Afterwards, in the street, cheering crowds surrounded him and Biggar and escorted them down Sackville Street to the Imperial Hotel, where Parnell eventually came out on to a balcony and addressed them. 'The work begun this night', he said, 'will be heard throughout the world and will strike terror to the Saxon heart.'

It is difficult not to think that, young and able to wait as he was, he could already see himself not just as an obstructionist in Parliament but as a potential leader of the Irish people in a wider framework.

The Rotunda meeting had been largely organized by restless Fenians. Two of these, Patrick Egan, the Dublin businessman, and Thomas Brennan, the young Dublin radical who had spoken with Parnell in Wexford and whose uncle was one of Egan's partners, were on the platform together with some of the more advanced nationalist MPs. A week later the annual meeting of the Home Rule Confederation of Great Britain took place in Liverpool. The Confederation had long been in the control of Fenians like Egan, though Butt was its nominal President. Now, on the first day of the meeting, a warm tribute was paid to Butt for his 'distinguished services to the national cause' in a motion seconded by Parnell. The next day, however, after Butt had returned to London, Parnell was elected President of the Confederation in his place.

One of the Fenians present on this occasion described Parnell as looking 'like a bit of granite'. In conversation beforehand Parnell had said to him personally, with outstretched hands and clenched fists 'and eyes that went through you all the time, "Something striking must be done."' His election as President of the Home Rule Confederation of Great Britain was a start.

The loosely defined character of the Irish national cause at that time, far from presenting him with a problem, may have been something which he found instinctively attractive. An easy detachment from accepted political thinking was something he had long ago acquired naturally from his American mother. A tradition of Protestant nationalism only sketchily remembered had been inherited from his father's family. Both sentiments merged easily with that other emotive tradition all about him in Ireland, that of Catholic folk memory, to give a sort of reality to a cause tantalizingly out of reach. Parnell was to make a series of rousing speeches in Britain that autumn from his new position of President of the Home Rule Confederation, but the most significant of all was delivered in Castlebar, Co. Mayo, just before Christmas 1877. 'Let no man lightly define the measure of Irish independence. Let no man', he said there, 'assign a *ne plus ultra* to the march of our nation.'

He was to repeat this phrase in turbulent times ahead, when he would add the words 'Let no man say: "Thus far shalt thou go and no further."' But already, as early as this winter of 1877, his mind was open to the possibility of any national future that might prove feasible. However much expediency might require the compromise involved in precision, imprecision was to be his fundamental strength. Such flexibility now brought with it an immediate tactical advantage of importance.

Those Fenians, often politely termed 'advanced nationalists', whose dogma was a separate independent Irish Republic only to be won by force of arms, had come to seem embarrassingly irrelevant to modern politics. The noble-minded, half-deaf, half-dumb novelist Charles Kickham still sat in splendid self-immolation as Chief Executive of the

Irish Republic 'now virtually established', denouncing as anathema all compromise on the purity of that dogma, and expelling from the Supreme Council those like Biggar and O'Connor Power who continued parliamentary activity after the end of the three-year period for which he had sanctioned it in 1873. But the real importance of the Fenian tradition at this time lay exactly in the fact that so many men possessed of the zeal which had formed it were dissatisfied with its irrelevance for the foreseeable future. Patrick Egan and Thomas Brennan were typical examples. Disillusioned with the wait for a call to arms that was too impractical ever to come, they were ready to put their energies elsewhere. No less devoted to the nationalist cause than before, they looked about for real ways of being active to promote it. A hard core of potential activists was thus available in Ireland for anyone who could find a way to make use of them.

Such men had a natural appeal for Parnell, who knew even more calmly than they did that an armed rebellion was out of the question but who shared with them a wish to 'do something striking'. He, on the strength of his performance in the House of Commons, had a natural appeal for them. At a Glasgow meeting Parnell had attended earlier in the summer, one of the Fenians there, John Ferguson, had pre-empted the *Freeman's Journal*'s phrase by signalling Parnell's and Biggar's parliamentary tactics as heralding 'a new departure in Irish politics'.

It is possible that as early as 1873, when Parnell was only beginning to consider entering politics, he had discussed with one known Fenian the way in which a projected cooperation between Fenians and parliamentarians might work out. Certainly in 1875, when he was looking around for a constituency, he had hoped to get a Fenian to back his application, and two years later he had written of this same man as a possible recruit to the parliamentary party: 'I think with twenty such men here we can have things at our mercy.' And Parnell had certainly never hesitated, when he felt it appropriate, to indulge in the sort of high-flown martial rhetoric beloved of Fenians with no alternative field for action.

One Fenian still in prison was soon to express graphically the state of mind in which he found himself at this time:

I found myself in prison for sending a few rifles to Ireland, without the consolation of knowing that one of them was ever shouldered to smite an enemy of my country. I was in prison only for *resolve*, not for an act whereby a single link of Ireland's chain was broken ... The years I had laboured in the national cause ... were therefore barren of practical results ... and I resolved that no other period of my life should be so ... if I ever ... regained my liberty.

This man was Michael Davitt, of whom Parnell had twice spoken in the House of Commons, lastly that summer, when arguing for special recognition for political prisoners. Davitt was now thirty-one. His family had emigrated from Co. Mayo to Lancashire in the aftermath of the Famine, when the cottage from which they had been evicted was burned down and their furniture thrown into the road. His right arm had been amputated at the age of eleven after an accident in a Lancashire cotton-mill where he worked. He had taken part in an abortive raid on Chester Castle at the time of the Fenian rising of 1867, and had remained in England as a Fenian agent until his arrest in 1870. Now, in December 1877, he was released on ticket of leave from Dartmoor by the Government as an act of clemency, two years early – a piece of accidental timing which was to prove of crucial importance in Irish history. Within a few days he met Parnell and some active Irish MPs in London to thank them for taking up his case with the Government.

Parnell had already had a number of private contacts with Fenians in the course of the summer. Some time apparently in July he and Biggar had taken a few days off from the House to go to Paris to talk to the Fenian John O'Leary, who had been amnestied but exiled in 1871. There they had run into another old Fenian, J. J. O'Kelly, now an American journalist, whose own contacts were with the one part of the Fenian movement capable of having real relevance to contemporary politics. This was that separate organization in the United States, Clan na Gael – also to be known as the United Brotherhood (or VC in the elementary code it favoured) – run by the New York journalist exile John Devoy and the Philadelphia-Irish doctor William Carroll. Though they had managed to effect one successful action, the escape of a number of Fenian convicts from Australia, their own practical plans for the future centred in classically remote Fenian style on attempts to exploit England's difficulty in the Balkans, where war with Russia looked possible. Clan na Gael's significance, however, lay not so much in its conspiratorial plans as in the very considerable sums of money it was in a position to raise for any Irish cause from the hundreds of thousands of Irish men and women who in the past thirty years had left Ireland for 'the land of the free' with bitterness for England in their hearts.

After this Paris meeting, O'Kelly wrote to Devoy that he had had 'a long chat' with Parnell and Biggar and found Parnell a man of promise who 'ought *to be supported*' (O'Kelly's emphasis). Observing that Parnell had the idea of combining all nationalists, both conservative and radical, O'Kelly thought that if supported by twenty to thirty men in Parliament Parnell could 'render really important services'. He went on, 'He has many of the qualities of leadership – and time will give him more. He is cool – extremely so and resolute. With the right kind of support behind him . . . he would so remould Irish public opinion as to clear away many of the stumbling blocks in the way of action.'

On 15 August, the day after Parliament broke up and just before Parnell's triumphant return to Dublin, O'Kelly had met him again, this time in London, and had had another 'long chat'. 'He is a good fellow', he wrote, 'but I am not sure he knows exactly where he is going. However he is the best of the parliamentary lot.'

William Carroll, writing to Devoy in the middle of that month, said that, though Parnell was 'doubtless a man of nerve and spirit', there could be no reasonable hope of such men getting anywhere 'without a military force to back them'. Carroll and Devoy were, as they had to acknowledge before long, in danger of being left behind by events.

No one could yet see clearly the way in which things were about to develop. A bad harvest that year had already made some impact on the lives of the Irish people. Parnell and Davitt were the two men who would determine much in the sequence of events of which this harvest was the forerunner.

At the moment of his release to London, Davitt was described by one eyewitness as a 'tall, dark, romantic-looking man, looking more like a starved poet than a revolutionist'. Many years later he gave his own description of the impression Parnell had made on him at their first meeting. He said how struck he had been 'by the power and directness of his personality. There was this proud, resolute bearing of a man of conscious strength, with a mission, wearing no affectation, but without a hint of Celtic character or a trait of its racial enthusiasm. An Englishman of the strongest type, moulded for an Irish purpose.'

When, Davitt wrote, Parnell spoke of the work which 'a few of us' were carrying on in the House of Commons, there was not a suspicion of boastfulness in anything he said, only confident promise for the future.

Speaking sympathetically of Davitt's ordeal in prison, Parnell said he himself would never be able to put up with its indignities and privations and that he would kill a warder and get hanged rather than endure them.

Three weeks later they met again, this time in Ireland, where Davitt had not been since he was four. There an upsetting incident occurred – a small prologue to their coming involvement in dramatic events. On the night of 12 January 1878 Davitt had sailed from Holyhead with three other released prisoners, ex-soldiers convicted of Fenian sympathies in 1867. They were met at Kingstown harbour the next afternoon by huge cheering crowds and a committee organized by Patrick Egan, headed by Parnell and containing many restless Fenians and strong nationalists, including John Ferguson – the man who had spoken earlier in the year of 'a new departure in Irish politics'. Also there was Thomas Brennan, who now in an address spoke of the prisoners' sacrifices which had not achieved Ireland's freedom but had saved her honour and vindicated her manhood. The list of signatories to this address, headed by Parnell, included the names of three men who before very long, as members of an extremist secret society, were to have a remarkable impact on his career: James Carey, Daniel Curley and Joe Brady.

Parnell accompanied the four released prisoners to Dublin on the boat-train, in a party which also included the proprietor of the extreme nationalist papers the *Irishman* and the *Flag of Ireland*, Richard Pigott. Parnell invited the four men to breakfast with him the next morning at Morrison's Hotel, where he was staying.

One of the three Fenian ex-soldiers, former Sergeant McCarthy, had looked particularly worn and broken by his prison experience on arrival, and had obviously been exhausted by the reception. However, he went to the theatre that night with Davitt to see Dion Boucicault's play about a Fenian returning to Ireland, *The Shaughran*. He came to breakfast next morning at Morrison's Hotel with the others. He had just joined Parnell's party, which included Biggar, Egan, Brennan, Pigott and others, when he was seen to grow pale and stagger. He was helped to a sofa, where he died almost at once of a heart attack.

It must have been in a state of some shock that Parnell went that same morning to another hotel in Dublin, the Hibernian, where he had just been told that the Clan na Gael conspirator Dr William Carroll from Philadelphia was staying. Carroll had come on a visit to Europe to try to assess for himself the general state of the advanced nationalist movement in Ireland.

Just over a year before, when Parnell had been on his visit to the USA with O'Connor Power to see President Grant, he and Carroll had been little concerned with each other, though Carroll had called at Parnell's hotel in Philadelphia at the time. Now things were very different.

The only documented account of this Dublin meeting was written by Carroll some thirty years later and so must be of doubtful reliability, though what he then reported of Parnell's part in the conversation sounds plausible. Carroll wrote that Parnell, asked by him if he was in favour of the absolute independence of Ireland, had replied that he was, and that as soon as the people declared for it he would go with them. Carroll then pledged Parnell the support of the Clan and their friends on that basis.

Parnell was back in the House of Commons four days later to speak and vote on an amendment to the Queen's Speech tabled by the Irish party. The amendment was mild enough in itself, though Butt had not wanted to move it at all. It declared that it was the duty of Parliament at the earliest opportunity 'to consider, in a wise and conciliatory spirit, the Irish demands which the Irish people have repeatedly raised'.

The effect of Parnell's experiences in Dublin four days before was discernible in his speech. He told the House indignantly that, though Sergeant McCarthy had long complained in prison of the symptoms of heart disease, he had been made to continue doing heavy work there, and that the jury at the inquest which he had attended had found that McCarthy's death had been hastened by his prison treatment. There was also an echo of the sort of thing he must have discussed with Carroll, when he said that, although the Home Rule programme pledged Ireland to help England in foreign difficulties such as the present Eastern crisis, it would only do so on one condition: namely, that England should allow it the right of self-government. He listed among the Irish people's grievances the need to settle the land question and to establish a university in Ireland which Catholics could conscientiously accept.

He also took the opportunity to enjoy himself at the House's expense by reiterating the serious purpose that lay behind all his performances there. 'I have been blamed by my friends', he said to some sympathetic amusement, 'for taking part in English legislation. I should infinitely prefer to devote the whole of my parliamentary time to considering and discussing Irish questions, but, coming over to London, I found that there were none to discuss owing to the great block of business. The number of Home Rule measures that can be brought forward during the session do not exceed five or six. Therefore I cannot employ myself better . . . than in helping the English Members to make their bills a little better. If they insist on keeping Irish Members idle they must not be surprised if they interfere in English business in a way they do not like.'

In his next speech in the House, nearly three weeks later, he was able to make it clear that, as a representative of the Irish people, he felt himself as separated from Her Majesty's Opposition as he did from her Government. Gladstone had been fulminating against the Turkish atrocities in Bulgaria. 'If', said Parnell, 'the Rt. Hon. Gentleman had carefully studied the history of Ireland, he would have discovered that Ireland had suffered more at the hand of the British Government than the Bulgarians at the hand of Turkey.'

For the next few months he worked hard to take up the House's time by making English Bills a little better. He fought in particular for humanitarian improvements in the conditions for women and children in factories and workshops and for prisoners subjected to military discipline. Obstruction took a less sensational form than in 1877, though the course of the Factories and Workshops Bill was certainly prolonged by a series of reasoned amendments, and a small group of Irish Members once again subjected the annual Mutiny Bill to far more rigorous scrutiny than had long been the House's custom.

Flogging could still be ordered as punishment in the Army on active service, and Parnell intervened a number of times to assert his passionate belief that it should be abolished altogether, or, if that were not to be immediately possible, that it should be inflicted in as humane a manner as possible, and not in addition to other punishments. An attempt by the Secretary of State for War to curtail such debate by promising a select committee was rejected by Parnell with words from the heart of his truly radical nature. 'It is contrary to the principles of constitutional freedom', he said, 'to prevent members from expressing their conscientious opinions. If such a system had always prevailed in this House, we would not have been in the proud position we are now. We would have been still very much as we were in the Middle Ages. A very slight acquaintance with history would convince anybody that reforms had always been due, in the first place, to the persistence and courage of a minority.'

Just over a week before, he had been in a minority of 63–263 which had voted for the abolition of capital punishment. The next week was that in which he suddenly took the Fenian John Barry off to watch the walking-match between the Irishman and the American at the Agricultural Hall, Islington, where he bribed the band to play 'God Save Ireland' in addition to 'God Save the Queen' after the Irishman's victory. He was in high spirits. It was in these days at the end of March 1878 that at his own request he had a further meeting with Dr Carroll of Clan na Gael.

The meeting this time took place at the Surrey Hotel in the Strand. On 30 March Carroll wrote to Devoy in New York to tell him merely that in the course of it Parnell and other obstructionists present had made clear that they were ready to cooperate for Irish independence ('at the firm's service for anything they can do in their line'). Presumably this was on the same sort of basis as that outlined at the Dublin meeting in the Hibernian.

From other later accounts of this second meeting, in which O'Donnell, J. J. O'Kelly and the Fenian literary man John O'Leary also participated, it seems that much time was spent in a long theoretical disputation between O'Donnell and O'Leary, and possibly also Carroll, during which Parnell remained largely silent. 'Slippy', even, was how O'Donnell described him, summing him up reasonably enough as an opportunist. 'He had no clear idea whatever', was what he wrote thirty years later, 'Except that you could squeeze a lot out of English politicians, if you were either troublesome or utilizable enough.'

Obviously he had been both silent and talkative enough to obtain Carroll's general approval and thus that of Clan na Gael. What was happening at these meetings was that Parnell and Carroll were quietly sounding each other out. What satisfactorily emerged for both of them was that each could recognize in the other an acceptably flexible approach to any serious nationalist opportunity the future might offer.

Meanwhile Parnell could continue to tease the House of Commons, telling it, when reproved by a Chairman of Committee on one occasion for 'taking a most unusual course which had never recommended itself to the House', that he was afraid it would often be necessary for him to do so, as it had been in the past. 'I have occasionally found', he added, 'that such a practice has been attended with very beneficial results.' Sometimes the House could tease him back. He appeared on 4 April with a collection of English newspaper cuttings critical of himself and his friends which, he said, citing the parliamentary authority Erskine May and a precedent of April 1699, raised a point of privilege. He was told, correctly, that he was out of order because the rule was that the whole newspaper in each case should have been shown beforehand to the Clerk of the House.

His vigour was undiminished, however, when the next day he rose to speak on the Budget's increase in tobacco duty. He said that, since there was really no middle class in Ireland such as existed in England, a disproportionate share of any increase in a duty like this which hit the poor would fall on Ireland, a country where, in the course of the present Eastern crisis, he had 'nowhere seen the same disposition to sing Rule Britannia so prevalent in the streets of London'. 'For the last two or three years', he said, 'the grain crops in Ireland have been bad or indifferent, so much so as to reduce many farmers to the verge of starvation, and of course this condition of things has reacted on the labourers. Therefore this new impost comes at a most unfortunate time when the people were particularly unable to bear it.'

It was to this aspect of life in Ireland that his attention was now to be directed.

Chapter 16

The Fenian with whom Parnell kept intermittently in touch through the spring and summer of 1878 was Michael Davitt, the young, one-armed Fenian convict on ticket of leave, almost exactly Parnell's own age, whom he had seen first in London and then welcomed to Ireland in January. A couple of days after Sergeant McCarthy's death in Morrison's Hotel, Parnell had gone back to London and the House of Commons, but Davitt, after a fortnight in Dublin, had crossed Ireland by train to see again his home county of Mayo, where he was greeted by cheering crowds. He spent a week there, mainly among the Fenian-minded.

Mayo was the county in which conditions for the landed poor had changed less since the end of the Famine than anywhere else in Ireland. More than four-fifths of Mayo's smallholdings had disappeared in that national trauma, and the greater part of these had been converted to pasture. Eighty-six per cent of the remaining tenants were now concentrated on roughly one-third of the agricultural land, the poorest in the whole country. Here survival, still largely dependent on the potato and on money earned by seasonal migrant labour in England and Scotland, was the only real political issue, psychologically sensitive at the best of times to the possibilities of eviction and rack-renting inherent in the landlord system. An integral part of that sensitivity was awareness that good times might not last. The harvest of 1877 had been disappointing. Well-documented reports had already been published that winter from a more prosperous part of Ireland, Co. Tipperary, telling of preparations for some fifty evictions on an English-owned estate there. The anxiety endemic in the landlord–tenant relationship – and it was the anxiety which was the relevant political factor – was easily awakened in the smallholdings of Co. Mayo.

In other counties earlier in the decade Fenians marking time had linked themselves to those agrarian 'Ribbon' secret societies which had long sought to offer protection to tenants by imposing their own rough justice on landlords, agents and those who took land from which another had been evicted. It was among men of similar outlook in Mayo that Davitt spent his first week for nearly thirty years in the county from which he and his family had been ejected. One of these men, Matthew Harris, a Fenian, a builder with wide contacts in the county, had been smuggling rifles into Connaught and had founded in 1876 a Ballinasloe Tenants' Association. He had been busy organizing meetings at which he denounced evictions, rack-renting and the continuing process by which tillage was being turned into grazing land. Davitt also spent part of the week with James Daly, Editor of the *Connaught Telegraph*, a paper prominent in the local agitation for tenant right. At a meeting to welcome him in Castlebar, Davitt heard Daly link the land question via the current Russo-Turkish Eastern crisis to the old Fenian slogan that England's difficulty was Ireland's opportunity. The atmosphere in the county can only have made a deep impression on him. He had been alone a long time with his disappointment over the progress of the Irish nationalist cause. But it was not until many months later, after the impact on him of influences on the other side of the Atlantic as well as of events in Ireland, that a strategy for the future fell into place in his mind.

Parnell himself was not unaware of the atmosphere in Mayo, for it was there that he had looked to the horizon with his *ne plus ultra* speech before Christmas. He saw Davitt in London at a meeting for political prisoners on 14 February 1878, and again at a great meeting at the St James's Hall in London on 9 March, when Davitt gave a long account of his own experiences in prison. They may well have met again at a meeting which Dr Carroll of Clan na Gael attended near Manchester that spring and at which, according to Carroll, Davitt 'and other Fenians met the parliamentarians and I.R.B. men'. They certainly saw each other at a meeting at St Helens, Lancashire, in May, to which they travelled together by train. During the journey Davitt – or so he wrote twenty-five years later – asked Parnell to become a Fenian and join the IRB. Parnell declined, while not apparently dissociating himself from an eventual final goal of total independence for Ireland. He preferred, he said, to work through Parliament in his present manner, while not ruling out the possibility that this would lead to the ejection of Irish MPs from the House of Commons, in which case they would set up their own parliament in Dublin – the theoretical possibility canvassed since the days of O'Connell.

Davitt's account of the conversation with Parnell also said that they agreed then on 'a war against landlordism for a root settlement of the land question'. In saying this he was almost certainly using hindsight to anticipate attitudes which only became clarified a year later. In speeches

towards the end of 1879 Parnell more than once referred to February that
year as the month in which a decision was taken to base a political
campaign on the land question; Davitt's later account may well misdate
the talk.

What is certain is that neither Parnell nor Davitt made a point of the
land question in their speeches at the St Helens meeting itself. This was
concerned with an amnesty for the few remaining Fenian prisoners.
Davitt spoke as an exponent of classical Fenianism. Parnell, speaking as a
man who thought skilled parliamentary obstruction a readier instrument
for opening up the future, said rather that progress might come about by
the expulsion of Irish MPs from Parliament and the setting up of their
own parliament in Dublin with explicit repeal of the Union.

But what lingers in the mind from this encounter at St Helens is that
part of the conversation in the train in which Davitt asked Parnell to
become a Fenian. Nothing could reveal more strikingly how far and with
what confidence Parnell, the young Protestant landlord of five thousand
acres in Wicklow and a former High Sheriff of that county, had by now
come his own way than that his Catholic fellow-countryman, a convict
just released from Dartmoor and son of a small farmer driven out of
Ireland by the Famine, should now find it not out of place to ask him if
he wanted to join the Irish Republican Brotherhood.

There was little contact between them for the rest of the year. In July
Davitt sailed for the United States to see his mother and sisters who were
living in Philadelphia, the home town of Dr William Carroll of Clan na
Gael. Davitt was to spend his six-month stay in the USA under Clan na
Gael's political care.

On landing in New York he had been introduced to the Fenian exile
John Devoy. Devoy went down by train with him to Philadelphia, where
he met and was approved by the executive of Clan na Gael. For the rest
of this visit to America, which lasted until the middle of December 1878,
he remained in close contact with them and with Devoy in particular, and
embarked on a series of public meetings and lectures under their auspices.
In these he developed an argument for a modern version of Irish republicanism which would continue to collaborate with other nationalists than
Fenians – men of the type of Parnell – even though they might not
subscribe to the orthodox dogma of eventual armed rebellion. Increasingly
he stressed the relevance to nationalism of the land question.

The practical everyday problems of life on the land had long left the
Irish tenant farmer and labourer with little room for the loftier concepts
of nationalism. Nationalism, empty apparently of the real interests of the

people it claimed to embrace, had seemed just a matter of formal rhetoric. But the two interests, Davitt increasingly argued, were one and the same.

Davitt's own Mayo background, and particularly his visit there earlier in the year, obviously played a big part in bringing him to this view – not a new theory in Irish national thinking, though it had been out of fashion. But now in America it developed in his mind under the influence of John Devoy. At one of Davitt's first meetings, after Davitt himself had spoken, Devoy put forward a resolution, which was passed unanimously, to the effect that the land of Ireland belonged not to the present landlords but to the people of Ireland, who under an Irish Republic would hold it from the State. This crystallization of Davitt's thinking about the land was to contribute with great effect to events in the Ireland to which he returned at the end of 1878.

The year had seen a shift in Parnell's mind too, particularly in terms of tactics. Butt's leadership of the Home Rule Party, still nominally respected on all sides, had become virtually meaningless. For the first three months of the 1878 session he never appeared in the House of Commons at all. His health was deteriorating; the demands on his professional time as a barrister, essential for his financial well-being, were becoming more and more burdensome. When he did eventually appear in the House, on 11 April, there was a warm demonstration of affection for him in the Lobby, but this was partly because only a few days before he had announced his intention to resign as leader of the party.

The English newspaper the *Standard*, looking around for a competent successor to him, could see none. Parnell was not even among the possible candidates it considered and rejected. But he was still, as he had said of himself earlier in the year, a young man who could wait. He was just waiting in a more and more independent state of mind.

At the party meeting at which Butt's letter of resignation had been read, it had been decided at once to telegraph him to reconsider his position. Parnell then made a proposal of which everyone there knew Butt would have disapproved. He said that, in response to a message which the Queen had just issued calling out reserves in view of the tense Eastern crisis, the party should table an immediate critical amendment in the House stating that the Queen's interests could never be efficiently protected so long as the interests of the various countries which comprised the Empire were neglected. His proposed wording continued:

The experience of the legislative union between England and Ireland has conclusively shown that successive governments have been unable and unwilling to attend to the legitimate requirements of Ireland inasmuch as discontent is promoted and the poverty of Her Majesty's subjects in the country increased by laws which permit the eviction of the cultivators of the land and the imposition of unjust rents, and which leave the vast majority of the people without facilities for obtaining education of their children in accordance with their conscientious convictions, and that the only remedy for these grievances consists of the restoration to Ireland of her legislative rights.

After a warm discussion, in which several Members objected that to table such an amendment would be unconstitutional, the proposal was turned down by a decisive majority: 11 to 4. It was agreed, however – again after some discussion – that Parnell at least had a right to present such a resolution to the Clerk of the House on his own account, which he did. The small attendance of members at the party meeting (fifteen out of a possible total of sixty-five) at this important juncture in its fortunes could with reason be taken to suggest that not just the leader of the party but the party itself was moribund. It continued not to see itself in that way.

A few days later, at another party meeting in London, Mitchell Henry, a wealthy Englishman with property in Co. Galway, which he represented in Parliament, criticized Parnell for 'individualistic' behaviour in the House and complained of 'a treasonable and truculent document' advertising a public meeting and naming Parnell and Biggar as 'the true leaders of the Home Rule Party'.

Unconcerned by strictures from whatever quarter, Parnell continued to enjoy himself in the House. Reprimanded by the Speaker for his attempt one evening just before Easter to delay the Chancellor of the Exchequer by speaking in favour of an amendment of O'Donnell's, he raised a laugh by saying, 'If I am not at liberty to do that I do not know what I am at liberty to do. If I am not to criticize the Chancellor of the Exchequer what am I to do? I am really afraid to do or say anything!'

He went on to suggest that, since there were thirty-one Irish motions which had to be dropped for the Easter recess, the House should be placed at the disposal of the Irish Members for the relevant period.

Butt meanwhile wrote to the electors of Limerick saying that the reason he proposed to resign was that constant attendance was now needed in the House to exercise authority and control over certain members of his own party and he was unable to give the time for this. Nothing could have pointed up more clearly the nature of the difference between himself and Parnell, who saw the need to make trouble for the

Government as being the only point in attending the House. That difference, over which Butt retained the sympathy of the majority of the party, was, in the words of one member of the majority, 'wide and deep ... the difference between constitutional action and futile attempts at revolution'.

A futile attempt at revolution was in fact what Parnell was instinctively circumventing. But what may have troubled him was that, in terms of real political effect, the difference between him and Butt was not all that noticeable. It was true that Butt and his supporters had failed to make any progress with the constitutional claims of Irish nationality over a period of five years, but then Parnell and his supporters, while annoying the Government and thus pleasing a number of people in Ireland, had brought about no constitutional advance either. Nor did they look like being able to do so.

Parnell worked amazingly hard in the House of Commons that spring and early summer of 1878, researching with impressive industry a great variety of technical detail involved in the Civil Service Estimates, continuing to press for penal reform, and often, in the course of all this, as the Speaker was to observe during a debate on the Irish Estimates in June, 'repeating the same argument over and over again and ... thus trying very severely the patience of the House'. To this last rebuke Parnell replied innocently enough that he had no wish to do that, but it was almost impossible for him to say anything without doing so. It was his third year of doing this sort of thing. He was now far more expert at it than when he started. But liberation, in whatever form, of that Irish sense of nationality with which he now identified himself still seemed a long way off.

Butt was eventually coaxed into withdrawing his resignation from the party's leadership, on condition that he should not actually have to be in the House too much to exercise it. The party welcomed this at a meeting at which Parnell was present. But that same night Parnell addressed a meeting of the Home Rule Confederation of Great Britain in Islington and made clearer than ever before his own increasing contempt for the parliamentary business in which he was involved. He said that he was unable to go on contending against the House of Commons, the whole power of the English Government, and not only that but other members of the party. He would do it for the present session, but, unless the party showed at the next general election that it knew what work had to be done and that it was determined that its representatives should do it, 'I cannot consent to take part in the sham of Irish representation which exists, for it has been and is a sham.'

His words were greeted with loud cheers by the Irish of Islington but at a Home Rule Party meeting four days later he was censured for his use of the word 'sham' by Mitchell Henry, while Butt spoke lamely of the importance of party unity, the uselessness of 'mere political excitement and the need for patience in politics', insisting that the party 'which does not have patience in struggles for a political cause will never win'. It was the exact opposite of Parnell's approach.

In Dublin the *Freeman's Journal*, while praising Parnell's ability, patriotism and devotion – which, it said, no true Irishman could question – deplored the Islington attack on his colleagues as unjustifiable. Parnell's only response to all this, other than a cool letter to the paper pointing out that he had actually restrained himself from making any 'personal' attack on his 'brother members' because such attacks had so frequently proved fatal to the Irish cause in the past, was to table at the party meeting the motion 'That in view of the opposition of the Government during five sessions to all bills brought forward by Irish Members, it is the duty of the Irish Members to refuse supply to any such government.'

In the course of a long party debate on this, Parnell was much criticized and the resolution was called 'childish'. He was given the opportunity to withdraw it, but refused. It was then negatived by 16 to 8, with Butt leading the majority against him. The *Freeman's Journal*, whose present proprietor, Edmund Dwyer Gray, now a Home Rule MP, had voted with Parnell, stressed that the majority decision had to be respected, but added:

When all is said and done what do the Party intend to do or do they intend to do anything? We are convinced that the country expects action of some kind from them, expects that they will give expression as its representatives to the general indignation at the manner in which the Government has acted towards Ireland for the last few years. We regret to say we see very little indication of the Party as a Party doing anything ... All is not done when Mr Parnell is outvoted. The doings of the Honourable Member for Meath may be very disagreeable, but after all they are only symptoms of a widely existing, profound and increasing dissatisfaction which cannot and will not be ignored.

Such words were being read at Irish breakfast tables by men who were not in the main any sort of 'advanced' nationalist. 'Advanced' nationalists had their own papers, such as Richard Pigott's *Irishman* and local ones like that edited by Davitt's friend Daly in Co. Mayo, the *Connaught Telegraph*. Readers of the *Freeman's Journal* were, generally speaking, the more prosperous farmers and the respectable business and professional classes of Catholic Ireland. The effect of these words on them at this time may well have been to condition them to think that this was the way they were thinking, or at least the way they ought to think. There was a growing restlessness in the air, a preparedness to acknowledge that national identity required something more positive than the token respect conferred by gentlemanly representation in Parliament. This restlessness had been largely brought about by Parnell.

Such a mood was unlikely to be fully satisfied by a palliative measure such as that which was indeed passed for the benefit of Ireland towards the end of the 1878 session. It was the first constructive measure in almost five years of the Home Rule Party's existence: an Intermediate Education Act whose beneficial effect was to transfer a State subsidy to Catholic schools.

A subsidiary effect of this had been to make Parnell restrain himself from aggravated obstruction in order to ensure the Bill's safe passage in Government hands. But a bizarre twist was given to the latter part of the 1878 session by his own appointment to a committee set up by the Chancellor of the Exchequer with the very purpose of examining the rules of parliamentary business. The real object of this committee (though this was politely not spelled out) was to see what could be done about obstruction. Parnell had presumably been co-opted in the hope of in some way committing him to better behaviour in future. The committee sat all summer, and he was actually praised for his participation by the English *Daily Telegraph*, which spoke of him having 'recently become a master of parliamentary practice' and as someone who 'has proved himself a very intelligent and useful member of the Committee'. But it managed to make little progress, partly as a result of this very intelligence of Parnell. The *London Examiner* confronted the main issue: 'How is Mr Parnell to be put to silence?' And it continued, 'The fact that Mr Parnell sits beside them on the Committee, stern, lugubrious, melancholy as is his wont, with grim humour laboriously assisting them in their mission, puts the one grotesque touch on the sitting that is needed to make it supremely ridiculous.'

The *Freeman's Journal*, which agreed that the committee had done little but waste time and the Chancellor of the Exchequer's temper, took a less jaundiced view of Parnell:

It did not need Mr Parnell to render its labours barren . . . But his presence, grave, sardonic, cool, implacable, his remorseless cross-examination of the Speaker and Chairmen of committees not only overthrew Sir Stafford Northcote's fond hopes of finding a facile means of dealing with obstruction, but made the whole affair, including the chief officials and the leader of the House, ridiculous if not contemptible . . . He has found Mr Parnell too much for him, and the result has been that the Member for Meath leaves the Committee [at the end of the first week in July] a much stronger man than when he entered it.

He took little active part in the last weeks of the session. He was in any case looking beyond the present Parliament altogether. Some talk of the next general election, constitutionally due before long, was already in the air, though the Conservative whips were denying that it would be in 1878. The Home Rule Confederation of Great Britain, of which he had now been President for twelve months, with its power, however limited, to affect the Irish vote in British constituencies, was the body which had more immediate relevance to his thoughts. The air of Westminster, he told it that autumn, had an imperceptibly demoralizing effect on a man similar to that which the smoke and fog of London had on the walls of the House itself: 'we should try to make our stay there as short as we possibly can'.

Even before Parliament was prorogued in August, the Liverpool branch of the Confederation had urged him to consult with local leaders of opinion in Ireland about how to improve Irish representation in the next Parliament. When the Confederation held a meeting in Dublin that October, at which Parnell received a standing ovation, the tactical emphasis was on organization of Home Rule voting power for the next general election. Asking his audience to place this work directly in his own hands, Parnell promised that he would use the voting power of the Irish in England 'relentlessly against all the opponents of the Irish demand for self-government'. A resolution was passed thanking him for an offer to visit a number of English boroughs as soon as his parallel work in Ireland permitted. It was now reckoned that there were some twenty-seven constituencies in England in which the Home Rule vote held the balance. Only a week before, Butt, urged by O'Connor Power to call a Home Rule Conference with exactly this purpose of organizing for the next election, had replied that he saw no advantage in doing so. He accused Parnell of assuming a dictatorial attitude, a charge which Parnell in Dublin calmly rejected.

There were two ways of looking at what was happening. One was to see Home Rule 'languishing', as the London *Times* put it, and to infer that a certain amount of remedial legislation was all that was necessary to kill it off altogether. The other was to accept that Home Rule in the old gentlemanly sense as pursued by Butt was already dead and to regard the term in future as a convenient cover behind which to pursue the widest obtainable national aspiration. This virtually was what Parnell was doing. Realist enough to know that Butt still commanded the allegiance of the old party, he was by now little worried by that. He was taking over Home Rule in the new sense himself. Only the *Freeman's Journal* managed to position itself between the two points of view. 'The popular force', it wrote, assuming at least that there was one, 'is paralysed.' But it was being prepared for new life to be put into it.

In America John Devoy was giving impetus to the cause of Irish nationality by linking it, with Davitt's help, to the land question. He was also alert to the new state of affairs in Ireland. Stimulated, it seems, by reports of the Home Rule Confederation meeting in Dublin and their implication that the true future of the national cause in Ireland was in the hands of Parnell and his associates, he took a positive public step to associate Clan na Gael with him too. On 25 October 1878 he sent a telegram to Dublin to be shown to Kickham, as nominal head of the IRB, to the goals of which he himself still officially subscribed. If Kickham approved, the telegram was to be shown to Parnell. It proposed that American nationalists would support Parnell and his friends on certain terms. These included principally that the limited Butt-type demand for federal Home Rule should be replaced by one for self-government, that there should be vigorous agitation for a settlement of the land question on the basis of a peasant proprietary, with immediate concern to abolish arbitrary evictions, and that Irish Members of Parliament should all vote together in Parliament and adopt an aggressive pro-Irish stance.

There was nothing in any of this to which Parnell had not already been subscribing for some time.

Chapter 17

A 'new departure' in Irish politics was how Devoy, in the fashionable phrase, described the proposal he telegraphed to the Irish Republican Brotherhood in Dublin. He published it openly in New York the day after it had been sent. The phrase appeared in the headline of an article he wrote in the *New York Herald* two days later. The 'new departure' has since acquired some monumental status in Irish historiography. It has been repeatedly written about as if Devoy's move did indeed represent something significantly new. Even T. W. Moody, one of the soundest historians of the period, writing a hundred years later, acknowledged the 'new departure's' legendary character while effectively dismantling it into three separate identities. The truth is that, just as the phrase itself was not original in 1878 in being applied to Irish political currents, so, politically, Devoy's move signified nothing other than that the secret republican body in the United States, Clan na Gael, was coming to terms with the movement of events in Ireland in a way that the secret republican body in Ireland, the IRB, was failing to do. The immediate political impact was nil, for a new departure had already been undertaken by Parnell.

Kickham, President of the IRB's Supreme Council, rejected the proposal. Fenians who similarly adhered to the traditional orthodoxy were thus unaffected. Those who did not so adhere were looking to the future in 'new departure' style anyway and already supporting Parnell. Kickham merely forwarded the telegram to Parnell by post. Parnell took no notice of it other than to worry that it might unnecessarily frighten his more moderate supporters, though the moderate *Freeman's Journal* in fact rightly saw nothing in its terms to which any opponent of the Union who supported constitutional action could object.

All Devoy had done was to outline publicly a policy which Parnell himself was already following with unpublicized support from former Fenians. As someone who wanted Ireland to be a nation, he had argued for peasant proprietorship long before. He may well have been gratified to hear of this moral backing from a source his supporters would respect. Knowledge that in future Irish-American funds might well become available for political purposes other than military rebellion must also have been reassuring. But for him otherwise, as for Ireland as a whole, nothing was changed.

Disputes about the wisdom of Devoy's initiative from a republican separatist point of view, such as that which shortly took place between Davitt, who aligned himself with Devoy, and Richard Pigott, who saw a better financial interest for his newspapers in traditional Fenianism, remained on the esoteric sidelines. Parnell himself was looking pragmatically towards a coming general election in the light of a developing economic crisis on the land. Republican separatism, in whatever form, was a force which he could take or leave as he felt like it.

Three days before Devoy's telegram, the Home Rule Confederation of Great Britain meeting in Dublin had unanimously passed a resolution placing the direction of the Irish vote in England and Scotland at the next general election in Parnell's hands. Responding to his re-election to the Confederation's presidency by acclamation, he promised that he would use that voting power 'relentlessly against all the opponents of the Irish demand for self-government' – the very cause which Devoy was belatedly about to make a condition for support in his 'new departure'.

The whole emphasis of Parnell's speech that evening was on the need for the constituencies to speak in favour of 'energetic policies', and he received a standing ovation. He was obviously in jovial mood, saying that he had been in Ireland for the past two months (presumably at Avondale) and telling his audience what self-sacrifice it had been for him ('a very great piece of self-sacrifice') to have to retire into private life towards the end of the last parliamentary session and give up punishing the Government in order to permit the Intermediate Education Act to be passed – 'just as we had got them well and nicely into a corner', he said to laughter. 'Just as we were getting to the cream, why we had to go back into private life!'

As so often, particularly as his public persona increasingly dominates what we know of him, the lack of a further glimpse into that private life is tantalizing. It is a bonus even to be able to record that he spent that night at Dublin's Imperial Hotel.

His old travelling companion and fellow obstructionist MP, O'Connor Power, who only four years before had been assessing him as 'a mediocrity', was in Co. Mayo a few days later praising him at a meeting of a Mayo Tenants' Defence Association. This had been newly formed 'to defend the unfortunate down-trodden tenantry of Mayo harassed by rack rents and capricious evictions'. O'Connor Power told his constituents that they were 'under the influence of an abominable land system the like of which blighted no other country on the surface of the globe', and that 'the question of tenant right depended largely on the efforts of the people themselves'. He strongly advised all of them to take an active part in its settlement, concluding to loud cheers, 'Let us raise the cry: "the land of Ireland for the people of Ireland!"'

Parnell joined him at a tenant-right meeting at Ballinasloe on 2 November 1878, where he heard the neo-Fenian Matthew Harris propose two resolutions. The first one ran:

Seeing that the continuous depopulation of our country, if not put an end to, must result in obliterating this nation as the home of the Irish race, and knowing as we do that since the English connection a continuous effort has been made by various English governments to obliterate this nation from the number of distinct nationalities, we deem it to be the duty of every Irishman to use his best endeavours to protect and save the tenant farmers of Ireland from being forced from their homes by landlords who demand excessive rents or attempt to lessen their numbers by capricious evictions.

The second declared that 'nothing was more detrimental to the interests of a people desirous of achieving their liberty than indolence or apathy on the part of their representatives', and that it was therefore 'the duty of Irish constituencies to support none but men pledged to the policy of action initiated by Mr Parnell and the advanced section of the party'.

Both resolutions were passed unanimously.

Parnell himself – introduced as 'their second O'Connell, the man who would gain them their own Parliament, tenant right and everything else' – then rose to speak, to loud cheering. He told the crowd of some three thousand people that energy inside and outside the House of Commons was necessary to solve the land question, and that without such energy they would get nothing at all. They should lose no more time, 'but take the matter in hand for yourselves . . . decide on making an exertion when the time comes to strike'. The Irish people, he said, should do something for themselves on these questions, and he went on skilfully to link the land question with the nationalist cause in emotional populist terms.

'[The Irish people] have at stake the cause of their wives and children; they have their hearth-stones to protect, they have their roof-trees to preserve; they have their land to keep and their country to save and erect as a nation . . . There are five and a half million people in this country, enough people to win their own freedom, and if they are determined they will win it.'

A fortnight later he spoke at an enthusiastic Tenants' Defence Association meeting in Kerry. Introduced by a Chairman who said that, behind Parnell, he was 'determined to force his way against even the bayonets of England if necessary to fight for the independence of his native land', Parnell himself came out as he had done before for peasant proprietorship.

What was speeding up events was not Devoy's 'new departure' but the agricultural crisis and the opportunity this gave for greater coherence to a nationalist strategy. Market prices for cattle and wheat were falling in England and Ireland under the impact of transatlantic competition. In 1876 the number of head of cattle imported into the United Kingdom from the United States was 1,100. In 1877 it was 30,000; in 1878, 68,000. Wheat prices at the beginning of November 1878 were lower than for over thirty years. The last two harvests in Ireland had in any case been disappointing.

The Irish agricultural economy was particularly sensitive to such setbacks after the relatively greater prosperity generally enjoyed in many parts of Ireland since the Famine. Credit was being squeezed in the shops. Landlords in Ireland were on the whole not allowing reductions of rent as generously as were some in England. The old anxiety of Irish tenants-at-will, in many of whose families the Famine was still a living memory, was becoming a more vivid political factor than ever.

There were now in Ireland two quite separate political groupings both appearing nominally under the single banner of 'Home Rule'. One was that of the official party under the seriously ailing Butt. For all its minimal achievement over several years, most of its members still conducted themselves as if, within their respectable standing, they were politically relevant. This easily misled their English opponents into thinking that Home Rule itself was finished. 'After half a dozen years of parliamentary trial,' wrote *The Times* at the end of 1878, 'what is the result? Home Rule has been tacitly dropped ... The wave of national excitement is receding ... Home Rule will probably survive for a time ... But it will gradually fall into insignificance and oblivion.'

But the other group, a very small one, technically of the party though increasingly alien within it, was that of which Parnell was seen to be the leading light. Its size was in inverse proportion to its relevance. As an enthusiastic young supporter of Parnell, John Dillon, son of a Young Irelander of 1848, perceived at the beginning of December, the true reality of Irish politics now had only the most precarious footing at Westminster. 'No honest Irish nationalist', he wrote, 'can any longer continue to recognize Mr Butt as leader . . . The only hope that remains now is that Mr Parnell and the active party will take a determined line of action.'

It was a view which Parnell himself echoed when he wrote from Avondale a few days later to the Chairman of the Kerry Tenants' Association. 'For more than the past year,' he said in his letter, 'I have come to the conclusion that little or nothing is to be expected of the present parliamentary party and that its component parts must be largely renovated if the country desires results from any parliamentary action.'

There was a short extraordinary parliamentary session that winter called to discuss troubles in Afghanistan, but he took no part in it. He probably spent Christmas and the New Year at Avondale, where he could have taken heart from reading in the *Freeman's Journal* that in London the *Pall Mall Gazette*, the *Observer* and the *Economist* were all forecasting that Irish Members would hold the balance of power in Parliament after the coming election. He might also have noted that cross-Channel boats had been leaving Dublin without a single hoof of cattle on board and that agricultural prices were continuing to fall fast in the English markets too. On 18 January 1879 he himself crossed over to begin a tour of northern and midland cities of England to consult about organization of the Irish vote there. He was already beginning to function as unofficial leader of a shadow party.

He was back in Dublin at the end of the month to take part in meetings of the Home Rule League, including its annual general meeting on 4 February 1879, at which Butt himself appeared ill and sadly on the defensive even though his own supporters were in the majority. The meeting was poorly attended, and John Dillon looking round the empty seats talked of rats leaving the sinking ship.

Paradoxically, a meeting of the Ulster Home Government Association which Parnell and Biggar attended a week later in Belfast was in much better heart. Both MPs were welcomed with loud prolonged cheering, and Parnell himself with particularly loud cheers and the waving of hats and handkerchiefs. He had to apologize to his audience because as a result of what he called a 'bad bronchial attack' he had almost lost his voice, but his message came through clear enough as he spoke to a resolution that English government in Ireland was illegitimate, being founded on force, and that an Irish parliament was the only true authority for the people. The trouble with such resolutions, he said, was that the English Government was little interested in what Irish public opinion had to say. He reminded his audience that by Gladstone's own admission it was only the

Fenians who had made his Government listen, at least to the extent of disestablishing the Protestant Church and then passing his first Land Act. Of course, Parnell added, he was not advocating revolution now, but they had to find some way of making England listen or 'they might pass resolutions until they were black in the face'.

A way of making England listen was in fact to hand, in the form of the agrarian economic crisis, though the extent to which it was to alter Irish politics for ever would only become clear in the next few months with the assistance of other men. Many of them would be Fenians straying from the straight and narrow path of the IRB orthodoxy. Principal among these would be Michael Davitt, playing a major part in the organization of tenant defence in his home province of Connaught.

But the crisis was being felt not only in Connaught. Even in the relatively prosperous farming lands of Co. Cork, bad weather, falling butter and cattle prices, and the withdrawal of credit by bankers and shopkeepers had led to the serving of an unusually large number of eviction notices by early January 1879. The increasing number of bankruptcies of small farmers had an immediate effect on their labourers. The call for seasonal migrant labour in England and Scotland, literally often a life-saving stand-by for families from the West of Ireland in normal times, faded away as the depression hit equally hard on the other side of the Irish Sea. And the weather throughout the spring and summer of 1879 was the worst for decades. The third wet season in a row was to result in a disastrous harvest. The potato crop, still the staple means of livelihood for many of the Irish people, would be the smallest for thirty years – down over half on that of 1878.

In his speech at Ballinasloe in November 1878 Parnell had already shown his ability to take political advantage of such a situation. There he had directly linked his audience's family welfare with the cause of nationality, talking of 'their land to keep and their country to save and erect as a nation' in one breath. Since then he had concentrated on organization of the Irish vote for the next election. But on Easter Monday, 14 April 1879, at Kilnaleck in Co. Cavan, he addressed a crowd estimated at more than ten thousand on rising ground outside the town in terms which revealed even more strongly his awareness of the need to woo the Irish people towards a militant sense of nationality. For them a sense of nationality might normally be only of secondary interest in their daily lives; for him it had become the mainspring of his being.

He began by saying that Cavan, like Meath, whose population had been halved in forty years by 'landlords tempted by love of gain to consolidate farms and banish the people', had also 'felt the heel of the exterminator, yet [it] still maintained the remnant of a noble people to join in the struggle for Ireland . . . who could stand shoulder to shoulder to fight for their country'.

'I invite you', he went on, 'not to be faint-hearted, but to believe in your country and trust in yourselves . . . You have great principles to contend for, you have great interests to defend: you have your hearths and homes to protect, you have the future of your children to secure, the blessings of free education to secure for them, you have the right of living in the land that gave you birth, and lastly, though not least, you have the great duty of rearing up your country into a nation – a great and glorious nation.'

He again spelt out what he saw as the final settlement of the land question: 'the man who cultivates the soil is the owner . . . every tenant [is] to be the owner of the farm he at present occupies at will'. He admitted that this might not come for many years, but he insisted that united at home and abroad 'you shall gain all your rights one by one. You shall tear them and force them from England.'

And in his peroration he made clear, as he had done before, that in his mind there were no constitutional lengths to which Ireland should not be prepared to go. 'And when you have your country to yourselves . . . you shall be proud of what you have done, and your children after you will be proud of you and look back on the time when you made this struggle and insisted on your rights, and thank you for your exertions and your pains, just as the people of America thanked those noble men like George Washington and others who in 1775 secured the independence of America.'

He was cheered to the echo, and the echo, however faint, resounds today. There has seldom been a more effective simple expression of what Irish nationalism sought to be about than in this speech of Parnell at Kilnaleck at Easter 1879.

Under the impact of the agricultural crisis a new momentum was being given to Irish politics. Old rhetoric was making new contact with reality. Within seven years, as a result of what was to happen now and the use Parnell was to make of it, Home Rule would no longer be a mere Irish shibboleth which Englishmen could dismiss annually as a ritual nuisance, but an issue central to British domestic political life. Under Parnell, 'Home Rule' was to become a basis for Irish national feeling from which there could be no going back. From it the only movement, if there were to be any, could be forward.

★

The principal first-hand retrospective accounts of what was to become known as the 'Land War' have come from Michael Davitt and John Devoy. Of the two, Davitt was to be the closer to events through his passionate involvement in the organization of the most seriously affected area, Connaught. But events assumed a rather less ordered pattern than his account, published a quarter of a century later, sometimes suggests. Devoy was secretly in Ireland for some of the spring and summer of 1879, making contact with the IRB and even arranging for rifles to be smuggled into Ireland. In the background he was of great relevance to the Land War by reason of the American-Irish financial support he could command. But in his own later record he displays a misleadingly proprietorial view towards it, based on the significance he attached to his 'new departure'. It was Parnell, cooperatively in touch with both men but applying himself to events independently, who put himself in position to turn such events to political effect. Conscious as he had been long before Devoy's new departure of the value of neo-Fenian support, and already on terms of understanding with Clan na Gael after his 1878 meetings with Dr Carroll of Philadelphia, he would certainly have found the goodwill of an influential nationalist like Devoy reassuring. But it was hardly instrumental to anything that was happening in Ireland.

Devoy had crossed the Atlantic on his secret visit to Europe in February 1879, and Davitt had arranged for Parnell to meet him in Boulogne some time early in March – though not on 7 March, the date regularly given, since Parnell was in the House of Commons that day, speaking in favour of parliamentary votes for women. At the Boulogne meeting, as at two subsequent meetings between Parnell and Devoy which were to take place in Ireland in April and June, the two men got on well and found their general views in harmony. Devoy would have liked some more formal alliance, but this was unnecessary for Parnell since he had Devoy's support anyway as well as that of all extreme nationalists prepared to disregard Kickham's orthodoxy. Moreover, any explicit arrangement might have proved publicly embarrassing.

Devoy later recalled how Parnell, while not committing himself to any specific national objective at Boulogne, had left the distinct impression on him that 'he had not made up his mind as to which objective was the best, or the one most likely to be realized, but that he would go with the Irish people to the fullest limit in breaking up the existing form of connection with England'. There is every reason to believe this. Parnell was about to give an identical public impression in his Easter Monday speech at Kilnaleck, likening the Irish struggle to that of George Washington for his country's independence.

At the next Parnell–Devoy meeting, in Dublin (probably on 6 April), Davitt was again present, urging on Parnell the relevance of the agrarian crisis to the national cause in a manner that probably contributed to the effect of that speech a week later. By the time of the three men's further meeting in Dublin on 1 June that crisis had become more acute. With direct encouragement from Davitt, a powerful organized agitation for tenant protection and the reduction of rents was effectively under way in Mayo. Events were temporarily in control.

Chapter 18

A situation in which events are in control is also one in which men are seeking ways of controlling it.

Parnell had already understood and articulated plainly enough in his speeches at Ballinasloe in November 1878 and at Kilnaleck in April 1879 how discontent with 'landlordism' could be used as an inspiration for nationalism. For Davitt too the themes were inseparably entwined. But for the time being the emphasis was on what was actually happening on the land – over most of Ireland, and not just in the West.

Parnell was one of only two MPs present at a meeting of the Central Tenants' Defence Association in Dublin on 16 April. Two resolutions were passed. The first expressed the need 'at this crisis of universal depression to state plainly before the Empire, the disaster and perhaps ruin that is impending over the country'. The second, while reaffirming the traditional tenant farmers' call for fixity of tenure, fair rents and freedom to sell a holding on leaving it, declared that 'a reduction of rents amounting in the majority of cases to 25 per cent is absolutely necessary to preserve the credit of the occupiers'.

The *Freeman's Journal*, commenting on this meeting, made clear how far both the depth of the crisis and the concept of an important new principle in the light of it were now recognized. The paper spoke of the renewed activity for tenant right 'springing spontaneously from the circumstances of the times'. Two bad seasons, it continued, had 'reduced the farmers of this country to the saddest straits, and the people of Ireland have had brought home to them in the most painful way the question whether the agrarian system under which a single unpropitious season can plunge a nation into distress and a second such season into misery, is a sound or even a tolerable one'. The first necessity of the law, it concluded, was the reduction of rents, which, fixed before American competition had grown to its present dimensions, were now entirely out of the power of people to pay.

It was no radical source that was expressing this view but a paper which was still cautiously reserved in its attitude to Parnell. A letter in it a week later, from 'a farmer', supported its general approach. 'How', this correspondent wrote, 'can the farmers pay rents which in the palmiest days were heavy while they are forced to sell their produce at so low a price? Things all over the country are already beginning to look serious and in hitherto passing wealthy districts "Farms to Let" is the order of the day ... But there is a remedy ... landlords should lower rents sufficiently to enable the tenants to tide over the depression.'

Michael Davitt's much later account in his book *The Fall of Feudalism in Ireland*, published in 1904, gives the impression that it was in the West of Ireland that attention was principally directed towards the crisis. Obviously the crisis was more dramatically felt in the poverty-stricken West than elsewhere, but tillage, dairy and cattle farming all over Ireland were simultaneously affected. The *Freeman's Journal* noted that the very large quantities of meat imported to the end of January 'must have made a terrible inroad into the pockets of the home cattle-raising farmers'. Graziers were among the more prosperous farmers, but their difficulties thus had an even more serious effect on labourers than those of small farmers who employed fewer. By the end of May even in the normally prosperous farming land of Co. Kildare an urgent cry was going up for landlords to reduce their rents in proportion to their tenants' reduced ability to pay. At a meeting of the Guardians of the Naas Poor Law on 28 May a resolution was put forward expressing 'painful regret and astonishment that the landlords with very few exceptions hold to the hard and fast tone of rents only reasonable in just and better times'.

Such poor law unions were composed of both ex-officio members – Justices of the Peace and in most cases landlords – and elected members more widely representative of the local community. The ex-officio members of the Naas union in fact walked out in a body before this resolution could be passed. It was then passed unanimously. A further resolution, which stated that the landlords' want of sympathy called for greater union among the tenant farmers for their 'mutual protection and self-interest and for a more active and outspoken line of conduct', was finally withdrawn out of some surviving class deference to the gentry who had walked out.

In Co. Cork, where high prices for butter and generally good harvests in the early 1870s had led to a rapid extension of credit from banks and shopkeepers to prospering small tenant farmers, inability to maintain payments with the sudden fall in prices had been leading to bankruptcies and an alarming increase in court processes for eviction ever since January. By mid-June an estate manager there was writing that things were worse than at any time in his twenty-five-year management of the property. The small farmers in the region of Ballyvourney, Co. Cork, were, he wrote, 'in a most distressed condition . . . [with] no end to sheriff's sales'.

However, if the farming communities of Co. Kildare and Co. Cork were feeling the pinch, there was in the always poor lands of the West where Michael Davitt's attention was concentrated an unease which for many living memories carried with it the scent of death. Six days after Parnell's meeting for some ten thousand at Kilnaleck in Co. Cavan there had taken place the first of that year's meetings for Co. Mayo, on 20 April at Irishtown. This was to set the pattern for the whole of Connaught in the ensuing months. It was organized by the editor of the *Connaught Telegraph*, James Daly, with help from Davitt, who did not however take part. Some seven thousand farmers, many on horseback, heard calls for resolutions drafted by Davitt for 'unceasing determination . . . whereby our inalienable rights, political and social, can be regained from our enemies', for undying hostility to the landlord system, and for an immediate reduction of rents pending the system's abolition. Some reductions of rent began almost immediately to be granted.

It has been authoritatively stated that 'the Irishtown meeting was something quite new in the long history of agrarian troubles in Ireland'. In one sense this is patently not so. Quite apart from Parnell's previous week's speech at Kilnaleck, he had spoken as strongly in Mayo itself at Ballinasloe five months before. But the tone of the attack on the landlord system had an aggressive edge at Irishtown that transferred to the continuing tenants' campaign throughout Connaught. Because the distress was so dramatically noticeable there, it was this campaign which provided a sort of model for spontaneously organizing tenants' groups all over Ireland.

Parnell himself, while making occasional forays across the Irish Sea, still concentrated his activity largely in the House of Commons, and continued to do so until the session ended in mid-August. But he remained acutely aware of what was happening in Ireland and in close touch with events there. Speaking in the House at the end of May, he said that a collector of the cess tax had told him that he had not had such difficulty in collecting tax from farmers since 1847. He himself called for 'an exceptional measure of land reform' and said that if, over this, Home Rule Members might be 'disposed to hang back a little, the constituencies would not let them'. His own tactical plans centred more and more and more on efficient organization of the nationalist vote both in Britain and in Ireland itself ahead of the next general election, now widely thought to be imminent.

Against this background of change which lacked as yet any very clear indication of what the change might lead to, the decline in health and, on 5 May, eventual death of Isaac Butt seemed almost irrelevant. Proper tribute was of course paid throughout Ireland to the memory of this man who had in his day started the Home Rule movement, even if under his leadership it had quite lost impetus and effect. But it was a tribute on the sidelines of a new reality.

Parnell, who had long written Butt off as 'hopeless', was properly present at the meeting of the party in London at which grief at Butt's death was duly registered under the presidency of William Shaw, the moderate Home Ruler and Member for Co. Cork, generally regarded as Butt's most suitable successor. Parnell also attended the private funeral service for Butt in Dublin a few days later. But he did not take the train up to Stanorlar for the burial, attending instead a meeting of the Home Rule League in Dublin that afternoon to urge that a true Home Rule candidate rather than some mere Whig in all but name should be selected for Limerick in Butt's place. When, however, a JP named Gabbett was chosen, Parnell strongly objected. Gabbett, he said, was a man who 'never identified himself with the movement founded by Butt and is entirely unknown in connection with the National Cause'. He tried to pass a resolution of regret at the choice but found himself in a minority of three on the Home Rule League executive, with John Dillon and Patrick Egan. The *Freeman's Journal* criticized his action as 'ill-advised, ill-timed and hostile to the Home Rule cause'. Gabbett, the paper said, was 'a local gentleman of fortune and station and' – this clearly was the important point for the *Freeman* – 'backed by the Bishop of Limerick'.

Parnell, as if to emphasize his total independence of any easily identifiable political stance, appeared on the same day as his protest at a meeting at the Mansion House in Dublin on a platform with Sir Arthur Guinness, the Conservative MP for the city, to consider the best way of raising a fund for Butt's family. In the end he accepted an assurance from the *Freeman* of Gabbett's 'devotion to the National Cause' and wished him 'a great triumph' – which indeed Gabbett achieved a week later, actually slightly increasing Butt's former majority. What mattered principally to Parnell, with a general election possibly on him at any moment, was that devotion to the national cause should be seen as the necessary prerequisite for winning a seat.

In the previous week there had been a more genuine 'national' success when a seventy-nine-year-old Irish soldier of fortune, James Patrick Mahon, calling himself in the manner of an Irish chieftain 'the O'Gorman

Mahon', was for the second time elected at a by-election in Co. Clare caused now by the appointment of the other sitting member to a government post in Australia. Fifty years before, the O'Gorman Mahon had helped O'Connell win the election there which brought about Catholic Emancipation. To bring the present into line with the past was always to be an essential precondition for Irish nationalist success.

Parnell would have noted with pleasure that there had been a heavier turnout this time than at the by-election in Clare two years earlier, and that the O'Gorman Mahon had increased his vote.

His attention was equally sharply focused on electoral possibilities in Britain. In a speech in Glasgow in March he had again made clear how important it was going to be to organize the votes of Irishmen in Britain. 'Irishmen in England', he declared, 'are in the centre of the enemy's camp.' At the end of May a deputation from the North London Home Rule Association called on him by appointment to discuss the organization of Irish electoral strength in various London boroughs, in many of which little had as yet been done. Parnell admitted to them that until their visit he had been despondent about London, where only in Finsbury, Marylebone and Southwark had anything so far been done; but he said he now felt much reassured. He promised to pass their views to the executive of the Home Rule Confederation. He had a heavy cold at the time and was very hoarse in the House that day. Speaking on the Civil Service Estimates, he twice had to resume his seat when his voice failed him.

His energy was wonderful. While preparing in his mind for the election and watching, in touch with Davitt, the development of the agricultural crisis in Ireland, he was active in the House throughout the summer, applying himself seriously to the business of improving Bills while at the same time delaying them and implicitly conveying to the British Parliament that it would find life very much easier if it granted the Irish a parliament of their own. The Army Discipline and Regulation Bill was one which the Government was forced to keep bringing back before the House for over two months, and, in a reference to what had happened two years before over the South Africa Bill, Parnell at one point commented, 'I am not going to wear myself out as uselessly as I did then but intend to keep up my strength ... I can assure the Government that it will take them much longer than 25 hours to press this Bill through the Committee by physical force.'

He spoke out over and over again against flogging, calling for its total abolition or, if that could not be achieved, for at least the reduction of the maximum permitted number of lashes from fifty to six, or that the flogging should be stopped when the skin was broken, or that the word 'stripes' should be substituted for 'lashes'. Dogged persistence resulted in the Government agreeing to display in the House of Commons the four different types of cat-o'-nine-tails used. 'I do not see', said Parnell, 'how anyone who has seen the cats could support the inflicting of such a punishment. The tails of the cat are exceedingly long and there are a number of hard and solid knots in them which when the punishment of the cat is inflicted by a powerful warder must make a very considerable lacerated wound . . . The instrument seems specially designed to inflict as much pain and punishment as possible.'

Soon after this display of the cats the Liberal Opposition, which had hitherto supported the Government, swung round to vote for abolition, and the Conservatives were eventually grudgingly to agree to abolish flogging in the Army in all cases except where death was the alternative. Parnell remarked that the only reason he could imagine a victim preferring a flogging to death was so that he could afterwards shoot the officer who had ordered it.

The confidence he had acquired since the early days of obstruction was now very marked, and he continued to meet with the wary respect of a House to whose sensibilities he remained quite indifferent. He had no inhibition about referring to the war then being fought in Africa against the Zulu King Cetewayo as 'an unjust and flatigious war', though this was only a few days after the House had been shocked by the news of the disaster to British arms at Isandhlwana and though the son of one of his Wicklow landowning neighbours had been killed there. It was the sensibilities of the mass of the Irish people he cared about, and in Ireland popular sympathy was with the Zulus, regarded as another small people downtrodden by the British Empire. He was not afraid to release a cold passion when he felt like it. On the proposal to establish a new Irish Brigade of Guards, he thought that the recruiting sergeants found it far too easy to get starving Irishmen into the Army already without further inducement, concluding, 'At least half of the regiments now at the Cape are composed of young men from Connemara . . . sent to Zululand to become the holocaust of that imperialism which has lately become so much the fashion.'

On a bill to implement the recommendations of a recent Royal Commission on Law he again revealed his strong humanitarian concerns in supporting a proposal to abolish the charge of 'constructive murder', which had led to the hanging of three Irishmen – Allen, Larkin and O'Brien – after the shooting of a policeman at Manchester in 1867; also in supporting the proposal to establish a Court of Criminal Appeal (not in fact to be established until 1907). 'It has always appeared to me', he said, 'to be a relic of barbarity that they should never have allowed an appeal in criminal cases.'

This parliamentary activity was throughout that summer interspersed with long journeys by train and boat backwards and forwards to and from Ireland. On 1 June he had been in Dublin at Morrison's Hotel for his third meeting with Devoy, in the company of Davitt. The same air of harmony as before seems to have prevailed. All three shared aims more easily shared if details about them were left imprecise, and this was particularly true of Parnell, for whom imprecision was, consciously and unconsciously, an instrument of policy. All wanted the maximum achievable nationalist goal while using the present agricultural crisis to undermine the landlord system. There was less need than ever for a literal compact, though Devoy's much later account, when the shape of events was already history, suggests that his ego wanted to think there had been one. Parnell had support already from those Fenians prepared to discard the orthodox IRB ban on work with parliamentarians, and Davitt had anyway recently got the IRB to agree to Fenian activity in the land agitation provided ultimate Fenian separatist ideals were not compromised.

At this Morrison's Hotel meeting on 1 June, Davitt talked with Parnell about a land demonstration which he was helping to organize for Westport in Co. Mayo the following Sunday and for which Parnell's name had been advertised for weeks as one of the principal speakers. There was opposition to the meeting from local clergy. Parish priests had in fact been taking a prominent part in tenants' defence meetings in other parts of the country, including those at which Parnell had spoken, but the tone of the campaign for reduction of rents in Mayo raised the spectre of agrarian violence and secret societies – anathema to the hierarchy of the Church. Parnell, who was as aware of the need not to antagonize the Catholic Church as he was of the need to woo Fenian activists, had to balance in his mind the risks of offending either.

From Morrison's Hotel he went back to Avondale. According to his own account, it was only as he left Avondale for Dublin the following Saturday that he was told for the first time of the opposition to the Westport meeting by Dr John MacHale, the Archbishop of Tuam. MacHale had published a letter in that day's *Freeman's Journal* strongly condemning the meeting and, without mentioning Parnell by name, reproving 'a Member of Parliament' who was prepared to support it.

Regardless of this, Parnell met Davitt at Morrison's Hotel before going that night with him to Westport in time for the meeting, which was to begin at 3.00 p.m. in a field near the town.

The *Freeman's Journal* estimated that some four thousand people were present there, though there would have been even more had it not rained heavily up to about ten o'clock that morning and had the Archbishop's letter of the day before not had its local effect. The Archbishop had actually preached at early mass in Westport that morning without referring to the meeting. Those who did attend had come in bodies from different parts of Mayo and made an imposing enough impression, some eighty of them being on horseback. Many wore green ribbons and rosettes, and there were green banners proclaiming 'The Land for The People!', 'Down with Land Robbers!' and 'Ireland for the Irish!'

Rain began again just before the meeting started and continued pitilessly throughout the afternoon, but there were great cheers for all the principal speakers as they assembled, and further cheers for the Zulus, but also for the Archbishop of Tuam. A voice from the crowd crying 'Cheers for the priests!' was balanced by another crying 'Cheers for the French Revolution!', and in both cases the crowd obliged.

Davitt was the first speaker, proposing the resolution that 'whereas the Irish people have never ceased to proclaim their right to autonomy, we hereby reassert the right of our country to self-government'. Lest the word 'autonomy' – acceptable to the most moderate Home Ruler – should jar on the Fenian-minded, he added, to a cry of 'We will have total separation', that his own views on nationality were so well-known that it was unnecessary for him to define what he meant by self-government, though, just in case they had forgotten, he reminded them to more cheers, that he was for 'independence', like the Zulus. He went on to denounce the landlord system as being 'like a mill-stone round the neck of Ireland'; and, in a passage which reveals something of the understanding that must have existed between him and Parnell, he declared in front of him without embarrassment that the people 'should depend on themselves for the settlement of the land question and not upon the Irish party'. They should organize and combine to defend each other in their interests.

This was the heart of the message that now began to go out from the tenantry of Connaught to the rest of Ireland, and it was supplemented by the next speaker, Malachy O'Sullivan, a Fenian, who declared that moral force became strong by having physical force behind it. It was impossible to accept, he said, that a landlord parliament would settle the land question. Voices called out from the crowd, 'Down with Home Rule!'

and 'To the Dust with It!' There is no record of how Parnell looked as he heard this, but there is no reason to think that in the context he would have been displeased.

O'Sullivan went on to tell the crowd that they must meet together and propose fair rents to the landlords and if these were not accepted pay none at all. 'If necessary,' he concluded, 'you must be ready to lay down your lives to sustain the doctrine of the land for the people and the people of the land, you must be ready to lay down your lives to sustain it and rather die on the field of battle than in the ditch.'

The first clear verbal shots were being fired in what would become 'the Land War', and Parnell was there to be loudly cheered as he rose to add his own. He dealt first, masterfully and very typically, with the problem of the Archbishop of Tuam. He told how news of the Archbishop's disapproval had reached him only the day before. 'I am sure', he said, 'John of Tuam would not wish me to dishonour myself by breaking my word to this meeting by remaining away from it.' What he then said was not very different in substance from what he had said before at tenants' meetings in other parts of Ireland. But the heightened atmosphere at this Westport meeting, the succession of such meetings that was quickly to follow under Davitt's guidance in Connaught, and the increased notice taken of such events while a disastrous harvest made the agricultural crisis more and more painful all over Ireland ensured that his words this time went into history – a sort of early monument in the place events were making ready for him.

He restated the basic principle that the final solution to the land question was a buying-out of the landlords so that the occupier of the soil became its owner. In the meantime, however, there must be a reduction of rents proportionate to the tenant's ability to pay in such times. (He himself, though he did not proclaim this, had reduced the rents on his own five thousand acres in Co. Wicklow by 20 per cent.) What, though, if the landlord did not reduce the rents? Then, as he had said before and the Fenian Malachy O'Sullivan had just said again, they must help themselves: 'You must show the landlords that you intend to keep a firm grip of your homesteads and lands. You must not allow yourselves to be dispossessed as you were dispossessed in 1847.'

And addressing himself to the link between this, the all-important immediate practical problem, and the power of nationality within them which could help them solve it, he virtually lined himself up with the contemptuous view of the official Home Rule Party taken by Davitt. 'Above all remember that God helps him who helps himself and that by showing such a public spirit as you have shown today, by coming in your thousands in the face of every difficulty, you will do more to show the landlords the necessity of dealing justly with you than if you have 150 MPs in the House of Commons.'

The final resolution of the Westport meeting declared that any landlord who evicted a tenant for non-payment of rent was 'an enemy of the human race'. It gave a pledge 'to protect by every means in our power the victims of such oppression'.

Parnell was escorted back from the field to Westport station by a large cheering crowd who saw him on to the mail train back to Dublin. At Castlebar and Balla along the route, the platforms were packed with people applauding him, and at Claremorris a torchlight procession appeared in his honour.

Davitt wrote later that, by now, rather than William Shaw MP, who, he said, was officially known in England as the leader of the Home Rule Party but only known in Ireland as Chairman of the Munster Bank, it was Parnell who was the real leader of the parliamentary party. There was an unmistakable populist truth in this, of which Parnell was well enough aware. He was also aware, though, that, with the limited populist electorate of the day, any ability of his to manœuvre at Westminster – which was where the only present source of political power lay – was as yet limited too.

He was back in the House of Commons the next evening, having travelled all the previous night, and looking, as the London correspondent of the *Freeman's Journal* noted, 'as vigorous as any of his fellows'. He gave another demonstration that evening of his talent for combining obstruction of Commons business with constructive humanitarian thought, though on a matter and in a style light years away from the concerns of the Irish tenant farmers he had been addressing so effectively the day before. Speaking on the subject of salaries for prison warders, he said, 'If you give a low salary to a prison official you necessarily get an inferior class of man for warders . . . It has always appeared to me that the professional warder should be like the professional schoolmaster. The great majority of prisoners are first-time offenders . . . capable of reformation, and if warders of an inferior class are set over them these prisoners will be hardened in crime instead of reformed.' The next night he was attacking flogging, and two nights after that supporting O'Donnell in a protest against the massacre of Zulus.

But in Ireland it was the words spoken at Westport by himself and others that rang in the public mind. Neither the Archbishop of Tuam nor the London *Times* nor the *Freeman's Journal* liked what they had heard. Both the Archbishop and *The Times* thought that agrarian secret-society activity was being encouraged, with its inevitable threatening letters, woundings and murders, and the *Freeman's Journal* too spoke of 'violent and exaggerated language' and 'agitation threatening to overflow into mischievous and unwholesome channels'. Parnell replied sharply that this sort of comment was what one might have expected from *The Times* but out of place in the *Freeman's Journal*. 'Or', he wrote, 'does the *Freeman* possess in Mayo a detective force superior to that of the Government since the latter have not found it necessary to draft extra police into the country, or to adopt additional precautions to meet "the policy of illegality" which fills you with such alarm?'

He ended, however, on a more conciliatory note: 'I trust and believe it is not too late to unite everybody interested in the welfare of the tenants of Mayo, for I feel convinced that a movement has been commenced there which has taken a hold upon our people unequalled in our time.'

The movement was indeed swelling in the West, as Davitt continued to help organize meetings there throughout the summer and furious rainstorms put paid to any hope from the harvest. Calls for abatement of rent were going up from almost every county in Ireland. Though the Archbishop of Tuam continued to deplore the activities of people like Davitt – 'a few unknown strolling men who . . . seek only to mount to place and preferment on the shoulders of the people' – and urged his flock to 'be guided, as of old, by their faithful allies the priests', the populist tide was against him and priests were soon to be found taking part in such meetings in the West. The *Freeman's Journal* and its more moderate readers were also having to come to terms with the pressure of events and accept that, whether they liked it or not, their conventional patriotic thoughts had suddenly acquired a sharper, if perhaps less comfortable, edge.

It was not unreasonable to feel apprehension that at work behind the western agitation might be something akin to the old agrarian secret-society system, with activists, loosely known as Ribbonmen, prepared to use physical violence, or more often threats of physical violence, against landlords, their agents and particularly tenants who took land from which others had been evicted. What were officially known as 'agrarian outrages', consisting principally of threatening letters, did in fact quadruple in Connaught that summer compared with the year before, though none of the new violence was as yet homicidal. But the impressive evidence of organization and even something like a rough military discipline at the meetings was alarming for those troubled by Fenian memories of twelve years before, or the ghost of ''98'. At the largest public demonstration to date, which took place on Sunday 15 June, after mass, in a field outside Milltown, Co. Galway, with about fourteen thousand people present, the *Freeman's Journal*'s correspondent wrote that the proceedings seemed to have been 'peculiarly well organized'. Every district sent representatives, who arrived in almost military order. There was an 'immense' number of mounted men, and banners were carried bearing the Irish harp without the crown and slogans such as 'Down with the Tyrants', 'God Save Ireland' and 'The Land for The People'. Proposing the first resolution of the day, which was a call for what 'the people of Ireland have never ceased to demand, their right of Self-Government', Thomas Brennan declared that speeches should be short and decisive. The most eloquent and significant speech of the day was, he said, 'the tramp of the mighty multitude of earnest and determined men who they saw marching that day'. He added that they were determined 'to use the expressive words of Mr Parnell, to keep a firm grip on their homesteads'.

Someone in the crowd called for three cheers for Parnell, which were loudly given. And while Brennan also spoke about his audience being in 'open insurrection against the landlords' and, without justifying outrages, said that given the poverty and toil which marked their daily lives it was small wonder 'they should sometimes hear the report of the revolver in the night', his emphasis was on the nationalist cause: 'To make Ireland a nation should be the first duty of your lives and the best thing to do is to act so that Mr Parnell and others will be able to shake off the dust of Westminster from their feet.'

He was followed by Malachy O'Sullivan, who told them that for seven hundred years they had been deprived of their independence and before the God of Justice they now asserted that the principle of national independence was as strong as ever. 'We will fight for it,' cried a voice from the crowd, and there were three cheers for 'the French Revolution', 'the Irish Republic' and the Zulus.

Davitt followed, linking the present feeling of anxiety over rents with a 'national' past by calling for the 'restoration of the natural land system with the cultivator as proprietor'. It was again significant that, while enthusiasm greeted the name of Parnell at this meeting, only contempt was expressed for the Home Rule League and the party's new leader, William Shaw.

There were two more demonstrations in Mayo before the end of June, on successive Sundays at Castlebar and Carnacon. The fact that at all such meetings most of the crowd would have been to mass earlier helped emphasize the most easily recognizable feature of their historic national identity: their religion. Bringing the lofty and somewhat remote ideology of national aspiration into line with it and with the economic self-interest of everyday life became a more natural experience week by week. At Carnacon, where the meeting was held to draw attention to some threatened evictions, a green flag was carried at the head of a column of a thousand marching men who came into the field three deep and drew up in front of the platform. The first resolution they heard declared that they were prepared to resist such evictions 'at the sacrifice of their lives'.

By 1 July, which the *Freeman's Journal* described as 'the most extra-ordinary in recent memory', with a succession of furious rainstorms lasting for twenty-four hours, priests in many counties in Ireland were backing calls for reductions of rent, often supported by their bishops. At Claremorris on 13 July priests appeared for the first time at a meeting in Co. Mayo, and indeed a priest sat as Chairman. It so happened that this was also the only meeting which Devoy on his undercover tour of Ireland was able to witness. He of course was much impressed by the contingents 'marshalled by mounted men'. 'To-day the priests and people of Mayo are as one,' declared Canon Bourke, the Chairman. The new unanimity did not prevent Davitt from saying that so far the farmers had been too moderate, asking for no more than a reduction of rents which it was impossible to pay. The soil of Ireland, he reiterated, must be returned to the people of Ireland.

Parnell himself, while keeping in close touch with Davitt as this new undercurrent of popular power developed in Ireland, continued his activity in the House of Commons, where he might before long be able to turn such undercurrent to advantage. He was rising repeatedly on the Army Discipline Bill and any other matter which gave him and his few colleagues a chance for progressive obstruction. The London correspond-ent of the *Freeman's Journal* said that there was now actually talk of the Government going to the country on the question of dealing with obstruction. He wrote of Parnell on 12 July, 'One of the great secrets of the success of the Honourable Member for Meath is that he is always calm and collected and that he thoroughly masters his subject before he ventures an opinion. Yesterday he was at his best.'

This was the time when the battle over flogging in the Army was at its height, when Parnell was seen to get to his feet 250 times in twelve sittings – more than twice as often as any other obstructing Irish Member – and when, on 16 July, the Government finally agreed to retain flogging only for occasions when the alternative sentence was death, leading to wide recognition that it would soon have to be abolished altogether.

The whole campaign had been a masterly demonstration of the way in which Irish Members, if determined enough, could influence the power of Parliament. This, as Parnell knew, was the only realistic source of power to which Irish nationalists at present had some access, however remote. Even Davitt, together with many other 'advanced' men, now recognized that physical force had to be disregarded as a viable alternative.

There was one future alternative, less unrealistic than physical force but equally located in the realms of theory, namely secession from Parliament altogether and the formation of that 'Council of 300' in Dublin which had been the last theoretical resort in O'Connell's time. How effective such a self-styled representative body could be, should it prove possible to set one up, was problematical. But serious plans to implement it were soon to be under way with approval from Parnell and active participation from Davitt.

In the meantime, the only arena in which the pressure of events in Ireland could be turned to strategic advantage was that of Parliament. A dissolution was expected at any time. It was on the possibility of being effective in the next Parliament that Parnell concentrated. What precisely he might achieve there did not need to be defined too closely. He clearly had no doubt that he could achieve greater success than any that had come the way of the old Home Rule Party under Butt, or was likely to come its way under Butt's successor, Shaw. There can have been little doubt in his mind either that, once the party had undergone the vigorous renewal he was hoping to bring about, it would eventually come under his own leadership.

Meanwhile a new by-election was pending, this time in Ennis.

Chapter 19

He was to say later that had his man not won this Ennis by-election he would have given up politics altogether. It is not easy to believe this, since he was by now so wholeheartedly engaged in politics, with such reasonable hope for advance in an unpredictable future, that any incidental set-back would seem more likely to have spurred him to greater efforts. However, a rare contemporary insight into Parnell's private personality at this time is available to suggest at least some dilatoriness in character which may have made it difficult for him always to find the determination he wanted. Such a flaw could possibly have had a negative influence on his ambition in a moment of defeat.

A young man from Co. Cork, Timothy Healy – nine years younger than Parnell – who had worked in the Home Rule Confederation of Great Britain, was now parliamentary correspondent of the *Nation*. Parnell had helped him in the House – been 'like a brick' to him – and had won his admiration. Healy was Parnell's first choice as Home Rule candidate for the by-election.

The trouble was that there was another Home Rule candidate in the field, who would not be shifted, a former Whig lawyer named O'Brien, recently converted to Home Rule and backed by the priests. On being told that it would be a very difficult seat to win with two Home Rulers in the field and one Conservative, Parnell agreed to Healy's suggestion that an older candidate, another Irish journalist, a man of about Parnell's own age and of 'advanced' views, Lysaght Finegan, should be put forward instead.

Parnell tried to get O'Brien to stand down, to prevent a split in the nationalist vote giving the Conservative a chance in what would normally be a Home Rule seat. The *Freeman's Journal* thought that it was Parnell's man who should stand down. 'There are many', it commented, 'who doubt whether Mr Parnell has sufficient solidity and prudence for the part in Irish politics to which he seems to aspire.' It thought he was acting most unwisely in backing Finegan.

There was little time for the campaign, but Parnell promised that he would be in Ennis for its opening on Sunday 20 July. However, on the Friday night before, Parnell lingered long in the House of Commons, appearing to show some reluctance to move. It was only as a result of Tim Healy's insistence that he did so. Healy took him from the House to his own rooms in Doughty Street to stay there for the night, and the next morning took him on to Euston where he put him on the train to Holyhead. Parnell arrived in Ennis by the mail train at 4.00 a.m. on Sunday to be met on the platform by Finegan, who escorted him to Carmody's Hotel. The next day he threw himself into the campaign and gave himself over to it enthusiastically for the rest of the week.

At three o'clock that afternoon the first meeting was held before a large crowd waving green flags in a square dominated by a statue of O'Connell. Finegan declared himself for 'the principles of old' and the restoration of national independence. Parnell, who was greeted by the crowd with great enthusiasm, immediately started enjoying himself at the expense of the alternative Home Rule candidate, O'Brien, who had actually appeared in court at times as Crown Prosecutor. 'He comes before you and says he is prepared to fight against the Government. Can he fight against the Minister who gives him his daily bread . . . contend against a Government that pays him quarterly? No. I think not.'

Night after night for a week, similar great popular demonstrations were held all over the constituency, and Parnell, as the *Freeman's Journal* in a reluctant tribute conceded, 'threw his personal influence, his immense working energy and his thorough earnestness into the contest', acting throughout as Finegan's agent and, even at the poll, vigorously reprimanding O'Brien's assistants for following voters into the booth. At the same time he was passing out instructions to his own assistants and managing for all his 'careworn' look to exchange commonplaces with the local magistrates. Even so it was a close-run thing.

There were only 247 electors in the constituency but there was an 85 per cent turnout. Finegan won by five votes over O'Brien. The Conservative was a fairly close third. There can be little doubt that without Parnell's participation O'Brien, the merely nominal Home Ruler, would have won.

Finegan, who had fought for the French in the Franco-Prussian war, declared in his victory speech that 'as in 1829 [when O'Connell had won the election which led to Catholic Emancipation] Ennis has today struck a great blow in the battle of national independence so nobly and generously begun by the chief of the Irish people, Charles Stewart Parnell'. He said that when he took his seat in the House of Commons he would let them know that he was 'a messenger of war . . . a messenger of war until a full and ample measure of justice was done to our great, glorious and immortal country'.

There were calls for Parnell, with much cheering and waving of hats. Speaking obviously under the influence of great emotion, he thanked the electors and told them they had indeed 'sent out a messenger to England that she would tremble at'. They had, he said – and this was clearly the importance for him as he looked to the future – struck a note which would be followed in scores of constituencies throughout Ireland. 'The emotion which fills my heart – I know you will forgive me but I would say it if it were my last utterance – is "well done Ennis . . . Well done Clare!"'

That evening a crowd of about two thousand assembled in military formation with a brass band outside his hotel to escort him and Finegan to the station. There was a vast crowd on the station platform, spreading away down the line, and both Parnell and Finegan had great difficulty getting into their carriage. They had to be partly dragged and partly pushed through the crowd of admirers. Finegan got there first; it was some five minutes before Parnell could join him.

When they arrived at Limerick there was another crowd waiting and cheering for them, and they spent several minutes shaking hands with people on the platform. A soldier came up to Parnell to shake hands with the man who 'killed the cat'. There was a cheer 'for Home Rule' and an equally enthusiastic one 'for something Better', and then Parnell and Finegan were off to Limerick Junction, where they changed for the mail train to Dublin.

The next day Parnell took Finegan straight to a meeting of the Home Rule Party under Shaw in London. There they faced a different reality. They found themselves in a minority of 8 to 16 in proposing that the party should follow a policy of obstruction in Parliament until the Government had disclosed the full character of its pending Universities Bill for Ireland. Flushed with a sense of power in Ireland, they were back in a world in which Ireland had little power at all.

An all-too-typical incident of internal Irish backbiting now absorbed Parnell's attention for a few days. Possibly as part of a concerted attempt by moderates to make Parnell understand his isolation in what to moderates seemed the real political world, snatches of his alleged conversation both in victory on the platform at Limerick Junction and in defeat at the party meeting the next day were reliably reported to have given offence. It was said that at Limerick Junction Parnell had remarked of his leader,

Shaw, that he was 'an old woman unfit to lead any party', of Edmund Dwyer Gray, the MP who was proprietor of the *Freeman's Journal*, that he should be thrown out at the next election, and of Gabbett, the new Home Rule MP replacing Butt for Limerick, whom he had been lukewarm in welcoming in the first place, that he was 'a very good dancer but politically an ass'. Parnell's alleged comment after defeat at the party meeting was even more damaging, for this was said to have been that those in the party who had there outvoted him were a 'cowardly set of papist rats undeserving of getting anything'.

None of these sentiments were in themselves out of character for Parnell, and although to have expressed the last in particular in such terms would have been a surprising tactical blunder, this does not mean that in the heat of a disappointed moment he might not have done so, although he hotly denied it. Certainly it suited his opponents to try to make the most of the allegations. Specific denials of any such remarks immediately followed from Parnell and his supporters, to be rebutted in turn by those, including Gray himself, who maintained that they had heard at least something very like them. Certainly the row needed to be seen against the background of Gray's and other moderate Home Rulers' genuine apprehension at the way Parnell was going.

'In many ways', Gray was quoted as saying at this time, 'I have a sincere respect and admiration for Mr Parnell. But I must not be understood as holding myself in any degree committed to Mr Parnell's peculiar policy – if indeed he really has any definite policy, which I sometimes doubt.' In the end the matter was tactfully cleared up as a 'misunderstanding' by no less a mediator than the Archbishop of Cashel, whose very intervention was perhaps some further indication that politically the wind in Ireland was blowing in Parnell's favour.

Meteorologically this was certainly so. A correspondent in Drogheda had just written to the *Freeman's Journal* to say that:

even now at the end of summer, the weather is wintry, cold and cheerless with a constant downpour of rain . . . The harvest that used to be cut and gathered by the 15th August is as green today as it was six weeks ago. Other years new potatoes were plentiful early in July; this year the stalks are sickly and shrivelled and embedded in water . . . For the past few days a canopy of dark clouds like a pall of death has covered the land and people do not hesitate to say that the end is near.

This was a message not from the suffering West but the relatively prosperous North-East.

In the West, Davitt, who had been in constant touch with Parnell, suggesting to him that he should put himself at the head of some centrally organized national movement for land reform, now took the first step himself in the hope of finally bringing this about. On 16 August he and James Daly of the *Connaught Telegraph* formed an organization to be known as the National Land League of Mayo. Its ultimate objective was to abolish the land system of Ireland, pending which the defence of the tenants' interests against rack-renting, evictions and other wrongs would be centrally undertaken and given the maximum amount of personalized publicity. Parnell had simply been informed that the move was about to take place, and also presumably that the principal promoters of the scheme were the neo-Fenians Thomas Brennan, Matthew Harris and Patrick Egan. He had expressed publicly neither approval nor disapproval but privately wished the project success. A fortnight later he himself went to a big meeting of farmers, shopkeepers, priests and others at Limerick, where, arriving by the Cork train at 11.15 in the morning, he was met with prolonged applause and a band playing 'See the Conquering Hero Comes'.

When the meeting started in the Cornmarket at two o'clock that afternoon, a number of priests as well as known Fenians could be spotted in the dense crowd estimated at twenty thousand. There was a priest in the chair on a platform which was densely packed to the point of considerable discomfort. Possibly this made it a particularly inviting target for hecklers. When the priest in his opening address said that one of their objectives was to extend and simplify the land-purchase clauses in Gladstone's Land Act of 1870, a voice called out, 'Yes we will – by the rifle.' When the reverend Chairman warned that, if there were not an immediate reduction of rents, there would be a repetition of the scenes of the Famine, another voice called for 'Three cheers for Fenianism'. The Chairman said no, he did not want Fenianism. Whereupon there was a call for 'Three cheers for the Irish Republic'.

Parnell, received for several minutes with tremendous cheering and the waving of hats and handkerchiefs, began by saying that the particularly crowded wooden platform on which they were placed put them 'very much in the position of the struggling tenant farmer of the country because we find it so hard to maintain our footing'. But he went on to depict the crisis with great seriousness. No man, he said, could tell how it would end, but he firmly believed that good for Ireland and the Irish people would come out of it. Supposing, he asked, landlords refused to give any reduction of rent: what were they to do? 'Shoot them,' came a voice from the crowd to great cheers, and another, 'Drive a ball through them' – equally cheered.

'No, no,' remonstrated the reverend Chairman, but Parnell merely said they might as well look this question in the face, and he put forward just as strongly as anything being said in Mayo the following doctrine: 'It is the duty of the Irish farmers at the present time to ask for a reduction of rents, and if they get no reduction where a reduction is necessary, then I would say it is their duty to pay no rent.'

There was loud and prolonged cheering at this.

'And if', he went on, 'combining in this way and being refused a just and reasonable rent you keep a firm grip on your homesteads, I tell you no power on earth can prevail against the tens of thousands of farmers of their country.'

There were loud cheers and cries of 'Parnell for ever!'

He concluded, 'I believe the land of a country ought to be owned by the people of the country, and I think we should centre our exertions upon obtaining that end. You will find that after one or two seasons like this the landlord class will be only too willing to come and say, "For God's sake give us the value of our land and let us go in peace." Then we will have the farmers of this country occupying the position they ought to hold. We will have them independent in feeling self-reliant and national. We will have an Irish Nation which will be able to hold its own against the nations of the world. We will have a country which will be able to speak with the enemy at the gate.'

There seems little evidence here, or indeed in any of his speeches of the previous ten months, of that 'caution and indecision' which some historians, accepting perhaps too readily Davitt's later self-centred account, have often seen in Parnell in the summer and autumn of 1879. Parnell in fact, at a time when no one could see clearly where events were leading, was the one man acting as if he were confident of his ability to control them. Plans were being made for him to speak at Tipperary, Tullow, Cork and Navan in the coming weeks. The London *Pall Mall Gazette* wrote that his 'stumping tour' was a perfectly natural result of his recent success in the House of Commons. It was promoting a systematic agitation in Ireland in view of the coming election. The English public, said the paper, with an eye to some possible future Government action, were 'waiting with no little anxiety to discuss the length of Parnell's tether'.

Davitt meanwhile proceeded with plans for his own stumping in Connaught. He was the principal speaker at some of the six Sunday meetings held there between 21 September and 19 October. The two men were often in contact. However wary Parnell might have been in committing himself openly to the leadership of a nationally organized movement along the lines advocated by Davitt, their paths – long parallel – were now converging.

On Sunday 21 September, Parnell addressed a crowd estimated at twenty thousand on the fair green in Tipperary town. Many of them had been to mass that morning to hear their parish priest say that there was nothing more vitally important to the people of the country than the great land question, and he wished the meeting success. A priest sat on the platform as Chairman, together with Parnell and the former Young Irelander P. J. Smyth MP, with whose more staid and academic views on Repeal of the Union Parnell had before now been at variance. Smyth's presence alone was testimony to the nationalist breadth the land movement had already achieved. There were banners proclaiming 'Ireland for the Irish' and a large white one by the platform on which were inscribed the words 'In the name of God and the democracy of Ireland we demand the surrender of Castle Rack-Rent'.

Parnell, speaking to a resolution which declared that the occupier must become the owner of the soil, said, 'It is no use relying on the Government – it is no use relying on the House of Commons – you must rely on your own determination. I tell you if you are determined you have the game in your hands. Let there be no shrinking among you . . . I feel sure the time has come when you can strike and help yourselves by standing together. For God's sake strengthen those among yourselves who are weak and require strength, band yourselves together, organize yourselves, refuse to take farms from which persons have been evicted. Providence', he concluded to prolonged cheering, 'is fighting for you. The elements are fighting for you.'

And far away at Tuam in Co. Mayo that afternoon Davitt was telling a smaller but equally enthusiastic audience that Parnell was at that moment putting forward in Tipperary the only remedy for the present situation: an agreement made between the tenant farmers, the landlords and the State by which, in return for a certain compensation to the landlords for the loss of their proprietorial rights, 'the tillers of the soil should be proclaimed and recognized as the owners of the land which they had cultivated and improved by their industry'. He made clear that there was to be no question of defrauding landlords of their rights.

Arrangements for a new national political combination under Parnell's leadership based on the doctrines he and Davitt were propounding were already under way. They were at first rather more complex than Davitt's later account suggests. Though Davitt had certainly taken an all-important initiative with his foundation of the National Land League of Mayo in August, it was Parnell who took the first public political step when, having talked to Davitt, he gave notice at a meeting of the Home Rule League in Dublin on 6 September of the need for the Irish nation to have a chance of expressing its opinion in the present situation. This would be done by the holding of a 'National Convention' of three hundred delegates in Dublin before the next general election. Delegates were to be elected by manhood suffrage on the payment of a small subscription.

Patrick Egan, Thomas Brennan, John Dillon, James Daly and James Louden, President of the National Land League of Mayo, all met regularly in September to discuss the arrangements. William Shaw and other members of the official Home Rule Party were not interested. Davitt, who had been keen on a National Convention from the start, was to concern himself closely with the plans. As late in the year as 14 November, at a committee meeting in Dublin with Parnell, Dillon, Brennan and others, now joined by P. J. Smyth, he elaborated at length the detail with which the Convention was to function, projecting its meeting in Dublin 'not later than April 1882'. But the idea was for the time being to go into cold storage, eclipsed by a further product of Davitt and Parnell's collaboration which came to dominate events for the next two and a half years.

On 21 October 1879 in the Imperial Hotel, Dublin, the Irish National Land League was formed, to organize the tenantry of the whole country on the principles laid down by the National Land League of Mayo, which was absorbed into it. The extent to which even Davitt had not fully realized at the time the full potential that this Land League would be able to develop is suggested by the fact that, when outlining in November his plans for the Convention, he mentioned that the National Land League 'as a neutral body' would lend the Convention Committee its rooms in Abbey Street until it could find offices of its own. There was to be nothing neutral about the Land League.

It was after agreement with Davitt that Parnell, writing from Avondale at the end of September, had issued invitations to take part in the League's foundation. The invitations were accompanied by an 'Appeal to the Irish Race', written by Davitt and designed to prepare the way for a visit to America, which Parnell, as Land League President, agreed to undertake. Of the other six executives of the League, three – Davitt, Egan and Brennan – were neo-Fenians, two – Biggar and W. H. Sullivan – were 'advanced' Home Rule MPs and one was the former Secretary of the Central Tenants' Defence Association, A. J. Kettle. Kettle had been calling for a 'fair rent combination' to save the country since June, and his organization had been involved in most of the big land demonstrations outside Connaught. It was now to be absorbed, like the Land League of Mayo, into the Irish National Land League. A fifty-four-man committee was appointed which included Matthew Harris, O'Connor Power, Lysaght Finegan, John Dillon and a number of radical priests.

A force was now in being quite independent of the official Home Rule Party, with some potential, in Ireland at any rate, for revolutionary change. Significantly, it was known to have the sympathy of a number of bishops of the Catholic Church, one of whom was T. W. Croke, that Archbishop of Cashel who had cleared up the recent 'misunderstanding' between Parnell and the proprietor of the *Freeman's Journal*. Croke was actually being criticized in Rome for his support of Parnell, who was said there to be a 'violent man [who] used language of a socialistic tendency'. But even Church opponents of the new organization were aware that too much disapproval of a movement with such clear populist appeal could produce a harmful reaction against the Church itself.

Little was immediately changed. The Land League's mechanism needed to be worked out in detail. Expectations centred on the projected visit to America by Parnell to raise League funds. Since it was the extremist elements among the Irish in the USA who were the most likely to subscribe, it had been laid down, and Parnell had accepted, that none of the League's funds should be used either to help buy out any landlords' interests in the land or – and this had been a concession on Parnell's part – for furthering the interests of any parliamentary candidate.

Meanwhile all over Ireland a spirit which demanded change augmented weekly as the great land meetings continued and the effects of the disastrous harvest and the economic recession made themselves more grimly felt. From Galway it had been reported that few of the potatoes could be called edible, and the oat and wheat crops were as green as two months before. Even in Parnell's relatively prosperous county of Wicklow a priest had said that signs of distress there were 'manifest and alarming'. 'Next gale [rent] day', he went on, 'will find many of the farmers penniless . . . Our strong labourers are even now idle, tradesmen in parts are seen walking the roads. Who will feed their hungry wives and starving children during the coming winter?'

'With the coming of each day,' wrote the *Freeman's Journal* in an apocalyptic leader, 'the prospect begins to darken. The country is sunk in despair and the seeming apathy, born of hopelessness, which masks the beginning of a great crisis, may tomorrow be followed by recklessness and defiance. Where it will end now that the people are about to realize what is before them, no man can say.'

That it could end one day in a national Irish parliament of as yet unspecified constitutional status was the single long-term political thought fixed in Parnell's mind. He again made this clear after his usual standing ovation at a meeting in Newry five days before the official formation of the Land League. And he allowed himself to refer there to the always awkward but seldom acknowledged difficulty in promoting Irish national sentiment, namely the absence of support from so many Irishmen in the North-East, though he did so in typically rhetorical terms. He regretted, he said, that the Presbyterian Liberal Unionists were not there, because he could 'not forget that they had been the backbone of the United Irish Movement in '98'.

His present tactics combined agitation on the land question with efforts to increase support in Parliament. Flexibility was, as always, the essence of his political approach. It was this which made his collaboration with the more rigidly separatist Davitt, and even with Devoy, virtually carefree. Some remarks he had made at a Home Rule League meeting in Dublin that August, at a time when he was in regular contact with Davitt, are sometimes quoted as indicating an uncertainty of purpose which Davitt himself is not beyond imputing to him. But if quoted in full they reveal something else.

He had said first of all that he was hoping for about another dozen MPs of similar temperament to supplement the few existing obstructionists after the next election. He did not expect the bulk of the party to be of that temperament, though he did expect them to come to his support if they were in real trouble. A voice clearly sensing the sort of future trouble that might be coming Parnell's way here called out, 'We will invade the prison and bring you out!' Parnell then went on, 'If we cannot get a sufficient force of men to carry out our ideas it will be our duty to give up parliamentary agitation altogether. But when I give up parliamentary agitation I don't promise to take to any other agitation.' It is what then followed that is not always quoted. A voice called out, 'A pike!' Parnell then said simply, 'The future must be told to take care of itself.' In that understated ambivalence lay his strength in the developing crisis.

Working with Davitt to set up the Land League and make plans for the prospective National Convention while preparing for his all-important visit to the United States, he continued to address great meetings of tenant farmers all over Ireland.

At Navan in his own constituency of Meath on Sunday 12 October 1879, nine days before the League's official foundation, almost every house was decorated with evergreens as he arrived for lunch in a carriage from the station, passing through green archways to be greeted with banners inscribed with 'Irish Lands in Irish Hands', 'See the Conquering Hero Comes', 'Let Erin Remember the Days of Old', 'The Active Party Only Are Ireland's Representatives' and other such slogans. At mass that morning, a Father Connolly had told the congregation that the meeting that afternoon would be 'the greatest national demonstration ever held in Ireland'.

Thirty thousand people were reckoned to be there by two o'clock to hear another priest first move a resolution which welcomed Parnell back 'after all his labours and heroic struggles for Ireland in an alien Senate' and proclaimed 'our unaltered confidence in him and the noble policy which has won for him the admiration and devoted attachment of the Irish race at home and abroad'. It called on the constituencies to 'augment the power and numbers of the active section of our parliamentary party'. Only four years ago, this priest said, Royal Meath had given Parnell to Ireland, to glory, and it now welcomed the chieftain back again.

Parnell himself, rising to prolonged cheering and waving of hats, took pride in addressing 'a multitude unequalled since O'Connell addressed your forefathers on the Royal Hill of Tara'. (There were cries of 'A second O'Connell!') He told them to offer the landlords their own idea of a fair rent, and, if the landlord refused that, to ask him to appoint an arbitrator on each side, and, if he refused that, to 'hold the money in your pocket until he comes to his senses'. 'You are the hope of Ireland,' they called back.

At a banquet for four hundred people in his home that evening, a toast was drunk to the proposed National Convention.

Nationwide the enthusiasm which both the National Convention and the Land League were designed to marshal continued to assert itself. On the same day as Parnell's Navan meeting, Davitt addressed a meeting of some twelve thousand people at Annaghmore in Co. Roscommon, and another eight thousand were at Tubercurry in Co. Sligo.

Three days after Navan, Parnell was in the North again, at Belfast and Newry, harking back to other historic times and wishfully suggesting 'that a United Ireland was nearer than you might suppose'. In Belfast he outlined the various constitutional forms this might take – Grattan's parliament of 1782, Butt's federation, or complete separation. There were loud cheers for separation. He said that all this was a matter 'which must be left to the course of events for solution'. For once he defined a view of his own, saying that he himself believed that 'England and Ireland might live together in amity connected only by the Crown'. But, sheering away again from too much precision, he immediately added that 'whether the regeneration of Ireland is to be brought about in that way or some other it is perfectly unnecessary to discuss to-night'.

Just over a week later he was once more at a great meeting, at Enniscorthy in Co. Wexford, scene of bloody events in the rebellion of 1798. Here rhetoric could be let loose unrestrained. Listing the main points in 'the great struggle for the land of Ireland which we have initiated this summer' as abatement of rents, the reclamation of waste lands, and a peasant proprietary, he told a crowd of some fifteen thousand standing in drenching rain to 'depend upon yourselves and yourselves alone for the solution of this great Irish land question . . . Providence has given us the opportunity of asserting our vision . . . We stand under the shadow of a hill where your ancestors made far greater and sterner sacrifices than you are called upon to make to-day. Let it not then be said by your children that you were degenerate sons of great sires, but let the people of Wexford to-day, inheriting the glorious traditions of the past, keep alive the spirit of resolution, of courage and of determination that is the imperishable heritage of all Irishmen, that you possess and that you will show in this great and coming struggle.'

Perhaps the fact that his mother and sister Fanny were on the platform that day helped him rise to traditional heights of oratory with special verve. A priest moving a vote of thanks to Parnell and 'the two amiable and patriotic ladies' revealed that Fanny, with whom this priest had corresponded, had said that the one thing she regretted in life was not to have been born a brother to Parnell to make it easier for her to help him in his battle for the rights of Ireland. Parnell, clearly himself in amiable mood, concluded proceedings with one of his platform jokes, saying that he would now 'evict' Father Kenny from the chair so that he could move a vote of thanks to him.

Davitt, though a less publicly charismatic figure, was driving himself equally hard, addressing in the West at least six meetings that October while working on the organization of the Land League and the National Convention. He too could bring rhetoric effectively into service for the new Land League. 'You must not imagine . . .' he told his audience at Killaloe on the same day as that on which Parnell spoke at Enniscorthy, 'You must not imagine that you can be turned out by the roadside to die as in 1847.

There is a spirit abroad in Ireland that will not stand that a second time ... Therefore agitate, work, organize, persevere. Never give up the struggle until there is no landlord left in Ireland.'

It may seem surprising that Parnell's own status as a landlord should have caused virtually no difficulty at all for his supporters in a land agitation designed to effect the removal of all landlords. Except from time to time by his opponents, the fact was little commented upon. At a meeting once when Parnell was talking of the landlord's powers, a voice in the crowd had called out, 'Aren't you one yourself?' But it had been immediately answered by another which cried, 'One of the best of them.' His grant of a 20 per cent reduction on all his Wicklow rents was in fact lower than some Irish landlords were conceding, and below the 25 per cent demanded in many a public resolution, but it had to be seen in relation to the level of his rents before the reduction was made. A Government estimate of reasonable rentable value, known as Griffith's valuation, had been made of Irish farm lands over a period as long ago as the years 1852–65, based on farm prices ruling at the beginning of those years. In the interval such prices had risen considerably, and, though the fall in prices in 1879 restored some practical relevance to Griffith's valuation, it was still, in most places, arguably a low estimate. Parnell's approximately five thousand acres were all let for rents at or below Griffith's valuation and they had not been raised since the valuation was made.

There were altogether seventeen landowners of a thousand acres or more among the fifty-six members of the Home Rule Party before 1880, and Parnell was the only one to have come out unequivocally for peasant proprietorship. The personal consequences for himself of land reform seem to have worried him little, though his new colleague A. J. Kettle, years later, remembered a meeting in Dublin early in 1879 at which an attempt to pass a rent-strike resolution had made Parnell whisper into his ears, 'If you pass that resolution I will be starved!' This was almost certainly a joke, though it is not clear that Kettle understood it as such.

As for other 'Home Rule' landlords in the party, it became noticeable that even those who had distanced themselves most severely from Parnell's political attitude and from the strong language of the land agitation, in which landlords were 'held up to odium', began to manifest at least some altruistic concern as the autumn of 1879 wore on. In November Edward King-Harman MP, a 'Home Ruler' with large estates in the West of Ireland, who actually sat with the Conservatives in the House of Commons, wrote a letter to *The Times* from his house in Duke Street, St

James's, saying that, principally because of the sudden collapse of the credit system on which farmers had subsisted for the past seven years, 'famine was abroad' in the West, where the potatoes would not last till Christmas. He concluded, 'I see no means of avoiding a terrible catastrophe if the Government does not intervene.'

Mitchell Henry MP, one of Parnell's most tenacious critics within the party, holding nine thousand acres in the West, sent an apology for his inability to attend a large meeting of Davitt's at the end of October and appeared in person at one at Athenry two days later with Matthew Harris and John Dillon on the platform. There he manifested a rhetoric with which they could have found little to complain, saying, 'The angel of death in the shape of famine is hovering over a large portion of this our beloved land.'

But the true character of such western meetings was one with which a man like Mitchell Henry must have felt ill at ease. At one addressed by Davitt in Mayo ten days before, many of the crowd of some five thousand had assembled in uniforms of some sort. All wore green sashes, and some of the horsemen carried imitation swords and pikes. At a meeting at Kilmaine early in December, banners were carried with the words 'Unity is Strength' surrounding the emblem of a pike and supplemented by the words 'By this motto we conquer.' 'The tyrant's difficulty is the peasants' opportunity!' proclaimed another in a neat contemporary adaptation of the old Fenian slogan.

Parnell himself, looking first to the House of Commons as the instrument with which at least to start achieving whatever might be achievable, had to be tactically wary of public extremism. On at least one occasion on which a rhetorical question of his about what to do with a certain type of landlord had been responded to with a cry of 'Shoot him' he had judiciously replied, 'No I do not recommend that.' But he can hardly have been inwardly discouraged by such elementary displays of ardour for the cause.

When he arrived, rather late, by the Dublin train for a great demonstration in Galway on 2 November, several thousands were waiting for him, including a contingent of three hundred horsemen wearing green scarves. The Chairman of the meeting, a Galway priest, announced that they had on the platform with them that day 'one whom he would call the Achilles of Irish force'. Three cheers for Parnell followed immediately, and another speaker more simply described him as 'the leader of the Irish people'. A decent balance was struck at the dinner in Black's Hotel that evening when he was presented with an address saying his name should be linked in letters of green and gold in the pages of Irish history with those of Grattan, O'Connell and Butt.

With the date of his departure for the United States still not fixed, he led a hectic life over the next few weeks, with land demonstrations in Ireland and visits to England by boat and rail to try to help organize the Irish vote for the coming election. At a Home Rule meeting in Glasgow on 4 November, a speaker expressed concern that, though Parnell would make a name for himself in Irish history, he was afraid he was killing himself by overwork. A significant resolution was passed there, pledging support for his policy even though this might require tactical voting for Tory candidates. At a crowded meeting at the Free Trade Hall in Manchester, he was received with enthusiastic cheering and described what was happening in Ireland as 'a strike' against unjust rents. He was in Bolton the same night, and two nights later in Leeds, speaking of the importance of trying to hold the balance of power in Parliament after the next election. He reminded his audience that, while helping Ireland over the crisis on the land, it was essential to keep in mind the claim to the power of self-government.

He was back in Dublin on 14 November for the meeting of the National Convention Committee at which Davitt went into detail over that project's intended mechanism. He was at Roscommon on the 17th, escorted, as was now the custom, in a wagonette from the station through green arches by hundreds wearing green sashes and rosettes and welcomed with slogans such as 'Charles Stewart Parnell: Ireland Trusts and Loves You Well'. In his speech after delivering his now routine immediate advice to tenants to offer a fair rent and to hold it if the landlord refused to accept that, he spelt out his present idea of the way in which peasant proprietorship would actually be achieved. An agreement by the tenant to pay a fair rent for thirty-five years would in itself secure him the ownership of the land. The landlord would then be compensated by receiving a capital sum from the State equal to two-thirds of the fair rent compounded for twenty years and, in addition, for the next thirty-five years, one-third of that fair rent which the tenant would be paying to the State.

It must be doubtful whether many of his green-bedecked audience would have bothered their heads much over this mathematical view of the future. What was important for them was the emotion evoked by the principle, an emotion not just inspired by the prospect of relief from a system which in hard times like the present brought anxiety and desperation but one which echoed deep feelings from the dim past of their identity. It was on such feelings that Parnell, Davitt and the many neo-Fenians and advanced men who cooperated with them were working in order to translate them into political nationalism. And if sometimes the very sense of exaltation in their work carried them away from reality, this was no less than their audiences enjoyed.

'Victory', concluded Parnell at Roscommon, to great cheering, 'is even now dawning in the West ... Before long you will be in Ireland the possessors of Ireland really and truly entitled to make laws for your country, entitled to own the land on which you live, and having the proud privilege of asserting the great Irish Nation in her future years of honour and glory amongst the Nations of the Earth.'

Robert Emmet, hanged for his abortive republican attempt at rebellion in 1803, had stipulated that he should have no monument until Ireland could take her place among the nations of the earth. There would have been few in that crowd who did not recognize the allusion. Subscriptions for a monument to Emmet were in fact now being solicited in Dublin, and Parnell had been one of those to contribute. The gap between Emmet's aspiration and his own could seem already negligible. As Matthew Harris rounded off the Roscommon meeting by saying, they had one advantage which had not always been the case in revolutionary movements: they had a good man to lead them. They had such a man in Charles Stewart Parnell.

The arousal of revolutionary expectations was the principal achievement so far. A mechanism to implement these was indeed under construction, but the Irish National Land League was as yet only four weeks old and the ambitious project for a National Convention was still only in the planning stage. However, some indication of what future organization might achieve was already evident in the increasing number of rent reductions now being granted in response to the sense of crisis which the great land meetings had articulated.

Reductions sometimes a good deal higher than Parnell's own 20 per cent began to be publicized from the end of September onwards. Twenty-five per cent was not uncommon in many counties, including the West, while there were some exceptionally high concessions – 50 per cent on an estate in Co. Dublin in October and on one in Blacklow, and another of 37 per cent in Tipperary. Some were in the region of 10 or 15 per cent – the latter, for instance, being the figure on the estates of Biggar's father. But the figures themselves could be misleading unless the level of rent from which the reductions were made was also known. The extent to which fear, as Davitt maintained, rather than compassion lay behind the reductions is difficult to assess. Undoubtedly compassion played a part in the minds of many landlords. In the minds of others, anxiety may well have accompanied it, particularly as the organization of the Land League began to take shape in the last two months of 1879. The crudeness of many of the threats delivered to landlords did not necessarily make them laughable. A letter to a Cork landlord in November ran, 'Sir. Take notice that if you do not abate your rents 50% you will be shot, murdered or otherwise maltreated d.v. and may God have mercy on your soul.' It was signed 'Republican Garrison'.

The Land League, in need of the funds which Parnell was about to go to raise in the United States, was at first able to do little but carry out its stated aim of publicizing landlord threats of eviction and pay the costs of tenants financially unable to apply in the courts for compensation for their improvements under the Land Act of 1870. But its very existence was strengthening tenants' morale, and the knowledge that it was doing so was equally a factor in the new situation. The last quarter of 1879 showed both a noticeable drop in the official figures for evictions and a simultaneous increase in so-called agrarian outrages for all three southern provinces of Ireland. Significantly, both the largest drop in evictions and the largest increase in the number of outrages was in Connaught, where, because of its predecessor, the National Land League of Mayo, the Irish National Land League was temporarily strongest.

A further all-important feature of the Land League's policy – that of discouraging 'land-grabbers', or those prepared to take and pay rent for land from which another had been evicted – was also at work, having been given an early public lead by John Dillon, who had enjoined that if any man then took up such land, 'let no man speak to him or have any business transaction with him'. This principle – in later years known as 'boycotting', after the surname of one of its most notorious victims – received further specific commendation from Thomas Brennan in a speech he made in Parnell's presence at the end of November. 'We tell you,' he said, 'pay no rent until you get a reasonable reduction, take no land from which another has been evicted. Should such a mean wretch be found in Mayo then I say "Go mark him well, cast him out of the society of man as an unclean thing".' A voice from the crowd here shouted, 'Yes, as a mad dog!' And Brennan continued, 'Let none of you be found to buy with him or sell with him, and watch how this modern Iscariot will prosper.'

Parnell, speaking after him, praised 'the magnificent speech of Mr Brennan', and continued, 'As he has told you there are days not for work but for action . . .' Such words were something like a call to arms in the Land War.

Parnell of course took care to supplement his own words with his customary ambivalence. 'Let us', he said, 'remain within the law and the Constitution and let us stand even though we have to stand on the last plank.' He retained his double edge to the last, adding to loud cheering, 'Let us stand until the last plank is torn from under our feet.'

But the days when he could so effortlessly play the rhetorical double game were already numbered. The success he courted in the world of political reality was closing in on him. Only in these last few weeks before he left for America could he continue free from the restrictions which that success would bring with it.

The meeting at which he had spoken after Brennan was in many ways the most tense of all those he had so far attended, for it was convened on the scene of an eviction at Balla, Co. Mayo. The atmosphere was further highly charged by the Government's arrest two days before of Davitt and two others for 'seditious' speeches encouraging resistance to 'landlordism' at a meeting in Co. Mayo. Parnell had travelled overnight to Balla from a great protest meeting in Dublin the day before at which he had been swept on to the platform by a surging crowd amid tremendous cheering to tell them that Davitt had been imprisoned not for anything he had said but 'in an attempt to drive the people of Ireland to abandon the land agitation and drive them into armed conflict against the fortress of the Government'. He urged them not to be provoked into doing what 'the butcher of the poor Afghans and the destroyer of the Zulus earnestly desires us to do'. He afterwards addressed a cheering crowd in praise of Davitt from the balcony of the Imperial Hotel, and then left for Balla on a special train with John Dillon and Thomas Sexton.

There the next day some eight thousand men formed up in a column four deep, with two hundred mounted men bringing up the rear, and accompanied Parnell to the scene of the eviction where a hundred police with rifles had been assembled. A young journalist there, William O'Brien, wrote in his diary that it was the first time he had ever seen Parnell in a fury.

There was the now customary display of imitation weapons in the crowd. The day was the anniversary of the execution of the 'Manchester martyrs' of 1867, and banners commemorating them were carried alongside those which welcomed Parnell and called for 'No Surrender'.

A farmer named Dempsey with a wife and seven children were the subject of the eviction. This had been postponed once already because Dempsey himself was in bed with a fever and his children had measles.

Now, on arrival, Parnell learned that the Sheriff had once again post-poned the eviction, because Dempsey was still not well. The first resolution at the meeting welcomed this successful end to the action against which it had been called to protest, and Brennan and Parnell proceeded with their rousing speeches before departing for Dublin. Brennan, in his speech, made a point of repeating the words about resistance to landlordism for which Davitt had been arrested, and he himself was duly arrested for this a fortnight later. The Government, however, then lost its nerve, and also much face in Ireland, by deciding not to proceed further in either of their cases, presumably for fear of the unreliability of an Irish jury.

An unmistakable air of political optimism prevailed in these first weeks of the Land League's existence. But the distress caused by the failed harvest was being felt painfully in many parts of Ireland. In Skibbereen in Co. Cork of all places, the scene of terrible suffering at the time of the Great Famine of thirty years before, some forty tenant farmers were now reported to have gone to see the town commissioners bearing every appearance of 'pinching hunger' as they reported that their families were starving. In Parnell's own Wicklow parish of Rathdrum the unoccupied rooms of the workhouse were being cleaned and whitewashed, while bedding and clothing were being made ready for any likely influx of homeless paupers. Even so temperate a witness as Parnell's opponent in the party, Mitchell Henry, wrote in mid-December of 'black despair' settling on his part of Galway. He said he had 'never seen men so changed' as those who came in to sell their produce: 'pale, thin and bloodless, silent and without a smile. Their condition is absolutely without hope.' The wife of the Viceroy, the Duchess of Marlborough, launched a major charitable appeal. Her fund, together with one raised by the Dublin Lord Mayor and money soon to be supplied by the Land League itself, in fact prevented any catastrophe like that of 1845–9, but as the year ended it was by no means clear that this would necessarily be the case.

Parnell remained aggressively active in both England and Ireland until almost the last moment before he sailed for America. His last big land meeting was in the market square at Castlerea in Co. Roscommon a fortnight before. The *Freeman's Journal* described it as one of the largest and most enthusiastic such meetings yet held. Excitement ran particularly high because of the discovery in the crowd of police note-takers, 'more dead than alive with fright', whom the rest of the constabulary at first tried to protect from the threatening crowd with rifles levelled from the hip. Their eventual safety was only successfully guaranteed by Parnell after he had first protested strongly at the way the crowd themselves had been threatened.

In this speech he made one of his rare references to his own landlord status. Condemning the whole landlord system, he said it had brought 'incalculable evils on this country . . . we ought to strain all our endeavours to abolish it'. And he reminded his audience that he himself spoke as a landlord. A voice in the crowd here called out, 'I wish you had all the land.' To which Parnell replied in that curiously stilted style to which at every stage of his life he was periodically prone, 'I wish that Fate had cast my lot in life in some other position, but still the prejudices of my class ought not to blind me to the patent facts of the case.'

He ended on a wildly optimistic note which showed how happily he could still now let easy rhetoric before enthusiastic crowds blind him to realities that lay ahead. 'By taking advantage of the forces at present waiting,' he said, 'we should in all probability during the present winter, and in the succeeding year, be able to make a large number of tenants owners of the soil.'

Davitt, who also spoke at the meeting, was at least realistic behind the scenes, being prepared, for all his public rejection of violence, to discuss secretly the importation of rifles into Ireland with American money, to be used not for a conventional rising but for a shock force to support the land agitation. But he too now, while conceding that Parnell did not share his own clear separatist principles, said that 'as a humble follower . . . he thought [Parnell] was the man whom Providence had marked out to lead the Irish people to victory'.

But some indication of the land agitation's present shortcomings, for all the rhetoric, was revealed the same week by the final chapter in the Dempsey eviction story. On 12 December 1879, a bitterly cold day, a party of a hundred heavily armed police turned the family of nine out on to the road. Their furniture was smashed with sledgehammers. It was some twenty-four hours before temporary lodgings could be found for them. The Land League, for all the self-congratulation of the earlier meeting, had been unable to have any effect on the final outcome.

The only step it could now take was to arrange for payment of Dempsey's rent and legal costs. This it proceeded to do, though even this was a strain on its funds. The family was reinstalled just in time for Christmas, but the event hardly augured well for that prospect of early victory for national objectives which the speeches of Parnell and Davitt seemed to be holding out.

Parnell, for all the understandable pleasure he must have derived from the evidence of his personal success in Ireland, also retained at least a theoretical grasp on realities. At the meeting in Dublin a few days before he left for America at which the Land League and the former Central Tenants' Defence Association were technically amalgamated, he took the precaution of qualifying his own resolution for 'occupation ownership' or peasant proprietorship with the phrase, 'and where that may not be possible a claim for fixity of tenure at fair rents and free sale'. But in the mood in which he was leaving for the USA this was more likely precautionary afterthought rather than any carefully thought-out adjustment of policy. In general the situation was too volatile, the future too unpredictable, to seem to require excessive concentration on detail.

What might reasonably have given him more serious immediate concern were the intricacies of internal Irish-American politics with which he knew he was about to be confronted. The raising of money for the Land League was bound to involve a delicate balance of appeal between moderate sections of American opinion and the enthusiastic revolutionaries of Clan na Gael who deplored too much sidetracking of funds or attention from the revolutionary goal. In fact there is no evidence at all that he was in any way worried.

On 21 December Egan and Davitt went down by train with him and Dillon to Cork, where there was an enthusiastic crowd on the platform, including a man named James Carey, to see them off to the harbour of Queenstown. There another enthusiastic reception was only slightly marred by a display of opposition from an orthodox Fenian, Charles Doran, whom Parnell had at one time hoped to enlist in parliamentary collaboration but who remained intransigently disapproving of any truck with constitutional politics.

It may have served as a useful reminder of the sort of trouble he could occasionally expect to meet with in the United States.

Chapter 20

The journalist R. Barry O'Brien, who was to come to know Parnell well and wrote the first biography of him only a few years after his death, said that he set out for America with a light heart. This seems likely – the political future presented only opportunities; difficulties ahead were an exciting challenge. Certainly his mission presented him with difficulties of its own. Clan na Gael's support was vital to the success of the tour, and he was to enjoy it throughout behind the scenes, but some Clan na Gael supporters were wary of his parliamentary commitment at home, which was seen as a compromise of revolutionary ideals. He had to be careful to sound the right rhetorical note in speeches without compromising his own credibility for parliamentary manœuvre. But this was no more than what he had been doing in Ireland itself for over a year, and with the Atlantic between himself and the British press the need to avoid close scrutiny was actually less urgent.

On arrival in the USA another problem presented itself. Even while he and Dillon had been at sea, the situation in Ireland had deteriorated rapidly: the distress was becoming daily more severe and even desperate. They therefore decided on arrival to appeal for funds not only for the Land League, as originally intended, but also separately for the charitable relief of distress in Ireland. Three such appeals were already in existence: two from Ireland – those of the Viceroy's wife, the Duchess of Marlborough, and of the Lord Mayor of Dublin – and in the USA, one launched by the *New York Herald*, an opponent of Irish extremism and, as such, politically hostile to an 'agitator' like Parnell. Part of his great energy therefore had to be given to a bickering of cross-fund rivalry based on political differences. At the same time some of his Clan na Gael supporters resented him bothering about charity at all. What he did was to direct the main thrust of his energy towards raising enthusiastic support and money for the Irish national cause on the widest possible level. Audiences could consider that cause as embodied either in the Land League or in relief for an Irish population which English government had once again brought to the verge of famine as thirty years before – when many in his audience had themselves been driven to emigrate from Ireland to America.

In this sense the tour was to be an overwhelming success, though he would be criticized for his attacks on the rival relief funds and at times would cause disappointment by the untheatrical nature of his oratorical style.

The Cunard ship the *Scythia*, on which he and Dillon had travelled for eleven days through wintry Atlantic weather, docked in New York at 1.30 in the morning of 2 January 1880. At 7.00 a.m. a welcoming committee and a number of reporters came out to the ship in a revenue cutter but waited for Parnell and Dillon to have breakfast before going on board. Eventually Parnell appeared at the port rail, to be greeted by much cheering. They went up to meet him.

The *New York Times* man described him as having a fair skin with hair slightly inclining to baldness, adding 'his eyes are rather small, dark blue and keen . . . though his countenance has a certain nervousness of expression giving one the idea of his being a practical man'. He contrasted him with Dillon, who looked 'more the visionary and enthusiast'. As the formal address of welcome was read, Parnell stood looking quietly at the ground and replied with what was to be the underlying theme of his whole tour. 'We must hope and believe', he said, 'that the time is approaching when we may be able to speak of Ireland as other men speak of their own country, and that we may be able to speak of her as really and truly among the Nations of the Earth.'

Once again, few in his audience, especially the American Irish, would have failed to recognize the echo of the republican Robert Emmet's words from the dock. His mother, with Fanny, Anna and Theodosia, had come to meet him too, and after answering questions from reporters ('Are you here in an official capacity?' 'I have been sent by the National Land League of Ireland') he went with his family to the Fifth Avenue Hotel where they were staying and where he met more of the press for another two hours.

The first public meeting was held the next day in Madison Square Garden before about seven thousand people. The *New York Times* reported that the whole audience rose to greet him with 'wild tumult from thousands of shouting throats'. He was with his mother and three sisters, and as the party made its way to the platform 'hands stretched out in all directions to reach the young agitator'.

'The American people', he began, 'occupy today a proud position. They are virtually the arbiters of this Irish question.' He went on to tell them, to loud cheering, that victory was bound to come to the exertions of the Irish people in their great struggle for liberty, and that it was the solution of the land question that was the great step to freedom.

The speech set the tone for the confident style with which he was to address hundreds of thousands of Irish Americans over the next two and a half months. Again, the breadth of the Atlantic made it unnecessary to be too precise about difficulties. In a euphoric conclusion to this speech in Madison Square Garden he told the audience, 'We shall have the dreams of every patriot in all ages realized and the orange and green will be united.' There was a rush for the audience to shake hands with him, and according to the *New York Times* 'for a few minutes the gentleman seemed in danger of being dismembered'.

Before the week was out Parnell had spoken to great applause at the Catholic Institute in Jersey City – where he had a military escort of the 9th New Jersey Regiment – and at a packed Academy of Music in Brooklyn. He had also addressed the New York Stock Exchange, contrary to the usual practice by which politics were excluded there. The justification for his appearance was found in the charitable aspect of his appeal, though he was hissed once or twice by those stockbrokers who regarded him, with his views on landed property, as an unsuitable 'agitator'.

The next day he was in Philadelphia, where he was welcomed by that Dr William Carroll, Chairman of Clan na Gael, whom he had last met in Dublin and who was one of those firmly of the opinion that charity should be kept out of the campaign. In circulating all members of Clan na Gael at the beginning of the tour and asking for invitations to speak to be sent to Parnell and Dillon, Carroll had stressed that it was for the political purposes of the Land League that they should be supported and that it should be made clear that the money raised at meetings was to go towards these political objectives. Carroll's own secret concern at this time was to get arms to the West of Ireland – about which he was writing to John Devoy. This made clear the sort of political objectives he had in mind. It was the sort of thing which Parnell, who was to remain in close touch with Carroll in the following weeks, took care to know nothing about.

In Philadelphia, in the Academy of Music, the largest theatre in the world after La Scala in Milan, Parnell spoke, to a great ovation, of 'widespread famine over six counties of Ireland'. But he showed himself aware of Dr Carroll's susceptibilities. When he went on to talk of the struggle between the landlord and the tenant in Ireland and the need to change the system, a voice called out 'By revolution!' Parnell pointedly did not say, 'No'; he just reminded his audience that he had American blood in his veins too. There was nothing in the implication that he had not hinted at before, even stated more directly.

From Philadelphia he and Dillon moved on to Boston, where, escorted by the 9th Regiment of Massachusetts to a platform occupied by two hundred leading citizens, he made a masterly statement of his ambivalence on nationalist tactics. 'I am not in favour of revolutionary methods', he said, 'yet still, as a sensible man, I cannot help saying that if things are allowed to continue as they are in Ireland much longer our people will not be able to content themselves or to withstand the influences which drive them towards violent and revolutionary methods . . . [*Cheers.*]' He went on to deliver a neat thrust at British imperial government – always a popular target for Americans. 'To a Government that does not hesitate to spend 10 to 20 millions a year on childish and cruel wars in all parts of the world', he said, 'it would be surely a good change if they would devote their attention to domestic affairs and to securing the happiness and prosperity of their own people at home instead of destroying that of other people abroad.'

New words were being put to the tune of 'John Brown's Body':

> Says every true American, Parnell thy cause is ours,
> We pray for Heaven's blessing to strew your course with flowers,
> The land-sharks dare not harm thee with our united powers
> To set Ireland free!
> *Chorus:* 'Welcome!   Welcome!
>   Onward!   Onward!'

Parnell and Dillon went on to Indianapolis, Cleveland and Buffalo, were back in New York on 29 January, and on 2 February went to Washington, where by 96 to 42 the House of Representatives had passed a resolution that Parnell should be allowed to address it. He delivered a rather dull if unexceptional half-hour lecture on land tenure in Ireland, taking pride again, in conclusion, in his own American blood, and in the part America was playing by helping to make unnecessary in future such humiliating appearances as that of himself and Dillon 'as beggars and mendicants before the world'.

He was politely received. He apologized for having trespassed upon their attention at such length and thanked them for 'the very great kindness and attention with which you have listened to my feeble and imperfect utterances'. It was, even by his standards, a painstaking performance.

What was by this stage in his career Parnell's regular and well-established speaking manner was hardly what Americans expected of a public orator, least of all one whom they had been told was something of an 'agitator'. Even later, at the height of his career, he was to tell a friend that he was always nervous at public meetings and found it an effort to attend them, so one can imagine what a strain a tour like this must have placed on him. Yet it was always this very effort which gave power to his public presence and to the words he delivered so that these were able to impress audiences as diverse as the peasantry of the West of Ireland, the House of Commons and the people of the East Coast and Middle West of America. The dollars, both for the Land League and for famine relief, rolled in, and he was in much popular demand. Four days after addressing the House of Representatives in Washington he received an invitation to address the State Senate and House of Representatives of the State of Virginia.

Arrangements for the tour were at first in the hands of Dillon, though Carroll helped when he could and was sharply critical of Dillon's blunders and omissions in planning the schedule. The correspondence required to deal with invitations and appointments clearly overwhelmed Dillon. Three cities named Springfield (two of them a thousand miles apart) announced Parnell's arrival on the same day. Both Fanny and Anna Parnell, who were running the Central Relief Office in New York, were described as being 'acerbic' about Dillon's capacity for management. Fanny herself did what she could to help resolve the confusion. She told Devoy on 10 February, 'My brother writes that his engagements are Pittston Pa. 11th; Altoona Pa. 12th; Baltimore 13th; Pittsburgh 15th; Wheeling, West Virginia, 16th; Columbus, Ohio 19th; Cincinnati 20th; Detroit 22nd; Chicago 23rd. It will thus be impossible for him to be in New York . . .'

It was at Cincinnati that Parnell made a speech which was later to be seized on by British opponents as particularly notorious. Both the East Coast American-Irish nationalist paper the *Irish World* and one of the local Cincinnati papers reported him as saying there that the ultimate goal for which Irishmen were aiming and which alone would satisfy Irishmen whether in Ireland or America was the destruction of 'the last link' which kept Ireland bound to England. The unequivocal implication of separatism in this was later to cause him trouble, though in fact he had made clear often enough before, both in Ireland and the USA, that the total independence of Ireland, like that of other nations of the earth, was to his mind a desirable option if it could somehow be successfully achieved. It was over two years since he had proclaimed in Castlebar that no man could assign a *ne plus ultra* to the march of a nation. He had indicated as much again at Kilnaleck and elsewhere in 1879. Only a few weeks before the speech at Cincinnati he had declared in Cleveland, Ohio, that after seeing the armed regiments of Irishmen who had turned out to welcome him there he was reminded of the remark of the Catholic Irish exile Sarsfield, about to die for France on a foreign field in 1693: 'Oh that I could carry these arms for Ireland.' 'Well,' Parnell had added, 'well, it may come to that some day or other.' At Rochester soon afterwards he was again quite open when he said that it was indeed the duty of every Irishman to shed the last drop of blood for his rights, but 'at the same time we all recognize the great responsibility of hurling our unarmed people on the points of British bayonets. We must act with prudence.' As his first biographer said, such expressions, then, came from Parnell's heart.

Subsequent research has shown that a second Cincinnati paper in fact reported a more anodyne version of Parnell's peroration, with reference merely to Ireland taking her proper place among the nations of the earth, and that the reporter for the first Cincinnati paper and for the *Irish World*, which had an in-built need to appeal to extreme nationalist readers, may have been one and the same person. All this is only of marginal interest in the context of that time, though it was to assume some political significance later.

Meanwhile he had sent to Ireland for more competent help in the management of the tour. The young Tim Healy was to come out as an assistant. Parnell left Dillon in Pennsylvania and took a train for Chicago, Detroit, Minneapolis, St Paul and Dubuque, Iowa, where he arrived from St Paul on 27 February.

For nearly two months he had seldom slept two nights in the same town and had been subjected to endless official welcomes, enthusiastic receptions and meetings at which, though he often made the same speech, it was impossible for him not to deliver it in the grip of his own controlled nervous tension. He had taken catnaps on the Pullman cars whenever he could, but the *Dubuque Herald* could not help noticing that he was showing the strain of his mission. A salvo of cannon shots was fired to greet him, and these were followed by the usual welcoming speeches and a military escort to his hotel. The *New York Herald*, with its opposition both to the Land League itself and to its famine relief fund, was by now accusing him of going round America on the same speech, and indeed, as usual, in the Dubuque Opera House he attacked in the same terms as he had already done elsewhere not only the landlord system in Ireland as the cause of the famine but other relief funds such as that of the *New York Herald*, of which he urged a boycott. Some four hundred dollars was collected at the door, and this, together with individual donations for that night and money already raised by committees in the city for him, amounted to more than four thousand dollars there altogether.

This was creditable, for the young 'agitator' had not been getting good notices from the conservative Middle-Western press. A month before his arrival in Iowa the *Iowa State Register* had written that he was not meeting with the cordial encouragement in the country which sympathizers with the Irish movement had expected, and this, the paper said, was 'attributable chiefly not to his cause but to himself'. In Boston, it said, he had been 'cold as an iceberg, with a thin voice, an awkward manner, no animation and no style, delivering a speech committed to memory that does not even warm in its delivery and is failing to get to the hearts of his audience'. However, Parnell's individual style had had the very opposite effect on one young American reporter who had heard him speak for the first time in January in the Academy of Music at Buffalo. He wrote later:

Before Parnell had spoken six words I recognized his superiority to any man on the stage or in the audience . . . Sure, his voice was not loud but under perfect control. The dress, the action, the face of the man was regal. His plea was for a clear comprehension of the matter at issue, that it might be effectively dealt with without heat, or fear, or haste . . . He carried a superb reserve . . . The audience . . . soon forgot to applaud, but just listened breathlessly.

Something of this must have taken effect even in Iowa, though the *Iowa State Register* continued to be guardedly hostile and other local papers equally deplored Parnell's 'stale sedition', the way he intermingled politics with his appeal for famine relief, and his attacks on the rival relief funds. Nevertheless the dollars continued to come in, and he went on south, first by special train and then by ferry-boat across the Mississippi to Davenport, where Tim Healy caught up with him.

After a nine-day crossing of the Atlantic, Healy had spent two days in New York with Devoy and Fanny and Anna Parnell. His mission was to help put better order into the rest of the tour. At Davenport he was able to report to Parnell that the remarkable success of the two Dublin relief funds now made it reasonable to concentrate on the political, Land League, aspect of the tour. This was probably welcome news for Parnell, since to do so would make relations with Clan na Gael easier. Healy was 'touched' that night to see Parnell taking the collection for relief from the audience himself.

In New York Healy had found to his dismay that the Parnell sisters regarded him as a 'Heaven-sent genius' after Dillon, whom he thought they were blaming unfairly 'for not being what he never pretended to be' while otherwise doing Parnell good service speaking and lecturing. Certainly it seemed that a lot of people had been offended by not getting replies to letters and invitations, and no one ever seemed to know where Parnell was or what he was going to do next. 'Of course, I know he never opens a letter,' Healy wrote to his brother in Ireland, 'and rarely a telegram . . . In spite of their [the Parnell sisters'] present graciousness and compliments, I shall be the next victim if anything goes wrong.'

But what was soon to cause the tour to 'go wrong' was something out of Healy's control.

He moved Parnell successfully on to Des Moines, where they were welcomed by a thirty-two-gun salute and where Parnell was accorded the privilege of addressing the state legislature – the first person from beyond the borders of the state ever to do so. At Springfield, Illinois, he was given the freedom of the city and addressed a meeting in the opera house presided over by the State Governor. Of St Louis, Parnell afterwards remembered 'addresses, parades and receptions – enormous meeting at the Merchants Exchange – next largest success after Chicago'. At that meeting he replied vigorously to attacks which the *New York Herald* had been continuing to make against him, including a charge that he would not dare to make his American speeches in Ireland. He insisted that he had spoken far more strongly in Ireland than he ever had in America.

Then on 6 March they moved north to Canada for a meeting in Toronto on the 7th and another the next day in Montreal, where Healy himself spoke for the first time in the tour. He used a phrase about Parnell that had once been applied to O'Connell, calling him 'the uncrowned King of Ireland'. It struck an easy popular chord, echoing between aspiration and ancient glory, and evoked a destiny to which Parnell seemed due to be called. The call was in fact on the point of arrival. When they got back to their hotel that night there was a telegram from Biggar in London: 'Parliament dissolved. Return at once.'

In the United States, Parnell had raised, in today's terms, about £2.5 million for famine relief and another £500,000 for the political purposes of the Land League. As Healy wrote to his brother from the SS *Baltic* on the way back to Ireland:

The work was more than anyone will ever give Parnell credit for; and then the deputations at every roadside station, and the shaking hands in the train! It was awful for him, and we had cards and circulars to spread amongst them, letters to write, and speeches to compose, all in the cars! The moment an hotel was reached another crowd gathered, who thought you had nothing to do but listen to their talk. A quiet half-hour or a five minutes' rest was unknown.

And Healy had been with Parnell only a quarter of the time. During that time, however, he had had glimpses of Parnell and his family which are precious not only because they bring them to life with the magic of the contemporary word but also because they illuminate something of that assured but eccentric spirit which had now attached itself so firmly to the fortunes of the Irish people. 'They are', he wrote to his brother of the Parnells, 'the most extraordinary family I ever came across. The mother, I think, is a little "off her nut" in some ways, and for that matter so are the rest of them. The indifference of the family, one towards the other, is amazing, and there doesn't seem very much outward affection manifested.'

In this Healy may just have been registering his unfamiliarity with a reserve that was the social norm for families in a different Irish class from his own. But this ease of detachment which he had noticed was to play some part too in the equally close involvement which Parnell had now acquired with the Irish people.

Healy said in his letter that Fanny and Anna, who both worked very hard for the movement, were 'mutually jealous of each other's efforts – Parnell being sublimely indifferent to them'. Just after Parnell got to New York from Canada, Theodosia had quite suddenly announced that she had decided to go to Paris to see their sister Delia, who was married to the American millionaire James Livingston Thomson. '. . . neither of the others seemed in the least surprised or to care a damn, and Parnell himself said "Ah!" though none of them had ever heard of the project before.' Yet Healy noticed that on board during the Atlantic crossing 'Parnell showed a great deal of attention to his youngest sister' and when two years later Fanny, to whom he had been apparently 'sublimely indifferent', died quite suddenly in America, he was devastated.

He was a man whose emotions were as powerful as his ability to keep them under control.

Chapter 21

Up to this point in his life any attempt to find out what sort of a human being it was who, in the person of Parnell, was beginning to affect the course of Irish history has to depend almost entirely on external sources: on behaviour revealed in contemporary newspapers or parliamentary reports, or recollections compiled by family, friends and colleagues, mostly after he had already become an imposing figure and often after his legendary status had been enhanced by death. But soon, from the summer of 1880, a new source of evidence becomes available, shedding light for the first time, and spasmodically for the rest of his life, on some of his innermost feelings. Much of this evidence is provided by himself.

Nearly a quarter of a century after his death, the woman whom he was eventually to marry published over a hundred letters he had written to her over a period of ten years. With the possible exception of two of them, no one doubts their authenticity, though there was at least one typographical error in transfer from manuscript to the printed page, and there has undoubtedly been some editing – which raises a special question to be considered separately. There is, however, no doubt at all about the genuineness with which the letters reveal with almost embarrassing openness at times the depth of his emotional being. In the two volumes of memoirs in which they appear, less value attaches to some of the accounts of events than to the content of these letters. But there is also much in the memoirs themselves to reveal the sort of man Parnell was in private and the way in which this private person related to the role on the political stage that he was playing. The great good fortune for posterity is that this material becomes available only a few months after his reappearance on the political stage in Ireland at the end of his ten-day journey back across the Atlantic with Healy.

As their ship neared the southern Irish coast, Parnell seems to have been well aware that the most exciting phase of his political career now lay ahead. Still at sea on St Patrick's Day 1880, he had surprised Healy, who knew him as a 'temperate and economical' man, by ordering champagne for dinner and toasting the cause of Ireland. On arrival at Queenstown on Sunday 21 March he again surprised Healy by being disconcerted and petulant because no welcoming tender seemed to be coming out to meet them. But when it finally appeared, with old friends and colleagues like Biggar, Finegan and Davitt waving handkerchiefs on board, he became his old steady self again and after a quick visit to Cork for an enthusiastic reception – in the course of which the delay of the tender still seemed to rankle, for he mentioned it – he took the night mail train to Dublin to make his dispositions for the April general election. He had no more than three weeks in which to make them, and he immediately took advantage of the train's hourly stops through the night to address those on the platforms who had turned out to welcome him.

The United Kingdom's franchise was still a restricted one, confined to men, and based on a property qualification which was more restrictive in Ireland than in England. The male electorate had last been extended by the Reform Act of 1867; the likelihood of its being extended further in the foreseeable future, with the restrictions in Ireland removed, depended on a victory for Gladstone's Liberal Party and its radical elements at the general election. But this would not be the Liberals' first priority, and the prospect of a wider franchise to give the vote for the first time to the main body of Parnell's and the Land League's supporters in Ireland was not of immediate relevance. Parnell's concern for the time being was to ensure that as many vigorous nationalist Home Rulers as possible – rather than mere Whiggish Irish Liberals who mouthed Home Rule because it had populist appeal – were chosen by the limited electorate for the party of which, though he had as yet no right to command it, he was the most vigorous representative in Parliament.

On the same day as he arrived in Dublin he returned to Co. Kildare, where he had already stopped once during the night. On the day after that he was at Thurles in Co. Tipperary; on the day after that in Roscommon. The pugnacious style in which he was determined to battle against the Whigs was soon in evidence. But in Roscommon he may for a moment have found himself in a dilemma.

Two members were to be returned for the county. One of the candidates, a Whig Home Ruler, Charles O'Conor – the O'Conor Don – had been sitting for it for twenty years and was well-liked; the other, the Hon. Charles French, also a man whose 'Home Rule' views were anodyne rather than nationalist, was less difficult to remove, though he too had sat for the county for several years. A decade later, men who had by then turned against Parnell put out a story that, far from being as determined in his choice of candidate as he made out, he had at first been prepared to allow at least the O'Conor Don, well enough liked as he was, to be returned unopposed and that he had tried to prevent his activist supporter J. J. O'Kelly from standing against him. Whatever the full truth, this story is clearly much garbled and the plain facts are different.

O'Kelly, who had only just come back to Europe from America to help in the election, had originally had no intention of standing at all. On 25 March, only days before polling, he was there in Roscommon with Parnell, but to lend support and not as a candidate. Parnell himself that day actually inveighed sharply against the O'Conor Don, though he was careful to show he was aware of the respect in which the man had been held – not least because some of his supporters were in the audience. Quite disingenuously he did say that he had had no wish to influence the judgement of the electors in choosing their representatives; but, while recognizing that they must have been reluctant to abandon the O'Conor Don, whom they had tolerated out of generosity, he noted that they had now unanimously passed resolutions declaring that neither the O'Conor Don nor the Hon. Charles French any longer had their confidence as representatives. What he went on to say made clear that he can hardly have wished to favour the O'Conor Don.

'You now see . . .' he said amid some commotion, 'you now see that you have no right to be generous at the expense of the whole of Ireland!' [*Some cheers and some more commotion*]. 'The O'Conor Don is a sample of West Britonism in Ireland – he is a sample of the rights of England and Englishmen to rule Ireland. He is the representative of English party government . . .' And with typically Parnellian sleight of hand he wooed those moderates who might still wish to be O'Conor Don's supporters with the use of a name which no moderate 'Home Ruler' could allow himself to reject: '. . . and if you deprive him of the representation of Roscommon you strike the greatest blow that has been struck against English misgovernment in Ireland since Isaac Butt was elected for the city of Limerick.' There were loud cheers.

He asked them who they were going to elect in the place of the O'Conor Don.

'Anyone you say! Anyone you like! It is all in your own hands!' called the crowd.

It was just the sort of thing he had come to hear. He recommended two men already named in a resolution which he had probably approved before the meeting – Dr Andrew Commins, a friend of his and one of his predecessors as President of the Home Rule Confederation of Great

Britain, but also 'the confidential friend and adviser of the late Isaac Butt', and a Major D'Arcy – and both names received the required cheers. But before polling-day D'Arcy was in fact replaced by O'Kelly. Both Commins and O'Kelly were then comfortably elected above the O'Conor Don and another nominal Home Ruler who replaced the discarded French. Whether or not Parnell had, as was later to be suggested, at any time before the meeting considered letting the O'Conor Don go through because of the 'generosity' felt towards him, the election result was a tribute both to his direct personal influence and to his percipience in throwing caution to the winds when they seemed to be blowing his way.

He was not to have such an easy ride in every constituency.

In the three weeks of the campaign he needed to maintain a more subtle balancing act between extremism and moderation than ever before. Both moderate and extreme nationalist influences were opposed to him. He himself wished to press for the strongest possible nationalist position without having to define it. On his performance now would depend at least part of the power available to him in Parliament over the next five years.

He had been presented with a terse reminder of difficulties ahead on arrival at Queenstown, when representatives of the Irish Republican Brotherhood had handed him an address. This stated unequivocally that he could hope for no support from any of them in the election. They were, they said, convinced that 'it is utterly futile to seek for any practical good through the means of parliamentary representation'. This can hardly have been a shock to him. The Fenians of the IRB had, on similar dogmatic grounds of dedication to nationalist armed rebellion alone, already rejected the Land League. He knew that many of the most effective activists behind the Land League were those Fenians who were ignoring the IRB's ruling; they would also be his most active supporters in the election. Matthew Harris as well as O'Kelly had been with him at Roscommon.

But it was the attitude of the Catholic Church which presented him with his most serious problem. In the days of the limited franchise the Church was still, in terms of structure and leadership, the nearest thing to a popular political organization in Ireland. And its leaders were wary of Parnell.

Early in 1880, a papal circular warning Irish Catholics against the dangers of extreme views had received the support of the Archbishop of Dublin, Edward McCabe. He made it clear that he thought that Parnell, by his 'agitation' in Ireland the previous year, had 'done an enormous amount of mischief', adding perceptively, 'and I believe that the latent Fenianism of the country was called into life and energy by his action'.

'Latent Fenianism' was an apt term for what had provided the Land League with so much of its energy. The fact that official Fenianism in the shape of the Irish Republican Brotherhood was also against the Land League meant that Parnell's two opponents from opposite poles, the Catholic Church and the IRB, now at times found themselves unofficially in a curious sort of political alliance. This manifested itself in a strange scene on the following Sunday, 28 March – Easter Sunday – a week after he had landed from America, when Parnell went to Enniscorthy in Co. Wexford to speak in support of two of his candidates, John Barry, a one-time Fenian, and Garret Byrne, a good Wicklow nationalist. They were opposing a Conservative and the previous sitting Home Rule Member for the county, the Chevalier Keyes O'Clery, who had distanced himself from Parnell in Parliament and now had the support of the local Bishop.

At an extremely unruly meeting in the Abbey square of Enniscorthy, Parnell had a physically rough time of it in public for the first time in his life. A dispute between O'Clery supporters and Barry and Byrne support-ers as to who had the right to use the public platform erected in the Home Rule cause led to fights on and around it, in the course of which Parnell, 'pale as a sheet', pushed his way through past the pro-O'Clery priest in the chair to the front of the platform. He was then hit in the face by an egg thrown with great force, and was splashed by bits of an orange which had been intended for him but had struck the man next to him. A reporter nearby said he turned 'absolutely livid'. Several attempts were made to remove Parnell by force. He was caught round the waist a number of times by priests and others, and was pushed from the handrail in front of the platform, while those in front endeavoured to catch him by the legs and pull him down. At the same time several people reached up from the crowd to shake his hand.

He remained outwardly impassive, 'pale but determined looking', as, with his tie awry and a button torn from his coat, and wiping bits of egg and orange off his face and beard, he did his determined best to address the crowd. He was subjected to constant interruptions, some of them from priests on the platform – one of whom tried to drag him backwards. He made no attempt to retaliate, but his supporters pulled him forward again and he continued with his speech in favour of Barry and Byrne amid persistent cries of 'No dictation!' and even 'Down with Parnell', countered by equally persistent cheers for him and his candidates. A detachment of police with rifles arrived in the square to prevent any more serious disorder.

At the end of the meeting a compromise resolution was passed, by which both Barry and O'Clery, but not Byrne, the outsider from Wicklow who had aroused most antagonism, were adopted as the Home Rule candidates for the county. However, it is further evidence of Parnell's growing professional mastery that at the election itself, a fortnight later, both Barry and Byrne were standing as Home Rulers and defeated O'Clery decisively. The size of the majorities which the two achieved against him – each winning more than six times O' Clery's number of votes – suggests that, while the priests pulling Parnell about on the platform registered the official disapproval of their clerical superiors rather than any broad popular feeling in Wexford, the boisterous hostility with which he had been met was probably the work of orthodox Fenians. Such men had no inhibition about using physical violence and wished to register as forcefully as possible their dogmatic opposition to Barry, the ex-Fenian, taking part in Parnell's parliamentary venture.

Two first-hand glimpses of Parnell's reaction to the event are revealing. The first concerns what he may have felt about being hit by the eggs and bits of orange. He had kept his dignity on the platform for all the rough handling, but what had he felt like inside? The reporter who had been close to him when the egg struck was, two hours later, in the local post office telegraphing his account of the meeting to his paper when Parnell himself came in and asked politely if he could see what he had written. When he got to the passage about the egg, Parnell said to him merely, 'I think it was an orange.' He then read on to the end, handed the piece back with thanks, and left without further observation. The next evening the same reporter, who had followed him to a meeting at Navan, heard Parnell deny quite brazenly that he had been struck by anything at all at Enniscorthy. 'There is no place in Ireland', he said, 'where such an insult would be offered to me.' He was always to have a masterful talent for making the truth what he wanted it to be.

The other personal insight comes from John Barry, the Wexford candidate. After the Enniscorthy meeting he went with Parnell to have a meal in a hotel. Parnell's trousers had been torn by one of the men who had tried to drag him off the platform from below. Parnell ate heartily with a waiter busily stitching away at his trousers. Barry described it as 'a comical sight'. But, as always, Parnell was master of his own dignity.

Three days later he was at Athlone, where there was likely to be a knife-edge battle between Home Ruler Edward Shiel and a Liberal baronet, Sir John Ennis. Ennis had himself stood as a nominal Home Ruler last time and, after a dead heat, had lost on a recount. Addressing the crowd now, with Healy and O'Connor Power beside him, Parnell told them that Irishmen all over the world – in America, Australia and throughout Ireland itself – were looking to Athlone to do its duty and re-elect Shiel.

'Is Athlone', he asked, 'going to do its duty?'

'Shiel is the man,' called a voice from the crowd.

'I have heard', said Parnell, 'that a man called Ennis has come here . . .'

'To hell with him,' interrupted another voice, to cheers and laughter.

'. . . a supporter of British rule,' continued Parnell. 'And this man is seeking to mislead you and betray the interests of your country. I cannot believe that in this age of enlightenment the people of Athlone could stoop to such infamy as to return Ennis for this borough . . . I cannot suppose for a moment that the borough of Athlone would be so unmindful of every consideration as to return a miserable West British Whig to represent them in the coming Parliament.' And this time he was interrupted by loud cheering.

But, even if they thought of themselves as part of the age of enlightenment, relatively few of those cheering had the vote. When the poll was declared just over a week later, it was found that Shiel had lost by 162 to 161. The result emphasized the hard struggle that still lay ahead of Parnell on the parliamentary scene whatever the unenfranchised crowd might say. He was to experience another setback in Co. Leitrim, where he tried to foist a Presbyterian minister, Isaac Nelson, on the constituency against the wishes of the local Catholic clergy, to one of whom he abruptly showed the door after an abrasive interview.

The style of his public electioneering showed little respect for the susceptibilities of moderate opinion, though just enough to keep his basic lack of consideration for it within bounds. For instance, speaking in Limerick on 31 March he told cheering crowds of how the United States, which had contributed millions of dollars for the Irish people in the course of his recent tour, were ready in fact to do a great deal more, and he spelt out what he meant by this. He told how the Colonel of the 96th New York Regiment, whose nine hundred men, all veterans of the Civil War, armed with rifles and bayonets, had escorted him through the streets to say farewell, had promised that he and his officers and men would come over to Ireland whenever Parnell called. 'I mention this', said Parnell, 'not to say that it is likely or probable that any such movement is going to be made, but to show you what great sacrifices for your country they are willing and ready to make for you.'

It was at that time possible to stand for more than one constituency and, if elected, to choose which to sit for. Parnell himself was standing in Meath, as before, in Mayo and in Cork City, each of which had to elect two members. Polling took place on different days in different constituencies. Parnell, though an almost accidental last-minute candidate in Cork and opposed in a lightning two-day campaign by the *Cork Examiner*, won the second of the two Home Rule seats there on 5 April, and from then until the end of the campaign on 13 April he, in the words of his agent, 'kept flying around the counties of Cork, Mayo and Meath' – for, although he himself was already elected for Cork City, he was trying to get his Land League colleague A. J. Kettle in for the county, once more against strong clerical opposition.

Parnell's agent went on, 'I do not believe he slept in a bed for ten days. He was also much engaged in looking after his other constituencies all over Ireland.' But of course they were not 'his' constituencies, or anybody else's. There was no Home Rule Party organization in a modern sense, and if there had been it would have been for William Shaw, the official Home Rule Party Chairman, to determine the tactics. What Parnell was doing was to try to prepare the ground for a fundamental change in the party's character. But he failed to get Kettle in for Co. Cork.

The result of the general election for the whole of the United Kingdom was a victory for Gladstone's Liberals over the Conservatives by 352 seats to 237. A few of the Liberals elected were from Irish constituencies – Shiel's opponent Ennis, for example, in Athlone, though most of them were from Ulster. The important thing for Parnell was to see how many of the men he wanted had been elected for the Home Rule Party.

He himself had won seats in both Meath and Mayo, but he chose to sit for Cork City. Sixty-three theoretical Home Rulers were elected altogether, but two of these – one the Rowland Blennerhassett whose entry to Parliament in 1872 may have put the idea of a political career into Parnell's head – soon seceded to the Liberals. This left sixty-one, of whom some twenty-five could be reckoned 'Parnell's' men. These were to be supplemented at the end of the following month by the Presbyterian minister Nelson who, having failed in Leitrim, now assumed the seat that Parnell had won, but declined, for Mayo.

Among the new men were a number of particularly devoted followers, mostly of about his own age, who were to leave their names indelibly on Irish parliamentary history in the years to come: John Dillon, who had accompanied him to America; Thomas Sexton, a clerk from Waterford who became a leader-writer for the *Nation*; Arthur O'Connor, son of a well-known Irish doctor working in London, and himself previously a clerk in the War Office, but always a man of strong nationalist views which had brought him into contact with Parnell; T. P. O'Connor, a journalist who had worked for *Saunders Newsletter* in Dublin and then moved to the *Daily Telegraph* in London; and J. J. O'Kelly, the Fenian soldier of fortune who had fought for the French in Mexico and in the Franco-Prussian war, had become a special correspondent for American papers in Cuba and the Red Indian wars, and had just been elected for Roscommon. Tim Healy, Parnell's independent-minded but hitherto faithful acolyte who had helped him on the American tour and still remained close to him, was to enter Parliament later in the year after a by-election.

A supporter of Parnell's from the previous Parliament, of an older generation, now elected again, was accidentally to prove of greater future significance than any of them. This was James Patrick Mahon, who liked to call himself 'the O'Gorman Mahon', as if he were some ancient Irish chieftain. He was now in his eightieth year. In his youth he had been at one time a supporter of O'Connell, but had then become a soldier of fortune. He had fought for the Tsar against the Tartars, had been a General in the Uruguayan army, an Admiral in the Chilean navy and a Colonel under the Emperor of Brazil, and had served in the Federal Army in the American Civil War and under Napoleon III in 1870. A duellist of some reputation, he had already done Parnell good service in the House, backing obstruction soon after he first entered it as one of the two members for Clare following a by-election in 1877. In the general election his Home Rule colleague was originally to have been Lord Francis Conyngham, who had been a member for Clare in the past. But at the last minute Conyngham withdrew owing to illness, and Mahon, searching quickly around for someone who would stand with him for Home Rule and hopefully pay the expenses of both of them, lighted on a minor Clare landlord, a forty-year-old former Captain in the 18th Hussars who, with a certain overconfidence typical of his dashing and attractive character, agreed not only to stand but to pay both their expenses as well. This was William O'Shea ('Willie' to his many friends), the son of a prosperous Dublin solicitor, formerly of Limerick, and a devoutly Catholic mother who had been made a papal countess. He owned some five hundred acres from which he drew rents in Co. Clare, but since leaving the Army he had pursued with mixed success a number of businesses at home and abroad and was resident chiefly in England, where he had a wife and three children.

Willie O'Shea's election address was shamelessly opportunistic, being designed at all costs to secure the support of the farmers of Co. Clare, without which he had no hope of being adopted, let alone elected. He maintained that it had been the veteran Young Irelander John Martin – 'my lamented friend, political guide and teacher' – who had proposed him as a member of the Home Rule League, soon after its formation, and that he did 'not make a mere time-serving profession in declaring for Home Rule'. Pressurized by Lysaght Finegan from the neighbouring constituency of Ennis to commit himself to follow Parnell, he said that if elected he would 'work with the Active Home Rule Party, under its recognized leader, Charles Stewart Parnell . . . and speaking as an Irishman,' he added, 'our country can never rest until its Nationality is recognized in our own Parliament.'

It had been before his marriage in 1867 that, after nine years in the Army, Willie O'Shea had sold the commission his father had bought him. His business enterprises had been partly in Spain, where an uncle of his owned a bank and where for a time he had been manager of a sulphur mine, and partly in England, where, hoping to turn to good account his skills and renown as a horseman, he had at one time started a stud-farm and quite soon gone bankrupt. An amusing man of charm and vivacity who spoke good French and Spanish and liked to dress well, he had the inherently optimistic conviction of many such people in relative youth that his superficial personal talents could prove effective in almost any field of his choosing. At something of a loose end in London at the end of the 1870s, he began to think of politics as a way of furthering a more profitable future, and his wife had encouraged him in this. The immediate problem of paying for the debts incurred by the twin candidacies in the election campaign was the sort of thing Willie O'Shea (he liked to pronounce it O'Shee) had become accustomed to deferring, happily enough, until later.

It had been the sort of campaign to which his charm was well-suited. The O'Gorman Mahon, still handsome despite his age and with a boyish twinkle in his eye, afterwards related how they had made their way round the county, kissing the girls and drinking with the men, and how O'Shea had momentarily overawed the peasantry with his dandified appearance but had quickly won them round with his admiration for their babies and their cattle. His attempt on at least one occasion to address a crowd had been a total failure, but political exposition was not a major consideration. They stood for the Home Rule Party, which was to be taken for granted as the popular party, and that was enough. The O'Gorman Mahon had fought for Ireland in the House of Commons; the

Captain of Hussars was now to be in the fight with him. Both were elected by overwhelming majorities over their Liberal and Conservative opponents.

To what extent Willie O'Shea himself had felt the need genuinely to think out any political position other than that which it had been politic to put into his election address to please the Clare farmers is uncertain. It was primarily the personal opportunity which attracted him. But, as his early House of Commons appearances were to show, his temperament and his five hundred acres in Co. Clare inclined him to a well-trimmed moderation in support of the new popular nationalist feeling. Insofar as it was a nationalist wind that was now blowing, he was happy to go along with it, on the assumption that it would not blow too hard or anyone too far. Not long after the election he was staying in a high-Tory country house in Wales and much enjoyed stubbornly standing up for Home Rule in the smoking-room until four o'clock in the morning against other members of the house party, most of whom, he said, he 'converted or professed to have converted to Home Rule before they shaped their uncertain courses to their bedrooms'. 'Home Rule' represented for him, above all, the slogan he had decided to stand for. He seems to have been in the house party without his wife and family, though in the letter in which he told the O'Gorman Mahon of this story he said he was 'greatly worried' about one of his daughters who had rheumatic fever.

Parnell, counting up the number of candidates now elected whom he could consider sound, probably gave little thought to O'Shea's victory, reckoning that since he came in under the wing of the O'Gorman Mahon he could not be altogether unhelpful. He had no need to take any more notice of him until the next month when, on 17 May 1880, members of the party met in Dublin to elect their Chairman for the coming parliamentary session.

Forty-six members out of a possible sixty-three turned up. One of the new men, the journalist T. P. O'Connor, spotted O'Shea there – a figure 'slightly over-dressed, laughing with the indescribable air of a man whom life had made somewhat cynical', standing out among the plainly dressed figures around him.

Two principal motions were before the meeting: one proposed that Shaw should again be elected Chairman of the party; the other, in the form of an amendment from the O'Gorman Mahon, proposed that the Chairman should be Parnell. Long speeches were heard on both sides. On the whole these went out of their way not to be divisive, though one speaker deplored any implication that Shaw might be considered to be undermining the party's principles by not supporting the Land League. The Land League, the speaker declared, was not representative of the Irish people. The O'Gorman Mahon, on the other hand, while paying respect to Shaw, struck a rhetorical note which accurately reflected the breadth of Parnell's popular appeal. Having spoken of his 'character for interpreting, activity, energy and severe devotion to the country', he went on to say that he had taught Irishmen 'how we can successfully combat the hereditary antagonism which exists in the Saxon mind against everything appertaining to the welfare of this country'.

But, before a vote could be taken, another amendment proposed that no sessional Chairman should be elected, 'that we may avoid in the House of Commons the appearance of disunion'. On this, Shaw and Parnell both refrained from voting. The amendment was defeated by 24 to 16. Voting with the minority on this, in opposition to his colleague from Co. Clare, and thus demonstrating his ability to be his own man, was Willie O'Shea. When the main vote came, however, he voted for Parnell, though most of his colleagues on the previous vote were for Shaw.

The result was: for Shaw 18, for Parnell 23. Parnell was declared elected sessional Chairman. O'Shea sent a telegram to his wife to tell her that he had voted for him, though he wondered if he might not be too far 'advanced'.

Parnell, who began his speech of thanks that afternoon by saying that he had been 'prevented by the sudden apparition of lunch' from making it before, stressed humbly enough that he did not regard the honour of being sessional Chairman as conferring on him actual leadership of the party and said that he personally would have preferred it if neither he nor Shaw had been elected but, instead, Justin McCarthy, his London friend and neighbour and now MP for Co. Longford. There may have been some truth in this. He had indeed canvassed the possibility of a unanimous choice for McCarthy early that morning, and not just in order to show that he was not himself ambitiously seeking the office. For, as he also now said, 'I am sensible that it must tie my hands to a very considerable extent in future; and that possibly my utility may be diminished in that way.'

This was a shrewd appraisal of a situation in which political strength on the parliamentary scene was likely to derive mainly from an unparliamentary source, namely the Land League. Just how volatile and even complex were the sources of national feeling he was hoping to coordinate had been illustrated by an incident at a Land League Conference in Dublin even before his election as party Chairman. Orthodox Fenians, believing only in armed insurrection, tried to break it up in protest against former Fenians, regarded as renegades, having anything to do with the Land League and its parliamentary connection. To placate them and restore order, Parnell told them, evidently with a sort of approval, of the American at one of his meetings in the United States who had offered 'five dollars for bread and twenty dollars for lead'. As Chairman of the party he would have to be more circumspect about saying such things.

The remark was to be brought up against him with some relish many years later. But it was something as apparently innocuous as a fish supper for three in Greenwich, held some time between his election as party Chairman and the opening of Parliament, that was to have far more profound consequences for him and indeed for future Irish history. He was not present himself. The three taking part were the two Members of Parliament for Co. Clare, the O'Gorman Mahon and Willie O'Shea, and O'Shea's attractive wife, Katharine, known as 'Katie'.

Chapter 22

Katie O'Shea was then thirty-five years old. Someone who, as a child, saw her from time to time remembered her afterwards as a beautiful woman, tall and dark, with a mouth 'expressive of tenderness and sweetness', sad wistful eyes and a head 'crowned with a wealth of soft, glossy dark hair'. Photographs of the time seem to suggest that she was in fact rather short, and that she was sexually attractive rather than strictly beautiful; but children have a natural instinct for true presence, and such photographs give no reason to doubt the young contemporary's later description of her manners as charming and her voice as 'gentle and low'. She had been married to Willie O'Shea since she was twenty-one. They had three children: a boy of ten and two daughters aged seven and five.

She had first met her handsome husband when he was in the Army with her two brothers, one of whom – later to win a Victoria Cross and become a Field Marshal – told her that Willie was 'the only man who sat properly over the fences at the Aldershot races'. Her father, heir to a baronetcy, a distinguished Anglican clergyman, had as a young man been Chaplain to George I's estranged Queen Caroline; her mother had been a Lady of the Bedchamber. They had married young and had thirteen children, of whom Katharine, soon 'Katie', was the thirteenth.* The Lord Chancellor in Gladstone's first Cabinet, Lord Hatherley, was one of her uncles.

Her childhood and adolescence had been spent in a forty-roomed Georgian (once Tudor) mansion in Essex where her father had one of his livings; she often visited an even grander country house nearby, where an elder sister lived with a rich husband. It was in this household that she had come to see much of Captain Willie O'Shea of the 18th Hussars. He became a regular visitor to her own home. Writing romantic poems for her, sending her occasional bouquets and taking her into dinner on his

---

* She always signed her letters, even to the Prime Minister, with the name 'Katie'. No one who knew her ever called her 'Kitty', though this was the name later to be attached to her, often disparagingly, by many who did not.

arm, he came to be seen as her *beau*, planting a proprietorial kiss on her lips to emphasize the fact when he thought it necessary. She in turn acquired a 'dreamy sense of belonging to him'. But he was often away, both before and after he sold his commission, and she clearly enjoyed the social opportunities for innocent flirtation available to a pretty, not unsophisticated young girl of good family. Equally clearly she became strongly attached to him.

Her sophistication was a product not so much of conventional education, of which she had little, but of family background. Her mother was a cultivated woman, who had been a friend of Constable and Landseer, a good musician and the author of a number of three-volume novels published by Chapman and Hall, for whom her husband was a reader. Anthony Trollope was a friend who visited the house. Katie herself was literate, musical and spirited, a naturally gifted hostess for any ambitious, intelligent husband.

There was no doubt of Willie O'Shea's ambition, nor of his basic intelligence. He had been an above average pupil at the Catholic seminary to which he had been sent at St Mary's College, Oscott, in England, though he had not long stayed the course at Trinity College, Dublin, before going into the Army. A contemporary of his at St Mary's, where he acquired a clear, clipped English accent, remembered him there as already 'a bit of a dandy' but also 'a bit of a bully' who chased him with a fives bat. Katie too was a strong character, and was to turn out to be the stronger. Less than a year after the death of her father in 1866, she agreed to marry him. His Catholicism was unostentatious enough to be no obstacle. It was a love-match of some potential style. Even after thirteen years the memory of that bond was very real for both of them.

But the turbulence of Willie's business life and the consequent precariousness of his finances had not made married life easy. Her own parents were in no way rich for people of their social position. Willie had what was left of the £4,000 (some £190,000 in today's terms) he had received for his commission. Katie had £5,000 (now about £235,000) given on marriage by an elderly aunt, the extremely wealthy widow of a brewer, Benjamin Wood, who had once been Liberal MP for Southwark. This aunt – always known to the O'Sheas as 'Aunt Ben', after her late husband – was eighty-seven in 1880. Not unreasonable eventual expectations from her played an inevitable part in the O'Sheas' financial planning, and were to become an increasingly compelling factor in their lives. At the time of their dinner with the O'Gorman Mahon in Greenwich in the early summer of that year, present help from her had for some time been proving a godsend.

In the course of the thirteen years of marriage, the O'Sheas had lived in a number of houses in many different places, including Madrid for nearly a year while Willie worked in his uncle's bank. The failed stud-farm had been in Hertfordshire. They had then moved to Clarges Street in the West End of London, to Brighton (where their first child, Gerard, had been born early in 1870), to the Harrow Road, London (where they found the funeral processions to the cemetery at Kensal Green depressing), to Beaufort Gardens (where their elder daughter, Norah, was born in 1873), to the Isle of Wight, and in 1874 to Hastings, where their younger daughter, Carmen, was born a year later.

Though there were times when they were in the hands of moneylenders, there were also times – which may occasionally have been the same times – when they lived lavishly. For the house in Beaufort Gardens, for instance, Willie had insisted on expensive silver-and-blue wallpaper ordered specially from Paris. They had lived there with a staff of maids and a butler, and had entertained regularly. At other times it seems to have been only the occasional cheque from Aunt Ben that enabled them to take houses at all. It was when staying at the house which Aunt Ben had made possible in Hastings that Katie had decided, with something of that eye to the main chance which was the speciality of her husband, to go more frequently to see Aunt Ben in her large Georgian house at Eltham in Kent, then in countryside eight miles from London, and to make her closer acquaintance. She took Willie with her.

Aunt Ben, a woman of old-fashioned style and deportment and independent disciplined views, had of course known Katie before, though not well. She now took to her strongly. In need at her age of a constant companion, who could entertain her, read to her, drive in the countryside with her and be a daily solace, she proposed that Katie herself – her 'swan', as she called her – should take on this role, to which she might well feel attracted since her husband's enforced absences on business so often left her lonely too. In return Aunt Ben was prepared to buy her, as a family home, a solid Victorian house called Wonersh Lodge on the other side of Eltham's North Park, give her an income to maintain it, and pay for the education of her children. The arrangement could not have suited the O'Sheas better, and by 1880 it had already been in force for five years. She had further agreed to subsidize an apartment in the centre of London for Willie, who, when he had time, also took turns in reading to her at Eltham in his excellent French. Nor was this all. In gratitude for the success the arrangement proved, Aunt Ben had altered her will to leave the greater part of her very considerable fortune to Katie.

What effect these kaleidoscopic shifts of circumstance in the fourteen years of the O'Sheas' marriage had had on the quality of their personal relations is not easy to assess. The principal source from which any assessment can be made is the memoir Katie herself published more than thirty years later. The basic facts from the early period of the marriage related there can be accepted as broadly accurate, but in later parts of her narrative there are several detectable factual inaccuracies, the chronology is sometimes confused, and what seems an often calculated hindsight dominates the emotional content. In addition, more than one set of interests were involved in the publication. One of these was that of her son, Gerard O'Shea, then a man of forty-four and loyal to the memory of his father, who had died nine years before. Probably the most important interest is that of the author herself, who wanted to provide an acceptable personal explanation of her behaviour, as well as a tribute to a great experience of love.

Thus, although the affection which she undoubtedly maintained for her husband is clear enough in her account of events down to 1880 – and indeed beyond – there is also advanced a reiterating sense of disappointment with their relationship which may retrospectively have been given more emphasis than it had definitely acquired at the time, in order to excuse what followed. There is even a dismissal of the 1867 honeymoon as one of mutual '*ennui*', spent in a loaned country house with too many servants and 'little or no occupation for us'. There appear phrases such as 'I think Willie and I were beginning to jar upon one another a good deal now' and 'the wearing friction caused by our totally dissimilar temperaments'. There are pointed references to his forgetfulness of her; his business absences and the consequent loneliness for herself hang ominously over the years. Nevertheless, what may be of more significance today in the light of later events is the care she took at the same time not to omit her continuing fondness for him. 'Willie and I were very comfortable in Brighton.' She had wanted to be with him more, which was why they had moved from there to London. 'We were pleased to see one another again' (in spite of their 'totally dissimilar temperaments') after his eighteen-month absence on an optimistic mining venture in Spain. And while he had been away there she had been working in London loyally and sympathetically on his behalf – though possibly, it seems, having an affair there with an old friend and business associate of his.

By 1880 the arrangement by which the family home was at Wonersh Lodge, Eltham, and Willie conducted his business life from his apartment in central London was working smoothly. It was a 'seemly' arrangement in Aunt Ben's eyes in view of his business commitments. He came down 'fairly regularly' at weekends to see Katie and to take the children to mass, and she 'often' helped him with his entertaining in London, giving dinner parties at Thomas's Hotel in Berkeley Square, where she used to stay as a child. It was a not unconventional arrangement in the financial circumstances, after thirteen years of marriage. Certainly it satisfied her conventional aunt.

There seems no reason to doubt that the O'Sheas were having normal sexual relations in this year of 1880. After their celebratory dinner with the O'Gorman Mahon in Greenwich, they would almost certainly have spent the night together at Eltham, which is not far off.

More than thirty years later she wrote of the strong encouragement she had given to Willie to enter the political world. It would, she knew, 'give him occupation he liked', but she added, 'and keep us apart'. This last thought may well have been a convenient product of hindsight. Even so, she said that she had known she and Willie would stay good friends. That they were to remain good friends off and on for six more years is shown beyond doubt by letters to and from Willie included in the memoirs, and may provide an explanation for much in the ensuing story that otherwise seems obscure.

Parnell's name had come up at the Greenwich dinner naturally enough. Willie O'Shea was entering the political world to find advantage there one way or another. It was the O'Gorman Mahon, she was to write years later, who turned to her with the words: 'If you meet Parnell, Mrs O'Shea, be good to him,' adding that his trip to America had 'about finished him' and he did not think he would last the session out.

That Parnell had had an exhausting time in America was beyond doubt. But as the two MPs at Greenwich who had helped him become the Home Rule Party's sessional Chairman knew perfectly well, far from being finished, he was only just beginning. Whether the O'Gorman Mahon actually phrased the suggestion in that form, there is likely to have been mutual agreement that it was desirable for the O'Sheas to cultivate Parnell. Katie agreed to invite him to one of their dinners at Thomas's Hotel in Berkeley Square. A more immediately important decision was also taken that evening: that Katie should apply to Aunt Ben for a cheque to get Willie out of the embarrassment of having committed himself so rashly to pay both his and the O'Gorman Mahon's election expenses. The application was, as usual, successful. Aunt Ben was always pleased to see Katie solicitous for her husband. In the light of the developing seriousness of Irish affairs and the arrival in office of a Liberal

Government, his new career could be seen as promising. The new Chairman of the party was invited to dinner. For some time he failed to reply.

How was this new Liberal Government going to treat Ireland? When last in office Gladstone had shown some understanding of Irish problems. He had recognized that it was wrong for the Church of the Protestant minority to be the State Church and had disestablished it. He had passed a Land Act which for the first time recognized some interest in the land for the tenant as well as the landlord, and had given him some possibility of eventually buying his holding by instalments with State aid. He had begun his ministry then by declaring that his mission was 'to pacify Ireland', coming into office as he did just after the failed Fenian rising. Now, with the Land League asserting its own law in Ireland in the tenants' interests and one-time Fenians consorting with agrarian secret societies to help it do so, Ireland needed pacifying more than in 1868.

The Liberals, it could be hoped, would be more inclined than the Conservatives to think of pacification in terms of conciliatory measures rather than repressive ones. The Queen's Speech on 20 May in fact stated that the Peace Preservation Act which expired on 1 June would not be renewed. While stressing that it was the first duty of every Government to provide security for life and property as a 'sacred obligation', the Queen was now persuaded that 'the loyalty and good sense of my Irish subjects will justify me in relying on the provisions of the ordinary law, firmly administered, for the maintenance of law and order'. There was no mention of any need for legislation on the land. Indeed, Ireland itself ranked in the speech as of lower priority than the problems of Turkey, Afghanistan and India, and only just ahead of controversial public burials.

The Liberals' tactical position in Parliament did not look like causing them any difficulties. They had a majority over all parties of more than fifty, and this was made larger by the decision of Shaw, the former Chairman of the Home Rule Party, and other moderate Home Rulers to sit on the Government side of the House. With the Liberals now in power, this seemed to them the proper place for the Irish. Indeed Shaw, rising to speak in the debate on the Queen's Speech, having found no room on the Government benches, went out of his way to stress that his temporary appearance on the other side of the House was simply because he could find nowhere else to sit: it had no political significance. He made clear that he had nothing to complain of at this stage about the Government's failure to produce a new Land Bill.

Parnell, on the other hand, though he had specifically disowned any claim to party leadership on becoming sessional Chairman, did assert what was to become new leadership by sitting with his own supporters among the Conservative Opposition. Of the two members for County Clare, the O'Gorman Mahon sat with him; Willie O'Shea, in spite of his election address, chose at first to sit on the Government side, where influence lay.

Parnell in his speech in this debate, while conceding with some sarcasm that it was quite right to wait for land legislation since the new Chief Secretary for Ireland, W. E. Forster, was still 'ignorant of one of the greatest questions affecting that country', hoped that, if the Chief Secretary's need for time meant that thousands or more tenant farmers ran the risk of being driven from their holdings, some temporary legislation, at least, to remove pressure on the people of Ireland, would be introduced.

On the wider perspective of Home Rule, the chances of bringing Gladstone round to any sympathetic consideration of it were for the time being remote. The state of Gladstone's own mind on Home Rule was as clear as such a skilled moral pragmatist could then allow it to be. Some words he had used nearly three years before may still have been in the back of his mind. 'Had the Home Rulers a real leader whom they were disposed to follow,' he had written to Lord Granville, now his Foreign Secretary, 'I can't think it would be difficult to arrange a *modus vivendi* with them. As far as anything more than that I am not sanguine even if I suppose my own feelings about Local Government to be those of the party, for I go much further than the average Liberal.'

For the present, as he was soon to have to admit, Ireland was to catch him on the wrong foot altogether. No one was eventually to put this better than one of the two members for Co. Clare, in the following year. Willie O'Shea, who by that time had crossed the floor to sit with Parnell in opposition, then bluntly told the House that, when the Government came in, its mind had not been on Ireland as it should have been. 'Not even the Prime Minister himself', he said, 'had an adequate idea of the extreme pressure of the agricultural question in Ireland. He only thought English interests were jeopardized in the East, from Bulgaria to Kabul. His mind was on the temples of Benares when it should have been on the cabins of Connemara.'

In the summer of 1880 this situation was to Parnell's advantage. The more the crisis in Ireland became out of control, the greater was his own tactical freedom to try, with help from the Land League, to make something of it. 'They will do what we can make them do' was still his guiding principle.

Actually it proved possible to make them do something almost at once. O'Connor Power, sitting with Parnell on the Opposition benches, put forward a Bill to meet a deficiency in the Land Act of 1870 which was aggravating the crisis in Ireland. That Act, which provided financial compensation for a tenant evicted through no fault of his own, did not provide it for a tenant evicted for non-payment of rent. Due to the economic crisis and the previous bad harvests, there were now a considerable number of tenants who through no fault of their own could no longer pay their rents. O'Connor Power's Bill proposed to make compensation on eviction available to them too. It was making progress through the Commons when the Government decided to adopt it as its own measure. That summer the Bill passed all three readings in the Commons and went on to the House of Lords – an encouraging demonstration of the Parnellites' ability to affect Government policy.

It had been on the second reading of this Compensation for Disturbance Bill that Willie O'Shea, then still sitting on the Government benches, had made his maiden speech in the House, on 29 June 1880. Speaking as a minor Irish landlord, he used the opportunity to define carefully the role he now saw for himself in national affairs.

The Bill, he assured other landlords, was nothing to be alarmed about – no more an infringement of the rights of property than had been the Land Act of 1870, which few would deny had been applied satisfactorily. Moreover, turning to the present state of agitation in Ireland under the Land League, he urged that, in the spirit of compromise, some sacrifice had to be made to allay it. 'As the proverb tree escaped injury by bowing to the storm,' he said, 'so landlords would do well to make some sacrifice now.'

To display his concern for the tenant as well as for the landlord, he added that, while the Bill was indeed a small and temporary one, they – the Home Rule Party – looked forward to the Government bringing in a much larger measure in the next session. Again, as if to make clear his own personal position of balance within the Home Rule Party, he pointed out, correctly, that most of the so-called agrarian outrages consisted of threatening letters and notices. The figures could give a false impression, he said. His hope was that the agitation would die down and that what had indeed been a curse to social order would turn out to have been a blessing in disguise by causing Members of Parliament to look more carefully into the state of Ireland.

The parliamentary correspondent of the Unionist *Irish Times* wrote that Willie's was 'the ablest and most effective defence' of the Bill he had heard, and that both Gladstone and Forster had been 'profuse in approving plaudits and repeated hears'. The Clare Farmers' Club, which had sponsored Willie's candidacy, had just merged with the Land League. But it too may have approved, for the nationalist *Clare Freeman and Ennis Gazette* reproduced the *Irish Times*'s praise. 'Captain O'Shea has made his mark,' it said, 'and if he continues as he has commenced Clare County will have no reason to regret having conferred on him representative honours.'

However, as a Whiggish moderate actually sitting on the Liberal Government benches opposite the Home Ruler he had pledged himself to work with, his continued good standing in his constituency could by no means be taken for granted.

It is possible that the day of Willie's maiden speech at the end of June, for which Katie O'Shea might well have attended the House of Commons, was also the day on which she first saw Parnell. Parnell was certainly in and out of the House that week. In her memoirs, written over thirty years later, she gives a romantic account of going to the House of Commons specifically to ask Parnell why he had not replied to the repeated invitations she had been sending him since the middle of July.

In the context of the summer of 1880 it is necessary to remember that her only concern then was to get him into her husband's social net. She wrote in her memoirs of Parnell's emergence from the House to see her: 'He came out, a tall, gaunt figure, thin and deadly pale. He looked straight at me smiling, and his curiously burning eyes looked into mine with a wondering intentness that threw into my brain the sudden thought: "This man is wonderful – and different."' If, as seems probable, the account reveals some back-projection of later emotion, this is understand-able after all that was to happen; it is immaterial whether it is literally accurate or not. The important thing about the meeting was that something was soon to come of it.

He explained his failure to answer her invitations by saying that he had not opened his letters for days. A number of witnesses throughout his political life confirm that it was a habit of his to leave letters unopened – not so reprehensible, since he only had one secretary and these were days before the telephone and general use of the typewriter. She relates that he said he would in fact come to dinner with her when he came back from Paris, where he had to go for his sister Theodosia's wedding.

Whether the incident of a rose falling from her bodice on to her skirt as she said goodbye to him, to be picked up, touched lightly with his lips and placed into his buttonhole took place at this first meeting, as she related, or on some other occasion is also unimportant. Whenever it happened, something of that sort became a memory to stay with her to the end of her life. Her account of what he actually said at this first meeting is at least confirmed by his first letter to her, beginning 'My dear Mrs O'Shea'. It is dated Saturday 17 July, and comes from the House of Commons. He said he would be going over to Paris for his sister's wedding at the beginning of the following week and would write to her on his return, to 'ask for an opportunity of seeing you'. That she had been putting some pressure on him seems clear from the letter; it is clear too that, since meeting her, such pressure was no longer unwelcome.

'We have all been in such a "disturbed" condition lately', he wrote, 'that I have been quite unable to wander further from here than a radius of about one hundred *paces allons*. And this notwithstanding the powerful attractions which have been tending to seduce me from my duty towards my country in the direction of Thomas's Hotel.'

For a man who made a habit of not replying to invitations from social hostesses, he had been impressed.

It had indeed been a busy week in the House. In the course of it, Willie himself, while hoping that his wife would succeed in cultivating Parnell socially, had been quite active and uninhibited about showing his personal independence within the party. He had even voted on a number of procedural points against motions supported by Parnell. After one such motion, which Parnell had lost and on which most Irish MPs had voted on the other side, Parnell maintained with typical brazen calm that the majority of Irish MPs had voted with him, explaining that the only Irish MPs who counted were those truly nationalist Home Rulers on his side of the House. Those on the other side, he said, were mere 'West Britons' – a familiar term of abuse for those Irishmen who looked to the larger island for their interests, among whom Parnell was including, in this instance, Willie O'Shea.

On 13 July, while Katie O'Shea was still trying to get Parnell to come to dinner and four days before that first letter she had from him, Willie had taken up this 'taunt of being a West Briton' from his party Chairman. He said it 'fell harmlessly on him, one of the most Catholic of the Irish members'. There was an implicit rebuke here for Parnell and his own 'Ascendancy' background. The incident is of some value in showing how Willie, while anxious to cultivate Parnell, also saw it to his advantage to distance himself from him when he felt like it, and to maintain a standpoint from which he could be seen to be effective in his own right. At a time when power and influence so clearly rested with a Government which, while sympathetic to Ireland, regarded Parnell and his close supporters as extremists, it was a shrewd position for someone seeking personal advantage from politics to adopt.

Exactly when, after Parnell's return from Paris, his first dinner or luncheon with the O'Sheas took place is not clear: though Katie is precise in her memoirs, an alternative version is given by Justin McCarthy. But the detail is not important. Her memoirs are presumably reliable to the extent that at some early meeting – she says the first – when after dinner she and her husband took Parnell to the theatre, Parnell told her about the American girl with whom he had been in love in 1870. According to her, he told her he had sought out this girl again on his recent visit to the States and they had been at a dance together, though this sounds improbable given the hectic nature of his American tour. In any case, the point is that he seems to have gone out of his way to convey to Katie O'Shea that all passion in that direction was now spent.

That summer the House of Commons was to sit on until Tuesday 7 September, when Parliament would be prorogued. Katie says Parnell came to see her frequently in the Ladies' Gallery, where presumably she would go on her husband's ticket.

On Tuesday 3 August the House of Lords threw out Gladstone's Compensation for Disturbance Bill, immediately heightening tension in the land crisis. It was the first indication of trouble ahead for the new Government. Tim Healy, who remained in close touch with Parnell, was disappointed that he did not at once make more of a fuss in the House. 'I certainly thought that he would keep fighting to draw attention to the subject,' he wrote in a letter that week, 'but he absolutely discouraged anything approaching obstruction. Why is this? There must be a lady in the case, else he would not have been in such a hurry to leave the House as he has been, two or three times this week.'

There was a lady in the case; Healy's contemporary observation tallies with what Katie wrote in her memoirs. While Parliament was still sitting that summer, Parnell was taking her out for drives in a hansom cab to the river at Mortlake and elsewhere. Whether her interest in him was yet as personal as her memoir maintains must be uncertain, but there can be no doubt that he was forming a personal interest in her. She herself admits that what they chiefly discussed on these drives was 'Willie's chances of being returned for Clare in case another election was sprung upon us. Both Willie and I were very anxious to secure Mr Parnell's promise about this, as The O'Gorman Mahon was old, and we were desirous of making Willie's seat in Parliament secure.' Her concern for Willie to feel happily secure in Parliament certainly predates her love affair with Parnell, and was to continue far into it.

Distracted as he already seems to have been by Mrs O'Shea, Parnell was not in fact neglecting his sense of political commitment. Certainly, it was Frank Hugh O'Donnell, now increasingly critical of Parnell, who asked the Government what it was going to do about the rejection of the Bill by the Lords. He was told that there the matter would have to rest at present. But before the week was out Parnell himself had tabled a motion calling attention to the parliamentary relations between England and Ireland in the light of the Lords' rejection. 'It adds', he said, 'one more to the many proofs afforded since the Union of the necessity for such a radical change in these relations as will permit legislative effect in future to the voice of the vast majority of electors of Ireland constitutionally expressed.' And though after speaking at Newcastle on Monday 9 August he does seem to have been silent in Parliament until Monday 23 August – possibly away at Avondale – he was back in his place on that day to defend with spirit a familiarly ambivalent speech he had made in Liverpool, where he had talked about a hundred thousand swords, Protestant and Catholic, leaping from their scabbards for the rights of the people to make their own laws on the soil of Ireland.

The next day, when the motion he had tabled earlier came up for a short debate, he began a wary examination of the way in which Home Rule might work. It was the first time he had done so in a fashion carefully tempered to the House of Commons. It would be necessary, he said, 'to define what things an Irish Parliament might deal with and what it might not' (an attitude at first sight at variance with the vision of a hundred thousand swords leaping from their scabbards). He took a noticeably detached look at Butt's idea, which he called 'a sort of federalism', along the lines of the American states' relationship with Congress. He did not propose to bring forward a plan himself, he said, because he thought the time was not ripe for doing so. He thought it was, before all things, necessary that the House should be first convinced of its inability to govern Ireland under the present system. He used the same phrase as Gladstone had done three years before when speaking tactically in his private letter to Granville. 'Some *modus vivendi*', Parnell said, was desirable 'by means of which Great Britain and Ireland might succeed in getting on better in future'. Some prefiguration of the future was thus in place in his mind, but tied to recognition that only the present crisis on the land would determine its more exact shape. And a lot was happening in Ireland.

Meetings either to found new branches of the Land League or to mobilize branches for action against eviction were multiplying all the time, and particularly at weekends. There were at least six such meetings in different parts of Ireland on the Sunday before Parnell gave his thoughts to the House about eventual Home Rule. The tone in Ireland bordered on the revolutionary, and was mirrored in the semi-military formations in which many marched to the meetings. Speaking in Kildare that Sunday, the Land League organizer Michael Boyton said it was 'imperative that the farmers of Ireland should unite and organize for self-preservation'.

Very different economic interests were of course contained within the broad term 'farmers'. It could cover both prosperous graziers and small marginal subsistence farmers. In addition there were labourers whose interests were often at variance with both. But for political purposes the general cry was effective, and for many Land League organizers the political and economic motivations were inextricably entwined. At another meeting that same Sunday, at Belclare in Co. Galway, a Land League speaker declared its purpose as being 'to denounce land-grabbers and landlordism and above all to revive and diffuse the spirit of national-ity'. At a meeting near Boyle in Co. Roscommon, also on that Sunday, another prominent Land League organizer, Patrick Sheridan, commented on the fact that at the recent election the electorate had indeed driven out their previous MPs and replaced them with better men but these too were now superseded. The people, he said, must now be determined to legislate for themselves 'in resisting both the law and landlordism'.

As the end of the parliamentary session for the year approached, Parnell prepared to return to Avondale, first for some partridge shooting and then to make what political capital he could out of the volatile situation in Ireland. At the same time, other compelling thoughts were on his mind.

Not long before the session ended on 7 September, Katie O'Shea's sister, Anna Steele, gave a lunch party in her London house to which both Parnell and Justin McCarthy were invited. We don't know whether Willie himself was there, but it seems likely. We do know from Katie herself that, when she had to leave early to go down to Eltham to see her aunt, it was Parnell who went with her to Charing Cross to see her off. But they arrived to find that the train had just gone. He picked out a horse from the cab rank for her and drove down with her to Eltham, where she said goodbye to him. She did not take him into the house, because, she said, it was in too untidy a state.

Soon after this, Parnell again dined with the O'Sheas at Thomas's Hotel. It was no longer difficult for her to get him to come. He had in fact earlier met his hostess at Cannon Street station on her arrival from Eltham and had taken her first to tea with him in the Cannon Street Hotel. He had rooms there now, in addition to his lodgings in Keppel Street, as a sort of meeting-place at which to keep in touch with Irish Members of Parliament. On this afternoon he first took her into the dining-room, but, seeing some of his Members there, decided 'it would be more comfortable for us in his private sitting-room'. There, by her later nostalgic account, they talked politics, though towards the end he 'lapsed into one of those long silences of his that I was already beginning to know were dangerous in the complete sympathy they evoked between us'. At the time it may have been their discussion of politics, and its value for her husband's new career, which seemed the more important.

On the day after this dinner party he left for Avondale. But as soon as he arrived in Dublin he wrote to tell her that he had arrived and hoped to hear from her before very long. 'I may tell you also in confidence', he added, 'that I don't feel quite so content at the prospect of ten days' absence from London amongst the hills and valleys of Wicklow as I should have done some three months since. The cause is mysterious, but perhaps you will help me to find it, or her, on my return. – Yours always, Chas. S. Parnell.'

This was on 9 September. On 11 September he wrote another letter, headed 'Avondale', just before leaving for his shooting-lodge at Aughavannah, the old British barracks block built to control the Wicklow rebels at the time of the 1798 rebellion. 'I am,' he wrote, 'still in the land of the living, notwithstanding the real difficulty of either living or being, which every moment becomes more evident, in the absence of a certain kind and fair face.' He said he was going off into the mountains for the shooting, 'removed from post offices and such like consolations for broken-hearted politicians', but hoped for a letter from her somehow even there.

The *Freeman's Journal* had noted that, on leaving London, Parnell was 'not looking at all as well as his friends would wish him to be' and put this forward as the reason why he would not immediately be able to take part in more than a small number of the meetings he had been asked to address in the country. 'Too much physical exercise at present', the paper wrote, 'might interfere with his participation in popular meetings for the remainder of the year.' It is possible that Parnell himself had fed this to the *Freeman's Journal*, feeling a wish to keep his options on future movements open. Certainly he was ready to plunge into a great deal of physical exercise after the partridges in the Wicklow mountains round Aughavannah without apparent fear for his health. He was away from everything for a week.

While he was away, some of his new lieutenants were busy at Land League meetings in Dublin. John Dillon MP presided at one of these to hear Thomas Brennan report that twenty-three new branches of the League had been formed in Ireland in the past fortnight. At another, presided over by T. P. O'Connor MP, a glowing tribute was paid to their new leader by Thomas Sexton MP, who said that, far from familiarity breeding contempt, familiarity with Parnell had enormously increased his estimation of his powers, of his honesty and of his uprightness of purpose. 'I know of no man', he went on, 'who has a higher title for character.' He stressed his 'freedom from personal vanity, his invariable good temper . . . willingness to receive suggestions from all quarters . . . absolute devotion to principle', and concluded, 'I know of no man in all my experience more entitled to be called a distinctly high-minded man, and intercourse with whom has a greater tendency to strengthen the honesty of one's purpose and devotion to one's principles.'

Such was the hero-worship with which men like Sexton, carried away by a new prospect for the cause of Irish nationality in their lifetime, were then prepared to invest in the squire of Avondale, now trudging over his Wicklow heather with his mind on his partridges and possibly on Irish nationality, but also on the Englishwoman who had begun to disturb it.

Many of those who attended these Dublin meetings composed the hard core of the Land League – men like Patrick Egan, the Treasurer, and Thomas Brennan, the Secretary, and organizers like Patrick Sheridan and Michael Boyton. A piece of business transacted at the meeting where Sexton delivered his eulogy of Parnell gives a useful insight into the sort of activity on which the League was increasingly engaged all over Ireland.

At Easky in Co. Sligo there was only one man who would not cooperate with a Land League order to refuse to have anything to do with anyone who had taken, and paid rent for, land from which another had been evicted. This was the local blacksmith. It seemed difficult to refuse to have anything to do with the blacksmith because he provided an essential daily service for the rural community. The difficulty had been met by importing another blacksmith, building a house for him, and thus successfully freezing out the sinner altogether. Patrick Sheridan was among those who wildly applauded the report of what he called this 'moral chastisement'. The sum of ten pounds was voted to the new blacksmith (some £450 in today's terms). The 'moral chastisement' of the old one may well have been included in the police records of 'outrages' under the heading 'intimidation'.

Agrarian outrages, which often included harsher forms of chastisement for both land-grabbers and their animals, were to rise to new unprecedented heights in the autumn quarter – four times as many as for the same quarter in the preceding year. The total for the whole year was to be by far the highest ever recorded.

Parnell's shooting-expedition in the mountains was a failure; the weather was too wet. He was back in Dublin on Saturday 18 September, due to open the post-recess political season with a speech at Ennis in Co. Clare the next day. Two letters from Mrs O'Shea were waiting for him – a fact which seems to indicate some quickening of her personal interest in him – but he found no time to answer them before catching the night mail for Ennis with Lysaght Finegan, the MP for the town, whose majority had increased comfortably at the general election, and T. D. Sullivan, one of the Members for Westmeath. They arrived at Ennis at four o'clock on the Sunday morning, but even at that hour there were hundreds of people waiting for them, and a procession formed up with lighted torches and a band playing to escort them to their hotel.

Crowds poured into the town throughout the morning from all over the countryside. The streets were decorated with slogans: 'Parnell gave the praties – not the landlords!', 'The Two Ps – Parnell and the People', 'United We'll Stand for Parnell!'

Finegan spoke first. His was a strong, stirring speech, and in the course of it Parnell must have received a momentary shock of which he would have revealed no trace and of which no one else except possibly Finegan himself, a close friend, would have been aware. Finegan had spoken boldly of squeezing from the Government 'that which belonged to Ireland by every means which God and man had placed in their power' and of 'the divine right of the appeal to the sword'. Ireland, he said, had too long listened to words, and too long floated one banner after another in the summer breeze, and he urged the crowds to 'stand to one another as soldiers stand in battle array'.

None of this would have troubled Parnell, who had himself long been master of such ambivalent revolutionary rhetoric. It was when Finegan moved on to a more immediate view of the contemporary scene that the surprise came. It came from the crowd. Finegan had just voiced a certain respect for Gladstone's Liberalism and the radicalism of some of his supporters, stressing however that there was an '-ism' which he must

cherish and love above all and that was 'Nationalism'. As the cheers died
away, he added that he would say nothing of the men who had broken
the promises they made at the hustings. Whereupon a voice from the
crowd called out, 'O'Shea!' Finegan merely said that he knew there was a
day of reckoning coming and he would leave it to the people to judge.

Part of the long speech which Parnell made that day contained an
impassioned definition of what was soon to be known as 'boycotting',
after the surname of a minor landlord and prominent land-agent in Co.
Mayo against whom it was about to be practised on a dramatic scale. This
speech has gone into history. Parnell was not in fact proposing anything
new – Dillon and Brenan had recommended it the year before, and it had
been standard in the Land League for months – but this was the first time
Parnell's belief in it had been so passionately expressed.

'Now . . .' he said to the twelve thousand or so in front of him at
Ennis, 'now what are you going to do with a tenant who bids for a farm
from which his neighbour has been evicted?' 'Shoot him!' came a voice
from the crowd. 'Now I think I heard somebody say, "Shoot him,"'
replied Parnell, 'but I wish to point out to you a very much better way, a
more Christian, a more charitable way which will give the lost sinner an
opportunity of repenting. When a man takes a farm from which another
has been evicted, you must show him on the roadside when you meet
him, you must show him in the streets of the town, you must show him
at the shop counter, you must show him in the fair and at the market
place and even in the house of worship, by leaving him severely alone, by
putting him into a sort of moral Coventry, by isolating him from the rest
of his kind as if he were a leper of old, you must show him your
detestation of the crime he has committed.'

Earlier passages in his speech are today at least of equal interest. At one
point he may even have been keeping in mind the voice from the crowd
which had called out the name of O'Shea. Stressing what he said was for
him the salient conclusion to be drawn from the recent parliamentary
session – namely that the more independence the Irish party showed, the
more respect it gained for itself and for Ireland – he said he didn't
complain of the party, which was a good and working one. 'It is true', he
added, 'that a very small section followed the Government across the
House of Commons [*Groans from the crowd*] but I trust that these members,
recognizing that the overwhelming opinion of their constituents is in
favour of union and unity, will retrace their steps and will join the great
body of their colleagues in presenting a solid front to every Government
that falls short of either its professions or its performances, that on that

day it will be the duty of the present strong Irish party to show that it can punish the Liberal Government as well as the Tories.'

And knowing that what really gave the Irish party its strength at Westminster was the growing and still excitingly unpredictable strength of the Land League in Ireland, he continued, 'The measure of the Land Bill next session will be the measure of your activity and energy this winter . . .'

It was hardly surprising that his opponents saw a connection between such remarks and the unprecedented increase in agrarian 'outrages' – particularly when he went on with his specific advice about what actually to do with 'land-grabbers'.

As for further precise steps to take, he remained encouragingly speculative. He had brought up the following thought in speeches before: 'How would they like it if we told the people one day not to pay any rent until this [Land] question is settled? . . . We cannot continue to allow this millstone to hang around the neck of our country, throttling its industry and preventing our progress. It shall be for wiser heads than mine [to decide] whether, if the Lords continue obdurate and refuse all just concessions, we shall not be obliged to strike against rent until this question has been settled. And if the five hundred thousand tenant farmers of Ireland struck against the ten thousand Irish landlords I should like to see how they would get police and soldiers enough to make them pay!'

Who can he have meant by 'wiser heads' than his? Most likely it was a convenient formula for permitting him to make potentially unwise remarks. He sat down to great cheering.

Altogether that Sunday marked a fine start to the post-recess political season in Ireland. And although the *Freeman's Journal* declared that Parnell had opened it with spirit 'though with caution', it was a defiant caution, the tone of which was echoed simultaneously at meetings all over Ireland and was soon to alter the whole balance between the Home Rule Party and the Liberal Government in the exact manner Parnell had in his public ruminations envisaged.

Even as Parnell was speaking, Michael Boyton, the Land League organizer, unsupported by MPs, was arousing great enthusiasm before a similar crowd of some twelve thousand at a Land League meeting over which a priest presided at Cahir, Co. Tipperary. 'God knows', said Boyton, 'that Irish Nationality is the essence of this movement. It inspires the men who are engaged in it in the same way as the soul inspires the body . . . You are substituting for servility and avarice the two most glorious graces of nationhood – love of home and love of freedom.'

This was the theme at which Parnell had been hammering away since well before the days of the Land League, but there now seemed nothing like the same difficulty in getting it across – the threat of famine, the evictions and the Land League itself had seen to that. Boyton could let himself be carried away confidently by his own rhetoric. This was, he said, a revolution they were engaged in, 'a rebellion against injustice, a holy war in a just cause'. In appealing to the crowd to stand together like men, he said, 'Ireland needs a united army to achieve her place among the nations: the obsolete cavalry of [O'Connell's] Repeal, the artillery of Home Rule, the rank and file of the Land League and, who knows, but they might want the brother engineer who with patient dint was working till the day when they would give the signal to fire the citadel . . .'

Parnell, when he got back to Dublin on Tuesday 21 September, found his mind dominated by thoughts of Mrs O'Shea.

Chapter 23

A wire from her was waiting for him. It expressed some anxiety at not having had a reply to the two letters he had had from her on his way to Ennis the previous Saturday. He replied:

I received your two letters quite safely, and you may write me even nicer ones with perfect confidence. I blame myself very much for not having written you on my way through Dublin on Saturday, as you were evidently anxious about your notes, but I hope you will forgive me as there were only a few minutes to spare.

I trust to see you in London on Tuesday next. Is it true that Captain O'Shea is in Paris, and, if so, when do you expect his return?

Did this last question mean, as it could well be interpreted to mean, that he wanted to know whether the coast was clear? Though he was obviously by now beginning to be obsessed by the thought of her, there was also a legitimate reason for asking. The main topic they had so far discussed together, on her initiative, had been Willie O'Shea's position in his constituency. The interjection he had heard at Ennis may have been fresh in his mind, and word had probably come to him from other sources of the constituency's dissatisfaction with its Whiggish Member. At a Land League meeting in West Clare a few days later, at which Parnell was not present, an indignant cry was indeed to go up from the crowd that 'O'Shea is in France'. If, as was clearly the case, Parnell wished to develop his relationship with Mrs O'Shea, an obvious way of doing so was to help her as much as he could over this matter of her husband's future which so concerned her. O'Shea was in trouble. Parnell would need to discuss things with him. He ended his letter by saying that he would try some more shooting the next day and she could expect some heather.

But the next day he did not go shooting. He was in Dublin, and the extent to which he himself was in trouble became apparent. 'My dear Mrs O'Shea,' he wrote – 'I cannot keep myself away from you any longer, so shall leave to-night for London. Please wire me to 16 Keppel Street, Russell Square, if I may hope to see you to-morrow and where, after 4 p.m. – Yours always, C.S.P.'

Readers of that day's *Freeman's Journal* could have noted that 'Mr Parnell intends remaining in Ireland this winter.' In response to invitations to address Home Rule meetings in the North of England, it was said, he was having to reply that his Irish engagements were too numerous and that it was impossible for him to address any meetings in England. In fact he crossed to England that night and arrived at Keppel Street on the afternoon of Thursday 23 September, hoping to find the wire he had asked for from Mrs O'Shea.

But for Katie O'Shea it was not a convenient moment. Her old nurse, who had been living with her at Eltham, was ill after a stroke and probably dying. In her memoirs she wrote that because of this she was unable to go to London 'even for an hour to meet Mr Parnell, so I telegraphed to that effect'.

Curiously a letter from him, written on Friday 24 September, tells a slightly different story. It is headed 'Euston Station'. It says that there had been a muddle over the telegram: it had arrived at Keppel Street before he did, but the boy had refused to leave it, as Parnell was not there, and Parnell himself had to go to the district postal office to find it. Having done so, he went next day to London Bridge Station at 12.15. This implies that the telegram had not in fact said that she would not be coming but had suggested that he should meet her at London Bridge. 'The train from Eltham', he wrote, 'had just left, so I came on to Charing Cross and sent a note by messenger to you at Thomas's [Hotel].'

This sounds as if she might not have felt sufficiently concerned to make contact with him once the original appointment had misfired. Or it could have been, as he himself suggested in his letter, that the post office had notified her that they had been unable to deliver the telegram and she had then acted after all on the supposition that he would not be there and had not come.

The incident demonstrates in a small way the disparity that can exist between the text of her memoirs and what is revealed in the letters she published with them. It also seems to emphasize that at this stage it was Parnell who was the more agitated by the developing relationship. His letter from Euston Station told her that he was 'very much troubled' at not having seen her, as he had to return to Ireland that night, having come to London on no other business than to see her. He signed himself 'Your very disappointed C.S.P.'

The next day, Saturday 25 September, he wrote to her from Dublin in a less self-centred frame of mind. He apologized for not having expressed his sympathy in her trouble over her dying nurse (he must meanwhile have had a letter from her), adding that he wished he could have seen her only for a few minutes to tell her 'how very much I feel any trouble which comes to you'. He was just starting off for a Land League meeting at New Ross, Co. Wexford, to be held the next day, but hoped she would write to him at Avondale, from where, he said, letters would eventually reach him.

His letters convey vividly the double excitement of what was happening to him: his mounting obsession with her against the exciting background of political events in Ireland. His meeting at New Ross was described by the *Freeman's Journal* the next day as 'perhaps the most imposing that has yet been held in any part of Ireland'. It estimated that there were not less than twenty thousand people there.

He had reached Ballywilliam by train at seven o'clock on the Saturday evening and then travelled the five miles by carriage to New Ross, which had been *en fête* for him, decorated with garlands and banners, one of which proclaimed:

> Let it ring out over hill and dale,
> God bless our noble chief Parnell!

At the meeting itself the Chairman was, as was standard now at Land League meetings, a priest; there were twenty other priests on the platform. Resolutions were passed which condemned the Lords' rejection of the Compensation for Disturbance Bill, demanded a Land Bill which would introduce peasant proprietorship, thanked Parnell for his 'distinguished and patriotic services', and condemned those in the Home Rule Party who sat with the Government, promoting disunion in the nationalist ranks. All resolutions were passed unanimously. The priest who moved the last one declared 'From Donegal to Cork, from Wexford to Galway, every true-hearted Irishman and woman is raising their hands to Heaven to invoke its choicest blessings on the head of Mr Parnell. No smile of a Minister could seduce him.'

Parnell, when he came to speak, made two points very clearly. The first reiterated his constant theme that the solution of the land question, by setting up a peasant proprietorship, was an inseparable part of the national question. He then went on to leave no doubt whatever about the view which he, a landlord himself, had of landlords in general.

'Some well-meaning men are saying to-day: "Don't continue this agitation . . . you are driving the landlords out of the national ranks!"' (There was laughter at this, to which he warmed.) 'I should like to know', he went on, 'when the landlords, since the Union, were in the national ranks. It is nonsense to expect them to be in the national ranks while they know that their only hope of maintaining their right to commit wrong lies in the maintenance of English power in Ireland. And if it is desirable to have them in the national ranks I tell you the best way of bringing them there is to take from them the right to do wrong – to destroy the system of landlordism which was planted here by England in order that she might divide Ireland's sons among themselves and so maintain her power. We will not – you will not – be demoralized by concessions, and although the Irish land question may be settled, and though our people may be rendered prosperous and famine banished from the land, I feel sure that the removal of suffering, and the increase of wealth and independence in this country will, so far from diminishing the determination of the Irish people to rule themselves, strengthen them and enormously increase their power for regaining their lost right.'

Here in a nutshell was the assumption on which his nationalist policy for the immediate future depended: the grand, if imprecise, sweep with which he could envisage progress towards a national Elysium through peasant proprietorship seemed still the only necessary definition of a future in these uncertain times. Rumours which were beginning to circulate to the effect that the Gladstone Government was considering legal action against the Land League and 'agitators' like himself merely increased the sense of excitement.

At least seven other big Land League meetings were held that same Sunday in different parts of Ireland. At Skibbereen John Dillon, also making a strong attack on 'landlordism', urged people to march to such meetings 'under the discipline of their leaders', not, he said, to fight, but to show their determination. The neo-Fenian Land League organizers Thomas Brennan, Matthew Harris and Patrick Sheridan were all at other meetings, sometimes in the presence of MPs, drawing an equally fine rhetorical line between encouragement and incitement.

Possibly the heightening tension made Katie O'Shea a less immediately compelling influence on Parnell's mind. He did not go to London on Tuesday 28 September, as in his last letter he had suggested he might. Instead he attended, as Chairman for the first time since the parliamentary recess, one of the ordinary weekly meetings of the Land League in Dublin. Parnell expressed his 'gratification' at how well the work of the

League had been going 'over here' while he and others were at work 'over there'. He said he found the results of the Land League's work to be 'of the most enormous and unexpected character'. An incidental point he made was the desirability of allowing police note-takers to sit on the platform at League meetings, as part of a deal to keep the police otherwise away from such meetings altogether.

He wrote to Katie O'Shea the next day from Dublin to say that he had received a wire from her but not the letter which she had said she was sending. Perhaps, however, she had sent it to Avondale, where he was going that evening. 'I suppose then ... that I may soon have the happiness of reading a few words written by you. I am due at Cork on Sunday, after which I propose to visit London again, and renew my attempt to gain a glimpse of you. Shall probably arrive there on Tuesday if I hear from you in the meanwhile that you will see me.'

He added that he would be at Morrison's Hotel in Dublin again on Friday (1 October) on his way, before going to Cork, to a meeting at Kilkenny on the Saturday, 'and shall be intensely delighted to have a wire from you to meet me there'.

A wire from her was duly waiting at Morrison's, and he wrote at once on the evening before setting out for Kilkenny: 'somehow or other something from you seems a necessary part of my daily existence, and if I have to go a day without even a telegram it seems dreadful'.

Her wire, in a reference to his abortive visit to London of the week before, must have said something about not coming to England specially to see her. He wrote chidingly, 'I want to know how you intend to excuse yourself for telling me not to come on purpose if I must return. Of course I am going on purpose to see you; and it is also unhappily true that I cannot remain long.'

He said he would be crossing the following Monday evening – on his return from Cork – and would call at Keppel Street for a wire from her.

Next day, accompanied by Dillon, Sexton T. P. O'Connor and T. D. Sullivan, he set off for the meeting at Kilkenny. They arrived there by the Saturday morning train to be greeted by a band playing on the platform and with a green banner bearing his portrait waving in welcome. They were escorted to open carriages festooned with flowers in which they drove through the streets in triumph to their hotel. As an English MP who visited Ireland at this time was to write of such events, 'Parnell's journeyings can be compared only to the progress of Caesar. Parnell sits erect in the open carriage, accepting the homage of emotional enthusiasm in the streets with almost an Imperial mien.' He said that the enthusiasm shown for Parnell far exceeded that which Gladstone had enjoyed in his famous pre-election Midlothian campaign.

At the Kilkenny meeting, which began at 2.00 p.m. in the hotel, there were, as Parnell had advocated earlier that week, police note-takers on the platform but otherwise no police present. As he got up to speak, the whole audience rose to greet him, cheering and waving hats and scarves and handkerchiefs. One of the resolutions to be passed was, he said, one with which he could not quite agree, since it was merely in favour of fixity of tenure and fair rents, whereas he was against any partnership with the landlords and for 'the complete extirpation of landlordism'.

At a 'monster' meeting of some ten thousand people at Carrick-on-Suir the same day (the old epithet from O'Connell's day was now being applied), bolder words still came from Michael Boyton on the national aspect of the campaign. The Land League principles and nationality, he said, were 'travelling the same road'. They were there that day to advocate the justice of giving the land to the tiller of the soil. Having done that they would tell them another day 'how to snap the last link of the chain'. This conscious, or accidental, allusion to what Parnell had said earlier that year in Cincinnati raised loud cheers.

At yet another meeting that day, to establish a branch of the Land League at Barntown in Co. Wexford, the effigy of a man, with boots hung round his neck, said to represent a man who had taken land from which another had been evicted, was shot and then set on fire. The two Co. Wexford MPs (John Barry and Garret Byrne) for whom Parnell had intervened and got his trousers torn in the election mêlée at Enniscorthy in April were both present. A Reverend Canon Foley was in the chair.

The next day, Sunday, was a day of many monster meetings. There were said to be forty thousand people at Boyle in Co. Roscommon, where contingents from the countryside, headed by bands in military uniform and squadrons of horsemen under identifiable leaders, carried imitation pikes. These, as the *Freeman's Journal* reported, 'gave the gathering a suggestive air'. The two former Fenian MPs, O'Kelly and Commins, addressed the crowds. And it was on this day that Parnell himself made his triumphal entry into the city of Cork, the constituency which he now represented.

The *Freeman's Journal* said it would rank as 'one of the most wonderful events of his career'. He was received with 'little short of idolatry'. However, the idolatry fell some way short at the start.

When Parnell landed from America that spring, a die-hard dogmatic Fenian group in Cork had marked their disapproval of his parliamentary and Land League alliance by telling him he would have no support from them in the election. Some of these men had recently taken part in a raid on a ship in Queenstown harbour from which rifles had been seized. Their action had been condemned by Land League officials in Cork, two of whom were among those now welcoming Parnell as he arrived with T. P. O'Connor, Egan and others at Blarney station to be driven in two wagonettes in triumph into the city. All had just got into their seats when a party of men armed with revolvers came up and, while paying respect to Parnell himself, forced the two men out of the carriages and prevented them from taking part in the procession. Parnell and the others then rode on into Cork, where they were greeted with tremendous enthusiasm and some calls for 'an Irish Republic'. Apparently unaffected by the incident with the revolvers, Parnell stood in his carriage waving back to the cheering crowds in windows and on rooftops. Bouquets of flowers overwhelmed him, and at one point he was presented with his sister Fanny's poem 'The Hymn of the Land League' embroidered on white satin. A hundred thousand people were estimated to be in the streets.

On his arrival at the City Park at sunset, he delighted the crowds by making as unequivocally clear as he was ever to do what he stood for. There was, he said, to be 'no tampering with landlordism', implying that no Land Bill to be introduced by the Government which conceded mere further instalments of 'tenant right' could be satisfactory. 'That institution,' he emphasized, 'created for the purpose of maintaining English rule in Ireland and for the interests of the few against the many, will have to fall.

'The people of Ireland', he continued, 'are today engaged in a great struggle – in a struggle for the land of this country which was wrested from them seven centuries ago by force of arms . . . We are determined to do our utmost to make Ireland great, glorious and free and to take the power of governing Ireland out of the hands of the English Parliament and people and to transfer it to the hands of our own people. Determined as we are to secure these ends, we believe that we can only achieve them by making the land of Ireland as free as it was when the waters of the flood left it.'

Afterwards there was a banquet at the Royal Victoria Hotel, where, responding to the toast to him, he said, 'If there is one thing I am determined to bring about it is the power of the Irish people to govern themselves so that in future they might not have to associate the prosperity of Ireland with the name of a ruler sent from England.'

The pace was quickening. There was continued speculation about how long the Government would allow it to do so. Parnell himself was booked up for weekend meetings a month ahead. He was announced for Roscommon on 10 October, Longford on the 17th, Galway on the 24th and Limerick, where he was to receive the freedom of the city, on the 31st.

As soon as he got back to Dublin the next day, on Monday evening, he wrote to Katie O'Shea 'on the only bit of paper to be found at this late hour (a scrap taken from one of your own notes), to say that I hope to reach London tomorrow (Tuesday) evening and to see you on Wednesday when and where you wish.' But a great gale was blowing in the Channel all Tuesday, and he had to postpone his crossing until Wednesday evening.

He had to be back by the end of the week, not just for the meeting at Roscommon on the following Sunday, but for a special meeting of the farmers of Co. Cork which he had called for Saturday morning, 9 October, in the Royal Victoria Hotel in Cork.

But he was not back at the end of the week. On the Saturday morning it was Dillon who appeared before the farmers in the Royal Victoria Hotel.

'I address you', he said, 'under considerable difficulties, inasmuch as I am here to take the place of your member, Mr Parnell. I came here at his request, because he is a man the demand for whose presence just at present in all parts of Ireland is so great that he is unable to keep all his engagements, and he asked me to speak here for him to-day.'

But Parnell was not then in any part of Ireland. Nor was he to be at Roscommon, as he should have been, on the following day. His failure to arrive there caused considerable disappointment, but no explanation was forthcoming from his MPs O'Kelly and Commins, who addressed the meeting instead.

He was not back again for almost another week. He reappeared in Dublin the following Saturday evening to travel by train with Justin McCarthy to Longford for the meeting he was due to address there the next day. His arrival in Longford caused something of an embarrassing sensation.

A complete change had taken place in his appearance, and a lot of people doubted that he was Parnell at all. He had shaved off most of his beard except for a narrow strip down each jaw and under the chin. 'The Hon. Gentleman's appearance is so changed', wrote the *Freeman's Journal*'s reporter, 'that even his most intimate friends meeting him casually in the street would not recognize him.'

It seems likely that this was exactly why, in the time he had been away, he had made the change. For, after the usual enthusiastic meeting at Longford and a drive across to Roscommon, escorted by a contingent of horsemen, to spend the night and receive next day an address from the Town Commissioners (it spoke of assurance that his regrettable absence the Sunday before 'could only have been caused by business of the utmost importance'), he returned to Dublin on Monday 18 October and sent a letter at once to the wife of Willie O'Shea.

'My own love,' he wrote. 'You cannot imagine how much you have occupied my thoughts all day and how very greatly the prospect of seeing you again very soon comforts me.'

He planned, 'if things are propitious on your side', to return to London almost at once.

He signed the letter, 'Yours always, C.'

It seems clear that something of the greatest importance for him had happened. His relationship with the cause of Irish nationalism would never be quite the same again.

Chapter 24

For all his changed appearance on arrival at Longford after the unexplained ten days away in October, nothing else about Parnell seemed different. The vigour of his attack on the landlord system, with all that this was to mean for the national ideal, was undiminished. Greeted as of old by contingents of men wearing green sashes and carrying the slogan:

> Welcome, Brave Parnell,
> Our Hope and Our Pride,
> United Determined,
> We Stand by your Side!

he addressed himself to the prospect of the projected Liberal Land Bill.

'We consider', he said, 'that the propping up of the system of landlordism by attempting to improve the relations between the landlord and the tenant is impossible and will only result in disappointment and we will take no part in it.'

After writing his 'My own love' letter on return to Dublin, he seems to have spent the next week at Avondale. From there he wrote to Katie again on Friday 22 October, before setting out once more, this time with T. P. O'Connor for Athenry and another great meeting at Galway on the Sunday. He hoped, he told her, to be going to England to see her again immediately on his return, and he sent her some heather that he had picked for her three weeks before, adding, 'also my best love, and hope you will believe that I always think of you as the one dear object whose presence has ever been a great happiness to me'.

He had a great welcome at Athenry, where he spent the night after being escorted in torchlight from the station by a crowd and a band. He arrived in Galway on the Sunday afternoon, to be greeted by streamers of green and gold with the simple words:

> We'll trample on oppression,
> Tyrants we'll compel

To show their great oppression
With the aid of great Parnell.

A comparison of the last line of the slogan with the first line of that displayed at Longford, indicates the alternate pronunciations of his name in common use.

A prominent landlord, Lord Mountmorres, had recently been murdered and, with papers like *The Times* beginning to write that meetings such as this should be prohibited, Parnell sailed close to the wind by saying he doubted very much that Mountmorres's death was in fact an agrarian crime; it was more properly the responsibility of the House of Lords for throwing out the Compensation for Disturbance Bill.

It was in this speech at Galway that he made the later much-quoted statement that, important as was the land issue for the majority of the Irish population, 'I would not have taken off my coat to this work, if I had not known that we were laying the foundations by this movement for the recovery of our legislative independence.'

One way or another, this had been implicit in his whole approach to the agitation on the land from the start. Parnell's biographer F. S. L. Lyons has focused significance on Parnell's use here of the word 'legislative'. He argues that, inspiring as Parnell's words might be for the national cause, 'legislative' placed an intentional qualification on the degree of national independence to be attained. But this seems to misread the genuinely ambiguous nature of Parnell's nationalist stance.

Parnell spoke again that evening, at a banquet given in his honour at the Railway Hotel, Galway, outside which a fireworks display took place in the square. He rose to respond to the toast of 'Irishmen abroad', with which his name had been coupled. He told of how impressed he had been on his American trip by the potential power – 'undeveloped' he called it, and not only in money terms – of the Irish in America, who had done so much to help save the Irish people from famine that winter.

'I was', he said, 'perfectly amazed at the extent of the sympathy which the name of Ireland obtained in every quarter of the U.S.A. I feel convinced that if you ever call upon them in another fight and in another way for help, and if you can show them that there is a fair and good chance of success, you will have their assistance – their trained and organized assistance for the purpose of breaking the yoke which encircles you. Just in the same way as you had the assistance last winter to save you from famine.'

This was addressed not to an audience of potential Fenian supporters, whom he might tactically have wished to keep happy, but to a hundred banqueting gentlemen of Galway, whose enthusiastic cheering showed clearly enough their understanding of the theoretical possibility he was talking about. Yet the words, by stretching a point, could be given a general emphasis to be interpreted harmlessly enough. Conversely, his daytime reference to 'legislative independence' could, by stretching a point, be given a general emphasis to cover the possibility of separate independence too.

There was nothing new here. In order to keep more moderate nationalists reassured, Parnell had often in the past suggested Grattan's parliament as the national goal; he had equally clearly seemed to leave that goal wide open. It was almost three years since he had said at Castlebar, 'Let no man lightly define the measure of Irish independence. Let no man assign a *ne plus ultra* to the march of our nation.' More than once, both in America and in Ireland, he had talked of an independence as complete as that of the United States. Such ambiguity reflected not just a tactical shrewdness with which to attract support from all but the most dogmatic Fenians, and to touch the emotions of a countryside where the myths of 1867 still held some poetic popular sway, but a genuine unresolved element in his own nationalist feeling. 'They will do what we can make them do,' was more than ever his policy in this phase of the Land War. Land League branches were multiplying weekly to organize the tenantry in social revolt; government in Ireland was becoming increasingly impotent. Anything could happen, and Parnell was careful to make sure it looked as if it could.

The joint nature of the Land League's campaign – for the end of landlordism and for an imprecisely aspiring nationalism – continued to be something of which he and the principal speakers at Land League meetings regularly reminded their audiences. In addition to faithful Members of Parliament like Sexton, T. P. O'Connor, J. J. O'Kelly, Healy (elected for Wexford at a by-election in November) and – on his return from a further visit to America – Michael Davitt, four of the most tireless of such speakers were the official Land League organizers Thomas Brennan, Patrick Sheridan, Michael Boyton and Matthew Harris. These four, now largely forgotten in the patriotic canon, are some of the unsung heroes of Irish nationalism who did at least as much to try to bring life to that cause as some of the more successful famous names of forty years later. At meeting after meeting, week after week, sometimes together with MPs and sometimes without them, they harangued tenantry and labourers in the countryside with moving sincerity and zeal. While necessarily devoting the greater part of their speeches to exhortations to organize for land reform, not to pay rent above the old Griffith's valuation, to refuse to take land from which another had been evicted, and to treat those who did so as social and economic outcasts, they also constantly reiterated that there was something nobler still at stake: the ideal for which Parnell, in any interpretation they liked to put on it, had taken off his coat.

'You must never forget', Brennan had told a meeting at Westport, the week before Parnell's Galway speeches, 'that there is a higher cause than even the land for the people, that we have a nationality and that we should never fail to ask for the restoration of that great nationality.'

Sheridan, calling for support for the Land League at Clonmacnoise in September, had said, 'Join hands to-day in this one great national movement, and so sure as God is in heaven we shall sweep in onward strides to independence.'

In the same month Boyton had said at Cahir, 'If you stand to us . . . a brighter gleam of Irish independence than was beheld by the immortal Grattan shall spring forth, an Ireland and her people who have never yet forfeited their right to take their place among the nations of the earth.'

Brennan again, only two days before Parnell's speeches at Galway, had said, 'In prosecuting this great social war I trust you will never forget that Irishmen have a higher duty still, and that is the sovereign independence of their country.'

'Self-reliance', the watchword that was to come to political life many years later with Sinn Fein, was often on Brennan's lips.

But of course those to whom he and the others were speaking were only incidentally concerned with these higher thoughts. Such words provided fine emotive fuel for the real business in hand: the furtherance of their immediate self-interest by lowering rents and by organizing to establish a new land system which would free them from the insecurity which had made the recent bad seasons so painful. By far the greater part of all Land League speeches at meetings were concerned with such matters. Even those on the land who were not tenants at all but labourers had their interests theoretically embraced by the Land League. Landlord attempts to sow division between farmers and labourers were firmly rejected by Brennan. Altering the status of the tenant would, he maintained, raise the status of the labourer too. In Brennan's concept of the sort of social revolution that was to go hand in hand with nationalism there is a trace of Marx which foreshadows James Connolly.

'This is not merely a movement on behalf of the tenant farmer of Ireland against the landlords of Ireland,' he had said at Clonmacnoise in September, with Sheridan and Harris beside him. 'It is a movement of the workers of Ireland against the class who have been robbing you . . . It is the uprising of the democracy of Ireland against the privileged few . . . There is a class in the community who do not work, who live upon the stolen fruits of your labour . . . That class can be got rid of by organization and determined action . . . The Land League is entitled to support in the name of nationality and humanity, and in these sacred and holy names I ask you to endorse the principles of the Irish National Land League.'

He concluded by talking of 'publicly sowing the seeds of, and the principles of, Republicanism which can alone raise an enslaved people'.

It was a fine amalgamation of the two Land League themes into something noble. But for those who cheered him to the echo it was the summoning of ancient national emotions to change their day-to-day existence that made the appeal, rather than the attempt to articulate such emotions in modern political terms. Sheridan, proclaiming at a Land League meeting in Ramsborough in July that the spirit of nationality in Ireland is 'like the soul of man, imperishable, indestructible, immortal', had received only a polite 'Hear, hear.' There can be small doubt that at this stage in the mind of Parnell it was the national aspiration, in whatever imprecise form, that was the dominant thought. He was not essentially an intellectual concerned with socio-economic theory. He had a serviceable intellect, but it was driven by his emotions. At the same time, he was well enough aware of the day-to-day reality in which his goal had to be pursued.

The *Wiener Allgemeine Zeitung* interviewed him at Avondale towards the end of 1880. Instead of the 'terrible' character the journalist had been led to expect he would find there, he found a man who 'would, in Vienna, be taken for an amiable cavalier; in Berlin for an officer in the Guards in private dress'. His beard had disappeared (which makes the date of the interview some time after 17 October) and the journalist saw before him 'a pale, finely chiselled countenance . . . mounted on a neck which did not seem much in favour of bowing; a large thoughtful brow over a pair of full and bright eyes, which in moments of intense emotion (which Parnell understands well how to master) sometimes assume a piercing and stern expression'. His voice was clear and sympathetic.

The Austrian asked him if he was sure he had got the balance between Home Rule and the land question the right way round in his political campaign. Might it not have been better, he asked, to put Home Rule first and then approach the complicated land problem, which would be less difficult to resolve if the battle for Home Rule had been won?

'The land question – a matter which concerns the daily bread of the people,' replied Parnell – 'is more easily understood by them; it finds its way to their hearts; it brings enthusiasm into the movement.'

But if enthusiasm for the national movement thus depended on the land question, what might happen to that enthusiasm if the land question were to become less urgent? This was a question the Austrian did not put.

Boyton had expressed the theoretical idealism well when he had said that nationality inspired the Land League as the soul inspired the body. But, as Parnell recognized, with the average tenant farmer it was more the other way round: the body, it was hoped, would inspire the soul.

It was physical activity, often of a crude kind, which was providing the dynamic for the revolutionary situation which Michael Davitt found on his return from the United States on 20 November. Davitt, who took for granted that social and national revolution went hand in hand, then reported back to Devoy in New York that the Land League, with some two hundred thousand members in all four provinces of Ireland, and its own courts in which local disputes were adjudicated, was virtually ruling the country. 'You would be astonished,' he wrote, 'to know how far some of our former timid people have advanced during the past few months. On the whole the outlook is splendid.'

Certainly Davitt's optimism was justified to the extent that landlords found themselves largely unable to collect rents higher than Griffith's valuation, which was, on the whole, unrealistically low. A Cork land-agent reported to one landlord that month, 'The country is in a most lawless state; in fact it is impossible to collect rents and where it is to end I know not.' He told the trustees of one estate, 'if the people were left alone they would pay willingly, but these Land Leagues are destroying the country'.

Pledges to pay no higher rent than Griffith's valuation were repeatedly asked for at public meetings and enthusiastically given. It was intimidation that enforced them. A typical instance of what the Cork land-agent meant occurred on an estate near Tralee one night in November when about fifty men with blackened faces appeared at the homes of tenants and made them promise on their knees not to pay any rents higher than the Griffith's valuation. They seemed to be strangers, but said that, if evictions followed, they would come to the tenants' assistance. Only the week before a farmer evicted from his farm near Mallow, Co. Cork, had been reinstated by a party of forty men carrying arms. Davitt, in his letter to Devoy, wrote, 'The courage of the people is magnificent. All classes are carrying arms openly.'

For those who did nevertheless pay the full rents asked, there was sometimes a grim warning and more often immediate trouble. A typical warning was that received in November by a farmer near Maryborough, Queens County, who had paid his rent in full: a coffin was placed in front of his door. Another, named O'Donnell, having supper at home in Kilrush, Co. Clare, with his brother and one of his daughters, had a blast of snipe-shot through his window; his daughter was hit in the neck. Two widows of Newmarket, Co. Cork, who, unlike the other tenants on the estate where they lived, had paid their rent in full, were visited by a party of women with blackened faces and were 'carded' – had sheep's combs drawn through their flesh. In Loughrea, Co. Galway, people were actually threatened with reprisals for not attending Land League meetings.

Landlords could of course be intimidated too. Sometimes they or their agents were shot at, though only eight 'agrarian homicides' were recorded by the police in 1880. One of these took place in October, when a Cork landlord, being driven in a wagon round his estate to try to collect rents, saw his driver shot dead beside him. More often landlords were dealt with by threats to their servants or by boycotting. When later in the year the tenants of Matthew O'Connell of Lurgan in Co. Armagh refused to pay any rents at all unless he reduced them by 50 per cent, threatening letters were sent to his servants, telling them to leave him. Local people were warned not to sell him turf. Both ears were cut off one of his donkeys.

The mutilation of an owner's animals – the 'houghing' (hamstringing) of cattle, the cutting-off of tails of horses – was a recurrent warning phenomenon. Human beings sometimes received the same treatment. In the same week as Matthew O'Connell's donkey lost its ears, a man named Hanson in Tralee, whom the local bailiff had put with his family as caretaker into a house from which a family of ten had been evicted, was visited at night by a large party of men armed with rifles and a penknife. They broke open the door, hauled him out of bed, and made him kneel on the floor. His right ear was then slit with the penknife, after which he was made to swear an oath that he would never come between landlord and tenant again. Another man then slit his left ear and made him swear 'loyalty to the tenant cause'. The party left him to think things over with his terrified family, although he had temporarily fainted from loss of blood.

As a notice put up but quickly torn down by the police in Boyle, Co. Roscommon, had it, 'Every man must be a friend or an enemy. The men who will not support the people's cause should not be supported by the people.' There followed a list of shopkeepers in Boyle who were supplying landlords. 'Avoid and cut these props of landlordism,' enjoined the notice. 'Leave the grass growing up the doors of these traitors and flunkies. God Save Ireland.'

Another pledge regularly taken at Land League meetings, in addition to one not to pay more than Griffith's valuation, was that not to take land from which another had been evicted. Although the violence which enforced such a pledge was taken out on the 'land-grabber' himself, its real effectiveness lay in economic damage to the landlord: his power to evict for non-payment of the full rent was rendered useless if he could find no one else to whom he could let the land.

Thus until the Government could recover the initiative on law and order from the Land League – or rather from those mysterious agents of the Land League in the countryside who operated in its name – landlords were effectively squeezed in a grip which gave some reality to the social revolution Parnell hoped to exploit.

One instance of a landlord who managed to escape this grip was recorded on the Co. Sligo estate of Sir Henry Gore-Booth, father of a future republican heroine. Informed by his tenants, in line with Land League principles, that they would only pay Griffith's valuation rents in future, he immediately agreed. He then opened his rent-books and showed them that they were in fact at present paying rents below Griffith's valuation. They agreed to go on paying their normal rents.

Bailiffs and those serving eviction notices now rarely tried to do their job without police escorts, and these sometimes were of little use. A bailiff and a process-server operating with a police escort for Lord Annesley near Enniskillen were set upon by hundreds of people before they could get down to business, and were forced to retreat with their escort into one of his lordship's shooting-lodges, where they were besieged all night by men surrounding the house and threatening to destroy it. They had to be rescued by reinforcements the next day. A process-server rashly trying to serve eviction notices without an escort near Castlebar had actually succeeded in a few cases before being set upon by a crowd of men, women and children and left with head and face disfigured, his clothes drenched in blood and deprived of all his legal documents.

Gentler treatment was reserved for a solicitor who had refused his tenants' demand for no rent higher than Griffith's valuation: the Land League banned him from hunting. But the steward of a landlord in Bruff, Co. Limerick trying to do business at Bruff fair and prevented from doing so because of a Land League boycott of his master made the mistake of drawing a revolver on the crowd which was hooting and jostling him. He was knocked down and had his clothing ripped off and torn to tatters. Another man at the fair, identified as one who had taken a farm from which a widow had been evicted, was in a way luckier. He was effectively prevented from selling any of his farm stock, and a local shopkeeper who had unknowingly already bought supplies from him was so terrified of reprisals that he simply gave them back to him. With something in hand at least from this transaction, the farmer went back home again in fear of his life.

Nor were things always comfortable for those to whose aid the Land League came. A man named Connolly of Cappamore, Co. Limerick, had just married a widow, Mrs McLaughlin, when he was evicted by the landlord and his house was levelled to the ground. One night a party of about two hundred men, some armed, took him back to the site, where they had built him a wooden hut in which they 'reinstated' him. They made him take an oath not to give it up on peril of his life. His subsequent history and that of the former widow is not recorded, but there were cases when those so reinstated were unable to avoid re-eviction and a fate worse than the first.

The case of a man called Murphy was brought up at an official meeting of the central Land League in Dublin, as were many such cases of distress where financial help was needed. After Murphy's eviction, a man named Talbot had paid the landlord £200 and had taken possession of the house and the land for his family. Some time afterwards, reported a young Land Leaguer, Timothy Harrington (later an MP), forty men came and 'stripped' the Talbots, even though they had arms, and 'sent them through the country', putting Murphy back into possession. Since then, however, Murphy had been thrown out again and this time had been arrested and put in prison, where he now sat without bail. The Land League awarded him ten pounds (some £450 today).

During Harrington's recital of this story, the Chairman of the Land League meeting, T. D. Sullivan MP, stopped him for a moment at the word 'stripped'. 'Stripped?' asked Sullivan. 'I suppose you mean they discovered them?'

'No,' replied Harrington. 'Stripped them naked and sent them through the country. It was an unnecessary thing to do, but when men's possessions are executed, you hardly know what will be done.'

The extent to which the Land League in its official capacity had any control over some of the things done in its name and the extent to which it was prepared, however embarrassed, to condone or at least turn a blind eye towards them were major issues of these times on both sides of the Irish Sea. There were certainly those who had little real doubt that even Parnell himself was implicated in the worst of the violence. When at the beginning of November 1880 it had been put to the vote in the Waterford Corporation that Parnell should be awarded the freedom of the city when he came there, the decision to do so was taken by only the narrowest majority, 18 to 17. When one alderman said he knew 'of no man more deserving of the honour than Mr Parnell', another interjected, 'Is it for shooting landlords?' He added that he had great pleasure in moving 'that Mr Parnell should go to hell'.

Parnell himself was soon receiving several threatening letters a day from Unionists in England and Ireland, couched in terms similar to those which it was inferred he was responsible for having had sent to others. One such letter spoke of him receiving his 'quietus from the hand of one upon whom the lot of hurrying you into the presence of an avenging God has fallen – steeped as you are in wickedness and damned Communism'. Another, from Liverpool, threatened to cut off his ears.

No one of any political sophistication supposed that Parnell himself had direct contact with the forces responsible for the violent actions behind the Land League campaign. To think this would have been stupidly to underestimate his sense of political flexibility, never more alert than at this time. But to suspect that the calls which Parnell and others were continually making for people to organize Land League branches had some connection with the organization of the criminal intimidation deployed on behalf of the Land League's objectives was not unreasonable or unintelligent, whatever the Land League itself might say.

Almost all Land League speakers at public meetings had for a long time been making a point of expressing disapproval of violence in their speeches, even if at times they sounded rather as if they were making a show of doing so. They often allowed some ambiguity into their injunctions to obey the law. An extreme version of this could be found in the speech Matthew Harris delivered in Parnell's presence after Parnell himself had spoken at Galway on 24 October.

There were, said Harris, 'two monstrous evils' between which they had to choose. 'I ask myself which is the greater evil – is it better that one bad man should be shot down than that thousands of families should be driven from the face of the fair land? If the tenant farmers of Ireland shoot down landlords as partridges are shot down in September, Matt Harris would never say one word against it . . . I tell the people that they will be supported by the Land League – that the tyrant and every tyrant like him will meet with strength and power enough to make them stay their hands.'

Remonstrated with by the Chairman of the meeting, but not by

Parnell, Harris replied that all he meant was that if landlords were shot down he would not, as he had done in former times, come forward and denounce the men. At which there was a murmured 'Hear, hear!'

In fact landlords were not being shot down like partridges, or at least only like the very occasional partridge. But to explain agrarian 'outrages' as an attempt to deal with landlord 'crime' could be a dangerous incitement to violence in the prevailing atmosphere.

Brennan, speaking the next week at Ballina, Co. Mayo, urged his audience to show their determination no longer to remain the willing slaves of a few idlers; they should join together and combine for the destruction of the powers of these idlers. He was, he said, not an advocate of strong words 'unless we are able to give practical effect to these words by strong deeds . . . They talk of assassins with horror, but do they ever think of those who are the real assassins? The landlords of Ireland are not less guilty because they are protected by the English law in the commission of their crimes.'

John Dillon, an MP since the summer and as active a speaker at meetings week after week as any other member of the Land League executive, was more circumspect about the use of violence, telling an audience at Fethard, Co. Tipperary, in November that victory could be achieved without resort to any at all. However, he added, 'I am not a man too much given to telling the people not to shed a drop of blood, because I believe it is worth a great deal of human blood. But the interests of the movement are best served, particularly as regards the good name of the Irish race in other countries, by maintaining a strictly defensive position.'

Michael Davitt, equally active after his return from the United States, was, as the Land League's founding spirit, possibly the most openly concerned about the use of violence in its name, particularly the mutilation of animals. 'These damned petty little outrages', he called them, and he boldly denounced the boycott if used simply to intimidate or to work off old scores. He hated tyranny, he said, whether it came from the landlords or from the ranks of the Irish National Land League, and he would set his face against boycotting being used against any man in Ireland simply because he would not join the Land League. If they denounced coercion coming from the Government, or injustice coming from the landlords, how could they sanction coercion coming from their own ranks? 'This is a great moral organization for a moral purpose,' he concluded, 'and it must be carried on on moral lines.'

Yet this was the same Davitt who had been proud to report to Devoy only a few weeks before that all classes were carrying arms.

Parnell, while sharing from a civilized point of view Davitt's distaste for unnecessary violence – particularly the mutilation of animals – was almost certainly more pragmatic in his thoughts about both its uses and its inevitability in present circumstances. As Brennan was to put it to a crowd before the year was out, 'While joining with my colleagues in imploring you not to ruin a cause that is already won, by having recourse to outrages, I at the same time know that human nature is human nature and that as long as outrages are practised on the people there will always be reprisals. The way to get rid of these outrages is to remove the cause of them.'

At a meeting of O'Connell-type proportions in a field near Limerick on Monday 1 November, a week after his Galway speech, Parnell would tell his audience that 'the nearness and completeness of this settlement depends entirely on your own exertions'. He urged them 'to bring the strong force of public opinion to bear on any man who does take a farm from which another has been evicted', and he told them that 'in this way you have the power of settling the land question this winter'. In saying such things he knew quite enough of the secret realities of rural Ireland, as well as of human nature, to sense the sort of action to which such words might lead, however much he might deprecate it. The next Sunday, 7 November, at Athlone, he was to ask the people 'to show that you have inherited some of the determination of your fathers, and that you are determined to hold by your homesteads until you have undone the conquest of seven hundred years ago'. In saying this, again he knew quite well that he was also calling up dark forces with a different concept of morality from that of the civilized world of modern politics in which he operated.

The tradition of individual secret societies in the Irish countryside – of people combining at local level for self-protection and self-interest in a society where the official laws were those of 'strangers' – dated far back in time. Periodically, as with the Defenders secret society of the 1790s, or the Ribbon movement of the nineteenth century, these had assumed a certain national scale. The Defenders particularly and to some extent the Ribbon movement had developed national aspirations aside from the conventional politics of the day. The earlier phase of the Irish Republican Brotherhood had had its own tenuous associations with the secret-society tradition, though it was itself the first such to concentrate on a purely political character. Only ten years before the Land League, in the county of Westmeath, the Ribbon movement had temporarily re-emerged to indicate again that it was to the land itself rather than to any concept of it as a political abstraction that the strong feelings of ordinary Irish men and women most easily attached. In now striving to bring the two sources of national feeling into one coherent movement, Parnell and the other Land League leaders, with their injunctions to organize and combine, were summoning powerful if primitive forces to new political effect.

A clash in Ireland, from which there might be no turning back, between English authority and Irish popular will now seemed increasingly imminent. It was becoming recognized that what was happening there was in a different dimension from a simple administrative problem of law and order. The *Pall Mall Gazette* had written on 18 October, 'We have really to face in Ireland a social revolt of formidable magnitude. The idea that more coercion and the abolition of liberty will suffice to set Ireland right is more and more clearly seen to be the shallow and inadequate thing it is.'

As Land League branches proliferated week after week and meetings continued to grow in size and number, accompanied by contingents of horsemen in green, sometimes carrying long staves tipped with tin to seem like lances, it became obvious that the Government would soon have to act. There had been discussion within the Cabinet as to whether or not to suspend habeas corpus. Gladstone wished if possible to act within the normal law. The decision to prosecute normally had been taken; action to implement it was expected any day.

Parnell made it clear that he was ready to exploit the inevitable increase in tension. 'If they manage in any way to commit the leaders of the Parliamentary party,' he had said in his speech at Galway, 'we shall resign our seats into the hands of our constituents as a solemn and sacred duty to elect men in our place to carry on our work in the House of Commons.'

It was a bold statement, and perhaps the first indication of the real danger that lay ahead for him. This consisted not so much in imprisonment itself but in the likelihood that positive Government action would force him out from the advantage of his flexible ambiguity into a commitment to action from which there could be no turning back. Were the Irish people really ready for such a commitment? Equally important – though no one then yet knew why it was likely to become a relevant question, and possibly it was only beginning to stir at the back of his own mind – was he himself ready? For him a very different, purely personal, commitment had already formed on the other side of the Irish Sea.

Even before the meeting at Galway on 24 October he had written to

Katie O'Shea to say that he hoped to go to London as soon as he got back. Whether in fact he did now do so for a lover's lightning visit between 26 and 30 October cannot be said for certain, though it seems unlikely. Katie wrote thirty years later that he visited her 'several times' that autumn, which could be taken to cover the three visits we know definitely he made before the end of the year, or this as a fourth as well. Her chronological precision is often unreliable. What can be said for certain is that wherever he was she must have been on his mind.

We know that he was in Dublin by 11.30 a.m. on Saturday 30 October to take the train to Limerick Junction with Dillon and O'Kelly for a meeting in Tipperary the next day. There, in his hotel, he was presented with an address which spoke of 'faith in his genius and ability to meet every emergency' and which cordially welcomed him to a town 'where the national flag of Ireland was never lowered'. He went on to a meeting in the town, where the Dean of Cashel was in the chair.

Possibly because of the character of the Chairman, or because Parnell was beginning to ponder the personal disadvantages of committing himself to too unequivocal a position in Ireland, his speech was rather more subdued than usual. Certainly he reiterated clearly 'the two main planks in our platform': that rents should not be rack rents and that no one should take land from which another had been evicted. He also stated his personal conviction that a peasant proprietorship was the answer to the land problem, but – with untypical moderation for this stage of the Land League campaign – he went out of his way to recognize that there were others who thought that a lowering of rents would be sufficient to make the land system acceptable. 'I do not', he said, 'wish to be drawn aside into a discussion of the best method.' He spoke of the matter as 'ripe for settlement in this year or next', until when 'it is simply a waste of time to think of formulating plans as long as the people and Parliament of England exhibit the temper they have been exhibiting'.

But he was back in sharper form at the banquet that evening, reproving Tipperary for the fact that the Royal Irish Constabulary appeared to have thought the town sufficiently quiet to make it possible to withdraw a part of its force to cope with the turbulent county of Mayo. 'If you don't have them back within a month,' he said, 'it will be an eternal disgrace to the city of Tipperary. Don't let me be misunderstood. I don't want you to go and shoot landlords but the fact that these police have been sent away shows the disorganized state of the city.'

The next day, 1 November, he was in Limerick for the meeting in a field to the south of the town. The *Freeman's Journal* reckoned this 'more representative, influential and enthusiastic' than any meeting since the days of O'Connell. This time there was again nothing remotely equivocal about Parnell's approach. He called on his audience above all to organize and combine, to offer only a just rent, and to bring the strong force of public opinion down on land-grabbers. As for any alternative to peasant proprietorship, he now repeated what he had implied before about the call for the 'three Fs' – fair rent, fixity of tenure and free sale: 'I believe that platform to be untenable.'

He received the freedom of Limerick the next day, and was back in the Imperial Hotel, Dublin, on Wednesday 3 November. There he was having lunch with J. J. O'Kelly, the American journalist James Redpath and the young Land League enthusiast Timothy Harrington when the waiter announced the arrival of a plain-clothes officer of 'G' Division of the Dublin Metropolitan Police. This man served him with a copy of his indictment for conspiracy on nineteen counts. They included conspiracy to prevent payment of rent, to prevent legal ejectments, to prevent the taking of farms from which a tenant had been evicted, and to create ill-will among Her Majesty's subjects. He accepted the indictment with a smile, and resumed his lunch. Thirteen others were named with him, including Egan, Harris, Boyton, Sheridan, Brennan, Biggar and Dillon. Interviewed by another American correspondent, for the *New York Herald Tribune*, the next day, he was asked what effect the prosecution was likely to have. He replied typically, 'If the movement had been in its infancy the result would undoubtedly be to stimulate it, but the organization is now in such a fair way to completion that I cannot think it is in need of the help which prosecutions usually afford such movements.'

He probably relished the indictment's definition of boycotting (not literally so named) as 'threatening to cut off and exclude from all social intercourse and communication, and from all intercourse and dealings in the way of buying, selling and other business, and to shun at all times as if affected with a loathsome disease . . . in contempt of the courts of the Queen . . .'

He attended a specially summoned meeting of the central Land League that afternoon. There he merely emphasized that the only thing that now mattered was 'organization', and he promised that it would not be his fault if before the next session of Parliament there was not a branch of the Land League in every parish of Ireland.

The *Freeman's Journal* called for a fund to be started at once for the defence of Parnell and the others accused.

He wrote on Thursday 4 November to Eltham, a formal letter of the sort that could be read by others: 'My dear Mrs O'Shea, – I take advantage of almost the first moment I have had to myself since leaving you to write a few hasty lines. And first I must again thank you for all your kindness, which made my stay at Eltham so happy and pleasant.'

Whether this refers to the all-important stay between 6 and 16 October in which he and Katie became lovers, or to the possible further visit between 26 and 30 October, cannot be established, though the tone is undoubtedly that of a thank-you letter for a stay of some significance. It was the sort of letter which would have made the visits seem quite in order with Aunt Ben, to whom he had not yet been introduced, particularly when he made the occasional polite reference to Captain O'Shea. Saying that he did not suppose he would get to London before the following Thursday, 11 November, he added, 'but [I] trust to be more fortunate in seeing Captain O'Shea then than the last time.'

It is uncertain whether Willie was at that moment at Eltham or still abroad. In either case, such phrases might prove helpful not only with Aunt Ben but also, if necessary, with Willie himself. At the same time there was another practical and innocuous reason for saying such a thing: Willie's rating in his constituency had been suffering noticeably from his long absence.

We have seen that Willie's honeymoon period with his constituents, marked by the plaudits for his maiden speech, had not lasted long. It is true that a few weeks after that speech and before the dramatic development of events in the autumn he had attended a large successful land meeting at Milltown Malbay (on Sunday 5 September) at which activity of his on behalf of the county was seen to have paid off. He had been instrumental in helping to get a Bill through Parliament to enable a railway company to build a line in Co. Clare. It was just the sort of business enterprise he had entered politics to further, along with his own interests. When he rose to speak at this meeting he had actually been received with loud cheers and a cry of 'He brought us the railway.'

A letter praising him had been read from the other Member for the county. 'I desire it to be recognized by all', the O'Gorman Mahon had written, 'that to the zeal, energy and perseverance of your young member Captain O'Shea is the county indebted for the advantages that must inevitably accrue – He achieved the affair himself and . . . to him alone should be accorded the well-earned merit of this favourable issue.'

When Willie himself spoke that day he had made the right sort of noises, such as saying that the meeting was 'worthy of O'Connell' and asking 'is the husbandman getting the due reward of his labours?' – to which he duly answered, 'No.' But he had also struck an optimistic note in praise of the still relatively new Liberal Government, to the effect that 'there never was a House of Commons more ready and more willing to settle the [land] question equitably than the present House of Commons'. Gladstone had even written to thank him for what he said.

But as the Land League, with which the Clare Farmers' Club had amalgamated in June, spread its agitation, that sort of flattering optimism had turned sharply sour, and was no longer the sort of thing that recommended itself to his constituents.

As far as his Westminster record was concerned, his attendance on divisions in the House had been good – almost as good as Parnell's, in fact, though this itself had been half the figure for a few other Irish Members. Willie had also been present at four of the eight meetings of the party that had taken place. But it was how he was rated in Ireland that mattered. In local affairs, apart from the Clare railway, he had written a number of letters to the local magistrate at Cappagh on the coast of West Clare in an attempt to get a much-needed pier built there. But this, as a local newspaper put it, was 'in the first full flush of success just after the Captain's return' for the county. Now he seemed to have disappeared in pursuit of his private business interests abroad.

Katie, who had made clear to Parnell in the summer her concern that Willie should be secure in his political career, now had an additional reason for wanting to see him contented in it. And signs had been increasing in the constituency that all was not well for Willie there.

While Parnell had been with her at Eltham on Sunday 10 October, a small but significant incident had taken place at a public meeting at Ennistymon in Co. Clare to indicate that unless Willie reformed his ways he could hardly hope to hold on to his seat for long. Letters of apology for absence from the meeting were read from both county Members, but, whereas that from the O'Gorman Mahon was judged satisfactory, a brief one from Willie was received with disapproval amid loud cries of 'We don't want him for the County again!' Someone in the crowd called out, 'He doesn't care; he's got what he wanted. Is there anyone now to come up and say a word for him?' To which someone else replied, 'He's not worth it.' And indeed there was no one to speak for him.

Fortunately, however, Parnell himself was available to help. It is time to look for a moment at the nature of the love affair in which he was engaged, and at the state of mind of himself and of the other two people concerned.

Chapter 25

Parnell's own state of mind is probably the easiest to determine. The emotional initiative had come from him; he seems to have had few if any moral scruples about letting it do so. By upbringing and temperament he had long taken a confidently independent view of his own actions. What many saw in him as pride was something subtler and more attractive: a sense of quiet personal detachment which seldom needed to be asserted, an achieved independence of mind which at some level he may have equated with the independence still to be achieved of the country with which he felt identified by birth and ancestry. He was never a man ready to concede that what he had done was wrong. At the same time, all who knew him well commented that with the strength to be his own man went a singular gentleness and consideration of manner. It is likely that, in this phase of his life particularly, he would have felt as much at ease in any course of action on which he had decided, whether in private or in public life. The danger in such self-confidence was its failure to realize that other people might not always judge his actions in the same light as he did himself.

But what then about the feelings of Willie O'Shea and the extent of any conflict of feelings in Katie herself, unmistakably fond of her husband as she was? The principal sources from which answers to such questions can be attempted are threefold. The first is Katie's own book of memoirs, flawed as these are by inaccuracy and the romantic sense of vindication by hindsight. The second is the evidence of the divorce court in the case of *O'Shea* v. *O'Shea* in November 1890. The third, a most interesting supplement to Katie's memoirs, is a first-hand account of what she said about the triangular relationship many years before she wrote about it. This is based on conversations with her held in 1891 by a young Balliol undergraduate, Henry Harrison, who had given up his university career to help Parnell politically, and who, after Parnell's sudden death, had gone down to Brighton to give Katie what help he could.

The book in which Harrison published his account of these conversations has its own flaws. The chief one is that his own deep personal attachment to Parnell, and to his memory, made him on the whole uncritical of the story as she told it to him. In addition, he did not write it down until nearly forty years later, by which time not only may his own memory have softened but he had also long been familiar with her own account in her memoirs, though he was at special pains to discount much of this. Moreover, the unorthodoxy of his own personal life in the interval, in the course of which he had himself entered into an unconventional relationship and fathered an illegitimate child, may have inclined him to place in an uncritical, even elevated, light any serious irregular liaison condemned by the conventional criticism of the world.

The eventual impact on public life of Parnell and Katie O'Shea's affair as scandal makes it difficult to see it at this early stage for what it was: in itself not all that extraordinary an event. It is perhaps best placed in perspective at the start by a comment made by the poet and traveller Wilfrid Scawen Blunt, who had some acquaintance with all three people involved. 'There was', he wrote of Parnell, 'nothing in his relations with the lady as things went in the society in which he was bred, for special reprobation.'

It is useful to remember this when looking back to the later Victorian era from an age more than a hundred years later which can mistakenly see sexual promiscuity as an un-Victorian speciality of its own time.

Blunt went on, 'He was on the contrary, and compared with most young men, austere . . . Anyone with a knowledge of life will understand . . . what a domination this first serious passion of his life had come to exercise over him.' So much can certainly be read into the early letters.

Katie O'Shea's response had not been long in coming. Her sexual commitment to him may be assumed to have taken place by the time he returned to Dublin on 16 October and wrote her the letter beginning 'My own love'. Such commitment on her part cannot be seen as just a tactical move to ensure his support for Willie; she had him involved on Willie's behalf already. Moreover, the large number of letters and telegrams she was soon sending him suggests her own early deep involvement.

But how did she reconcile this involvement with her own real affection for Willie? Was she deceiving him or, as she was later to suggest, had Willie encouraged her to have such an affair in the hope of furthering his own prospects within the Home Rule Party? In spite of scrutiny of such questions for over a hundred years by historians and others, it is still not easy to answer them with complete certainty.

Frank Hugh O'Donnell, Parnell's sometime collaborator in obstruction but a later critic, who was himself not unworldly, on one occasion in the early 1880s walked with all three of them from Hyde Park to Pall Mall. He talked to Katie most of the time, finding her clever and handsome, with 'a delicacy of feature and softness of charm', and was 'struck by her clever conversation while a little bored with her persistent questioning'. Writing many years later, he was quite certain that Willie had then suspected nothing and that he was warmly attached to Parnell. What Willie could have been warmly attached to, of course, was the prospect for himself that went with being on such close terms with Parnell. In which case, whether he suspected nothing or acted as if he suspected nothing might have been hard to distinguish. Possibly at that stage he did not even let himself know. At least until July 1881, nothing seems to have disturbed the apparent equanimity with which he viewed his leader's friendship with his wife.

What did his wife tell Harrison about her husband's attitude to the affair at the beginning? There are two clear indications in what she said to him of the truth behind the impression she wished to convey of straightforward condonation.

'Did Captain O'Shea know?' he reports her as saying to him of the affair in general. 'Of course he knew. I do not mean that I or anybody else told him so in so many words except once . . . There was no bargain; there were no discussions; people do not talk of such things . . . He knew too, of course, that Mr Parnell was staying with me when he was not. How could he fail to know? Do you think it would have been possible to bind my children to secrecy? Would he not have heard it from the children when he saw them on Sundays? Or the servants, if he cared to ask?'

In other words, there was, at any rate at first, no direct condonation. That he did not discourage, and indeed encouraged, an association in the interest of his own career is beyond doubt, but he did not necessarily encourage an affair. It could be said realistically that he did not need to. Katie liked to imply that he had done so indirectly. Speaking to Harrison of an occasion presumably in 1881 when Parnell and Willie had been discussing politics together, presumably in London, she cites her husband as saying, 'Take him back with you to Eltham and make him all happy and comfortable for the night, and just get him to agree.' But although she added that his air and manner 'made his meaning unmistakable', it is clear that condonation, even then, was rather something she chose to interpret than something that Willie positively expressed. The distinction may be a fine one, but it can turn out to be of some political interest.

What Katie said to Harrison and still more what she wrote in her memoirs about her long affair with Parnell had understandably assumed in her own mind a profound dimension proportionate to the great romantic myths of people like Tristan and Isolde. But in the autumn of 1880 it may well not have been quite like this in her mind. In fact she made it clear to Harrison that there had been quarrels between herself and Parnell over the extent to which in this early stage she should openly commit herself to him. Parnell, Harrison reported on the basis of what she told him, 'would have greatly preferred to have taken her openly before the world and to have paid such price by way of penalty as the broken laws and the outraged conventions might exact'.

The significance of this is that it shows Parnell here prepared to give up his political life altogether for her – which is what the ensuing scandal would then undoubtedly have involved. It was a prospect he had already aired once in a letter and which he was to air again. Because her will prevailed in the quarrel, the scandal had to wait ten years, when it broke with very different results. But the quarrel disclosed that what, up to this point, had been Parnell's passionate if often imprecise romance with Irish nationalism was ready to take second place in his mind to his romance with her. It also disclosed that, however she was to write about her own romance later, there were ties with Willie – partly financial but also partly emotional – that she was not at first prepared to give up for Parnell. Personal emotions often fail to run a very coherent or easily traceable course; but events would soon lock her and Parnell into attitudes for which the separate concerns of each – Irish nationalism in his case, fondness for Willie in hers – would need to be adjusted to their overwhelming tie to each other.

Harrison's further recollection of what Katie told him in 1891 was that 'sex love' between herself and Willie was 'long-since dead' when she met Parnell. But it is clear from what she further told him that sexual desire at least on Willie's part was not dead. Harrison recollected that she said she 'regarded any attempt to resurrect it [sex love] with definite repugnance. She did not believe in its reality on his side.' In other words, there were still such attempts, and, on his side, the appearance of 'reality'.

An occasional passage in some of Parnell's letters to her in following years seems to reflect an awareness of this, and there is evidence from both before and at the time of the divorce court to suggest that she may from time to time have surrendered to Willie's attempts at reality, and at least one suggestion from elsewhere that she did so quite purposefully. How much the possibility may have troubled Parnell is not easy to say, though in his letters it is mainly feelings of concern on her account that seem aroused. In his eyes, after all, it was she who had led him to think of himself as her 'own husband', and he was soon characteristically to be signing himself as such.

To what extent anyway did she and Parnell 'talk of such things'? At the time of the quarrel they must have done so to some extent. Given the retrospective emphasis in her memoir about the way she and Willie had grown apart, she would certainly have eased Parnell's conscience by emphasizing that sense of separation to him. She told Harrison that she did just that: 'He had taken my word for it that I was free.' Willie's separate apartment in London would have lent the notion plausibility.

On the other hand, her Aunt Ben, who was paying both for Willie's apartment and for Wonersh Lodge at Eltham as a family home, certainly did not interpret the arrangement as an accommodated separation. She was able to find the marriage openly respectable, even though occasional 'slanders' on Katie did reach her ears. Indeed, the conventional moral views on marriage held by Aunt Ben, who was now eighty-seven and on whom such very considerable financial expectations for the whole O'Shea family depended, were an all-important complicating factor in the delicate situation.

Such then was the emotional and material set of circumstances from within which Parnell was now to conduct his political life. And from it some benefit for Willie was soon forthcoming.

In his letter of 4 November in which he talked of returning to England the following week, Parnell made only a passing jocular reference to the Government prosecution: 'The thunderbolt, as you will have seen, has at last fallen, and we are in the midst of loyal preparations of a most appalling character.'

He was due at his meeting at Athlone on Sunday 7 November, but passing through Dublin on his way there the day before, he found time to write to her formally again: 'You can have very little idea how dreadfully disappointed I felt on arriving here this evening not to find a letter from either you or Captain O'Shea.' He had been hoping for a reply to his own last letter and a further telegram.

At Athlone itself, where he arrived in the field at about 2.00 p.m. on the Sunday, he delivered a particularly rousing, confident and defiant speech to respond to the impending prosecution. It was as if his mind were wholly concentrated on the great crisis which seemed at last about to break. 'I want to see every city in Ireland organized and pitted against this intimidating Government. When that is done they will see the uselessness of reverting to the old policy of repression and coercion.'

There could be no doubt that the hearts of his audience were with him. 'He is a grand man!' cried a voice from the crowd. 'The best in the world!' cried another.

It was then that he had gone on to ask them to show themselves heirs to the determination of their fathers and to undo the conquest of seven hundred years.

But that it was not only the Government against which he was pitted was demonstrated by a dramatic occurrence just before he spoke. As the Chairman and speakers assembled on the platform, decorated as usual with banners, streamers and evergreens, the whole centre of the structure suddenly collapsed with a loud crash. Most of those standing were thrown to the ground, including O'Kelly, who was accompanying Parnell. But Parnell himself, as the *Freeman's Journal* correspondent reported, 'had the good luck to step back to a safe position just as the woodwork gave way'. He and O'Kelly, examining the structure afterwards, found that one of its principal supports had been deliberately sawn through. It was the work of the same group of orthodox Fenians who, disapproving always of the Land League's parliamentary connections as subversive of the true national cause, had torn his trousers at Enniscorthy in the spring and so brusquely ejected some of his companions from the triumphal carriage on his visit to Cork the month before. Was there, as they dogmatically suspected, inevitable disaster for that cause in following a man who played for it with cards, including the constitutional card, so close to his chest?

When, a week before the Athlone meeting, he had spoken in response to his award of the freedom of the city of Limerick, he had given some indication of the way he now intended to proceed. Having repeated that in May he had had 'very great doubts' about accepting the nomination for chairmanship of the party, 'a position that requires great moderation, skill and experience', and having stated that he was not one of those who believed in the permanence of an Irish party in the House of Commons, he had made what seemed like another specific commitment to future tactics: 'if we fail after a reasonable time and after having been enabled to use those methods which we desire . . . if we fail by Parliamentary action in Westminster in obtaining the restoration of our Irish Parliament, I should consider it my duty to return to my countrymen to consult with them as to the action which we ought to take and to decide whether the representatives of Ireland ought any longer to continue participating in the sham of Parliamentary Government so far as Ireland is concerned'.

With the Government prosecution now officially hanging over him and other prominent members of the Land League, tactics for a more immediate eventuality than the refusal of an Irish parliament needed to be considered. What was to be the response to a clamp-down on the Land League? Withdrawal from Westminster and the setting up in Ireland of an alternative assembly had been a move proposed in the days of O'Connell. It had the advantage of sidestepping the constitutional process without commitment, at least in the first stage, to insurrection. At the same time, in the heady climate of late 1880, committal to any specific tactic in advance could seem unnecessary, even unwise, for someone of Parnell's pragmatic skill.

He had by now established an almost mythical reputation with the Irish people, creating a sense of confidence that whatever way he decided to work things out would be for the best. For all his temperamental coolness, he cannot have been wholly unaffected by such a mood. At meetings all over Ireland, often in places where he had never been, banners carrying his portrait and bearing slogans exalting him, accompanied by simple doggerel praising his name, proclaimed his unique powers, and orators who knew him personally spoke of his magic spell to tens of thousands of people who would never set eyes on him. Boyton, speaking elsewhere on the day on which Parnell told Athlone that organization itself would make the Government abandon its old policy of coercion, announced that he had come 'to represent your illustrious leader Charles Stewart Parnell who is worthy of all the trust you reposed in him. Parnell', he said, 'is the first man this century the intelligent British Government has feared. He has more means at his back than the shouts of the people of Ireland. He has at his back a reserve the British Government little dream of.'

Here a voice from the crowd interjected, 'The Irish Americans!'

But it was left more mysterious than that.

'A reserve', continued Boyton, 'that will one day make itself felt, for Parnell has not yet shaken his stick at the British Government.'

Exactly how the stick would be shaken when the moment came, and how the moment itself would be recognized, could still be left open. But for how much longer? And there were other concerns. In a few days after returning from Athlone, Parnell embarked on a whole new phase of the Land League campaign, the trickiest as far as the nationalist aspect of the campaign was concerned: its inauguration in Ulster. At the same time he was thinking about Eltham.

From Avondale, to which he returned from Athlone on Monday 8

November before setting out for Ulster, he formally sent back to 'My dear Mrs O'Shea' some keys he had taken with him by mistake on his previous visit. He was already planning to follow them himself almost immediately.

On Tuesday 9 November he launched the first major Land League meeting in Ulster, at Belleek on the borders of Co. Fermanagh and Co. Donegal. He addressed the special difficulties in that province head on from the start. Although he was a Protestant, he said, 'the Land League is not a sectarian movement and therefore the platform of land for the people is one on which all creeds and classes of Irishmen may unite . . . I am convinced that the day is not far distant when orange and green being united together we shall see the dreams of every patriot realized.'

In Ulster an appeal to Irish nationalism needed to be muted with regard to that part of the audience likely to be Protestant. At Belleek, where there were many Catholics, traditional national rhetoric could certainly count for something in support of the land agitation. But in Ulster generally, if the Land League were to make headway, it was the appeal to self-interest in the fight against the landlords which had to be stressed; many rents there, after the recent bad times, were regarded as oppressive. 'Combine and organize to protect yourselves against the land conspiracy which has condemned this country to poverty and degradation,' was how Parnell concluded at Belleek. This was in general the safer bet in the province.

Accompanied by Dillon and O'Kelly he moved on the same day to Ballyshannon, which, also predominantly Catholic, welcomed them with a torchlight procession. But on their way back to Dublin next day they stopped off for a meeting of some five thousand people in Enniskillen in Co. Fermanagh – 'Protestant and loyal Fermanagh' as Parnell tactfully put it. He trimmed his appeal appropriately.

He pointed out that he himself was a Protestant who was not afraid to live among a majority of Catholics, and said that, if he were, he would rather leave the country for good than ask a minority in the country to help him against the majority. Equally he told Catholics that they ought not to fear their Protestant fellow-countrymen. It was the class unity of the two different creeds that was emphasized rather than their shared nationality.

'We wish', he said, 'to organize the tenantry of Ireland regardless of all creeds. So that if the tenant farmer in the South is struck down by an unjust landlord, the tenant farmer in the North shall be ready to protect him. And if on the other hand the tenant in the North is injured the tenant in the South may also be ready to protect him . . . We ask you, the Protestants and Catholics of the North, to join hand in hand with us and help make an unbroken line from Cork to Belfast and to obtain for the people of Ireland their own land.'

This use of the word 'land' in a double sense was of particular value in the North. There was no mention here of the political status of the land in question, no word about 'independence', legislative or otherwise, and no wider invocation of national feeling.

'We preach the principle that the land of the country should belong to the people of the country' was the ambiguous way the full Land League cause could most conveniently be put in Ulster, where Orangemen themselves were demanding the 'three Fs' – fair rents, fixity of tenure and free sale.

The *Freeman's Journal* reported that Parnell had been received at Enniskillen with prolonged cheering. The *Cork Examiner* noted only that 'the gentlemen were respectfully received, but it can hardly be said there was great enthusiasm'.

No one doubted that Parnell's heart was in what he was doing. Yet the night he got back to Dublin, on 11 November, he wrote to Katie O'Shea:

My dearest Love, – I have made all arrangements to be in London on Saturday morning, and shall call at Keppel Street for a letter from you. It is quite impossible for me to tell you just how very much you have changed my life, what a small interest I take in what is going on about me, and how I detest everything which has happened during the last few days to keep me away from you – I think of you always, and you must never believe there is to be any 'fading'.

He added that he did not want her to send him any more 'artificial letters'; he wanted as much of her as she could put into words.

There was a postscript to this letter saying that telegrams had been sent both to her and to Willie ('W.') which were 'by no means strictly accurate'. The probability here is that they gave information about a journey other than the one he was about to undertake. If so they were probably designed to deceive not Captain O'Shea but the Government, which with some reason was suspected of keeping a watch on Parnell's movements and of using certain powers under the law to open and read letters and telegrams in transit.

Whether or not the Government agents were duped, people in Ireland certainly were, for he now disappeared from the political scene in Ireland altogether for the better part of three weeks. He spent it at Eltham with Katie O'Shea.

Some anxiety over the impending trial would have added intensity to their feelings for each other at this time. And there was a further apparent cause for tension: for the first time since they had become lovers, Willie was there too.

The evidence for this comes from the divorce court hearing ten years later. One of Katie's servants, Jane Lenister, there gave evidence that 'Captain O'Shea was there the whole time that Mr Parnell stayed at Wonersh Lodge in November or December 1880.' There is no reason to doubt that she was speaking the truth. Parnell stayed at Eltham only once in November 1880, on this occasion, between the 13th and the 30th. His only stay in December was to be at Christmas, when, as we shall see, Willie was, by his own contemporary testimony, in Madrid. So there the three of them must have been together, for nearly three weeks, on this visit in November.

Katie's cross-petition put into court in the divorce case ten years later began, 'The Petitioner constantly connived at and was accessory to the said alleged adultery from the autumn of 1880.' But was it as simple as this? What can the atmosphere have been like?

Certainly she gives no hint in her memoirs of how Willie's presence affected the stay, for she makes no mention of it at all. Her account is merely about the domestic happiness which she and Parnell were now beginning to enjoy together. Only in the opening line of the relevant chapter does she seem to confirm her servant, Jane Lenister's, later evidence. 'In the autumn of 1880', she writes, 'Mr Parnell came to stay with us at Eltham.' 'Us' could perhaps mean just the children or even the servants, but it certainly does not exclude the possibility of Willie's presence. It is an instance of the disingenuousness of much of her book, which withholds any aspect of the triangular relationship detrimental to the dignified romantic picture she wished to present.

Why, if, as she told Harrison, Willie tacitly accepted that Parnell was her lover, could she not refer to Willie's being there? Perhaps because in these early circumstances the possibility that she was deceiving her husband might look a little too likely. In fact, her account of how ill and exhausted their guest was on this visit may relate to the way she let it seem plausible to Willie that she was just looking after Parnell platonically in the interest of all three of them. But if so, she was deceiving him. And there is something else besides the deceit which she may have wished to conceal.

With the affair, in 1880, so recent, she cannot then have known how lasting or profound it was to be. Parnell's own insistence that he was prepared to sacrifice everything for it can hardly yet have developed. An early detail which reminded her that in this phase it might have been a mere surreptitious affair, however passionate, hardly fitted in with the romantic saga and role in it for herself she was concerned to portray in her book. She had therefore either conveniently forgotten Willie's presence or decided to leave it out.

What, though, of Willie? He was very much what was known as 'a man of the world'. For all Parnell's invalid status, would not some sixth sense over a period of many days have suggested to him that 'something was going on' between his wife and the leader of the party? It is not improbable that he would have heard of Parnell's October visit from one of his three children or even the servants. But it may be useful simply to remember the walk Frank Hugh O'Donnell took with the three of them early in the 1880s, when Willie either did not suspect anything or at least very convincingly did not appear to suspect anything, and leave it at that.

What must clearly have happened in the course of this triangular stay in November was some constructive conversation on the subject of Willie's political welfare in his constituency. He had to go abroad again on business almost immediately afterwards, but when he returned a month later, for the opening of the new parliamentary session in January, it was to be with a much more intelligent approach to the careerist opportunities offered by contemporary politics – one which was to distinguish him from other Whiggish Home Rulers with whom he had previously been too easily associated.

As for Katie, her memory of the visit was quite simply one of connubial bliss, but with her lover rather than her husband, and her account certainly conveys something of what their life was like when they were together at Eltham.

Characteristic of the many vague inaccuracies in the book is her remark that 'in the autumn of 1880' Parnell was at Eltham and 'only going to Dublin as occasion required'. Though this may have been suggested by a memory of his failure to go to Roscommon and Longford when due on the previous visit, it predates a casualness towards events in Ireland which was not to develop generally until later. More plausible for this occasion is her other implication that he came to her to enjoy a rest with someone with whom he was in love, to relax from the strenuous political activity, travel and speech-making to which he had been devoting his energies in Ireland. He had had three weeks of speeches at Longford, Roscommon,

Galway, Tipperary, Limerick, Athlone and in Ulster, quite apart from Land League business in Dublin and natural concern about the outcome of the forthcoming prosecution. All this may well have accounted for the exhausted daytime sleeps she describes him as falling into ('from sheer weakness on the sofa before the fire'), and for his need for a process of 'building-up', though to say as she does that he was near death's door seems an exaggeration and may again reflect the necessary invalid front.

Perhaps it was on this visit that he complained of a sore throat which, he only reluctantly confessed, he thought might be caused by her overwatering of house-plants or, another time, even by a green carpet. The detail certainly tells something about an obsessional quality in his character. He became, she says, so obsessive about the carpet that a part of it had to be sent to London for a chemical analysis before it could be pronounced harmless. Whether this actually took place in the autumn of 1880 as she implies (some events she relates as having done so certainly did not) is immaterial: the important thing is that such intimate glimpses into his personal character are to be found almost nowhere else. Another foible related by her seems at first so grotesquely improbable as to be a scurrilous interpolation of later enemies. This is the intense fixation of dislike in his mind for the colour green, that national colour which bedecked the banners and triumphal arches of all his meetings and was so proudly worn by enthusiastic supporters. But this can only be accepted as authentic when testified to by Katie O'Shea, who knew him as no one else ever did, and moreover was amply confirmed by political colleagues who knew him too. Whatever her failings in chronology, it is her revelation of personal insights into the childlike complexities of this apparently self-sufficient man which, with the letters she prints, give her memoirs their special value.

Her story of a drive with him further into Kent that autumn and an encounter with Irish hop-pickers who recognized him with cries of 'The Chief! The Chief!' seems like an inaccurate predating of an occasion in another year. If Irish journalists actually expecting him at Longford the previous month could not recognize him when they saw him with his beard shaved off, it seems unlikely that Irish families certainly not expecting him among the alien hop-fields of Kent would have done so that same autumn. Yet her account, whenever it should apply, gives a touchingly human picture of him, as he 'lifted his cap with that grave, aloof smile of his' and apologized for not feeling up to making the speech they called for from him, while showing his concern for the children scrambling dangerously under the horses' legs.

What did they talk about together? Probably not much about detailed party politics at this stage, for her limited personal role in this was only to come later; but, with Willie there, inevitably about Willie's difficulties with his constituency, about the prospects for the coming trial, and also about the evictions. She describes Parnell during this period (and her chronology here may well be right) often sitting 'far into the night at Eltham speaking in that low, broken monotone, that with him always betokened intense feeling strongly held in check' of the cruelties of the evictions. She has him calculating 'afterwards' that there had been fifty thousand evictions in Ireland, but the span of time to which the figure refers is not clear. Official figures show that there were just over two thousand families, or ten thousand people, evicted in 1880 by the end of the year, of whom some 10 per cent were readmitted as 'caretakers'. Significantly, evictions had dropped sharply in the autumn to less than a quarter of what they had been for the previous six months of the year – a change undoubtedly brought about by the effectiveness of the Land League's 'organization' – but they were still running at an average rate of more than one a day, and there is no reason to doubt her when she says that the tales of them made her heart sick.

In her account over ten years of the intimacy of their life together, it is often not possible to say which detail applies to which period. But it seems clear from the fact that he was writing to her as 'My dearest Wife' before the end of 1880 that the domestic nature of their relationship was quite soon in place. Avondale too may already have been one of the things they talked about in private, and she recalls their discussion of 'his stone quarries at Arklow, his saw-mills, etc. . . . what Kerr, his Irish agent, was doing at Avondale, [and] some of his hobbies at home'. The latter were to include prospecting for gold in the Wicklow hills.

Whether or not either of them could ever seriously have thought that they might one day be able to share the home in Ireland he loved so much is impossible to tell. They were to become so close that they must at times have wished for this. And yet the impossibility of them living together in a Catholic Ireland of which he was the political leader, while Willie was alive, must always have been painfully clear. And Willie was very much alive, not just in those weeks at Eltham in November 1880 but for a foreseeable future in which Katie's fondness for him and care for his interests were an integral part.

Parnell seems to have shown little concern for the curiosity which his inscrutable disappearances might arouse among his colleagues. Katie gives one glimpse of his attitude which may be relevant to this period at the end of 1880 and possibly account for his failure to turn up at Roscommon in October. It happened more than once, she said, that he was due and ready to leave Eltham for a meeting in Ireland when at the last moment he would decide after all not to go but throw himself into a chair and spend the evening opposite her talking and 'always watching me with that intent, considering gaze that was my bewilderment and my joy'.

She would want him to telegraph or at least write an apology or some excuse. 'Never explain, never apologize,' he would reply, adding – though this comment suggests a relevance to later years only – 'I could never keep my rabble together if I were not above the human weakness of apology.'

In this early crucial phase of both the liaison and the political battle for Ireland which one way or another was to occupy him for the rest of his life, he once again demonstrated that what was important for him was important just because he had decided that it was to be so. This applied equally to his adoption of the cause of Irish independence and to his love for Katie O'Shea. Both were in the keeping of a single will.

But the question cannot help arising: what, if anything, had he told, and to whom, about these sudden disappearances? What, for instance, had Dillon been told in explanation of his need to deputize for his leader at the last moment in Cork? And what went on in the minds of Commins and Byrne when they had to appear without Parnell, so eagerly expected, at Roscommon and without being able to account for his absence? What were the assurances about unavoidable business which were unquestioningly accepted when he did turn up the following week? Who formulated them, and how much of the real truth did this person know? From available accounts it looks as if the O'Shea liaison itself was not suspected until February 1881, though the evidence concerning even that date is not quite certain. What seems certain is that someone then had to do some covering-up for his movements. But how much did they know, and who was it? If Parnell made anyone a full confidant about his personal life at all at this stage, it could have been his friend O'Kelly, or possibly Finegan, but on balance perhaps even these seem unlikely: the only full confidant Parnell ever had, apart from Katie O'Shea, was himself.

Chapter 26

The *Freeman's Journal* of Thursday 2 December 'understood' that Parnell had 'passed through' London on his way to Dublin the night before. And on that day he wrote from Dublin to 'My dear Mrs O'Shea' to tell her that he had caught the train at Euston 'with just ten minutes to spare'. 'I need not tell you', he added, 'how much I regretted leaving Eltham so suddenly . . . My stay with you has been so pleasant and charming that I was almost beginning to forget my other duties . . . Trusting to see you again next week on my way to Paris.'

This last phrase could be a reference to some proposed future meeting with Willie there, but it could equally be used to provide plausible justification for further trips across the Irish Sea, should anyone find the letter and read it. Parnell after all had a married sister living in Paris.

This was a formal open letter. But there was also a postscript: 'I have been exceedingly anxious all day at not receiving your promised telegram to hear how you got home.'

Home from where? Katie cannot have gone with him to Euston, or he would not have told her that he had caught the train with only ten minutes to spare. Perhaps they had been together for a time beforehand at Keppel Street, an eventuality to which she never makes any reference in her memoirs. But why was he 'exceedingly anxious'? It was about six weeks since they had first become lovers, and this could possibly have had something to do with it. Did Katie perhaps think she might be pregnant? Or was it straightforward anxiety about Willie? Similar unresolved uncertainties continue to haunt the story of the triangle for many years.

Parnell wrote to her, again quite formally, two days later to say how pleased he had been to get letters (*sic*) from her in the interval: 'to say the truth,' he wrote, 'I have been quite homesick since leaving Eltham, and news from you seems like news from home.' He added that 'Since writing Captain O'Shea it does not look as if I could get further away from Ireland than London, as Paris is inconvenient from its distance.'

It is difficult to see why there should have been any need to see Willie in Paris, unless simply in response to a friendly invitation. But it certainly seems as if some sort of political accommodation to involve Willie more closely with the party had been effected between them in the course of the long November stay. In a few days' time he was asking Katie to pass on the message to 'Captain O'Shea' that a meeting of Irish Members preliminary to the coming parliamentary session would be held in Dublin on 4 January.

The 'homesick' letter had been written in Dublin on his way to Kilkenny, where he was to spend the night before moving on to Waterford for his first big public meeting since his return. He had some reassuring news for her about the coming trial. The defendants (or, 'traversers' – those who were 'traversing' or denying in plea the Government's allegations) had requested a postponement; the court had refused this, but this, he now said, did not really matter because it turned out that they did not have to attend the proceedings unless specifically directed to do so. Moreover, from an assessment of the names on the panel from which the jury was to be chosen, it looked as if there was every chance of the jury being likely to disagree on its verdict, though this could not be said for certain.

Arriving at Kilkenny at the end of the day on which he had written this letter, he found only a small crowd on the platform as there had been no more than a rumour that he might be stopping there for the night on his way to Waterford. And those that were there, not having seen him lately, were in for the same sort of surprise as had struck the waiting crowd at Longford the month before. The *Freeman's Journal* reported, 'his appearance as regards his whiskers being changed tended to mystify'. Next morning he caught a special train, with two engines decorated with laurels and green flags, which had been hired to take people from other parts of Ireland to the Waterford meeting. It was said to be the longest train that had ever left Kilkenny. As it eventually drew into Waterford, it was as if Parnell had never been away.

In fact it was his first visit to Waterford.

A great cheering crowd waited for him at the station, and on the platform itself stood the Mayor and Corporation to welcome him with a formal address which, after noting 'the numerous sacrifices you have made in the cause of our country' and thanking him for his efforts in America, expressed the hope that his efforts to raise Ireland to her true position would soon be crowned with success.

A procession was then formed to escort him, with bands playing national airs, through streets full of triumphal arches and past shipping in the harbour decorated with bunting and green emblems, to a field outside the town where what was reported as one of the largest crowds ever assembled for such meetings was waiting for him.

When the prolonged cheering and waving of hats had died down, he began by saying that he thought it was indeed 'the largest land meeting yet held in Ireland' and used this thought effectively to sweep away at once any lingering questions there might possibly have been in people's minds about his recent silence.

'I have been absent from the country for three weeks,' he said, 'and during that three weeks this great movement has made more progress, has accumulated more force, than during the eighteen months of its existence.' And the great crowd laughed and cheered as he added, 'Nobody can henceforth charge me with having been the cause of this movement.'

He was in exuberantly confident mood. There is no trace of that sense of conflict between political and personal interest he had expressed in his letter to Katie of 11 November and even hinted at in his two letters on return. One might have expected the agreeable domesticity of this last stay to have reinforced the unease, particularly if Willie had also been in evidence. But it was as if the happiness of the stay and of the love affair and the rest from politics had given his political attack new vigour.

Partly this must have been a reflection of his growing confidence about the result of the coming trial. The prosecutions, he told the Waterford crowds, were undertaken by a Government which knew that it was beaten, to pass away the time, to postpone the moment when its disgrace and defeat would be revealed to the world. As to the charge of encouraging assassination which was being consistently levied against the Land League by its opponents, he simply emphasized that it was effective organization along Land League lines alone 'that would prevent assassination and other things in the country more than any British law ever did'.

But he went on to commit himself perhaps more dangerously than he realized to a tactical position which could impair future room for manœuvre.

It seemed certain that if the Government were to start a new coercive policy against the Land League, it would try to compensate with a measure of land reform designed to appeal to rank-and-file Land League supporters. Some intervention to control rent, inevitably a popular move, was not beyond possibility. But Parnell was now as intransigent as he had ever been against the acceptability of anything less than outright peasant proprietorship. His whole tone was one of uncompromising national self-reliance. What was the use, he asked, given the Whiggish element in the Liberal Party and the need anyway to get every Bill through the Lords, what was the use of expecting a really satisfactory measure of land reform through Parliament in the coming session?

'No use,' came an obliging voice from the crowd.

He went on to ask what was the use of expecting from such a Parliament a rent revaluation that would not be enormously biased in favour of the landlord. This, he said, was why he had always been against the 'three Fs', for the fairness of a fair rent would be determined by a Government tribunal. As to the exact terms on which the peasant proprietorship for which they stood would be established, 'Let me leave to the enemy the offer of compromise, let the first offer of compromise come from them, for they are the beleaguered and isolated garrison and I warn them that if they waste too much time and delay too long to settle with the enemy who is now at the gate, the day will soon come when they will find that their power of proposing, of obtaining any compromise has been taken away from them.'

Peasant proprietorship was, in his mind, only one goal on the way to the nobler, larger one of Irish nationality. First stressing that those farmers who were obtaining abatements of rent should pass on some of the benefit by giving employment to the labourers during the coming winter, he concluded by saying that, if organized branches of the Land League were pushed on in every parish in Ireland, he promised that 'before a very long time has elapsed – perhaps much sooner than any of us expect now – the people of Ireland will be enabled to enter for the first time on the path of prosperity and national independence'.

If any of his audience were left wondering about the precise constitutional nature of this national independence and what it might involve them in, he gave as clear an answer as he ever had when he spoke that same evening at the Lord Mayor's banquet in Waterford Town Hall, whose walls proclaimed 'God Save Ireland', 'Parnell for Ever' and 'Parnell: Ireland's Hope and Trust'.

'It is impossible', he said, 'in these days of enlightened public opinion to continue the governing of this country against the will of the majority of the people ... who stand to-day in the same position as our ancestors stood. We declare that it is the duty of every Irishman to free his country if he can ... we will work by constitutional means so long as it suits us. We refuse to plunge this country into the horrors of civil war when she has not a chance, but ... I ask any true Irishman, whether he be priest or layman, whether he would not consider it the first duty of an Irishman to do what he could to enable his country to take her place among the nations of the world. If it could be shown to him that there was a fair prospect of success from the sacrifice, I ask my reverend and lay friends whether they would not consider it their highest duty to give their lives for the country that gave them birth. I call for no vain, no useless sacrifice. I don't wish to be misunderstood for a moment. Our present path is within the line of the Constitution. England has given us that Constitution for her purposes. We will use it for ours, and if I ever, or if anybody over whom I have any influence, calls upon the people of Ireland to go beyond the lines of that Constitution, we should do so openly and above board.'

Perhaps he was remembering for a moment that an alderman who had introduced him at the afternoon meeting had referred to him as 'General Parnell'.

'But,' he concluded, 'for the present, taking our stand within the limits of the Constitution, relying upon organized Parliamentary action, relying upon organized national action at home, I believe that we have sufficient forces to achieve our ends . . .'

Was he just saying this sort of thing, as can be argued, to ensure as much neo-Fenian support in Ireland as possible and, in particular, the all-important financial support of nationalists in the United States? Certainly the useful political effect of such words cannot have been absent from his mind. But to put them down solely to tactics seems a misjudgment of his late-1880 mood, the back-projection of a more considered attitude of later years. The independent state of mind in which he had first committed his personality to politics had, psychologically, been revolutionary, and in these exciting days of the Land League a misty but potentially revolution-ary prospect was undoubtedly in view. For those in the vanguard for the cause of Irish nationality a glimpse of bright morning lay ahead, and he was happy to be leading them into it.

Next day he received the freedom of the city of Waterford which had only been so narrowly voted him some weeks before. Perhaps aware of this, he struck a steadier note in his acceptance speech.

'I may perhaps be too sanguine in my estimate,' he said, 'but I feel that . . . if we can organize the people and maintain the independence of the party in the House of Commons . . . in five or six years' time at the outside we shall have broken the power of the English government.' The London *Times* that week had no doubt what his scarcely concealed aim was: 'The absolute separation of one island from the other'.

He stayed on that night in Waterford, and on the following day, 7 December, he was lent a horse by one of his local MPs and took the field with the Curraghmore hunt, assimilating at once easily enough into his old Ascendancy background. The meet was fixed for 11.00 a.m., but an hour before a crowd had collected outside his hotel, hoping to see him in his red coat. When he emerged, they were disappointed to find that he was dressed much as usual, except for a pair of gaiters. But once in the field he won respect even from the most die-hard of political opponents, incidentally seeming to give the lie to Katie's later recollection that he had been 'at death's door' only a few weeks before. He was the first to jump one particularly daunting stone ditch of which most others fought shy. Lord Waterford jumped it close behind him, calling out 'Good man!' as they both landed.

'It's the horse, my Lord, that is good,' Parnell replied.

'No doubt, but I like a little pluck in the man who is mounted on a good horse and you have shown that to-day, sir.'

Or so at least the *Freeman's Journal* reported the conversation, and, authentic or not, it was evidence of the sort of spirit which that middle-class nationalist paper was happy to attribute to him.

Later in the four and a half mile run, it further reported, 'always in the van was to be seen the graceful figure of Mr Parnell who led nearly the whole way and would have been awarded the brush if the fox hadn't gone down a sewer and escaped'. The paper was pleased to note that he had displayed 'the same indomitable energy and courage in the hunting field as in Parliament'.

By Thursday 9 December he was back at Avondale and writing to Katie to say that he hoped to be able to start for London on the following Sunday and to go down to see her at Eltham on the Monday. He said he was not going to attend any more meetings until after the opening of Parliament, 'as everything now can go on without me'.

This was, at least temporarily, a reasonable assessment. On the same Sunday as he had spoken at Waterford, Dillon and Boyton had been at a great meeting at Fethard in Co. Tipperary, a county in which there were now fifty branches of the Land League and where 85 per cent of the landlords were said to have accepted the old Griffith's valuation as the basis for rent. A small army of horse and foot marched into the meeting from the surrounding neighbourhood. Its contingents were headed by clergy and carried flags which bore Parnell's portrait. Total respectability was conferred on the meeting by the presence in the chair of the Archdeacon of Fethard himself. He heard Dillon tell of the 'immense advance' the Land League had made in the previous month (for most of which Parnell, of course, had been away) and declare that if the Land League were suppressed the house of every landlord would be built over a volcano and 'he cannot tell the hour when the volcano may burst and sweep him and all belonging to him away to a far worse fate than the Land League had intended for him'.

'To hell!' came a voice from the crowd.

Davitt on the same day at Mitchelstown poured scorn on any 'lame measure' that might be about to come from the Government in the form of a Land Bill granting the three Fs. These, he said, could fairly be interpreted as promising 'fear, feud and failure . . . security of rent and comfort to the landlord with assurance of poverty and rags to the tenant'. But such rhetoric obscured the likelihood that fair rents – provided they were fair – fixity of tenure and free sale would seem satisfactory enough to most tenants.

Meanwhile Parnell was trying to complete arrangements to spend Christmas at Eltham. After getting back to Waterford on 8 December he had told Katie that he would probably be able to start for London on Sunday the 12th and see her the next day. But instead he had to write to her on the 12th to tell her that the jury panel for the trial was about to be struck and that he must be there to give final directions for conduct of the defence. He would now leave on the Monday evening for London, he said. But this he could not do either, for, as he wrote again to tell her in another formal letter, the trial of Tim Healy for allegedly threatening a 'land-grabber' with violence was due to be heard on Thursday 16 December in Cork, and he would have to be present in his own constituency for that. The case was of the utmost importance as the first of such State trials; he clearly thought that his presence there would make an acquittal more likely. In the meantime he changed the date of the pre-session meeting of the party, bringing it forward from 4 January to 27 December. Willie was informed.

But Healy's trial was unexpectedly brought forward by a day. A wire was sent to Parnell asking him to come a day earlier. Parnell wired back to say that he would be there by the Wednesday afternoon. But he was not there to witness Healy's acquittal, which took place during the day. The incident is chiefly interesting because it sheds some light on what people thought was happening when Parnell disappeared. The *Freeman's Journal* said that he had 'postponed his visit to Paris in order to attend the trial'. Healy, speaking that evening to the crowd celebrating in Patrick Street outside his hotel, told them correctly that Parnell would have been there to celebrate too and thank his constituents had the Crown not brought the case forward by a day, but, he added, it would have been a pity to take him away 'from his other duties' when the fight had already been won.

By the weekend Parnell had gone to England dutifully but happily to spend Christmas at Eltham with the woman he now thought of as his wife.

Part II: 1881–1882

ELTHAM, DUBLIN, WESTMINSTER, PARIS, WESTMINSTER, ULSTER, AVONDALE, LEINSTER, MUNSTER, KILMAINHAM

Chapter 27

What we know for certain of this Christmas Parnell spent at Eltham is that, after staying for just over a week, he left for Ireland again on Boxing Day; also that he and Katie had a 'squabble' in the course of it, and that Willie was not there. Katie, in her memoirs, has a brief description of a Christmas which she suggests was this one, but she is confused because she has him at Eltham on New Year's Day when he was in fact in Ireland. But her account of him being worshipped by an excited new Irish cook from Co. Tipperary, who fell on her knees and kissed his hands, may apply to this Christmas of 1880, and it is probable that always at Christmas he tipped her staff 'generously'. His strangely ambiguous attitude to popularity in Ireland is revealed by his 'horror' at the cook's behaviour: he told Katie that he 'disliked it extremely', and that he had expected to be 'quite free from that sort of thing' in her house.

A feature which must have been common to every Christmas he spent at Eltham was the presence of Katie's three children, Gerard, Norah and Carmen. She never mentions his relationship with her children, though there is positive evidence that, as they grew up, both Gerard and Norah felt ill at ease about his association with their mother. Gerard was to be ready to give evidence against him in the divorce court ten years later, and Norah was never to view him with more than, as she put it, 'inimical toleration'.

That Parnell and Katie O'Shea's love for each other was strengthened by this last stay of 1880 is clear from the letters he wrote her very soon after his return to Dublin. Monday 27 December had been an important day, that of the rescheduled Home Rule Party meeting before the opening of Parliament on 6 January. At it he was unanimously elected 'leader', and Justin McCarthy was elected Vice-President. A unanimous decision was taken by the party to sit in opposition to any Government, including Gladstone's which refused Home Rule to Ireland.

Among the letters of apology for absence was one from Willie O'Shea, written from a Madrid address. He said that he greatly regretted the change of date for the meeting, since, having made his business arrangements on the calculation that the meeting would be held on 4 January, he was now unable to change them, particularly as they involved the presence in Madrid over Christmas of 'eminent counsel' from England. But his letter seemed to show something of the new mood Parnell had been able to induce in him. He hoped and believed, he said, that 'the absence of a unit will be of no importance owing to the unanimity with which I am sure the whole party must be inspired at the present crisis'. Whether he would now consider sitting with Parnell on the Opposition benches or whether that would be carrying unanimity too far was not to be known until Parliament met on 6 January. But it seems clear that thus far at least Parnell's influence had had effect.

On Parnell's journey in the middle of the day from the Dublin City Hall, where the meeting was being held, to his hotel, an enormous crowd which had gathered in Sackville Street took the horse from his cab and drew him there themselves. They repeated the exercise when he returned to the City Hall an hour later. That evening he wrote Katie a short formal note beginning, 'My dear Mrs O'Shea', saying he had been 'exceedingly anxious' at not getting the telegram she had promised to send to tell him how she had 'got home'. He trusted to hear next morning that it had been all right. The next day, from Morrison's Hotel, he wrote calling her 'My dearest Wife'.

It was the first day of the State trial in which he and the other thirteen Land League names were appearing, and he gave her excellent news about the composition of the jury. 'The jury sworn to-day', he wrote, 'cannot possibly convict us, and there is a very fair chance of an acquittal.' He did not think the Government would try to stop him attending the opening of Parliament but was not sure; he thought he would have to be 'prudent'. A postscript said that he had both wired and written to Willie in Madrid to explain that what he had said at the previous day's meeting about possibly not being in Parliament when it opened was 'intended to throw dust in eyes of Government' and should not be interpreted literally.

The postscript is further evidence of his consideration for Katie's concern for Willie's political career. Willie needed to be warned not to stay on in Madrid in the mistaken belief that there would be no real parliamentary action.

The most important sentence in the letter, however, may have been just before the end: 'I was immensely relieved by your letter this morning. You must take great care of yourself for my sake and your and my future.' This seems a curiously personal liberty for an otherwise formally addressed letter.

The second greatest love of Parnell's life, Avondale (built 1777), near Rathdrum, Co. Wicklow, in 'the garden of Ireland'.

Delia Parnell, Parnell's mother, daughter of the American naval hero Commodore Charles Stewart, son of an Ulster emigrant. He had 'whipped the British' in the war of 1812. She had her daughters presented at Queen Victoria's court.

Parnell at the age of six.   Parnell at the age of sixteen.

Parnell's favourite sister, Fanny, a beauty who wrote passionate Irish nationalist verse, and founded the Ladies' Land League in New York in 1880. Her sudden death in Bordentown, New Jersey, in 1882 deeply upset Parnell. (Courtesy of the National Library of Ireland.)

Parnell pointing the way to his constituents a month after his sudden death at the age of forty-five. (Courtesy of the National Library of Ireland.)

Parnell at twenty years of age, as he was at Magdalene College,
Cambridge.

Clare (1883–1909), daughter of Parnell and Mrs O'Shea. (Courtesy of the National Library of Ireland.)

Katharine ('Katie') (1884–1947), daughter of Parnell and Mrs O'Shea. (Courtesy of the Rev. J. V. F. Maunsell.)

Assheton Clare Bowyer-Lane Maunsell, Parnell's grandson through his daughter Clare, aged sixteen. He died in the British Army in India in 1934.

Parnell in late 1880 or early 1881 sh after he had cut off his beard, possibly at first to make himself less recognizable in England. (Courtesy of the Mansell Collection.)

Katharine (Katie) O'Shea, born Wood in 1845. Divorced by Captain Willie O'Shea in 1890, she married Parnell six months later in 1891. He had had this photograph with him in Kilmainham jail.

Parnell about to be arrested in his bedroom by Detective Superintendent John Mallon at Morrison's Hotel, Dublin, on the morning of 13 October 1881. (Courtesy of the Mary Evans Picture Library.)

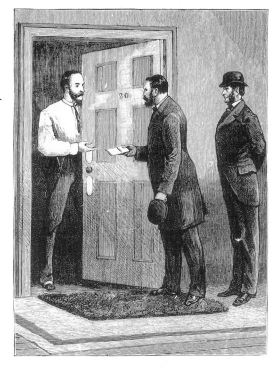

THE LAND WAR!
NO RENT!

NO LANDLORDS GRASSLAND

Tenant Farmers, now is the time. Now is the hour. You proved false to the first call made upon you. REDEEM YOUR CHARACTER NOW.

NO RENT

UNTIL THE SUSPECTS ARE RELEASED.

The man who pays Rent (whether an abatement is offered or not) while PARNELL, DILLON &c., are in Jail, will be looked upon as a Traitor to his Country and a disgrace to his class.

No RENT,   No Compromise,   No Landlords' Grassland,
Under any circumstances.

Avoid the Police, and listen not to spying and deluding Bailiffs.

NO RENT!   LET THE LANDTHIEVES DO THEIR WORST!

THE LAND FOR THE PEOPLE!

The 'No Rent' Manifesto was issued by Parnell and others from Kilmainham jail on 18 October 1881. It was a failure. Tenant farmers were already hurrying to obtain the benefits of Gladstone's Land Act.

An invitation to the O'Gorman Mahon, Willie O'Shea's fellow member for Co. Clare in August 1880. This was possibly the occasion on which Parnell first dined with the O'Sheas (see postscript, top left). (From the O'Gorman Mahon Papers, courtesy of the University of Chicago Library.)

The Ladies' Land League run by Parnell's sister Anna in Ireland (here seated at desk) 1880–82. The Ladies' Land League carried on the work of the main Land League when this was suppressed in October 1881. It was closed down by Parnell himself in 1882. (Courtesy of the Mary Evans Picture Library.)

SUPPLEMENT TO THE WEEKLY FREEMAN OF 18TH DEC., 1880.

PORTRAITS OF THE FOURTEEN TRAVERSERS
IN THE
STATE PROSECUTION
OF THE
LAND LEAGUE.

(Courtesy of the National Library of Ireland.)

THE DEFEAT OF OBSTRUCTION IN THE HOUSE OF COMMONS: REMOVAL OF MR. PARNELL BY ORDER OF THE SPEAKER, FEBRUARY 3, 1881.

Resistance to eviction in Co. Mayo in the days of the Land League. (Courtesy of the *Illustrated London News* Picture Library.)

Parnell assaying Wicklow minerals in his laboratory at Wonersh Lodge, Eltham, Kent.

Some key figures of the Irish parliamentary party.
(Courtesy of the Mary Evans Picture Library.)

Conditions in Kilmainham were not harsh. Parnell wrote Katie over a hundred letters there, often in invisible ink. They were smuggled out by warders. (Courtesy of the Mary Evans Picture Library.)

SUPPLEMENT TO THE
WEEKLY IRISH TIMES
THE IRISH SPHINX.
SATURDAY
29th September 1883

Parnell, with the Land League and Kilmainham jail in the past, and two and a half years before the Home Rule Bill. 'Where he was going was always more interesting than where he had got to.' (Courtesy of the National Library of Ireland.)

In the days of the 'Union of Hearts'. Within a year they were at each other's throats. (Courtesy of the National Library of Ireland.)

Parnell electioneering in the first of three by-elections of his last year of life (1891), after he had been rejected by his Irish party as leader. Lime had been thrown at his eyes in an earlier meeting. (Courtesy of the Mary Evans Picture Library.)

Captain Willie O'Shea in later life –
sometime of the 18th Hussars, MP for
Co. Clare and for Galway, and husband
of Katie, whom he divorced in 1890.
(Courtesy of Topham Picture Source.)

Parnell's first public meeting after the
divorce and the party 'split'. (Courtesy
of the British Library.)

An American reaction to news of the O'Sheas' divorce.
(Courtesy of the National Library of Ireland.)

Parnell comes to Cork to rally support after the divorce.
(Courtesy of the Hulton-Deutsch Collection.)

Why was he again so worried about her going home from Keppel Street, or this time perhaps from Euston, or even Holyhead? It sounds like primarily a concern for her health, and this seems confirmed by his words in a tender letter two days later, beginning 'My dearest Love':

I fear I was very foolish to allow you to come with me the day of my departure; I felt sure it would do much harm, and until your first letter arrived I was in a continual panic lest some dreadful disaster had happened.

That my poor love should have suffered so much makes my heart sore, and she must take great care of herself for the sake of *our* [Parnell's emphasis] future.

It was three months since the early-October visit on which they had become lovers. If she were now pregnant, or at least thought herself to be, his anxiety for her and the reference to his 'poor love['s]' having 'suffered so much' would be explicable – the suffering being the result of the physical discomforts of early pregnancy. The anxiety for a man so wholeheartedly in love would not have been unreasonable if she had had to travel back from as far as Holyhead or even from central London by train, or by horse-drawn cab the eight miles or so to Eltham. Certainly the anxiety can hardly be attributed to the presence, experienced or apprehended, of her husband, for Willie, as both of them knew, was busy with his expensive lawyer in Madrid – and indeed with this very letter Parnell enclosed a letter he had just received from him (possibly his apology for not attending the meeting).

We know for certain that Katie bore no living child in 1881. We know that by about June 1881 she was pregnant with a child of Parnell's to which she gave birth in February 1882. It is quite feasible that she may have been pregnant for the first time by Parnell at the end of 1880 and then have suffered the miscarriage which he seems to have dreaded. Certain phrases in his letters to her during the later pregnancy seem to confirm that such a thing may have happened earlier. All that needs to be noted is that whether there was a real pregnancy or perhaps only a false one, or possibly neither, the bond between them was by now extremely close.

Parnell had gone to the first day of the State trial in Dublin's Four Courts in style, arm-in-arm with the Lord Mayor of Dublin, Edmund Dwyer Gray MP. He took his seat with Sexton and Brennan immediately opposite the Attorney-General, who began his long and often tedious indictment of the Land League as a dangerous conspiratorial organization.

Parnell's face was reported as having its usual austere composure, his eye 'the same penetrating fix'. He read a newspaper as the Attorney-General recited at great length extracts from different defendants' speeches at Land League meetings in Ireland throughout the year.

Greeted with tremendous popular enthusiasm each time he arrived at or left the Four Courts, Parnell attended the proceedings regularly for the first six days. On the second day he had listened imperturbably to the tables being turned on him for his cleverly ambivalent use of the word 'land' in a speech at Cork. 'The people of Ireland', he had said there, 'are to-day engaged in a great battle for the land of their country which was wrested from them seven centuries ago by fraud and violence. We believe we shall in a short time obtain the restitution of the land of this country.' This was now singled out as an example of seditious talk. But it ranked tame beside the citation in court of something Brennan had said on the national theme in the same month: 'It is the duty of every man now to make Ireland a Nation and when I say Ireland a Nation I mean no mockery of freedom. I mean the mistress of her own destinies – Ireland with a national army to guard her shore – Ireland with a national Senate and Ireland with a national Government that will know no higher authority than the will of the Irish people.' And elsewhere Brennan had talked of 'sowing the seeds of, and the principles, of Republicanism which can alone raise our enslaved people'.

It could be argued that if the Crown seriously thought it could get a Dublin jury to condemn political rhetoric in Ireland as illegal, it was revealing the degree to which it was out of touch with the people it claimed to rule.

Another defendant, J. W. (Scrab) Nally, came closer still to the mood the Crown was contesting. He was quoted as saying to a meeting, 'You all have rifles now and any of you who are not able to buy a rifle or a gun can have a pitchfork. But you must pay 10/- for a licence if you want to shoot vermin. You all know the vermin I mean. I believe the words of the Act read crows and magpies, but this includes vermin.'

The best way of combating such a mood was, of course, not by prosecutions at all, but by a combination of firmness with conciliatory land reform – a strategy which in fact, within a week or so, the Liberal Government was tentatively to unfold in the Queen's Speech to Parliament. Meanwhile, until Wednesday 5 January, when he sailed from Dublin to attend the opening session of that Parliament the next day, Parnell chose to continue to appear in court.

Lord Randolph Churchill had been sitting near him on the first two days, but on the third day an American lady was seen sitting in that place instead. The *Freeman's Journal* noted that between her and Parnell 'several apparently gracious messages passed during the day'. At the New Year weekend he went up to Avondale, having felt 'tempted', he wrote to Katie, 'to run over and spend the New Year and Sunday with you, but feared you might not be alone'. (Parnell himself, after all, had just warned Willie to return.)

Down in Dublin again on Monday 3 January, Parnell found three letters and some telegrams waiting for him at Morrison's Hotel. Katie had read the account in the *Freeman's Journal* of the messages passing between him and the American lady and it had upset her. (He had, of course, told her soon after their first meeting of the American girl to whom he had once been attracted.) In the letter he now wrote, he told her it pained him very much to know that this had made her unhappy and he gave his own version of what had happened:

An old and ugly woman with whom I was very slightly acquainted, but who wanted to put herself *en evidence*, perched herself just behind me, and got a gentleman sitting next to her to hand me down a slip of paper, on which was written some message of congratulation. I only rewarded her with a stare, did not even bow or smile, and certainly sent no communication of any kind in reply. That was all. I will ask my own dearest to believe in me while I am away, and never again to feel unhappiness from want of confidence.

Whatever the exact truth – and the benefit of some doubt may lie with Parnell on the grounds that you can't believe everything you read in the newspapers – it seems obvious that Katie O'Shea was now as much in love with him as he had been with her almost from the start.

He ended his letter by saying that he was coming over on the Wednesday morning, 5 January, 'and shall be with my own wifie on Wednesday evening about eight'. Willie's visits to Eltham were normally at weekends. Parnell was probably there when he said he would be. He left Kingstown that Wednesday morning with two of his MPs, Edmund Dwyer Gray and T. D. Sullivan, thus disappointing a considerable crowd which collected in the evening to see him off on the night boat, for which his departure had been announced.

He had caught a slight cold at the turn of the year and had been appearing in the court-room, already noisy with coughs and sneezes, wearing a dark purple 'turban' as some sort of eccentric comforter. The cold seemed better the day before he left. He knew in any case that he was about to be well looked after.

The prosecution meanwhile ploughed on in the absence not only of himself but also of most of the other 'traversers', towards what many confidently predicted would be a humiliation for the Crown. The Parnell Defence Fund raised by the *Freeman's Journal* had already reached over twelve thousand pounds (some half a million pounds today).

On his arrival in London, Parnell – according to Katie's memoirs – went to spend 'some days together' with her at Eltham. Once again questions about the exact nature of the triangular relationship present themselves, for Willie was now back in London, about to attend the House regularly, and therefore presumably to pay his usual regular Sunday visits to his children at Eltham. This of course helped to make Parnell a perfectly respectable guest of the married couple in Aunt Ben's eyes, and he was now introduced to her for the first time. She found him charming. 'His quiet manners and soft, clear voice pleased her greatly,' Katie recalled, 'as also did his personal appearance.' They had walked up and down in one of the rooms of her house, and she had told him how once, long ago, she had met O'Connell. 'I much prefer your voice, Mr Parnell,' she had said, 'for Daniel O'Connell's enunciation was startling to me.'

Willie too, of course, spoke with an easy English accent.

She was pleased when her niece told her that Parnell had commented on her pretty arm, noticed through old-fashioned net sleeves fastened with bracelets. Aunt Ben was eighty-seven that year, and it must have been a relief to both husband and wife that the new friend went down so well with the benefactress who gave the family an income of some £160,000 a year (in today's terms), who provided Willie with his rooms in London, and whose wealth before very long Katie was due to inherit.

As well as his own rooms in Keppel Street, Parnell now used rooms in the Westminster Palace Hotel as a sort of unofficial base for the Home Rule Members. This was where he was to rest when Parliament sat late, as it was often to do that January, though even then he and Katie at least once had a secret rendezvous elsewhere – probably at Keppel Street – before she drove down to Eltham. Some insight into the way the triangular situation adjusted itself may be gleaned from her information that sometimes Willie would give the seats he secured in the Ladies' Gallery of the House of Commons to friends of his, but she always knew then that Parnell would ballot for one for her. It implies an easy if unspoken tolerance of Parnell's interest in her, as also of Willie's interest in his ladies.

The Queen's Speech with which the parliamentary session opened dealt with Government concerns in Turkey, Montenegro, Greece, the Transvaal, Basutoland, Afghanistan and India, and then Ireland. Of Ireland it was stated that the social condition of the country had assumed an alarming character, but proposals would be submitted to give the Government powers additional to the ordinary law in order to deal with this. Proposals for land reform were less explicit: it was simply said that the principles of the 1870 Land Act would be developed 'both as regards the relation of tenant and landlord, and with a view to effective efforts for giving to a larger portion of the people by purchase a permanent proprietary interest in the soil'.

As the Home Rule Party settled down to debate this, it was noted that only four of the moderate Whiggish members who had in the previous session sat on the same benches as the Government had now obeyed the recent party ruling and had moved over to sit with Parnell and the others in opposition. One of these was Captain O'Shea.

Parnell's audacity in absenting himself from the court where he was being prosecuted in Dublin, to appear in London in order to take on the Government in the House of Commons, was, as Davitt was to write later 'unprecedented, but so was a leader so resolute and a combination so strong in a modern Irish movement'. That resolution was about to be put to a test which in its consequences was one of the most critical of his political career.

The elements of crisis were unmistakable. Whether or not the jury in Dublin convicted him and his colleagues, the Government, once it had got through the business of the Queen's Speech, was going to introduce a Bill in Parliament which would enable it to imprison anyone it wished, and thus break the Land League. Davitt had already told Devoy in America that if habeas corpus were to be suspended 'the Land League would be crushed within a month and universal confusion reign'. Would Parnell, himself almost certainly by then in prison, be able somehow to take control in that revolutionary situation? If so, he might determine the future of the two islands in a way unthinkable for at least a century – a century in which the majority of the Irish people had become an effective political force as they had not been when restless Protestant colonists stood for Irish nationalism a hundred years before. There was even a possibility he might eventually succeed in breaking the mould of seven centuries altogether.

Such speculation was hypothesis, bordering on fantasy. What was not in doubt was that the majority of the Irish people, one way or another, were supporting the Land League. Even among the Protestant minority in Ulster there was a strong feeling at least for the 'three Fs' and against the Government for concentrating first on coercive measures. Yet what exactly was to be done? Government measures including the suspension of habeas corpus were inevitable. The most that Parnell and his supporters could hope to do in Parliament was to delay them.

They were to manage in fact to hold up the introduction of the first Coercion Bill for a fortnight, by spinning out the usually formal debate on the Queen's Speech with two remorselessly argued amendments. This was the beginning of a new bout of obstruction, more sophisticated and on a greater scale than that at the end of the 1870s, for there were now some twenty active obstructionists at work in place of the previously dedicated three or four, and inflated argument rather than procedural tricks and unnecessary reading from parliamentary reports now absorbed the impatient Commons' time.

Parnell himself displayed immense vigour and resource. His speech on 7 January in which he moved his amendment that 'the peace and tranquillity of Ireland cannot be promoted by suspending any of the constitutional rights of the Irish people' was hailed by the *Freeman's Journal* as 'a specimen of marvellously irresistible logic and historical research'. He rose, the paper said, 'above himself to the great height of the occasion and was received in silent respect'. A still more persuasive compliment was heard in the Commons itself from a political opponent, the Conservative Member for Dublin University, who described it as 'about one of the most adroit, intelligent and sagacious speeches I have ever heard delivered in this House showing a thorough knowledge of the men he sought to convince'.

It is often difficult to sense the full impact of a speech from Hansard, which, unlike newspaper reports of big public meetings, seldom conveys atmosphere. Most accounts of Parnell's speaking style emphasize that it was the deliberation and strength of his search for the right words with which to pin down his meaning rather than rhetorical fervour that made him at his best so impressive. As a Liberal MP who had watched him in the House over many years put it, he had always had 'the rare talisman of being in earnest and the gift (no one could exactly say how) of impressing his hearers with being so'. And by now his House of Commons style had matured into something highly compelling. His early obstructionist colleague but later opponent Frank Hugh O'Donnell, while disparaging his political character, went out of his way to say that by this time he had something 'really eloquent in his speeches. It was', he said, 'a gross error to represent him as deficient in speaking power. He made a clear statement clearly.'

He could also use this power of compulsion to skate masterfully over awkward truths and misleadingly convey clarity with the sleight of hand of oversimplification. Often in the questionable attitudes which he was to strike so confidently at intervals throughout his career it is difficult to say whether he was aware of the veiled deceit he was sometimes practising or whether he was able to carry conviction to the extent he did just because he had somehow managed to convince himself that no deceit was involved.

Thus in this speech on his amendment to the Queen's Speech his attitude to the House was one of almost fatherly concern in his wish to help what he hoped was the majority of Members 'who are desirous of being informed on the question of alleged agrarian crime and outrages, and are desirous of giving fair play to Ireland'. He was not at all surprised that 'Englishmen and foreigners' should have been led astray by the conspiracy of the press against the good name of Ireland. He had, he said, been coming over to England 'occasionally' since Parliament last met and reading the English papers had found himself tempted to think that in the few days of his stay some sudden change had arisen in Ireland 'and that instead of a state of disturbance and outrage below the normal condition of the last thirty or forty years, as I shall prove by statistics, some extraordinary epidemic of crime had arisen there'.

In the manner of a sympathetic lecturer, he outlined the objects of the Land League without wishing to 'in any way prejudice the trials which are now proceeding': the prevention of rack-renting and the establishment of a peasant proprietorship. 'Hon. Members will admit there is nothing so very dreadful in those objects.'

Henry Lucy, who watched this performance from the Press Gallery for the *World*, wished those Irish people who went to Parnell's meetings could see him now:

What a revelation to their simple minds! What a useful lesson for their contemplation! [The] Mr Parnell they know is accustomed to stand before them with pale face and quivering lips, denouncing England and all that is English. [The] Mr Parnell, who presented himself to the House of Commons last night, was a quietly-dressed gentleman, with hair carefully brushed, beard neatly trimmed, and mincing manners that might have allured to his touch the most timid mouse. There was a delightful unconsciousness about him of all that had happened in Ireland since the House last met, and of all that might be happening at that very hour. The whole thing was, according to his way of putting it, an abstract question to be argued quietly in the House of Commons in the languid hour that succeeds dinner.

To charges that he had incited outrage, Parnell replied that at every meeting at which he had spoken he had taken care to reprove it, and that other prominent Members – he mentioned Davitt – had even exceeded him in the vehemence with which they denounced it. He did concede that 'some members belonging to the League may have said incautious, foolish and hasty expressions calculated to mislead the people', but these, he said, had been very exceptional. (Brennan, Boyton, Egan and Harris were thus tacitly demoted from their prominence in the League and, though all on trial with himself in Dublin, were little enough known in the House for the sleight of hand not to be spotted.) In any case, he said the outrages themselves were 'enormously exaggerated': half of the 2,500 or so reported for the year were merely threatening letters. This certainly was accurate, but he blandly brushed all types of threat aside as absurd with a recent story from his own experience.

'The other day,' he said, 'I was travelling to London and a man who sat beside me but did not know me, said: "I tell you what ought to be done with that Parnell; he ought to be shot for the way he shoots the landlords in Ireland."' The Prime Minister, Parnell added, would surely have been surprised if as a result he had applied for protection when travelling on the North Western Railway.

The statistics he had promised were equally misleading, though bewildering in complexity. Somehow he managed to make out that the number of outrages for 1880 was below the average for the years 1844 to 1880. The plain fact was that it was more than six times the average of outrages since 1848. The gist of his argument was that, by its open organization, the Land League – 'which undoubtedly has committed some mistakes, whose action, in some respects, is open to blame and criticism – I do not wish to deny for a moment' – was a force for keeping outrages down. The choice was 'whether you will have an open organization, or whether you will have a secret conspiracy', to which he added the surprising statement 'Secret conspiracies do not now exist in Ireland.'

This was of course quite literally untrue, for the Irish Republican Brotherhood was as secret as ever, as he and the Land League were periodically made aware to their discomfort. If, however, it could be assumed that what was under discussion was the existence of agrarian secret societies in the form of the eighteenth-century Whiteboys or the later Ribbon movement, then there was some truth in his general statement, for nothing on that scale any longer existed. On the other hand, he knew perfectly well that secret sources for violent action in agrarian affairs in Ireland remained permanently in place as part of Irish history, and that the Land League benefited from their activity for all its official reprobation. Indeed, at a point later in his speech he used this very fact as a further argument against British rule in Ireland.

The agricultural labourers and tenants of Ireland, he said, who had 'now been stirred in a quite unprecedented way . . . have been taught to rely on agitation and organization, to rely upon combination among themselves, and upon the force of public opinion, to prevent persons from offending against the unwritten law of the majority of the people of Ireland . . . And when I say the unwritten law, I wish to point out to you that the majority of the people of Ireland do not make their laws themselves, they are made for them by a nation outside themselves, entirely unacquainted with the wants and wishes of the people of that country. The result is that if there are unjust laws pressing upon them, as the agrarian laws of Ireland are admitted to be, the only way the people can protect themselves from them is by their own unwritten laws, which they have striven to enforce, and have successfully enforced, so far, up to the present occasion, by the strong force of public opinion.'

This of course was exactly what his opponents were saying was happening, and he was blandly turning the argument on its head to his own advantage. He even compounded the trick when, after saying that it was *not* intimidation that prevented tenants from paying rent, he insisted it was 'the public opinion of the majority of the people'. And what did he mean by 'public opinion'? He explained honestly enough.

'I regret', he said, 'that tenants have not yet sufficient moral courage to go to the landlord and say, "We won't pay you more than the Government valuation because by so doing we believe we shall injure the settlement of the Land Question." I regret that on the contrary many of the tenant farmers go and say, "If we paid more than the Government valuation we should have our houses burned down, our cattle houghed or ourselves injured." But where is the intimidation? The intimidation is on the part of the landlords to whom the tenant is afraid to speak the truth. The intimidation is not on the part of the Irish National Land League.'

It was a dazzling performance. With the exception of the last two sentences, there could hardly have been a clearer description of what was happening from any of his opponents. And yet he could make it seem like an argument against them.

He had reminded the House that there had been forty-eight 'Coercion Bills' altogether in the past half century, including five suspensions of habeas corpus. And he rounded off with something as near to a peroration as he ever normally came. 'I entreat the House', he said, 'to pause before it plunges into the abyss before it . . . You have never been able to rule the Irish people by terror and coercion and you never will be able so to rule them.'

The next speaker declared with understandable feeling that Parnell's speech was 'the most misleading statement and most incorrect interpretation that had ever been laid before the House of Commons or the English public'. The Chief Secretary, W. E. Forster, made play with Parnell's devious references to 'the unwritten law'. Even the Conservative Member for Dublin University who complimented his speech as 'adroit, intelligent and sagacious' and as 'showing a thorough knowledge of the men he sought to convince' did so in order to point out that what Parnell was doing was to try to make the House forget what the true position in Ireland was.

But what Parnell had demonstrated was not something of any real importance in terms of argument. Everyone knew that there could be no question of persuading the Gladstone Government to change its mind over the introduction of coercive measures; the Conservative Opposition was not going to oppose it on this. Even the delay he had caused could be only of temporary value. But what had been unmistakably demonstrated was that, as the Government embarked on confrontation with an Irish crisis as dangerous as any in living memory, it had in Parliament an opponent as resolute as itself who not only held sway in Ireland but could command attention and even respect in the House of Commons as no Irish leader had done since the days of Daniel O'Connell. He already had a political power out of all proportion to his parliamentary representation. He was still only thirty-five, so the eventual likelihood of further democratic electoral reform made his future presence on the political scene formidable indeed. And, for the present, a question even lay over whether he would continue to bother with Parliament at all.

On the weekend after this brilliant *tour de force* on the first amendment to the Queen's Speech, he and Willie may well both have been together at Eltham on Sunday 9 January. They were certainly both in the House of Commons the next day when Willie too spoke on the Speech. He made clear his essentially moderate position in the party, but, speaking now on the other side of the House from his former moderate associates, also went out of his way to show his loyalty to Parnell and pay tribute to him. He had heard, he said, 'with great regret' the Chief Secretary for Ireland say that 'my honourable Friend the Member for the City of Cork has by speeches knowingly incited people to commit outrages. Now, I would not call, even in the conventional language of the House, the honourable Member for the City of Cork my honourable friend if I did not know that he is utterly incapable of conduct of that kind.' In the same speech he declared that Ireland was in fact in a most dangerous state of revolution, and that, although he himself was 'not a Land Leaguer', it was the Land League which had brought the land question, 'one of the most dangerous to the Empire, nearer settlement'.

The speech is useful not only as evidence of at least a superficially agreeable relationship between the two men but even more as an indicator of how exactly Willie saw himself fitting into the fast-developing political scene and was finding there a real place for himself which he could turn to his personal advantage. He had already demonstrated a minor example of how business and politics could be rewardingly combined by setting up the railway company for West Clare. But his eye for the future was now on something much more ambitious. Such ambition needs to be seen in the light of the future as it appeared likely at that time and not in the light of the future as it in fact turned out to be.

In this speech on 10 January Willie referred back to that meeting at Milltown Malbay the previous September when he had looked expectantly to Gladstone's new Liberal Government and had actually earned the Liberal Whip's gratitude for saying such things as 'there never was a House of Commons more ready and more willing to settle the [land] question equitably than the present House of Commons'. Now, he said, though this meeting had been 'but a brief while ago, yet it seemed a cycle in the history of Ireland'. They were, he said, now oscillating between hope and fear, but he still hoped that the Prime Minister would, with a Land Bill, rise equal to the occasion and provide 'a great measure, a worthy rival of the mightiest feats of statesmanship and would, without coercion, restore law and order in Ireland; law founded upon justice, order and upon contentment of a hopeful people'.

For all the possible dangers of the present crisis, it was still reasonable to look to the foreseeable future in terms of some *modus vivendi* between the Government and the Home Rule Party. Gladstone's political position for the next five years was impregnable. He enjoyed an overall majority in the House of Commons. He still wished in a general way to do justice to Ireland. Parnell, for all his magnetic popularity in Ireland, had no effective political power except through the House. Irish politics as seen from there could only be worked out within a structure of compromise. This could contain an important place for an Irish Catholic Member on close terms with his more extreme leader, from whose views he often differed significantly, but whom he, unlike other moderates, was prepared up to a point to support. It could be just that position of valuable influence from which Willie instinctively saw his fortunes likely to thrive. It was a position which he would endeavour to exploit for over five more years.

When, after over a week of successful delaying tactics, Parnell's amendment to the Queen's Speech was predictably lost by a majority of 378, Willie O'Shea voted with him in the minority. So in fact did William Shaw, with most of the rest of a Whiggish group of eleven. But these then all decided to leave the party altogether after the weekend. Willie O'Shea did not. He continued to see his future with Parnell, the leader who stayed periodically in his and his wife's house at Eltham. He would, incidentally, almost certainly have known by now from his children of ten, seven and five, if he had not been told before, of Parnell's stay there over Christmas.

Parnell's energy throughout that week had been unflagging. Apart from his own speech, he had intervened eighteen times on one point or another in the debate itself, and had risen to intervene on other issues before the House twenty-four times as well. On Monday 17 January he rose again to speak to a second amendment tabled by Justin McCarthy. On the same day the Prime Minister's son, Herbert Gladstone, noted in his diary that O'Shea, whom he knew well, had told him something about Parnell. He said that, although a puppet in the hands of three former Fenians now in the Land League, Parnell was 'thoroughly honest and not touching a penny of Land League money'. This is hardly the sort of thing Willie O'Shea would have gone out of his way to report if he had been harbouring personal resentment against him. The conclusion must again be that at this point he did not want to think too closely about his wife's relationship with Parnell, given its value for himself, or that he genuinely did not much care, or that he did not see the austere and rather withdrawn figure of Parnell as at all a likely pairing for his vivacious and attractive wife and therefore accepted at face value her account that his general state of health and well-being needed looking after for the sake of all three of them. The statement he was to make ten years later that until the middle of 1881 nothing had happened to excite his suspicions could even be taken as not very far short of the truth. If, of course, he himself was continuing to have conjugal relations with her, as both she and he were later to imply, any suspicions that may have arisen from time to time would have been more easily laid to rest, or at least tolerated.

Chapter 28

The Home Rule Party's second amendment to the Queen's Speech, tabled by Justin McCarthy, was to the effect that naval, military and constabulary forces of the Crown should not be used to enforce ejectments for non-payment of rent until Parliament had decided on a future Bill on land ownership. The terms of the amendment gave the party a conveniently wide field to range over, and Parnell took good advantage of this. He first spent as long a time as he could, before being reprimanded by the Speaker for irrelevance, replying to the charges of obstruction which Gladstone and his deputy, Lord Hartington, had already thrown at the party. He then proceeded to another technical irrelevance, namely a personal reply to charges that in his pursuit of the Irish national goal he wished to break up the Empire. Typically, his explanation did little to make it clear that this was not indeed his object. But his remarks throw some interesting light on the sort of options he was keeping open.

Arguing first that the abolition of 'landlordism' and the removal from the landlord class of the temptation 'to place themselves in a position of antagonism to the rest of their country' would leave no class interested in maintaining English supremacy in Ireland, he went on, 'and we should in a natural and peaceable way, without any violent revolution, in my opinion, and without jingle of arms, but by the union of all classes in Ireland, obtain the restoration of our legislative independence'.

It is debatable how far he really believed that traditional Unionists, former landlords, would be more rather than less likely to give up their emotional links with Britain if they had already had to give up their land. But the idea certainly appealed to something in his own ancestral folk memory about late-eighteenth-century Protestant nationalism.

He then added a rider which, though intended to help clear him of the charge of wishing to break up the Empire, came unashamedly close to substantiating it. He would not venture to say this at a public meeting in Ireland, he said, because he would be prosecuted for it, but, relying on the generosity and fair play of the members of the House, he would say it. 'I believe', he declared, 'it would be the duty of every Irishman, if circumstances could so come about that a fair chance presented itself of obtaining the freedom of their country, I believe it would, under those circumstances be the duty of every Irishman to do that which it would be the duty of every man to do, and which the people of every country are proud to do – shed his blood; but it would be a crime to plunge the Irish people into an unequal and useless struggle.'

It was of course quite untrue to say that he would not dare say such a thing in Ireland. He had said almost exactly the same thing at Waterford a few weeks before, and on a number of other occasions. But Members of the House were doubtless flattered to have their generosity and fair play relied on. In other words, he was admitting that he did not have any objection in principle to a rising in arms against the Empire for Ireland's freedom other than that it had no physical chance of success and was therefore, at least for the time being, wrong. Which was why, he said, he had never gone beyond the constitutional lines of agitation. These could make it possible for Ireland to remain friends with England and, 'as Grattan used to say, there would be the link with the Crown. You would have lost the right to make confusion and mischief in Ireland, and inflict bad and unjust laws upon us, and you would then see that we were not so terribly hostile to you as you found was the case before.'

One Member had already pointed out that Parnell's personal explanation about what he did or did not mean to imply for the future of the Empire was in fact quite irrelevant to the amendment they were meant to be debating. But the Speaker tolerantly granted some of that indulgence traditionally permitted to a Member making a 'personal explanation', trusting that he would soon get back to the amendment. This Parnell eventually did, and, in winding up, looked for a moment at what the successful obstruction over the Queen's Speech was in fact concealing, namely the question of what was likely to happen when in due course the Protection of Persons and Property Act and the suspension of habeas corpus inevitably passed.

Parnell's most thorough biographer, F. S. L. Lyons, says that in this speech Parnell 'publicly stated . . . that the first arrest under the Protection of Person and Property Act would be the signal for a general strike against rent, with the implication that in such a crisis the Irish Members would return to their own country to organize the demonstration'. But this interpretation of what Parnell said gives an impression of singleness of purpose. Hansard shows that it did not in fact come out quite like that.

Parnell liked to keep options open not only to retain for himself freedom of movement but also to bemuse his opponents, and at this moment he had every reason, both public and private, for wanting to feel free. At the very beginning of his speech he had certainly hinted at the possibility of withdrawal, but this was part of an indignant, almost petulant, protest against the Government's charges of obstruction. He said that to try to get a fair hearing for Ireland in the House was 'almost a hopeless task'. This, he said, might be the last session in which any large body of Irish Members would come to the House, and that in Ireland many were saying, 'What is the use of going to the House of Commons at all?' It would be far more dignified, he added, for Irish Members to retire in a body by themselves than tell their countrymen that it was a farce to seek redress from the English Parliament. However, this was more an expression of exasperation than a positive statement of policy.

Something much more like policy – but still not precisely that – came some time later, close to the end of the speech, when he made the House face up to the future with a threat, though of course first disavowing that it was any such thing.

'If', he said, 'you adopt coercion in Ireland, the first man that is arrested will be the signal for the suspension of the payment of all rent in Ireland. Such a proposal was made at the end of the last session . . . I am glad to say,' he continued, 'that I have successfully resisted it up to the present moment but it would not be possible for me, if you insist on taking the leaders of the people and put a stop to this organization – it will not be possible for me to resist it any longer.' In other words it would not be his signal, simply one that could not be resisted. 'The most moderate men in Ireland,' he went on, 'the Catholic Bishops and the Catholic priests will recognize its necessity, and you will find yourselves face to face with a far more formidable movement than that which preceded it – most probably a secret movement. Let no Right Honourable Gentleman suppose that the tenants, who have found out how to organize themselves, will not be able to carry on an organization in such a way as to baffle any attempt to stop them, in spite of all his spies and policemen . . . He does not recognize the nature of the force he has got to deal with.'

How probable was this view of the immediate future? It was a view at least partially shared, with apprehension, by his nationalist opponents in the Irish Republican Brotherhood, who, on the principle that they had the monopoly on any decision for rebellion in Ireland, were preparing to post all over the country a proclamation addressed to the 'Men of Ireland' to dissuade them from taking any action. There was an evident fear of being upstaged. The crisis, they said, was 'full of danger to the national cause' because the British Government and 'its aiders and abetters' meant to provoke premature resistance. 'You have a cause for revolt,' the proclamation went on, 'but you are not yet prepared, and crushing disaster now would leave to the next generation the task of beginning anew the great work so far advanced . . . The time to strike has not yet come. Beware then, of being misled by false and foolish friends.'

Parnell, unlike the IRB, had to live in the reality of the present, for, again unlike the IRB, he had the support of the majority of the people of Ireland. His alarming prediction of what might happen was certainly made partly to scare the Government into thinking again about bringing in some Land Bill before coercion, but at the same time it was not unrealistic. How far, then, had he worked out any real policy for leadership in what, if his prediction were right, would be rebellion possibly even on the scale of 1798 but with more sophisticated coordinates? His speech had actually clarified little about future policy. All he really made clear was that he understood the situation better than the Government. His authority, at least, had impressed the House. The former Conservative Chancellor of the Exchequer, Sir Stafford Northcote, who followed him in the debate, said that Parnell had spoken 'as if he were an equal power addressing the Crown and Parliament, as if he were . . . supreme over the organization which is now the virtual ruler of a portion at least of Ireland', and 'with an authority almost co-equal with the Queen of England'. Events were about to call this impressive bluff.

The debate on the Queen's Speech finally came to an end on Thursday 20 January with the dismissal of the second Irish amendment. Both Parnell and Willie O'Shea voted together in the minority of thirty-four. Parnell was in the House the next day, Friday, but not on the following Monday, when Forster sought to introduce his Coercion Bill, the Protection of Persons and Property (Ireland) Bill, which would suspend habeas corpus. It is possible that Parnell spent at least part of that weekend at Eltham, where again he may or may not have seen Willie on one of his Sunday visits to take the children to mass. Willie was not in the House of Commons on either the Friday before the weekend or the Monday after, so it is possible he may have spent it away from London. It is difficult at times not to become obsessionally curious about such movements, in the hope that they may disclose something more exact about the nature of what was going on. On the other hand, the fragmentary evidence where once so much must have been available may usefully reflect a real inexactness at the heart of the triangular relationship itself.

Whether Parnell was down at Eltham at all on this Sunday 23 January or not, the reason for his absence from the first day of the Coercion Bill debate on the following Monday was made plain when he turned up in court in Dublin that morning to hear the final charge to the jury in the case against himself and his Land League colleagues. He had arrived from England by the night boat. He came into court to a burst of cheering, but could find only a back seat, where he was consoled by a bouquet of flowers from one of the ladies in a better one. 'There', wrote the *Freeman's Journal* reporter, 'sat the Irish leader all day, waiting to meet his fate, with the same grave sweet tranquil earnestness as if the fate of a nation as well as his own were not in the balance.'

There was an element of dramatic hyperbole about such journalism, for it was known that there was a majority of Catholics on the jury; disagreement was confidently predicted. The prediction came true the next day, though the jury were out for nearly five hours before the foreman returned to tell the judge that they were 'unanimous about disagreeing'.

Parnell had sat there all day, buried in a newspaper most of the time 'with that pale, clear-cut indomitable face of his', but he was almost mobbed by excited crowds when he went out to the coffee-room for his lunch. The *Freeman's Journal* said that the crowds 'had fastened their eyes on him in semi-adoration' and that when he came back into court from lunch while the jury were still out he was received with thunderous applause which the jury cannot have helped hearing. When they did return, the judge in fact sent them out again to try to resolve their 'unanimous disagreement', but to no avail, and Parnell left the court just before 7.00 p.m. in triumph to pass through immense cheering crowds on his way to catch the 7.35 boat back to Holyhead. He had had a threatening letter in the course of the day addressed to 'The Scoundrel Charles Stewart Parnell'. 'You rogue,' it ran, 'if you are acquitted we shall shoot you. God Save The Queen.'

He was back in the House of Commons next day to fight the Protection of Persons and Property Bill with wonderfully renewed vigour and zest. He found that the House had been up all night as his supporters tried for twenty hours to prevent the Government giving the Bill precedence. He was in time to vote in a minority of thirty-three, along with Willie O'Shea.

Some twenty resourceful Irish Members under Parnell's command now succeeded in delaying the first reading for five nights. The writer R. Barry O'Brien, who was to be his first biographer, helped Parnell with his research for the debate in the House of Commons library and gives a vivid picture of his untiring energy behind the scenes. O'Brien spent hours walking up and down the corridors of the House with Parnell as the debate proceeded. Encouraged by O'Brien's account of O'Connell's obstruction over coercion in the 1830s, Parnell confessed he was really 'very ignorant' of Irish history. 'I am very quick though at picking up things,' he added. They went off to the library together.

O'Brien was amazed to see him calmly marking the books with a blue pencil as they pored over them afterwards together in the Reading Room. 'Do they allow you to mark books here?' O'Brien asked. 'I don't know,' replied Parnell. 'By Jove! This is very good.' And he again put a mark in the margin.

Any tiring members of the Home Rule Party, Whiggish or not, who temporarily withdrew from the debate to be caught by him in the corridors or the Reading Room were sharply coaxed into a return to the Chamber. 'Desperate man! Desperate man!' one of them managed to mutter to O'Brien behind Parnell's back.

Granville, Gladstone's Foreign Secretary, came down the corridors towards them one night at the height of the excitement in the House over the Home Rulers' obstruction. Parnell took no notice of him. 'A pleasant face, Lord Granville's,' said O'Brien after he had passed. 'I did not see it,' replied Parnell.

When he came to speak himself, on the fourth night of the debate, he had a long extract from one of O'Connell's speeches to read, written down for him by O'Brien. But after a while he had some difficulty in reading O'Brien's writing. Parnell hesitated awkwardly. An Irish Member near him who knew O'Brien's writing well offered to read it for him. But Parnell insisted on going on himself. Afterwards O'Brien apologized for causing him embarrassment.

'A. M. Sullivan tells me you could scarcely make out my handwriting.'

'Not at all. I read it very well and produced a very good effect.'

The Speaker had indeed complained that in reading so many extracts Parnell really was trying the patience of the House very severely. And, as in the obstruction times of the late 1870s, Parnell again took the opportunity to enjoy himself in his most straight-faced manner at the Speaker's and the House's expense. He would not for the world transgress the ruling of the chair, he said, but he was bound to say that he would have to try very severely the patience of the House. He was not, however, aware that trying the patience of the House was a breach of Order . . .

Old comrades of the 1870s – O'Donnell and Biggar – were now ably assisted by young members brought in at the election the year before:

T. P. O'Connor and Tim Healy among others. The House had already been sitting for forty-one hours in this unprecedented first reading of a Bill and Biggar was once again on his feet when the Speaker, who had been replaced for a time by his deputy, returned to the Chamber and delivered the first of two shocks with which the Government was about to discountenance Parnell and force him to look beyond tactics and rhetoric to a precision of strategy on which he was surreptitiously short.

Citing a threat to the dignity, credit and authority of the House, the Speaker said that under the accustomed rules and procedures its legislative powers were now paralysed. A new and exceptional course was required. He arbitrarily closed the debate and called an immediate vote on the Irish amendment, which was overwhelmingly lost. There were indignant cries of 'Privilege! Privilege!' from the nineteen Irish Members in the House. He then put the main question for the first reading, and this was at last agreed to, without a division. At half past nine in the morning of 2 February, after forty-one and a half hours continuous sitting, the House adjourned.

Parnell himself had not taken part in the final vote – he had retired early to the Westminster Palace Hotel, to be fresh to continue the debate next day. But when he got up he went off to meet Katie O'Shea, she tells us, before she drove back again to Eltham.

A historic forty-eight hours lay ahead of him. The ability seriously to delay legislation for Ireland, coercive or otherwise, had been removed at a stroke by the Speaker. He had deprived the Home Rule Party of its one effective parliamentary weapon. The question of the value for Irish nationalism of any parliamentary action at all now posed itself more acutely, and not just in rhetorical form. The eventual passing of the Bill, with its suspension of habeas corpus, had been brought much closer. Anxiety for the future more personal and immediate than before took possession of many minds. In Parnell's mind, thoughts about his deep private commitment at Eltham must have played a powerful part.

There was one plausible Irish strategic alternative to Parliament: that long-postponed democratically elected Convention originally planned by Davitt, Parnell and other Land League figures for the autumn of 1879–80. At that date the rapidly worsening distress of the winter had turned minds to more immediate things, including Parnell's journey to the United States and then the general election. The consequent postponement of the Convention and the events of the interval had given the idea a redundant air, though it had not been forgotten. But curiously there seems to have been no thought given to using it to break new constitutional ground.

On walking out on the morning after the long night of 1–2 February, the nineteen Irish Members who had so vociferously cried 'Privilege!' at the Speaker's arbitrary closure had, it was reported, considered leaving the House of Commons altogether and returning to Ireland. They had gone to consult Parnell about this, but he, either still asleep in the Westminster Palace Hotel or with Mrs O'Shea elsewhere, was unavailable. He appeared in the House when it met again that afternoon, moving in vain first that the Speaker's decision should be debated as a matter of privilege, and then arguing, in a forceful but characteristically roundabout fashion which laid all the blame for the previous night's scenes on the Government, that the House should adjourn so that they could discuss the new rules which Gladstone was planning for the next day in line with the Speaker's decision. This motion for adjournment was predictably lost.

The next day brought a new, more dramatic crisis of its own.

Parnell had given some thought to future strategy in Dublin on the day the Government's attempt to convict him had broken down with the jury's disagreement (25 January). The possibility of arbitrary arrest in the near future had brought urgency. At lunchtime in the Four Courts, Davitt had proposed to Parnell that he and others likely to be arrested should go at once to America to collect funds, while Davitt himself, who favoured a general strike against rent, should stay in Ireland to face coercion. A. J. Kettle, the tenant farmer and Land League activist, had been there too and had thought that not only should the whole party leave the House of Commons, but all, including Parnell, should stay in Ireland to face coercion, while calling for a strike against rent until Parliament dealt with the land question. Parnell had told Davitt and Kettle to come to London to talk again in two days' time.

In the past he had on a number of occasions in public looked favourably on giving consideration to the possibility of a strike against rent. But events were fast taking him out of the realm of rhetoric. At a meeting of the Land League executive in Dublin the day after Parnell left for London, Davitt got support for a no-rent strike from Egan and Brennan as well as Kettle. These four were in the Strangers' Gallery of the House on the evening of both 27 and 28 January, and it was on the 27th that a further informal discussion took place with Parnell in attendance, though he arrived late.

Kettle again proposed his more revolutionary plan, and the talk went on the next day with most of the Land League executive there and Parnell again presiding, though again late.

He had said little at the meeting the day before, but this time, it is said, he produced a proposal of some sort which, according to Kettle, was similar to that which Kettle himself had put forward. The most detailed account of this meeting – of which no contemporary record exists – is that written by Kettle himself some thirty years later, when his mind, though still acute, was probably oversimplifying the past. In Davitt's account, itself written twenty years after the event, his dates are confused but he says only that Parnell 'was not averse to this extreme policy'. Kettle has Parnell more positively delivering a paper in favour of action, but it seems unlikely that he was in fact doing more than taking note of a feasible option. The impression that when he subsequently adopted no such plan he was performing a volte-face is incorrect.

After the trial and on return to London, but before that meeting, he had sent a cable to supporters in New York, where approval from strong nationalist opinion was essential for maintenance of the Land League's flow of funds. 'The Land League has won a victory,' the cable began, with reference to the trial. It went on to look to the immediate future. 'The Irish Party', Parnell said, 'are doing their work well. I am entirely satisfied with them.' He said they would fight the coercion proposals for as long as they could and that when the proposals came into force the Government hoped 'so to exasperate the people as to provoke rebellion'. He praised the Irish people's 'perfect discipline [as] worthy of all admiration'. He went on, 'As we stand at present, passive resistance to unjust laws is the stronger weapon in our hands.'

The tone was firm, but calm and unrevolutionary. There was no mention of 'suspension of rent', or even of the party's return to Ireland. If a spectacular change of policy had been in Parnell's mind, some suggestion of this would have been at least partly reflected in a message to people so receptive to such thinking.

But the pace was quickening. That cable had been sent on 26 January. On the same day there officially came into being in Dublin an organization which was the brainchild of Davitt: a Ladies' Land League, modelled on the American Ladies' Land League that Fanny Parnell had founded in New York. In Dublin it would be able at least to continue to distribute funds to evicted tenants should the Land League itself be effectively suppressed and its leaders imprisoned under the coming Coercion Acts. Its very active President was to be Parnell's other unmarried sister, Anna. Parnell himself was strongly opposed to the idea, on the grounds that putting women into a position of danger was inviting ridicule. He was to have other reasons later.

After Parnell's meetings with Davitt and the others in London on 27 and 28 January, Davitt went back to Ireland, where, at a Land League meeting in Carlow on 30 January, he made a speech attacking 'the Chief Slanderer of Ireland [the Chief Secretary] Mr Outrage Forster' and stirred traditional echoes from Irish history with the words that the fear of arrest had no terror for 'the Young Ireland of to-day'. The next evening he was back again in London to discuss with Parnell the National Convention idea of December 1880 and its use now for pronouncement on the Government's land proposals when they should eventually appear.

Davitt spent two hours on Tuesday 1 February sitting in the Gallery of the House of Commons listening to that historic forty-one-hour debate which the Speaker was to bring to an abrupt end. For part of the time he found himself sitting there next to an official of Scotland Yard. The radical MP Henry Labouchere introduced them to each other with the words 'You two men ought to know one another.' But Davitt left before that dramatic session had run its course, and was back in Dublin on 2 February.

Davitt had now been on ticket of leave from his treason-felony sentence for three years. At about two o'clock on the afternoon of 3 February, after leaving the Land League offices, he was crossing O'Connell Bridge with Brennan and Matthew Harris, his revolver in his pocket as usual in case of threats from possible orthodox Fenian assassins, when he was arrested by detectives on a warrant issued in London by the Home Secretary the day before. His ticket of leave was withdrawn. He handed his revolver to the police who at his request gave it to Brennan. He was taken over to Holyhead by the night boat, and the next day was back in Millbank prison where he had begun his sentence ten years before.

News of the arrest reached the House of Commons by telegraph within hours. The atmosphere there was already strained by recent excitement. The mainland itself was tensely expecting some sort of 'Fenian' trouble. There had been an explosion at a barracks in Salford; extra guards were being placed on barracks in different parts of the country. The news of Davitt's arrest itself proved explosive. It had been made by simple withdrawal of ticket of leave and not under the new Coercion Bill still being debated. What, in the language of Parnell's warning of some days before, would it turn out to be the signal for?

Chapter 29

Parnell was faced with a crucial decision. This has been properly described as 'a turning point in the history of the party and the country'. It was what did not happen that was the event. The manifestations of a revolutionary situation were to continue in Ireland for another eight months, but this was the one moment when, with whatever consequences, Ireland's political leaders might have ignited it. They did not. The opportunity was not to occur in Ireland again for nearly forty years.

Parnell's prediction that the first arrest under the new coercion legislation would be 'a signal' for upheaval did not technically apply, because the coercion legislation had not yet been passed and Davitt's arrest was in the form of the withdrawal of his ticket of leave for violation of its conditions. Confirmation of this in the House by the Home Secretary, Sir William Harcourt, was greeted with 'a tempest of cheers' from the Liberal and to some extent the Opposition Conservative benches. Very calmly Parnell got up and asked what were the conditions that had been violated. Harcourt simply sat there without replying, his arms folded across his chest. There was an outburst of anger from the Irish Members, but the Speaker merely called on the Prime Minister to propose formally the new resolutions which would enable debates held up by obstruction to be brought to a summary end. Henceforth if a motion which declared the business under discussion to be urgent were supported by forty Members rising in their places, then the motion would be put to the House at once. If such a motion were then carried by a majority of three to one, the Speaker would control further business for the time being.

The drama of the day before was now eclipsed. Gladstone had only just begun to speak when Dillon rose angrily on a point of order to try to return to the subject of Davitt's arrest. The Speaker told Gladstone to proceed. Dillon refused to sit down and, against uproar from the House, insisted that he had risen to a point of order. He remained standing facing the Speaker, who was also on his feet. After some minutes of this confrontation the Speaker managed to shout above the din that he was 'naming' Dillon, whereupon Gladstone moved that Dillon should be suspended and the motion was passed by a large majority. Dillon, ordered to withdraw, refused. The Serjeant-at-Arms was called with his attendants and put his hand on Dillon's shoulder. 'If you employ force,' said Dillon, 'I must yield,' and did so. This was only the beginning.

Parnell had encouraged Dillon in his defiance. He took his turn next. When Gladstone began to try again, Parnell moved that the Prime Minister be no longer heard. The Speaker refused the motion. Gladstone got up again, but Parnell persisted. The Speaker named him. Now when the motion that Parnell be suspended was proposed, most of the Home Rule Members remained in their seats, defying the Speaker and refusing to move into the division lobbies. One of the few who did go to vote was Willie O'Shea, who thus again could draw attention to the special position he wanted to be seen to occupy on the Home Rule side. He was one of a minority of seven who voted against Parnell's suspension. The majority for it was 385. 'I respectfully decline to withdraw,' stated Parnell, 'unless compelled to by superior force.' Superior force now again arrived in the form of the Serjeant-at-Arms, who touched him on the shoulder. Parnell slowly descended the gangway, bowed to the Speaker and walked out of the House with head erect and amid the ringing cheers of his supporters. The same performance was now repeated in the case of the thirty-four other Home Rule Members after each in turn had similarly defied the Speaker.

They were suspended only for the duration of that day's sitting, but theatrically at any rate the event had significance. Was it to be anything but theatre? Withdrawal of Irish Members from Westminster before return to Ireland had long been discussed as a possible tactic on the road to Irish freedom; thirty-eight years later it was to prove to be the first sure step. On the day before the expulsions of 3 February the Home Rulers, in Parnell's absence, had walked out voluntarily, but this had been in instant protest against the Speaker's closure ruling, a spontaneous reaction in reply to a surprise development. The party meeting held immediately afterwards, to which Parnell had eventually turned up, had made clear, by its unanimous rejection of a motion from O'Connor Power to withdraw to Ireland, the lack of any collected political design in the gesture. But the present move in response to Davitt's arrest and under Parnell's specific leadership was of a different, deliberate order. The withdrawal was not technically involuntary, but it had been brazenly invited and could reasonably qualify as the first symbolic step into a new political future. If, in the light of the recent tentative discussions with Davitt, Kettle and other Land League officers, a policy of withdrawal were ever to be implemented, the occasion for implementing it seemed to have arrived. The Government was still not in possession of the coercive powers it sought from Parliament.

On the other hand, it could be argued that the Government would get such powers all the sooner if the Home Rule Members were no longer in Parliament to delay them. More to the point was to ask how many Members would back a move for permanent withdrawal, even in the new circumstances. The most authoritative estimate is twenty, even if Parnell had wanted to call for it, while only five would actually have advocated it. In Ireland itself, what was there in terms of strength with which to face the Government's new powers? Militarily, if it were to come to open rebellion, clearly very little. The Irish Republican Brotherhood was surely right about that, for all the increase in locally held arms which Davitt had noted with approval and for some of which J. J. O'Kelly, the Hon. Member for Roscommon, was responsible. The most likely outcome would be a form of anarchy in which refusal to pay rent would be backed by 'outrages' more frequent and on a scale greater than ever before. An active political leadership based in Ireland, receiving probably greater support than ever from America, might seek to exploit the Government's embarrassment and trade Home Rule with the Government for a return to order. It would have been a long shot in any case, but without positive political will in the party it was no true shot at all.

Even with Parnell appealing for calm and restraint in Ireland, as he now did, the ensuing months did see some such anarchy come about. But, because of that appeal, the possibility of extracting political advantage from the situation was small. By appealing for calm and restraint he had rejected that particular gambler's hand. Still without quite knowing where he was going, he played for time. In fact he went first to Paris and to Eltham and only after just over a fortnight to Ireland, and then only for one day.

'Outrages' for 1881 were in fact to be almost double those for 1880. 'This country is in a state next to rebellion,' a Cork land-agent was to be writing later in the year; 'but for the number of troops and constabulary no-one would be safe who had any connection with the land.' Small isolated incidents of something like guerrilla warfare did take place from time to time. In Co. Limerick in May 1881 five hundred troops and a hundred police on their way to help the serving of an eviction notice were forced back by rifle fire from a ruined castle and had to send for artillery to try to reduce it. On their return they found all bridges on roads leading to the castle destroyed and were again forced to retreat. Ballylanders on the edge of the Galtee mountains in the same county was turned into 'virtually an independent agrarian republic'. A body of men wearing military-style uniforms, carrying military ranks and calling themselves 'The Royal Irish Republic' operated in the Millstreet area of Co. Cork. A certain similarity to the first disparate elements of what was to become the Irish Republican Army of forty years later can be detected. The difference was that forty years later the Irish politicians had moved to Ireland and it was the nationalist goal that was the coherent inspiration; in 1881, the politicians remained in England and it was the need to reduce rent and stop evictions that provided the dynamic, reinforced by ancient emotions about deprived identity.

Now, with only parliamentary leadership and voices but no power in the House of Commons, and with a new factor in the form of a conciliatory Government Land Bill to weaken the agrarian drive, it was inevitable that for all the temporary increase, 'outrages' would lead nowhere on the trail of political nationalism. Indeed before the end of the year Parnell was to find himself in something of a political blind alley. Ironically, it was to be the Government itself which would rescue him from it, with finally a little help from their and his friend Captain Willie O'Shea.

What had decided Parnell not to advocate the rash step into an unpredictable national future? His independent temperament and his rhetoric might have been thought to incline him to such a move. In the first place, his rhetoric and its ambivalence were now so much a part of his independence of mind that to have abandoned them for a new reality would have required a severe psychological wrench. Moreover, there was one overriding personal reason why extreme measures at this juncture were unattractive to him: his heart was now in England with Katie O'Shea.

It was already nearly three months since he had told her that as a result of her changing his life he detested the political part of his life that kept him away from her. The passage of time since had only intensified his feelings for her. He seems to have had no hesitation at all about what to do.

The expulsion of the thirty-six Irish members ran for only twenty-four hours. A party meeting was held immediately, and next morning, 4 February, the *Freeman's Journal* was briefed on what had gone on at it. It reported that there had been a fear 'that the people of Ireland would become excited by Davitt's arrest . . . They [the party] felt it their duty to call upon the people of Ireland not to overstep by one inch the limits of constitutional agitation.' And an official message to the people of Ireland rang out on a note of triumphant caution: 'Fellow countrymen, we adjure you in the middle of all these trials and provocations to maintain the noble attitude that has already assured you ultimate victory. Reject every temptation to conflict, disorder or crime. Be not terrorized by a brief reign of despotism ... We ask you by self-restraint, your unshaken organization, your determined perseverance to strengthen our hold on the struggle we maintain.'

The decision seemed to have been taken calmly enough, but it hardly left the protagonists on the Irish side in a calm state of mind. Even though coercion had still to be passed by Parliament, there was an almost panicky feeling that coercive measures might be taken immediately. Dillon left for Dublin on the Thursday afternoon of his expulsion, and on arrival cabled London for a special Land League meeting to be held in London the next day, for which he was prepared to return with Brennan. The meeting was in fact held in Dublin, whence he issued instructions to members that if there were large-scale arrests of Land League organizers in any area members should withhold all rent. Otherwise he did not advise a general strike against rent, 'because I wish to give every landlord the opportunity of taking his stand for or against coercion'. The Land League also sent a message to Parnell asking him to go at once to America to raise funds. Parnell that day, Friday 4 February, asked by a reporter of the *Freeman's Journal* whether the expelled members would return to Parliament, replied, 'If we consulted our own feelings we should retire, but we must do our duty.' He said nothing about going to America. The next day Patrick Egan, the Land League treasurer, left for Paris with the Land League funds, to keep them out of the hands of the British Government.

Some of the story of the next ten days, particularly where Parnell is concerned, still remains mysterious, though much of the usually accepted version of the story can be shown to be false. That version emanates from the publication of memoirs nearly fifty years after the event by Tim Healy, who had by then achieved a sort of eminence as England's first Governor-General of an Irish Free State, but whose political career, after early devotion to Parnell, had later flourished on public disparagement of his former chief, strong traces of which survive in his book. According to Healy, what happened was that he and most of the Land League executive, including Biggar, Dillon, T. D. Sullivan and O'Kelly, went at once to join Egan in Paris for an emergency meeting at which Parnell undertook to join them the following day. Matthew Harris and another member of the executive, James Louden, joined them there, but the next day came and went and there was no sign of Parnell. There was no sign of him and no word from him for over a week. After eventually opening a letter addressed to Parnell at the Hôtel Brighton, 218 rue de Rivoli, where they were all assembled, Healy and Biggar were about to set off for England and the address in the letter (which Healy, writing all those years later, remembered as being in Holloway, London, but others remembered as Eltham) when they saw Parnell arriving in a cab.

A good part of this story is untrue, as can be seen easily enough by reading Hansard and the newspapers of that week, even though it has in general continued to be accepted by historians. But while it is easy to show that Healy's facts are astray, Parnell's own movements remain characteristically hard to determine.

In fact, of the members of the Land League executive, both Dillon, who had stayed in Dublin until Wednesday 9 February, when he came to England to address a meeting at Manchester, and Biggar, who had been in and out of the House of Commons all week and attended a meeting at Clerkenwell on the same Wednesday were voting in a division as late as one o'clock in the morning of Saturday 12 February and left only later that day for Paris. Brennan, Harris and Louden – all members of the League executive, due at the Paris meeting – were spotted in the Lobby of the House as late as Thursday night, 10 February. A. J. Kettle, another member of the executive, crossed to London from Dublin only on the Saturday morning itself. In his own memoirs, written long after the event, though not as long afterwards as Healy's, Kettle says that Parnell himself came on board the boat at Dover that morning and that they travelled together from Calais in a crowded train to Paris. There, in the Hotel Brighton, Healy asked Kettle – indeed in amazement – where he had found Parnell and said that 'we' had been going to get detectives to look for him, thinking he had been 'done away with'. 'We' were probably himself, Egan and O'Kelly, but the account of the whole executive waiting for him for a week in Paris is clearly wrong. Both Dillon and Biggar had also arrived only that day, straight from the House of Commons. So what had been happening? Why did at least Healy and perhaps Egan and O'Kelly too feel they had lost Parnell?

Certainly Egan is known to have been in Paris with the funds since the previous Saturday. O'Kelly, who was a fluent French-speaker, had very probably gone with him to help to deposit them. There seems to be no contemporary trace of Healy anywhere in England or Ireland during that week. Though not a member of the executive, he was then acting as an assistant to Parnell. All three may well have been expecting Parnell earlier; but, as we shall see, there is some evidence that he had already been in Paris once that week, in which case they would at least have seen him, because it was them he had come to see.

How true is Healy's story that he had opened a letter addressed to Parnell at the Hôtel Brighton for a clue to where he might be? And was it written from Holloway? Davitt, though not present in Paris because he was in prison on the Isle of Wight, knew something of the story twenty years later, and T. P. O'Connor, who had also not been there, wrote of it only ten years later, hearing like Davitt that the letter had come from Katie at Eltham. It was indeed said to be the first knowledge the party had of the liaison.

Eltham was where Parnell had been at least some of this time, but it does not look as if he had been there all the week. There was to be some positive evidence that he had been in Paris already at the start of the week, and it is odd, if he had been at Eltham all the time, that a letter from Katie there should have arrived in Paris before he did. It seems likely that this was a letter which had been written to him when he was in Paris in the early part of the week and had arrived in the interval. What is clear at least is that Parnell's movements had throughout the week been a public mystery, as they were so often to be. To try to sort them out is once again an oblique way of savouring his enigmatic character.

Katie O'Shea's memoirs, written many years later, only serve, as so often, to complicate the puzzle. She does have an account of a time when Parnell, fearing arrest for sedition, came down at night to her at Eltham and asked her to keep his stay secret, even from the servants, before going off to a Land League meeting in Paris. But she places this inaccurately 'in 1880' and makes his length of stay a fortnight rather than the week it would have been if he had stayed there for the whole of this period in February. Her report of him discovering *Alice's Adventures in Wonderland* to read on this occasion, reading it 'earnestly' and finding it 'a curious book' may be said to have a convincingly characteristic ring, however. Her account too of him setting out at first with her on a circuitous route for Paris via Harwich in order to throw off possible pursuit, but then changing his mind to return to London and travelling via Dover in the usual way, could also be true. But that does not mean he was with her all week.

The last firm sighting of him in the newspapers at the beginning of the period was on the night of Friday 4 February, when he gave his interview to the *Freeman's Journal*. It was reported after the weekend that he had gone to Paris to help Egan deposit the Land League funds there. Egan, said the *Freeman's Journal*, would stay in Paris, but Parnell would return for the Coercion Bill debate in the House on the night of Tuesday 8 February. But he was not back in the House that night. The weather in the Channel was, in any case, so bad that the Captain of the mail-boat refused to leave Calais.

Parnell, it was then reported, had started instead for Frankfurt am Main, where some of the Land League funds were in safe-keeping. But the *Frankfurter Allgemeine Zeitung* sheds no light on such a visit other than to reproduce this same report. If he had in fact gone to Frankfurt on Land League business, it is unlikely that Healy would have been mystified by his absence.

It seems more probable that the Frankfurt story was devised in embarrassment to give some public explanation of his otherwise perplexing disappearance. A surmise could be that he in fact returned to Eltham as soon as the mail-boat did sail, and indeed his return to England from the Continent was reported in some papers on Thursday 10 February. This was denied again the next day, when there was no further sign of him.

All sorts of rumours and suggestions began to circulate. He could be expected in the House on Friday night, the 11th – but he was not there. He had been arrested for high treason – the Central News Agency was immediately authorized to deny this. He was about to retire – immediately denied by the *Freeman's Journal*. He had 'bolted with the Land League funds'. He was 'showing the white feather'. In fact, in not unreasonable apprehension at first that the Government might be about to follow the arrest of Davitt with the arrest of himself, he had almost certainly been enjoying conjugal seclusion for a few days in the comforts of Eltham and reading *Alice's Adventures in Wonderland*.

Two questions remain. The first, to which there can never be an answer, is one of pure curiosity: did Willie, voting loyally as he was in the House that week against the Government in divisions during the Coercion Bill debate, know that Parnell was with Katie? The second question is the still unresolved one: was Parnell in fact in Eltham all through the week? There is quite a lot of circumstantial evidence to suggest that he was not – quite apart from what the *Freeman's Journal* had originally said: namely, that he was with Egan in Paris during the early part of it. The Press Association too had reported his arrival there on Saturday 5 February.

An extreme Clan na Gael activist, William Mackey Lomasney, who wrote to Devoy in the USA on Friday 11 February from Paris where he had just arrived, said among other things that Parnell had been there earlier 'but I could not make out where he stopped'. The French paper *Le Figaro*, which on Monday 14 February reported that Parnell had just arrived, also said that he 'had already been there recently'.

Kettle's information of his own joint arrival with Parnell that day can incidentally be apparently confirmed by the Press Association which reported seeing them together at Calais on Saturday 12 February. Less reliable may be its further report that Parnell had in the interval been in Frankfurt on hearing that in England he would be arrested. If there had ever been any truth in that, what was he doing now at Calais? Here its information can only have come from Parnell himself: he had been down the coast at Boulogne, he said, to see his sister, who was married to a banker. Such arcane wanderings, real or alleged, were in one context or another to become standard routine for much of the rest of his life.

The executive meeting which now took place in the Hotel Brighton on Sunday 13 February confirmed the unrevolutionary approach which Parnell had expressed through the *Freeman's Journal* the week before. In an open letter to the Land League in Dublin, he said that 'after full and grave consideration' he had decided not to go to the United States as had been requested but that it was his 'duty to remain in Ireland and in Parliament during the present crisis'. He could, he said, not agree that there was very little to be expected of Parliament. Coercion had to be fought and, where the promised Land Bill was concerned, help had to be given 'in pointing out in what respects it may fall short of a final settlement of the land question, should it fail to offer an adequate solution'. This suggested a tame approach to the coming Bill by contrast with the rejection of any compromise on peasant proprietorship categorically proclaimed at public meetings.

Perhaps to make up for the generally unarousing tone with which things were now being brought down to earth, a new political note was struck in this letter to the Land League, echoing some of the Marxist and English radical thought with which Davitt in particular had been in touch, and with which Brennan, then in Paris, was particularly sympathetic. There was talk, in the light of approaching household suffrage, of 'appealing to the working men and agricultural labourers of Britain who verily have no interest in the misgovernment and persecution of Ireland' and of 'a junction between the English democracy and Irish nationalism upon the basis of the restoration of Ireland's right to make her own laws ... and the enfranchisement of labour from crushing taxes for the maintenance of standing armies and navies'. Parliament, it was said, was at present governed by the landlords, manufacturers and shopkeepers of

Great Britain, where at election times 'the springs are set in motion by the wirepullers of the two political parties, and the masses of the electors are driven to the polling-booth to register the decrees of some caucus of place and power . . . and not the good of the people'. Public opinion in England was also deliberately and systematically perverted with regard to Ireland, but vigorous radical agitation would change all that.

Populist dogma of this sort was hardly Parnell's style. It did not come naturally to the cast of his mind, never much inclined anyway towards political theory. Later he was to dismiss such talk as irrelevant. For the present he could perhaps accommodate this vein in Land League executive thinking all the more easily because of the comforting personal symbolism to be found there for himself in the expressed need to keep close ties in England. From now on it was impossible that thoughts about the woman he regarded as his wife and with whom he wanted to spend the rest of his life should not always have a part in the background to his political thinking. Both his head and his heart had long been devoted to the pursuit of whatever form of Irish independence he could manage to bring about. His head would continue to pursue it as tenaciously as ever, but his heart would now often be elsewhere – at Eltham, or wherever else in England Katie happened to be.

Inasmuch as his heart was in this Paris letter to the Land League in Dublin, it was in that section which dealt with the present responsibility of the tenant farmers of Ireland. 'Upon their action during the next few months', he wrote, 'probably depends the future of Ireland for a generation.' They were not called upon to make great sacrifices, nor to run much risk themselves. They were asked only not to pay unjust rents and not to take farms from which others had been evicted for such refusal.

'If they collapse and start back at the first pressure they will show themselves unworthy of all that has been done for them during the past eighteen months . . . If on the other hand they remember our precepts and bear themselves as men, willing to suffer a little for the good of all, they will make for themselves a name in Irish history and their children may speak proudly of them as the precursors of Irish liberty.'

This was the way he had long been talking, and it had suited both himself and those who heard it. In the past, a generalized emotive tone had well suited a situation in which future reality seemed unpredictable. But reality had now come sharply into focus. It could be seen that, in a crisis, Irish leadership actually had remarkably little new to offer. The initiative lay with a Government which, armed with new repressive powers, was about to offer a Land Bill promising concessions to the tenant farmer. Parnell and the other active Home Rulers could only offer the same as before: minority talk in a Parliament which had just deprived them of much of their effectiveness, and, in Ireland, semi-revolutionary rhetoric which, while applauded, was increasingly seen to be to one side of real events.

As if tacitly acknowledging this, after the Land League executive meeting in the Hotel Brighton at which Matthew Harris reported 'the most perfect union had prevailed', Parnell did not at once go back to the House of Commons like Biggar and Healy. Accompanied by his friend and interpreter O'Kelly, he decided to make the most of the Paris scene in which he found himself. There at least there was no difficulty in making immediate impact. As early as the next night, so the *Freeman's Journal* reported, he had made contact with a number of prominent statesmen, journalists and other figures of influence, including Victor Hugo. The impression he made on the correspondent of *Le Figaro* was much the same as that which he always made superficially on strangers, but expressed in the French language acquires fresh verisimilitude. He was found to be *'quelqu'un et quelque chose. Sa main est blanche et soignée et l'habitude générale de son corps trahit la correction et la netteté qui semblent être l'apanage des Anglais.'*

The week before, when Davitt's arrest had seemed to *Le Figaro* to be the spark which would set off an explosion in Ireland ('the general uprising, long prepared, will soon break out') the paper had shrewdly doubted whether in fact Parnell would be prepared to go as far as Dillon, saying it 'slightly mistrusted the sincerity of his convictions'. Now it saw him, in the flesh at any rate, as impressive. He had an eye 'remarkable for the size of the iris, a dullish black but with subtle reflections of steel . . . Parnell, usually stands motionless with head bent forwards, but his eye ranges everywhere with the slow rolling gaze of a wild animal at rest following the movements of all who pass before his iron cage.' He also reminded the reporter of a thoroughbred horse.

It was being said in Paris that Parnell had 'a distracted air', but the man from *Le Figaro* thought this wrong. Parnell had hardly been seen there except in public, which meant that most people had seen only a bored Parnell. But in two hours now spent alone with him the reporter decided that the thing about him was not that he was distracted but that he was doubly preoccupied, both listening to what you had to say and at the same time listening to another voice which no one but he heard. The journalist became rather carried away by this idea, and likened him to a condemned man being visited in the death cell, or to an orchestral conductor listening to two different orchestras at the same time. Reverting to his physical traits, the journalist found him to have a politely mechanical smile and a mouth which expressed serenity but in no way resignation, and two rows of small, well aligned, excessively white teeth.

Part of their conversation was about Davitt. 'What a man!' said Parnell. 'I'm sorry you couldn't talk with him. I admire him. He came to see me two days before he was arrested. And today he's wearing a yellow number on his convict's sleeve.' Parnell showed him on his own sleeve where the yellow number would be.

Looking out of the window at the burnt palace of the Tuileries, still a ruin after the troubles of the Commune ten years before, the journalist pointed out to Parnell the plain-clothes police on the bridge stationed there to keep watch on him, and Parnell told him how he had given them the slip the day before in the rue Vivienne. For the first time in the interview he laughed out loud.

The next day Parnell got up late – which, said *Le Figaro*, keeping as sharp an eye on him as the plain-clothes police outside, was understandable because he had been 'receiving as many visitors as the late lamented Shah of Persia'. That evening he and O'Kelly went to dinner with Victor Hugo. There was a party for fifteen, including Victor Hugo's grandchildren and the former communard Henri Rochefort, now editor of *L'Intransigeant*, whom Parnell had already met the day before in a café near the rue Drouot. Rochefort said that on shaking hands with him he was as moved as he had been shaking hands with Garibaldi a few months before. At Victor Hugo's the two Irish agitators, Parnell and O'Kelly, were wearing white ties and tails – the only two guests who were. Victor Hugo, speaking after the dinner, compared Ireland's situation with that of occupied Poland.

Another figure, then of the left, who met Parnell in these days was the young Clemenceau, who called on him at the Hôtel Brighton, as also did figures of the right such as the royalist Comte de Flavigny and the Vicomte O'Neille de Tyrone, the well-known Bonapartist descendant of a great seventeenth-century exile. The two latter were to prove of some use to Parnell to offset against Rochefort and Victor Hugo when he was criticized by the Archbishop of Dublin, Dr McCabe, for seeking allies in France among 'impious infidels'.

But what actually was he doing there, staying on like this in Paris? The Land League funds were safely lodged. His presence was needed to fight the Coercion Bills in London. He gave two reasons for his stay. One was that the Continent was now the only safe place from which the Land

League could communicate with America without its cables being intercepted by the British Government at the transatlantic cable station of Valentia Island in Co. Kerry. The other was the need to inform the Paris press of the true situation in Ireland, of which hitherto they had seemed sadly ignorant. So in Paris at least he could feel that the role of potential revolutionary was still his, while in effect he was marking time.

It may have been in this mood that some time during that week he met the Clan na Gael visitor of die-hard Fenian views who was in touch with John Devoy, William Mackey Lomasney. Lomasney, who had already been imprisoned in Ireland once for his part in the Fenian rising of 1867, was indeed to die hard only three years later, blowing himself up on the Thames while attempting to destroy London Bridge. Now he was particularly happy to meet Parnell, having missed him the week before. He wrote at once to Devoy to give some account of the conversation. 'I feel', he said, 'that he is eminently deserving of our support, and means to go as far as we do in pushing the business.' He had sent the Fenian exile John O'Leary to see him, and he had got the same impression and had said he was 'pleased with him'.

Within twenty-four hours of this conversation, or possibly even on the same day, Parnell had an interview with a reporter of the Paris newspaper *Le Gaulois* in which he took care to distance himself totally from such Fenians, saying that, whereas they wanted a brutal revolution, he wanted only economic reform and an Irish parliament but no separation. In each case it was what the man from *Le Figaro* had spotted: Parnell's ability to conduct two different conversations at the same time, one with the person he was talking to and the other elsewhere inside his own head. To which voice he was really giving his attention was perhaps something he himself could not always say. Of course there was a tactical need to give an impression of extremism in America, where the financial support came from. Of course there was a tactical need to appear to remain within constitutional bounds at home, where the constitution was all he had to work with. But it is likely that the most important consideration with which he needed personally to identify was the freedom to keep every emotional option open for Ireland. In one way such freedom was to remain buried deep within him for the rest of his life, to emerge again under pressure many years later when personal and political restraints long built into his consciousness were subjected to unprecedented crisis. For the present it was a state of mind which he could allow to persist consciously for several months more.

In May in the House of Commons he was to meet another emissary from Clan na Gael, Henri le Caron, to whom he gave the same impression as he had given Lomasney, namely that he and they shared the same final goal of total separation between England and Ireland. This time, however, he was talking to someone who, though Parnell was to have no idea of it for many years, was also playing his own game of conducting a quite different conversation inside his own head. For le Caron was a secret agent of the British Government, long working close to the inner councils of Clan na Gael in America. The same afternoon he reported to British intelligence what Parnell had said to him. He also wrote at once in his role as a loyal Fenian to John Devoy, reporting in appropriate language that Parnell had delivered 'a veritable bomb-shell'. He said that Parnell had said that he had long ceased to believe that anything but the force of arms would accomplish the final redemption of Ireland. He saw no reason why, 'when we were fully prepared, an open insurrectionary movement could not be brought about'.

In this case the tactical element in Parnell's statement clearly played a significant part. Le Caron stressed the extent to which Parnell was complaining of hostility to him from the more extreme elements in Clan na Gael and was anxious to ensure the free flow of American funds on which the Land League was so dependent. But at least some of Parnell's heart was in what he said too.

Chapter 30

Like most turning-points, the non-event of February 1881 did not necessarily appear a turning-point at the time. At the end of the month it was still uncertain what effect the new Coercion Bills, soon to become law, would have on Land League Ireland. Equally uncertain was the shape of the coming Land Bill and the effect this might have on the tenant farmers whose material interests Parnell and others had entwined with nationalism. Michael Davitt, before his arrest, had written to John Devoy in New York, 'The Government Land Bill will not be enough, but it will satisfy a great number inside the League and be accepted by the bishops and priests almost to a man. I anticipate a serious split in the League when the Government measure comes out.' It was to prove an accurate prediction.

Parnell, adjusting with difficulty to the continuing uncertainty of a situation about which he had already made up his mind, resorted to a display of nervous energy. He arrived back in the House of Commons from Paris on the afternoon of Friday 18 February and entered at once with spirit into the battle which some thirty Irish Members had been fighting all week against Forster's Protection of Persons and Property (Ireland) Bill. Willie O'Shea had figured loyally in the Irish minority while Parnell had been away, standing up on Monday 7 February to elicit from the Home Secretary reassurance about Davitt's treatment in prison, and being counted regularly against the Government in subsequent division lists. He was in the House the day Parnell returned.

Parnell, speaking to an Irish amendment which required reasons to be given for arbitrary arrests under the Bill, made good use of his Paris visit. The Bill covered offences *wherever* committed. 'During my stay in Paris,' he told the House, 'I was always followed when I went out by two detectives who, I was informed on good authority, were sent by the Chief of Police at the request of the British Embassy . . . Since the Bill stipulates that people can be arrested for an offence whenever committed, I myself could have found myself thrown into solitary confinement on the basis of information from French detectives.' To which Forster rather weakly replied, 'Not solitary.'

Possibly Parnell spent that night and part of Saturday at Eltham, but he travelled overnight to Ireland and on the Sunday morning went straight to a meeting at Clara in King's County. He was welcomed along the route with all the old popular enthusiasm. It was as if things were still just as they had always been.

He responded in kind. At Mullingar a band was playing 'See the Conquering Hero Comes', but it was drowned out by the cheering which greeted him. 'Keep to the lines which we have preached', he told the crowd, 'and depend on it that the struggle that we have commenced will in a very short time be carried to a victorious and glorious end.'

At Clara itself, he went even further than usual, inciting positive action on behalf of that 'unwritten law' of the countryside of which he had spoken in more circumspect tones in the House of Commons the month before. While on the one hand continuing to call for passive resistance and no retaliation, in line with his instructions to the Irish people at the beginning of the month, he now advised them to plough up land from which any tenant had been evicted, so that the evicting landlord would be unable to let it to anyone else. (Since this in fact turned out to be an indictable offence under the Whiteboy Acts, he hurriedly withdrew the advice the following week.)

In general the tone of his speech carried as triumphant a note as if Davitt had not been arrested, as if the moment to bypass Parliament altogether and embark on some bold new course into a better future had not yet come and been rejected, as if the most important feature in his own life did not now tie him and his own future to the other side of the Irish Sea.

'This', he told them, 'is perhaps the last great struggle that Ireland has ever made ... Victory is almost shining in your banners ... I am confident that you will be equal to the occasion and in a very short time at the end of our battle, we shall have the satisfaction of looking around us, and of seeing the fair plains of green Erin once more made free.'

He was greeted by loud and prolonged cheering. Few can have bothered to wonder how all this, particularly now, was to come about.

They were not to know that the colour green was in fact personally abhorrent to him; or that, for all his love of his own house, Avondale in Co. Wicklow, it was his English 'wife' who could never come there who held his heart, at Eltham in Kent. Yet he was not deceiving them. His Irish national feelings came from such a very different social, historical and personal source from theirs that the surprise is not the extent to which their minds moved in different worlds but that they genuinely shared such a strongly felt emotional Irish identity. And, for all his apparent political sophistication, he shared with them too some incoherence about where that strength was to take them.

But together with the emotion of this speech at Clara went some precision about how he proposed to treat the coming Land Bill. He had often before dismissed its prospect with something like scorn. Here now was one reality to bring his visions more sharply into focus.

'As regards the Land Bill,' he began, 'I have always expressed my belief that the present Parliament and Government would fail to settle the Irish land question, and the fact that they have placed coercion before their Land Bill shows that they do not intend to settle it. But whatever measure they may bring forth, even though it be very inadequate, provided it passes, it will put the tenant in a better position to continue the struggle against landlordism. Although it may not be a permanent settlement of the Irish question, yet it gives the tenant a legal defence against ejectment. I shall look upon it as something not to be refused or rejected, while at the same time I shall take care to point out in what respect it must fail to be accepted as a final solution of this problem.'

It was a position from which he was hardly to waver, though at intervals giving some appearance of doing so while managing to make it seem wholly consistent with the Land League's highest principles.

This new wariness echoed Davitt's fear, already expressed in his letter to Devoy, that some tenant farmers might feel attracted to the benefits of the Bill and thus wane in their support of the Land League's agitation. As so often, Parnell was careful to ensure that all options were left open.

'We cannot', he said, 'say anything for certain with regard to the Land Bill until we see it.' And in case this should sound too compromising, he added, 'I only thought it advisable to tell you today what I have said on many other platforms, that I believe the Land Bill will fail to provide a permanent settlement of the Irish question.'

He moved more happily towards his peroration: 'I expect you then finally to be worthy of the occasion. The eyes of the world are fixed upon you ... Your forefathers spilled their blood on many a field of battle. Step by step and inch by inch they contested the possession of the fair land of Ireland with the myrmidons of Henry and Elizabeth and the troopers of Cromwell ... Will you be worse than they?'

'Never! Never!' came the stirring reply.

But the present could no longer be so easily oversimplified as the past. It was as if, aware of this, he was seizing every opportunity to pretend that it could be. On his way back to Dublin on the evening train, he

stopped to speak at almost every station along the line. At Moate he said,
'The settlement of the Irish land question seems to be so near at hand, you
will have little else to do than stretch forth your hands to be saved . . .
Prove superior to intimidation. Fear them not and trust me that you will
see as a result that we shall have gained the great cause of the freedom of
Irish land and have taken the first step to our national independence.' (He
had of course been careful also to talk of 'legislative independence' in the
course of the day.)

Back in London the next afternoon, he arrived at the House of
Commons just as the division bell was ringing for a vote on a second
Coercion Bill. He hurried in to vote in a minority of forty-eight along
with Willie, and appeared with him again in five other divisions that
evening in which the Irish minority was always around that number. The
next day Parnell himself spoke vigorously against the Bill in the House,
discoursing with something of the touch of an academic lecturer on the
Fenian movement and its hostility to the Land League. He stressed how
the Fenians both in Ireland and up to a point in the United States opposed
the Land League as a movement of social character calculated to draw
people away from the Fenian object of national independence, rather
than, as he put it, building up a nation in Ireland. The Americans
complained that the Land League diverted funds away from revolutionary
purposes. The last thing the Land League was, it appeared, was revolutionary. As for the Fenian movement which was, that movement was of small
consequence: 'at no time in the last seven to eight years less powerful than
now'. This was all used as reassuring argument for taking the crime of
treason-felony out of the Bill.

Willie did not speak that day, though the day before he had, as a former
military man, asked a question about the failure to land marines to help
General Sir George Colley in the difficult war then being fought against the
Boers in South Africa. He was, however, with Parnell again the next day,
Tuesday 22 February, in seven more Irish minorities of between twenty-nine
and forty-five against the Bill. Parnell himself spent that night at the
Grosvenor Hotel, near Victoria, and next morning wrote a formal letter from
there to 'My dear Mrs O'Shea' to tell her that he was just leaving for Paris,
where he would be for a few days. He followed this with another formal letter
(signed 'Yours always, C.S.P.') from Dover, asking for his portmanteau and
other things of his in his room 'or in the wardrobe' to be sent to him at the
Hôtel Brighton, rue de Rivoli, Paris. As this was a formal letter plainly
available for Willie or Aunt Ben or anyone else to see, it was clearly assumed
that there was nothing inappropriate about his belongings being at Eltham.

O'Kelly travelled to Paris with him this time, and they stayed for just over a week, seeing prominent French personalities like the Archbishop of Paris (much reassured to hear from them that the Land League did not believe in physical force), the French engineer of the Suez Canal, de Lesseps, who invited them to dinner, and the Vicomte O'Neille de Tyrone, who was disturbed that the Archbishop of Dublin had been so put out by Parnell's previous interview with the communard Rochefort, but was told by Parnell that Archbishops of Dublin were always pawns of the English Government anyway. Marshal MacMahon, whom they went to see with Egan, received them most cordially. A portrait of Parnell appeared on the full-page front cover of *Le Journal Illustré*, and photographs of him and other Irish leaders were in many Parisian shop-windows. He and O'Kelly were particularly honoured by the Archbishop of Paris, who saw them personally to the front door after their visit and said goodbye to them with good wishes for the Irish cause. In Paris at any rate the Irish revolution could be felt to be under way.

Parnell wrote a formal letter to his eminent host of the previous week, Victor Hugo: 'To you, honoured sir, who have known how to arraign the sympathy of mankind for Les Misérables, I feel that we shall not appeal in vain when we ask that your voice should be raised on behalf of a brave but unfortunate nation.'

Soon after he arrived he had also written to Eltham a letter beginning 'My dearest Katie'. He had had three letters from her already at the Hôtel Brighton, and his reply now contained a sentence which reveals something of the intimacy between them now lost to history. 'I never had the slightest doubt of my darling,' he wrote, 'and cannot imagine why she should think so.' What doubts did she think he might have been having? Had this anything to do with the presence of Willie in London and probably also at Eltham while he had been away?

Mystifying in a different way was another sentence in a letter from him two days later: 'Have received following telegram which do not under-stand: "Motive actuating latest arrival worthy consideration – telegraph all right." Please explain who is latest arrival. Yours very truly, C.S.P.' A formal letter followed the same day: 'My dear Mrs O'Shea, I cannot understand your telegram received to-day at all, although I have been thinking it over all the evening. I wired back as you appear to request in it, "All right."'

What can this have been about? Fear of some Fenian plot against him? Had she perhaps got wind of the arrival in Paris of William Mackey Lomasney through Anna Parnell, whom Lomasney had certainly telegraphed in an attempt to get in touch with him? Or was it fear of a British Government plot? Parnell was certainly apprehensive on that score. He told her in his letter that his departure from London had been sudden because he had heard his arrest was intended for something he had said at Clara (presumably the advice to plough up land), and that he would have been held until the suspension of habeas corpus, after which he could have been held indefinitely. 'I think, however, they have now abandoned this intention, but will make sure before I return.'

Before he wrote again from the rue de Rivoli ('My dearest Love'), he had already received four more letters from her.

'Your letters make me both happy and sad,' he wrote. 'Happy to hear from my own, but sad when I see how troubled you are.' And he signed himself, 'Always yours, Charles'.

What was troubling her? The strength of their commitment to each other perhaps, and the effect of this on her relationship with Willie.

He was back in London towards the end of that week, on Thursday 3 March, when he went into the division lobby against the Government in an Irish minority of fifteen. Willie O'Shea did not vote that day, but he was there the next day to hear Parnell deliver a powerful speech against Forster's second Coercion Bill, which proscribed arms in certain areas of Ireland.

'I cannot', Parnell said, 'imagine anything that the most ardent nationalist could do to make the breach wider between England and Ireland, and to conduce eventually to the disruption of the Union between the two countries worse than the course the Government is taking in forcing coercive legislation on our country. But you have done more to create and preserve a chasm between England and Ireland than all the American Fenians from New York to San Francisco.'

He again took the opportunity, for the House's benefit, to put himself in perspective to the Fenian movement. It was a perspective in which he managed to distance himself equally clearly from the Union. He said he had 'the greatest respect for many Fenians ... who believe in the separation of England from Ireland by physical force'. He qualified this only by adding, 'though I have this respect for these men I have never been able to see that a physical force policy was practical or possible to adopt'. In other words it was the impracticality, not the ideal, of their policy to which he was opposed.

Typically he also managed to put in a plea for the Union as an argument against the Bill. 'If you think that the people will be the sufferers,' he said, 'you make a mistake; because it is important that you should maintain the link between the two countries . . . The more you tyrannize, the more you trifle with the Irish people, the stronger will burn the spirit of nationality, the more they will free themselves from the yoke which renders such things possible.' In which case, it could be said, he should have been voting for the Bill. But no one said it. He held the House as always now in a sort of respectful hostile thrall.

Whether he and Willie spent that weekend together with Katie at Eltham is not known. But they were together a lot in the House of Commons after the weekend, appearing in the division lobby for a large number of minority Irish votes against the Arms Bill for most of the rest of the week. Some of these minorities were as small as 17 to 253, and almost all others less than forty.

It was of course only a matter of time before Forster got his second Coercion Bill through Parliament, and on 18 March it received the royal assent. It had taken just three weeks, the *Freeman's Journal* commented, to disarm Ireland. But the arms had hardly been employed for conventional patriotic purposes. A fortnight before, Michael Boyton had declared in a speech at Tralee that he was bound to say that if he had a home and family he would shoot everyone that came to evict him, and if there were a more effective mode of getting rid of them he would carry it out. He was careful to add that of course he was not actually giving that as advice. But the caution did him no good: three days later he was arrested under the Protection of Persons and Property Act and imprisoned in Kilmainham jail. A number of lesser-known Land League activists had already been imprisoned, but his was to be the first of a long list of notable arrests.

Political tension for Parnell now centred on the coming Land Bill. The difficulty for him lay not so much in the attitude he was to take to the Government as in the attitude he was to take to his own supporters. In the past he had been on the whole unequivocal: anything less than peasant proprietorship was unacceptable. But a new Land Bill which was to offer serious improvements in the pattern of everyday life to the tenant farmers would undoubtedly seem attractive to them regardless of whether or not it strictly conformed with the principles of the Land League and the nationalist sentiment the Land League invoked. Yet to compromise on principle was to make difficulties for himself with the most articulate and fervent of his nationalist supporters.

The problem now was different from that at the beginning of February, when Parnell had confronted a major strategic dilemma. The dilemma now was a tactical one: whether to contest the Land Bill on the highest principles or whether to accept it as a compromise while trying to limit the extent of the compromise. The personal consideration was no longer acute: either way his presence was wanted in the only effective field of action he now had – the English House of Commons – and England was where he wanted to be. It was of course the strength of his support in Ireland that was the source of his strength in the House, but he had to be in England to use it. And in England he could lead the life he wanted with the woman he regarded as his wife, without abandoning the cause for which he had entered politics.

Since he first entered politics, his heart had ruled much of his dedication to Irish nationalism. His heart was now elsewhere. His head was freer to rule his politics. In private life his head was much interested, even fascinated, by science and engineering. Irish nationalism was to become for him increasingly a matter for political engineering.

Gladstone rose to introduce his Land Law (Ireland) Bill in the House of Commons on Thursday 7 April, two days before the House adjourned for the three weeks' Easter recess. Parnell thus had time to sound out opinion in Ireland before seriously committing himself. Gladstone began his two-and-a-half-hour speech by saying that he thought he was dealing with 'the most difficult and complex question which in the course of my public life I have ever had to deal'.

The Bill, which was to be considered by the House of Commons one way or another for over four months, had been based on the general recommendations of a Government Commission headed by the Earl of Bessborough which had just reported. One paragraph of this had read:

A thorough and very general change in the system of land tenure seems imperatively required; such a change as shall bring home to tenants a sense of security, shall guard them against undue increases of rent, shall render them no longer liable to the apprehension of arbitrary disturbance, and shall give them full security for their improvements.

Another paragraph recognized that:

An ejected farming tenant in Ireland has nothing to turn to, except the chance of purchasing another holding, the offers of which are limited and the prices high. Not to come to terms with his landlord means for him to leave his home, to leave his employment, to forfeit the inheritance of his fathers and to some extent the investment of his toil, and to sink at once to a lower plane of physical comfort and social rank.

The Land League itself could hardly have put the basic concerns better. It was exactly to bring about changes in this state of affairs that most people had joined it. If then the Bill were to correct it, what would become of the call to the principles of nationality also embraced by the Land League? The Bessborough Commission had nothing to say about that.

The Bill conceded the 'three Fs' that had long been regularly rejected as inadequate by the Land League and by Parnell himself. The fair rents were to be fixed by an independent tribunal. But would the Land League rank and file be so ready to reject them now that they were actually coming their way?

Fortunately there were obvious defects in the Bill as presented, and doubts about how its provisions might work. These usefully enabled Parnell to refrain from committing himself at first. Leaseholders were excluded from the operation of the Bill and – a vital question that had often come up at public meetings and sometimes been voiced by Parnell himself – would not an inevitably Establishment-minded rent tribunal be in favour of the landlord rather than the tenant?

He played for time, awaiting the Easter recess. In a short reserved speech, the tenth to follow Gladstone that day, he confined his criticism to the section of Gladstone's speech which had outlined the Bill's incidental provision of subsidy for emigration. Every man in Ireland, he said, was required there for developing the industrial resources of the country. As for the main proposals, he simply generalized by saying that his opinion in the past had always been that it was extremely difficult, if not impossible, to reconcile the respective interests of landlord and tenant in the soil. It was too delicate a relationship. Any friction, however slight, he said, would destroy the practical utility of such a scheme as that proposed.

He left London the next day and almost at once began, however tentatively, to express an opinion. The following days gave further proof of the apparently untiring physical vitality he was capable of putting into politics. He had four meetings in England and Scotland scheduled for the next ten days, to be interrupted by a visit to Cork and a meeting of the Land League in Dublin at which that body would officially pronounce its judgement on the Bill.

At Birmingham on Friday 8 April he called the bill 'an honest and sincere attempt to deal with the land question'. He then left for Cork, where he again gave the Bill a not unsympathetic welcome, though he drew attention to the fact that the 1870 Act had not always worked as well as it had sounded as if it were going to. At the meeting of the Land

League in Dublin he went so far as to say he was 'inclined to rejoice that it [the Bill] admits what is practically the programme of the League'. This was optimistic indeed. He went on to stress the Bill's most promising aspects. He found that it admitted 'the existence of rack-renting, eviction and landlord oppression, and acknowledges the necessity of such a radical change in the law as will put it in the power of the farmers to become owners of their land – the land they till'.

The latter comment was only true inasmuch as there were certainly some provisions for land purchase within the Bill. The Land Commission which was to be set up could advance to tenants from the State between two-thirds and three-quarters of the purchase money required by the landlord, such sums to be paid off over thirty-five years at an interest rate of 5 per cent. Between a third and a quarter of the purchase money therefore still had to be raised by the tenant. This was hardly a return to the people of Ireland of the land of which the myrmidons of Henry and Elizabeth and the troopers of Cromwell had deprived them. He understandably found it necessary to qualify his approval by saying that 'while the Bill appears to admit the justice of the objects of the National Land League it provides a very inadequate means for the purpose of gaining these objects'. Skilfully he managed to get a resolution carried to this effect, together with instructions that the Bill should be examined at the great Convention now called to debate it on 22 and 23 April.

It was a characteristic effort to rally people on both sides of a potential political divide at the same time. In the meantime he went back to England, to Manchester, apologizing for having had to postpone his visit by twenty-four hours, and being greeted at the station by ten thousand Irish and other supporters who held him up there for five minutes before he could leave.

In keeping with the approach outlined in his letter to the Land League from Paris and its talk of the desirability of uniting democratic forces in both islands, he was there to address the Democratic League of Great Britain and Ireland. He told them suitably that the Irish land question was really a labour question, again making clear that he did not wish to adopt an unreasonable attitude to the Land Bill.

On Saturday he was at Newcastle, where he made the rather loose statement that Gladstone was going to make an attempt at peasant proprietorship and 'supposing it to be a *bona fide* attempt' . . . he thought it should be given a fair trial. At the same time, in order to emphasize that, while not against the Bill, he was firmly on the side of the Land

League, he stressed that he believed the only way by which the land question could be settled was 'to make the tiller of the soil the owner'.

It is easy to see how his mind was working. He knew that the Bill would pass anyway and that any improvements he and his MPs in the House of Commons could achieve would be minimal. His instinct was that the average tenant farmer would welcome it. Another instinct told him that those behind him who had done most to give the Land League its power would fight any abandonment of its highest principles. He knew that both instincts were right. He did what he could to balance them. It was an impossible task, but he summoned rhetoric to help him sort it out.

He ended his speech at Newcastle by saying that 'no one could predict whether the result of this Bill will be to make the interests of the landlord more secure, or whether it will lead to the establishment of a peasant proprietary, but if I think it will strengthen the present system or obstruct the establishment of a peasant proprietorship I would rather cut off my right hand than accept it'.

After a meeting at Glasgow on 18 April, he sailed for Ireland and the coming Convention.

In Dublin he signed the Land League's report on the Bill which, while not rejecting it, described it as 'an imperfect measure'. This report, while maintaining that it was fundamentally impossible to place the relationship of landlord and tenant on a sound economic basis because it was 'impossible to sustain it on any other basis than bayonets', said that nevertheless the Irish people wanted a peaceful solution of the land question and were willing to make concessions. However, it added somewhat ominously, 'Tomorrow they may insist upon rigid justice.'

The next day a thousand democratically elected delegates from all over Ireland met in the Round Room of the Rotunda to take up a position on the Bill. The Rotunda was the hall in which, almost a hundred years before, the Volunteers of Protestant nationalist Ireland had met with flashing swords to dedicate themselves to their country's legislative independence. But no one now, publicly, asked why these delegates were not meeting for a more fundamental democratic political purpose than to examine a Land Bill offered by the British Government. Parnell did, however, draw attention to the fact that this was the first representative assembly held in Ireland for the last hundred years. Among other things, he said, they would be able to show the world that the Irish people were fully fitted for the great duties of self-government. And there was an implication too that, in deciding on how Ireland would deal with the Bill, the Convention had superior status to the party.

But only a year before he would have been proud to proclaim to the world that such a body was fulfilling those very duties of self-government already. Now, the die cast in February had determined that for the foreseeable future the only battleground for Irish nationality was the floor of the House of Commons.

The Convention did display independence, but towards the lead which Parnell seemed to be giving rather than to the British Government. Its attitude was largely summarized in a letter severely critical of the Bill read from Patrick Egan in Paris. He wrote disparagingly of the innumerable vital blemishes and omissions of what he called the tactic of the present attempt to patch up the land question. The original two-faced resolution based on the report presented by the Land League was adroitly withdrawn by Parnell, noting what the *Freeman's Journal* called 'the tide of feeling which set in with the speeches of several delegates'. A new, stronger and longer resolution was substituted, declaring that the Bill failed to give effect to the just principles of the Land League and declining to make the Convention support it in its present shape. It doubted whether it was possible by any amendment to render the Bill acceptable to the Irish people; but without amendment by the Land League, it should be 'unhesitatingly' rejected.

A further resolution was proposed by Dillon, and passed, to the effect that another Convention should be summoned before the Bill's third reading in Parliament, 'in order to give the people an opportunity of determining whether the amendments passed in committee are adequate'. Dillon left his audience in no doubt about what he himself thought would be the outcome. 'The Bill', he said, 'is from beginning to end a thoroughly dishonest measure . . . passed in its present shape or in anything resembling its present shape [it] would leave the tenant farmer more helplessly, more hopelessly than ever at the mercy of the landlord than ever he was in the history of this country.'

Parnell at public meetings moved continually from one side of the fence to the other. On Sunday 24 April he worked out a neat argument which managed to be on both sides at the same time: 'If a really fair rent could be fixed,' he said, 'landlordism would disappear in a few years because, deprived of the right to plunder, landlords would be only too glad to surrender and sell out . . . But the whole question hinges upon this: . . . is it likely that any [Government] tribunal will give the tenant farmers fair play in fixing rent? I don't believe that they will!'

And while Willie O'Shea in London went about his own business, pressing the Treasury, in the House of Commons, to assist with the construction of a pier at Cappagh, near Kilrush, the left wing of the Land League continued to stress in Ireland that they themselves were in no mood to compromise over the Bill, whatever their leader might say. They seemed determined to use the Bill to drive the political situation once again towards climax. Brennan at Claremorris, Co. Mayo, on Sunday 1 May told the crowds, 'Make no mistake about it – you are now at a crisis in the history of your country. If you have the courage to act as you have acted up to the present, if you show that you are men and not cowards, then the system which is already reeling will go down before the might of the people. But if you turn away from the path that you have already pursued, if you stop by the wayside, then all your past work is of no avail and the brave awakened manhood that is now in the country will not obtain much for the benefit of it.'

He referred to the principles which first guided them when the Land League raised its banner for the people. 'Every principle we then advocated is as true now as it was then. We then asked you to be self-reliant, not to look to the English House of Commons for amelioration of your condition – we told you to rely on your own stout hearts, and strong right arms, and that in Ireland and not on the floor of the English House of Commons was the strength of the power of the people . . . Well, I tell you the same today – I tell you that the moment you remove the scene of the struggle from the hills and plains of Ireland to the English House of Commons or to Irish law courts, you sound the death-knell of this movement.'

John Dillon at Grangemockler, a village some ten miles from Clonmel, was saying much the same thing that afternoon: 'Now is the time when the landlords have thrown in their last card in their endeavour to destroy this organization and to leave the people at their mercy. If we can live through this summer, if we can resist successfully . . . the evictions of the landlords for the summer until the autumn comes, then the victory is in our hands and we have it.'

Dillon was to be arrested and taken to Kilmainham jail the next day. Brennan and others were to follow him not long afterwards. There they were secure in more ways than one, having no further responsibility for whatever might happen in this critical moment to which they were summoning the people of Ireland. For Parnell it was, at least for the present, still not so easy.

Chapter 31

In the busy fortnight between the introduction of the Land Bill on 7 April and Parnell's second trip to Ireland, where he stayed until the end of the month, he obviously saw little of Katie at Eltham. But Willie was probably there quite a lot. A letter Parnell wrote her from Glasgow before leaving for Dublin on 19 April contained the sentence 'I trust my own wifie has not permitted herself to be too unhappy and that she has not been worried.'

There was no reason why she should have been worried on his account: the Government was not going to arrest him while it hoped for his help on the Land Bill. The likelihood is that the reference is to Willie. There is no indication in the letter that such a likelihood worried Parnell. His conviction that she was his own 'wifie', and his alone, seems to have been total. His letter also sent her some written 'authority' for her to collect letters addressed either to herself or to bearer at what was presumably some previously agreed address. This too suggests that Willie was around at Eltham and that knowledge of letters passing between them needed to be kept from him.

Willie continued dutifully to attend the House of Commons, marking out for himself a political role more constructive and ambitious than that of former members of the party like Shaw, who, though they appeared from time to time in the anti-Government lobby over the Coercion Bills, continued to sit loyally on the Government side of the House. Willie, loyal in general to Parnell, stayed on the Opposition benches. At the same time he asserted a personal political individuality, asking questions of the Secretary of State for War about military matters, and once in March drawing attention to his brother-in-law, General Sir Evelyn Wood, and the way his arrival in South Africa had 'inspired the troops and affeared the Boers'. A few days later he was pleading with the Chief Secretary for Ireland to allow women the option of being searched at police stations rather than immediately on the spot.

On 5 April, two days before Gladstone introduced the Land Bill, Willie took an initiative on a quite different matter. He had already been instrumental in getting a railway company to operate in West Clare; he was doing what he could to get a pier for Cappagh, near Kilrush. In both enterprises he doubtless had some degree of personal material interest. He now wrote to the Irish Lord of the Treasury enclosing a petition from Sir George O'Donnell, Bt, to have revived in his favour the old title of Tyrconnell, last enjoyed by the Deputy whom the exiled James II appointed in Ireland in 1689.

He emphasized that O'Donnell's petition had the strongest support of the Catholic hierarchy and enclosed letters from Dr John MacHale, the Archbishop of Tuam, and from the Bishops of Killala, Achonry, and Dromore. 'This unanimity among the Bishops', he added, 'is all the more remarkable because Sir George O'Donnell is not a Catholic.' And he hinted broadly at the sort of party advantage he himself was capable of seeking out for Gladstone by pointing out that Sir George had rejected help offered by 'a personage connected' with the previous Conservative Government, being himself 'a consistent Liberal'.

Sir George O'Donnell's petition was eventually to be turned down despite further persistence by Willie. But Willie had demonstrated plainly enough the capacity in which he hoped to make his mark in politics. The style of his recommendation made clear the role he saw for himself: that of an agent for the Government between traditional moderate nationalist Ireland and the emergent radical nationalism represented by Parnell. He was indeed about to venture into this field far more ambitiously and significantly, on the land question itself. His position on the Land Bill, though almost certainly favourable, had not yet been disclosed.

This, however, was the least of Parnell's concerns for the moment. He now had to make up his own mind more precisely than hitherto, because the Bill's second reading was approaching. A lead of some sort in the House would be required. Bearing in mind the degree of hostility to the Bill shown at the Convention, he now devised a piece of political engineering to enable him to be unfavourable to the Bill without opposing it. At a party meeting on 5 May in London, he forced through a resolution to the effect that, as part of a protest against Dillon's arrest, the party should, when the time came for a vote on the second reading of the Land Bill, not go into the division lobbies at all. This served the treble purpose of protesting against Dillon's arrest, marking dissatisfaction with the Bill, and at the same time doing nothing to prevent it from passing. The resolution, which expressed a sense of the Bill's 'inadequacy', was passed by only a small majority in a vote of 18 to 12. Willie O'Shea walked out of the room rather than take part in the vote.

There followed a short exchange of differing views between Parnell
and the nationalist Archbishop of Cashel, Dr Thomas Croke, who thought
it was wrong to seem to be opposing the Land Bill without first trying to
improve it. The majority of the Irish population, he said, were in favour
of giving the Government a fair chance to pass the Bill.

Parnell replied that he would indeed have hesitated to urge the course
he was taking until it had been made abundantly clear by Tory tactics
that there was 'little fear of its being endangered on the second reading
. . . Nor', he added, 'is the course proposed by us indicative of hostility to
the measure.'

This was the sort of thing he had to say to a prominent and influential
figure like the Archbishop of Cashel. And when Croke replied, realistically, that there seemed little point in splitting the party so early if voting
or non-voting made no difference, Parnell let the matter rest.

He was looking more to the mood of the democratically elected
Convention when he finally made his speech on the second reading. This
certainly indicated 'hostility to the measure'. Indeed, he began by saying
that, while most speeches so far had been concerned with details of the
Bill, he could not approve its principle, because it did no more than
simply reaffirm the principle of partnership between tenant and landlord
already introduced by the 1870 Act.

The important question was, as Parnell had more than once indicated
in public speeches: would a Government-appointed tribunal really be
likely to take the tenant's view of what should be a fair rent rather than
the landlord's? He addressed himself to the former party Chairman
William Shaw, who had broadly supported the Bill from the Government
benches: 'I now ask the Hon. Member for the County of Cork who is
doing so much to lubricate the larynx of the Irish people in order to
induce them to swallow this Bill, amended or unamended, as best they
can, I ask him whether he considers anything but a very large and general
reduction of rent will be or ought to be satisfactory to the tenants?'

It was a long speech, occupying almost fifteen columns of Hansard, but
it was less equivocal than anything he had said before. He managed, as so
often, to conjure quite a lot of tortuous nationalist argument into a speech
which was technically about an administrative measure.

He reminded the House that the Land League's doctrine of peasant
proprietorship was linked to the higher call of Irish nationality. And
turning, as he had done on the first day of the Bill, to the Government's
proposal to subsidize emigration, he cited instances of how well Irishmen
had done outside their own country, particularly in the United States, and

turned this into a major nationalist point. 'Now the reason that the Irish do not succeed in Ireland', he said, 'is because a nation governed by another nation never does succeed. Under such circumstances communities lose their feeling of independence which to them is just as necessary as to individuals, in order to promote exertion. Because your rule, a horrid rule in Ireland, overshadows everything.'

He ended on a note he had struck before in public speeches about Irish landlords. It was one which is rendered confusing by his use of the term 'landlord' as continuing to identify a class in future, even after the land they had owned had been exchanged for peasant proprietorship. But it clearly expresses a personal wish to see himself reunited with his own class in the old eighteenth-century Irish nationalism of his ancestry. It has emotional but not economic or political significance. 'We do not want the Irish landlords and the Irish tenants continually to live in opposing camps,' he said. 'As individuals, the landlords are well fitted to pick their place as the leaders of the Irish nation.'

He concluded with a pluckily optimistic gloss to complete what was virtually his last chance to be able to seem in control of the matter. He entreated the Government 'to make the measure, in committee, more healthy for the poor people and less hurtful, and to bring about such improvement in it that we, the Irish Members, may vote for it without feeling that we are compromising the position we have hitherto occupied and sustained'.

At least it expressed his predicament honestly enough.

The second reading was, as he had predicted to Archbishop Croke, comfortably passed, by a majority of 176. Thirty-seven members of the party had obeyed the party resolution and abstained, though the London correspondent of the *Freeman's Journal* said that the majority would not have done so had not Parnell threatened to resign. Among those who ignored the party resolution and voted for the Bill was Willie O'Shea. An argument put forward by one of the other party members who did likewise was that in the first place by no means all the members of the party had been present when the vote on the party resolution had been taken, and, second, that he had called a meeting of his constituents in Ireland and they were in favour of the Bill and of an attempt simply to get it improved.

To judge from a report in the *Freeman's Journal* of the following week, the strain of all this may have been beginning to show on Parnell: 'Mr Parnell, I am sorry to say, is looking very pale and weak and utterly unfitted for any active exertions. This I believe he attributes principally to the bursting of some drainpipes in the neighbourhood in which he lives and the consequent escape of noxious gases.'

The story may have been planted in the paper specifically to explain Parnell's absence from the parliamentary scene for much of the following week. It was to turn out to be an important one in Parnell's life.

In her memoirs, Katie describes how 'in the early summer of 1881' her aunt had an old friend to stay, and she herself was able to go away to Brighton for a month, where she took rooms for herself and her children. She describes Parnell coming down to see her with his beard just cut off, though this detail must be one of her chronological confusions, since he had been beardless in France as late as March of that year. The important thing is that he did go down to see her, and, since at no other time that summer did he spend time away from the House of Commons without explanation as he did in this week at the end of May, it may be supposed that he spent much of this week at Brighton.

Apart from Katie, one aspect of Brighton particularly fascinated him. The railway station there was then being rebuilt, and his engineering interests were compulsively engaged. According to Katie, 'He spent hours at odd times pacing the station, measuring distances, heights, depth of roof, etc. etc., and in drawing up plans in order that he might build a cattle shed on the same lines at Avondale.' This he eventually did.

It seems likely that it was in this week too that their first child was conceived, for she was to be born exactly nine months later. Willie probably stayed in London at least most of the time, for he appeared in Parliament on three successive days that week and voted in eight of the divisions held, whereas Parnell voted in none.

Parnell was back in the House on Monday 30 May, voting again in the same anti-Government lobby with Willie for the rest of that week. They must in any case have been in still closer contact in the days that followed, for on the afternoon of 10 June Willie had a conversation with Gladstone in the House which, though no one could possibly have realized it at the time, was to be the first preliminary step in a series of developments that were eventually to play a dramatic part in British and Irish history.

That evening Willie wrote Gladstone a letter enclosing an outline of what he had spoken to him about that afternoon, namely a plan to facilitate the passage of the Land Bill. In essence this proposed compensation from the Exchequer for landlords who agreed to reduce their rent to an average of the Griffith's valuations, and was put forward with at least a suggestion that it might prove a possible alternative to peasant proprietorship. It was to be politely but firmly turned down by Gladstone after he had referred it to his Cabinet. But the significance of the proposal lay in the wording of the letter with which Willie accompanied it. He wrote:

In order to avoid all possibility of misunderstanding, I have read it to Mr Parnell who expressed himself satisfied that it embodies the principles by which he yesterday promised that he would stand. I am therefore in a position to promise that the opposition of Mr Parnell's party in the House of Commons will immediately cease and that he will give the Bill an effectual support in Ireland, such support to be loyally afforded even if outwardly and for the moment prudently veiled.

There is an unmistakably authentic Parnell-type stamp on the last part of this sentence. In the course of Willie's spasmodic attempts over the next few years to act personally as mediator between Parnell and the Liberal Government there were times when he exaggerated the extent to which he carried Parnell's confidence, but it seems more likely than not that in this first instance he spoke the truth when he said that the plan had Parnell's approval. This was his first major effort in that field of political manipulation from which he sought personal advantage, and he would have been careful not to prejudice his credentials so soon. The whole episode is an instructive indication of the direction in which Parnell's mind was now moving, whatever he might say in public. A *modus vivendi* with the Liberal Government from which he might try to achieve at least some form of Home Rule was now the only realistic nationalist option open. But he had been careful not to tell any of his supporters either in Parliament or the Land League of this approach through O'Shea.

The Land Bill, after its second reading, went into committee for nearly two months, during which Parnell intervened more than a hundred and fifty times while the Irish did what they could to improve a Bill they both opposed and favoured. The only significant improvement was achieved by Tim Healy, with a sharp clause which prevented a landlord from increasing rent on the basis of a tenant's improvements. On the third reading, on 29 July, carried by 306 to 114, Parnell and most of his close supporters did not vote. But there were two surprises. Willie did not vote either, although given the bridging role he was allotting himself he might have been expected to back the Government. Unexpected also was the vote of J. J. O'Kelly, one of Parnell's closest supporters, in favour of the Bill – a symbolic expression perhaps of the party's tactical acceptance of the Bill despite its failure to acknowledge the Land League's principles.

Parnell was aware of the need to prepare a special position for himself if he were going to keep control of events in the months ahead. Early in July he had written to William O'Brien, one of the staff reporters of the *Freeman's Journal*, asking him to become the editor of a newspaper he was about to set up. Parnell had bought, from the by now slightly shabby nationalist journalist Richard Pigott, his two declining, old-fashioned Fenian and anti-Land-League papers, the *Irishman* and the *Flag of Ireland*.

O'Brien had written in his diary, nearly three years before when he first met Parnell: 'He has captured me heart and soul and is bound to go on capturing.' He now consulted some of the Land League extremists then in Kilmainham jail about this, in particular Dillon, whose opposition to the coming Land Act on principle and to Parnell's trimming policy continued steadfastly. When Dillon declared himself against the idea, O'Brien realized for the first time that Parnell's paper would not have a unanimous Land League executive behind it. He therefore communicated his doubts about taking the editorship to Parnell, who revealed how he intended to use the paper to keep his options open. He said he did not think this sort of opposition would last if the paper were managed on 'straightforward and advanced lines'. He would see to it that all sections of opinion in the movement were conciliated, he said, and that there would be 'no room for complaint of backwardness by anyone'. He then sent a telegram to O'Brien to come to London, and took him to dinner at his favourite restaurant, Romano's in the Strand.

Talking late over their dinner, Parnell sent O'Brien home with real insight into the ambivalent nature of his mind's workings on the national question, and 'with a certitude that discontents in either of the extreme sections could not seriously disturb the calculations of such a leader, and that nobody was less likely than he to give up the revolutionary potentialities of the movement until they had accomplished a radical and permanent change in the relations between the two countries'.

The first issue of *United Ireland* appeared on 13 August 1881, nine days before the Land Bill, conservatively revised by the Lords, received the royal assent.

Throughout these weeks nothing on the surface seemed to have interfered with Parnell's concern for the delicate internal political situation in which the Land Bill had placed him. But a disturbing incident had just occurred in his private life. It provides a strange if still somewhat indecipherable landmark in the story of his relationship with Katie and with her legal husband, Willie. As usual there is more than one source from which to try to construct an account of what actually happened, but none of them leaves a totally satisfactory sense of having learned the truth. The most clinically factual is that later disclosed by the evidence in the divorce case of November 1890.

The central fact is that on 13 July 1881, Willie suddenly wrote to Parnell as follows:

Sir – Will you be so kind as to be in Lille, or in any other town in the north of France which may suit you or your convenience, on Saturday next the 16th inst? Please let me know by 1 p.m. today where to expect you on that date so that I may be able to inform you of the sign of the inn at which I shall be staying. I await your answer in order to lose no time in arranging with a friend to accompany me.

I am your obedient servant,
W. H. O'Shea.

He was challenging his leader and house guest to a duel.

What had happened? If Willie's own evidence is to be trusted – and it is confirmed in all but accuracy of dates by Katie's – it had come for the first time to Willie's ears in London that Parnell had been staying at Eltham without his knowing of it. On 12 July Willie went down to Eltham to see Katie about this, and on arriving there he found Parnell's portmanteau in the house. A furious row between legal husband and wife followed. After a painful scene, he left the house that night and walked all the way back to London in the early hours of the morning. He went straight to St James's Street, where Anna Steele, Katie's sister, lived, and after talking to her he wrote the letter challenging Parnell to a duel. Why exactly he went to Anna Steele was never made clear. She was then on good terms with her sister, but it seems mildly strange that Willie should have immediately gone to her in the early hours of the morning. It can be seen as evidence of some genuine human desperation, as can the walk all the way back to London from Eltham when he might have found a cab.

Whatever else was going on in his mind, it seems genuinely to have been a shock to him to discover that Parnell may have been having an affair with his wife. If, on the other hand, he had up to this point been virtually conniving at an affair which suited him, it still might have seemed necessary to go through the motions of challenging the man who made a cuckold of him in current London gossip to a duel, but he would surely have set about the charade in a less agitated fashion.

He returned to Eltham in the afternoon, with Anna Steele, to talk to

Katie. She, he later said, gave him 'assurances with regard to Mr Parnell', but he does not seem to have been content to accept these at once. When he got back to London he wrote again to Parnell, not having had any reply to his first letter: 'Sir, I have called frequently at the Salisbury Club today and I find that you are not going abroad. Your luggage is at Charing Cross Station. Your obedient servant, W. H. O'Shea.'

Next day, a letter from Parnell dated 14 July from the Westminster Palace Hotel said that he had indeed replied to Willie and would now like to hear from him, since 'you will find from the contents of the letter referred to that your surmise that I refuse to go abroad is not a correct one.'

Parnell had in the meantime seen Anna Steele and had given 'assurances' that there were no grounds for jealous suspicion. These were apparently enough for Willie 'eventually' to accept them, and no more was thereafter heard of the duel.

Katie's account of this sequence of events in her memoirs and earlier to Harrison virtually confirms it. She says that it was after this incident that she and Parnell 'were one, without further scruple, without fear, and without remorse'. This may well be true, but it is unlikely to be the whole truth. What is certain is that after this incident it can no longer be said that it had not occurred to Willie that his wife might be having an affair with Parnell. Whether he genuinely accepted the 'assurances' as valid or whether it suited him to do so in view of the potential value of having the leader of his party so close to him now becomes the question.

It is of course not possible to say whether Parnell and Katie genuinely thought that they had been successful in putting their 'assurances' across. But that they seemed to feel it necessary to continue to put up some smokescreen of deceit is shown by a short series of letters which she herself publishes in her memoirs – four to be precise, between 20 and 26 July from Parnell to her, beginning 'My dear Mrs O'Shea' and preserving a tone of distant correctitude. He told her in one of them that he was thinking of going over to Paris so he would like her to send him his travelling-cap if it were at Eltham. The next day he wrote to her to tell her not to bother to do this since he was not going to France.

One further small detail of this incident remains to perplex and even to suggest a possible element of unreality on all sides in the conduct of the matter. This is that on 14 July, the very day on which Parnell wrote back to Willie, he and Willie were in the division lobbies of the House of Commons together, voting in a small Irish minority of twenty-three. To have been able to see them there might have made clearer what was actually happening.

The most important thing for both may have been that Katie from now on managed to convince each in his different way that she was his, for all her insistence in her memoirs and to Harrison that she had been 'swept into the avalanche of Parnell's love' and that she could not fight against it any longer. This in itself was certainly true, but it does not necessarily mean that her attachment to Willie was broken or that the preservation of their marriage was a mere formality. As Willie himself was later to put it, 'Having accepted the assurances I became reconciled to my wife.' Or, as his counsel in the divorce case was to put it for him, 'The affectionate relations which had always existed between Captain O'Shea and his wife were resumed.'

Nor was such testimony necessarily the humbug which some commentators have assumed. Though he was not to be cross-questioned in court, Willie O'Shea had put into the court evidence in the form of his diaries to suggest at least that those affectionate relations did last off and on for almost another five years. And when Katie gave birth to a child early in February 1882 Willie was to assume it was his own. Certainly nothing again seems to have troubled him on the lines of his former suspicions for a long time. However, even if these had returned, it seems likely that he would have found a way of dealing with them. For political events were about to place him in the position he had always hoped might come his way.

Chapter 32

The Land Bill received the royal assent on 22 August, after three weeks in which the Lords' amendments, naturally in favour of landlords, were considered by the Commons. The Irish naturally saw the amendments as mutilations of the Bill. But the Government was in some cases prepared to accept them, though conflict between the two Houses did arise and at one moment produced enough tension to make Healy think the Lords might actually throw the Bill out rather than give way.

Parnell, as so often in his career, demonstrated an ability for hard work behind the scenes which enabled him to intervene authoritatively on the detailed complexities of the amended clauses. He did so thirty-three times altogether in these three weeks. But a weight was temporarily off his mind. Though the Act fell far short of the Land League's uncompromising principles, a restructuring of the Irish landlords' property rights in favour of the tenants was now about to become law. Responsibility for an awkwardly uncommitted attitude was no longer his. He could be hostile to the Act without either endangering its benefits or occasionally having to look prepared to compromise. How far the hostility should go was the next problem, but it would be a more straightforward business.

In intervals between attention to the Lords' amendments, he had found time to enjoy himself in the House, sometimes along agreeably ir-responsible lines. In a debate on 1 August, theoretically about the order of business, he had tried to discuss treatment of so-called 'suspects' arrested under Forster's Coercion Acts. For the last three months, he said, he had been receiving dozens, even scores, of letters from prison cells in Ireland – 'as the Government must very well know, as they have been opening them'. There was a revealing echo here of the previous two-faced attitude to the Land Bill: 'These captives', he declaimed, 'cry to us and ask us whether we are going to leave the men who won the Land Bill?'

But the Speaker's interest was in telling him he was going beyond the question before the House. Parnell said he would be very sorry to do that; he wanted to confine himself within proper limits. He at once started to protest again about the arrests of the 'suspects'.

Reprimanded twice more by the Speaker, he said that if he and his fellow Irish Members were not to be allowed to bring the cause of their imprisoned countrymen before the House he would 'boldly say that all liberty and regard of private right was lost to that assembly'. He accused Gladstone of transferring himself from a constitutional Minister into 'a tyrant'. The Speaker named him for 'language utterly unparliamentary and improper' and for disregarding the authority of the chair. Gladstone rose to move his suspension, but before he could do so Parnell rose too and said that he would not wait for 'the farce of a division'. He walked out of the House, in order, he said, that the public might see 'that there is no longer freedom of discussion left to the Irish Members'.

Gladstone said he had never heard such words addressed to the Speaker. Parnell's suspension for the rest of the day was carried by 131 to 14.

Willie does not seem to have been in the House. He certainly took no part in the vote. He was, however, present for the rest of the week, and Parnell himself returned on Thursday 4 August.

It is just possible that the suspension may, on Parnell's side, have had something contrived about it. Two days before this he had written to Katie apparently for the first time since the strange incident of the duel a fortnight before. Exactly how far that unpleasantness had been resolved to the true satisfaction of all three parties remains obscure, though some awkwardness at least between the two men might have persisted as they continued to see each other daily in the division lobbies.

Parnell was probably keeping away from Eltham at weekends for the time being. The letter he had sent Katie on the Saturday before his Monday suspension was a formal one ('My dear Mrs O'Shea') — the sort of letter which she was later to describe as 'formal though friendly that anyone could have been shown'. It said that he thought she had some books of his at Eltham and that unless he heard otherwise from her he proposed to come down to look for them on Monday at 'about eleven or twelve'. He said he would call at the House of Commons on Monday to see if there was word from her.

We do not know whether there was word from her or not. We do know that the House was not due to meet that day until a quarter to two in the afternoon. So, assuming that he had intended all along to take part in the debate from which he was suspended, he is unlikely to have meant in his letter 'eleven or twelve' in the morning. But, suspended, he would have had a perfect excuse for leaving early a House which sat on, though not discussing Irish matters for long, until one o'clock next morning. Not that he ever seems to have worried about absenting himself when he felt like it, but on this occasion he could do so without reproach. Certainly a coded imprecision about timing would not have been out of character in the formal but friendly letters that were so often to pass between them over the years.

Certainly too, by a fortnight later, they were again in constant touch in spite of all 'assurances'. On 17 August he wrote her a note to say that he had been 'rendered very anxious by not receiving any news from you to-day' – as if such a day were, by now, exceptional. He trusted nothing had happened to her and that she was not ill, and added a cryptic note: 'I had a very satisfactory conversation yesterday, and things look much straighter.' This was presumably a reference to Willie, though what exactly the word 'straighter' meant in the triangle at this stage can now never be known.

Proof that he was not allowing personal concerns to interfere with the meticulous research he put into his parliamentary work is shown by the fact that on the same day as he wrote this note he delivered a long and detailed attack in the House on Forster for the type of arrest he was making under his Coercion Acts. He accused him of using these not to stop outrages but to put down public opinion and to set up 'a reign of terrorism' in the minds of every peaceably disposed person who took part in the land agitation.

He must have seen Katie over part of the next twenty-four hours or so, for, although he was in the House on both 18 and 19 August, he wrote her a note from there on the evening of the 19th to say he had arrived home all right, presumably from Eltham, and that he was very much pleased to learn that evening of her 'good hopes'. What were these? He signed it merely 'C'. The 'hopes' may well have been that Willie would be away for the weekend and beyond. Willie was in fact about to go to Ireland to visit his constituency. He was to make no further appearance in the House before the end of the session.

'Very much pleased' as Parnell was, he again did not let his personal state of mind interfere with his work. In a debate on Supply that night, he delivered a substantial speech about the salaries of the Chief Secretary and his officials which even Forster, whose position he was attacking, called very able, interesting and, he had to say, from Parnell's point of view, 'moderate'. Forster presumably could say this because, although Parnell described him in his speech as being looked upon 'with horror and detestation by the great body of the Irish people' and occupying a position 'more despotic than that of the Czar of Russia', he considerately stated that this was not so much Forster's personal fault as that of the entire system he represented, which elected people to govern Ireland 'unacquainted with the wants and aspirations of the Irish people'. As the parliamentary correspondent Henry Lucy had commented of his speech on the second reading of the Land Bill, he could have a manner persuasive in conveying that 'he was sorry – really sorry – if the course he was about to take, gave pain or inconvenience in any direction'.

Parnell's final performance for the session took place on 20 August. He moved a challenging resolution in committee: that the rearrest of Michael Davitt had not been warranted and that he ought to be freed. In reminding the House of Davitt's original sentence, of his release on ticket of leave by the Tory Government and of his part in politics after his liberation, he made what can now be seen as something like a Freudian slip which showed the way his mind was moving. For, saying that Davitt had been practically the founder of the Land League movement, he added, 'During the last twelve or eighteen months *which that movement lasted* [my italics] Mr Davitt took a very prominent part . . . in aiding the organization and objects of the Land League.'

No one took him up on this unconscious hint that the Land League's day might be over, and he went on to show how moderate Davitt's speeches had been since his return from America in November 1880, and how he had consistently deplored outrage and the use of intimidation. He quoted Davitt's 'This is a great moral organization for a moral purpose, and it must be carried on on moral lines.'

Finally he made a telling and embarrassing point against the Liberal Government when he reminded it how earlier legal proceedings they had taken against Davitt in November 1880 had failed. He could hardly have had time to 'overturn Ireland' in the interval between the dropping of those proceedings and the passing of the Coercion Act. After that it could have arrested Davitt under the lenient conditions of a 'suspect' instead of withdrawing his ticket of leave and returning him cruelly to penal servitude. 'I now', he said, 'call upon the Government for the defence of their action – Mr Davitt's conduct needs none.'

Attendance on the debate had been poor, sinking once below the quorum of forty and never rising much above a hundred. The principal Government reply came from Harcourt, the Home Secretary, who reminded the House that Davitt, convicted of Fenian activity in his youth, had in his recent speeches given just as much indication of continuing Fenian views as he had of disapproval of outrage. Just over a fortnight before he was arrested he had spoken at Mallow of 'the wolf-dog of Irish vengeance' bounding over the Atlantic if ever the patience of the Irish people became exhausted by Government brutality. The Irish Members routinely cheered this quotation, and Harcourt routinely identified it as Fenian language.

'Throughout the whole of this language . . .' he said, 'whether it be the language of the Fenian conspiracy or of the Land League organization – there is always this menace about ulterior force, a threat to resort to this ulterior force . . .'

But the menace seemed sufficiently harmless to be able to be left to a House only one-sixth full. Ambivalence about the use of force was reduced to a mere debating point on both sides of the club-like atmosphere of the House of Commons. Parnell's motion was eventually lost in an insignificant division of 61 to 19.

He probably enjoyed himself more in the debate which immediately followed in committee that day, on Civil Service Supply. In proposing to limit the sum being paid to the Royal Irish Constabulary, he desired 'to call attention to the harsh and cruel conduct of the constabulary in Ireland'.

In a Supply debate like this, he was certainly within his procedural rights in making the most of the fact that the RIC, unlike the police in England, were 'encumbered' with rifles and bayonets, handled their bayonets 'in a most savage fashion' to disperse crowds, and in at least one instance used their rifles to 'beat out a man's brains', at Bodyke in Co. Clare. In evictions, police charged into houses with fixed bayonets, sometimes through the windows, and 'were very frequently excited by drink when sent on these eviction expeditions'. When Forster queried this, asking for a specific instance, Parnell replied that he did not suppose, did he, 'that he could get even Irish policemen to knock women and children about unless they were excited by drink'?

A further complaint was that, being accoutred like soldiers, the RIC did not wear numbers and so could not be identified by the people on whom they were 'daily making attacks and assault'. The manager of a gasworks in Cork, trying to cross a bridge on his way to the races during some rioting, had been rushed at by three policemen, knocked down and stabbed in the groin by one of them but could not identify him because he wore no number.

Parnell's own sister Anna had been on a train to Limerick two months ago on which there were also constables returning from an eviction, and on arrival at Limerick they had set about the crowd on the platform waiting to greet her, 'indiscriminately right and left without the slightest provocation'. A respectable Protestant farmer 'was knocked down and brutally beaten like a dog, and the young lady with him was also knocked down'. Anna Parnell herself had only managed to escape injury by getting out of the carriage on the other side and crossing the line to leave the station that way. Irish Members were now about to go to Ireland and, as all were now probably to be exposed to this sort of treatment on the part of irresponsible constables, they were 'entitled to ask, that if they escaped being killed by these attacks upon them by the police, they should have some opportunity afforded them of being able subsequently to identify their assailants'.

This was a Saturday. He almost certainly spent a few days with Katie at Eltham. She was three months pregnant with his child, who Willie was also to think was his. His new weekly newspaper, *United Ireland*, said that it was in a position to announce that Parnell would be spending a few days in Paris (a usual cover of his for Eltham, though the paper might not have been expected to know that) before going to address a meeting of the Land League of Great Britain at Newcastle upon Tyne at the end of the week. But a by-election taking place in Ulster seems to have changed his mind. By the time that paragraph appeared in *United Ireland*, Parnell had already been a day in Co. Tyrone.

This journey to Ireland was to be his last either way across the Irish Sea for more than seven months. It was to lead to a turning-point in his career as decisive as that of February, and far more dramatic. Before eight weeks were up he was to fall into police hands himself. They would not, however, be armed with rifle and bayonet, and he was to have no difficulty in identifying them, for they were to introduce themselves to him personally. He was not to see Katie again until after their child was born.

His political concern now was to help determine the Land League's attitude to the new Land Act. It had been evidence of his continually maturing political adroitness that he had managed to get the second meeting of the Convention postponed until after the debatable clauses on which it had originally been convened to pronounce had become law and unalterable. This postponed meeting was now set for 15–17 September. He could expect strong words for total rejection of the Act.

In the meantime he turned his attention to the by-election in Ulster. There the Land League had managed to attract more support than might have been expected, given its equal concern for both nationalist and agrarian principles. By the weekend he was campaigning for the Home Ruler and Land League candidate for Co. Tyrone, a Unitarian clergyman named Harold Rylett opposing both a Conservative, and, more important, a Liberal named T. A. Dickson. The previous Member, a Liberal, had had to resign on being appointed to the Land Commission.

If Parnell had been reading the *Freeman's Journal* attentively that week, as he usually did, he might have noted with relief on more than one count that Willie, who had also come to Ireland, was attending conscientiously to his constituency duties. Captain O'Shea, the paper said, had been visiting nine 'suspects' from Co. Clare imprisoned in Limerick jail for whose release he had for some time been 'exercising his influence'. He had come specially to see them in order to find out more particulars of their cases. His interviews with each subject were of 'very long duration'.

In the Liberal constituency of Co. Tyrone it was obviously essential to identify Home Rule and the Land League as far as possible with the traditional Ulster Liberal cause. An early emphasis of Parnell's when he spoke at Newtonstewart in Co. Down on Sunday 28 August was on the need for Dickson to retire in Rylett's favour and 'not split the Liberal ranks'. The Land League was made to seem somehow a subsidiary, if an important one, of the Liberal cause, though the Liberal cause also had somehow to be made independent of the Liberal Government. It was a tortuous exercise, but he had long become a master of such work.

Speaking next at Dromore and Enniskillen, he again performed the feat of rolling different objectives into a single cause. 'What', he asked at Enniskillen, 'is the end and object of the Land League for which we struggle? We aim at abolishing rent and making the people the owners of the land of this country. The Government passed an Act in the session just gone by for the purpose of establishing the courts to fix rents. We do not aim at fixing rent because, as I have said, we aim at abolishing it altogether, and as far as the Land Law may reduce the rents, so far will it go in our direction, and if the result of the Land Act should be to reduce the rents by 30% we can fairly call on you to rally again. And with this proof – that a reduction in your rent is the result of two years' work by the Land League – we can call on you to rally behind us and press on with this work until we have reduced the rent to nothing at all.' He added that the final success of what he called 'your movement' might take a few years, but his audience would have left with his cry ringing in their ears that 'the attempt to reconcile the interests of idleness and industry, of the toilers in the fields and the dwellers in the castle, is utterly impossible'.

This could not fail to be an attractive note in Ulster, where, though the farms were more prosperous than in most of the rest of Ireland, rents were felt to be high. Nothing was said at Enniskillen about the nationalist cause also discreetly lodged in the Land League programme, and in areas where the landed gentry tended to be regarded as more relevant enemies than nationalists there was something strongly appealing about his assurance that the Land League was concerned to see that land should be transferred 'from the oligarchy who hold it, the ten thousand landlords, to the six hundred thousand tenant farmers who with their families constitute the great majority of the Irish people'.

He did go so far as to talk about 'national force' when he admitted that he disagreed with Michael Davitt's view that 'the Land Act would disintegrate the national force'. But here in Ulster the 'national force' could be taken to produce a disappearance of rent rather than the disappearance of British rule.

A clear picture began to emerge of the attitude he intended to take towards the Land Act once it came into operation. At Strabane, after first telling the crowd that the Land Act had been obtained mainly through the exertions of the Land League, he said, 'If we can teach the tenant farmers how much of it they can possibly use, and how much they ought to reject, then this Land Act properly used and carefully guarded against – insofar as it is likely to produce demoralization into our ranks – would be of importance in encouraging the people, in putting them in a better position to push forward and gain the full platform.' In other words, if the Land Act turned out to work beneficially, so much the better; but the important thing was that it provided a new stage from which to push further ahead to total peasant proprietorship.

He had originally been due to preside over a Land League meeting in Dublin the next day, Wednesday 31 August, but had already sent a letter from the White Hart Hotel in Omagh to say that he was too busy canvassing to attend. Sexton, who read his letter to the meeting, added, 'I observe with rejoicing that Mr Parnell is exhibiting in this contest that marvellous energy and that stern and uncompromising Irish spirit which has won for him the leadership of the Irish Party.'

On Thursday 1 September he was at Dungannon, where, a hundred years before, the legendary Volunteers of Protestant nationalism had first come together to give a nominal legislative independence to their Irish parliament. He linked that event to modern times by saying that the tenant farmer had made more progress in the two years of the Land League than in the eighty years since the Union which had removed that parliament. It was an indication of at least temporary success in that widely Protestant locality that the crowd drew him back in a wagonette to his hotel after the meeting.

He weighed up judiciously what it was tactful to say and not to say in

Ulster, depending on the composition of the local population. At Fintona, where there were many Catholics, he told them with reference to the Land Act to 'beware of the concealed evil which lies in every gift which we get from England'. But at Ballygawley he was in trouble. Speaking from a small platform in the main street, he was continually interrupted. 'You are not wanted here!' came shouts from the crowd, followed by cries for Dickson, the Liberal candidate. He had temporarily to suspend the view he had expressed in Parliament about the work of the Royal Irish Constabulary: 'If you continue to interrupt I will give the offenders into the hands of the police.'

There was more interruption. The *Freeman's Journal* reported, 'Mr Parnell then called the attention of the constabulary to the affair and the head constable removed the chief offenders.' And when interruptions broke out again, he addressed himself in his sternest Ascendancy tones to one of the young men in the crowd, telling him that if he did not behave himself he would have him arrested.

Parnell's canvass for the Home Ruler here was more than just an electoral campaign. It was only the second time he had made a foray into Ulster since becoming nationalist leader. Assuming a responsibility, as leader, for the whole island, as he increasingly saw it necessary to do, he was tackling the trickiest aspect of all in the nationalist aspiration; namely, that a sizeable proportion of the Irish population from the North-East no longer wished to have anything to do with this aspiration. Thus the aspect of the Land League's platform to be emphasized here, to the temporary exclusion of much of the rest, was its achievement in bringing into prospect lower rents and even finally a total peasant proprietorship. What Land League organizers like Boyton, Sheridan and Brennan had constantly emphasized, the movement's aspiration for Irish nationality, could be left to look after itself for the time being.

At Cookstown, the weekend before the poll, Parnell went as close to the nationalist wind as was appropriate. First he told them what they most wanted to hear. 'The landlords of Ireland', he said, 'have reaped where they have not sown, they gather where they have not toiled. It is time to put an end to them.' Then he exhorted his audience to show the determination and courage of their race with the words 'Let the North join with the South, Presbyterians and Protestants and Catholics, till they hold such a united Ireland as will show every English Government that they can no longer dare to oppose the irresistible advances of Irish democracy.'

Certainly there was a slight echo of Wolfe Tone here, but Tone after all had had some success in that part of Ireland in his time.

He was not always successful in blurring the issue. At the eve-of-poll meeting at Dungannon he had a rougher reception than before, finding it difficult to get a hearing at all. The mood of Ulster was, unlike that in the other provinces, unpredictable. Returning to Ballygawley, where he had had a bad time before, he now found cheering crowds and blazing tar-barrels to greet him. But how successful would the actual campaign for his candidate turn out to be?

The *Freeman's Journal* on the day of the poll paid him a special tribute: 'Even those', it wrote, 'who best know Mr Parnell's indomitable energy and determination have been astonished at the marvellous display of these qualities on the present occasion. When he went into battle it had appeared hopeless . . .'

Hopeless the battle turned out to have been. On 7 September the Liberal, Dickson, was elected with 3,168 votes over the Conservative, Colonel Knox, who won 2,084. The Home Ruler, Rylett, trailed far behind with 907 votes.

It was disappointing. Gladstone in particular took great comfort from the result. But in the longer-term interest of Irish nationality Parnell could reasonably think that his time had not been wasted. When he addressed the Land League in Dublin the next day, he even managed to analyse the vote quite optimistically. There were in any case, he said, only 1,700 Catholic voters on the electoral list; Tyrone used to be one of the blackest of the northern counties; and, considering that most of the priests would have gone for Dickson, there was something to be proud of about this first contest which the Land League had ever fought in the North. 'Two years ago', he said, 'it would not have been possible for me to have gone through the country and preach the doctrines we preach there and have escaped with our lives.'

He had to return to what was now going to be the main problem. As he put it to the League meeting in Dublin, 'It is of the utmost importance that the farmers should maintain an attitude of reserve in order that they may not be demoralized by those parts of the Act which have been intended for their demoralization.' He meant those parts of the Act intended to seduce them with the prospect of reduced rents and to make them forget everything else about the Land League programme.

The extent to which Parnell was himself envisaging that programme in terms not only of the land question but of wider national aspirations was shown by his growing concentration on other national themes. One was the need to look to the interests not only of the tenant farmers themselves but of the labourers, artisans, shopkeepers and others whose improved status also figured within the context of a true Irish national society. Another was the need to develop Irish industries. But he had more immediate matters to concentrate on first.

Though colleagues like Dillon and Egan would have preferred him to denounce the Act totally, the basis on which he now presented its acceptance was hardly something to which they and what *United Ireland* editor William O'Brien called the 'Kilmainham party' could reasonably object. This of course did not stop some of them from objecting, particularly in the confinement of Kilmainham itself. One of the 'suspects' then held there told Parnell's first biographer many years later how a clique among them, which was already finding fault with Parnell for his moderation and complaining that he wanted to work with the Act and unite with the Liberal Party, had met in a shed in the recreation yard to decide what message to send to the National Convention on 15 September.

Proceedings in the shed were opened by one of those present suggesting that a box of matches should be sent to the Convention as a gesture towards the burning of the Land Act. But in fact the Convention passed off smoothly enough, thanks largely to Parnell's adroit and sympathetic handling of the vociferous left wing.

'The Land Act settles nothing,' he said. 'It leaves everything in an unsettled condition to be a continual source of contention between the landlords on the one side and the tenants on the other ... The Land Act was undoubtedly intended to break up the organization, to produce individual, even sectional contentment, while the grievances of the great mass of the tenant farmers and the people of Ireland were still left unresolved.' And now, among other people of Ireland, he particularly pressed the cause of the labourers omitted from the Bill.

Expanding further on the national theme, he stressed the need for Irish industrial development: self-government, he said, would provide protection for Irish industry. In the meantime they should try to impose a protectionist system for themselves – buying, wherever they could, Irish goods rather than those made in England. 'The cause of the political and social evils which afflict and impoverish our country,' he said, 'is to be found in the detestable system of alien rule so injurious and oppressive to our people.'

He was not in Ulster now. He could stress the national theme as much as he liked, and he well knew that the Convention liked it too. Resolutions were passed unanimously, securing Ireland's right to national self-government without qualification of that self-government's extent, condemning coercion, reasserting the need to abolish landlordism, and confirming the unacceptability of the landlord–tenant principle behind the Land Act. As to policy towards that Act, after the long debate in which out-and-out opponents were allowed to have their head, Parnell asserted his authority and a resolution authorizing the executive to select tenancies in various parts of Ireland to be made the subject of test cases before the courts was carried by acclamation. Finally, whereas the Act said that fair rents should run for fifteen years, the Convention recommended only yearly tenancies, on the grounds that the ability to pay even a fair rent could well vary considerably with changing economic and weather conditions over so many years.

It was the sort of occasion that made people feel that they had the power over events which they claimed to have. O'Brien, editing *United Ireland*, had been quite carried away, calling the Convention 'in all but name the Sovereign Parliament of the Irish nation'. That might conceivably have been true of a Convention called the previous February. But if it had been a sovereign Irish parliament now it would have been laying down its own prescription for the Irish land question and not having to debate one already made for Ireland by a British Government.

But the general effect of the Convention's success was quite enough to worry traditional Unionists. The former Conservative Chief Secretary for Ireland, Sir Michael Hicks Beach, said in the Conservative stronghold of Cheltenham the following week that anyone who had studied speeches at the Convention would find that 'the delegates to it regarded the Act as little else than waste paper, and made no secret that what they wanted was the separation of Ireland from the United Kingdom'. And certainly in Ireland's capital there was felt to be cause for celebration. While Tim Healy went to Cork to begin to select the first test cases to take to the land court, Parnell came to Dublin from Avondale to receive a hero's welcome as if he were somehow on the eve of a great national victory.

It was a demonstration organized with theatrical panache but no great efficacy by the Land League. It was dark by the time the train reached Harcourt Street Station at 8.10 p.m. on Sunday 25 September, and tens of thousands of people were waiting for him in the streets. The *Freeman's Journal* next day described how, as his carriage slowly made its way through the masses of people, 'the glaring lights of the flambeaux made the scene both weird and remarkable'.

At the junction between Harcourt Street and St Stephen's Green the horses were taken from his carriage and he was drawn by strong men down Grafton Street to College Green, where he dramatically brought the procession to a halt himself, pointing at the Bank of Ireland to declare that it was 'a place of memories which no Irishman would ever forget'. Ten years later almost to the day his coffin was to be halted at the same spot. The throng was now so great around him that, although he had been due at the Land League offices in Sackville Street at 9.15, it was not until more than an hour later that he eventually arrived there. He looked exhausted and had to have a rest before he could address the crowd.

Sexton stood in for him on the balcony for a while, telling the masses filling Sackville Street before him, 'Tonight this ancient city has covered itself with glory. It has given to the greatest statesman the Irish race has ever produced the greatest demonstration of enthusiastic feeling ever shown in the history of Ireland or of any country in the world.'

An illuminated address presented to Parnell on arrival had ended after much fulsome praise with the words 'We ask you to lead us on to that glorious consummation, the dream of Tone, Emmet and Fitzgerald – National Independence.' And the cries from the crowd below were for three cheers for the Irish Republic.

Parnell himself, by now refreshed and speaking with what the *Freeman's Journal* called 'a considerable amount of energy and evident feeling', contributed to the occasion in the same spirit. 'Those not yet born', he said, 'will thank you who are alive today who have taken part in the great work of the Land League . . . The spirit shown in the jails and in every quarter and every corner of Ireland will never die until it destroys the alien rule which has kept our country impoverished and in chains and sweeps that detestable rule with its buckshot and its bayonets far away over the Channel whence it can never return.'

For a moment he brought himself back to reality with care. 'But we are warned by the history of the past that we must fight these people within the lines of the Constitution . . . We shall not permit ourselves to be tempted for one instant beyond our strength.'

It would in any case not even be necessary, it seemed: 'As we have succeeded in bringing the national movement and the cause of Ireland up to its present point in a few short months we are confident that before many months have elapsed we shall put on the completing work and finish the edifice which Irishmen have striven during long centuries to build. And today for the first time Ireland believes in the probability of completing it.'

Anyone listening to him might have thought the time had already come.

'We say to England: You have endeavoured to rule us for 700 years and your failure is more disastrous than it has been at any time during those long years ... And we say to England: You have been tried and you have been found wanting, you had better give it up, for if you don't give it up soon the united voice of the civilized world will bear it no longer.'

But the immediate reality to be faced the next day revolved around the question: would the tenant farmers be seduced by 'fair rents' into forgetting the higher national principles of the Land League?

A number of local County Conventions were planned. At the first of these, held at Maryborough, Queen's County, on Monday 26 September, Parnell went straight to the point, asking tenants not to show a selfish spirit by rushing into the land courts and taking advantage of them when they came.

He seemed to be putting his heart into the attempt to convince the tenant farmers that they were involved in the building of a new Ireland. Again he stressed the need to include the labourers in this new society they were building. And lest such an appeal should seem too altruistic, he took care to point out that it should not cost them anything to do this. The 'fair rent' would have to take into account the tenants' need to pay good wages to their labourers, so that 'liberality to your labourers will come not out of your pockets but the pockets of the landlords'. Even this, however, was taking an optimistic view of human nature. The counter-argument could be that the liberality having got into their own pockets should stay there. And how, a cynic might further argue, would the liberality to labourers not have to come out of the tenants' own pockets when they eventually became the owners of their own land according to Land League principles?

The appeal on the land question, like that on nationality, lay on a border between idealism and self-interest.

There was further evidence in his speeches at this time of idealistic thinking he had picked up from socialist-minded radicals in the Land League like Brennan, with their contacts in Britain with the Marx-reading H. M. Hyndmann of the Democratic Federation. 'It is our determination to insist that all the working classes of this country, be they farmers, labourers, artisans or shop-keepers – everybody who lives by his hand or his brain shall earn a fair substance.'

Later he stated categorically that the Land Act was 'quite inadequate even as a settlement of the question between landlord and tenant in Ireland'. And he reminded them that the present plan was clear. No one should go into the land court without the sanction of his local branch of

the Land League. It was important that only average cases should be
tested – not those with high or very low rents. Very high rents would
make it easy for the land court, wanting to make a good impression, to
lower them ostentatiously and thus undermine confidence in the Land
League. 'It would', said Parnell, 'call upon the tenant farmers of Ireland
to admire it and say, "See what fine fellows we are, and how we are
reducing your rent!"'

Presiding over the weekly meeting of the Land League in Sackville
Street next day, he reiterated the hope that no tenant would apply to the
court on his own account without first consulting his local branch. He
said the Land League's selection of cases to be tested would be ready by
the first day of the court's sitting. And he added a personal touch to give a
special note of confidence to his support of the League. He said a
shopkeeper in his own county of Wicklow was in trouble with the police
for putting up a notice to the effect that no one should go into, stay in, or
have anything to do with a house which had entertained the so-called
Emergency men, recruited to help landlords with their problems over
evictions. When he got back to Avondale in a day or two, he said, he was
going to put exactly the same notice up on his own door and see if the
police would come.

But that very week he received a disturbing indication of the sort of
difficulties that lay in store. The Catholic hierarchy at Maynooth issued a
manifesto earnestly exhorting the Irish people to avail themselves of what
they described as 'the advantages derivable from this Act'. Their belief
was that 'if rightly used, it will bring substantial benefits and help them to
obtain their rights social and political which they justly claim'. This
Catholic backing to the tenants' natural wish to pursue their own interests
was likely to prove a formidable counter to Parnell's plea that they should
do no such thing.

He was not a man to underestimate political problems in his way, and
he now stepped up the intensity with which he promoted his theme. It is
possible that in the near-euphoric mood in which he was now being
received round Ireland – ironically, partly a result of the 'inadequate'
Land Act being seen as a welcome achievement – he overrated his chances
of success.

By no means all the clergy were of a different opinion from his. On
Sunday 2 October, Father Sheehy, a popular priest who had been one of
the first 'suspects' imprisoned in Kilmainham, was released as a gesture of
goodwill by the Government. Parnell, taking Sheehy with him, on that
Sunday made something like a triumphant entry into his own constituency

city of Cork. They drove together in a coach from the station into a garlanded city, both themselves laden with flowers, through cheering crowds whose applause, according to the *Freeman's Journal*, broke out on every side, 'like the rattle of musketry' and through 'a hurricane of agitated handkerchieves'. It was, said the paper – and this was the sort of thing that was now being said all the time about Parnell – an ovation such as he had never had before. It might have been difficult in these circumstances not to think he was truly on the threshold of victory.

In the course of his speech at the banquet in his honour that evening at Cork, he allowed himself to give a fair idea of what he might consider a fair rent to be when adjusted by the land courts. Estimating the true rental value of the land of Ireland as being then between two and three million pounds, he noted that the rent actually being paid was seventeen million pounds. An adjustment in proportion to that discrepancy was thus signalled as the sort of thing the Land League might deem a fair rent. It would of course still only be regarded as a stage on the way to the true goal of a peasant proprietorship and not in any way a final settlement.

Such a suggestion was unlikely to receive serious attention in England, and indeed before the week was out Gladstone had singled it out for particular scorn and reprobation. Not that Parnell was in any mood to care what Gladstone had to say. He wound up his speech at the Cork banquet with the words 'Our English governors must yield to the rational demands and aspirations of our people. This struggle is simply a renewal of the old battle which has lasted so long. You were never nearer winning it than you are today. You never had such an opportunity of victory as you have today.'

But the immediate struggle was to be with his own people. The next day he was in Mallow, where he was also welcomed with a great demonstration, although he had arrived on a private visit. He came in fact with a list of those evicted tenants whose cases had been selected for investigation by the Land League with a view to them being taken as test cases. The warmth of his welcome did not prevent him from delivering a sharp rebuke to the League's local Mallow branch, which he described as a rotten one for using its Land League grants to pay rents demanded in order to prevent evictions. He moved from there to Waterford, where another County Convention was about to sit and where the whole town was hung with flags and evergreens to welcome him.

At the Convention he referred to the possible tactic of paying no rent at all, and he made a gesture in the direction of the Catholic hierarchy which had so recently cut across his purpose with their manifesto. He said untruly that though people of influence had put forward this 'no rent' idea, he himself had always been opposed to it on the grounds that to do so would be to lose the support of the clergy and cause division in the Land League ranks. But he again stressed strongly that 'no tenant must go and make his little huckstering bargain with the landlord by himself'. It was a phrase of which he had become fond; he repeated it a number of times in the course of that week.

Behind everything he said and did there was now a lively awareness of the need to keep the confidence of his more extreme but influential supporters – men like Egan, Brennan and others in the Kilmainham party. With their continued support came even more important support from America and, most important of all, the money that came with that. The extreme nationalists in the United States were the people who raised most of the money, among them Patrick Ford, the editor of the widely read *Irish World*, and his own much-loved sister Fanny, who ran the New York Ladies' Land League. She had sent a poem to William O'Brien for *United Ireland* about the Land Act which began:

> Tear up the parchment lie,
> Scatter the fragments to the hissing wind . . .

Of course there were such tactical considerations for him to bear in mind, but it is difficult to think that he was being half-hearted about what he was saying: he could hardly otherwise have been saying it so power-fully. Or was his chief concern to convince himself?

The reasoning with which he had brought the Dublin Convention unanimously to back the policy of testing the Act had been immaculate. As he had said there, he did not believe the Act would stand the test, but only when it had been shown that it did not would they be justified in the eyes of world opinion in whatever stand they might take for the future – whether this were to be a 'no rent' policy or otherwise. There seems no reason to think that he personally was then considering compromise on the final principle of peasant proprietorship. The Act did make certain provisions for that, but on a scale which, viewed realistically, was insignificant. It was no charade he was playing with the policy of testing the Act, though the likelihood of failure must have been strongly in his mind. For the real question was not whether he would continue to hold his more extreme supporters on both sides of the Atlantic together, but whether his moderate supporters, the rank-and-file tenant farmers, would continue in line. Would they have the moral fibre to resist the attractions of a lowered rent, even though lowered by much less than the six-sevenths figure he was suggesting?

There was also working in his mind a factor of which the outside world had no knowledge: how would the uncertain consequences of an uncertain situation affect what was by now unquestionably the one firm reality in his own life, namely his love for Katie O'Shea? Serenity and stability were what he found with her, whatever problems might arise from him doing so. But he was clearly now courting disturbance to that serenity.

As early as 26 September, when Parnell addressed the County Convention at Maryborough, Chief Secretary Forster had written to Gladstone to suggest that Parnell should be arrested. Gladstone had demurred. But that was before Parnell's triumphant progress through Munster and Leinster. The Prime Minister's view was changing. As the Dublin street ballad-maker was soon to have it:

> It was the tyrant Gladstone
> And he said unto himself:
> I will never be aisy,
> Till Parnell is on the shelf.
> So make the warrant out in haste
> And send it by the mail
> And we'll clap the pride of Erin's isle
> Into cold Kilmainham jail.

Chapter 33

On Friday 7 October while Parnell, flushed with his triumph at Waterford on the Thursday, went off to his shooting-lodge at Aughnavannah with O'Kelly for a day's shooting before leaving for Wexford on the Sunday, Gladstone, addressing Liberals on a number of subjects at Leeds, turned to Ireland and in so many words accused Parnell of wanting to sabotage the Land Act. He at least had no doubt that Parnell was doing much more than papering over his own internal political cracks: he saw him as presenting a policy which would have to be tackled head-on if his own skilful device of the Land Act were to pacify Ireland as he intended. As he said in his speech at Leeds, 'We are convinced that the Irish nation wishes to take free and full advantage of the Land Act.' And Parnell was telling the Irish nation not to do that. To tumultuous cheering, Gladstone now told his audience in what could only be heard in Ireland as ominous tones that 'the resources of civilization are not exhausted' in dealing with what he had called 'the immoral and degrading doctrines' which Parnell was preaching.

The very day of this speech of Gladstone's at Leeds, Parnell, acting as Chairman of the weekly meeting of the Land League in Dublin, had shown himself quite unperturbed at the thought of anything Gladstone might say or not say about him. He told the meeting that the executive was busy filing applications for hearing before the land courts of two cases involving evicted tenants in Co. Cork, four in Co. Donegal, two in Co. Derry, two in King's County, one in Tyrone, two in Fermanagh and two in Co. Roscommon. He said a hundred more such cases should be ready in a few days' time. Such cases had been specifically chosen as ones in which the courts would not find themselves able to reduce the rents.

Certainly it looked as if Parnell, if not primarily rejecting the Land Act, as Gladstone in his speech implied, was doing his very best to see that it would not work. Small wonder that Patrick Egan, the Land League Treasurer over from Paris for the meeting, went out of his way to say that, whatever slight differences of opinion they had had over questions of policy in the past, there was none now as regards the ultimate object of the League in getting rid of landlords.

Parnell moved calmly off next day by the morning train from Avondale's local station, Rathdrum, for another triumphal welcome awaiting him at Wexford. With him was O'Kelly, closest to him of all his MPs, together with Healy, still close but never a companion, and the local Wicklow MP, Byrne. They stopped on the way at Enniscorthy, where Parnell received a welcoming address and delivered the now routine injunction to do 'no miserable huckstering bargain' with landlords behind the backs of their neighbours. They moved on towards Wexford.

His movements about Ireland had recently been so continuous that it is easy to forget the attraction which his own house at Avondale still held for him despite all other concerns and commitments, including Katie at Eltham. Sometimes he managed, as it were, to marry her to him at Avondale, writing to her, as he had done in the early part of that week, as 'my own Wifie', to tell her that two separate tests carried out on the dark stone in the old silver mine on his estate had shown there to be a good deal of silver there and that miners were already working on it. He thought he might be able to get six or eight ounces to the ton out of it, which would make it a viable proposition to work. This information was the sole content of his letter, which revealed no personal emotion other than the opening words and the signature 'Your Own King'.

They had clearly been keeping up an intimate correspondence, by letter or wire, ever since he had left for the by-election in Tyrone, when he had had to be away for nearly a fortnight. Shortly after he returned from that he had sent her a bogus formal letter from Morrison's Hotel, Dublin, where he was staying after presiding over that week's Land League meeting. The letter said that he had 'quite recovered' from some 'attack' and the doctor had said he would be able to travel in a few days. This unnecessary and even improbable information was doubtless there to help with the useful picture of a political leader, friendly with the O'Sheas, whose troubles with delicate health made him fragile in his bachelor state and in need of sensible care and attention whenever it could be provided for him in England. The enclosure with this letter, addressed and to be posted to someone else, in fact began, 'My own Wifie' and made no reference to his health at all but was concerned that he had not been able to write to her as much as he had wanted, if only a few words – 'but', he wrote, 'my Beauty will forgive her own husband'. He said the wire that he had just received from her would have an instant answer. He also wrote, 'It gives me so much pleasure to know that your trouble has not returned since I left, and that my wires give you pleasure.'

Was this a reference to Willie? Or to some problem with her pregnancy?

This was in fact now four months advanced and beyond the normal phase of particular discomfort. But something was making her sad. Was this her conscience over Willie? Or her King's absence? He told her that her King thought 'very, very often of his dearest Queen' and wanted her to be happy for his sake. As for his own activity, 'Everything is going on very well here,' he said, 'and your King is much satisfied.'

On the day before Gladstone made his speech at Leeds, Parnell sent Katie a long, intimate letter from Morrison's Hotel. It is a letter which seems to make many things clear about the state of their affair at this moment, one of which being that Willie, then in Ireland, was in no conventional sense of the word 'condoning' it. The letter is worth quoting in full.

My own Wifie, –

I called to-day to see him on my return from Dungarvan, but he was out, and I waited for him three hours. [In reprinting this letter in her memoirs, Katie placed a footnote to make clear that 'him' meant Captain O'Shea.] Calling again at eleven to-night, he was again out, but returned just as I was writing to make an appointment for the morning. He *says* that he leaves to-morrow (Friday) evening, and stops to shoot on Saturday in Wales, and goes on Tuesday to Paris to see the Papal Nuncio, who he says has requested him to come. This, then, is the last letter I can send you for the present through Eltham, so I hope to have the other address from you to-morrow morning.

My dearest Katie must have been very lonely ever since. Did she get my three letters? Her husband has been so busy, he has not even had time to sleep, but he has never been too busy to think of her.

I can go to London early next week if I may see you. Should I remain in London or go down to you?

With numerous kisses to my beautiful Queenie.

C.S.P.

He was not to be in London early next week, or indeed for several months to come, though an immediate visit was clearly what he was planning.

He wrote again the next day to 'My dearest little Wifie', saying that her husband had been 'very good since he left you, and is longing to see you again. He has kept his eyes, thought, and love all for you, and my sweetest love may be assured that he always will.' As soon as he got back from Wexford he hoped to be able to go over and see her by Wednesday at the latest. Everything in Dublin, he said, had been settled up 'pretty satisfactorily, and I trust only to have to make an occasional appearance in Ireland during the rest of the autumn and winter.' He signed himself 'Always Your King'.

The meeting on the Sunday at Wexford went off with the now customary *élan*. With the town decorated in the customary triumphal tradition of arches draped with laurels and other foliage, Parnell's carriage, drawn by four grey horses with postilions, moved to the Windmill Hills outside the town, where the great insurrectionary events had taken place in 1798. At the place where he was to speak, a scarecrow-like effigy wearing a tall white hat to represent a landlord had been tied hanging to the chimney of a tumbledown cottage.

Parnell told the crowds that they had gained something in the last twelve months, but only a fraction of what they were justly entitled to. 'The Irishman who thinks that he can throw away his arms just as Grattan disbanded the Volunteers in 1782,' he said, 'will find to his sorrow and destruction when too late that he has placed himself in the power of a perfidious and cruel and unrelenting English enemy.'

There were groans for Gladstone.

It was a relatively short speech for these days, but one splendid sentence was to ring down through history. Addressing himself to what could only be interpreted as the threat Gladstone had delivered at Leeds, he said, 'It is a good sign that this masquerading knight-errant, this pretending champion of the rights of every other nation except those of the Irish nation, should be obliged to throw off the mask today, and stand revealed as the man who, by his own utterances, is prepared to carry fire and sword into your homesteads, unless you humbly abase yourselves before him and before the landlords of the country.'

The next day Parnell received the freedom of Wexford. At a banquet in his honour that evening, it was his own name instead of 'the Queen' which was coupled with the prosperity of Ireland in a variation of the traditional toast. He commented that he could not but think this a happy augury for the future of Ireland and for the downfall of English institutions in the country. 'We won't', he said, 'get anywhere until we remove English misrule.'

Asked after his speech of the day before whether he thought it was likely to lead to his arrest, he is said to have replied, 'I think I am likely to be arrested at any time – so are we all. A speech is not necessary.' Indeed it was not. The decision to arrest him had already been taken in principle. When one of his Members of Parliament was talking to Parnell's first biographer some fifteen years later, he said he had asked Parnell that evening if he had any instructions for them if he were to be arrested. 'Ah!' Parnell is said to have replied deliberately, looking through a glass of champagne which he had raised to his lips. 'Ah! If I am arrested, Captain Moonlight will take my place.' The story has sometimes been judged apocryphal.

Captain Moonlight, an overall synonym for the small secret agrarian groups busy with 'outrages' in the countryside, had long been independently at work in the cause of the Land League. It remained to be seen whether the Captain would be able to work so effectively without the oblique sense of authority he could claim when Parnell was there.

Parnell got back from Wexford on Tuesday 11 October and wrote to Katie from Morrison's Hotel, Dublin, to thank her for the two letters and two wires 'from your King's Queen' which had been waiting for him. He added a phrase that must be cryptic for posterity but would not have been to her: 'Your telegram this morning took a great weight off my mind, as your silence made me almost panic-stricken lest you had been hurt by that ——— [*and this was how she printed it in her memoirs*] and had not been able to try to get to town.'

Willie, we know, had just returned to England from Ireland, and the reference must have been to him. Some fear that he might have been pressing his 'conjugal rights' could have accounted for it.

However that might be, Parnell, seeing himself as her own true husband, intended to start for London at the end of the week, after a visit to a meeting in Kildare on Thursday 13 October. 'If I arrive London Friday night shall go to some hotel and shall wait for my darling. Will she mind asking for my number?'

But he did not even get to Kildare. Intending to catch the 10.15 train from Kingsbridge station, he had himself woken at 8.30 by the porter of Morrison's Hotel. This porter told him that two gentlemen were waiting below to see him. Parnell sent him back down to ask their names, and the porter returned with the information that one was the Superintendent of Police, John Mallon, and the other a police constable. With characteristic *hauteur* Parnell sent a message that he would see them in half an hour, when he was dressed. He used the time to scribble to Katie a few words of 'comfort and hope', for he knew the shock would be terrible for her. But the porter meanwhile gallantly told the police that Parnell was not after all stopping at the hotel. He came back to advise Parnell to escape through the back of the house. Parnell appreciated this, but declined on the sensible grounds that the police would be watching every exit. The porter then went down to show the detectives up. Superintendent Mallon presented the warrant for Parnell's arrest courteously, and they were courteously received. Parnell was told he could post his letter on their way from the hotel to Kilmainham jail.

The party travelled in an ordinary cab until they reached the Bank of Ireland on College Green, where Parnell had made his grand rhetorical gesture only just over a fortnight before. There a group of Dublin Metropolitan police were now waiting and jumped on to two jaunting-cars to drive ahead of the cab. Mounted police were waiting as they turned the corner from Parliament Street on to the quay that ran along the river Liffey; they escorted the procession up towards Kilmainham. Few people in the streets paid much attention at that time in the morning; this was the sort of activity that had come to be seen as fairly routine since the introduction of the Coercion Acts. It was to be a few hours before the news of Parnell's arrest excited a great outburst of furious indignation all over nationalist Ireland.

In England the news was greeted with wild enthusiasm as Gladstone, at the Guildhall that morning to receive the freedom of the City of London, theatrically had himself presented with a telegram and announced to an excited audience that 'within minutes' the resources of civilization had been put into effect. The man who 'had made himself prominent in the attempt to destroy the authority of the law' was under arrest.

On arrival at Kilmainham, Parnell did what he could to destroy authority there by refusing to allow himself to be searched, but he did agree to empty his pockets on to a table. Seven pounds was taken off him for safe custody. He was placed temporarily in a bare but medium-sized room with a table and two chairs but without any carpet on the floor. There a few hours later a reporter from the *Freeman's Journal* found him reading that paper in an apparently relaxed state of mind. When the journalist asked him if he thought the Government would now suppress the Land League, he said he thought not: there were too many people for them to be able to do that. 'If they do,' he added, thus giving some authenticity to the story of his alleged remark about Captain Moonlight at Wexford, 'the people will be driven back upon secret organizations as in former times.'

As for himself, he thought he would ask to work in the carpentry shop.

The letter he had written to Katie told her she 'must be a brave little woman and not fret after her husband. The only thing that makes me worried and unhappy is that it may hurt you and our child. You know, darling, that on this account it will be wicked of you to grieve, as I can never have any other wife but you, and if anything happens to you I must die childless. Be good and brave, dear little wifie, then.' But, after signing it 'Your Own Husband', he added a most significant pointer to the way in which he thought everything was likely to change for them in the future. 'Politically', he wrote, 'it is a fortunate thing for me that I have been arrested, as the movement is breaking fast, and all will be quiet in a few months, when I shall be released.'

Given the intensity with which he had for the past few weeks been promoting the Land League policy and principles, as if a great victory were at hand, his apparent total reversal of attitude now would have produced a devastating public effect had it got abroad. And this was apparently the letter he had posted in an open letter-box on the way to jail. Even now it can have a bewildering impact after everything he had been saying. What the postscript reveals is the sense of desperation that must have lain behind the energy he had put into the Land League cause over the past few weeks, aware of how likely it was that the average tenant would want to take advantage of the Act. The awareness may have hit with particular force now that his arrest seemed to bring a whole era of his work to an end. He might even have been accepting that fact with some relief, since the new phase might eventually make it possible to be closer to Katie.

The truth was, as he had hinted at Mallow when he criticized the local branch for simply using funds to pay rents, that the Land League was not as well-structured as it should have been. Many local branches were inefficient, sometimes spending money with little reference to the League's true principles, and running their administration in slovenly fashion. Parnell's sister Anna, whose Ladies' Land League was very different – highly motivated and efficient – was later to castigate the Land League itself in a work whose title encapsulates her argument: she called it *The Great Sham*.

On the very day of Parnell's arrest, Timothy Harrington, a Land League branch organizer, then himself in Galway jail, had written to Parnell with complaints about the way the organization was being run, and he made suggestions for its improvement. More detail was needed, he said, about the numbers of branch offices, many of which were not recorded at all in the books of the Land League. On the other hand there were branches in the books which met only when a grant was wanted for someone in the locality. Of the main office, he said that Brennan worked very hard – was indeed the most hard-worked man of all – but the clerks did not work nearly hard enough. They seemed more concerned to parade their political correctness than to get on with their real work. He was always hearing complaints about neglect of correspondence. And in the legal department there was 'room for an immense saving of money'. No one now fought a landlord in court unless the League gave him money, he said, whereas in the past tenants had often done so. Moreover, he said, money should be given to a tenant to fight a landlord only when there were other tenants on the estate who would also benefit from a successful result. Many isolated tenants were now getting money simply to fight actions on their own behalf.

There can have been little of this which Parnell had not sensed already. It was a picture of Land League morale very different from that which he had been at pains to encourage and project. As he well knew, such morale was not likely to maintain the principle that application should be made to the land court only in the interests of the tenantry as a whole.

Where then to go from here? If Gladstone's Land Act were successfully to undermine the League's authority by introducing the 'three Fs', sending the ideal of full peasant proprietorship into abeyance, what became of that higher ideal which had always theoretically been of the essence in the Land League cause: the claim of Irish nationality? Parnell now had a period of enforced rest and reflection in which to prepare for a new era in pursuit of this goal. But events were temporarily to get in the way. Within days, new Government action had forced him into a position inside Kilmainham in which he had no choice but to present a more militant Land League front than ever.

On the day after he had written his gloomy postscript to Katie – though implying some personal compensation for them both – he had written more soberly, if marginally less honestly, to Dillon – at liberty once more since early August – who was to take charge of the movement in his absence. He warned him that 'some of our friends' were now in favour of a radical change of policy – presumably a general rent strike – but he was 'very strongly of the opinion that no change should be made until we can see whether we can keep the tenants out of court'. He recommended that the test cases should be proceeded with, and thought that 'if the Government do not suppress the organization we can I am sure maintain and strengthen the movement'. There was nothing here about the movement 'breaking fast'.

Dillon, who had resolutely refused to accept the Act even to the extent of testing it, bravely now took on responsibility for passing on Parnell's recommendation. But the arrests next day of Sexton and an Acting Secretary of the Land League, together with the issuing of a warrant for the arrest of Tim Healy, further exacerbated outside feeling in favour of a rent strike. Even Parnell in Kilmainham reluctantly came round to think that there was no other option, if for no other reason than that the removal of such all-important officials made it impossible to proceed with the test cases. Dillon, unaware of Parnell's changed view, at a great meeting in Dublin that evening continued loyally to urge restraint, though he did add that the League executive had 'no intention of coercing or intimidating people into paying rent'.

The very next day Dillon himself was arrested for the second time that year, and with William O'Brien, the editor of *United Ireland*, and J. J. O'Kelly, also arrested, joined Parnell in Kilmainham. An additional factor now bearing on the decision about what to do next was the need to satisfy the all-important American supporters who were urging a rent strike – as was Egan, the Treasurer, from Paris.

On 18 October a manifesto calling on all tenants to pay 'no rent' until the Government restored the Irish people's constitutional rights was issued from Kilmainham, signed by Parnell, Dillon, Sexton, Brennan and Kettle from the prison, with the names of Davitt and Egan added for good measure. It had been written in what has been well described as 'flaming prose' by O'Brien, but none of those signing there – with the possible exception of Brennan – can have really believed it would work. As Parnell was to say years later, there was really nothing else to be done after the arrest of all the leaders. It was a way of preserving face. But he must have known as he signed, straightening himself up and looking hard at Kettle after he had done so, that O'Brien's flaming prose had small chance of igniting anything. It was Kettle who had urged a 'no rent' course in February, when it might possibly have set all Ireland ablaze. He himself signed now after asking Parnell not to blame the people if they failed to carry the policy out.

Two days later the Catholic hierarchy in the form of the most nationally minded archbishop of all, Dr Thomas Croke of Cashel, gave the people a lead in the opposite direction and condemned the manifesto. Within weeks tenants were going to the land courts and testing them for themselves, finding them prepared to lower rents without any further help from the Land League at all.

In fact by then the Land League no longer officially existed, having been suppressed by the Government on the same day as Archbishop Croke's pronouncement against the 'No Rent' manifesto. But it was little more than a ceremonial Government decision: such effective control as the League had maintained had virtually disintegrated with the arrest of the political leaders. The Ladies' Land League, though locally effective in bringing aid and alternative housing to the evicted, could hardly command a political dimension.

A skeleton network of sorts did, however, continue underground. The American economist Henry George, who arrived in November as correspondent of the extreme nationalist New York *Irish World*, described something of this in private letters to his editor, Patrick Ford, in which he put matters he could not put into his articles for the paper. He said that 'the men in Kilmainham' were managing to keep in touch with people outside but communication was becoming 'increasingly difficult'. Outside, a man named Moloney, with whom he was in touch, was in the Fenian jargon 'a sort of head centre'. He had formed a committee which included two MPs, Edmund Leamy and John Redmond, while the former League solicitor, Gough, dealt with legal business; Egan in Paris was supplying money from funds which he continued to receive from America, but was neither receiving reports nor giving any directions. Sixteen men were 'out travelling the country', but George did not seem excited about their activity. 'It seems to me', he wrote, 'that a great deal of energy and ability might be utilized that is now going to waste. It seems to me that this has been a weak point and is still a weak point.'

Several weeks later he told Ford, 'Sometimes it seems to me as if a lot of small men had found themselves on the head of a tremendous movement and, finding themselves being lifted with importance and power they never dreamed of, are jealous of anybody else sharing the honour.' He excluded Parnell of course.

It was what Harrington had complained of about the clerks in the office before the League was suppressed: the terminal disease of second-rate conformity to which revolutionary movements are often subject.

Boyton, jailed but released after claiming American citizenship, was the man outside Kilmainham whom George found 'the most intelligent and best informed' of those he met. Boyton confirmed his view that it was the leaders' ideas that had given the Land League its force, rather than any good management. He told George that the loss of Davitt had been an enormous blow and had never been repaired. Parnell, he said, was a true man, a magnificent parliamentary leader, but did not have Davitt's grasp of detail.

It was Anna Parnell's Ladies' Land League, not suppressed, which was now carrying on the whole business of relief and support for the evicted tenants, and indeed harassing bailiffs, police and the landlords who evicted them. Because, as George reported, she was very much 'the boss', her organization was run, with able companions, on much more businesslike lines than had been the League itself. Of Anna's ardour, wrote George, there was no question – though he was not so sure about her judgement.

Nor was her brother, whose affection and indeed admiration for her were mixed with mistrust for what he saw as her erratic behaviour and extravagance with the American funds. However, those to whom she so vigorously and with such determination brought relief and assistance adored her and regarded her as a delivering angel.

What had always given the Land League's policy its edge in the countryside was, of course, the grey area between boycotting and intimidation which much of the leaders' rhetoric had inspired, however much they denied it. And such activity continued after the arrest of the leaders and the suppression of the Land League. Small local agrarian secret societies now had the field to themselves, and early in November Captain Moonlight made a personal appearance in *United Ireland* to confirm the prediction said to have been made at Wexford. There was a report in that paper of a notice pinned to a door which ran, 'As I am Captain Moonlight I will visit you by an early date and leave youse as an example to all.' Two coffins were drawn at the bottom of the paper. It was said to be written in a female hand.

This was directed at a couple called Kavanagh in Chapel Lane, Athy, Co. Kildare, but he – or she – was everywhere. In the last quarter of 1881, for most of which Parnell was under arrest and the Land League suppressed, the number of outrages rose sharply to almost exactly the same number as in that quarter of the previous year. They were not to fall noticeably until the summer of 1882.

Part III: 1882–1891

KILMAINHAM, WESTMINSTER, ELTHAM, BRIGHTON,
WESTMINSTER, CO. GALWAY, BRIGHTON

Chapter 34

Parnell's life in prison was in no way arduous. By comparison with average conditions for a late-twentieth-century political prisoner it was even luxurious. After only one night in a standard cell twelve feet by six he was moved to a larger room which he immediately described in a letter to Katie on 14 October 1881 as 'a beautiful room facing the sun – the best in the prison', saying that he was 'very comfortable'. Fellow-suspects, with whom he could associate all day long, were in adjoining rooms and he assured her that time did not hang heavily on his hands, nor did he feel lonely.

He was of course presenting conditions in the best possible light, because, as he went on to say in his letter, 'My only fear is about my darling Queenie. I have been racked with torture all to-day, last night, and yesterday, lest the shock may have hurt you or our child. Oh darling, write or wire me as soon as you get this that you are well and try not to be unhappy until you see your husband again.' He had her photograph with him and said he kissed it every morning. He signed the letter 'Your King'.

His life in Kilmainham was in fact to be as reasonably civilized as any life within the stone walls of a Victorian prison could be. His room, for which the Ladies' Land League had soon provided furniture and curtains for the barred windows, looked out on a small courtyard in which suspects were free to exercise and play handball for some six hours a day. Free association within the building was virtually limitless. He could see almost as many visitors as he liked, often without a warder present, and could receive newspapers and books. Within five days of being there *The Times*, *Engineer*, *Engineering*, *Mining Journal*, the *Pall Mall Gazette* and the *Universe* had been sent to him from London; he had the Irish papers too. William O'Brien later gave a warm personal account of the life in Kilmainham and said that, though Parnell did read the occasional book of history, or even Roman law, he used to say that 'Literature has no chance against the *Freeman*.' The essentially scientific bent of Parnell's mind was made charmingly clear to O'Brien by the way he treated an expensive musical box playing 'The Wearing of the Green' which had been sent him by some outside well-wisher. He was only interested in dismantling it to explain its mechanism to his prison companions.

Parnell, O'Brien, O'Kelly and Dillon, with Kettle and Dr Joseph Kenny, Parnell's doctor, both of whom had been arrested too, and Brennan and Boyton, still there at first, formed what O'Brien called 'a pleasant little company'. Kettle too in his memoirs recalls 'a very pleasant time as prisoners' in Kilmainham.

Food could be sent in from the outside, though to save the Land League funds, which often paid for it, they sometimes made a show of going on prison fare, in which case, as O'Brien noted, it was the scientific aspect of how to make the most of it which mainly interested Parnell. From the available ingredients he constructed a skilfully variegated if rigorous Irish stew. O'Brien, writing nearly a quarter of a century later, also said Parnell had a set of keys to Kilmainham made by a locksmith in Dublin so that he could escape if there were ever any question of moving the prisoners to England, but this may be just a fanciful projection of something that was merely discussed. Certainly the picture of Parnell happy in the thought that he could always walk out if he wanted to, but not necessarily doing so, is in character. In her memoirs, published in 1914, Katie claimed still to have those keys.

On the whole, such personal details as O'Brien gives of their time in Kilmainham together are likely to be as reliable as memories can be after twenty years or so, for even when years later he became opposed to Parnell he always remained tenderly disposed towards his 'Chief'. Among Parnell's favourite topics of conversation were his admiration for the United States and interest in the history of the American Revolution, particularly Washington's cautious early revolutionary tactics.

O'Brien also took note of Parnell's superstitions, which he put into perspective by saying that they always seemed to be 'whimsicalities that amused him, rather than beliefs that had any real influence'. His dislike of the colour green O'Brien diagnosed as linked to slightly obsessional hypochondria; it was akin perhaps to that with which he had confronted Katie over the watering of her house-plants. Green, Parnell seemed to think, could be a source of arsenic poisoning. As to the strange absurdity of disliking the national colour of the country for which he cared so much, he faced this head-on with a jocular 'How could you expect a country to have luck that has green for its colour!'

Inevitably a large number of green gifts from lady well-wishers arrived for him at the prison – 'embroidered smoking caps, tea-cosies and even bright green hosiery'. Many of these were given away to his fellow-prisoners, but one particular eiderdown quilt covered in green satin with his monogram worked in gold was, according to O'Brien, pushed away carefully beneath a cupboard in his room, where the mice soon got at it. This may or may not have been the same quilt as that, also green – 'a colour I detest' – about which he wrote to Katie. He said he was sending it to Wicklow (Avondale presumably), which suggests that he cannot have detested the quilt itself all that much. The colour, anyway, was not the only reason it was going: 'I don't want it here at all, as there are too many things on my bed as it is. Ever your own King.'

It is through the many very loving letters that he wrote to Katie from Kilmainham – over the six months of his imprisonment nearly fifty, including a few formal 'Mrs O'Shea' letters within which the others were enclosed – that it now becomes possible to come closer to his innermost self than at any other stage of his life. Only very occasionally do the feelings there reflect politics – as in the postscript about 'the movement is breaking fast'. Mostly they reflect only his very real concern and love for her, to which his whole being is bound. The simple genuineness of the emotions expressed – not extravagantly, and all the more moving for the absence of literary quality or style – convey the quite ordinary humanity of the man in a way not always possible in those memoirs which look back upon him as a legendary hero. And by reading these letters it is possible to confirm at least one truth about the position of Willie: one way or another, he was being deceived.

Willie had seen Parnell in Dublin only a few days before his arrest and wrote to him immediately on hearing of it – presumably to commiserate, although Katie has an account of him at Eltham, 'joyful' at the news. What comes unmistakably out of Parnell's many Kilmainham letters to Katie is that the assurances they had given Willie after the duel episode had been worth nothing.

Of the formal letters, Katie says specifically in her memoirs, 'If Willie were at Eltham I would show him this note asking me to post enclosure on a certain date. The enclosure was, of course, to me.' She writes that at this time 'the deception I had to practise towards Captain O'Shea, seldom as I saw him, told upon my nerves just now'.

It was the contention of Henry Harrison, the champion of Parnell and Katie's ethical probity in this affair, who talked to her at length immediately after Parnell's death, that Katie's book was published under the dominating influence of her son, Gerard O'Shea. It is true that Gerard, who had disliked Parnell and wanted to defend his by then dead father's honour, played a positive role in prompting his mother to write. But Harrison maintained that, because of this, the book did not give an authentic picture of what had gone on and that it concealed the real truth: namely, that the affair had been condoned from the earliest days by Captain O'Shea.

Harrison based this conclusion principally on his belief that at the time of writing Katie was not 'fully aware' of the implications of what appeared in her book; that she was not responsible for the book as it appeared, nor for those implications; and that she was not anyway 'capable in 1914 of writing a book about the 1880–91 period'. But this argument ignores two overwhelming objections. First, Parnell's letters in the book, the authenticity of which no one, including Harrison, has ever doubted, reveal the deception of Willie clearly, quite apart from what she wrote herself. Second, on the occasion of the publication of her book in 1914, she attended, with Gerard, a Press Association meeting where journalists from leading newspapers and magazines were able to question her. Her intellectual alertness as well as her charm was evident to all.

Gerard O'Shea was indeed by her side, and would certainly have been pleased with much that she had published. But suggestions, such as Harrison makes, to the effect that she was 'incapable' and virtually senile in her 'old age' – 'a broken and helpless old lady' at sixty-eight – are unsustainable. The most conclusive piece of evidence for the deception of Willie, at least well into 1882 – Katie's admission that Willie thought himself the father of Parnell's child born that year – is one with which Harrison's notion of the realities of human life seems unable to cope. Such a possibility is dismissed by him as 'vile', 'an enormity', 'unbearable shame' and, more curiously, as having 'her womanhood . . . rolled in the kennel'. Harrison's understandable, if unrealistic, concern to portray only an unconventional purity in the Chief's relationship with his mistress led him to distort the picture of the way things actually were almost as seriously as some of the eventual evidence in the divorce court may have done.

Parnell had not been in Kilmainham more than a few days before he had found a means of smuggling letters out of and into the jail uncensored – through a warder and by one of his regular visitors. Within a few weeks he had also elaborated a system by which he wrote to Katie between the lines in invisible ink, and instructed her to do the same. He was concerned to reassure her about his health, and, although from time to time he was writing from the prison infirmary, he emphasized that this was principally to give him more comfortable quarters and that Dr

Kenny collaborated over invented 'little maladies' to keep him there. 'The latest discovery is heart attack affection,' he told her flippantly.

Kenny's own reports to the prison doctor confirm this, with further accounts of 'violent spasms', 'severe abdominal pain' and 'an alarming tendency towards syncope'. Whatever truth there may have been in any of this, Dr Kenny clearly enjoyed making the most of it. Certainly Parnell's own concern for his health was evident in his letters, but only in such a way as to reassure Katie that there was nothing very seriously wrong. In a formal letter at the beginning of November he told her, 'I was rather indisposed yesterday, but am very much better to-day. I am told that everybody gets a turn after they have been here for three or four weeks, but that they then become all right.' And in a private letter the next day, 'I have quite recovered. My illness did me good, and I have a first-rate appetite.' Referring to the photograph he had with him, he reminded her of how he looked 'at my beautiful Queen's face every night before I go to bed and long for the time when I may be with you again. Only for that I should be happier here than anywhere else.'

Health faddist as he was, he clearly took some pleasure in letting her share the details, though this was nearly always linked to his wish to reassure her in her pregnancy.

'My darling,' he wrote in a letter of 14 December, 'you frighten me dreadfully when you tell me that I am "surely killing" you and our child [by being in prison]. I am quite well again now, my own, and was out to-day for a short time, and will take much better care of myself for the future. It was not the food, but a chill after over-heating myself at ball.'

He played a lot of handball, particularly with O'Kelly. He said he had missed it for the last few years of his life, and it suited him, for, as he also said, 'strong exercise always agreed with me'. In general he seemed to suffer no physical ill-effects from his six months' imprisonment and actually put on six pounds in weight towards the end, which, combined with the exercise, appeared no bad sign for his general state of health.

Imprisonment does not seem to have affected him psychologically. There are virtually no signs of depression. The nearest he ever comes to this recurrent prison phenomenon is at the end of November, when he notes that 'The time is passing rather more slowly this month than the first, but still it is not yet monotonous.' The prospect of seeing her again and the thoughts about her which fill his letters seem to have kept his spirits up throughout.

He worried a lot about her and her unborn child. Some of this worry is concerned with the presence of Willie. Since Parliament was not sitting, it is not easy to trace Willie's movements and whereabouts at least until the last phase of Parnell's imprisonment. But there were clearly times when he was about at Eltham, and neither Parnell nor Katie liked it. Or rather, her dislike seems to have been confined to one particular aspect of his physical presence. We know, however – both from the letters in her memoirs and from the evidence in the divorce court – that a bond of some sort was to continue between Willie and Katie for several years more. Curiously, jealousy of Willie does not seem to figure in Parnell's letters to 'his own Queenie', though he is extremely concerned for her discomfort at Willie's presence.

Willie was staying at Eltham for some days up to the weekend of 18 to 21 November. Parnell wrote to her on 21 November to say that he was relieved to know that she was less miserable than she had been, 'yet I am still very much troubled and anxious about you. Has he left yet? It is frightful that you should be exposed to such daily torture.'

The use of the word 'torture' – though it obviously does not signify literally that – seems to imply something more than boredom or irritation. Willie was after all her own husband, even though Parnell was constantly signing himself as such, and it is not impossible that he could have been insisting on what, in the manner of that day, he would have considered his conjugal rights of one sort or another. Her lover in his letters enjoined her to 'get some sleep for her husband's sake [by which he meant himself] and for our child's sake, who must be suffering much also'.

One might have expected that, imprisoned as he was, the torture would have been for Parnell in having to consider such things, but there is no sign of this in any of the letters, although references to Willie in one form or another recur quite often. Ten days later he told her that he was trying to make arrangements for her to visit him in Kilmainham as soon as Willie had left for Madrid. It seems Willie must have stayed on some days longer at Eltham. Parnell's plan was that Katie should pose as one of his cousins, a Mrs Bligh, coming from England. He would see her, he hoped, in the Governor's office with only the Governor present, so that there could be no danger that the MPs in Kilmainham, like Dillon or O'Kelly, might recognize her.

As the weeks went by he became more and more concerned for her. Writing to her just before Christmas he said how 'very, very happy' he was 'that my own Wifie is better', and that she had been 'relieved from some of the intolerable annoyance for a time'. 'Your husband is quite well,' he added flatly. He meant, of course, himself.

On Christmas Eve he sent her a present which, apart from the love he sent with it, is not specified in his letter, but he hoped it would make her forget some 'squabble' they had had last Christmas Day which he said he had long since forgotten. 'My darling,' he added, 'you are and always will be everything to me, and every day you become more and more, if possible, more than everything to me.' On 30 December he said he was getting 'very nervous about the doctors'. She should, he said, 'tell one of them the right time, so that he may be on hand, otherwise you may not have one at all. It will never do to run this risk.'

What can this have meant? She was some seven months pregnant at the time, but it could be that she had so far managed to conceal this from everyone, including Willie, and therefore had not contacted doctors. It might just have been possible.

He began the New Year with a note which said that she must take great care of herself and be sure to have 'at least one doctor in February. It will never do to let it trust to chance.' And a few days later he wrote again:

You must tell the doctor, and never mind about———. Could you not go to London or Brighton about the beginning of February? London would be best, if you could get him away on any pretext; but if you could not, Brighton would leave you most free from him.

It is perfectly dreadful that Wifie should be so worried at night. I had hoped that the doctor's orders would have prevented that.

But again there is no hint of personal jealousy. His letter continues with details of how well he is being fed: 'Chops or grilled turkey or eggs and bacon for breakfast, soup and chops for luncheon, and joint and vegetables, etc., for dinner, and sometimes oysters.'

In the first letter of the new year, on 3 January, there had been a first hint of the political background, to which so far – at least in the letters which Katie publishes in her memoirs – he had made almost no reference at all. He wrote, 'There is every prospect of my being able to see my darling soon, but it does not do to be too sure, as things change so much from day to day.'

This clearly did not refer to his plans for letting her visit him in the presence of the Governor. He must have realized that she was by now too far advanced in her pregnancy for that. What he was referring to was the prospect of his eventual release. What had been happening in Ireland during the almost three months in which events had been virtually out of his control?

Agrarian outrages had continued at an unusually high rate for that quarter and were to show few signs of fluctuation for many months to come. But they were, as they had not been in the days of the Land League, outrages in a political vacuum. With the political leadership impotent, there was no chance of turning the embarrassing anarchy to political advantage. However, the Government was equally at a loss. Use of the Coercion Acts could certainly be more severe than ever, and a number of strongly motivated and determined special resident magistrates were seeing to it that this was so. But the Government, though not like the Irish leadership impotent, was potent to no point, for the outrages did not diminish. Logically, both sides should have been looking for some way out of the vacuum.

Two personal accounts from opposite ends of the political spectrum give some insight into what this vacuum looked like. One comes from the American economist Henry George, still writing for the *Irish World* and still maintaining contact both with activists and with others outside Kilmainham and at least on one occasion seeing Parnell within. The other is that of Gladstone's son Herbert, who had gone to Ireland on a tour of investigation for his father, arriving there on the very day on which Parnell was arrested. He noted then, incidentally, that Forster, the Chief Secretary, who had ordered the arrest, expressed some personal sympathy for Parnell as a man, and at the same time that Forster himself was permanently under threat from possible assassins. A telegram had arrived from England a few days after Herbert Gladstone to say that two men, whose names and descriptions were given, were said to be on their way to Dundalk specifically to assassinate Forster. Herbert Gladstone found himself carrying a loaded revolver to protect Forster when he moved about with him.

He noted in his diary for 19 October, the day after which the 'No Rent' manifesto appeared, that this was received 'with satisfaction' by the authorities because it would bring the conflict to a head and 'decide waverers in the Land League'.

The next day was historic too. It saw not only the appearance in the *Freeman's Journal* of Archbishop Croke's letter condemning the 'No Rent' manifesto but also the opening of the land court in Dublin. Disregarding Parnell's injunction to wait for the testing of the Act by the Land League, tenants started to bring in their own individual cases fast. Within less than a week 1,322 applications for fair rents had come into the court, and they continued to arrive at the rate of around 200 to 250 a day. So much for Parnell's injunction to wait for the Land League to test them. The Land

League was suppressed the same day. The sending of Dr Kenny under arrest to Kilmainham that week had also contributed to a general raising of Government spirits. There was, said Herbert Gladstone, no doubt that Kenny had been using medical consultations with the prisoners as a means for enabling them to communicate with friends outside. Herbert Gladstone lashed out in his diary at Anna Parnell – 'that insane cat and her silly crew'. She herself was to refer in time to him as a 'sneaking spalpeen'.

Ten days after his arrival he set off for the South to collect facts for his father. At once he found that in the course of the week there had been a sea change in the atmosphere. One agent in Cork who the week before had been unable to collect any rents at all now reported that he had just had the best day for rents he ever remembered. One of the toughest of the new resident magistrates specially appointed earlier in the year, Clifford Lloyd, was saying that people had begun to touch their hats to him again and that tenants were coming to the land court in their thousands. The number of applications had indeed almost doubled in four days, but there was now something of a danger that the courts might become blocked with applications. The only bad news came from Kerry, where they were still having difficulty in collecting rents. One very big landowner there had just served three hundred writs on his tenants.

Herbert Gladstone left Ireland early in November for a five-day visit to his father at Hawarden but was soon back in the South of Ireland, trying to find out in Cork what people were thinking of Parnell. He gathered that he was still immensely popular but thought that out of sight might mean out of mind. He found the 'No Rent' manifesto condemned everywhere; on the other hand, he probably went to few places where it might not have been. He found quite a lot of Parnellite intimidation in the town. On the day of Parnell's arrest, apparently, it had been more than shopkeepers' windows were worth not to shut up for the day and bring out a picture of the 'Uncrowned King'.

Travelling a good deal around the South-West in Co. Cork and Co. Kerry over the next fortnight, he found the picture by no means evenly improving. He came across one embattled if fearless landlord, a harsh man, who dared his tenants to shoot him and went about with two or three revolvers prominently displayed in his belt, calling for three cheers for the Queen. Extensive evictions were being planned in the neighbour-hood, and two or three companies of infantry together with police were going to leave Bantry in gunboats for Castletown, still a very disturbed district. Gladstone reckoned that all the tenants due to be evicted could pay rents if they chose to do so.

At Kenmare a police sub-inspector told him that all was very quiet and that the Land League, always feeble there, had collapsed entirely after it had been suppressed. On the other hand on travelling to the vast estate of Lord Kenmare himself, in the area of Killarney, he found his agent, Samuel Hussey, despondent about the state of the country. He thought it was worse than the year before and that the land courts, by reducing rents, would in fact ruin large numbers of landlords. He said the tone of the tenants to the landlords was as hostile as possible. He was expecting to be shot, and when in the countryside carried a revolver and a Winchester rifle. The police sub-inspector there confirmed that the state of his district was as bad as ever.

On Tuesday 29 November Herbert Gladstone set out on an eviction expedition in Co. Cork with a hundred police, fifty of whom were armed. It was in a wild region above the coast, nearly all stones and bog. He watched as families were ejected from eleven cabins, but 'there was little work for the crowbars'. All the families were readmitted as caretakers. He personally thought the rents were too high. There had not been much fuss – a few girls had cursed Forster with cries of 'To hell with Buckshot,' and a few stones had been thrown at the police – but he had more trouble really back at his hotel, where the waiter, who he had already noted was 'approaching *delirium tremens*', was drunk again and incapable and had to go to bed.

Two days later he set out again with another eviction party, escorted this time by a hundred and fifty men of the 36th Rifles and fifty police. There were only two houses to be visited, but there had been serious trouble there last year, when the police had been fired at. This time the trouble was provided by a Miss Reynolds of the Ladies' Land League, whom the escort prevented from getting to the first house. There the tenant was allowed to pay as much of his rent as he could and to remain as caretaker. Miss Reynolds did, however, get to the second house before the bailiffs and the police. With about a hundred people watching, she told the tenant not to pay anything, to get all his possessions out of the house, and that the Ladies' Land League would build him a better one. As Herbert Gladstone said, since all this had been said in public it would have been more than the man's life was worth not to agree and he was consequently ejected.

The picture continued to be uneven. He went to the Limerick area, where the Resident Magistrate and the police county inspector told him that there was still a lot of intimidation and that rents were not coming in at all. They did say that people seemed rather tired of 'the extreme men and doctrines', but he saw a lot of boys marching about the streets singing Land League songs. A few days later a landlord in Co. Clare told him how tenants were more prepared to pay rents but still finding it risky to do so. This man had to make an assignation with one old tenant in a wood to receive his rent. He told him that on another estate tenants had met determined to ask for a 50 per cent reduction and when one had spoken up saying, 'Why not offer decent terms?' another had said to him, 'Do you want this stick down your throat?' The would-be mediator did not speak again.

There were certainly enough of such incidents to show that the agrarian climate was not changing all that fast. But it was changing. It was a different situation from that in which Parnell had gone to prison, in which the 'No Rent' manifesto had been issued and the Land League suppressed. New forces which could not be reversed were at work.

A new question to be discussed was the plight of landlords whose rents the courts had much reduced. There was talk of compensation having to be paid to them. But this, it was thought, would be impractical because unfair to those landlords who had already reduced their rents and could get no compensation because they had not been taken to the courts.

On his return to Dublin, Herbert Gladstone found the Special Resident Magistrate Clifford Lloyd staying in Phoenix Park with Forster. Lloyd had no doubt that the tough coercive powers that existed, properly applied with the sort of determination he himself was showing, could deal with the agrarian problem. But the fact remained that outrages were not noticeably being reduced, though Herbert Gladstone, perhaps influenced by Lloyd, was optimistic about present policies succeeding. He left Ireland finally at the end of January 1882 for the coming parliamentary session, being a Member of Parliament for Leeds.

On 23 March 1882 he made some notes in his diary about a conversation he had just had with his father. The Prime Minister was suddenly saying that he had all along been opposed to this kind of coercion by suspension of habeas corpus. He would have preferred, he said, to alter the ordinary law to make it more severe; but he had had no support for this in the Cabinet. A logical deduction to make from this (though his son did not make it) might have been that Gladstone was searching around in his mind for a new policy.

But how had all these months looked to someone observing the situation outside Kilmainham from a Land League point of view? Henry George arrived at Queenstown, the port of Cork, almost exactly a month after Parnell's arrest. He had received a shock even while still on the tender taking him from the liner to the port. The shipping-agent who had the passenger list for the liner called him aside and asked him if he was indeed Henry George, and then told him that he himself was a Land Leaguer and advised him to change his name. He said he would certainly be dogged by detectives from the moment he landed, and possibly arrested.

'I of course refused any such kindness,' George told Patrick Ford in the personal letter he wrote to him from Dublin. 'I can't well describe to you the reign of terror I found here', he said, 'and the difficulty . . . of getting at the truth about things.'

He said people were afraid to talk, and that it was the most damnable Government outside Russia. Miss Taylor of the Ladies' Land League went so far as to say outside Turkey. Like Herbert Gladstone on the other side of the fence, he tended to be over-optimistic about his cause. He said that Archbishop Croke's condemnation of the 'no rent' manifesto had struck an even harder blow than any that came from Gladstone. As the strongly nationalistic Bishop of Meath, Dr Thomas Nulty, had said, it was a case of '*Et tu, Brute?*' Those George talked to told him that it was the clergy who were the real problem for the Land League, but he was inclined to think that very many of the clergy were with the people and for 'no rent', though being 'bulldozed' by the hierarchy.

He had found a good deal of pessimism about the future, but he himself felt that things were holding up better than might be expected – 'at least after Dr Croke's fulminations'. He felt respect for Parnell's political sagacity and for that of the other men in Kilmainham, but wondered whether they were not too afraid of delegating authority to the outside. He said Parnell had put his foot down about creating a specific organization on the outside ('It would be presumptuous of me to say unwisely').

Writing again ten days later he was able to tell Ford about such continuing underground organization as did exist, under the man named Moloney. Like Herbert Gladstone, he tended to see people who reinforced the optimism of his own side. Duggan, the nationalist Bishop of Clonfert, told him just after Christmas, 'Nothing can stop this movement.' But George himself was becoming concerned about what he called 'a great amount of Whiggery in this Land League movement, more than I thought before coming here. And I think this is especially true of the leaders.' He saw a much more radical phase coming.

He saw Parnell himself at the end of January in Kilmainham. He played the interview down when writing his column for the *Irish World* because anything he said about it might ruin the warder who had been present, and make enforcement of the rules more strict. Parnell, it is clear, revealed none of the thoughts about the future in his mind, thinking probably only of the need to keep financial supporters in the United States happy. George told Patrick Ford that Parnell was 'in magnificent spirits, says the country is standing splendidly and that the Government is killing itself'.

In fact, whatever impression George had taken, Parnell's mind was beginning to move along different lines. While the old Land League movement had lost direction, he could see that the Government too was getting nowhere. This certainly would have been the basis for some of his new thinking. Equally in his mind was his concern for Katie.

There was very little in his many letters which one way or another did not reflect their intimacy. Almost nothing reflected directly the present situation and the political future as Parnell was thinking of it. There were, however, certain clues to the way he might be going, for all the conventional enthusiasm for a traditional stance expressed to Henry George. Thus, in the middle of December, after receiving a letter from Katie in which she had told him that he was 'surely killing' herself and her child by being in prison, he had written, 'Rather than that my beautiful Wifie should run any risk I will resign my seat, leave politics, and go away somewhere with my own Queenie, as soon as she wishes; will she come? Let me know, darling, in your next about this, whether it is safe for you that I should be kept here any longer. – Your own Husband.'

In other words, if necessary he would make terms and get out of Kilmainham. It was just over a fortnight later, on 3 January, that he was to tell her that there was every prospect of being able to see her soon, though things changed from day to day. The inference that some development might be afoot was supplemented by what he wrote eight days later, on 11 January 1882:

My own Queenie, –

Yes, I will go to you, my love, immediately I am released. There is nothing in the world that I can do in Ireland, nor is it likely that I shall be able to do anything here for a long time to come. Certainly until the Coercion Act has expired I will not speak here again, so Queenie need not be afraid that when she gets me again she will lose me.

I am disposed to think that Government at present intend to release me shortly before opening of Parliament, but, of course they may change their minds and hasten or postpone my release.

The first clue to what was happening both in Parnell's mind and elsewhere seems to have been in a letter he had written her as early as 7 December 1881. In this he had simply said that she would see a paragraph about his health in the *Freeman's Journal* in two days' time which might worry her, but she was not to be worried because it was going to be very much exaggerated for the purpose of preventing their prison rooms being changed for others that were not so nice. He had in fact only got a slight cold, but the doctor thought nothing of it.

This paragraph in the *Freeman* turned out to contain an account of an interview on the day following this letter with Frank Hugh O'Donnell, who had come to see him in Kilmainham. As published it was innocuous enough, and certainly made the most of Parnell's cold. He had had to wire her at once to prevent her getting too worried, and followed this up with a letter saying, 'You must not pay any attention to O'D's account, as it was carefully got up.'

What it had been got up for was not just to present some reason for the prisoners not having to change their rooms, but so that Parnell and O'Donnell could have a talk about the future. O'Donnell had in the past month been publishing a series of articles in *The Times* which virtually provided a policy for conciliation between the Government and Parnell over the Land Act. O'Donnell was concerned that, with the great rush to the land courts for the reduction of rent which was undoubtedly taking place, landlords should where necessary receive compensation for the reductions they had made. Linked to this was what O'Donnell rightly saw as the major problem from the tenants' point of view: namely, that of the arrears of rent which so many had necessarily accumulated as a result of the bad seasons of 1877–9.

The important thing was that conciliation was now in the air. O'Donnell wanted to sell it to the Liberal Government, and of course he needed equally to sell it to Parnell. Possibly when he visited him in Kilmainham he did not know to what extent, for his own private reasons, Parnell might be ready to think along the same lines.

Parnell's January letters indicate increasingly that something is in the air. On 21 January he wrote, 'It looks like our release shortly.' A week later, 'It looks as if they were going to keep me here for a while longer, probably till a month or so after the opening of session,' and at the end of the letter, 'It looks to-day as if D. [Dillon] would go out soon; in that case it would facilitate our release.'

As the likely date of their child's birth approached, he became more and more anxious that Katie should not worry about him: 'I really cannot remember when I have ever felt so well in my life.' He felt a real sadness not to be with her: 'It is very, very hard not to be able to see each other, and that my poor Wifie should not have her husband with her now'. He sent his 'best love to our little child'. A week later, on 10 February, expectation of his release was becoming more precise: 'I think that we shall probably be released by the middle of March, as it will be known then which way the tenants intend to go, and we shall be able to decide whether it is worth our while remaining here any longer.' In other words, it was his view that an initiative from him could secure his release.

On 14 February he was blaming himself for the unhappiness which she had obviously been expressing to him in her letters: 'Wifie is very good indeed to write her husband such beautiful letters; if she only knew what a pleasure and happiness every word from her is to her husband it might make her feel a little less unhappy . . . I often reproach myself for having been so cruel to my own love in staying so long away from her that time.' (He meant the weeks he had spent entirely in Ireland after leaving England for the Ulster by-election.) If on 13 October he had not made the arrangement to go to Kildare, he would have been 'safe with Wifie. Until then I had settled that I should leave Ireland after Wexford.'

He went on to say something which, though it was probably said primarily to reassure her about his closeness to her as their child's birth approached, amazes as much as the offer to leave politics of two months before:

At least, I am very glad that the days of platform speeches have gone by and are not likely to return. I cannot describe to you the disgust I always felt with those meetings, knowing as I did how hollow and wanting in solidity everything connected with the movement was. When I was arrested I did not think the movement would have survived a month . . .

To what extent this denotes genuine disgust at his meetings, to what extent disappointment at the way things turned out and to what extent simply a personal longing to get close to her is hard to determine. Certainly it is partly the last, because in this letter, so close to the birth of their child, he was thinking about the time when she had been conceived. 'When I get out', he wrote, 'I hope to have a good long rest with my own little Wifie somewhere, and to listen to the waves breaking as we used to those mornings of spring last May.'

He was talking and thinking about Brighton the previous year. Now, in this time and place, it was not surprising that the political half of of his life should in retrospect seem a terrible intrusion. He thought constantly of getting out: 'next month, when the seeding time comes,' he wrote, 'will probably see the end of all things and our speedy release'.

It still remains almost impossible to accept that his presence at those meetings and the splendid performances he had so consistently given at them were part of a false prospectus. Perhaps the explanation is that here in Kilmainham he had for the first time the leisure in which to confront the problem of reconciling the two commitments, one public and one personal, to which his life was dedicated; perhaps he momentarily despaired of solving this. After his eventual emergence from Kilmainham, most of the rest of his life was to be based on an adjusted balance between the two ideals which possessed him: his love for Katie and his equally total commitment to some form of Irish freedom. Perhaps here in Kilmainham, by wrestling *de profundis* for a moment with the conflict that these could bring for him, he drove his mind to an extreme in an attempt to break out of that conflict altogether. In fact out of that struggle came the equilibrium which, though it was to disappoint many of his former supporters, allowed him to maintain that sense of ability to control the world around him that was at the very centre of his being.

Again, on 17 February, when their child had just been born at Eltham – though he did not know this when writing – he reassured her, 'It is exceedingly likely that we shall all be released about the end of March.'

Their child, a girl, was born apparently strong and healthy with the brown eyes of her father. Her birth was announced in *The Times*. The form in which it was fashionable to make such announcements was in this case peculiarly appropriate:

On the 15th February, at Eltham, the wife of W. H. O'Shea Esq. M.P. a daughter.

Meanwhile there had been a straw in the wind from another quarter. In London the new session of Parliament had opened at the beginning of February, and Gladstone, speaking in the House of Commons, and implying that it would not be long before he retired, aired what he described as his 'very strongest opinions upon matters in the nature of local government'. He said he had the strongest objections to the prevailing tendency for centralization of government 'not for Ireland merely but for England ... I believe that local institutions – the institutions of secondary authority – are a great source of strength and that in principle the only necessary limit to these powers is the adequate and certain provision for the supremacy of the central authority.'

He was talking partly, in only a thinly veiled manner, about the possibility of some sort of Home Rule for Ireland. And should the veil not have been thin enough, he went on to make it clear that, in his mind, Irish control of Irish affairs need not necessarily be a step towards separation. He said it was time to find out what provisions people might be prepared to make for the supremacy of Parliament, should some form of devolution come about. He had deployed some of the same tone the week before in the House, when he had talked about the need for a plan 'under which the local affairs of Ireland could be, by some clear and definite line, separated from the Imperial affairs of Ireland'.

All this was enough to send *The Times* into a state of great consternation. Examining what Gladstone had said, it declared, 'We must emphatically dissent from this view which has never before been advanced in the House of Commons by a responsible Minister.'

Though there is no reference to any of this in his letters, none of it would have been lost on Parnell, avidly reading his newspapers in Kilmainham. Further information about how people were thinking on all sides may also have been coming to him from O'Donnell and the O'Gorman Mahon, who also visited him in Kilmainham and who may well have reported back on the way Parnell was thinking, at least on politics, to his fellow Member for Co. Clare, his friend Willie O'Shea.

To what extent thoughts about his daughter were also in Parnell's mind at this time is not easy to judge. There is a virtual break of almost a month between a second letter he wrote from Kilmainham on 17 February, the day after the birth, to tell Katie how relieved he was to know, after anxiety which had driven him to tears, that 'everything was quite right', and the next, beginning 'My own darling Queenie', which virtually repeats what he had said in the letter of 17 February, namely how hopeless and miserable he had felt until she had been able to tell him that 'all was quite right'. But now – and it is as if it were for the first time – he was able to tell her how happy he was 'that our little daughter pleases you . . . I shall love her very much better than if it had been a son; indeed, my darling, I do love her very much already, and feel very much like a father. What do you intend to call her? Will you not give her papa's best love and innumerable kisses?'

There is only one break in the gap: a formal letter, which may have enclosed an intimate one, merely saying that it was a long time since he had heard from her and that he sometimes wondered 'whether you have quite forgotten me'. He did say that he had had trouble for a week with his system of communication. A letter of Parnell's towards the end of March contains a reference to suggest that Willie had been at Eltham much of this time. Willie himself was now about to play a part in events to put out of his mind for the time being any thoughts about his wife which may or may not have been troubling him.

Chapter 35

An opportunity such as even Willie can hardly have hoped might one day come his way now presented itself. There is no preliminary hint in the Kilmainham letters – secret as they were, with their invisible ink – of any suggestion that he might be useful as an intermediary with the Government. We do not know what letters Katie chose not to publish, but by the date of her book's publication in 1914 these events were not the sensitive political issue they had once been, and there was no reason why she should have withheld any such suggestion had there been one. In fact such references as Parnell makes about Willie in these letters are always guardedly hostile. Willie's later avowal that until 8 April 1882 he had taken no initiative may probably be accepted.

The opening sentence of the letter Parnell wrote to Katie on 5 April 1882 may, however, have referred to a contact at some level which Willie knew to be going on: 'My own dearest Wifie, – I think it very likely that something will be done by the Government shortly on the arrears question.' This was the question of tenants' arrears of rent, which O'Donnell would have discussed with Parnell when he came to see him in Kilmainham in December.

Later in this letter of 5 April Parnell sent 'kisses to our little daughter', though he was much troubled by something Katie had told him about the baby's health. He also wrote again about how he saw the future:

I am longing very, very much to see my own Wifie. I love you, my darling, more and more every day, and I should feel quite reconciled to giving up politics for ever and living with my sweet Katie all by ourselves away from everybody and everything. I do not think anything will ever induce me to speak from a platform again. I always disliked it excessively, but I should loathe it now.

But he seems to have realized that something about what he was saying needed correction:

Wifie must not, however, suppose that I am annoyed with the way things have gone. On the contrary, everything has succeeded remarkably, and much better than anybody could have expected.

Part of the success in his eyes must have been that he would now be able to see much more of her.

On 7 April he wrote again expressing further anxiety about what she was telling him of their daughter, though he admired very much a lock of the child's hair which she had sent him. 'I am so glad it is more like Queenie's than mine, although there is enough of mine in it to spoil it somewhat and render it less beautiful than Wifie's. Still, there is a splendid golden tint in it which is quite exceptional.' Later in the letter he spoke of his mother's health being 'very much broken latterly' and that he thought of applying to go over to see her. But he wanted to try to get O'Kelly released first. O'Kelly, with whom he had been playing a lot of handball until recently, had become ill. The idea of release was in the air. Dillon had also been ill, and, in his letter of two days before, Parnell had said it was thought Dillon would be 'released to-morrow'. Dillon's illness had indeed earlier provided some grounds for consideration of his release by the Chief Secretary. Forster had told Dillon's brother, 'The doors of Kilmainham are open if he likes to go to the Continent, but he must not stop here.' Dillon had refused to accept any terms and had taken pains to have his refusal published in the *Freeman's Journal*. This had been in January. It is significant, therefore, that in this letter of 7 April Parnell was writing to Katie, 'D. is going abroad and will not even appear in the House for a couple of months.' But he was a little premature with this information.

The very next day, 8 April, a letter of greater historical importance was written, not from Kilmainham but from Willie O'Shea's London rooms at 1 Albert Mansions, SW, and it came from Willie himself. It was addressed to Gladstone.

It began by referring to the proposal he had made to Gladstone the previous summer, with Parnell's approval, while the Land Bill was being debated in the House – the scheme by which landlords, in return for reduction of rent, might be compensated proportionately by the Exchequer. Gladstone, after consulting the Cabinet, had politely but firmly rejected it. But the important part of that letter in retrospect was that section in which, in return for acceptance of the proposal, Parnell was prepared to cease opposition to the Land Bill then before the House and to give it 'an effectual support in Ireland, such support to be loyally afforded even if outwardly and for the moment prudently veiled'. In other words, something approaching that *modus vivendi* between the Liberals and the Irish party for which Gladstone even some years before had expressed a hope was on offer. In the light of what Gladstone had recently been saying about Home Rule in the 1882 parliamentary session, this was an intelligent moment at which to venture a new approach on similar lines.

It was particularly intelligent if anything was known of Parnell's mood in Kilmainham. Willie, in this letter, told Gladstone in so many words that he had not been in touch with Parnell: he was 'without any recent communication elsewhere . . . But', he went on, 'terms might still be possible, although of course now sibylline.' He may not have been in touch with Parnell, but he was certainly in touch with Katie at Eltham. Relations between them were at this stage closer than could be inferred from the occasional references to Willie in the letters Parnell was writing to her, and even they imply regular contact. At the very least Katie wanted Willie to be successful and happy in his political career, and the moment was certainly opportune on all counts for her to encourage him to act. It is unlikely that Parnell's mood in Kilmainham would not somehow have been conveyed by Katie to Willie. The reference in Willie's letter to 'sibylline' terms was the exact equivalent of the 'prudently veiled' attitude which had been described as necessary in the proposed accommodation of the year before; it caught a touch of Parnell's political character aptly.

Willie's letter to Gladstone had begun, 'I have sometimes wondered whether, in the pressure and anxiety of Irish affairs, your mind has ever reverted to the compromise which I proposed to you last year.' It continued, 'Last year all that was needed could have been done on a mere matter of detail. To save the situation now, great audacity would be required, but great audacity has often proved to be great statesmanship.' Though the proposal was, as the year before, concerned with financing the land settlement, Willie's tone in this last sentence was clearly intended to suggest that collaboration in present circumstances was likely to prove of the widest political worth.

Many years later, in quite different circumstances, Willie was to be asked whether this approach to Gladstone was made without the direct authority of Parnell. He replied, 'Without any authority whatever from Mr Parnell, direct or indirect.' The use of the word 'indirect' here, though in the form of a denial, probably indicates it to be less than the truth.

No immediate reply was received from Gladstone.

A sad but propitious event now occurred. In Paris, Parnell's young nephew Henry Thomson, son of his rich married sister Delia, had fallen ill at the end of March. He lived alone, spending much of his time composing music; and his mother had discovered that he was ill only by accident. The illness was not taken very seriously at first, but he developed a high fever and, after a week of constant delirium, died. Parnell's sister was devastated. Parnell seized the opportunity. He applied to Forster by telegram for permission to attend the funeral. It is indicative of something in the climate on the Government's side that permission was granted at once.

At six o'clock in the morning of 10 April Parnell left Kilmainham on parole and, travelling by Holyhead, was by the afternoon at Willesden Junction in London, where he was met, by arrangement, by the deputy leader of the party, Justin McCarthy, and by Frank Hugh O'Donnell, by the former Acting Secretary of the Land League in Ireland, P. J. Quinn, already released from Kilmainham, and by the Secretary of the Land League organization in Great Britain, a man named Frank Byrne. Byrne, though none of the others then knew it, was closely connected with a new Irish secret society formed for the purpose of assassinating leading members of the Government administration in Ireland.

Parnell had agreed by the terms of his parole not to take part in open political activity, and he retired to McCarthy's house in Jermyn Street to discuss the failure of the 'No Rent' manifesto and the need to do something about the tenants in arrears. Afterwards, not wishing to arrive in Paris by night, he went down to Eltham, where he saw his child for the first time and found her desperately ill. Willie was not there; he was in his rooms at 1 Albert Mansions. Parnell spent the night with Katie at Eltham. He would almost certainly have heard from her about Willie's letter to Gladstone.

The next afternoon, on his way to Paris at last, he called on Willie at Albert Mansions. Presumably it presented no problem that he had first been to Eltham, since it could be thought reasonable to have expected to find Willie there. This in itself perhaps indicates that he was there a lot. What the two of them had to say about the recent birth of Katie's child can never now be known.

In fact Parnell and Katie's daughter was seriously ill. Katie later wrote in her memoirs that Willie, at Eltham, was being 'very good; I told him my baby was dying and I must be left alone. He had no suspicion of the truth, and only stipulated that the child should be baptized at once . . .' Katie had her baptized in Willie's Catholic faith in the drawing-room at

Wonersh Lodge. She was named Sophie Claude, after a sister of Parnell's who had died and, oddly, an old friend, Lord Truro. It is likely that Katie had told Parnell of this, but she publishes no letter of his showing awareness of it. He had in fact suggested 'Sophie' earlier, but was afraid it might arouse suspicion.

Parnell told Willie that he was pleased that he had made his overture to Gladstone. The possibility of his eventual total release was discussed, and it was decided that, were it to be granted, it should in no way be accepted with any conditions attached. Willie told Parnell that he would communicate with him in Paris if he got an answer to his letter to Gladstone. They dined together and then Parnell left by train for Dover.

Gladstone's reply was sent the same day, 11 April. It was discouraging, but there was something non-committal at least about the last few words. 'I do not see any mode of proceeding upon the lines which you have drawn,' he wrote, 'but the finance of the Irish Land Act must be dealt with during the present year and I hope that the plan will be such as to suit itself to whatever may be the scale of any possible operation.'

It is not clear whether Willie sent this reply to Parnell in Paris or whether he waited until he had tried to obtain an improvement on it, which he now proceeded to do. He replied to Gladstone on 13 April to make clear that the part of his own letter of 8 April that really mattered had been not that part which concerned the land question but the wider implication behind it to the effect that some sort of collaboration might be possible 'elsewhere' on terms however 'sibylline'. He built up his credentials by telling Gladstone how on Monday 10 April, the day of the release on parole from Kilmainham, Parnell had not wanted to go on to Paris immediately and arrive there at night but had spent Tuesday 'partly at my house at Eltham . . . and partly here [Albert Mansions].'

This was the most important and exciting moment in Willie's political career to date, and he was determined to make the most of it. He wrote, 'The person to whom Mr Parnell addresses himself in many cases (much as I differ from him in serious matters on politics and policy) is myself.' The reason for this, he said, was that Parnell knew that none of his MPs had nearly so much influence with the clergy of the county he represented as himself.

There then followed a sentence which showed how far his present excitement was getting the better of him and even endangering the basis for confidence he was trying to establish. 'Eighteen months ago', he wrote, 'Mr Parnell used every effort to induce me to take over the leadership of the party.' He said that this was known to only two or three people besides themselves. He said he mentioned such things only to explain what might otherwise appear to be 'fatuous officiousness'.

The statement that Parnell could have asked Willie to take over the leadership of the party is so obviously absurd that some explanation needs to be looked for. The most likely one is that Willie was thinking of the time of their November stay together at Eltham in 1880, some eighteen months before, when Parnell certainly induced him to see that it was well worth his while to figure on his side of the party rather than with Shaw and the other Whigs. The inducement may well have left a flattering impression on Willie which he now allowed himself to exaggerate. Certainly he now saw himself, with some reason, as in a position to urge that he had a special relationship with Parnell – though Gladstone was not to know the full truth of it for at least some weeks – and 'By the use of this influence,' Willie wrote, 'I brought Mr Parnell within the spheres of moderate counsels in June.'

He said that when he had seen his leader on the previous Tuesday, 11 April, Parnell had commented that the Government must now be regretting having refused the earlier offer of collaboration, but Gladstone's reply had made clear that this was not so. 'However,' Willie said, 'I will try to mediate again. This time, of course, Mr Parnell has no part in the initiative.'

This was later to be admitted as untrue, though it was reasonable for Parnell to wish at that stage not to be seen to have any part in it. The essence of the proposal now put forward was that 'in consideration of certain amendments to the Land Act ... and of some understanding of other matters ... a return would be made advantageous in the higher sense to the country, and in the lower to the Government'. Willie said that 'moral support of great power might be enlisted to aid very actively against agrarian outrage, and that effectual steps might be taken to hasten the acquiescence of the tenants in the spirit of the Land Act'.

The latter part of this offer was of course a total reversal of everything Parnell had been saying on platforms in the eight weeks before he was sent to Kilmainham. However, in the six months he had been there, the overall failure of the 'No Rent' manifesto and ever-increasing successful applications to the land courts had made it possible to see that what he had been saying on platforms belonged to a different world from the political reality of April 1882.

There was no compromise over the Land League's fundamental principle of peasant proprietorship, but here too in Willie's letter there was a significant indication that the political world was very different from six months ago. 'Either you must carry it out to the full extent,' wrote Willie to Gladstone, 'or the Tories will take the wind out of your sails.'

Gladstone's secretary, John Morley, wrote a note across this letter from Willie, saying shrewdly that it appeared to be 'an admission of acquiescence of his [Parnellite] party in state of outrage in Ireland – in an effort to get as much credit as possible in a losing game'.

But if the game was one which the old Land League movement was losing, it was not exactly one which the Government was winning. Gladstone sent Willie a reply which, while still guarded, coming from such a skilfully wary politician, could be said to carry a positive note. 'I am very sensible', he wrote from Downing Street, 'of the spirit in which you write and I think you can assume the existence of a spirit on my part with which you can sympathize.'

It was presumably this letter of 15 April from Gladstone which Willie sent as an enclosure with his own to Parnell staying in Paris at the Grand Hôtel, 12 boulevard des Capucines. The tone in which Parnell thanked him for it the next day ('My dear O'Shea') makes clear that he had indeed had a part in the initiative, and that he was in no way discouraged. 'Very interesting,' he called it; '. . . I trust that something may come out of the correspondence and certainly the prospect looks favourable.' He discussed for a moment the terms which might make three-quarters of the tenants owners of their land at fairly remunerative prices to the present landlords; a permanent settlement was, he said, 'most desirable for everybody's sake'. This was the nearest he came to acknowledging a practical political dimension in the negotiations.

He thanked Willie for inquiring after his sister, and told him that she had been 'very much cut up' but was somewhat better now. 'My presence here', he added, 'has been a great help to her in every way.' Curiously, but in character to the extent that it represented his straightforward disregard of being thought vain, he said almost exactly the same thing in two other letters: one to his sister Emily, and the other to Katie at Eltham.

He wrote to Katie three times from Paris on this visit, twice formally and once beginning 'My own Queenie' and signing himself 'Your own loving King'. But the content of this one was hardly more intimate than that of the other two formal 'My Dear Mrs O'Shea' letters. All three spoke mainly of his health. It seems his nephew had died of typhoid, and that a great many people in the American colony were down with it. But his sister's house – to which he was 'obliged to go' – had been well

disinfected. The two formal letters were mainly concerned with a cold he
had caught. His sister had insisted on him seeing a doctor, who said it was
nothing. But he thought it was unwise to travel too soon in case he
caught a fresh cold. He thought he had caught it from leaving off a
flannel jacket which he always slept with in prison. It would have been a
bad chest cold 'had I not taken two Turkish baths immediately I felt it
coming on'.

A curiously flat impression of personality is created by these letters. He
was, after all, in an extraordinary situation. He was temporarily a free
man in a foreign capital after six months in a prison to which he was in
honour bound to return, though he seemed to have free choice as to
when he did so. He had, only a few days before, been reunited for a day
and a night with the woman he loved so passionately that it seemed at
times as if nothing else would ever be of importance to him again. He
would have to leave her almost immediately after his return to England
and go to jail in Ireland. Their two-month-old child, whom he had only
just seen for the first time and was his own first child, was desperately ill
and might even be dying while he was away. The political life on which
for the past six years he had with considerable success concentrated all his
prodigious energy to help make Ireland 'a nation' was on the threshold of
a quite new chapter. The shape of his movement's recent failure looked as
if it could now be transformed with some understanding from the British
Government itself into a new form of success. And yet here he was,
sitting in his hotel in the boulevard des Capucines thinking chiefly about
his cold, his vest and the taking of Turkish baths. Even the intimate letter
to Katie was obsessed with the prospects for his health. It made no
mention at all of their dangerously sick child. It would be possible to
see the continuing obsession in the two formal letters as useful backing
for his presenting himself as a bachelor invalid in need of the care and
attention he got at Eltham. In which case it was the clearly genuine
obsession revealed in the inimate letter that helped make the cover so
convincing.

The only other subject touched on in these short letters is the matter of
his future movements. He had told Willie to expect him back at the end
of the week ending Saturday 22 April. The formal letters refer vaguely
to some plan 'to spend a few days in the south or elsewhere' and 'a
journey into the country' which he could start on the morning of
Tuesday the 18th. It seems quite possible that these were coded references
to his real intention, which was to return to Eltham during the week in
the hope that Willie might come down only at the weekend.

Parnell, having telegraphed to Eltham that he was coming, did indeed arrive there on Wednesday 19 April. But Willie showed up at Eltham too. There was much to discuss. In the first place, after receiving Gladstone's temporizing reply of 15 April, Willie had felt sufficiently encouraged to take a new step. On the same day, he had written to a member of Gladstone's Cabinet, the President of the Board of Trade, the radical Joseph Chamberlain, after speaking to him in the House of Commons.

As you appear to be a Minister without political pedantry, I take the liberty of enclosing a copy of a letter which I have written to Mr Gladstone . . . I ask you how the Liberal Party is to get in at the next election and at the one after and so on against the Irish vote? And if by any chance it did get in, how on earth it is to get on? . . . You have to deal with men and things as they are, and although time and many hateful incidents have aggravated the difficulties, still I believe that it might be to the advantage of the Liberal Party if its leaders were to try to compromise honourably, and that such an effort might be made by the most influential Irishman of the day in a candid and moderate spirit.

He had approached the heart of the matter.

Willie and Chamberlain were then hardly acquainted, though occasionally exchanging a few words in the House. Chamberlain later reflected on how Willie's letter had struck him. 'It seemed to me', he said, 'to offer the possibility of a new departure and of an understanding with the Irish representatives which might lead to a permanent and satisfactory settlement.'

His reply, on Monday 17 April, had been encouraging. He had emphasized that of course he was in no position to commit any of his colleagues, and had some reservations of his own, but 'I think I may say that there appears to be nothing in your proposals which does not deserve consideration, and which might not be the basis of a subsequent agreement.'

However, Chamberlain stressed that, if the Liberals were to show 'greater consideration than they had hitherto done for Irish opinion', the Irish too must pay some attention to British public opinion about outrages in Ireland. 'Since the present Government has been in office,' he added, 'they have not had the slightest assistance in this direction.' Willie in his immediate acknowledgement of this letter had, as he himself might have put it, struck while the iron was hot: 'What the French call the psychological moment ought not to be lost,' he said.

Chamberlain wrote to Gladstone the next day: 'Mr Parnell is tired of prison life, and would, I think, be found reasonable. Might it not be worth while to open negotiations . . .?' He suggested he might be permitted to approach members of the Irish party, including Healy and O'Shea, to find out 'whether they are now ready to unite with us to secure the good government of their country'.

And thus began the delicate and urgent process by which Parnell's own strategy was to be reorientated towards alliance with the Liberals and to stamp a new political pattern on the British parliamentary system. That pattern would last in general for over thirty years, during which Irish nationalist hopes could remain concentrated on the possibility that there was at least a practical hope of realizing Home Rule. But that is a different story.

The machinations which were to lead eventually within this fortnight at the end of April 1882 to what came to be called 'the Kilmainham Treaty' were necessarily extremely delicate on both sides.

On the Government side the Chief Secretary, Forster, while not wholly opposed to the release of Parnell and the other prisoners in return for definite Irish commitments, became increasingly adrift from Gladstone and the rest of the Cabinet as he required from Parnell commitments more definite than the Government saw politic to demand. This was to lead to Forster's resignation.

On Parnell's side there was a paramount need to minimize as far as possible a sense of disappointment, disillusion, even betrayal among some of his supporters, if the new direction in which he was going to work for Ireland while living out his life with Katie was to be effective.

But he had another internal political problem of which the outside world was not aware, and that concerned Willie O'Shea.

There was no question but that so far Willie had been extremely useful. No other member of Parnell's party could have been, literally, so well placed either to receive indications of Parnell's preparedness to explore negotiations with the Government or, once these had been set in train, to work out with Parnell before he returned to Kilmainham how they might be further implemented. His independent distance from Parnell within the party as a moderate gave his status as an intermediary a special credibility. He had performed his task competently, with a tact which bordered more or less acceptably on both self-confidence and obsequiousness but, except possibly for his strange reference to Parnell's offer of the leadership, lapsed into neither.

Only Forster, apprehensive as he was about where the Government's 'new departure' might be leading, expressed doubts about Willie at this stage. 'I do not believe he has the influence either with Parnell or with the priests he claims,' he had written to Gladstone on 18 April. Parnell himself can have had no lasting belief in him as an intermediary, quite apart from any views he may have formed by now of his character. The mistrust which others in the party were certain to have for him on account of his moderate, former Whiggish views made him unsuitable in the long term. Still, his initiative had just brought negotiations valuably closer, particularly by his contact with Chamberlain; this link needed to be maintained.

In the course of talking over developments with him this weekend at Eltham, Parnell had to undergo the harrowing experience of knowing that his child was dying in another room of the house while he needed to appear sympathetic to both Willie and Katie but sufficiently detached to give Willie no grounds for suspicion. If Willie's worldly instincts did not penetrate their secrecy in these circumstances, perhaps Parnell's natural ability to assume a personal coldness at times had something to do with it, or perhaps Willie was just too absorbed by his own role in the negotiations to care to return to last year's anxieties about Parnell and his wife. His exact state of mind on the matter continued to remain an enigma for years.

Sophie, the two-month-old baby girl, was to die before Parnell left, but, as Willie had left Eltham before he did, he and Katie must have had some time in which to share their grief together, contrary to the account in her memoirs.

In line with Gladstone's letter of 15 April, the terms of the deal to be worked out concerned principally a settlement of the arrears of rent in exchange for Parnell's agreement to denounce agrarian outrages and to encourage tenants to pay rents where necessary as adjudged by the land courts. Behind this lay the question of the release of those imprisoned. Parnell's own release did not need to be a matter for negotiation, because, if agreement were reached, his release would be necessary in order to make it effective. He could with easy dignity make it no part of negotiations. But there were important questions about others. One of these, not in Kilmainham but now in Portland, was Davitt, whose release – and goodwill – was essential, though Parnell was anxious it should not take place until he had himself been able to talk to him.

Some time during the day on Saturday 22 April, Willie came up to London to see Chamberlain at his house in Princes Gate to give him a résumé of the way things had gone in conversation with Parnell, and

Chamberlain himself wrote out for them a memorandum to summarize the way things were now to proceed. Parnell was to advise all tenants to pay rent and would denounce outrages of every sort, including any resistance to law and all processes of intimidation, whether by boycotting or otherwise. Tenants in arrears with rents would have them compulsorily wiped out by a composition of one-third payable by the tenant, one-third by the State and one-third remitted by the landlord.

That evening Chamberlain went to the Reform Club as the guest of a member who had also invited Henry George, then in London from Dublin. George was a personal friend of Davitt's, on whom he had had some influence with his ideas on land nationalization. While in London he had been agitating for Davitt's release and had been to see Harcourt, the Home Secretary, who had turned him down. He now asked Chamberlain if he couldn't see to this. Chamberlain replied that he could not, because Harcourt would be jealous of any interference. However, he did say that he thought George would be able to see Davitt before he returned to America, which George took to mean that Davitt would be released before that. Chamberlain also said that he was in favour of going further with amendments to the Land Act and of relaxing the reins of coercion, although he complained that the Irish had not helped by refusing to condemn outrages. Thus did the correspondent of the New York *Irish World* come unwittingly within reach of a major journalistic scoop about the biggest Irish story of the year: the 'Kilmainham Treaty'.

The very real nature of the negotiations that had begun on Saturday 22 April made Parnell now seriously take stock of the suitability of his present intermediary as a sole agent for dealings with the Government. His private difficulty was that, whether he liked it or not, the personality of Willie O'Shea was obviously going to be an inseparable feature of his own life for as far ahead as he could see. Willie's personal susceptibilities, which included his vanity and his ambition, were going to have to be taken into account, along with his usefulness or otherwise.

Perhaps even while Willie had been seeing Chamberlain at Princes Gate that Saturday afternoon, Parnell had written to the deputy leader of the party, Justin McCarthy, with whom he had last talked over matters in Jermyn Street more than a week before. A lot had happened in the interval, and he now arranged a meeting for three o'clock next day at which he could put McCarthy in touch with all that had been going on. Starting on his way back to Kilmainham that Sunday, he called at Jermyn Street and discussed matters, including Chamberlain's memorandum, with McCarthy for such a long time that he missed the night boat-train for Holyhead and had to spend the night at Crewe before sailing back to Ireland the next day and re-entering Kilmainham.

'Everything went off very nicely and quietly,' he wrote to Katie, 'and I have not caught any cold this time. O.K. [O'Kelly] had aired my bed very carefully, etc., and they were all very glad to see me again, with the exception of the authorities.'

He was writing on the day of their daughter Sophie's funeral, and ended his letter:

I have been thinking all day of how desolate and lonely my Queenie must be in her great sorrow. I wish so much that I might have stayed to comfort her, but I have indeed every hope and confidence that our separation will not now last very long. It is too terrible to think that on this the saddest day of all others – and, let us hope, the saddest that we *both* shall ever see again – my Wifie should have nobody with her.

Good-bye, my own darling, Your loving King.

But he had enclosed with this letter one which he had received from Willie. We do not have this, but it clearly contained a reproach for lack of confidence in having seemed to switch the role of intermediary with the Government from himself to McCarthy. Parnell asked Katie in this letter of 25 April what he was to say to Willie, adding that he had told 'my friend in Jermyn Street' what to do – meaning that he had sent him a letter encapsulating their conversation to be shown to Chamberlain. He said he was thinking of writing to Willie to say that the letter he had sent to him from Paris on 16 April should have been 'sufficient indication of confidence'.

Willie meanwhile had been continuing activity on his own account. He had contacted Chamberlain again and had rather clumsily let him feel that he was being pushed too far by having to discuss concessions on matters other than the so-far agreed matters of arrears. It became necessary for Willie to explain, 'My note was in no way intended to spring any fresh demand on you.'

Chamberlain, however, was himself already conveying something of the conciliatory spirit in the air to other Irish Members, including Healy, who sensed from this, as he was to put it much later in his memoirs, 'that Parnell was about to give in'. Chamberlain informed the Cabinet of his conversations with Healy and Justin McCarthy as well as with Willie O'Shea.

Forster, the Chief Secretary, was becoming increasingly uneasy about what was happening. He thought it necessary that, before any question of a deal, Parnell should make a public statement condemning all agrarian outrages – including every sort of intimidation – and that even before the prisoners were released there should be fresh powers for the Government in a new Coercion Act.

Chamberlain, though no party to this last suggestion, recognized that some binding commitment by Parnell would help, and suggested that Willie should apply to Forster for permission to visit Parnell in Kilmainham. Forster, in spite of his reservations expressed to Gladstone about Willie's qualities, agreed to this, and on the morning of Saturday 29 April Willie arrived at Kilmainham to spend the greater part of the day talking to Parnell.

What came out of this encounter was, from Parnell's point of view, principally part of a face-saving exercise to pacify Willie and perhaps to make Katie happier too. Parnell saw no need to see him. He had even written and wired to Willie two days before, telling him that if he came to Ireland he should not come to see him. But there he was, and, though the basis for the negotiations had been spelt out carefully in Parnell's letter to McCarthy, the essence of those arrangements was now spelt out again in a letter to Willie – and, it so happened, rather more fully. Again, presumably to save Willie's face, the letter was dated the day before the meeting, 28 April, in order to show that Parnell would have written it even if Willie had not come to see him. As Parnell was to write to Katie, Willie would have been dreadfully mortified if he had had nothing to show.

The letter to Willie began with an apology: 'I was very sorry that you had left Albert Mansions before I reached London from Eltham, as I had wished to tell you that after our conversation I had made up my mind that it would be proper for me to put Mr McCarthy in possession of the views which I had previously communicated to you.'

The rest of the letter repeated the need to settle the arrears question, to admit leaseholders to the fair-rent clauses, and to extend land purchase; all this would 'enable us to show the smaller tenantry that they have been treated with justice and some generosity'. The settlement of the arrears question in particular, he wrote, would, he had every confidence – and it was a confidence shared by his colleagues – mean that 'the exertions which we should be able to make strenuously and unremittingly would be effective in stopping outrages and intimidation of all kinds'.

What was in this letter which had not been in the letter to McCarthy, however, was a passage which was to make it historic. After saying that the accomplishment of such measures as had been outlined would in Parnell's judgement be regarded by the country as a practical settlement of the land question, Parnell continued, 'and would, I feel sure, enable us to co-operate cordially for the future with the Liberal Party in forwarding Liberal principles' and would enable the Government to feel 'justified in dispensing with further coercive measures'.

Willie returned happily to London.

Gladstone was already excited. On Saturday 29 April, the day Willie was in Kilmainham, he wrote a note to Forster to make sure that when the Cabinet met the following Monday they would hear 'all that O'Shea (and anyone else) can tell us about Parnell and the interview today'.

Willie on his return went to see Forster and handed him Parnell's letter, which in turn was handed to Gladstone on the Sunday. Gladstone took a much more optimistic line than Forster about its contents. He said he thought it was the most extraordinary letter he had ever read, adding, 'I can't help feeling indebted to O'Shea.'

When the Cabinet met on Monday 1 May, the possible release of the Kilmainham 'suspects' was discussed. Gladstone commented, 'There has been *no* negotiation. But we have obtained information. The moment is golden.'

The Lord Lieutenant of Ireland, Earl Cowper, had for some time been wanting to resign, and had in fact done so on the very day on which Willie saw Parnell in Kilmainham; but he was still at his post. Gladstone wired him in Dublin, 'MOST SECRET': 'We know authentically that Parnell and his friends are ready to abandon No Rent formally and to declare against outrage energetically.' The following day he wired him again: 'Cabinet has decided for release.' All this, it seems, came as a surprise to Cowper, who had had no information about what was going on. Even Gladstone's Chief Whip, Lord Richard Grosvenor, had heard little of what was afoot. Gladstone, when he wrote to him that day, expressed something of the guarded sense of elation he felt: 'I do hope you will be better about Ireland when you know what has taken place. Of a "new departure" we know nothing, but of new hopes and prospects much.'

A 'new departure' was exactly how Forster saw it, and he did not like it. 'It is in fact', he wrote, 'a concession to Parnell.' He resigned.

On the same day, 2 May, Parnell, O'Kelly and Dillon were set free. Davitt was to be released in due course. O'Kelly went up to Avondale with Parnell. The servants rushed out of the house to welcome them, crying with joy, but, according to O'Kelly, Parnell was quite unmoved.

An old woman seized him by the hand, kissed it and covered it with tears. 'Oh Master Charley, are you back to us again?' O'Kelly said Parnell was like a statue: he made a casual remark as if out for a morning walk and went through into the drawing-room, where his sister Emily was waiting.

'Ah, Charley, is that you? I thought they would never let you back again!'

'Well, what did you think they would do to me?'

'I thought they'd hang you.'

'Well, it may come to that yet,' Parnell said with a smile.

Or so at least the conversation went as reported by O'Kelly to Parnell's first biographer, who thus reproduced it more than fifteen years later. Inasmuch as it reveals Parnell as easily in command of his emotions in an entirely new political situation as he had been in the old, it seems to have a certain valid ring.

Two days later Forster was giving his personal reasons for resignation to the House of Commons – a crowded House, with the Prince of Wales in the Peers' Gallery. He was just saying why he had had the three released Members of Parliament arrested in the first place when Parnell himself pushed his way through the crowd of Members at the Bar of the House and walked up the House to cheers from his own party. Forster said that while he could not regard the release of the Honourable Member for Cork as advisable, he was glad to see him there, because he would be having to allude to him – which he did by accusing him of intimidation of Her Majesty's subjects and, in so many words, of having given inadequate undertakings that this would stop while blackmailing the Government into releasing him and his companions. Parnell, when he spoke, stated only that there had been no bargain of any sort and that a settlement of the question of arrears of rent would make it easier for him and his friends to try to diminish agrarian outrages in future.

The next day, Friday 5 May, Willie asked for an interview with Gladstone and went to see him at about six o'clock in the evening. He had, Gladstone noted, been up all night, and had had a long and in his opinion most satisfactory conversation with Parnell, who, he was confident, would do what he had said he would do – namely, help reduce the number of outrages. Among those who he thought would help Parnell do so he named Egan and Sheridan. It emerged that Parnell had consulted with his colleagues in Kilmainham before writing the letter which Willie had brought back.

It was obvious that the Government would be in for trouble with the

Conservative Opposition, which would take up Forster's insinuations that, in return for tactical political advantage, Gladstone had too easily surrendered to the forces of outrage in Ireland. But, in spite of this, the outlook for both parties to an agreement which promised such very considerable advantages to both seemed fair indeed.

The principal difficulty ahead for Parnell would be opposition from the left wing of the former Land League movement. Disappointment was already being expressed at what could look like a sell-out to the Government for personal advantage and the compromise of the principles for which the Land League had stood.

Henry George, still writing for the *Irish World*, had begun to be apprehensive even before the official release of the three from Kilmainham. On the morning of the day on which he had had dinner with Chamberlain at the Reform Club, he had heard of a conversation of Justin McCarthy's reported from a dinner the night before. McCarthy – who had then not yet had his meeting with Parnell, though he had of course talked to him the day before he left for Paris – was saying that Irish Members were already disposed to help the Government.

George himself had some weeks before formed an unfavourable impression, from a revolutionary point of view, of the quality of Irish Home Rule Members – 'the worst I ever saw', he wrote to Patrick Ford. They were, he said, quite out of touch with their constituents in Ireland. As Boyton had told him, 'When they cross the Channel they become completely cut off until they get back again, and however much the Irish people might advance in thought, these Members could not feel it.' Even a man like Healy was essentially a Conservative. Such Members had been frightened by the lengths to which the movement had gone in Ireland and were, he told Patrick Ford, disposed to unite with the Government over the land question. He had been uneasy about Parnell's stay in Paris. It seemed to signify something, although he wasn't quite sure what. 'It may be natural, for Kilmainham is not a pleasant place, but it don't seem to me wise.' And now that Parnell was out of Kilmainham he was more worried still. Within a matter of weeks George was to be writing, 'Parnell seems to me to have thrown away the greatest opportunity any Irishman ever had. It is the birthright for a mess of potage.'

But this was a judgement far removed from the necessary realities of current nationalist politics in Ireland. A real difficulty for Parnell, of course, was that one of these realities was that the finances came from just those incipient revolutionary forces in America, represented by George and Ford, which disliked the way he was heading. Nevertheless, Parnell's adroitness in handling internal pressures within the movement had been demonstrated clearly enough in the past. There was no reason why he should not deploy it as effectively now that he found himself steering the movement towards its objectives by constitutional collaboration with the Government rather than in semi-revolutionary opposition to it.

Though it was a *modus vivendi* between Liberals and nationalists to which he was now committing himself – and still only a tentative one – there was no reason in his mind why it should in the long run be a *modus vivendi* convenient only to Gladstone. If the Liberals were to be worked with, they were also in the course of time to be worked on. It would still be a matter of getting them to do what they could be made to do. With perhaps at the most some twenty to thirty Members of Parliament prepared to work in close harmony under his leadership towards a nationalist objective through a Liberal Party as yet quite uncommitted to Home Rule, and in the main largely opposed to it, it was not going to be a fast process. But an extension of the franchise, which many Liberals wished to see come about, was likely to be in place by the next general election, and there was no knowing how much more effective the political power of Irish nationalists both in Ireland and England would then be. There was no reason why Parnell's original concept of an Irish party independent of all parties should not continue in spirit, even though the party was temporarily tied to one. All sorts of possibilities could be seen to open up in the new course which he had decided to run. But, before he could get his bearings to run it, something happened to shatter for the immediate future any prospect of either an Irish nationalist party or the Liberal Party making anything out of a *modus vivendi* at all.

Chapter 36

The assassins who Herbert Gladstone had heard were after Forster were still about. They had in fact come dangerously close to Forster a number of times, but, either through incompetence or, on one occasion, because they were afraid of killing a woman in the carriage with him, they had failed to carry out the 'execution' as planned. Their last failure had been on the very day Forster left Ireland for the last time as Chief Secretary, 19 April, when he drove to Kingstown harbour for the boat to England instead of going by train from Westland Row station where they were waiting for him.

His would-be executioners were members of a newly formed small secret society called the Irish National Invincibles, rather more sophisticated, at least in its connections with the Land League leadership, than the diverse agrarian bands operating in the name of Captain Moonlight. It was by definition a shadowy organization, and the evidence about it, though not insignificant, is itself indeterminate, being an amalgam of police informers' and convicts' reports, court-room accounts and one unreliably self-glorifying memoir. Its origins seem traceable to a meeting which took place in London soon after the arrest of Parnell and the other principal leaders of the Land League, at which Biggar, John Barry M P, also a former Fenian, and Egan were present. At this the need for some new initiative to rally active nationalist morale after the recent set-backs was discussed, together possibly with the desirability of using assassination as a political weapon. A Directory of three was formed, of which one member may have been Egan and another the Land League organizer Sheridan. Another, certainly, was Frank Byrne, Secretary of that Land League of Great Britain, which shared offices with the parliamentary party, now in Bridge Street, Westminster. Byrne was to be one of the group to meet Parnell at Willesden on 10 April, the day of his emergence on parole from Kilmainham. Liaison had long been made by then with an assortment of the many restless ex-Fenians in Dublin keen to react in some way to the Land League's suppression. A Dublin Invincible Directory had been formed.

Interestingly, Henry George of the *Irish World* seems not to have had wind of this development to report in his private letters to Patrick Ford. There he described the only alternative to the imprisoned leadership as being the former Land League clerk Moloney, who was clearly outside the counsels of the Invincibles, though some of those he sent travelling about the countryside may have been members of the new secret society on their own account. It seems almost certain that Egan, with his access to the American funds, played some part with the Dublin Directory, though, as has been neatly said in the most comprehensive study of the Invincibles to date, 'it is not at all clear to what extent he who undoubtedly paid the piper called the tune'.

On the other hand, one member of the London Directory who undoubtedly knew the tune was Frank Byrne. Byrne it was who under the supervisory eye of an American Civil War soldier, Captain Macafferty, a formerly imprisoned Fenian exiled in 1871, had smuggled a dozen twelve-inch-long surgical knives into Dublin in the skirts of his pregnant wife, as more suitable silent instruments of assassination than revolvers. On Macafferty's advice, cord was later wrapped around the handles to give a better grip.

Forster was now beyond reach, but the Under-Secretary, T. H. Burke, was still there, having been in that post since 1869. Burke was one of the relatively few Irish Catholics to have made a successful career in Dublin Castle, but he was for that very reason regarded by nationalists as something of a traitor, or at least a 'Castle Rat', and thus almost as appropriate a target for assassination as the Chief Secretary himself.

The most likely successor to Forster had, in many people's eyes, been Joseph Chamberlain. Willie O'Shea, on hearing that Chamberlain was hesitating about accepting the post, sent him a note to say that if he accepted it would be 'a point of honour with Mr Parnell to work as if for himself to ensure the success of your administration'. Next day, 3 May, Chamberlain himself was expecting a call from Gladstone. It did not come. Instead Gladstone appointed as Chief Secretary for Ireland Hartington's brother, Lord Frederick Cavendish, previously Financial Secretary to the Treasury.

Cavendish had hitherto seemed a conscientious and likeable figure but of no great political weight, a man of whose nervously excitable manner of speech in the House *Punch* had once said, 'In calmest moments his words tumble out at fourteen to the dozen.' It reported Harcourt as saying of him, 'all his words are conjunctions' as he watched him with interest at the dispatch box, 'trembling in every limb and pouring forth his torrent of tumbling speech'.

On the morning of Saturday 6 May Cavendish made his entry into Dublin with the new Viceroy, Lord Spencer, and met his officials in the offices of Dublin Castle. Afterwards, Spencer rode off with his usual small mounted escort to the Viceregal Lodge in Phoenix Park. Cavendish, who knew and liked Dublin from the time when, ten years before, his brother Hartington had been Chief Secretary, decided to walk there, to dine with the Viceroy that evening. Inside the Park as he continued on his way to the Lodge a cab came up behind him and stopped. His Under-Secretary, Burke, was inside and got out to walk the rest of the short way in conversation with him. It was about seven o'clock on a normal Saturday evening. There were a lot of people about. There was a polo match going on. Spencer, on his way there ahead of them, had stopped to watch it. A middle-aged Dublin builder, James Carey, the owner of slum tenement property and a candidate the previous year for Dublin Town Council, had watched it for a moment too on his way in the direction of the Lodge. He was a member of the Irish National Invincibles.

Spencer reached the Lodge and went in to settle down with some papers at a window overlooking the front. He was talking there with his half-brother when he suddenly heard a shriek which he said afterwards he would never forget. 'I seem to hear it now; it is always in my ears. This shriek was repeated again and again.' He got up and saw a man rush towards the Lodge and jump over the railings, shouting, 'Mr Burke and Lord Frederick Cavendish are killed.'

They had been hacked to death in the roadway by twelve-inch-long surgical knives.

Their assassins got away in a cab and were not apprehended until early the following year. But the Invincibles' deed had in an instant done more than destroy in gruesome fashion the lives of two high-ranking representatives of the 'enemy' administration in Dublin: it had shattered all prospect for the time being of that collaboration between Irish nationalists in Parliament and the Liberal Government from which Parnell, Gladstone, Chamberlain and even Willie O'Shea had had such high expectations in consequence of the so-called Kilmainham Treaty. It was to be two years and more before Parnell could seriously hope to be in a position to do much more to advance the cause of Irish nationalism. It was the first time in the eight years since he had first decided to enter politics that the foreseeable future looked devoid of potential change.

The horrified outcry in Britain was full of anger. It could look so easily as if the murders were the result of Government weakness in freeing Parnell and his associates for its own political advantage. Fortunately for both Parnell and Gladstone, the link between the Invincibles and Frank Byrne, the man whom Parnell had met at Willesden immediately on getting out of Kilmainham, was not then known. But Forster could now be seen to have been quite right in not wanting to release the 'suspects', Gladstone wrong in putting him into a position where he had to resign. If it were to save its face, the Government now had no possible political alternative but to revert to an even more severe pattern of coercion than before. Parnell was put in a position where he had no political alternative but to understand its need to do so, while trying to ameliorate the measures in Parliament as far as he could. But the *modus vivendi* and whatever might eventually come out of that for the benefit of Ireland would have to wait.

The one person who could now view the immediate future with a certain optimism in the light of the opportunities for influence which might represent themselves in the malaise was Willie O'Shea. There was for a start the advantage he hoped to be able to derive from the useful link he had forged over the Kilmainham Treaty with Chamberlain, the most brilliant and ambitious member of Gladstone's Government.

Parnell had spent the morning of the fateful day – a bright and sunny one even inside the walls of Portland prison, where Davitt had now been for over a year – on his way down to see Davitt with Dillon and O'Kelly. They brought him back to London in the afternoon. Davitt, who had been able to pick up very little political news from the outside world the whole time he was in Portland, had been told only that morning that he was to be released. Parnell, Dillon and O'Kelly were now able to tell him why. It had been an intelligent move on Parnell's part to get at him before anyone else could. In the light of the semi-revolutionary climate prevailing when his ticket of leave had been withdrawn in February of the year before, Davitt, like many of the more active former members of the Land League, could be expected to see the Kilmainham Treaty as a surrender and publicly question the direction Parnell was taking.

In the train going up to London, Parnell explained.

'We are on the eve of something like Home Rule. Gladstone has thrown over coercion and Forster, and he will legislate on the land question. The Tory party are going to advocate land purchase, and I see no reason why we should not obtain all we are looking for . . . The No Rent Manifesto [Davitt had only heard of it for the first time three months after it was issued] has failed and been withdrawn.'

Davitt asked about the Ladies' Land League, and defended it strongly when Parnell said that it had done much harm along with some good.

But Parnell said he would explain everything about the future more fully the next day.

They spent part of the rest of the journey allotting themselves posts in the coming Home Rule Cabinet in Ireland. O'Kelly was to head the police, Sexton to be Chancellor of the Exchequer, Dillon Home Secretary and Davitt himself, putting to good use his long experience, Director of Prisons. The light-hearted mood was not to last for more than a few hours after their return. Incidentally, the new Chief Secretary, Lord Frederick Cavendish, also figured in the general optimism. He was described to Davitt as 'one of the most modest and best men in the House, and a thorough supporter of the new policy'. It would have been just about as their train was coming into London that Cavendish set out on his walk from Dublin Castle to Phoenix Park.

On arrival in London they all went to the Westminster Palace Hotel, where Parnell had his rooms, and celebrated Davitt's release with toasts to 'the Home Rule Parliament of the immediate future'. Parnell took himself off to Katie at Eltham. Davitt and Dillon stayed in the hotel, and some time after eight o'clock that evening a journalist came in with a cable sent from RIC headquarters in Dublin to the Central News Agency. It said that Cavendish and Burke had been assassinated by a band of men outside the Viceregal Lodge in Dublin. They literally could not believe it, assuming it to be 'a bogus outrage for to-morrow's Sunday papers'. But at five o'clock next morning Davitt's old friend Henry George came into his bedroom with a telegram in his hand, confirming what he called 'one of the worst things that has ever happened to Ireland'.

Parnell himself read the news next morning, Sunday 7 May, in the *Observer* as he went into Eltham station to catch the train to London to see Davitt. Katie, waiting by the door to the station, watched him as he opened the paper and noticed 'a curious rigidity about his arms' as he held it open. He stood so still that she felt suddenly frightened and called out to him, 'King, what is it?' He came back and showed her the headline. She put her hand into his and he crushed it so hard that her rings cut into her fingers. His face was ashen. The train was coming in and she hurried him on to it. 'I shall resign,' he said, to which she replied, 'No, you are not a coward.' He half disregarded this.

Willie, with his established channel to Gladstone of the previous month, was put to use at once. Before going to see Davitt, Parnell called at Albert Mansions and gave him a message to deliver to Gladstone, through his secretary, in which he said that if Gladstone thought it necessary for him to resign 'for the maintenance of his position and for carrying out his views he was prepared to do so at once'.

He then went on to the Westminster Palace Hotel, where in Davitt's room he sat down on a sofa 'deadly pale, with a look of alarm in the eyes which I had never seen in any expression of his before'. Davitt, in his account of more than twenty years later, has Parnell saying he was going to send his resignation into Cork that night and retire into private life. But the message which he had got Willie to give to Gladstone had been more judicious than that. And in the answer he got back through Willie almost at once it could be said that he had obtained as clear an expression of continued goodwill towards the Kilmainham commitment as he could hope for in the circumstances.

'My duty', Gladstone told Willie, 'does not permit me for a moment to entertain Mr Parnell's proposal ... but I am deeply sensible of the honourable motive by which it has been prompted.'

Parnell now knew a little more clearly where he might stand than when he had crushed the rings into Katie's fingers that morning or sat down so deadly pale on Davitt's sofa. But the atmosphere among Irish Members in the hotel was still depressed. Healy, who was among them, said at one point that they should all resign because the cause was lost for a generation.

Though Willie had his uses, there was the same reluctance as before to use him more than was strictly necessary. After agreeing to a manifesto very strongly condemning the murders which had been written by Davitt, it was Justin McCarthy whom Parnell took with him to see first Sir Charles Dilke and then Chamberlain. One or the other of them was now expected to be appointed Chief Secretary.

There was talk with Dilke of the prospects for Home Rule despite the blow the cause had suffered. Dilke made an interesting distinction between his own and Chamberlain's position on the subject. Dilke said he would be inclined to press Home Rule on the Irish people even if they were not fully inclined for it – which demonstrated a shrewd perception of the contemporary realities of Irish nationalism – whereas Chamberlain, Dilke said, would only give Home Rule if the Irish people refused to accept anything less.

As they left Dilke to go to Chamberlain, Dilke took McCarthy aside and said it was unwise to let Parnell walk about the streets, as someone might recognize him and hold him responsible for the murders.

When they saw Chamberlain, he said he was once again quite prepared to take over as Chief Secretary if Gladstone were to appoint him. No one, of course, could have been more pleased to hear this than Willie O'Shea, who came in while they were talking. In the end, disappointingly for

Willie, Gladstone was to offer the post not to Chamberlain but to George Trevelyan, then a parliamentary secretary to the Admiralty.

But it was to Chamberlain that Willie had now tied his fortunes, and in the immediate future and throughout the next three years he was to hover about his political presence, hoping always to make the most of this allegiance in political terms to his own advantage – particularly because of his curiously special position with Parnell where matters bordering on eventual Home Rule for Ireland might be concerned. Chamberlain, for his part, whatever view he may have come to take of Willie's character over these years, knew of the special quality of his association with Parnell, without perhaps letting himself inquire into it too closely, and was happy to make use of him as a very special channel to the man who constituted an unavoidably effective factor in British politics.

Some years later when, for a number of reasons, Chamberlain took a less sympathetic view of Parnell than he did on this day after the Phoenix Park murders, he wrote an account of their afternoon meeting in which he described Parnell as being 'as white as a sheet, agitated and apparently demoralized. Throughout he was abjectly afraid for his own life.'

'They will strike at me next,' Chamberlain quotes him as saying. 'What shall I do – what can I do?'

Such a demonstration of personal fear seems, on the face of it, uncharacteristic – though Dilke, who never had any reason to express hostility to Parnell, also noted that he was 'white and apparently terror-stricken'. There is a conflict of evidence over how the meeting ended which makes it difficult to decide whether Parnell's dismay was as extravagant as Chamberlain's later memoir maintained. Willie, some six years later, when he had every reason to express antagonism to Parnell, stated that they had left Chamberlain's house in a cab together and that Parnell had asked him to get police protection. Parnell later categorically denied this. He is supported by McCarthy, whose own memoir, written before Willie's account, specifically says that he suggested to Parnell that he should take a hansom cab on leaving, for the reason Dilke had given earlier, but that Parnell replied rather sharply that he would do nothing of the kind and intended to walk the open streets like anyone else. Which they did. In fact one person shouted from the top of an open bus, 'There's Parnell,' but it was impossible to tell whether in friendship or animosity and they were otherwise unnoticed.

This certainly seems more characteristic of Parnell's behaviour in normal times – though this was not a normal time. Willie's memory may have genuinely become confused by the fact that he did unquestionably secure that day police protection both for Parnell and for himself, not only in London but at Eltham too. Which again raises a matter of human interest about the nature of the continuing relationship between the two of them and Katie. It was to be several years more before anything like a resolution of that relationship appeared – a resolution which, characteristically, was still to leave much of the enigma unanswered for posterity.

But in the meantime, for all the apparently devastating impact of the Phoenix Park murders, Ireland, led by Parnell in a different role from that in which he had figured so far, was to move closer than ever before to Home Rule. The Kilmainham Treaty was to be ratified, in its fashion, after all.

Chapter 37

It is at this point that Parnell, already an acutely effective political figure, can be seen poised to enter British domestic politics as a determining force. But in the aftermath of the Phoenix Park murders he was to be kept waiting.

Within less than five years of his release from Kilmainham in May 1882 he had in fact helped turn out two British Governments – one Liberal and one Conservative – and, by manœuvring the Liberals into adopting Home Rule, had borne some indirect responsibility for the demise of a third. The effects of that Liberal commitment to Home Rule continue into our own day. But for the first two years after Kilmainham nothing very much seemed to happen.

He was eventually to achieve this position by a combination of his independent will-power, practised Parliamentary skills and masterful handling of a new political body, the Irish National League, which was founded in October 1882 to pursue the national aspirations of the suppressed Land League. After a major franchise reform in 1884, which more than trebled the number of Irish voters, the Irish National League was to provide him, after the general election of 1885, with the first disciplined democratic political party of modern times. The votes at Westminster of this Irish nationalist party, whose eighty-six Members were pledged to vote together and who received in some cases payment through American funds, became crucial for any British Government whose majority did not appreciably exceed that number. It was to be a far cry from the day in February 1881 when the semi-revolutionary option of withdrawal from Westminster, had he chosen to exercise it, could have commanded no more than the obedience of twenty Members.

The revolutionary option had now, it might reasonably be supposed, disappeared for ever as a serious means for trying to satisfy Ireland's national aspirations. It was to constitutional action alone that Parnell was apparently irrevocably committed, both publicly and privately. Quite apart from personal inclinations, which pointed him in the same direction, this was the only practical political choice open to him after the overwhelming success of Gladstone's Land Act.

By the time he came out of Kilmainham, the land courts were already swamped with applications for fair rents. There had been more than 75,000 while he was still there, making nonsense of the 'No Rent' manifesto, and, although the courts had only been able to deal with some 7 per cent of these applications so far, almost 90 per cent of cases heard had resulted in a lowering of rent for the tenant. The sense of urgency about the national question, so long linked with the land question by himself and other Land League leaders, receded.

It was fortunate that the only political choice was one that suited him personally so well. His one personal wish was to be able to pursue a happy domestic life with Katie. There was not even any need for him to work out which of the two reasons for his new stance was the more important. In only one respect was his viewpoint unchanged: however much it might now seem that it was to be in England that the future of Ireland would be decided – and it did so seem – he was not a man ever to forget that it was the effect in Ireland of what was done in England that would count in the long run. For the time being, however, in the aftermath of the Phoenix Park assassinations, there was little chance of being able to do very much at all.

Thus was to begin a quite new phase in the surface nature of Parnell's relationship with Irish nationalism. At one level it was to remain as it had always been from his earliest days in politics – a cause deep in his own personal being, an emotional expression of a need for independence which identified with often inarticulate aspirations of the Irish people. Politics were the manner in which he made all this articulate. Now, under the twin pressure of public events and his other great emotional need, which was to be with Katie O'Shea, that manner assumed a more technical character than hitherto. The engineering man of science, who was also a lover, was now in charge. One way or another, it was a phase which was to last eight years – almost to the end of his life. It is a period in which the events are much more familiar from the history books than the earlier part of his life, for he and the Irish party now become an essential part of British history. But an account in some detail of this part of his career is essential in order to understand how Irish nationalism came to follow the course it did in the next century.

It had rightly been sensed from the moment the news of Phoenix Park broke that feeling in England against the Irish would run high. Davitt later recalled the anxiety with which he had entered the dining-room of the Westminster Palace Hotel on the morning after the murders to face the stares of those already breakfasting there. A new Coercion Bill had in any case been intended by the Government, and it was inevitable that this would now have to be brought in as soon as possible and in a more severe form than originally planned. This was something Parnell realistically accepted. He admitted to the radical MP Henry Labouchere that the Bill was politically necessary for Gladstone on account of English opinion, though he did not want it applied to himself and thought it would not be really effective against 'the outrage-mongers'. Labouchere passed this on to the Cabinet through Chamberlain, as Parnell had known he would.

The main thrust of Forster's speech on 4 May, the day when he first confronted Parnell in the House again, was directed not at the leader of the Irish but at the leader of his own party and at his former colleagues in the Cabinet from which he had just resigned. Reciprocally, Gladstone's main political concern now was to dismiss the charge being made against him that with the Kilmainham Treaty he had undermined the authority of the law by striking an advantageous deal with Parnell for party political purposes.

In this battle, to one side of him, Parnell remained more or less neutral, emphasizing that he had made no conditions for his own or anyone else's release but that it was indeed the prospect of being able to deal with the arrears question which had brought him back to the House. The total effect, as so often with Parnell in the House, was to leave him a dignified figure able to put Ireland above the level of the cut and thrust of local debate.

Willie too took the opportunity that day to enhance the political role he now seemed to be pursuing so successfully. He defined in his speech the part he had seen for himself in politics ever since he had entered the House, namely to make friends 'on both sides of it and amongst every party and every section . . . to use the opportunity of correcting any misunderstanding as to opinions held here and there', and he hoped he should not be thought too officious if he 'endeavoured to put matters right'.

'It is most natural', he went on, 'that a person, wishing his information to be constantly and continuously correct should occasionally refresh it at the fountainhead' – which was why on 29 April he had visited Kilmainham. He laughingly refuted any suggestion that he might have had his return fare to Kilmainham paid out of secret-service funds.

Within less than a fortnight it was to become less of a laughing matter.

The charge against Gladstone was of course pressed with particular hostility and even viciousness after the Phoenix Park murders on 6 May.

Arthur Balfour, for the Conservatives, although long a personal friend of the Gladstone family, spoke of 'a government of infamy'. Outside the House, Tory opponents were even more outspoken. 'Would to God the assassins' knives had been plunged into Mr Gladstone!' and 'Fancy! Mr Gladstone went to church the day after the murders and actually stayed for the sacrament!' were some of the things being said.

In such a climate, the chance for some time of being able to implement any *modus vivendi* between Liberals and Irish was obviously remote. On the Monday after the murders, Parnell made an appropriate impression when he appeared in the House dressed in mourning and spoke in a low voice of his 'unqualified detestation of this horrible crime . . . committed by men who absolutely detest the cause with which I have been associated', but this did nothing to dispel the talk of surrender and of Gladstone's 'compact with traitors'.

'No arrangement, no bargain, no negotiation. Nothing asked and nothing taken,' was how Gladstone had put it, which, if not strictly a falsehood, was certainly to one side of the truth. Such prevarication could be sustained only by moving warily.

Gladstone had to take account of the fact that he was ahead of many Liberals in that part of his mind already feeling its way towards some moderate accommodation to Irish aspirations. His words at the beginning of the session to which *The Times* had taken such objection had been evidence of this. Nor was it only those who confronted him from the Tory Opposition and those Liberals sharing Forster's misgivings who took an intransigent view of Parnell and any tendency to move towards him. Distinct reservations were felt by one of Gladstone's own secretaries, Edward Hamilton, who was to become his principal secretary in the summer of 1882. When Willie O'Shea, the previous year, had made his first confidential approach to Gladstone with Parnell's scheme for settling the land question with rents based on Griffith's valuation and State compensation for landlords, Hamilton had written in his diary, 'It is needless to say the Government will not look at such a proposal. How could they demean themselves to bargain with such a fellow as Parnell?'

When, in April 1882, before the Kilmainham release, Willie had begun his new overtures to Gladstone, Hamilton had been able to reconcile himself with what might be happening only by telling himself, 'It may be as well to know what the views of the Irish Party are. But it seems impossible to have any direct dealings with them.'

As for Willie himself, a further hint comes from Hamilton's diary of the way he was likely to be assessed from the inside: 'I expect O'Shea himself is, though a gentleman by birth and a brother-in-law of Sir Evelyn Wood, not of the "straightest".'

After Kilmainham, Hamilton's reservations remained undiminished. Possibly provoked by Willie's note of self-satisfaction in the House of Commons, he commented on 9 May, 'I have the greatest apprehension of anything which implies a belief in the integrity and straight-forwardness of any one of the Parnellites, including O'Shea, though he does seem to be like a gentleman.'

Three days later he came to the conclusion that 'the Government should have declined to lend an ear to their advances'. It had been right to release Parnell and the others on the strength of their undertaking to try to stop outrages, but the Government should have 'declined to give Parnell any idea of its intentions'.

With such misgivings on the part of as loyal a supporter as Hamilton, it was not surprising that Gladstone's position should become even more sensitive after a disconcerting incident in the House for which Willie was at least partly to blame. Gladstone was asked at Question Time on 15 May to produce the documentary evidence relating to the intended conduct on release of the recently imprisoned Members. Gladstone replied that certain letters had indeed passed between Members of the House but there was no reason why they should be produced, as this would be 'open to an objection as tending to diminish the responsibility of Her Majesty's Government'.

'Perhaps', intervened Parnell, 'it may be better if I am permitted to read the letter . . . which as I understand forms the documentary evidence alluded to.' And he then read out his letter to Willie from Kilmainham, dated 28 April, in which he had outlined the need for the arrears question to be dealt with and for leaseholders to be admitted to the Land Act as a means of ensuring that efforts to stop outrages would be effective.

'Yours very truly,' he concluded; 'then there follows my signature.'

Another Member then asked the Prime Minister if that was the only letter to constitute the documentary evidence. But before Gladstone could reply, Forster jumped up and asked Parnell if he had read the whole of the letter.

Parnell said he had not kept a copy of it himself, but the member for Clare (Willie) had given him a copy from which, he said, it was possible one paragraph might be missing.

It was not a paragraph, but some words about future collaboration were indeed missing. Parnell said he had no objection if Willie wanted to communicate the whole letter to the House.

This was a good example of his cool House of Commons style. It was not of course Parnell himself but Gladstone who, in the present situation, might have cause for objection.

Willie then got up to admit that he thought he ought to take an early opportunity to give some explanation, but since he did not have the document with him he sat down again. As he did so, Forster came and put a copy of the letter into his hands.

Willie rose again to be greeted with cries of 'Read!', and eventually he did just that. He read the letter all through again, but this time with the missing words included – with their reference to cooperating 'cordially for the future with the Liberal Party in forwarding Liberal principles' and to the Government feeling 'justified in dispensing with further coercive measures'.

What now looked like a maladroit attempt to obscure something that was already an embarrassment made things much worse for Gladstone, who could only repeat what he had said before: namely, that 'there never was the slightest understanding of any kind between the honourable member and the Government'. He was technically correct, since the understanding had been tacit and the release which appeared to ratify it could be made to seem a separate occurrence. But his resort to such a casuistical position did not look good, and the Conservative Opposition made the most of it.

Again, Parnell could stand largely to one side of the English political squabble. It affected him only inasmuch as it lengthened the time before Gladstone could be seen to develop a *modus vivendi* with the Irish. However, Parnell himself could at least try to pursue some such thing behind the scenes.

He told Labouchere that, if the Government would meet him and the party in the conciliatory spirit of certain amendments they were proposing to the Prevention of Crime Bill, he would 'promise that the opposition to the Bill would be conducted on honest Parliamentary lines'.

It was indeed a tough Bill: among other strong measures, it replaced trial by jury with trial by three judges, it gave magistrates further powers to convict, and it extended police powers of search. Gladstone's difficulty in being seen to accommodate Parnell after Kilmainham was compounded by the fact that his Home Secretary, William Harcourt, who was seeing the Bill through the House of Commons, particularly regarded concessions as a dangerous sign of weakness and was determined that if possible none should be made. Parnell, on the other hand, having just antagonized men like Davitt and Brennan, together with many American supporters, could not afford to let the Bill go unamended without a real fight. For some weeks, attempts on the Irish side to mitigate the Bill and on the Government side to mitigate opposition to it continued behind the scenes through intermediaries.

The line to the Cabinet ran through Joseph Chamberlain, the President of the Board of Trade. Chamberlain had long held a pragmatically balanced view of Irish affairs: he was determined to oppose what he saw as Parnell's ultimate goal of separate national independence; while disliking coercion, he disliked violence and disorder more; but at the same time he saw the need to go as far as possible within such parameters to meet undoubted Irish grievances.

As the Prevention of Crime Bill came up for debate, Parnell spent an hour on 22 May telling Labouchere that he did not in the least complain of Gladstone, that he really was 'most anxious to get on with the Government if possible', and asking to be told as soon as possible the next day whether there was to be any concession. Labouchere wrote to Chamberlain, 'He says that he is most anxious for a *modus vivendi*, and believes that if the present opportunity for establishing one be let pass, it is not likely to recur. He and his friends are incurring the serious risk of assassination in their efforts to bring it about.'

And, again according to Labouchere, Parnell put the inducement to the Liberals in even plainer language than the Kilmainham Treaty had done: 'He points out, not as a bargain but as a matter of fact, that the Liberals may – if only there be concessions on the Coercion Bill and a few modifications of the Land Bill – count on the Irish vote, as against the Conservatives, and suggests that this will make the Government absolutely safe even though there be Whig defections.'

But whether it was for concessions over the exclusion of treason and treason-felony from the Bill or over a precise definition of 'intimidation' in the clause which dealt with that crime, there was almost no change to be had from Harcourt, to whose attitude Gladstone was umbilically tied. The Chief Whip, Grosvenor, described Harcourt as looking 'sulky as a bear' as he tried on one occasion to get him to meet a point of Parnell's: 'with regret' Harcourt had to turn it down.

As public parliamentary battles over the Government's Bill continued, Parnell's personal preference for a *modus vivendi* continued to be expressed privately. 'He is most anxious that Gladstone should not think that obstruction arises from any ill-feeling towards him,' Labouchere told Chamberlain. But, he went on, Parnell did want Gladstone to know the facts. Egan in Paris was furious at the idea of the League being converted into a mere moderate tenant-right organization with its headquarters in Dublin. Every day the ultras in the party were telling Parnell that nothing was to be gained by conciliation. When, in the middle of June, Harcourt did agree to accept one minor amendment of Healy's both Healy and Parnell wanted Labouchere to tell Gladstone how grateful they were.

Unfairly, in view of the minimal return the Irish were getting from the Government, the Government was passing through Chamberlain to Labouchere continual reproaches about the extent to which the battle over the Bill was being spun out. Labouchere gave Parnell's reply to Chamberlain on 24 June, representing him in these words:

I acknowledge that Mr Gladstone and Mr Chamberlain have acted fairly, and so far as I can I should always be ready to meet their wishes. But I deny that we have obtained the concessions we expected ... Let us know what amendments will be accepted in future. I am most anxious to carry out what I understand was the contemplated policy when I was released from Kilmainham and to work with the Government in bringing the active faith of Irish agitation to a close. But this I cannot do if I am suspected of ulterior motives and I cannot show that something is given for my Party.

This merely confirmed to Chamberlain what he had heard from Parnell himself in the Lobby of the House a fortnight earlier and which he had reported to Gladstone. The message was that 'if all his proposals are rejected he cannot keep his Party from violent opposition.' There was, of course, a personal side to this: the possibility of assassination by extremists, of which he had already spoken, could seem real enough. He was not a man to let personal fear play much of a part in his thinking, but he had told Labouchere that he never went about without a revolver in his pocket, and even then he did not feel safe. We know that at this time he was practising his revolver-shooting at Eltham.

Parnell's anxiety to get on to some sort of working terms with the Liberals made itself felt through other intermediaries besides Labouchere.

Willie and Parnell were at this time both at Eltham a good deal together as well as seeing each other continually in the House of Commons. Although Parnell had expressed clear reservations about using him as an intermediary at the time of Kilmainham, the personal link Willie had formed with Chamberlain could obviously be helpful. Willie had written to Chamberlain before the end of May to tell him that he was doing all he could to make Parnell see that it was a critical time for him to assert his authority and 'to put it to the Irish people whether they mean to follow him or not'. The balanced way in which, on 19 May, Parnell spoke in the House on the need for a reasonable interpretation of 'intimidation' in the Bill, much impressed Gladstone and even Harcourt. It would certainly have added something to Willie's credibility with Chamberlain.

But anxiety on Willie's part that he might not be able to deliver Parnell's cooperation to the extent the government hoped for led him into an apparent impatience with Parnell almost as unreasonable as the Government's own.

On the day in late June 1882 before Labouchere delivered Parnell's almost desperate plea that he must have something in the way of concessions over the Prevention of Crime Bill to show his party, Willie was complaining to Chamberlain that 'Parnell is frequently in a "moony", drifting state of mind nowadays, with which it is difficult to keep one's temper.' He enclosed a copy of a sharp note which he said he had given to Parnell the same day, complaining that it was a long time since, at Parnell's request, he had told Gladstone there would be no obstruction over the Bill and reminding Parnell that he, Willie, had therefore 'a special right' to beg him to carry out his engagement 'in its spirit as well as in its letter'. These strong words may have been intended chiefly to display Willie's credentials to Chamberlain. After all, if he was to be an effective intermediary he had to keep in with Parnell too. And it is significant that Willie was all this time and into July continually appearing in the division lobbies with Parnell to vote with him on Irish attempts to amend the Bill, usually in minorities of between thirty and forty but on one occasion, at the end of June, in a minority as small as twenty-one.

Nevertheless, as the Irish, including himself, continued to dispute the Bill in the House, he told Chamberlain, five days after his last communication, that he had spoken to Parnell in the very strongest terms that afternoon and could not understand him. Chamberlain replied satisfactorily: he spoke of the confidence he had always felt in Willie's 'good faith and honour' and wished he could say the same about Parnell's conduct, which was most disappointing. 'He was', he said, 'in danger of destroying all hope of the *modus vivendi* about which we had been hopeful.' The day after that, Willie sent Chamberlain a copy of another letter he said he had written to Parnell complaining of the 'deplorable' consequence of not being able to meet the Government's wishes. He wrote, in this letter to Parnell, of 'the graver question as between you and myself – the honourable fulfilment by you at any risk of an important pledge'.

It could be thought that Willie, whether consciously or not, was here asserting some very special personal right to have Parnell honour a pledge to help the Government. What is certain is his concern that failure to prevent continued obstruction of the Bill might lose him the place he had contrived for himself as an influential go-between. It is equally clear that Parnell was not opening his political heart to Willie as he had been doing to Labouchere. Though the impasse created by his own need to humour his party and by Gladstone's need to humour his Home Secretary now seemed total, there had been a further attempt to get round it. This involved another intermediary with Gladstone – not Willie, but Katie herself.

On Tuesday 20 June Gladstone's secretary, Edward Hamilton, had made a reference in his diary to Parnell's attempts behind the scenes to come to some working arrangement with the Government, mentioning Labouchere 'as a sort of ambassador' and Willie as having 'tried his hand again and with prudence and moderation, though not with equal success'. Hamilton continued:

Mrs O'Shea has also been making some attempts and actually enveigled Mr Gladstone into seeing her. She seems to be on very intimate terms with Parnell; some say his mistress. It would have been far better for Mr Gladstone to decline point blank to see her or communicate with her; but he does not take the view of the 'man of the world' in such matters . . . Were the fact of his having seen this woman known, it would give encouragement to the supposition that the Government paid too much attention and heed to the Parnellite party.

This diary entry arouses immediate interest on more scores than one. Gladstone himself had in fact already heard the rumour that Katie was Parnell's mistress: his Foreign Secretary, Granville, had mentioned it to him in a letter a month before, and his Home Secretary, Harcourt, had earlier revealed it as a fact at a Government meeting, based on his police surveillance. Gladstone maintained that he could not believe it, and it certainly did not prevent him from seeing her, as Hamilton now noted with regret.

Gladstone himself had been regularly receiving letters from one O'Shea or another from the very moment of the Kilmainham release.

Willie, anxious to cash in on the apparent success of his Kilmainham intervention, had written to him on 3 May to make clear that he was still in place for direct influential dealing with Parnell. 'If Mr Chamberlain goes to Ireland [to become Chief Secretary under Forster] I can undertake that Mr Parnell will work for his success as heartily as if he were working for his own.' Writing again on 6 May, although presumably before the news of Phoenix Park had broken, he made clear that he was ready to provide intelligence to Gladstone straight from the horse's mouth. 'Mr Parnell has called a meeting of his friends for 2 p.m. on Monday at which it will be decided to give unanimous support in the division on Sir Michael Hicks Beach's [Conservative Opposition] motion. There are a few grumbles but they will be immediately silenced.'

He wrote six more letters direct to Gladstone between then and 13 May. There then came a pause until 9 June, when he wrote asking for an interview with him. 'I am much troubled by the course with which affairs have drifted and I am anxious to be of use in setting them right.' He asked for 'a few minutes' interview early today. I believe that I might possibly do some good.'

Hitherto Gladstone had been sending him considerate replies. This time Willie was merely requested to communicate with Chamberlain.

Meanwhile his wife had actually seen Gladstone. Whether or not Willie was aware of this must be uncertain. From the first letter she had written to Gladstone on 23 May it seems unlikely. She wrote on North Park, Eltham, writing-paper but from Thomas's Hotel in Berkeley Square. She was 'very anxious' to ask him if he would let Parnell have 'a five minute *private* conversation with him':

I believe that if you would kindly manage to see me for a few minutes after the morning sitting today you will forgive my troubling you, when you hear my reasons for being anxious that you should see him but I would prefer not to write on this subject. Mr Parnell would of course wait on you at any place and time that may suit you. If you kindly grant my request I am writing in perfect confidence that you will not mention the subject of this letter to *anyone*. I have not, and shall not, not even to Captain O'Shea.

In the light of what Gladstone had been hearing so recently from Harcourt and Granville about Parnell's rumoured relationship with her, but which he had in unworldly fashion dismissed from his mind, it would be surprising if this last sentence had not struck some sort of chord there and brought the rumours back again. Indeed it is possible that it attracted a certain indecipherable interest. For the moment, however, he was firm. He wrote back, the same day, a very polite letter saying that ever since Parnell's release he had been careful 'to avoid any act or word that could injure his position or weaken his hand from doing good . . . I do not think I ought to see him in the manner you have described.'

Katie was not to be put off. She wrote again two days later, begging Gladstone to see her for a few minutes because of the 'over-riding importance of what I have to tell you'. Again he turned her down. But by the end of the week her persistence was rewarded: he went to see her at Thomas's Hotel on 1 June.

What precisely took place at this meeting is not known, except that it did not lead to the meeting between Gladstone and Parnell for which she had hoped. Katie records in her memoirs simply that they had a long talk about Parnell and politics and Ireland, but it is clear from subsequent correspondence – she had written him twenty-one more letters altogether by the end of the year – that the main purpose was to reassure Gladstone of Parnell's wish to make the tacit understanding of the Kilmainham Treaty work as well as it possibly could in the awkward circumstances. The desire on Parnell's part – and she made it clear that she was writing with his authority – was to mark out an incipient personal political alliance. A fortnight after the first meeting Katie was sending proposals for amendments to the Prevention of Crime Bill and subsequently other meticulously worked out documents in Parnell's handwriting.

Before the end of June she was trying to see Gladstone again, and on his failing to comply she was 'asking not to be "boycotted" altogether'.

Irish obstruction under Parnell's leadership was proceeding simultaneously, and when, in July, Government plans for tightening up the procedure for arbitrary closure of debates were under discussion, she revealed the cooperative nature of Parnell's advances behind the scenes clearly enough when she wrote on 11 July, 'I have had some further conversations with Mr Parnell and I find his plans are to meet your views regarding the *clôture* in every way he can.'

The immediate practical results of all this were virtually nil, and Hamilton's relegation of Katie's intervention to mere irritable asides in his diary puts it in its proper place in terms of practical politics. But in the longer view it is important on two counts: first, as showing how wholeheartedly Parnell was now committed in his mind to the principle of working with Gladstone towards whatever national goal for Ireland it should prove possible to push him towards; and, second, as inducing a generally favourable personal response in Gladstone's mind towards Parnell for any such future possibility. When in three years' time Gladstone's mind did begin for tactical reasons to turn further in the direction of satisfaction for Irish national aspirations, this previous sense of a personal contact already achieved through Katie's communications may have helped.

One simple human factor in all this remains to be questioned. Why, given the very peripheral nature of this contact now taking place, did Gladstone actually bother to see, rather than just receive communications from and write to, Katie O'Shea? He was in fact to see her twice more after the Thomas's Hotel meeting, both times at Downing Street. (Katie in her memoirs, where she exaggerated the significance of these contacts, implied wrongly that it was more than twice.) But why, despite his very strong but courteous early refusal, did he within a few days reverse his decision and see her at all?

In the previous month, Hamilton had noted in his diary the recurrence of something about Gladstone which troubled him: 'the most disagreeable question of the night walks has come to the front again,' he wrote. On Saturday 6 May, when, unknown to him, his nephew Lord Frederick Cavendish and the Under-Secretary Burke had already lain dead for some hours in Phoenix Park, Gladstone was seen by a Conservative MP being accosted by a woman with whom, so the story at London dinner parties was running, he was actually arm in arm. The Prime Minister's occasional habit of wanting to talk to prostitutes in central London with the avowed intention of redeeming them from their trade had already proved a source of some embarrassment. Hamilton this time had a talk with Gladstone, in the course of which he was allowed to make his point about the inadvisability of such good works. It is perhaps not overfanciful to suggest that, having heard what he had heard so recently about Mrs O'Shea's reputation, Gladstone had some personal interest in meeting this superior class of fallen woman face to face. But of course there was never any question of trying to redeem her. In fact in her memoirs she stressed his great charm of manner and found 'his wonderful eagle's eyes showed just sufficient admiration in them to savour of homage without offence'.

Certainly she was anxious to use any influence she might be able to exert over him. Hamilton noted that on the morning of 29 August Gladstone gave her another interview (at Downing Street this time) 'at her earnest solicitation'. Her main concern then seems to have been first to press for clemency for a condemned man whose case Willie had taken up, and to ask Gladstone to consider an appointment for Willie as Under-Secretary in Ireland. 'This or some other plan', thought Hamilton – and not altogether implausibly – 'is very likely what has been at the bottom of O'Shea's overtures and negotiations all along.'

In fact both the O'Sheas got short shrift from Hamilton. 'Mrs O'Shea will continue to volunteer writing under the inspiration of Parnell,' he wrote on 23 September. 'It is a great piece of impertinence, and yet difficult for Mr Gladstone to forbid it.' And in November, 'That bother-some woman Mrs O'Shea is at it again, writing for an appointment for her husband.' Hamilton thought it most unfortunate that Gladstone felt that Willie had some claim on the Government for his services. In Hamilton's view, 'motives of self-advancement' were the heart of the matter. And in that, where Willie was concerned, he was not far wrong. Neither for her lover nor for her husband did Katie in fact manage to achieve anything concrete with Gladstone. But Willie had other irons in the fire.

Politically the fight over the Prevention of Crime Bill came to a dramatic climax on the morning of Saturday 1 July when, after an all-night sitting, twenty-six Irish Members – including Parnell but not Willie – were suspended for obstruction as in the old days. But of course they were not the old days, however much surface events like this might make them seem so. They no longer took place against the background of a potentially revolutionary situation in Ireland.

Perhaps what most clearly illustrates the distinct change of climate after Kilmainham is the conspicuous drop in the number of agrarian outrages that had taken place after Parnell's release. These fell continuously to the end of 1882. There had been 462 in April, of which 287 were threatening notices or letters. By October the monthly total had fallen to 111, with 36 threatening notices or letters. In 1883 the monthly total never rose above 100.

Of course it was in the nature of the continuing Irish rural social structure of landlord–tenant relations that periodical assertions of what Parnell had called 'the unwritten law' of the countryside should also continue: disappointingly few tenants were able to take advantage of the land-purchase clauses in the Land Act. In a few years' time there was in fact to be a renewal of tension on the land of some consequence, but on a much smaller scale and more localized than in the days of the Land League. Significantly, Parnell would then choose to play almost no part. With the gradual introduction of more generous land-purchase arrange-ments in succeeding decades, the land question was in fact never again to be the instrument of nationalism which it had been in the days of the Land League. A situation analagous to what had been the state of Ireland in 1880–1 would not recur for another forty years, and then in a differently emphasized context.

In 1882, the Prevention of Crime Bill became law in the middle of July and the Arrears Bill became law in the middle of August. Almost all the more than 100,000 tenants in arrears of rent who applied to be admitted to the benefits of the Land Act were successful. Parnell now waited calculatingly for the day when the general election due for 1885 should give him the power one way or another to exploit for Irish purposes that *modus vivendi* which Gladstone by then could no longer afford to hold back. He used the interval to fashion his hold on the apparatus of the new Irish National League, and to consolidate his relations with that other all important political apparatus in Ireland, the Roman Catholic Church.

One further necessary political consideration, that of sufficiently placating his own left wing while at the same time subduing its more extreme elements, was made easier by fortuitous circumstances outside his control, and in one important instance by his old enemy Forster, the former Chief Secretary. Parnell knew well how to make the most of such advantages as presented themselves.

Suppression of the Ladies' Land League, though it cost him for life the affection of his sister Anna, of whom he had once been so protective in childhood, was easy. He cut off its funds. Control of the former Land League's funds in Paris had been secured in June 1882, and Egan resigned as Treasurer in October. There had been one great advantage of the failure that summer to achieve the *modus vivendi* for which Parnell had been striving so hard behind the scenes: the fight in the House of Commons had given him continued credibility in Ireland as much the same sort of figure as he had been for the past few years. In this respect the murders in Phoenix Park, while disrupting the intended *modus vivendi* and shattering the immediate prospect to which he had emerged from Kilmainham, had done him a service, by making Harcourt persevere with an uncompromising Prevention of Crime Bill against which he could protest so vigorously.

If Parnell had been more successful in his overtures behind the scenes, it is likely that the protests of the left wing of the old Land League might have presented him with more difficulties than they did. As things were, both Dillon and Brennan, for example, who were with him at Avondale before the Convention which founded the Irish National League in October 1882, could now be seen to be to one side of the main course of politics. Dillon, actually thinking that he was giving up politics altogether, was to leave for the United States, as was Brennan, soon to be joined there by Patrick Egan after he had handed over the Paris funds. The steady unrevolutionary policy which the Irish National League laid down gave Parnell's new course accepted status.

But, embarked as he now was in pursuit of political advantage in a

technical spirit suited to much of his temperament, he never lost sight of
the truth that an emotional power, also part of his temperament, identified
itself with something in the historic cause of the Irish people whose
victory he was hoping to engineer. Thus, even in the national doldrums
in which the cause was becalmed for nearly three years after 1882, part of
his mind was well enough aware of the storm which might one day blow
up to support that cause.

In January 1883 the Dublin police made their first arrests for the Phoenix
Park murders. It soon became clear that they were getting several of the
right people: including James Carey, Joe Brady and Daniel Curley, all of
whom had signed an address headed by Parnell welcoming Davitt to
Ireland on his release in 1878. The British press and the Conservative
Opposition took full advantage of the news to revive details of the crime
which had so shocked the nation, including the Liberal Party, nine
months before, and to refresh the sensations of dismay at the terrorism
which apparently so easily associated itself with Irish nationalism. Parnell's
old opponent Forster was not slow to seize his opportunity.

On 22 February 1883, in the debate on the Queen's Speech for the new
session of Parliament, Forster delivered a blistering attack on Parnell,
accusing him directly of connivance in Irish crimes. He said he did not
accuse him of planning the murders, but he had either connived at them
or chose to remain in ignorance of what was going on.

There may have been some indirect substance in this charge in relation
to some of the Land League agrarian outrages of the 1881, but to reiterate
it at a time when the Phoenix Park murders were once again in
everybody's mind was challenging indeed.

'It's a lie,' cried Parnell. But that was all. In the succeeding uproar,
O'Kelly was suspended. Parnell chose to say no more for the time being,
although there were calls from the House for him to do so. He simply sat
silent, much as he had sat opposite Forster throughout the attack, 'trying,'
said Henry Lucy, 'not altogether successfully, to seem at ease with a sickly
smile on his face'. Hartington, Gladstone's deputy, said that his silence
was a prima facie case for support of the charge.

Next day, at five o'clock in the afternoon, Parnell rose in his place as
Members waited intently for his defence. He gave none. With that
masterly dismissal of the House's fundamental relevance to Ireland which
had first brought him to prominence in the days of Isaac Butt, he made it
clear that he saw nothing to defend himself against. Nothing he might say
could affect the opinion of the House, so, in Lucy's words, he 'spoke only

for Ireland'. Lucy observed his hands twitching nervously in his pockets, but noted too that he had complete command of his voice.

There was no suggestion of any sort of regret for anything, only accusation of Forster for what had happened in Ireland when he had been Chief Secretary. He even made a macabre joke at Forster's expense which would only really have been appreciated in Ireland. Referring back to the Parnell letter to O'Shea, a Cabinet document which Forster had produced the previous May when O'Shea had given Parnell an incomplete version to read, he said that Forster had acted to his previous associates as the informer James Carey had done to his fellow assassins in Phoenix Park, only without even the pretext that he was trying to save his own skin (Forster had already resigned as Chief Secretary).

Parnell ended by inviting the Government 'to fill up your ranks and send your ablest and best men to push forward the task of misgoverning and oppressing Ireland'. He said he himself was quite confident as to the future of Ireland. 'Although her horizon may appear at this moment cloudy, I believe that our people will survive the present oppression, as they have survived many worse ones, and although our progress may be slow, it will be sure and the time will come when this House and the people of this country will admit once again that . . . they have been led astray as to the right method of governing a noble, a generous, a brave, and impulsive people.'

Willie followed with a short, sharp dig at Forster for an inaccuracy in his account of the Kilmainham negotiations. This was much applauded on the Irish benches.

To remind the House that, although he might scorn its criticism of him, he was not going to spare his reciprocal criticism in the name of the Irish people, Parnell delivered three days later a speech more than twice as long as that in which he had replied to Forster, now castigating the Government in detail for the workings of the Prevention of Crime Act.

This Forster incident had been one which in Ireland enabled Parnell to sustain his semi-mythical status while his politics continued on a mundane and seemingly rather uninspiring course. It also helped him recover something of his old image with American supporters. It is useful too in reminding us of Willie's active presence on the political scene.

Willie's eventual part in the Parnell story, in which he is conventionally viewed as a man of questionable moral worth the dimension of whose character seems in inverse proportion to the catastrophe he provoked, makes it too easy to forget that at this stage he could seem a figure of some political potential. To those in the know, his readiness to engage in politics in his selected role was given special point by his apparent friendship with Parnell. Whatever he might feel about Parnell's friendship being directed primarily towards his wife was his own affair. His emergence on the public scene with a seemingly central function at Kilmainham had been a natural extension of his activity in 1880 and 1881. He had plausibility in his own right, even though an unflattering opinion of him was already forming in inner Government circles, with Forster once describing him to Gladstone as 'clever but vain and untrustworthy'.

From the beginning of the 1882 session Willie had continued to stand up for right in Ireland, criticizing Forster for not letting out the suspects, for not maintaining sufficient discipline in his police force, for exaggerating outrages, and for giving in too much to his 'infatuation' for new magistrates like Clifford Lloyd. He had been over to Ireland more than once to try to secure the release of some of the suspects.

He had, of course, not neglected certain personal concerns, showing an interest in March in a commercial treaty being negotiated between Britain and Spain, displaying his military background with the occasional question about the Army, and pursuing the interests of his constituents in an effort to get government money 'to counter the inadequate protection to the lives, canoes and gear of the sea fishermen of the County Clare owing to the unimproved state of the creeks and jetties on the dangerous coast'. A short speech in March about the safety of steam for tramways may or may not have been connected with an interest in some commercial enterprise; for it he drew on his knowledge of tramways in Rouen, which the next speaker said were not in fact relevant. His voting record for the session of 1882 had been consistently very fair.

The eventual passing of the Prevention of Crime Bill and the Arrears Bill in the summer had for a time left him little scope to act as an intermediary with Government. But he was not beyond putting an oar in when he thought it might be useful for him to be seen prepared to help.

His wife had meanwhile continued to write to Gladstone – two or three letters a month through the autumn of 1882, sometimes enclosing memoranda from Parnell on technical matters such as parliamentary procedure and defects he identified in the working of the Arrears Act. She kept in touch with him at intervals in 1883, with at least one request for him to see her again either at Thomas's Hotel or at Downing Street. It seems certain that this must have been known to Willie, although not perhaps in its full extent. At one point she had even enclosed a letter from Willie to herself in which he threw out, 'I should like to be Under-Secretary very much and I think I might make a useful one.' In March

1883, shortly after Parnell's audacious treatment of Forster's attack, she enclosed a letter from Willie to Gladstone designed to show the Prime Minister how useful he might be in keeping Parnell on the right lines when others might try to get him to stray towards extremism. Parnell was at this time thinking of going to the United States, where, for his purposes, the balance between extremism and moderation had to be nicely held. Willie wrote to Gladstone:

Now, Parnell, with all his talent, is about the worst judge of character I ever met. Remember that even after he knew [that] Egan was intriguing against him and after I had obtained evidence in Ireland as to Sheridan's doings, I could not induce Parnell to disbelieve in Egan's trust-worthiness as to Land League funds. Who will get the upper hand with Parnell in the United States? Mr Gladstone knows what my influence with him has done (Parnell's judgment in my case being lucid.) But with an ocean between us, what power can I have?

Two days later London was startled by a dynamite explosion in Whitehall, beside the Local Government Board's offices in Charles Street. Edward Hamilton, Gladstone's secretary, went over the next day to look at the damage, which he found far greater than he had expected, and was amazed that no lives had been lost. 'The breakage of windows', he wrote, 'was appalling, and the force of the explosion both inwards and outwards must have been tremendous . . . Doors shivered to pieces, ceilings lifted up, floors torn up, tables and chairs smashed, large wall stones thrown with great force many yards.'

This was the work of an extreme American-Irish dynamiting group which had some personal links with Clan na Gael though was not part of it. Parnell's projected trip to the United States was connected with the foundation of a new American League to replace the American Land League, just as the Irish National League had replaced the Land League in Ireland. It was a sensitive situation, since the new League would be in the hands of Clan na Gael. Probably disconcerted by the bombing, he decided to let the Americans sort out their own affairs without too direct an association with himself and he went on a short visit to Paris instead.

He was, as always, skilled at keeping blurred his attitude to the extreme nationalism to which the American Irish were prone. He was under attack for his moderation from Patrick Ford; but now in Paris he could suggest to an American woman newspaper correspondent that his bitterness towards England was unbounded. 'We must vomit her forth,' she quoted him as saying, and added, 'His aims seem vague but no less determined.'

Clemenceau saw him again on this visit to Paris and confirmed this account of his hostility to England, saying that 'his greatest hopes were that England would get its glory in war with Turkey over Egypt'.

Willie's attempts to warn Gladstone of what might happen to Parnell in America had proved unnecessary. There was now a lull before he could again see himself playing an important role in the British Government's involvement with Ireland.

What do we know for certain about the triangle in the period 1882 to 1886? Perhaps the most immediately useful evidence is to be found in that statement which Parnell was to make in 1890: namely, that Willie had always been aware that he, Parnell, was at Eltham in his absence between 1880 and 1886, and that *since 1886 he had known that he 'constantly resided there from 1880 to 1886'* [my italics]. In other words, before 1886, Willie did not know that Parnell had constantly resided there with Katie in his absence. In this period he was being deceived. He certainly knew of his wife's continuing friendship with Parnell, though: it was an essential component of his careerist outlook, a fact to be taken for granted. When in 1883 Katie rented two houses, one after the other, in Brighton for the O'Shea family, Willie knew that Parnell visited her there, because he himself came down from Albert Mansions and all three of them were there at times together. He must also have known that when Parnell called there he was known to the servants as 'Mr Stewart', in order to avoid publicity.

But the two lovers felt unsure enough about his reaction to their living together to make them want to keep knowledge of this from him. Reinforcing the impression that there was nothing to worry about was the fact that between 1882 and 1886 Willie and Katie frequently exchanged letters in which they used the affectionate nicknames for each other which stemmed from long before the appearance of Parnell. 'My Dick,' Willie called Katie; 'My Boysie,' Katie called Willie. Moreover, affectionately addressed letters of this sort from Willie sometimes contained unflattering references to Parnell which it is difficult to think Willie did not expect her to share, or at least to accept with equanimity. 'P for Pig', in reference to Parnell, even if to be taken as a sort of joke, could imply a closer relationship between the writer and the recipient of the letter than between the recipient and the 'Pig'.

We also have one more essential piece of evidence, although this can lead to different conclusions. In March 1883, the very month in which Willie had been stressing his close understanding of Parnell to Gladstone and Parnell's susceptibility to American influence, Katie gave birth to another child, Clare, announced in the conventional way in the newspapers. Although Clare and a further daughter, Katherine, were both later to be accepted by everyone – including Willie – as Parnell's children, there are indications that for a while Willie thought that Clare at least was his own.

If Katie was going to bed with both of them from time to time until 1886, a lot that is otherwise difficult to explain falls into place. Whether Parnell knew or suspected anything other than that Willie occasionally tried to force his attentions on her must remain hidden in that enigmatic aura which surrounds much of his personality for all time. But on balance it seems likely that it did not occur to him that she might sometimes succumb willingly, or at least not after the conclusion of the duel incident in July 1881. For from then on, as Katie made a point of saying in her memoirs, they 'were one, without further scruple, without fear, and without remorse'. Which they were, though perhaps only in her fashion.

The total omission from these memoirs of the birth of her two last daughters, who were Parnell's, may have been because the truth about them could not have been revealed without explaining how she had been able to keep Willie happy. For above all it is helpful to remember what she had told Harrison late in 1891, namely that she and Willie never explicitly discussed together what in fact was going on. This information may be the most valuable single piece of all in that entire puzzle of which some pieces will always be missing.

One further feature figuring permanently in the situation until 1889 is the need, accepted by all three of them, not to scandalize Aunt Ben, whose great fortune was an essential consideration for both the present and the future.

When Parnell first entered the O'Sheas' lives it could not have been anticipated that Aunt Ben would live so long. But if Willie did eventually come to accept that he was sharing Katie with Parnell, it would have been easier for him to do so in the knowledge that a resolution of the affair could wait with advantage for the old lady's death. At the same time, it was essential to ensure that nothing about Parnell's presence at Eltham should disturb her before she died.

In such remonstrances from him as followed the duel episode, it was the fear of unwelcome publicity that was always his central concern. Katie and Parnell, who lived closer to her, may at first have felt it easy to keep Aunt Ben's mind at rest; later, either because they wanted to placate Willie's increasing anxiety or because they themselves saw a danger of disrupting the bequest, they were to go to considerable lengths to conceal how close they were.

What was Parnell like in this closeness? Katie's memoirs, for all their periodic confusion and other blemishes, give an invaluable insight into the years of domesticity which settled into shape after Kilmainham.

We have him doing many ordinary things in an extraordinary way: laying tiles in a house by the sea while the workmen employed to do it were away at their dinner hour; dictating 'A Proposed Constitution for the Irish and English Peoples' while rolling a lawn; and, while digging in the garden, working on a poem for her which went:

> The grass shall cease to grow,
> The river's stream to run,
> The stars shall ponder in their course,
> No more shall shine the sun;
> The moon shall never wane or grow,
> The tide shall cease to ebb and flow,
>   'Ere I shall cease to love you.

The sleepwalking to which he had been subject as a child seems to have turned later into a tendency to powerful nightmares, though he did tell her that when in America in 1880 he had locked himself in his room at nights for fear of wandering about the hotel in his sleep.

He liked swimming, and once insisted on carrying Katie, who did not, fully clothed into the sea at Eastbourne, in broad daylight.

He enjoyed riding, describing one of his horses as going 'just like an india-rubber ball'. But he did not drive well, leaving the reins too slack on the horse's back for proper control.

His old interest in cricket seems to have faded. Katie was to have a cricket pitch made for him in a two-acre field at Eltham, but she gives no account of him or anyone else playing on it.

He was always interested to watch men doing manual work – 'a man with a hammer or a pick-axe was almost an irresistible attraction to him'. He would stop in the street to talk to them about their lives and homes. A rapport with ordinary people was natural to him; sometimes after a late sitting of the House he would take Katie, who had been in the Ladies' Gallery, to a workmen's street coffee-stall before driving down to Eltham. Yet he could combine this with the thoughtless *hauteur* which once let him forget all about a groom left waiting for him on a London pavement for hours.

That he should have taken up revolver practice at Eltham after the Phoenix Park murders is not in itself remarkable – Davitt had been carrying a revolver to protect himself against the old-guard Fenian hostility more than a year before. It was not unreasonable to suppose that the Invincibles who had struck at Burke and Cavendish in a conspiracy designed to show that Parnellite policy was inadequately advanced might one day decide to strike at him. At the same time there was hostility from anti-nationalist sources. This was not confined to threatening letters, of which he received many. On one occasion ornamental bronzes above the main gates at Eltham were cut through overnight, to fall upon anyone opening the gates in the morning. A groom received injuries. More than once when driving back to Eltham from London with Parnell late at night across open countryside Katie thought she spotted a man running alongside them in the darkness, and once she saw a man waiting in a ditch beside the road with a revolver which went off as he appeared to slip there.

The detail she gives of Parnell's own revolver practice has its characteristic touch. The repeated sound of his shots at a target much irritated her aunt's bailiff. Parnell placated him in his own fashion by inviting him to compete with him, and then continued to score bull's-eyes while the man shot wider and wider of the mark.

His pleasure at shooting with an airgun (he had even somehow been allowed to get in some airgun practice in Kilmainham) is further evidence of that childlike simplicity to which she refers more than once as so straightforward a part of his complex character. He liked to shoot at a lighted candle, but got bored with repeatedly having to relight it.

What does she tell us of what was actually going on in his mind apart from politics? Although brought up a Protestant and maintaining a special respect for the Catholicism that was the religion of the majority of the Irish people, he seems to have had no orthodox faith of his own. He believed, she says, only in some unknowable first cause and final end in which the elemental forces of nature played a part – a part to which he responded by embracing high winds and storm and seas, but also – while lacking any expert knowledge of botany – wild flowers and, for a time under Katie's tuition, astronomy. He found the thought of death painful and disturbing, convinced as he was that it separated souls who had come together on earth and returned them to the different planets under whose influence they had been born.

Whatever the intellectual quality of such beliefs, they show an intensity of feeling which those who knew only a cold and reserved personal exterior may never have suspected. Even his numerous superstitions – dislike of the number 13, dread of the colour green – which were widely known about, had a private background in the Irish peasant lore which he had absorbed deeply from the Avondale servants and others in his Wicklow childhood. Once when his fingers had been hurt in one of his Arklow quarries his old nurse, Susan Gaffney, had dressed them in cobwebs from the Avondale cellar walls, and when he cut his finger at Eltham he expected the same treatment from the cellars there.

Outsiders saw only a cold if courteous dignity. When, long after his death, Katie published his love-letters, their intimacy surprised and shocked by the embarrassing incongruity of such words from a figure by then of legendary status. He was, as Katie says she once told Gladstone, 'a volcano capped with snow'.

The snowcap itself was a deep one. Healy, when he had been with the family in New York in 1880, had noticed what to him seemed a rather unfeeling climate among them, a too ready taking of each other for granted. Emily's reported reception of her brother at Avondale after his six months in Kilmainham certainly reflects something of this. When the baby Sophie Claude died in April 1882, Parnell's letters appear to have had little to say about it; but six months later a stray line in a letter to his 'own darling Wifie' between political and business matters ran, 'Has anything been done about the monument yet? I hope there will not be any hitch.' When his much loved sister Fanny, the poetess, died suddenly in New York that year, he broke down completely and Katie had had to stay with him all day.

His ties with his family were strong if undemanding. Avondale was open to them. He kept in touch with his surviving sisters, though Anna's break with him over his change of course after Kilmainham was to be final. To his mother in America he remained a good son for all her eccentricities and troublesome variations of financial fortune.

What of his own finances?

Katie's account of their life together gives little hint of any shortage of ready money for everyday living. Travel, continual hire of cabs, the upkeep of horses, the renting of houses at the seaside and the transport of objects when necessary backwards and forwards across the Irish Sea – all such expenditure seems taken for granted. She does, however, say that he was 'careful' about small money matters and indulged in no luxuries for himself other than scientific books and instruments. Her own affluence reflected from Aunt Ben may well have played some part in this comfort.

But he did have financial problems of his own. His Wicklow estate including Avondale was heavily mortgaged – to the tune of some three-quarters of a million pounds in modern terms – and at the end of 1882 it became public knowledge that he could no longer keep up the payments.

An order for the sale of the entire property was made in February 1883. But there was one fortunate detail about the timing of this news: it coincided with Forster's attack on him in the House of Commons and his own strident counter-assertion in the old style that it was only the way things looked from Ireland that mattered. The way things looked from Ireland with regard to Parnell's loss of his home and the land held by his family for a century was that he had already done so much for the nation that the nation should now do something for him.

With enthusiastic support from William O'Brien in *United Ireland*, a financial testimonial was launched to which the nationalist Archbishop of Cashel, Dr Croke, gave immediate enthusiastic approval and support. The power of the Catholic Church was now combined with that of the Irish National League to give impetus to the fund. The testimonial gathered pace all over Ireland, and received a great stimulus when the Vatican condemned it, in response to the Pope's disapproval of the Irish Church's involvement in politics (partly under British Government influence). By the end of the year, around a million and a half pounds in modern terms had been collected for Parnell. And a fortnight before Christmas he went across to Ireland to collect it.

A much-repeated story about the apparently ungrateful manner in which he received the cheque and responded to this astonishing expression of affection and admiration from the Irish people needs to be adjusted. It derives from what occurred at two ceremonies to mark the occasion, on 11 December. The first was a brief private meeting in Morrison's Hotel, where, at a prelude to a great public banquet afterwards at which Parnell was to speak, the cheque for £37,000 was presented by the Lord Mayor in the presence of some twenty other MPs, including Davitt, Healy and Sexton. By their account, the Lord Mayor's few words preceding the hand-over of the cheque were interrupted by Parnell, who asked simply if the cheque were made out 'to order' and crossed. The story got passed on as an example of impatient lack of gratitude on Parnell's part, and his first biographer, R. Barry O'Brien, recorded it as such. This account was followed by subsequent writers and was given further apparent substance by Healy's memoirs published in 1929.

It is significant, however, that another contemporary, though not present at the time but writing her own memoirs a few years before Healy, countered O'Brien's version by saying that she had always heard Parnell's action on that occasion cited as 'an example of saturnine humour on Mr Parnell's part'. It might well have been a characteristic means of dealing with a certain embarrassment in the situation, in view of the greater occasion which he knew was about to follow, and indeed what happened at the banquet seems to confirm that he was reserving real response for that public event.

Curiously, Professor Lyons, accepting the Healy interpretation of the story, extends Parnell's alleged ungraciousness to the banquet itself, writing, 'All that he said to the expectant audience, and to the expectant nation outside, in return for this great outpouring of trust and affection were two cold sentences.'

But this is not so. As even O'Brien had related, Parnell made a long speech at the banquet after the Lord Mayor had proposed the toast of 'the Irish nation' and both Davitt and Sexton had spoken first. When Parnell eventually rose, he was greeted with a standing ovation lasting several minutes and much waving of hats. He spoke for five times as long as Davitt and Sexton had done and gave the audience what they wanted in return for what they and the rest of the Irish nation had given him.

With dignity and, in the circumstances, appropriate sentimentality and exaggeration, he gave a picture of the miserable condition of the Irish people as he had found it when he first took to politics. 'Artisans struggling for a precarious existence . . . The tenant farmer trembling before the eye of his landlord, with the knowledge that in the landlord's power rested the whole fate of himself and his family . . . His position . . . not so good as the lot of the South African negro . . . The Irish labourer, slave of the slave . . . with not even a dry roof over his head . . .' And he told how, wherever he looked 'the irresistible conviction was borne back on me that here was a nation carrying on its life, striving for its existence, striving for nationhood under such difficulties as had never bent any other people on the face of the globe'.

Many others had seen this too, and he said how happy he was to see many of those present that evening who had 'joined in the resolve that these things should no longer be'. History would say of the Land League movement that there had never been a movement which had contested against such an infamous and horrible system with so much moderation and such absence of crime.

The cheers with which his speech was punctuated were not just for what he had to say about the past: he looked forward to the future with a passion such as they had hardly heard from him for a long time. It was just what they wanted from him.

Freely attacking the present Government for its iniquities, he outlined a clear course to be pursued should it fail to mend its ways. 'Beyond a shadow of doubt it will be for the Irish people in England . . . and for your Independent Irish Members to determine at the next General Election whether a Tory or a Liberal ministry shall rule England. This is a great force and a great power: if we cannot rule ourselves, we can at least cause them to be ruled as we please.' There was great laughter and cheering at this. It was, he said, a force which had already gained for Ireland inclusion in the coming Franchise Reform Bill, and this generation would bequeath 'the great birthright of national independence and prosperity'.

It was for this sort of thing and the unresolved feelings that went with it that the splendid testimonial had been collected, and he was giving a fair return for it. The London *Times* was in no doubt whatever about this. The speeches at the banquet, it said, came to remind the British people that there was still an Irish question. 'No more uncompromising defiance was ever flung in the face of a nation or a Government than that in which the chief of the Land League has declared war upon constitutional principles and the connection with England.'

But there was no Land League. How this time was the war to be conducted?

Chapter 38

Ever since Parnell had been talking publicly about Ireland's national aspiration he had been defining it, and the word 'independence' itself, in different ways at different times. Sometimes, for instance, it encompassed Home Rule, sometimes vague self-government, sometimes legislative independence (Grattan's parliament), sometimes Emmet's 'nation of the earth', sometimes the example of the United States of America. The link with the British Crown was at times to be the only link, at other times to be something more, but more than once it was to be done away with altogether – a development certainly necessary if Emmet's ghost were to be laid to rest, or the United States' example followed. Such variations in thought had in fact usually been occasioned by the need to humour one type of supporter or another. But while there had been variation, it did not amount to inconsistency, for one eventuality had never actually been ruled out – namely, total separation. The imprecision at least was consistent. As to the means by which the ultimate goal, whatever it might be, was to be obtained, here also there was no inconsistency: it was always to be obtained by constitutional means, unless by those means it should prove unobtainable.

It was therefore not surprising that many political realists opposed to Parnell should assume his true goal to be separation from the United Kingdom altogether and should decide that at all costs this must not be allowed to come about. One such was Joseph Chamberlain, Gladstone's radical President of the Board of Trade, anxious to go some way to meet the Irish sense of grievance in the hope of stopping it becoming anything more. He had maintained a regular contact with Willie as a useful channel to the Irish party long after the feelers for a *modus vivendi* in 1882 had come to nothing. Parnell himself, as usual keeping open as many options as possible, was not beyond communicating directly with Chamberlain over matters of parliamentary procedure in the spring of 1884. But it was later that year that Chamberlain took an initiative which, while again ending in failure to bring about a Liberal/Irish *modus vivendi*, was to have significant subsidiary effects. Willie, concentrating much of his ambition now on the chance of becoming Under-Secretary for Ireland should Chamberlain get the Chief Secretaryship, played an eager supporting role.

The approach of a general election, to be fought under a newly reformed franchise likely greatly to increase the Irish nationalist seats in the House of Commons, ensured that after the relative stillness of the Irish question for the past two years a number of people with political ambitions were on the move.

The previously disputed Prevention of Crime Act of 1882 was due to expire at the end of 1885, and this gave added incentive to the search for an arrangement which could make it unnecessary to renew it. During October and November 1884, Willie had a number of conversations with Chamberlain in the House of Commons and at Chamberlain's home. In these, as Chamberlain later remembered, they 'discussed the possibility of some *modus vivendi* being found which might enable the Irish nationalist party to work with the Government and offer a chance of the settlement of the Irish difficulty'.

Willie put himself forward as a spokesman for Parnell, who, he said, was 'getting sick of agitation'. In these conversations with Chamberlain there had been some talk of applying a system of county councils to Ireland, and Willie conveyed that this must mean something more extensive than that also envisaged for the rest of Great Britain. At the same time it was made clear that if the Prevention of Crime Act were simply to be reviewed on the same terms as before, the Irish party would fight it 'to the uttermost'.

That Willie was at this stage reliably representing Parnell seems likely. On 27 November 1884 he brought Chamberlain a detailed note of Parnell's views and a copy of the Prevention of Crime Act with certain clauses marked. If these were deleted, Parnell would not oppose its re-enactment provided either a considerable measure of county government were introduced or the re-enactment were limited to one year only. Chamberlain was particularly interested in the county government idea; but the fact that Parnell offered it only as an alternative to limiting the Prevention of Crime Act to one year might suggest that from the start it was not of such great importance to him.

In the creation of one Administrative Central Board for Ireland, elected either by the proposed new county councils or by a separate process, and combining the work of those former boards which dealt with local government, education, land and transport, Chamberlain saw a perfect solution to the problem of giving the Irish control over their own affairs without incurring the risk of separation. As he wrote to a long-time correspondent, a Walsall solicitor who had recently visited Ireland:

I consider that Ireland has a right to a local government more complete, more popular, more thoroughly representative and more far-reaching than anything that has hitherto been proposed . . . I am willing to go even further. I believe that there are questions, not local in any narrow sense, but which require local and exceptional treatment in Ireland and which cannot be dealt with to the satisfaction of the Irish people by an Imperial parliament.

Chamberlain's Central Board would be 'altogether independent of English government influence' and would have powers of taxation in Ireland for its strictly Irish purposes.

The Walsall solicitor was so pleased by Chamberlain's readiness to meet the nationalist feelings of the many people he had been talking to that he showed the letter around to a number of friends in Ireland, where it was much discussed. The Central Board was identified as providing an alternative to that Irish parliament which in one form or another had been the Irish political goal since the days of Butt.

In fact, in this same letter Chamberlain actually stated his objection to the Home Rule notion as first introduced by Butt: 'because I believe it . . . would infallibly lead to a demand for entire separation'.

William O'Brien, who soon got wind of the letter, castigated the whole idea in *United Ireland*. Parnell, about to visit Ireland early in January, needed no warning of the difficulties which Chamberlain's ideas might create for him among his more advanced supporters. Before leaving for Ireland on 6 January 1885, he took care to send an unmistakably clear message to Willie:

My dear O'Shea,
. . . In talking to our friend you must give him clearly to understand that we do *not* propose this local self-government plan as a substitution for the restitution of our Irish parliament but solely as an improvement of the present system of local government in Ireland. The claim for the restitution of parliament would still remain.

He signed himself 'Yours very truly'.

This was where things started to go wrong.

Parnell got an immediate reply telling him that his letter complicated matters. 'You indicated verbally the wide system of self-government now under confidential discussion as a solution would be sufficient to satisfy the Irish people.' Now, Willie said, he did not know how to act. Just as they were really beginning to get somewhere in the negotiations, Parnell appeared to convey that he had wide further demands to make.

How Willie did act was to keep all knowledge of Parnell's letter and its contents from Chamberlain.

From this point onwards, though it did not immediately become apparent, disaster of a sort was inevitable. Willie was taking chances that he was incapable of handling, though it was in his character to carry on as if this were not so.

A week later Parnell replied magisterially to his rebuke: 'The two questions of the reform of local government and the restitution of an Irish parliament must, as I explained to you from the first, be left absolutely separate.' He added that Chamberlain's Central Board was being conceived as a substitute for an Irish parliament, actually having greater local powers than he himself had claimed for it.

This letter too, Willie kept from Chamberlain. Two days later he went to see him, bringing Parnell's own detailed Central Board scheme which Chamberlain indeed found to his surprise was more conservative than his own. It did not, for instance, put forward any claim for control of the police. But this did not seem to alert him to the fact that in no way did Parnell regard a Central Board as a substitute for an Irish parliament. Nor apparently did the speech which Parnell delivered at Cork on 21 January, in which he repeated in bolder terms something he had said already seven years before at Castlebar: 'no man has the right to fix the boundary to the march of a nation. No man has a right to say to his country, "thus far shall thou go and no further", and we have never attempted to fix the *ne plus ultra* to the progress of Ireland's nationhood, and we never shall.'

If the speech did come to Chamberlain's attention, he may have dismissed it as conventional rhetoric. Willie, in any case, playing his dangerous game, had taken the precaution of preparing Chamberlain for this sort of thing. As he told Parnell by letter, some days before he had explained to Chamberlain 'the position in which you are placed, and as long as you are practical for the time being, Chamberlain does not appear to mind the determination which you are expressing in your speeches of recovering Grattan's Parliament'.

In this letter he confirmed that Chamberlain accepted generally Parnell's plan for the Central Board and would prevent the renewal of the Prevention of Crime Act for more than one year in return for Parnell's giving 'the new democratic power a chance'.

He concluded his letter by stressing what for him was the real point of the negotiations as if it were also Chamberlain's own. 'Chamberlain', he said, 'might fare better politically were he to concentrate on English reforms and leave Ireland to the Whigs and the Liberal Party, but he was himself anxious to settle Ireland and will work steadily and fairly with us if you will put him in a position to overcome objections by the argument of 80 votes.' And he added what was for him a further personal point in the negotiations: 'besides, there will be a good many appointments to distribute.'

Willie was by now feeling so pleased with himself that he sent a copy of this letter to Parnell to Chamberlain, who was, however, much irritated by some of its tone and particularly by the whole of this last passage. He remonstrated with Willie sharply, protesting that 'a cut and dried treaty of alliance' had been constructed on the basis of what had been an off-the-record 'chat'. He concluded:

One thing, however, I must make clear: the time has not arrived for any negotiation or agreement. I am very glad to know Mr Parnell's views on local government which, in principle, seem to be the same as my own. If this turns out to be the case I shall be glad to find that we are working on the same side ... Experience alone can show if there is any possibility of co-operation between the Irish party and the English democracy.

There the matter rested between the three of them for the present, with a temporary postscript only to be found in a letter Chamberlain sent John Morley, expressing a certain unease about Willie's role as an intermediary. 'I believe him to be perfectly honourable and sincere,' he wrote, 'but he has a perfect mania for diplomacy, and seems inclined to press matters as if he were actually negotiating a treaty between two high contracting parties.' He said he had been pleased 'and perhaps a little astonished' to get from him Parnell's approval of his Central Board scheme, but added, 'my impression is that a solution of Irish difficulties will be rather delayed than hastened by his [Willie's] officious but well-meant interference'.

Parnell was equally wary of Willie. In fact he had taken the precaution of sending a copy of his own terms for the Central Board scheme to Gladstone using Katie as intermediary. But it is at least some testimony to Willie's reliability that, as Gladstone told Chamberlain (who had sent him the version he had received), the two schemes were similar.

The Central Board scheme came to life again, though to no constructive effect, three months later. For Parnell it was no more than a possible stepping-stone to better things. For Chamberlain it was an ambitious personal bid to lead a Liberal break-through on the troublesome Irish question. It can also be seen as only one, though the first, of a number of tentative moves by English politicians ahead of the general election to exploit the expected increase in nationalist seats to personal and party advantage. Parnell needed to do no more than extract what advantage he could for the nationalist cause from their manœuvres.

Chamberlain's difficulty proved to be with his own party. Though Gladstone was in favour of the scheme and for a time Spencer, the Viceroy, seemed in favour of part of it (a local-government extension but no Central Board), opposition within the Cabinet was becoming solid. At the end of April Chamberlain made an approach to Parnell through Willie. He and Dilke, his radical colleague, the President of the Local Government Board, would threaten to resign over the Cabinet's failure to accept the scheme if he, Parnell, would undertake not to obstruct a one-year renewal of the Prevention of Crime Act provided it were preceded by an Irish Local Government Bill. Willie and Parnell talked the matter over at some length in Willie's apartment at Albert Mansions and the proposal was accepted.

It was no great gesture for Parnell to make, though Chamberlain would not have appreciated this for he was still under the impression, carefully fostered by Willie, that Parnell regarded the Central Board scheme as an acceptable substitute for an Irish parliament. Moreover, by that stage there was something else of which Chamberlain was unaware: Parnell was in contact with representatives of the Tories to see if something altogether larger than the Central Board scheme might not be on the cards were the Tories to win the coming election.

In any case, neither Parnell's acquiescence in the resignation deal nor his furtive moves in a quite different direction had any bearing on the eventual fate of Chamberlain's Central Board scheme. This was decided by the Cabinet itself, which rejected it on 9 May 1885, thus revealing, even as late in the day as this, that Parnell's attitude still seemed to them something they could afford to disregard. 'Ah, they will rue this day,' Gladstone's son Herbert reports his father as saying to one of his Cabinet colleagues as the meeting broke up; and to another, 'In six years they will be repenting in sackcloth and ashes!'

Chamberlain and Dilke did not immediately offer their resignations, thus suggesting that they thought of Parnell primarily as an instrument to be used against their colleagues. They did threaten to resign some days later over further manœuvres around the Prevention of Crime Act, but their resignations had been neither accepted nor withdrawn when on 9 June 1885 the Liberal Government fell on a vote over a minor clause in the Budget which the Tories, under Lord Salisbury, won with the support of Parnell and his party. It was the end of the first act in the drama by which, within a year, the prospects for Irish nationalism were to be transformed.

One year later, on 8 June 1886, the first Home Rule Bill for Ireland ever put forward by a British Government was lost in the House of Commons by 341 votes to 311. It had been introduced by Gladstone, back in power since the previous January with Parnell's support. In any assessment of Parnell's career, the rejection of the first Home Rule Bill is not what was important. The spectacular achievement had been to engineer the introduction of any Home Rule Bill in the first place.

When Parnell first entered Parliament eleven years before, the idea of such a Bill ever coming before the House at all had seemed to political realists no more than a rhetorical chimera which enabled a few Irish Members to make nuisances of themselves. In 1876, after an Irish motion to look into the subject had been lost, the London *Daily Telegraph* proclaimed Home Rule's total disappearance, and as late as the early months of 1886 other British newspapers were referring to the notion of an Irish parliament as 'impossible' and 'not worth discussing'. Now, if it was not yet on the statute-book, there was a place waiting for it there. It could be said with reason that but for Parnell this could not have happened. And yet to see all this as a peak of success in terms of what he had entered politics to do, and in terms of that sense of personal fulfilment he sought in politics through Ireland, would be quite wrong. With him, where he was going was always more interesting than where he had got to. But how, first, had it been possible for him to switch between parties to get as far as he had?

Both the Liberal Party and the Conservative Party at this time contained internal stresses brought about by younger men's restless impatience with older leadership. There is evidence to suggest that the defeat of the Liberals in June 1885, if not actually engineered by Chamberlain and Dilke, was at least the result of their not striving to avoid it.

The figure in the Conservative Party then in a radical position analogous to Chamberlain's among the Liberals was Lord Randolph Churchill – in his aristocratic style as ambitious and restless with his party's traditional leadership as was Chamberlain in his businessman's mode. Unlike Chamberlain, Churchill had formed some personal sympathy with Ireland when he had been private secretary to his father, the Duke of Marlborough, the Viceroy there in the 1870s. He had made friends in Ireland, had got to know the countryside, and had seen the miserable condition of the peasantry in the West. His mother's relief fund during the winter of 1880–81 had done much to prevent the dreaded repeat of a Famine like that of thirty years before. His political interest in the country had been sufficiently aroused for him to attend the unsuccessful Government trial of Parnell and others early in January 1881. He was seen then on at least one occasion sitting in court close to Parnell, with whom he may well by then have made some acquaintance, though this was not to stop him later in the year saying that no one feared Parnell's influence more than he did. He had been on friendly terms with Isaac Butt but had consistently been opposed to Home Rule, while working on the principle that by conciliating Home Rulers he might induce them to abandon their objective. He had shown an instinctive dislike of coercion and had become an early convert to the inclusion of Ireland in the Franchise Reform Bill of 1884 in a way that had disconcerted some conventional Tories. During the summer of 1885 he saw Parnell at his own house in London a number of times and on at least two occasions before the combined vote against Gladstone in June. There was no question of a compact between them, but it suited Churchill's ambitious mentality to show a radical Tory initiative towards Ireland against the grain of the Salisbury leadership, just as it suited Chamberlain to be progressively ahead of the Liberal Cabinet to which Gladstone was bound. Parnell managed to make use of both of them, even simultaneously.

There were immediate gains to be had from the Tory Government which took office with Parnell's support, and these soon took shape. In return for that support, Lord Salisbury, the Prime Minister, decided not to renew the Prevention of Crime Act when it expired at the end of the session; he decided also to bring in a further measure of land purchase, to amend the Labourers' Act, and to make new funds available for Catholic education. A further bonus for Irish nationalists was a chance Parnell was given to urge, with Churchill's support and to some effect, the case for an inquiry into a celebrated case of probable miscarriage of justice in which, it seemed, an innocent man had been hanged after a horrific agrarian murder at Maamtrasna in Galway in 1882 under the Gladstone Government.

But the real value of all this was to be its effect on future Liberal considerations.

Parnell was now in the advantageous position of playing each party off against the other without having to do very much except see what might emerge. Elements in each party were using Ireland as a piece, if an important one, in their own game. Only a few days before he had helped put the Liberals out of office, and when he was already in close touch with Churchill at his London house, he had let Willie convey a scheme to Chamberlain by which the Liberals might agree to use the powers of the Prevention of Crime Act only following a specific Cabinet proclamation, thus depriving Dublin Castle of its *carte blanche* powers. And soon after the change of Government Chamberlain was again in touch with him through Willie.

Freedom from the constraints of Cabinet membership had given Chamberlain a chance to strike out boldly on his own. While attacking the Conservatives for taking advantage of Parnell's support, he made a public speech in which he talked of Britain's rule in Ireland being 'founded on the bayonets of thirty thousand soldiers encamped permanently as in a hostile country', and compared it with Russia's government of Poland or Austrian rule in Italy. He contacted Willie to know whether Parnell still stood by the agreed local-government proposals and to say that, if so, he and Dilke would refuse to join any future Liberal Government which was not prepared to implement them. He added that he and Dilke were ready to go to Ireland to speak about such proposals and 'to study the question there with a view to further discussions'.

Willie answered unashamedly on his own account, saying he thought there was a danger that Salisbury might compromise with Churchill and make him Chief Secretary with a seat in the Cabinet. Because of Churchill's sympathetic links with Ireland, Salisbury might then have some success there. 'Altogether,' he added, 'he might dish us.' By 'us' he meant Chamberlain, Dilke and himself. He told Chamberlain he would let him know everything Parnell had to say about the projected visit to Ireland, but it was 'too long to write at this hour'.

Parnell's game being essentially a waiting one, Chamberlain had to wait for over a fortnight for a clear view of his and Dilke's projected visit to Ireland. When it came, on 17 June, it came not from Parnell at all but from his Dublin paper, *United Ireland*. And it came in the form of a series of savage and contemptuous tirades against the two radical ministers for trying to make use of Ireland for their own radical ambitions within the British political system; it told them not to come, because they were not wanted.

Indignant and amazed, Chamberlain cut out the article, which talked of radical ministers who had abetted the horrors of the Gladstone Government trying to curry favour with the Irish people, and sent it to 'My dear O'Shea' in a letter which contained nothing but exclamation marks.

Willie scribbled in pencil an immediate reply saying he had seen Parnell who had simply said that when O'Brien, the editor of *United Ireland*, returned from abroad he would 'talk the matter over with him ... and that it might yet be put right'. But Parnell, he added, did not want to cause internal dissensions in his own party on the eve of the general election coming in November. Exasperated and embarrassed as he was, Willie almost made things worse, saying:

Although for more than three years, you have worked loyally, always doing, or doing your best for, everything I asked you on his behalf, and although I laid particular stress on the many assurances of (in my opinion) a most binding nature which I had taken to you from him regarding the present business, he did not appear to be disposed to go any further. I cannot doubt that on reflection he will see the necessity of altering a position of political and personal *cruelty* to you and myself.

The day of that letter was a Sunday, 28 June. Willie was off to Madrid on business for just over a week the next day, but before leaving he wrote to Chamberlain again, at five o'clock in the morning: 'Although my temper is not that of an angel but of an archangel, I made believe to losing it yesterday afternoon. Mr Parnell sat under a tree for an hour and a half reflecting on all my observations.' Willie added that if 'we' should think it advisable to drop the whole idea of the visit to Ireland, it should be done quietly and without announcement when he got back.

On the Sunday when the long conversation with Parnell took place, the tree under which they talked was presumably at Eltham, where both of them must have been staying for the weekend. It is a midsummer mental picture to hold for a moment in historical memory.

In this moment, not only was much left intentionally unresolved on the political scene, but also much in the triangular situation at Eltham. Willie, we know, liked to go down to Eltham at weekends to see his children. But by June 1885, when this conversation took place, not only his own three children, Gerard, Norah and Carmen, could have been there, but also the two daughters born to Katie in the last two and a half years: Clare, born in March 1883, and the baby Katie, born seven months before, in November 1884. As these two men talked under the tree that summer day, apparently only about politics, what were their feelings for the two smallest children whom their mother herself never even mentions in her memoirs?

The political scene at least had a decipherable clarity.

Parnell, having decided temporarily where to go next, was continuing to look to the Conservatives. They had appointed as Lord Lieutenant of Ireland Lord Carnarvon, a man who had thought more constructively about the problems of Ireland than most Tories and had earlier in the year actually written to Salisbury to say that he thought 'some fair and reasonable arrangement for Home Rule' was the best solution for a 'most thorny' problem.

Home Rule could of course be defined as loosely as anyone wished to define it. Chamberlain had at one point even been able to refer to his Central Board scheme as Home Rule. But the thrust of Carnarvon's comment on Ireland was that the best policy for the Conservatives was 'to take the initiative'. It said something for Salisbury's readiness to go along with him to some extent that he had in fact appointed Carnarvon as his Viceroy.

It was just eight days after Willie and Parnell had sat under that tree that Carnarvon made his first statement of policy in the House of Lords. It was then that he announced that the Prevention of Crime Act would not be renewed and that there would be a new Land Purchase Bill and another to amend the Labourers' Act. That morning he had met Parnell's deputy, Justin McCarthy, in a house in Grosvenor Square, where he had told McCarthy that he himself was prepared to go as far in the direction of Home Rule as Parnell could want. McCarthy did not attach too much importance to this, since Carnarvon himself admitted that he was ahead of the rest of his party, but it made it plausible for Parnell to adopt a show of being wooed, and Carnarvon's tone in the House of Lords that afternoon helped substantiate such an impression. He said he wanted to bring the rulers and the ruled together and to understand those questions of discord which had torn the two nations apart, and that he could not believe that to combine good feeling to England and good government to Ireland was a hopeless task or that 'with honesty and single-mindedness of purpose on the one side and the willingness of the Irish people on the other, it is hopeless to look for some satisfactory solution of this terrible problem'.

Just over three weeks later, on 1 August, Parnell met Carnarvon in a temporarily unoccupied house in Hill Street, Mayfair, though very typically he had only the day before issued a strong public denial of any communication with any members of the Government either directly or indirectly other than across the floor of the House of Commons. The conversation seems to have followed the same sort of pattern as that between Carnarvon and McCarthy, the basis being that no sort of engagement was being entered into by either side. Home Rule was fully discussed, and Parnell laid down clearly that Ireland must have a central legislative body with jurisdiction over all purely Irish affairs, including the right to protect Irish industries. Carnarvon found Parnell both more moderate and 'not so absolutely cold' as he had expected.

The meeting was to remain secret for almost a year. Though theatrically intriguing, with its detail of the dust-sheeted house in Mayfair, its political significance was not in fact great. But it did provide useful confirmation for Parnell that the association with the Tories carried some plausibility: it did not just depend on his contacts with the brilliant but erratic Churchill. Realistically speaking, there was one respect – if only one – in which the Tories were the more suitable party with which to try to establish a Home Rule legislature: they could carry the support of the House of Lords.

But at this stage Parnell was not thinking primarily of anything but short-term realism. His tactical design was to manoeuvre into place the one man who both his instinct and his scientific mind told him was capable of carrying through the principle of Home Rule with the moral power genuinely to convert both his party and his British electorate. For all Willie's protests, he had not minded antagonizing Chamberlain, for he saw Chamberlain's bid for a limited Irish initiative as primarily a bid with which to manoeuvre Gladstone over the brink of final retirement. And with Chamberlain now went Willie. A far more sympathetic and trust-worthy intermediary with the Liberal Party was at hand.

Intermittently over the past two and a half years Katie herself had continued to correspond with Gladstone, often receiving replies not from him but the Liberal Chief Whip, Lord Richard Grosvenor. That Parnell saw this correspondence as a useful way of trying to influence Gladstone behind the scenes is already clear from the detailed nature of many of her earlier communications. In June 1883, in a letter deeply regretting his refusal of a request three days before for another interview, she gave him some of Parnell's suggestions for future legislation. In the following month she sent him a paper in Parnell's handwriting which outlined headings of a Bill for the Reclamation and Improvement of Land in Ireland; a week later came a more immediate request: 'Pray forgive my writing to beg that you will not take the Irish estimates on Thursday . . .' In May 1884 she sent him another enclosure in Parnell's handwriting arguing for inclusion of leaseholders in the operation of the Land Acts.

It was clear from all these letters that she was speaking with Parnell's full authority, and she periodically emphasized this in her bold, confident hand which was often spread over many pages of small writing-paper headed 'North Park, Eltham'. The papers in Parnell's handwriting came sometimes from the same address and sometimes from the Irish Parliamentary Offices in Bridge Street, Westminster. In January 1885 she had, as we have seen, sent Gladstone a copy of those ideas of Parnell on local government which Willie had conveyed to Chamberlain. However, at that time Gladstone had been content to leave the matter in Chamberlain's hands. It was only when the Irish question began to sharpen in intensity for British politics, after the change of Government in June 1885 and Parnell joined the Conservatives in some sort of alliance, that Gladstone turned his mind to what in fact that paper might have said and what precisely Parnell's ideas might be now. He got Grosvenor to write to Katie. He asked her whether this 'document written by a typewriting machine containing Mr Parnell's views on local government in Ireland' still represented Parnell's views. She did not reply for a week.

On the very day that Grosvenor had written to her, Gladstone's son Herbert had made a public speech at Leeds declaring himself for some sort of parliament in Dublin. Katie, writing a week later, said she thought that nothing less than what Herbert Gladstone had outlined in that speech 'would be acceptable now, or considered calculated to settle the Irish question'. However, she said, this was only her own idea, and she would write again in a few days' time if he cared to hear from her. Gladstone's quickening of interest was made clear when Grosvenor wrote again two days later to say he hoped that Parnell's present ideas would be expressed in as 'plain and categorical' a manner as his local-government plan.

By 4 August Gladstone was becoming sufficiently impatient to write to Katie himself. His letter began by referring to the fact that Lord Richard Grosvenor had written to her several times, 'last I think about a week ago to learn whether the important paper forwarded by you to me early in the year on the subject of local government in Ireland as an explanation of the views and desires of Mr Parnell was still to be regarded as in any manner bearing that character'. He stressed that he felt it his 'absolute duty to learn, if I am able, whether it still exists for any practical purpose'. He picked on her reference in her last letter to Grosvenor to his son's speech at Leeds, wishing to make it clear that this was in no sense a proposal of any sort, but simply an opinion of his son's. He asked for early attention to his letters.

Katie replied the next day, saying she had only just returned from Folkestone and had been moving about lately without having letters forwarded.

Parnell's voice in the letter was soon audible. Of the local-government plan, she wrote, 'This method of procedure was only thought of in order to make it more easy for English statesmen to approach the question of a central legislative authority for Ireland when the difficulties of such approach appeared much greater than they now are.' In view of recent events, what now needed to be considered was a constitution similar to that of one of the larger colonies, with certain guarantees for the Crown and the landowning interests and fair treatment for the minority by the majority.

She asked Gladstone, as she had asked Grosvenor, not to mention her name with reference to the correspondence, 'and you must not mind me expressing a hope that it may not be mentioned to Mr Chamberlain'. This may have been because she did not want Willie to know what was going on.

But if the main purpose of the letter was to lay out the minimum terms within which future negotiations must be conducted, she also introduced a significantly concessionary note. 'Of course,' she wrote, 'if a scheme based on what I have written to you could be carried at all, you alone could carry it and render it in a practical form.'

A tactical reality was now at work on both sides of this correspondence. Gladstone answered skilfully and most characteristically in kind, calling her letter 'very interesting . . . too interesting, almost, to be addressed to a person of my age and too weakened sight, since it substitutes for a limited prospect a field almost without bounds'. This was a neat reminder of the fact that his own retirement from the leadership of the Liberal Party was very much on the cards, and that, as Katie had virtually conceded at the end of her last letter to him, if Parnell could not manage to do a deal with him he was unlikely to find anyone else well suited to conclude one.

There was an edge on his amiable letter throughout. While in reality now bidding for Parnell's support, Gladstone was skilfully at pains to make it clear that he was not doing so:

You do not explain the nature of the changes which have occurred since you sent me a spontaneous proposal, which is now, it appears, superseded. The only one I am aware of is the altered attitude of the Tory Party, and I presume its heightened bidding. It is right I should say that into any counter-bidding of any sort against Lord R. Churchill, I for one cannot enter.

If, of course, he said, it were a question of negotiation, he would have to 'take into view' when considering any project recommended by

Parnell 'the question whether two or three months hence, it might be extinguished like its predecessor on account of altered circumstances'. And he concluded by saying, 'I shall look therefore to such a paper as you describe, and appear to tender, as one of very great public interest.'

But, as was not altogether surprising, no paper was immediately forthcoming. It was high summer. The parliamentary session was at an end. Within a few days Parnell was off to Avondale for the shooting. Both he and Gladstone now knew where they stood in relation to each other. Although on the surface there were three sides to the British political aspect of the Irish question, only two of these were really relevant as each knew in their heart, and both had now drawn up their positions from which to manœuvre, with the Tory Party as a common pawn. One phrase in particular in Gladstone's last letter must have settled satisfactorily into Parnell's mind as he tramped after the grouse from his shooting-lodge at Aughavannah: what was being substituted for the superannuated local-government idea was not a limited prospect but 'a field almost without bounds'.

As if to celebrate the new prospect, in a public speech in Dublin on 24 August Parnell talked of 'a platform with one plank only and that one the plank of national independence'. A few days later he played confidently with the same theme: 'They will have to grant to Ireland the complete right to rule herself or they will have to take away from us the share – the sham share – in the English constitutional system which they extended to us at the Union . . .'

As usual, this sort of thing when noticed in England caused sharp anxieties, some of which Gladstone sought to allay in his fashion in his address to the electors of Midlothian in the middle of September. He stressed there how, while it was now safe to give some form of self-government to Ireland, the aim was 'to maintain the supremacy of the Crown, the unity of the Empire and all the authority of Parliament necessary for the conservation of that unity'. This was, at the same time, an encouraging speech for Parnell, who went some way to meet him and to help both of them when in a speech in Wicklow on 5 October he advised English statesmen to 'give our people the power to legislate upon all their domestic concerns and you may depend upon one thing, that the desire for separation, the means of winning separation, at least, will not be increased or intensified'.

Analysed carefully, this was not in fact quite the total reassurance for constitutionalists which it affected to be. Indeed, Parnell went on to say that, while the concession of a full and free right to manage their own affairs was the one way of restoring the affection of the Irish people to England, 'it is impossible for us to give guarantees'. However, as English rule in Ireland was now more unstable than it had ever been, such a concession was the only hope, and he pointed to the success achieved for the Austrian Empire by the grant of autonomy under a dual monarchy to Hungary and to the fact that the disaffection which had once shown itself in Canada and Australia had now disappeared.

This adroit balancing act was partly Parnell's response to his permanent need to encourage moderate constitutional support while not discouraging advanced nationalists – particularly those in the United States who were a major source of funds. But it can be a mistake to look at Parnell as a political phenomenon solely within the conventional context of the political scene. This was indeed where he had to operate for the foreseeable future – and where he was in fact to operate for the rest of his life – but it is impossible to have come as far as this, watching him operate within such a context, without being aware that always a part of his mind was reserved for something that did not fit into that context: something related only to what he saw as the needs and undefined aspirations of the Irish people and with which he identified part of himself. A technically minded man in many ways, he had the advantage of being able to turn the strong romantic forces within him to practical use and at the same time retain a sense of personal liberty rare in a hard-working politician. What could be seen in his politics as a tactical balance of right and left should also be seen simply as non-resolution of the difference between right and left in his own mind. The power to be like this put him one step ahead of almost everyone with whom he had to deal except Gladstone, whose own pragmatic skills were entwined with deeper, moral forces within him.

But all parties were now looking chiefly towards the general election.

Chapter 39

The voting was to take place in the third week of November. But Katie's letter which began a new, all-important bout of correspondence with Gladstone, on 23 October 1885, was concerned not with the delicate two-sided political probing of the summer but with 'a personal matter' which, she told him, was of great importance to her. Gladstone had by now heard quite enough from others, and indeed from her, to be able to realize that if something was of great importance to her it was also of importance to Parnell. To Parnell, her happiness – or rather the happiness they shared together – was the most important thing in his life. And, to an extent he was quite prepared to accept, her happiness required reassurance about the well-being of Willie, who was still her 'Boysie', as she was still his 'Dick', though Parnell may not necessarily have realized this.

She now told Gladstone that there was 'so much opposition to Mr O'Shea in the County Clare that the difficulty of getting him elected for Clare is very great – in fact so great that I do not feel justified in asking Mr Parnell to urge his claims as a candidate for that County any longer.'

Willie's position in his constituency had been the subject of some of their first conversations together when Parnell had taken her for drives down to the river at Mortlake soon after their first meeting in the summer of 1880. But Willie had not in fact really been so bad a constituency member once Parnell had pulled him into line at the end of that year. Both in his moderate – though not conventional – Whiggish views and in his personal dandified ways and business ambitions, he was of course very different from the main run of Irish Members – the 'bhoys' as he sometimes patronizingly liked to think of them. But while politically he had carved out an individual position for himself and had recently made a point of tying himself particularly to Chamberlain, he had fairly regularly over these years voted with his fellow Irish MPs. He had hardly been a prominent member of the House of Commons, but he was not a silent one either and had concerned himself spasmodically with the interests of his constituency. The implication in Katie's memoirs of his total detachment from and even hostility to the Irish party conveys a very inaccurate picture, as the full House of Commons division lists for these years demonstrate clearly. A nationalist Irish Member, discussing close to that time the state of the House of Commons in June 1885, noted that 'in Irish divisions [Captain O'Shea] usually voted with the Irish Party'. And the division lists confirm this, showing him voting during these years often with Parnell and often in quite small Irish minorities.

Unrepresentative in personal character of the tenant farmers of his constituency as he might be, they could not really complain that he had totally ignored their interests. Even before his emergence into the public limelight over the Kilmainham affair in 1882, he had as we have seen, spoken up from time to time on behalf of 'suspects' in Clare imprisoned under the Prevention of Crime Act, had cited incidences of police indiscipline there, and had asked for Government money to further the safety of the sea fishermen of the county. He had expressed dissatisfaction over the working of the Land Act in Clare and had pressed for those in arrears to be included under it. He had had a Bill standing in his name and that of five other Irish Members to facilitate further loans from public funds to Irish county fisheries. His activity in the Kilmainham affair itself had at least caused some amusement in the county; a local newspaper had likened his comings and goings to those of a Turkish intermediary then continually on the move in the Eastern question.

In the Hansard index for the entire 1882 session, he figures almost as much as the nationalists J. J. O'Kelly and T. D. Sullivan and even half as much as Parnell himself. He is to be found at least once in every volume of the session for 1883, though he is absent altogether from two of the eight volumes for 1884. Nevertheless, in the index for the whole 1884 session he again has up to about half as much space as Parnell. He seems to have been away, partly on business in Madrid and Lisbon, for much of the time from March to the beginning of June 1884, though perhaps surprisingly we do find him spending two days with Parnell at Avondale at the end of May. But it is probably his fairly consistent absence from duty during this period which accounts for the fact that in the third week of June the National League in his constituency registered a vote of no confidence in Willie O'Shea.

A curious sequence of events then took place. One of its side-effects was to lead to drama on a major scale.

Within the constituency Willie began to explore a strange alliance with men for whom in other circumstances he would have had no time: the old-style 'advanced' nationalists or orthodox Fenians of the county.

Inasmuch as these were opposed to the parliamentary policy of the National League machine which dominated the county, and inasmuch as that machine was opposed to Willie, there was indeed an alliance of interests of sorts to be fashioned between two such unlikely partners. Willie set considerable store by it for a time. He wrote to Katie ('My Dick'/'Your Boysie') in October 1884 to say that the Fenians had 'now shown such an extraordinary support that, as they themselves say, there will be murder in the County Clare if I am opposed'. It is of some interest that after some persuasion he actually got these Fenians to pass a vote of confidence in Parnell personally.

Two months later, writing from the Shelbourne Hotel in Dublin, he had still had been optimistic, saying he was 'wonderfully popular . . . amongst all the respectable people and amongst the Fenians. What a man I should be to take up the "Small Farmers' and Labourers' League"!' Again, it was a 'My Dick'/'Your Boysie' letter.

But Willie's enthusiasm for himself was not a reliable indicator in practical politics. It seemed little short of grotesque to imagine that such a ramshackle partnership could seriously challenge the National League's political machine. And so, obviously, by the date of Katie's October 1885 letter to Gladstone it had proved.

At this stage, more than ever before, Willie could see the serious possibility of a valuable political career for himself in the offing. The first half of 1885 had been marked by his increasingly close association with Chamberlain. From this, however clumsily he may have acted while thinking of himself as a subtle intermediary, he could see a bright future looming both for himself and for his family. Though at times also concerned with obscure financial negotiations, sometimes in Madrid, of which Katie seems to have had some knowledge, he was chiefly excited by the prospect, which he seriously seems to have thought Chamberlain held out to him, of becoming Chief Secretary for Ireland in a future Liberal Government. Gladstone, with reason, was thought to be on the verge of retirement, and the future of the Liberal Party could be viewed as lying eventually with Chamberlain.

As the local-government negotiations had shown, Willie was prepared to put up with all sorts of exasperating difficulties from Parnell in order to please. Of the Chief Secretary possibility, he had written to Katie ('My Dick') to say, 'This is an enormous thing, giving you and the Chicks a very great position.'

There is no clue in her memoirs to what Katie thought of such a prospect, though the absence of any comment may suggest that she was at the time undecided. But clearly it was extremely important to Willie that he should have a seat in Parliament. And, though she did not say this either, she was still sufficiently close to her 'Boysie' to want him to have what he wanted. Or perhaps she just wanted him to think she felt close to him.

Parnell was the obvious man to help. She had pretended to Gladstone that she could not ask Parnell to do so, but in fact he had already tried and failed, having found Willie's refusal to take the party pledge an insuperable obstacle. And Willie's bitterness with Parnell for first, as he saw it, letting him down over the local-government negotiations and then allowing *United Ireland* to attack his patron on the eve of his projected visit to Ireland in the summer was now compounded by a feeling of resentment that he had not tried hard enough to help him keep his seat for County Clare.

Exasperation with Parnell had been expressed plainly and forcibly enough during the summer in a letter to Katie. 'Mr Parnell is very unsatisfactory,' he had written on 8 May from the House of Commons:

He told me last night, with a sort of wave of chivalry, that I might convey to Chamberlain that he didn't hold them to the bargain [over Chamberlain's and Dilke's one-sided agreement to resign if the Central Board scheme were turned down by the Cabinet]; that they were free to compromise with their comrades if they chose. He does not much care for anything except the vague and wild politics which have brought him so much money.

And after the attack in *United Ireland* in the middle of June he had been more than ever uninhibitedly outraged with her friend:

My Dick, – We are of opinion that the formula holds good. 'No rational beings who have had dealings with Mr Parnell would believe him on oath.'
We know that he has recently said that he is under no obligation or promise to me!!!!!
The marks are of admiration, not of surprise. He has not told the lie to my face but . . . I have already told the *scoundrel* [Willie's emphasis] what I think of him.

This is a curious letter. The second sentence could be read to contain a nuance which related to the personal position of the three of them. But this, on balance, may be rejected. Willie was not much of a man for nuances. The letter conveys straightforwardly his sense of having been made a fool of by Parnell for being encouraged to lead Chamberlain on.

There is a touch of personal self-pity in it too as well as injured pride. He tells Katie that he is losing his hair: 'I am balder than a coot is. Such fun. I wonder whether I shall die soon, or if the day will come. Would I had understood it had come when I was asked to go to Kilmainham. Your B.'

Since Parnell's concern was to help Katie help Willie, he had clearly already discussed with her what she now proposed to Gladstone, namely that Willie should be given the Liberal candidacy in mid-Armagh, where he had a chance of success, and that, in return for this, Parnell would see that the Liberals got the nationalist vote in four other Ulster constituencies, and also in Wolverhampton, where a Liberal looked like being in difficulties. This was more of a concession than it might have looked, for Parnell had not yet decided whether to commit nationalist votes at the coming election to the Tories or to the Liberals. 'Mr O'Shea's being elected for a seat in the next Parliament is a matter of *great* importance to me,' Katie had written to Gladstone in her letter of 23 October. Then she added, almost as a postscript to what they had been talking about when they last corresponded in August, 'I have the plan I mentioned to you respecting a scheme, ready when you care to receive it.'

Gladstone replied immediately to say that that sort of electoral arrangements was really the province of the Liberal Chief Whip, Lord Richard Grosvenor; but he would not fail to tell him what he thought he knew already, namely that he would be very sorry if Captain O'Shea did not get a seat.

A week later Katie, as evidence that the really serious election business was getting under way, sent Gladstone a long document devised by Parnell with no less a title than 'A Proposed Constitution for Ireland'.

But in the meantime something had had to be done about Willie. It had not proved easy. On 25 October he had written to her sulkily from the Shelbourne ('Dear Kate'):

I have kept my temper more or less well so far. Mr Chamberlain, with his knowledge of what I did at various times for Mr Parnell, considers the latter – well, thinks very ill indeed of him. He (C) and all my life friends say that if he had any feeling, any spark of honour, he would have told his party that he was under such a promise and such an obligation that my seat must be secured, or he would resign his leadership.

In fact Parnell was to show before very long that he was prepared to do exactly that. It was to provoke the greatest internal crisis in the history of the Irish party to date, and to usher in a whole new, more delicate and dangerous era for the continuing three-sided relationship.

To begin with, it turned out that the Ulstermen were not prepared to accept Willie at all, and some other expedient had to be found. He, still in the Shelbourne, where he had been ill and where, he said, the doctor had said that 'the slightest cold would bring on a relapse which might be fatal', was at his wits' end. He told Katie he had known nothing about 'your political movements and arrangements':

All I know is that I am not going to lie in ditch. I have been treated in blackguard fashion and I mean to hit back a stunner. I have everything ready; no drugs could make me sleep last night, and I packed my shell with dynamite. It cannot hurt my friend [Chamberlain], and it will send a blackguard's reputation with his deluded countrymen into smithereens.

He ended with a touch of self-pity too absurd not to be genuine:

I wonder the little girls have not written to me; no one cares a bit for me except my poor old mother. I am very tired from writing a lot of letters. – Yours, W. H. O'Shea.

What his 'stunner' portended was at this stage obscure, though the threat was later to receive a veiled airing in as yet unforeseeable circumstances. For the time being, Willie, who had at all costs wished to retain an Irish seat – even as a Liberal – had to agree to cooperate with some arrangement for him to get a seat in England. But before he was prepared to do that, a strange and disturbing scene had taken place in the Shelbourne Hotel.

Parnell, along with most of the Irish Members, was then in Ireland making preparations for the general election. On the afternoon of 7 November he called on Willie at the Shelbourne and, as Willie told Chamberlain in a letter the next day:

began to mumble something about sorrow that I had not seen my way to contest mid-Armagh and hoped that an English seat might yet be found for me. I soon cut matters short by telling him that I did not want any more beating about the bush, that no man had ever behaved more shamefully to another than he had behaved to me, and that I wished to hold no further communication with him. He enquired whether I wished him to leave and I replied 'most certainly'. He then crossed the room and held out his hand. I informed him that I would not touch it on any account.

I do not suppose he has feeling enough to have felt the blow long, but I never saw a man slink out of a room more like a cur kicked out of a butcher's shop.

He wrote to Katie too the next day to say that everyone in Dublin was saying that Parnell's treatment of him had been 'loathsome'.

Parnell had to swallow all this unpleasantness as best he could. But he was prepared to do virtually anything to help Katie, and Katie was striving desperately through Grosvenor, the Liberal Chief Whip, to find a seat for Willie in England, with the general election almost on the country. Further to complicate the difficulty, only a few days before polling began, Parnell had finally decided to issue instructions to the Irish in Britain to vote Conservative: an overt ploy in that tactical manœuvring to bring Gladstone to adopt Home Rule.

Where Willie was concerned, it was only Katie's desperate persistence with Grosvenor which finally secured him the Liberal nomination for the Exchange Division of Liverpool. First there had to be some complicated horse-trading of nationalist votes worked out by Parnell in return; then Parnell himself had to be nominated as a candidate, to give plausible cover for the otherwise unaccountably strange appearance of Willie. Parnell was then able to withdraw. He got no thanks for his pains from Willie, who continued to complain to Katie (now 'My Dick' again) about what a treacherous liar Parnell had been in not supporting him for Clare.

Nor did any thanks come Parnell's way for the hard work he now put into the attempt to get Willie elected. It was a peculiar situation, for here was the leader of the Irish nationalist party, who had told Irish nationalists in Britain to vote for the Conservatives against the Liberals, supporting a Liberal against a Conservative in the Exchange Division of Liverpool. In the end the tortuous labour was in vain. Willie lost, though only just – by fifty-five votes.

The general election as a whole left 86 Irish nationalists holding the balance between 335 Liberals and 249 Conservatives, who temporarily took office. But before examining the all-important consquences of this, we may pursue the digression of Willie's parliamentary frustration, all-important too for Parnell in its way, through to its compromising end. Parnell now had to start all over again, for Willie, with moral support from Chamberlain, was as determined as ever to get back into Parliament, and already had his eye on a seat in Ireland. At that time it was still possible to stand for more than one constituency, and the only English seat to be won by an Irish nationalist had been won by the journalist T. P. O'Connor in the Scotland Division of Liverpool, a constituency with such a significant Irish population that the Liberals had abandoned the seat to him. Willie had earlier been pressing Katie to try to get it allocated to him.

However O'Connor's victory there now opened a new prospect for

Willie. O'Connor had also been elected for Galway, but he chose to sit for Liverpool. Willie now argued with Parnell that he should be put up for Galway by the party. Parnell asked if he were prepared to take the now requisite pledge to sit with them in the House and to back majority decisions. Willie said no, and Parnell replied that that was then the end of the matter. But it was not.

Willie put pressure on Katie. He said that he would get someone else to put him up for Galway if Parnell refused. This was a threat which could prove awkward. He seems to have got offers of support from those 'advanced' nationalists he had earlier contacted when hoping to stand for Clare. He told Katie of a 'Fenian Chief' who had been to see him at Albert Mansions, saying that, though their political views were poles apart, the Fenians would stick to him through thick and thin. 'I fancy', Willie wrote, 'that their admiration for me may be somewhat influenced by objection to certain members.' He signed 'Your B.', and added, 'The real boys want Galway "fought" . . .'

He also sent Katie a letter he had received from a 'Fenian Chief' showing that the Fenians there were seriously ready to help him. The man – a 'Colonel' – had talked to a man who had talked to an all-important member of the Irish Republican Brotherhood about it ('P.N.F.' – P. N. Fitzgerald) who was 'willing to do all he can', though he thought that the movement for Willie should start from Clare. Another Fenian, who was considering standing for Galway and who, if he were to stand, would be hard to beat, was ready to meet Willie and to stand down in his favour, which would, the Fenian Chief said, virtually ensure Willie's success there.

It seems that the Fenians' support for Willie was in gratitude for some influence he had exercised on their behalf as an MP – possibly obtaining the release of 'suspects' imprisoned under the Prevention of Crime Act, or even intervening (vainly as it turned out) on the part of a man due to be executed. A curious scene had taken place in a public house in Wardour Street in London at which a number of Fenians had presented a signed parchment testimonial to Willie, protesting at the fact that he was being excluded from political life. A copy of this was being shown to Fenians in Ireland.

The prospect of Willie thus appearing for Galway, backed by Fenians as he attacked Parnell for treachery, was bizarre and one which might bring embarrassment on a number of counts. Not least of these was the scurrilous interest it might arouse in the relationship between O'Shea, Parnell and his wife. In this respect a strange incident had occured a month before in the November general election in Ireland.

Parnell had spent some of the time he could spare away from his complex activity in the election in Liverpool personally opposing the re-election for County Louth of a member of his party named Philip Callan. He publicly accused Callan of being too often the worse for drink in the House of Commons and of leaking party secrets to the newspapers. But the real reason for Parnell's dislike of Callan and for his wish now to get rid of him was almost certainly something which had happened two years before. In the course of a by-election in Monaghan, a compromising telegram from Katie to Parnell had been opened and passed to this unreliable Member, who had thus been given access to the secret which, since the opening in Paris of that other communication from Katie in February 1882, had been restricted to very few Members in the party.

At the end of the inevitably unpleasant campaign in the general election, in which he was defeated by Parnell's own candidate, Callan suddenly turned on Parnell in public and attacked him for what he had done to him in contrast with what he had done for Captain O'Shea in Liverpool. In a cryptic rhetorical question which even those not in the know might have begun to decipher, Callan asked what there was in Captain O'Shea's political character or private history that was superior to that of Phil Callan and his wife that Mr Parnell should malign and traduce him but support with his best exertions Captain O'Shea.

It was the first public sign that the edges of Parnell and Katie's well-kept secret might conceivably begin to fray. And now, in the middle of January 1886, Parnell, still wondering what to do about Willie's insistence on Galway, met a member of the party who told him that Callan, planning it seems to raise a matter in court about Parnell's influence on his candidature, had asked if a certain 'lady in London' had ever spoken about him. As Parnell explained to Katie in a letter from Avondale, the point Callan intended to make was that he had been opposed at the election not on account of character and conduct but because the 'lady in London' wanted it.

The letter, which was addressed to 'My own little Wifie', was signed 'Your own loving King'. There was an untroubled postscript: 'Nothing will be done about any vacancies till I return.'

It might be asked whether Willie, bearing in mind the essential need to prevent any breath of scandal about Katie reaching Aunt Ben's ears, would really have risked an open anti-Parnell row over his Galway candidature and the uncontrollable consequences this might have unleashed. His whole tentative project with the Fenians may have been primarily a form of blackmail of Parnell; he had taken pains enough to keep Katie well-informed about it. On the other hand, he may not have been thinking too clearly about the matter at all in his petulance; he was suffering severely from gout at the time. But if intended as a sort of blackmail, it worked.

On his return to England for the new parliamentary session in January 1886 Parnell came down to Eltham one evening and told Katie quite suddenly that he had told T. P. O'Connor that he was going to run Willie for O'Connor's discarded seat of Galway. He must have calculated that that way the inevitable row would at least be under his control.

Writing even more than forty years later about his conversation with Parnell outside the railings of Palace Yard that evening, O'Connor could still very vividly convey the sense of shock with which Parnell's words had hit him. He said he had already had his suspicions that 'the incredible and the impossible was going to happen', but when he heard the decision 'my blood ran cold'. Forty years after the event, when the public consequences of Parnell's and Katie's liaison had long been history, he possibly exaggerated with hindsight his sense of the impending disaster of which the Galway election was to be only the first distant tremor. He wrote of 'the sophistries and false pretences with which Parnell sought to rationalize his decision'.

Parnell himself might not have had all that much faith in his rationale. He saw as his priority the need to deal with the chaos Willie threatened to unleash. But there was a grain of political sense in having Willie in Parliament – a man with special reason to be close to him, yet ambitious to make use of his own good connections with Chamberlain. Chamberlain's attitude to the sort of Home Rule that Gladstone might be brought to introduce was still not determined. At the beginning of 1886, Willie could be seen as a useful if minor agent in the Home Rule manoeuvres that lay ahead. Chamberlain was no fool; while he had already identified Willie's limitations, he continued to regard him as a man with whom it was useful to keep touch.

At any rate, Parnell, confident still of his mastery of the party, returned to Eltham that night as 'the King' he felt himself to be there, and showed no sign of concern about the way he had made up his mind. Telling Katie what he had told O'Connor, he laughed and said, 'You should have seen his face, my Queen; he looked as if I had dropped him into an ice-pit.'

There was a short, tense and terrible time to be gone through. Although it ended with a display of Parnell's mastery over the Irish party more impressive than any that had gone before, the fact that his mastery needed to be exercised in such a delicately personal situation meant that it could thereafter be exercised only with diminishing returns.

There were others in the party – men like Healy, Sexton, O'Connor and William O'Brien – who already thought of themselves as more important to its working than Parnell. They certainly appeared in the House more often, stayed there longer, and devoted their lives more whole-heartedly to the parliamentary scene. But part of Parnell's hold over the party derived precisely from the fact that, though he did not seem so essential in this run-of-the-mill way and got his strength from the true centre of his life elsewhere, his ability to cope when necessary, to devote himself assiduously to detail, and above all to seem somehow a cut above the atmosphere of the House of Commons which was the centre of their own lives gave him a natural air of superiority from which, still, derived his sway.

The intensity of feeling generated among the leading figures of the party in the period between Parnell's words with O'Connor outside the House of Commons and the declaration of the Galway poll on 10 February 1886 is chiefly explicable on two accounts.

In the first place, his dominance over the party was much more nominal since the days of Kilmainham. Men like Healy, Sexton and Dillon (whose reversal of his initial decision to give up politics after Kilmainham was itself an indicator of what was happening) had assumed greater and greater everyday responsibility for the running of the party machine, both in Ireland and in the House of Commons. In wider political circles during the dog days of 1883 and 1884 there had even been rumours from time to time that Parnell might be going to give up the leadership of the party altogether. Edward Hamilton, Gladstone's principal secretary, noted such rumours in his diary in April 1884, adding that there was no doubt that Parnell was not the man he had once been. It was certainly true that he had by then an agreeable alternative stability at Eltham, though few knew this.

Hansard's index for the session of 1884 shows Healy taking up nine and a half columns, Sexton six and a half, T. P. O'Connor two and a quarter, and Parnell himself just under two. Even Willie occupied three-quarters of a column. With the approach of the general election in November 1885 and the feasibility at last of some realistic manœuvring for Home Rule, Parnell's concern with the political scene had properly quickened. But, taking now what seemed to many in the party a quite outrageous step by running Willie for Galway, he found himself facing a resistance less easily overcome than ever before.

Second, and it was this that gave the crisis its peculiar virulence, there was the sexual undercurrent which pervaded it – all the more pervasive for being largely suppressed.

Both Biggar and Healy, alerted to the Galway situation by T. P. O'Connor and indignantly contemptuous anyway of Willie for his political views and resentful of the airs he gave himself, were quite aware that the candidate's wife was their leader's mistress. A politician's private life was still, in the late Victorian era, the sort of secret which could be open to people 'in the know' but remain a public secret. Wilfrid Scawen Blunt, an English Home Ruler, though a Tory at this time, found it astonishing that no one seemed to know that personal relations were at the bottom of this whole Galway business. Biggar and Healy knew well enough.

They set off for Galway to support against Willie the candidature of a sound nationalist named Lynch whom the party machine there had already selected. Their original hope had been to block Willie behind the scenes, but Parnell had got ahead of them. He had already sent a semi-coded telegram to the editor of the *Freeman's Journal* saying that, on the basis that Chamberlain would adopt Gladstone's Home Rule views, O'Shea, as Chamberlain's man, would have his own strongest support and that he would resign his own seat in Parliament if O'Shea were not returned. As a result, Willie's election address had appeared in the paper on the morning Biggar and Healy set off by train for Dublin.

Parnell had played his strongest card before they could get into action. It had been too strong for O'Connor himself, who now backed away. But Biggar and Healy were sufficiently aware of the indignation which so many others shared with them to feel confident. They arrived in Galway to find Willie already there. That was no problem. But two days later Parnell himself arrived. He was taking no chances, though he had in fact already won. His threat to resign had had an overriding effect on his *United Ireland* editor, William O'Brien, who otherwise totally shared Biggar's and Healy's feelings about Willie – 'loathing' as he put it – but had managed in two days to marshal the main bulk of the party in opposition to them now that they seemed on the point of leading that party to destruction.

T. P. O'Connor, who had started the protest against Willie, now actually arrived in Galway on the same train with Parnell to support him, accompanied by Sexton and J. J. O'Kelly on the same errand. Dillon's acquiescence had already been obtained by O'Brien. On the journey, Parnell had remarked calmly to O'Connor that Healy had been trying to stab him in the back for years, but he added 'with an easy smile' that he intended to use 'the resources of civilization' (as Gladstone had once put it) against him.

Healy, only two months before in a letter to the radical confidant of the Irish party, Labouchere, had boasted, 'Parnell is half mad. We always act without him. He accepts this position; if we did not we should overlook him. Do not trouble yourself about him. Dillon, McCarthy, O'Brien and I settle everything. When we agree, no one can disagree.'

But Parnell had now arrived in Galway to prove how wrong Healy was, though the uphill nature of the task he had set himself was made clear on arrival at the station when a hostile crowd jostled their former popular Member, T. P. O'Connor, and Parnell, rushing to his side, took him by the arm into the nearby hotel.

There is a conflict of evidence between two eyewitnesses about the extent to which the sexual undercurrent was allowed to surface in public. One young Galway journalist said he heard Biggar, addressing a crowd in the main square, bring up 'in the plainest language' the position of Mrs O'Shea; another, who was also there on that occasion, said that the nearest anyone got to the subject in public was when Healy, looking up at O'Shea, then sitting in a window of the Railway Hotel behind him, told a crowd, 'We may yet have to raise other issues in this election and we shall not fear to do so before we allow the honour of Galway to be besmirched.' However, one of these journalists, attending the private conversations between Biggar, Healy and the local nationalists whom they were trying to persuade to defy Parnell, said that both Healy and Biggar referred in them to what they saw as the heart of the matter, Biggar continually repeating, 'The candidate's wife is Parnell's mistress and there is nothing more to be said.'

Perhaps Biggar, who had mistresses of his own, found it easier to be more straightforward than Healy, for whom a certain puritanical concern with sex was later to find its intellectual outlet more easily. In both cases the implication was that Parnell was backing O'Shea as the price for being able to keep Mrs O'Shea as his mistress, or alternatively just as the price of O'Shea's silence in the matter. What, clearly, neither of them had divined was that silence was as important to Willie as it was to both his wife and Parnell, because a large fortune to benefit all of them (Aunt Ben's) depended upon it. Nor reasonably could Parnell's support be seen just as the price of Willie's connivance, which was either tacitly there anyway or, if not there, was no more required than it had been before. In fact they were of course on the right lines, generally speaking: the basic cause of the event was a simple human one. Parnell would not have wanted to put himself into such an extremely difficult corner if he had not loved Katie, whose concern for her legal husband was still very real. The fact that by getting Willie in for Galway he kept a convenient line open to Chamberlain in the already developing Home Rule manœuvres was a bonus, but no more than that.

Willie himself had to deal with the sexual context behind the scenes. He found it necessary to reassure the priest who was proposing him that there was no truth in what Biggar had been suggesting.

As for Healy, confronted now by Parnell himself, by T. P. O'Connor, Sexton and O'Brien, by a telegram with fifty signatures from other members of the party calling upon the electors of Galway to uphold Parnell's authority, and by an editorial in the *Freeman's Journal* stressing that Parnell had Home Rule 'almost in the hollow of his hand', his claim to be able to run the party as he chose looked paltry indeed. He caved in. Biggar was left in a minority of one. It was agreed that Lynch's candidature should be withdrawn.

But Parnell still had to face a disgruntled public meeting of Lynch's supporters. 'If you dispute my decision now,' he told them, 'there will rise a shout from all the enemies of Ireland: "Parnell is beaten, Ireland no longer has a leader."' Earlier he had reminded them of what the *Freeman's Journal* had said about him having Home Rule 'almost in the hollow of his hand'. This, followed by a particularly ardent and effective emotional speech by William O'Brien, did the trick.

Next day Willie was overwhelmingly elected as a Home Ruler without any pledged obligations to the party. And that, for the time being, could be said to be the end of the matter. Willie was in fact to be found in the House by the beginning of the next month, voting sometimes with a Liberal majority against Biggar, Healy and Parnell but also voting together with the party, including Parnell, in a minority of 84 to 200 on 2 March and on 5 March twice in a minority against Gladstone – on the first occasion with Healy, William O'Brien and the Irish Whip, Richard Power, on an issue which had clearly evoked some traces of Willie's occasional radical feelings. This was a vote to the effect that it was 'inconsistent with the principles of representative Government that any member of either House of Legislature should derive his title by virtue of hereditary descent'. On the same day he was in a much smaller Irish minority which also included O'Brien and Power.

This evidence is of interest in the light of a letter which Biggar wrote to Frank Hugh O'Donnell on 3 March. He complained that Willie was now voting 'regularly against the Irish Party', which was plainly not the case. But the letter is of greater interest in two other respects. One paragraph ran, 'We have plenty of personal jealousy between the different members of our Party. I mean the prominent members. No doubt you can name them. Neither would like to see any other of their number leader, and this assists Parnell to hold his place.'

This usefully defines the dented but secure position in which Parnell found himself after the Galway election.

But the concluding paragraph is of more interest still. It mentions something of which no hint had appeared in public in the course of the Galway election but heralds what was in many ways to be the most sensational public event outside the House of Commons of the following year. This paragraph began, 'It is thought by some that the Galway seat was a case of blackmail, O'Shea having possession of incriminating letters, and insisting on the seat to save exposure.'

Willie had indeed got wind of at least one letter apparently incriminating Parnell; he had almost certainly heard talk of others that were said to be around. All these, one way or another, implied Parnell's involvement with the men who had planned and carried out the Phoenix Park murders.

Willie's contacts in this field were those Fenians with whom he had so strangely formed an alliance while still hoping to be nominated with their support for Clare. In particular, he had struck up acquaintance with a London Fenian, George Mulqueeny, who had been working for many years as a clerk in the Victoria Docks. Mulqueeny maintained his Fenian contacts in Ireland; he had gone there for the funeral of the Head Centre of the Irish Republican Brotherhood, Charles Kickham, in 1882. In London he had been a member of the executive of the National Land League of Great Britain, whose secretary had been that Frank Byrne whose wife had smuggled into Ireland in her skirts the long surgical knives with which the Phoenix Park deed had been done.

Early in 1886 Mulqueeny got to know of a letter from Byrne, thanking Parnell for a cheque signed by him for £100. This was said to have been the money Byrne had used for his escape to France after the Invincibles had struck. Mulqueeny had told Willie that Parnell had paid for Byrne's escape; others seem to have told him the same thing. The police, it was said, had got hold of the letter. Willie afterwards stated definitely that he had been told this by Mulqueeny before he became a candidate for Galway. He also stated that he had not then believed it could be true. However, he did admit that there had been sufficient doubt in his mind at the time for him to inquire at the Home Office whether or not such a letter had been found by the police. Such doubt could have been communicated to Parnell. Since Parnell did in fact back him for Galway, Willie had to say afterwards that he had never doubted him. Inquiries at the Home Office, at Chamberlain's suggestion, were eventually to elicit that the authorities had no knowledge of any such letter, but it is interesting to note that, when later Willie was asked if he had believed the information to be correct, his reply ran, 'As I have intimated, when we enquired into the matter and found that the letter was not supposed to be in the hands of the authorities, I did not, I presume, pay much more attention to it.' He could have given a more convincing reply.

The explanation of this matter seems to have been that there did indeed exist a cheque for £100 signed by Parnell given to Byrne, previous to the Phoenix Park murders, but this was in fact no more than the forwarding from the Dublin Land League to the Land League of Great Britain of a contribution to it which had been raised in Ireland. Perhaps Willie was to *presume* and not pay *much more attention* to it because, as was to emerge, even more allegedly incriminating documents were at the time being discussed.

Certainly it seems that Willie's relations with Parnell and therefore with Katie too were moving into crisis. After the cumulative feelings of disgust with Parnell's 'treachery', first over Chamberlain and then over nomination for County Clare, the discovery of an apparent association with the Invincibles must have seemed to Willie to necessitate a dramatic parting of the ways. If such an allegation alone was to become public knowledge, what was likely to be the effect on Aunt Ben and her legacy – quite apart from the effect on his own standing in a political world where he owed so much to his ability to be close to Parnell?

The parting of the ways of any triangle has its own geometric problems. This one was particularly complex. It cannot even be certain that Willie saw it as a conventional sexual triangle at all.

In many ways it continued to be hard to see how he could not. The circumstances were such that only a husband either accepting that his wife was having an affair or pretending that he did not accept it could have behaved as he did. Certainly he did not know to what extent Parnell was residing at Eltham, but as early as the summer of 1884 he had already shown that he was again worried at least about how other people might see it. He had made the sort of fuss he had made in 1881 at the time of the threatened duel.

As we have seen, he had been away in Spain and Portugal for a fortnight in March 1884, and an attack of gout seems to have kept him away from the House of Commons for much of the next two months, although it had not prevented him from spending a couple of days with Parnell at Avondale at the end of May. From the first week in June, however, he was appearing regularly in the House of Commons in small Irish nationalist minorities – on 5 June in one of seven – and often too in Liberal Government majorities which the nationalists shared. He thus often found himself together in the same lobby with Parnell.

On Saturday 2 August 1884 he voted with Parnell in an Irish minority of 33 to 90 – backing a Parnell motion. This is of some interest because of the letter he wrote Parnell the following Monday. It seems he had heard something he did not like, possibly at Eltham on the Sunday, when he may have been down to see Katie and the children. Wherever he had heard it, on Monday 4 August he wrote to Parnell on House of Commons Library writing-paper: 'You have behaved very badly to me. While I often told you that you were welcome to stay at Eltham whenever I was there, I begged of you not to do so during my absence, since it would be sure at the least sooner or later to cause scandal.'

There follows one of those pieces of evidence which consistently puzzle just when it seems that some coherent picture of the triangular situation is emerging. 'I am making arrangements', Willie went on, 'with a view to taking my family abroad for a long time, and I hope that they will be sufficiently advanced to allow of my asking for the Chiltern Hundreds before the end of the session.'

A reply came from Parnell on Thursday 7 August ('Dear Sir'), couched in Parnell's highest dismissive vein:

I do not know of any scandal, or any grounds for one, and can only suppose that you have misunderstood the drift of some statement that had been made to you. If you finally decide upon vacating your seat before the autumn session, it would, I think, be most suitable if you could do so a few days before this present session closes, so as to enable the writ to be moved and the election held during the recess.

He said that if Willie wanted to communicate with him he could do so at Avondale, where he would be after 9 August for the shooting.

The circumstances of the triangular relationship often seem so enigmatic that one has to look in different directions for explanations of what might be happening. Could this conceivably be a contrived exchange of cover letters to be left around for Aunt Ben to find? Or even to be shown directly to her? The answer in this case must be no. For on the same day as Parnell wrote to Willie, Katie wrote too ('Dear Willie ... Yours K. O'Shea'):

I am very sorry that you should have waited in on my account, but after our conversation on Tuesday [5 August] I could not imagine that you would expect me – in any case, I was feeling scarcely strong enough to travel again in the heat yesterday and for the children's sake I should not like to die yet, as they would lose all chance of Aunt's money, and, however good your appointment they will scarcely have too much, I imagine, and certainly we have a better right to all she has to leave than anyone else.

There are two comments to make on this letter. First, she does not say she is averse to going along with Willie's 'arrangements with a view to taking my family abroad' on the occasion of his 'appointment'. Second, Willie had been seeing her at close quarters, and in that month of August 1884 she was between five and six months pregnant with her fifth child, to be born in November 1884. Her reference to her state of health seems to assume that he would have noticed this, but did he then think it his? He was to maintain this for a time, though later he conceded that it was Parnell's. Katie concluded in conciliatory tone, saying she was going up to London and hoped to see him before he left (for Ireland? for Spain?), but not to continue the conversation they had had on Tuesday. 'I will call', she said, 'about four o'clock if that will suit you.' And she added a postscript: 'Please telegraph early if any other time will suit you better.'

Only two sets of explanations fit in easily with all this; both stretch credibility, at least in the light of Katie's subsequent memoirs. The first is that Willie continued to let himself appear to think her relationship with Parnell platonic, even though it could 'cause scandal' in the world at large. The second is that she continued to let him think that he was her husband in more than name, and had at times over the past two years acted accordingly. The two explanations are not incompatible.

However, if Willie had gone abroad with her and the children, there would have been disturbing emotional consequences for Parnell. These remain totally unconsidered in her memoirs, which omit the incident altogether. Parnell, curiously, seemed quite unconcerned as to whether Willie and his family were going abroad or not.

The whole thing blew over as suddenly as it seemed to have arisen. Perhaps the meeting between Katie and Willie at four o'clock on Friday 8 August 1884 settled the matter again for a time. By the autumn of that year, Willie was, as we have seen, again happily appearing as Parnell's spokesman in conversations with Chamberlain. His 'appointment' abroad seemed to have vanished with the Chiltern Hundreds into thin air. By November he was bringing Chamberlain Parnell's thoughts on the details of possible local-government developments in Ireland, while on Christmas Eve 1884 Parnell, happy to address him now as 'My dear O'Shea', wrote to say he much regretted that he had opened an invitation to dinner from him too late but would look for him on Christmas Day at Eltham. In the following year it was only Parnell's political deceit and 'treachery' which seemed to upset Willie, though this was bad enough and brought only a somewhat uneasy reconciliation with the Galway election.

Katie herself, even before the problem of a seat for Willie had been finally dealt with, had once again resumed her correspondence with Gladstone on affairs of State. On 30 October 1885 she had submitted to him the so-called 'Proposed Constitution for Ireland' drawn up by Parnell, for whose return from Ireland she had waited before sending it. It detailed a 300-member elected chamber with 'power to enact laws and make regulations regarding all the domestic and internal affairs of Ireland, including her sea fisheries', but without power to interfere in any imperial matters. Direct taxation, customs duties, the appointment of judges, magistrates and all other officials, together with its own police force, were all to be in its power. The assent of the Crown would be necessary for all its legislation, and the right of the imperial parliament to legislate for Ireland would remain but would be held in suspense, 'only to be exercised for weighty and urgent cause'. Representation of Ireland in the imperial parliament was to be discussed. Naval and military forces would be maintained by the Crown in Ireland; no volunteer force could be raised in Ireland without the consent of the Crown and enactment of the imperial parliament.

All this was really a bait for Gladstone. For although Parnell and his party were still ostensibly with the Conservatives, it had been clear from the probing correspondence of the summer that Parnell saw in Gladstone the one real hope for effective Home Rule. Gladstone equally had shown a discreet leaning towards Parnell, without committing himself, and was to continue in this position some time longer, understandably refusing so easily to take the bait.

'Thank you for the interesting paper,' he replied. 'As the development of an idea that plays its part in national politics it cannot but be useful. I think a good deal on the subject and it will help me.' And he added gently enough, though this was what he was to make his sticking-point until Parnell himself was to move, 'Moreover I have seen it argued that Mr Parnell ought to seek a settlement of this from the Ministry in office.'

It was partly to call Gladstone's bluff that on 21 November, just before the election, Parnell had finally decided to instruct Irish voters in England to vote Conservative. The election result (335 Liberal to 249 Conservative seats and 86 Irish nationalist seats) put the Liberals in a position to have an overwhelming majority, if supported by Irish votes. The tone and pace of what was going on behind the scenes altered accordingly, though the Irish technically remained with the Conservatives, who therefore remained in office.

On 10 December Katie wrote to Gladstone once more, asking if such a scheme as Parnell had put forward in his Proposed Constitution was at all possible. A little gentle pressure was applied: 'I have to inform you that Mr Parnell is to see Lord Carnarvon.'

This was easy for Gladstone to deal with, and he did so with characteristic and consummate tactical high-mindedness. He replied that he was glad to hear that Parnell was about to see Carnarvon. He placed the whole matter of such Irish settlement as might be in the offing virtually above party politics altogether, saying that it was overwhelmingly a matter of public honour. In the circumstances, no plan could come from him but only from the Government of the day. At the same time he took care to ask a few detailed questions in elucidation of the paper of Parnell's which she had sent him.

She replied three days later saying that she was *extremely obliged* and enclosed a letter bearing on the four detailed subjects he had raised and asking for a reply if he found himself critical of it. He replied at once, on 16 December, with a very long letter making it unmistakably clear that he was now in business for Home Rule with Parnell. In the course of this he stressed that 'any letters now passing between us are highly confidential, I would almost say sacred. At the same time I shall not write a word without being prepared to stand by the consequences should it at any time become public.' And the next day, 17 December, she returned a letter of reciprocal engagement:

I believe I am justified in saying that Mr Parnell feels that any communication with the present Government would be useless as, however well disposed they may be individually towards the subject in question, they cannot settle it. As they must go out before it can be settled he could not make any communications to them that would be likely to be acceptable.

She enclosed a letter from Parnell to herself saying that he had no intention of bringing about competition between the two parties over a Home Rule settlement.

Thus the essential part of the negotiation by which eventually, under the pressure of the figures from the general election, Gladstone was to be brought by Parnell to commit himself to a degree of Home Rule was conducted behind the scenes in this correspondence with Katie dating back to the summer. (The degree was vague enough not as yet to antagonize Chamberlain, who was before long to be again a member of Gladstone's Cabinet.)

Of course there had been some open negotiation in the form of public speaking. In Dublin in August Parnell had not hesitated to stake his bid at the highest possible level, calling for a platform 'with one plank only and that one the plank of national independence'. A few days later he had stressed what to him was important: the power to give customs protection to Irish industries. And he had met the central fear of those who opposed Home Rule, namely that it would lead to separation, by saying that it was the failure to grant Home Rule that created the danger of a demand for separation. And he had pointed to the advantageous result to the Austrian Empire of giving self-government to Hungary.

Gladstone had also in the period before the election given some public evidence of the mood developing in his mind when he had said that, if the vast majority of those elected for Ireland should be for Home Rule, 'the satisfactory settlement of that subject . . . will become the first duty of Parliament'. But of course the most public gesture in the bidding had been Parnell's manifesto just before the election in which he had instructed Irish voters in England to vote Conservative, combining this with an aggressive attack on the Liberals for having been the party of coercion. It has been calculated that this gave an extra twenty seats to the Conservatives. That additional strength to his opponents may be said to have decided Gladstone to go without further ado to call for the Irish vote. But the process by which he was making up his mind remained a secret to almost everyone. Neither the Liberal Party nor anyone in Parnell's own party had any notion of Katie's correspondence.

Indeed in many ways the most notable aspect of Gladstone's eventual declaration for Home Rule was the general public ignorance, even bemusement, about what in fact might be going on. This is well illustrated by the entries in the diary of Edward Hamilton, who, although no longer Gladstone's secretary, was a man with his ear as close to the political ground as anyone in London in that day.

As late as 10 December 1885 Hamilton was seeing the political future unclearly. With the parties evenly balanced if Irish nationalists were put together with the Conservatives, some thought of a Tory Government on Liberal sufferance as being the best thing for the country. 'But apparently this is not Mr Gladstone's view,' wrote Hamilton. 'He is evidently bent on putting his hand to the Irish plough. He has incubated a plan and he wants now to hatch it.'

Two days later he was writing that Gladstone had 'Ireland on the brain', and that once he had made up his mind to a thing he was not to be deterred 'by personal considerations, by the fear of obloquy, by the prospect of a fall'. The next day he recorded that Gladstone was putting out a feeler to Parnell, but through the radical Labouchere. 'Nothing will tend to create a more uneasy feeling than an idea abroad that Gladstone is parleying . . . Parnell would wriggle out of any secret understanding.'

Then on Thursday 17 December, the day after Gladstone's letter to Katie clearly committing himself to cooperation with Parnell, 'All London', Hamilton wrote, 'was agog.' Going into Brooks's Club for dinner, he had been met by a storm of comment and questions: 'What does this mean?' 'Impossible to concede so far!' 'The country is not ripe for it!' 'The Ulstermen are ready to rise to a man if there is any paltering with Parnell.'

What had caused all this excitement was an article in the evening papers based on an interview with Gladstone's son Herbert in which it was implied that his father was about to come out in favour of Home Rule. Gladstone himself issued an immediate statement to the effect that this was simply his son's opinion, but the cat was out of the bag.

The dissension in the Liberal ranks appeared at once. Hamilton wrote, 'Lord Hartington has put his foot down, and, as the *Pall Mall Gazette* says, it remains to be seen whether he will take it up again.' Hartington repudiated any 'local government for Ireland' extended as a federal parliament. The price of Bank of Ireland stock was falling.

Behind the scenes, although committed in principle, Gladstone was still wary over detail in his correspondence with Katie. She had written to him on the very day of the so-called 'Hawarden kite' – Herbert Gladstone's interview – enclosing the letter from Parnell addressed to herself ('My dear Mrs O'Shea', on North Park, Eltham, writing-paper) saying he had no intention of taking any offer of Gladstone's to the other party to try to get it to compete, that he only wanted any outlines Gladstone might have for a future basis of settlement as guidance to himself for his own actions, and that no public declaration by Gladstone was necessary for the moment.

But Gladstone played Parnell along. He replied accepting absolutely Parnell's explanation of why he wanted 'some development of the ideas I have often publicly expressed', but he emphasized, and wrote three days later to do so again, that in the eyes of the world the Irish nationalists were 'in practical alliance with the Tories' and he did not wish to make what could look like an offer by way of a bribe.

Katie responded for Parnell at once, on 23 December. She said that in the 'alliance' between the Irish nationalists and the Conservative Government, both sides had carried out what was expected of them. The Conservatives had got the Irish vote in exchange for abandoning coercion, but there was no more to it than that:

I know [Katie wrote] that Mr Parnell never at any time expected them to attempt any scheme of the kind I sent you, for he never has at any time wavered from the belief . . . that you alone could carry it, and even at the eleventh hour he asked me on the eve of that division which brought in the present Government if I thought it possible to ascertain if you would consider a scheme for the settlement of the Irish question, as in that case . . . the Irish vote would not have been given to the Conservatives.

Parnell's own implicit commitment to the Liberals was now unquestionable. She added in a postscript, 'May I hope that you will let me hear again in a day or two if there is any step you consider it desirable for Mr Parnell to take immediately.'

But Gladstone still told her, partly at least out of some genuine respect for parliamentary tradition, that the Irish nationalists should continue in amiable relations with the Government for the present, to see whether or not Conservatives proposed 'some adequate and honourable plan for settling the question of Irish government'. He described himself as 'a man in chains, waiting to see if they would do so'.

Gladstone's wariness to commit himself was understandable enough. Although Irish cooperation was no longer in doubt, his difficulties were going to be with his own party. Chamberlain was unlikely to accept anything more than a variation of his local-government scheme of the year before; Hartington had already made clear that he could not accept a federal parliament for Ireland. Yet Gladstone could offer nothing less to Parnell.

Gladstone now saw it as the culmination of his life's work to be able to welcome Home Rule for Ireland. If the Tory Government could offer a scheme which he could support and perhaps improve, it would make things very much easier for him than if he had to bring this about himself. His determination to give the Tories every chance to do so was not just a reflection of his honourable beliefs in the traditions of parliamentary government according to the Constitution.

'I am doing all I can to get the Government to the point,' he told Hamilton on Christmas Eve 1885. 'And this is all I am doing. I do not doubt that they are seriously divided. If they will not act, there may be consequences.'

Katie replied to his last letter by saying that Parnell appreciated his difficulties; she said he had discussed the subject very fully with her since receiving that letter – 'in fact we have scarcely talked of anything else'. She enclosed a letter from Parnell to herself on the writing-paper of the Irish Parliamentary Offices saying he did not think there was the slightest possibility of the Conservatives offering any settlement under the present circumstances. But – and here there was just a touch of Parnell's own tactical fencing skill in the air – 'But possibly Irish members might prefer to pull along with [them] and keep them in office as long as they can rather than run the risk of fresh coercion.' He said it would be a serious responsibility for him to counteract this without more distinct information from Gladstone than had been discernible in his address to the electors of Midlothian of the previous September. (This had contained only high-minded generalities about the need for greater vision in meeting 'any just claim of the Irish people'.)

There was no immediate reply.

Hamilton saw clearly enough Gladstone's dilemma and did not feel happy for him. Indeed, on 29 December – Gladstone's seventy-sixth birthday – Hamilton wrote that he feared that he might come 'an imperial cropper'.

The extent of the disarray in the Liberal Party itself was revealed to Hamilton the next day when Harcourt came to see him and 'characterized the Irish plan as revealed [in Herbert Gladstone's "Hawarden kite" interview] with every imaginable adjective short of insane; took the most alarmist view of the situation and prophesied absolute ruin to the Liberal Party'. He spoke of 'excessive sourness among Mr Gladstone's colleagues at their never having received any intimation of their leader's wishes and intentions at the present critical juncture ... What they want deftly to hear is whether Mr Gladstone has a plan formulated, and if so what its main features are.'

Harcourt thought that any plan along the lines of the rumours so far heard would fail to find acceptance by his colleagues and that civil war in

Ireland was inevitable. Lord Rosebery, who came to see Hamilton the next day, however, thought that there was no alternative for the party other than to give Gladstone's scheme, whatever it might be, a trial, because what was in fact the only alternative – coercion – would be opposed by nine-tenths of the party. The most Hamilton himself could get out of Gladstone personally was the characteristically Gladstonian statement that, while his son Herbert's interview had not pledged his father to anything, he did not disapprove of his son giving his view of what his father's ideas might be.

But the moment for decision could not be delayed much further. Parnell knew there was nothing to be had from the Tories. Chamberlain was a man in the Liberal Party who, trying to sight his own future ambitions, wished to see movement of some sort. Now, for all the disappointment and recrimination of the previous summer, he put out an independent feeler to Parnell in the form of a memorandum. The emissary who delivered it was again none other than the man Parnell was backing against all the odds for the Galway seat, Willie O'Shea. The gist of the memorandum was pragmatic: the Tory Government wanted to get out of office but to do so on the issue of Home Rule, so that it could appeal to the country and return with a majority. Chamberlain now suggested that 'in the interests of a fair solution of the Irish question' an amendment which he had devised on an agricultural issue to be put forward by a radical henchman, Jesse Collings MP, could be used instead. He said it was up to Parnell to decide what line to take, and he warned him that Gladstone could not give him assurances on Home Rule because 'in the present state of opinion he would be defeated, and an appeal to the country would in all probability result in a Tory majority'. (It may, incidentally, have been about this time that Willie asked Chamberlain's advice about pursuing the Frank Byrne letter with the authorities.)

The next day, 23 January, Katie wrote to Gladstone again to say she had been 'authorized to say that the Irish would "assist in ousting the Government" if Mr Parnell could have reasonable assurance that the Queen will send for you and you will form a ministry'. She made out that this was on the strength of a favourable speech which Gladstone had made that week. Three days later she got a letter back from him, marked 'Secret', which said he had now determined to speak and vote for Jesse Collings's amendment. Early on the morning of 27 January 1886 the Tory Government was defeated on it. The Queen sent for Gladstone.

On 29 January Gladstone wrote to Katie to say he could understand why Parnell had been apprehensive lest on taking office he, Gladstone, should continue to make his views known only in public. He was now writing to say that this applied only to the time when he was hoping that the Tory Government would take up the Irish question. Now, he wrote, 'the full interchange of ideas' with the Irish Members through their leader was an indispensable condition for examination of the subject which he, Parnell, had well called 'autonomy undertaken by responsible ministers'.

After twelve years in Parliament, Parnell had been instrumental in bringing a British Government to legislate for a Home Rule parliament in Ireland – a notion which had been little more than a rhetorical dream when he had first been elected for County Meath in 1874.

Chapter 40

Looking back now on the fate of Gladstone's first Home Rule Bill, it is difficult not to see it as doomed from the start. Hartington and Chamberlain, while prepared to consider some devolution of local government to Ireland, had their minds closed to anything like that noble intent to meet Irish national aspirations (without endangering the Empire) on which Gladstone's mind had been working. He kept them officially in the dark for six weeks, not raising the Irish question in full Cabinet until 13 March 1886.

When on 30 January Gladstone offered Chamberlain the Local Government Board, an elliptical exchange had taken place between them on the subject of Ireland. Chamberlain was assured of 'unlimited liberty of judgement and rejection' of any scheme Gladstone might ultimately propose and full consideration of his own limited proposals; he in turn assured Gladstone of his own 'unprejudiced consideration to any more extensive proposals . . . with an anxious desire that the result may be more favourable than I am at present able to anticipate'.

Chamberlain did not resign until 27 March.

Meanwhile Parnell was backed by solid support from within his party and from Ireland. For the first time the Irish Catholic Church publicly expressed its 'conscientious conviction' that Home Rule expressed the legitimate aspirations of the Irish people. Parnell was now negotiating directly with Gladstone's Chief Secretary for Ireland, John Morley, who found him 'of striking, though not rapid insight'.

The basic principles of Gladstone's Home Rule Bill were outlined to him. Ireland was to have her own national parliament and (an improvement, this, on the legendary Grattan's parliament) its own executive to manage everything in Ireland except the armed forces, the police for a time, and customs and excise. All foreign relations were reserved for the imperial parliament, from which Irish Members were to be wholly excluded. Ireland was to contribute one-fourteenth of the money needed to run the Empire. On 5 April Parnell met Gladstone for the first time to discuss the details, and Morley, who was there, found him 'extraordinarily close, tenacious and sharp on money matters'. He succeeded in reducing Ireland's contribution to the Empire from one-fourteenth to one-fifteenth. He reminded them that there could be arguments in committee but he accepted, in spite of what he had said in public, that Ireland should not have control over customs and excise.

The sense of achievement in bringing a British Government to this point obscured almost totally the gap between what Ireland was now being offered and the sort of national aspiration to which appeal had often been made in the past – not least recently in extravagant terms by Parnell himself.

On 8 April, to an excited and packed House of Commons with chairs covering the central floor between the benches, Gladstone introduced the Bill in detail. Parnell spoke only briefly on this, the first, reading. Reserving his right to improve on the Bill by amendments in commit-tee, he said that he looked upon it as a final settlement of the Irish question and believed that the Irish people accepted it as such.

The House was to adjourn for the Easter recess on 19 April, for a fortnight, to return in the week of 3 May ahead of the second reading. But, before MPs left, Gladstone brought in a new Land Purchase Bill to accompany Home Rule. Its proposal was for the State to buy out landlords for a sum equal to twenty years' rental, and for the new peasant proprietors to pay the State back in annual sums 20 per cent lower than their present rent – a not ungenerous arrangement. But Parnell took exception to one detail of the Bill: a 'Receiver-General' was to be appointed in Ireland to collect the money, as if the Irish could not be trusted to pay it to England otherwise. It seemed a trivial matter over which to seek a quarrel, and it has been plausibly suggested that this was 'an inconvenient [to Gladstone] row . . . staged in order to make his connivance at a rather tame Home Rule Bill credible to his supporters'. His supporters, however, seemed quite content with the Bill; it was as if they themselves had never really taken the rhetoric too seriously. The row may have been more to reassure himself that the springs of the new constitutional arrangements did in fact run deeper than their literal form suggested, and that when he had talked, as so often he had done in the past, of independence as in the American example, or Emmet's epitaph, or his own 'the march of a nation', he had at some level meant what he said.

Something else in the interval before the second reading also concerned him personally. On 16 April Gladstone received another letter from Katie at Eltham. Her work in manœuvring for the Liberal alliance was long over, but this now was something that concerned both her and Parnell too. It was a plea for a job for Willie. He was on the verge of bankruptcy. Though the Member for Galway, he could apparently no longer see a role for himself with influential prospects in politics. Chamberlain would now hardly require an intermediary with Parnell; he was likely to leave the Liberal Party just because Parnell was tied to it. So Katie was turning to Gladstone for help.

She said that her aunt would 'assist my husband out of his present difficulties, for my sake, if she can see any hope of his getting any lucrative occupation – *but* if not, she will not help him, so you will understand how important your answer is to us in every way'.

What did this augur for Parnell and herself? If Gladstone were able to fix Willie a job in one of the colonies, for instance, would she and 'the chicks' go too? Or would she be glad to see him out of the way? If Gladstone had found an appointment for him, much in the triangular relationship that for so many years never becomes quite clear might perhaps have done so. But Gladstone merely replied politely that he never interfered with his colleagues' power to make appointments; he just made a note on the back of Katie's letter to the effect that Willie was indeed deserving of some gratitude for past services – presumably over Kilmainham.

That Willie was to remain at home and at large was to have significant consequences for them both. The 'letters' which at the time of the Galway election were said to suggest that Parnell had been involved with the Invincibles over the Phoenix Park murders were still said to be in circulation. They were indeed getting nearer home in the shape of the London *Times*. Someone as surprising as the former Liberal Chief Whip, Lord Richard Grosvenor, had even been involved in supplying some funds so that they could be pursued more closely. Of the progress of this pursuit, Willie himself, through Mulqueeny and his other strange friends, was soon to become more aware.

In the meantime he, like the rest of the political world of which he was still a part, awaited the second reading of the Home Rule Bill, which Gladstone introduced on 10 May in a long eloquent speech with the high moral undertone that was his speciality. He faced head-on at once the question at the centre of all doubts about the proposal to give Home Rule to Ireland: namely, whether it was 'a thing compatible . . . with the unity of Empire'. Yes, he answered, pointing out that in a speech at the beginning of the present session Parnell had said that what he wanted for Ireland was 'autonomy'. Autonomy, said Gladstone now, was a term internationally recognized as meaning management only of the specific territory to which it was applied. He said nothing of the things that Parnell had said at other times in other places.

After summing up much of the history of England's Irish question, and hinting that he was open to reconsider in committee details like the exclusion of all Irish Members, he concluded by saying the Bill would put an end to the controversy of seven hundred years, 'knitting together, by bonds firmer and higher in their character than those which heretofore we have mainly used, the hearts and affections of this people and the noble fabric of the British Empire'.

The crack in the Liberal Party appeared at once. He was followed and opposed by Hartington, the man who had temporarily led his own party when he himself had prematurely retired some years before. Hartington picked up the autonomy point. He reminded the House of all the other phrases Parnell had used for what he wanted for Ireland. And this was to be the crux of the issue around which much argument was to revolve over twelve nights of the second reading. Tellingly, Hartington quoted Gladstone's own words from the days just before Kilmainham when he had drawn attention to Parnell's ambivalence about whether the Crown was to be the only link between the two countries or not even a link at all. Hartington concluded by describing the Bill as 'fraught with mischief and disaster both to this country and to Ireland'.

But perhaps the most effective expression of the doubt about whether Irish Home Rule would enable the unity of the Empire to be maintained came from another Liberal, Sir Henry James, a former colleague of Gladstone's who reminded the House of 'the statements of eloquent men who are dead and gone, and who made one claim for Ireland which was that she should be a nation'.

At this point Parnell spoke for the first time on the second reading. He simply said what he had said in his maiden speech ten years before: 'She *is* a nation.'

'I understand', replied James, 'that the claim was that Ireland should be an independent nation with its own Flag ... Will the Honourable Member for Cork forgive me, as he says Ireland is a nation, if I ask him whether this is the nation which Irishmen have meant, when under this Bill her legislature will be brought lower than that of any province of any colony of the Crown, when Ireland will have no Flag, no army, no navy, when she cannot deal with her foreign affairs, or with her trade and commerce or even protect her coast? I cannot believe that the Irish nation will accept this as a final settlement.'

As the moment for the final decision approached in that early summer, Edward Hamilton's diary vividly reflected the growing excitement in London's social circles. The Prince of Wales, he reported, found Gladstone's Bill more than he could accept, though, perhaps surprisingly, given his mother's known views, he was not opposed to some sort of Home Rule. Two days later, on 26 May, Hamilton dined at the Rothschilds' and went on to an evening party at the Duchess of Manchester's. 'One certainly hears in society plenty of abuse of Mr Gladstone,' he wrote. It was said Gladstone was moved only by love of office and power. Queen Victoria, on the other hand, while 'dead against Home Rule', accepted that Gladstone in his error undertook his task for the highest motives.

As May ended, society could not make up its mind which way the vote was likely to go. The common belief, Hamilton wrote on 29 May, was that Gladstone would get a majority on the second reading, but, he added, 'people chop and change so much from day to day'. A few days later, on the 31st, he was writing, 'There never was anything like the shifts and changes – a most discreditable amount of shilly-shallying.' At a dinner at Downing Street, Gladstone himself had observed that the guests there that night might have carried a vote of confidence against him by three to one. The betting switched from day to day: odds on Gladstone one day, and the reverse the next. At the Rothschilds' (where Patti was singing before the Prince and Princess of Wales), Hamilton met Sir Henry James, who had spoken so effectively in the early stages of the debate. James told him he thought Gladstone was assured of his small majority. Would Chamberlain vote against the Government? Hamilton heard at Brooks's that he was thinking of abstaining.

On 2 June he wrote that he thought 'the smash-up of the Liberal Party' was inevitable. Two days later there was still thought to be a chance of Gladstone pulling through. At Marlborough House on Sunday 6 June, the day before the vote, he met Hartington, who said he was very confident about the way the division would go; but Hamilton still bet at odds of 6 to 4 from Nathan Rothschild that Gladstone would win.

Parnell spoke in the House on the last full day, 7 June – 'a remarkable speech', wrote Hamilton, 'every word carefully weighed and marked with conciliation'.

Certainly to anyone hearing the speech from an English point of view there was a balanced tone to it, well calculated to appeal to those who did not really like the idea of an Irish parliament at all but who might be persuaded to take this particular one. But, in the light of so much that he had said in the past, how could it not seem hollow and suspect to say that this parliament, limited and subordinate to the parliament of the British Empire, as he admitted it to be; with neither ultimate supremacy nor sovereignty over its own territory – and not even allowed to run its own post office – could possibly be seen as 'a final settlement' of all that noble struggle for an independent Irish identity, the past heroism of which he had so often evoked in the present to rousing cheers? Yet that was what he said it was: 'a final settlement'. Or rather, and thus possibly he provided himself with an escape clause, 'I believe it will be a final settlement.' The escape clause, if such it was, could not be used in the present situation. With the one proviso that there was of course also work to be done on the Bill in committee, he was accepting it as a measure which could 'close the strife of centuries and give peace, prosperity and happiness to suffering Ireland'.

Those who liked what they heard could nevertheless discount it as insincere, though it seemed sincerely expressed. But, viewing Parnell at that moment from our own time, it seems unhistorical to raise the question of sincerity at all. On the Irish benches, in Ireland itself and even in America on the whole, the Bill was accepted as the only attainable and therefore the only desirable objective. It was an integral part of its character that it was to be 'a final settlement'. Parnell, the political engineer, had it in hand.

The rest of Parnell's speech has some interest for our own time because he concerned himself, as he did only infrequently, with Ulster. In Belfast there had been serious riots against the prospect of the Home Rule Bill. Chamberlain, in his speech earlier in the debate, had proposed a separate legislature for Ulster. Parnell firmly rejected this. He could seem in a strong position, because at the recent general election there had emerged for the nine counties of the province a majority of one in favour of Home Rule. One of his arguments against Chamberlain's idea had much more validity then than it has today, for he pointed out that a separate legislature for Ulster would be isolating the 400,000 Protestants who then lived outside the province altogether. Events of a later time were to reduce that figure to an insignificant consideration.

But his essential argument about Ulster was an idealistic one. Its validity too has been destroyed by events, though even in his own time it was questionable in a way which, like most nationalists, he seldom troubled to face. 'We cannot', he said, 'give up a single Irishman. We want the energy, the patriotism, the talents and the work of every Irishman to ensure that this great experiment shall be a successful one.

The best system of government for a country I believe to be one which requires that government should be the result of all the forces within that country.' What was ignored was what has been ignored by nationalists ever since: namely, that 'all the forces within that country' did not see it that way.

What, that night, attracted more attention to another part of his speech was when the former Tory Chief Secretary, Sir Michael Hicks Beach, later in the debate queried a passage in which Parnell had said that he had every reason to suppose that if the Tories had won the election they would have offered him an Irish parliament with power to protect Irish industries. Parnell interrupted directly to say that, yes, a minister of the Crown had certainly conveyed this to him. Hicks Beach strongly denied this. There were cries of 'Name! Name!' Parnell did not then name Carnarvon, but he may have hoped by his intervention to engender enough disarray among the Tories to rally Liberal Party feeling among those whose support for the Home Rule cause was known to be fast ebbing away. If so it was to small avail.

Nor did Gladstone's own final attempt to appeal to all-party English patriotic tradition in doing justice to Ireland succeed in stemming the tide of deserting Liberals. 'Go into the length and breadth of the world,' he concluded. 'Ransack the literature of all countries, find, if you can, a single voice, a single book, find, I would almost say, as much as a single newspaper article . . . in which the conduct of England towards Ireland is anywhere treated except with profound and bitter condemnation. Are these the traditions by which we are exhorted to stand? No; they are a sad exception to the glory of our country. They are a broad and blank blot upon the pages of its history; and what we want to do is to stand by the traditions of which we are the heirs in all matters except our relations with Ireland, and to make our relations with Ireland conform to the other traditions of our country.'

The second reading was lost by a vote of 341 to 311 – a majority of thirty. Some time before the vote was taken, the Home Ruler Wilfrid Scawen Blunt, who had been in the Lobby of the House of Commons, had seen the old schoolfellow who had once chased him with a fives bat, Willie O'Shea. Willie had come over and shaken hands with him, and Blunt wrote in his diary next day that he had had it on the tip of his tongue to ask him whether he was going to 'vote square'; but he did not. In fact Willie walked out of the House without voting, one of the very few MPs to do so. Writing in his diary, Blunt called him 'a blackguard . . . the traitor we expected him to be'. And, with a certain strange prescience of which he could not then have been aware, he wrote of him, 'His name will be handed down in infamy through Irish history to the remotest generation.'

There seems to have been something more than just his desertion of the nationalist cause to make Willie walk out of the House of Commons. Next day he applied for the Chiltern Hundreds. Possibly it could be seen as a sort of loyalty to his old colleagues in the party that he had not followed Chamberlain and voted against Home Rule too. But Home Rule seemed to have had little to do with it. Why did he see it necessary now to bring his political career to an end?

Twice in the next few years Willie was to state on oath that in May or June 1886 he had learned something which completely changed his opinion of Parnell. That was his official statement. We know that his opinion of Parnell had long been, for one reason or another, flexible. But clearly something new had happened. What could it be?

The question has been asked many times but never convincingly resolved. It seems most likely that the most obvious answer is the correct one: that he had learned something more along the lines of what he had learned just before the Galway election from his friend Mulqueeny. Though there has been speculation that the event to which he referred may have been to do with Parnell's friendship with his wife, he in fact specifically stated in one of his court appearances that whatever it was that had changed his mind had nothing to do with her. And though reliability, as everyone who had anything to do with him, including Chamberlain, had discovered, was not always the most attractive side of an otherwise reasonably attractive personality, there is a good chance that he was speaking the truth on this point. But there is a confusing factor: there had indeed recently been something to disturb him, along the old lines, about Parnell's friendship with his wife.

Whatever exactly it was he had previously taken offence over in 1884 was, as we have seen, apparently resolved by the turn of that year. From what happened then he can again be seen to be resigned to the nature of their relationship for a time. And Parnell and Katie clearly felt confident enough together at Eltham. In February 1885 Parnell had actually brought some horses over from Ireland to be stabled at Wonersh Lodge. One of them, called President, was to be for himself; the other, Dictator, for Katie. That summer at Eltham a new room was built on to Wonersh Lodge where the conservatory had been, for Parnell's convenience. It communicated with Katie's room. Their equanimity in making these arrangements seems on the surface curious, because what happened towards the end of May 1886 has to be regarded as an embarrassing incident.

A brougham in which Parnell had been travelling from Eltham station to Wonersh Lodge collided on the road with a Sydenham florist's market cart and the brougham was slightly damaged. Three days later a paragraph appeared in W. T. Stead's *Pall Mall Gazette* headed 'Parnell's suburban retreat', detailing that accident and incidentally relating that while Parliament was sitting the Honourable Member for Cork usually took up his residence at Eltham, 'a suburban village in the south-east of London'. He could often be seen out riding round Chislehurst and Sidcup. There was no reference in the paragraph whatever to Mrs O'Shea. Willie, however, saw the paragraph and wired Katie, in some concern.

'My Boysie . . .' she replied:

I have not the slightest idea of what it means, unless, indeed, it is meant to get a rise out of you . . . I do not see that it has anything to do with us, and I am inclined to agree with Charlie, from whom I heard this morning, who says, in respect to Healy, that 'It is better to put up with a great deal of abuse rather than retaliate, for it is ill fighting with a chimney-sweep, for, right or wrong, you'd only get soiled.' I should say the paragraph has been made up by Healy and co. to annoy you, but I don't see why it should do so . . . I should advise you to hold on to your seat, for I am sure you will annoy the sweeps most by doing so. I am sure there would be no end to their spite after your Galway success. We will call early tomorrow and talk it over.

Your K.

The 'we' was not the royal 'we', which she never used. It can only have meant herself and 'Charlie'.

The air of enigma surrounding the relationship of the three of them persists. This letter, with its undoubtedly affectionate tone, could be read as taking for granted her 'Boysie's' knowledge that Parnell was at Eltham and that what the three of them had to deal with was the problem of Healy and others in the party making something embarrassing of this in order to compensate for their Galway failure. The formal letter, in the style of old times, which Parnell then wrote to Katie from the Irish Parliamentary Offices and which she gave to Willie could be read as merely a cover letter which could if necessary be shown to Aunt Ben. On the other hand it could also be seen as a classic example of deceit against Willie. As so often with incidents in the triangular relationship, either possibility – tacit connivance or deceit – seems plausible. Parnell's letter ran:

Your telegram in reference to the paragraph duly reached me. I had a couple of horses at a place in the neighbourhood of Bexley Heath, but as I am not able to be much away from London, I turned them out to grass for the summer. I am very sorry that you should have had any annoyance about the matter, and hope to see you on Sunday . . . Yours very truly, Chas. S. Parnell.

Their next action was to remove the horses, together with their harness and saddles, from the Wonersh Lodge stable to another stable, but one very close by. Whether this was to prevent 'Healy and co.' from being able to make any more trouble over the matter or whether it was to implement deceit of Willie – as was later to be maintained in the divorce court – remains part of the perpetual enigma. There is something strange, though, about the action if it were indeed taken in order to deceive Willie. The horses had been in the Wonersh Lodge stables since February 1885. In the fifteen months between that February and 24 May 1886 when the *Pall Mall Gazette* paragraph appeared, Willie would certainly have been down to Eltham more than once to be with the children and would have been capable of seeing for himself that Parnell's horses were there.

Whatever interpretation this sequence of events leaves us with, it seems much more likely that it was the other matter that had come to Willie's attention that was causing him the greater alarm. For if the chance of Katie inheriting Aunt Ben's money were to be forfeited by unpleasant publicity over Parnell's friendship with Katie – which she certainly must have known continued in some respect anyway – how much more devastating would the scandal be if it were revealed that Parnell had been in contact with the Phoenix Park murderers? For this was what there was now said to be evidence to prove.

This evidence had emerged from the twilit world of the Fenian and neo-Fenian underground, with its sterile presence in parts of the Continent – Paris, Brussels and even Lausanne – as well, of course, as in America. In this instance that world was made to seem doubly murky by the nature of the agent who had produced from it the evidence. The accusation that there had been a connection between Parnellism and crime had, of course, been common in the days of the Land League. What this agent claimed to be able to obtain were documents directly associating Parnell not just with agrarian crime but with the murders in Phoenix Park.

The agent in question was one Richard Pigott, sometime nationalist proprietor of the newspapers the *Irishman* and the *Flag of Ireland*, which

Parnell had bought for him in order to start his own paper, *United Ireland*. Though he had fallen on hard times financially and had acquired a dubious reputation for honesty, Pigott had once been thought reputable enough to attend among those who, with Parnell, welcomed Davitt and the Fenian soldier McCarthy to Dublin in 1878 after their release from imprisonment. His financial embarrassment had become increasingly acute over the years, and he had tried to turn a dislike of Parnell and his policies to advantage by at one time applying even to the former Chief Secretary Forster for money – and indeed got a certain amount. In the autumn of 1885 he had published a pamphlet, *Parnellism Unmasked*, which had had to be withdrawn for libel reasons and reissued in an amended form.

Pigott had come to the notice of a young former *Times* journalist, Edward Caulfield Houston, now secretary of a group called the Irish Loyal and Patriotic Union, whom he had told in December 1885 that he thought he could get material to confirm directly the connection between the Parnellites and crime. He came to an agreement to be paid a daily rate plus expenses, and set off abroad on a number of journeys to bring some of this material back. By April 1886 he was able to supply Houston with copies of five incriminating letters allegedly written by Parnell and six written by Egan. Houston, understandably, went off to see his old boss, the Editor of *The Times*, George Buckle, to tell him what was going on. Buckle, at this stage, declined to have anything to do with it.

Pigott went off on a number of journeys to Paris, and eventually returned in June to say that he was now able to buy the original of the letters if Houston would come to France with the money. This was to be paid to mysterious figures he was never to see who allegedly were to bring the letters to a hotel in a black bag. Houston did as he was told and, having handed this money over through Pigott to 'the men downstairs', together with a bonus for Pigott, was back in London in July with originals of the incriminating letters. He again went to see Buckle, who this time was much more interested. By the end of the year the letters were in the possession of the Manager of *The Times*.

Willie, who knew Houston, may very likely have known as early as June of his negotiations with Pigott. In June, after it seems spending two days in the Queen's Hotel, Eastbourne with Katie, he himself went off to Karlsbad, presumably to treat his gout. He may probably be believed when he said later that at the time he had no knowledge of the fact that Katie had taken a house at Eastbourne. In which case he would also not have known that Parnell was staying there with her. What he can be supposed to have known, however sketchily, about the Houston–Pigott transaction would naturally have heightened his anxiety about any news of Katie's continuing association with Parnell reaching Aunt Ben's ears.

It must be significant that when, in August that year, Hartington in a public speech made some not particularly veiled reference to Parnell's influence being used on Willie's behalf in the Galway election, Willie wrote to Hartington to point out that he had no wish to be thought to have owed his seat to what he called Parnell's 'terrorism'. And earlier that summer, on a picnic near Karlsbad, he had had his attention drawn by a lady to a paragraph in an American paper referring to Parnell's visits to Eltham and his 'Aspasia' there in the absence of her husband. On 2 July 1886 he had written to Katie to tell her of this in a remarkably straightforward way, not directly remonstrating with her but simply referring at the end of his letter to 'filthy swine like Parnell and his crew'. This final phrase may well have been an oblique pointer to what he knew, though she did not, of the material Pigott and Houston claimed to have got hold of about Parnell.

From this time forward his attitude to Katie's continued association with Parnell is consistently definite and hostile. It is most probable that it was in conversations Katie and Willie were having at this time, as revealed in their correspondence, that 1886 became the date from which it was known to Willie that Parnell had been constantly residing at Eltham in his absence since 1880.

Katie reminded Willie that a friend, Christopher Weguelin, had always been at Eltham in his absence in Spain in an earlier year and he had not seemed to mind. On 20 August Willie dismissed this and repeated what presumably he had been saying in their conversations: 'I forbid you to hold any communication, directly or indirectly, with Mr Parnell.'

In their exchange of letters during this period there are occasional mystifying references to a possibility that they might live together again in one form or another. For instance, on 13 September he wrote to her from Albert Mansions after she had appeared to be ready to meet his views: 'All I want is that you should engage not to communicate, directly or indirectly, with Mr Parnell and that you should take Norah and Carmen to Eltham and prepare a room for me so as to live in the house.' What may be significant here, possibly revealing that by now he had accepted the sexual nature of her relationship with Parnell, is the fact that there is no mention of her two daughters, Clare and little Katie, both of whom by now he may have acknowledged as Parnell's. (Gerard was then staying elsewhere.)

The pattern of the next three years until Willie finally – after Aunt Ben had died – brought his action for divorce is one in which he repeatedly insisted that Katie should have no communication with Parnell. But it is also one in which she and Parnell repeatedly tried to avoid Willie discovering that they were together, followed by Willie's repeated disappointment, usually as a result of items in newspapers, to find that this was so.

Frenetic as some of the action they had to take inevitably was later to appear in the divorce court, the domesticity of Parnell's and Katie's life together, so firmly established already, shows no sign of real disturbance. Outside events seemed to impinge remarkably little on the private tranquillity they had long ago successfully made theirs. This is partly because, with one exception, outside events over the next three years were not to be particularly demanding for Parnell – or rather he was not to allow them to be so.

Parnell's political life divides easily into recognizable phases. The individuality of his personal commitment to Irish nationalism had made itself felt as a public force both in Ireland and in Parliament even before the days of the Land League. He had then come forward naturally to lead and give political effect to the strong Irish interests and emotions which that organization was able to accommodate. Faced at the beginning of 1881 with something like a revolutionary brink, he had not crossed it but had walked beside it in search of a direction. The Liberal Government of that day had helped him to find this by imprisoning him in Kilmainham. The fact that he had by then found himself domestic happiness had further helped confirm in him the conclusion that the only way forward to wherever he might be going for Ireland was through some *modus vivendi* with the Liberal Government. The killings in Phoenix Park were long to blur the process by which this was to be realized, but eventual changes in English political forces had brought not only a *modus vivendi* in reach again but a point where he was able to extract from an English Government the first offer of some sort of independence to have come Ireland's way in that century. Though the Home Rule Bill had been defeated, Parliament had dissolved and, after a general election in early July 1886, a Conservative Government with a majority of 117 over Liberal Home Rulers and Irish nationalists had taken office, that offer of Home Rule remained in place until a Liberal Government came back again, provided nothing were done to imperil it.

It so happened that just as the Conservatives came back to power, naturally disposed to see the maintenance of law and order in Ireland as their principal concern, a situation was developing there which was likely to bring law and order once again to the test. A recession in the agricultural economy, with lower prices for tenant farmers, was recreating conditions in which some were finding it difficult to pay even the new judicial rents fixed by the land courts. Evictions were on the increase, particularly in certain areas like Co. Galway and Co. Tipperary, and with evictions came the agrarian discontent which led to reciprocal violence.

There had been signs of this happening even while the Liberal Government was in office. With a Home Rule Bill in prospect, Parnell had taken care to instruct the National League in Ireland to maintain discipline in the countryside, in order not to awaken traditional English fears of Irish 'outrage'.

Now the Conservatives were in office. The agrarian economy continued to deteriorate. Evictions increased. In Ireland a spontaneous movement came into being, encouraged by traditionally left-wing members of the party like Dillon and O'Brien, to be known, after the headline in William O'Brien's *United Ireland* which put the idea forward, as the 'Plan of Campaign'. Its principle, adapted from the days of the Land League, was that tenants should organize to offer landlords such rent as they felt able to pay in present circumstances; if this were not accepted, they were to place the money in a fund to help those subsequently evicted.

From this Plan of Campaign Parnell took care to remain aloof. His principle was that, above all, the sensibilities of both Liberal Home Rulers and Liberal Home Rule voters in the next general election should not be offended by that Irish party with which they were allied having any involvement in the sort of crime which had disturbed them in the days of the Land League. Thus, inevitably, both in the eyes of the party and, in the affected areas particularly, in the eyes of the Irish people, Parnell's authority was shifted into something like a neutral position. This became particularly noticeable as the Conservative Government, at the hands of its Chief Secretary for Ireland, Arthur Balfour, introduced stringent coercive measures allowing many offences such as boycotting, intimidation and resistance to eviction to be dealt with by courts of summary jurisdiction. In September 1887, after the police had shot into a crowd at Mitchelstown and three people were killed, the Chief Secretary was to earn for himself the name of 'Bloody Balfour'.

Coincidentally, or perhaps not, Parnell's aloofness from the Plan of Campaign, or rather his concentration on preserving the Liberal alliance at all costs, was accompanied by a prolonged bout of undefined ill-health during the winter of 1886 and the spring of 1887. William O'Brien, coming to try to discuss the Plan of Campaign with him one evening, had a bizarre encounter with him in Greenwich Park at which he was appalled and disconcerted by Parnell's strained and even awful appearance. As late as May 1887, the undramatic Justin McCarthy wrote about him thus as he appeared in the House of Commons one day after a long absence, partly spent at Avondale: 'Appeared', he wrote, 'is a fitting word to use, for no apparition – no ghost from the grave – ever looked more startling among living men ... The ghastly face, the wasted form, the glassy eyes gleaming ...'

However, in the spring of that year, something had happened which was eventually to do his standing a power of good in both Ireland and England in the estranged political position into which he had allowed himself to drift. For in March 1887, just when the tide of agrarian crime was attracting attention again in Ireland, *The Times* had decided to finish him off altogether with the use of those 'incriminating letters' Houston had bought through Pigott.

The paper first produced a series of coruscating articles condemning Parnell and his party outright for the crimes in the days of the Land League. 'Murder' was the charge directed against 'Mr Parnell and his friends' in the first of three articles in the week beginning 7 March 1887. The following week began with a leader scornfully challenging them to bring an action for libel against it: 'If our charges could be shown to be unfounded and not for the public benefit, we presume Mr Parnell and his friends might ask for heavy damages.'

It was on 18 April that *The Times* produced its trump card, supplied by Pigott: the facsimile of a letter written in longhand on one side of a folded sheet of paper and on the other side signed at the top 'Yours very truly Chas. S. Parnell'. The text, which was dated '15/5/82', nine days after the Phoenix Park murders, and in a different hand, ran:

I am not surprised at your friend's anger but he and you should know that to denounce the murders was the only course open to us. To do that promptly was plainly our best policy.

But you can tell him and all others concerned that though I regret the accident of Lord F Cavendish's death I cannot refuse to admit that Burke got no more than his deserts.

You are at liberty to show him this, and others whom you can trust also, but let not my address be known. He can write to [sic] House of Commons.

Katie in her memoirs said she saw the paper first that day and told him about it before showing it to him over breakfast at Eltham. He was quite unperturbed. McCarthy sitting beside him later in the House of Commons turned to him and said, 'Of course it is a forgery?' Parnell looked at him 'in a wondering way': 'Well, I shouldn't think you had much doubt in your mind about that?'

It was not until one o'clock next morning that he was able to intervene in the debate to ridicule *The Times*'s letter as a 'precious concoction'. He said that he had heard about it before he had seen it and had imagined then that an autograph he had signed had fallen into the wrong hands, but when he had seen it he had recognized at once that it was 'an atrocious fabrication'. He could not understand how 'what used to be a respectable journal could have been so hoodwinked, so hoaxed, so bamboozled . . . as to publish such a production as that as my signature'.

Superficially, in fact, it seems even today a passable version of his signature, though he went into some detail about where it was wrong. Where he was more immediately convincing was in his description of the subject-matter in a different hand as 'preposterous on the surface. The phraseology is absurd – as absurd as phraseology could possibly be.'

There was indeed a curiously inelegant, un-Parnell-like clerkly tone in the wording which must have struck for a moment even those who refused to accept his denial of the genuineness of the signature – of whom there were many, including the Prime Minister, Salisbury. But he did not sue *The Times*. It was not in fact until a year later that the matter came to a head, when the paper, in a burst of overconfidence after winning a libel action about the articles brought by Frank Hugh O'Donnell MP, published another letter allegedly signed by Parnell in the same way. This letter, purportedly written from Kilmainham to Patrick Egan, contained the words 'what are these fellows waiting for? This action is inexcuseable [*sic*] . . . Let there be an end of this hesitency [*sic*]. Prompt action is called for . . .'

After the failure of an attempt by Gladstone to get a parliamentary committee to look into all this, the Salisbury Government set up a full judicial Special Commission to examine the whole nature of the Land League, the circumstances in which it operated and the involvement within it of the parliamentary party. It hoped thus to turn the subject into a major indictment of the Irish parliamentary party and of the Liberal Party which could still maintain a close alliance, as it was doing, with such men.

In this political objective, though the Commission which sat for over twelve months in the new Law Courts was to make an effective case against much of the Land League operation in terms of condoned outrage, the Government was to fail. Less than halfway through the Commission hearings, after a brilliant cross-examination by Sir Charles Russell, in which Pigott, in the witness-box, revealed that he spelt 'hesitancy' in the manner of the alleged Kilmainham letter, with an 'e', the letters could be plainly seen to be forgeries. When the Court closed at four o'clock that Friday afternoon, 22 February, the total demolition of Pigott as a witness was expected for its next meeting, the following Tuesday. On the Saturday morning, however, he went to call on the radical MP Henry Labouchere to say that he wished to make a full confession. Labouchere insisted on a witness being present, and in front of them both Pigott then admitted to having forged all the letters, using genuine letters which he himself had had from Parnell at the time of the sale of the *Irishman* and the *Flag of Ireland*. He had put these letters up to a window, traced the signatures on to tissue paper, and then copied them through that on to writing-paper.

He was staying at Anderton's Hotel, near the Strand, and went that Saturday evening to the Alhambra music-hall. He was, theoretically at least, under police watch over the weekend. On the Monday afternoon he sold some books at Sotheby's and used the money to buy himself a ticket to Paris and Madrid. Successfully evading such watch as the police were keeping on him, he eventually arrived in Madrid on the Thursday and shot himself dead the next day in the Hôtel des Ambassadeurs.

Strangely, Willie O'Shea was in Madrid that day too. Parnell had for a time been convinced that Willie himself was the forger.

When Parnell appeared again in the House of Commons at the end of that week, 1 March 1889, everyone on the Opposition benches, Irish nationalists and Liberals, led by Gladstone himself, rose to their feet to cheer him. The Tory Solicitor-General, watching from the other side of the House, said later, 'It was an incident which might have disturbed the balance of mind of a smaller man. I saw Mr Parnell erect among the whole standing crowd. He took no notice of it whatever . . . I thought as I looked at him that night, that that man was a born leader of men.'

This humiliation of *The Times* at the Special Commission in February 1889, and thereby too of the Salisbury Government whose Attorney-General acted as prosecutor there, did much to confirm for Parnell that legendary status as leader which during recent years had sometimes faded as Ireland battled with Balfour's coercion, and Irish MPs were imprisoned in harsh conditions while Parnell remained isolated at or around Eltham or, if in Ireland, at Avondale. He had been speaking at no public meetings in Ireland, and aroused no national expectations as in the old days. The national expectation was now wholly contained in the prospect of the next Home Rule Bill. Gladstone, still keen and active in his eightieth year, could not last for ever. No likely future leader of the Liberals had the same near-religious commitment to do something for Ireland. The present opportunity would not be easily re-created.

Ever since the defeat of the 1886 Bill and the general election which had followed, Parnell had been careful not only to present as moderate a reaction to harsh events under Balfour as was compatible with being Irish leader at all, when Dillon and O'Brien were the people's heroes in Ireland, but also to restrain those periodically ambiguous expressions of the national claim which had always been his speciality. In that general election of 1886, he had, reasonably enough, concentrated on winning English votes to the Home Rule cause. Since the principal English fear about giving Ireland her own parliament was the danger of ultimate separation which this could conjure up, he had gone out of his way to allay it. At Plymouth that year he had emphasized that, were a move towards separation to develop in Ireland once she had her own parliament, England would have not only all the necessary power of ultimate sovereignty but also 'the moral power' to suppress such a move. Anyway, he said, separation was 'the hollowest and most absurd talk ever given utterance to'.

In March 1888, a year before his apperance at the Special Commission, he had met Gladstone in private to talk about the future. Gladstone thought he looked not ill but far from strong, and wondered, particularly when discussing how far the powers of a Dublin parliament were to go, whether the 'energies of his political pursuit were somewhat abated by his physical condition'. It is possible, of course, that Parnell wanted Gladstone to think this. That there should be nothing short of a Dublin parliament was his main point; limitation of its powers might not prove a problem and might be accepted. 'I understood him to mean', noted Gladstone shrewdly, 'might be accepted as a beginning.' There seemed general agreement between the two of them that an arrangement along the lines of the American federal system could be worked out. Gladstone's note of the meeting concluded with the observation, 'Undoubtedly as a whole his tone was very conservative.'

John Morley, Gladstone's Chief Secretary for Ireland, writing to a newspaper editor a few weeks later, said of this meeting, 'Like many other meetings of remarkable men, this was not distinguished by any remarkable occurrence. All went very easily. Mr Gladstone was as usual full of life and go. Mr Parnell was much more genial than usual, composed, intelligent and better informed upon general things than I had supposed him to be . . . It was all very easy and pleasant.'

Two other subjects they had discussed were the Plan of Campaign and a recent solemn pronouncement from the Vatican condemning it together with the practice of boycotting in Ireland.

This Papal Rescript concentrated immediate attention on the Plan of Campaign in a way which, particularly for a Protestant leader, required some definition of attitude such as he had been reluctant publicly to give to the Plan. To retain his authority in the strongly aloof position in which he had been content to place himself as Irish leader in these years was, by definition, not easy. But this presented him with something of a test. He had not spoken in Ireland for years. His lieutenants found it difficult to reach him, even in England. His appearances in the House of Commons were spasmodic, even rare. In the Hansard index for the session of 1887, his interventions occupy only one column, whereas those of Healy occupy nine columns, Sexton more than seven, and Dillon four. What was he to say now that the Papal condemnation of the Plan of Campaign demanded a stance?

He said it brilliantly in a speech to the Liberal Eighty Club in May 1888, effortlessly reminding people of his mastery. He had, as Conor Cruise O'Brien has succinctly written, two main groups in his movement in Ireland to deal with: the agrarian left and the clerical right. Now, writes O'Brien, 'with consummate self-confidence, [he] reached out and knocked their heads together, lightly but firmly'. He dismissed the Papal Rescript as only making matters worse: of course it was not his business as a Protestant to interfere with whatever the Church might choose to say, but it was going to make it more difficult for him to replace the Plan of Campaign, to which he had never been a party, owing, he said, to his illness at the time, though he would then have advised against it.

Home Rule, he was really saying, was the only thing that mattered – that and the reliance all Ireland must place on 'the great Liberal Party of England'.

This was the period of the 'union of hearts' between the Irish nationalist party and the Liberal Party, and – to hear Parnell speak – there was little need to think or worry about anything much more than the election which would bring about Home Rule for Ireland. There was to be no more convincing display of the way in which that union of hearts beat together than the moment on 1 March 1889 when he entered the House of Commons after the total collapse of *The Times*.

Only once in these years is there something of a significant reminder of other ways in which his thoughts might go. Careful always when speaking to English audiences to stress the harmony that would prevail between England and Ireland once Ireland had her own parliament, unusually in June 1889 he reverted in public to an earlier line of thought. He was speaking, as usual in this time, in England, but to an Irish audience – members of nationalist town councils of Ireland who had come to pay their respects. The Special Commission, although it had long ago dealt with Pigott, was still in session after more than ninety days, accumulating its attack on the Land League movement as a whole, and he chose the occasion to express his contempt for it.

The Commission's essentially political character was manifested in the Attorney-General's frequent concentration on the neo-Fenian origins of the Land League's work. Parnell now said he could not remember ever having considered that the constitutional movement might fail (a convenient lapse of his memory), but then in something like his old style he went on to say that 'if it became evident that we could not by parliamentary action and continued representation at Westminster restore to Ireland the high privilege of self-government . . . I for one would not continue to remain for twenty-four hours longer in the House of Commons at Westminster . . . I believe the Irish constituencies would not consent to allow us to remain . . .' All sections of Irishmen, he said, had always thoroughly understood that the parliamentary policy was only to be a trial.

However, it was to such a trial that his mind was now totally committed. Next month, at Edinburgh, he was saying all the right things again, stressing the 'strong and enduring bonds of friendship, mutual interest, and amity' between the two countries which were now on their way, and saying that nobody could for a single instant pretend that Irishmen were not justified in looking for constitutional means alone for the future prosperity of their country.

But what exactly this time were the terms to be on which Ireland was to obtain Home Rule? The situation between him and Gladstone was totally unlike that of early 1886: there was nothing veiled, retiring or obscure about Gladstone's total and open commitment. Indeed, in August he had suggested to Parnell that they should meet again to discuss how the future they approached together might work out.

Parnell finally came to visit Gladstone at Hawarden on 18 December 1889. They spent two hours together that evening, and two hours more on the following day. Gladstone's daughter Mary sat next to him at dinner, and they talked about the Special Commission. She recorded a vivid impression of his presence, speaking of his 'cool, indifferent manner, in sharp contrast to the deep piercing gaze of his eyes, which look bang through you, not at yours. He looks more ill than any other I ever saw off a death bed,' she added. The precise details of the discussion are not available, but Gladstone wrote shortly afterwards that he had carefully prepared all the points that he could possibly think of from which to fashion a good Home Rule Bill and an accompanying Land Bill and they had been able to discuss these fruitfully together. One detail which needed to be resolved because it had caused difficulties with doubtful Home Rulers last time was the retention or otherwise of Irish representation at Westminster. Neither of them was confined to hard and fast opinions about this. Parnell, wrote Gladstone, 'emphatically agreed in the wisdom and necessity of reserving our judgement on this matter until a crisis is at hand'. Nothing at the time seemed less likely.

Chapter 41

The Hawarden meeting was, in the view of both parties at the time, an unqualified success. There can be no doubt whatever about that, although before long it was to become a matter of amazing dispute.

'Nothing,' reported Gladstone of Parnell at the time, 'could be more satisfactory than his conversation, full of good sense from beginning to end.' No positive conclusions over details of the future Home Rule Bill were arrived at, but the important thing was, as Gladstone wrote, 'nothing like a crotchet, or an irrational demand, from his side was likely to interfere with the freedom of our deliberations when the proper time comes for practical steps'.

He and Parnell had taken a long walk together in Hawarden Park on the morning of 19 December. On leaving, Parnell went straight to Liverpool, where, that evening, at a meeting of the Liverpool Reform Club, he was introduced to the audience by his host the Chairman with the words: 'We see the head of the Irish race and the head of the majority of the English race facing each other with no distrust, shoulder to shoulder, with perfect confidence engaged in a common cause ... to settle the quarrel of centuries.'

And Parnell, welcomed by the Liberals there with the singing of 'For He's a Jolly Good Fellow' and a large cheque for the Parnell Defence Fund raised for the Special Commission proceedings, referred towards the end of his speech to the prospect of the next Home Rule Bill.

'I do not believe for a moment,' he said, 'that the land question will be the same difficulty and the same impediment in the way of a settlement of the national question, as it constituted in Mr Gladstone's Bill of 1886 ... You people of England now see, under the guidance of your great leader, the way to terminate the strife of centuries ... the great Liberal Party has come to the help and the rescue of Ireland ... I know enough of my countrymen to know that they recognize and join with you in recognizing that we are on the safe path to our legitimate freedom and future prosperity and that they will accompany me and accompany you in the path until you have helped your great leader to win the battle.'

His Liberal host was to write to Gladstone – though admittedly a year later, when the matter had become one of dispute – that Parnell had been much impressed by both the cordiality and the content of his visit to Hawarden, 'but more than all with the thoroughness of your proposals in regard to Ireland which went really further than he could have expected from any great English statesman and that they meant a most satisfactory solution'.

The omens seemed set fair at last for a resolution of those ancient problems of England with Ireland which had bedevilled British politics for so many centuries and, in the present one, had been such an awkward thorn in the imperial side. The next Liberal Government, it could be assumed, having come to power with the country's expressed support for Home Rule behind it, would have the moral sanction to make the House of Lords acquiesce in the people's will.

Within days a shadow had fallen on this prospect from another quarter altogether, portent of a storm which in little more than a year would engulf it and defer any sort of resolution for a generation.

In May 1889 Mrs Benjamin Wood – 'Aunt Ben' – had died at last, peacefully, at Eltham, aged ninety-six. She had left some seven million pounds in today's money to Katharine and her five children. It was left in such a way that Willie himself could make no claim upon it.

Six months before her death, Willie had written to Chamberlain stressing his anxiety that, for his children's sake, nothing should be published about the state of affairs between his wife and Parnell, of which he imagined 'a great many people have some notion'. (If Willie, preserving his self-respect, put it this way, it was clearly, in some circles, common knowledge.) He added, 'a very large fortune for them may depend upon it not coming into print'. It was he himself, he said, who had 'begged' that Mrs Wood's will should be arranged this way, so that he could not inherit any of the money. What he meant was that he had accepted that her all-too-plain awareness of his spendthrift ways would have deterred her from making the bequest at all if she thought he might be able to get his hands on it. The important thing had been that she should get no wind of her 'Swan's' adulterous relationship with the man whose voice she liked and whom she had accepted as a good friend of the family. 'I believe', wrote Willie, 'Mrs Wood is worth £200,000 or more [£9 million today] all left to them, and . . . Mrs O'Shea's relations would use any weapon to change her will.'

A knowledge of this background is essential for any understanding of what was soon to happen. Now Aunt Ben was dead. Even before she died, the relations had in fact made an attempt to have her declared of unsound mind. This had been thwarted by both Katie and Parnell writing, somewhat extraordinarily, to Gladstone himself for the assistance of his own private doctor in declaring her not so. Both Gladstone and then his doctor obliged. After her death, the relations did indeed proceed legally to contest the will and Katie's right to be sole heiress.

Willie's own attitude now went through a 180-degree turn. Publicity could no longer harm him. By joining forces with the other relations in an action to dispute the will, he would eventually be able to get his hands on at least part of the fortune; alternatively, he could sell his interest in it to the highest bidder before the lengthy probate case could be resolved. Planning now for a divorce, he went in October 1889 as a good Catholic, priding himself on the best possible connections, to regularize his decision with the Archbishop of Westminster, Cardinal Manning. He showed him the celebrated paragraph of the *Pall Mall Gazette* of May 1886 about 'Mr Parnell's suburban retreat'. The Cardinal, doubtful about the significance of this evidence, suggested a deed of separation, but Willie replied that this would be 'useless'. Whereupon the Cardinal asked for time to think about it, which Willie granted him.

However, five weeks later he was getting impatient. He wrote to the Cardinal to say he was having to wait about in England 'to the detriment of *other interests*' [my italics]. Personally, he added, he now had 'everything to gain by the completest publicity'.

He may well have felt more at ease writing to Chamberlain, whose man-of-the-world approach suited his purpose better than the theological circumspection he was to get from the Cardinal. Chamberlain replied reassuringly to the effect that 'the boldest course' was often 'the wisest'.

The remark has fuelled speculation that there was a politically manipulated element in Willie's decision to go for a divorce – that it was a calculated attempt by Chamberlain to ruin Parnell where Pigott's letters had failed. But this seems an unnecessarily conspiratorial view of what was anyway working in Willie's mind for his own purposes and simultaneously providing, free of all moral compromise, a welcome bonus for the cause of those Liberals who, as 'Liberal-Unionists', had now joined the Opposition.

Whatever feelings Willie may have had earlier in the decade about somehow re-establishing his marriage with Katie, these were by now extinct. She was at last no longer 'My Dick' to him, and he had ceased forever to be her 'Boysie'. But because of his fondness for Norah and Carmen, who lived with their mother, while Gerard lived with him (what were his feelings about little Katie and Clare?), there were still occasional meetings. It was one of these which led just before Christmas 1889 to what Willie, writing again to Chamberlain, described as 'a dreadful scene' and impelled him to take action whatever Cardinal Manning might say.

On the death of Aunt Ben, Katie had first taken a damp house at Mottingham, a few miles from Eltham, and then, longing with Parnell for the sea, had moved, not this time to Eastbourne, but to Brighton. Her account of their life together in the period is, as so often, confused, but at least at one stage Parnell was staying in a hotel near the old Chain Pier while she was in a house with her children. On a day just after Parnell's return from Hawarden and Liverpool on 19 December, Willie came down with Gerard to Brighton, perhaps with Christmas presents for the daughters. On 27 June 1887 Katie had given Gerard – 'her dearest Gerardie' – a written assurance that she would have no further communication, 'direct or indirect', with Parnell. The dreadful scene occurred when Gerard, coming into the house and going up to his mother's room, was told to wait downstairs because she was dressing. He did not go downstairs but into an adjoining room; there he found some clothes hanging up with Parnell's name on, some medicine bottles of his on the mantelpiece, and ointments and dressing things on the table. In a fury he began to hurl them out of the window. His mother, hearing the noise, came in and they had a violent row. According to W. T. Stead, to whom Willie himself related the event only three weeks after it happened, she admitted her guilt in the course of it. 'Mr Parnell', Willie said to Stead, 'is a gone-er and the first witness against Mrs O'Shea will be her own son.' Willie was back in London with Gerard by Christmas Eve and instructed his solicitors to petition for divorce, citing Parnell as co-respondent.

The news became public on 28 December. The *London Evening News* had sent a representative to Willie's rooms at 124 Victoria Street that morning to get confirmation of the report it had received. He found breakfast on the table there and his son Gerard with the Captain. He saw Willie as 'still a soldier in his bearing and movement. One would judge him to be a man of fifty [which he was],' he reported, 'and be prepared to credit him with the vigour of forty. Six feet in height, stout in proportion, heavy moustache and short-cut hair well turned to grey.'

Asked if he could be seen privately, Willie replied, 'You can speak before my son.'

Obviously Willie must have known the reason for the visit, but he affected ignorance. When the journalist, feeling awkward, urged that the matter was so private that only the Captain himself ought to hear, Willie agreed to see him alone and offered him a cigarette. When told about the report that the paper had received and which it did not want to publish without corroboration, he looked straight into the man's face and said, 'I may as well state that it is true.'

'And that Mr C. S. Parnell is the co-respondent?'

'That is true too, but how the deuce did you know?'

'And true that you are not claiming damages?'

'Of course I do not claim damages.'

He was a very model of correct behaviour. 'I am most grateful to your editor for having the courtesy to ask me before publishing.'

Adultery was stated in the petition to have taken place from April 1886 to the present date at Eltham, at 34 York Terrace, Regent's Park, at Brighton, and at Aldington, Sussex.

Parnell immediately struck a totally confident note to sustain the popular myth of his irreproachable character and allay any possible consternation. The action, he said, was all part of a plot on the part of *The Times* to get its own back for the Pigott fiasco and thwart the libel action he was bringing against it. This sat a little oddly with the rest of his statement, which said that Willie had been threatening to bring divorce proceedings ever since 1886 – long before the Special Commission. An even more oddly ambiguous remark was the admission that Willie had always known that he (Parnell) had lived at Eltham in his absence from 1880 to 1886, and that since 1886 he had known that he had constantly resided there from 1880 to 1886. On reflection this seems to substantiate rather than repudiate a prima facie case if not for adultery, at least for deception of Willie between 1880 and 1886. There can be no clearer proof of the mesmeric power which Parnell was able to exercise in Ireland than the fact that for more than sixty years no one seems to have been struck by the contradiction. Attention was first drawn to it in 1957 by Dr Conor Cruise O'Brien.

Uppermost in Parnell's mind was the need to make clear what concerned him: namely, that Willie had only brought the action now for his own devious reasons. What primarily concerned the public was not Willie's timing but whether his charge of adultery was true. Yet such was the spell Parnell had by now contrived to exercise over the Irish people, so overwhelming was the popular need to believe that the man to whom they had given their belief was all that such a man should be, that, in the eleven months between the serving of the divorce writ and the hearing, trust in him became an article of faith comparable almost to those of that

Church which sustained most of the Irish people. 'With regard to Mr Parnell,' wrote the *Freeman's Journal* on 30 December 1889, 'Ireland trusts implicitly what he says.'

All over Ireland local bodies like the Limerick Municipal Council, the Ennis Board of Guardians and the Killarney Town Commissioners spoke of Parnell's 'successful struggle against the infamous intrigues contrived to defame and overthrow him' and of his enemies 'playing against him with loaded dice' and confidently made statements such as that 'nobody holds any other view of the vile accusation sprung upon him than that it is a piece with the forgeries of Pigott'. The fact that Parnell's action against *The Times* for libel was imminent seemed of obvious relevance, and Parnell himself was quoted as saying that Houston was in some way involved. A meeting of Liverpool Irish pledged that they would 'look with contempt on the present miserable effort to withdraw public attention from *The Times* libel'.

In England as a whole, reaction was inevitably more quizzical, though apprehensive of another vindication for Parnell in the style of the Pigott affair. 'A party whose chief is a prospective co-respondent is rather like a waterlogged ship,' wrote the *Pall Mall Gazette* on the same day – adding, however, 'but charges can be brought against any man.' What Edward Hamilton wrote in his diary two days later was probably a fairly typical view of those Englishmen who knew anything of the situation. He said that the affair had been known about for almost as long as it had been going on, that O'Shea had 'winked at' the relations between Parnell and his wife so long as he thought Parnell could help him, and only when 'the friendship' between them came to an end did O'Shea find anything wrong – that was really all there was to it. Give or take a few nuances, the most important of which was the significance of Aunt Ben's longevity, this was not an inaccurate summary. But Hamilton was an Englishman and a Protestant; in Ireland such sophistication was not easily acceptable.

There were doubtless many who thought like Parnell's doctor, Joseph Kenny. On the same day as Hamilton wrote that entry in his diary, Kenny wrote to Dillon to say that he neither knew nor cared whether the allegations of adultery were true but they must stand by Parnell as leader at all costs. For those like Healy, O'Brien, Sexton and T. P. O'Connor who had known quite well what was going on even before the Galway election, this need to concentrate on loyalty to the leadership banished the allegations themselves to an obscurity which amounted to a sort of faith. It was a party faith which received immeasurable comfort from the unequivocal, if somewhat Delphic, reassurances given by Parnell himself to leading members that everything would turn out all right in the end and he would triumph just as he had done over the Pigott forgeries. He told Davitt, who was widely considered the most openly honourable member of the party, that he would come out of it all 'without a stain on his name or reputation'; and Davitt believed him. He told O'Brien, 'If this case is ever fully gone into, a matter which is exceedingly doubtful, you may rest assured that it will be shown that the dishonour and the discredit have not been on my side.' And this message, passed on by two such respected figures as Davitt and O'Brien, was enough for a party which so much wanted to believe that what Parnell said was true.

That Parnell himself believed what he said is unquestionable. He could not otherwise have been so successful in convincing others. This ability to transmit his own way of looking at things, regardless of the realities, to people who were looking to him for a lead had long been one of his greatest strengths. The way in which he looked on his relationship with his 'wife' did indeed involve no stain or dishonour for him – though this was hardly the way most Irish Catholics were likely to look at the matter. But it was here that the reassurances he had given to Davitt and O'Brien worked their all-important effect, for it was not now only his own authority but that of the party that was behind his 'innocence'.

Over the years, and particularly since the general election of 1885, the party had acquired from Parnell a real authority in its own right in Ireland. In February 1890 it passed a resolution unanimously expressing confidence in 'the wisdom, honour and integrity of our great leader'. There was thus a double conviction behind the majority of the Irish people's faith in their leader – that provided by Parnell personally and that by the party. The faith could reasonably be called blind. For the nine months that now elapsed before the case was heard, Parnell's reputation in Ireland remained intact and was even enhanced by what many saw as this new dastardly English threat.

The inevitably abject surrender at the beginning of February by *The Times* in its response to his libel action, involving it in a payment of £5,000 (£225,000 in today's terms) and costs, followed by the publication less than a fortnight later of the Special Commission's report, which, for all its criticism of the party and the Land League, unequivocally exonerated Parnell of the most serious charges against him, strengthened the illusion that the divorce action too could only end in triumph.

When on 11 February Parliament met, in the knowledge of *The Times*'s capitulation, he was received with wild enthusiasm by the sixty Irish Members present, and the meeting of the party that day was judged by the *Freeman's Journal* to have been 'a demonstration of . . . confidence in his wisdom, honour and integrity'. Two days later the Special Commission Report was made public and he received another great welcome as he entered the House of Commons. As he walked along the benches to his place, the whole of the Liberal Party, above and below the gangway, stood and bowed in respect to him, including Gladstone himself, turning towards him with one hand leaning on the table. 'Always mysterious, always inscrutable, always enigmatical', as the *Freeman's Journal* correspondent described Parnell that day, he took not the slightest notice of them and when he rose to speak later that afternoon, again to wild cheering from his own Members, he made no reference to the incident at all. In such a climate of personal triumph it was hardly surprising that people came to think of him as incapable of anything less. Even the Catholic Church voiced no serious qualms. Dr Walsh, the Archbishop of Dublin since 1885, was told simply of Davitt's report that Parnell was 'quite certain that he is going to come off with flying colours and that the whole thing is to break down'.

What reason could Parnell possibly have, apart from self-confidence in his own view of the truth, for allowing people like Davitt and O'Brien to believe such a thing and to pass on their belief without reservation? The answer was: his accurate enough assessment of Willie's character and his financial susceptibilities. Willie had indeed allied himself with the other O'Sheas in their contest of Aunt Ben's will and had on the one hand, as he had unabashedly explained to Cardinal Manning, had everything to gain from publicity on the affair now. On the other hand, the expectations he might have from a divided action against the will were by definition uncertain, limited and, above all, subject to the law's delays, whereas ready money was always his principal need. The settlement he would clearly prefer would be a private one by which, in return for a substantial sum in hand, he would agree to drop the divorce case, or even – and this was clearly the far more desirable solution for Parnell, being one which would remove all further need for furtive cohabitation and permit Katie to become Mrs Parnell – agree to be divorced on grounds of adultery, which might well not be hard to prove.

It was a not unreasonable hypothesis, and over the next nine months certain elementary steps were taken to secure its implementation.

The only possible flaw in the reasoning was the practical one that, although Katie was now nominally a wealthy woman, and far more likely to win her full inheritance from the contest over the will if no longer a respondent in a divorce case, she would not actually be able to get hold of the money until that contest was settled. It is odd that no steps seem to have been taken, in the form perhaps of arranged loans, to prepare for this.

A similar error of omission seems hard to understand on the side of the party. As Conor Cruise O'Brien has emphasized, it is not in itself odd that Ireland and the party, in the circumstances, should have been able to display the faith they did; what is odd is that astute politicians, particularly those with some inside knowledge of the affair, should have developed no contingency plans for the possibility of Parnell proving wrong about the divorce court. Their leader's self-confidence had almost somnambulistically become their own.

On other matters the gap between Parnell and his party could seem at times in the intervening months as wide as ever, though, in the curious way that had by now become the norm, there was no outward sign of division. His absences both from the House of Commons and from political activity in Ireland continued both to mystify and to be accepted. His no longer even ambiguous distance from the Plan of Campaign retained its sharpness, and was indeed given a new edge in the summer of 1890. After a phase of absence from the House in no way now unusual, even though the Irish Estimates had been under discussion and had involved Irish Members in vituperative clashes with the Government, he unexpectedly turned up and made an offer to Balfour about which he had consulted none of his colleagues and which now shocked and amazed them, proposing to cooperate with Balfour rather than fight him, and bring this agrarian agitation to an end by giving the tenants the benefits of the last Land Purchase Act.

The general amazement was compounded by the half-hearted way in which he made this approach to the enemy of Home Rule whom he and the Liberals were trying to get out of office so that Home Rule could be passed.

'I dare say . . .' he said, referring to the Irish Members he was supposed to be leading, 'I dare say my Hon. Friends would prefer to fight it out . . . I have little doubt that my suggestion will have been made in vain, but I shall have the satisfaction of knowing that the responsibility will not rest on me.' Curious words for a leader about his own party. John Morley commented, 'It is difficult enough for him to be absent and inaccessible, but if besides that when he does appear . . . to plunge into unexplained politics – it's too bad!'

But the significant thing about the episode was that when the *New York Times* published a highly critical article, written by an American journalist friend of Healy's, in which it was suggested that this 'astonishing and contemptuous act of treachery of Parnell's towards his colleagues was the product of mental disturbance' and that he might be about to retire from the leadership, a strong denial and rejection of any such thoughts was immediately issued in the name of the party and signed by three of its most prominent men – Sexton, Dillon and O'Brien – though not Healy.

Through other events of that summer, Parnell continued aloof. Aloofness turned out no apparent disadvantage, which perhaps helped him justify his wish to remain so. Dillon and O'Brien were prosecuted for their activity in the Plan of Campaign and skipped bail, escaping first to France and then to America to raise money. Parnell, who seems to have had wind that they intended to do this, took care to keep out of everyone's way at the time, being dissociated anyway from the Plan of Campaign, so that he could be accused neither of encouraging nor of opposing the move. Similarly, though the party for which he was nominally responsible was in trouble that summer with the Church, both for a certain raggedness in its political behaviour and for its insufficient regard for the Church itself, he took care totally to ignore such criticisms so that his identification with the party was able to seem as complete as ever without actually being so.

In this curious manner his authority in Ireland prospered by default. Ireland waited not for the divorce court but for that Home Rule which he had made a near reality and which was to be implemented when Gladstone and the Liberals won the next election. Even his long absence from Ireland could be rationalized, for, unlike those early Home Rulers in the days before the party came under his control, he had not, it appeared, been corrupted by the English scene. It could be seen as necessary for him to be there – it was the place where he had to be to see Home Rule through. But it was of course also the place to which with Katie O'Shea he was now, as it were, wedded. And the extent of that commitment was still, on the whole, a public secret.

At the same time it is remarkable, in view of the shock with which the news of their association was to hit public life, that, according to Katie's memoirs, it was by no means unknown to the man in the street. The *Pall Mall Gazette* article had brought souvenir-hunters for Parnell relics to Eltham. They devastated the garden. Later, when the two of them had moved into Walsingham Terrace in Brighton, with its view westwards over cornfields all the way to Shoreham, she says that, though they used to go out walking at special times to avoid attention, she was nevertheless always rather proud of the popular interest in him.

How else were they spending these months in which they waited to deal with Willie's petition for divorce at the end of the year, and during which Parnell's attendances in the House of Commons were so much less demanding than once they had been? They lived the lives more of a retired middle-aged couple than of figures at the centre of events. Such political work as engrossed him he did at a roll-top desk in the dining-room, but in the basement he had a furnace where he assayed for gold in the ore from his Wicklow hills. Katie feared that the heat there was bad for his health, but used to have difficulty getting him to leave the place for rides on his horse President with his dogs on the Sussex Downs. The blurred chronology of her narrative does not make it clear whether he went over in this year to Avondale for the shooting at Aughavannah which she says he liked to do for a few days every year – but only for a few days, 'because he could not bear to be away from me for longer'. She in turn liked to pack him hams and tongues and rugs to take with him, always with a new spirit-kettle for tea.

Books on mechanics and engineering were probably still largely his leisure reading, and it is possible that his touchingly boyish experiments with the design for a boat to be fitted with some form of stabilizer for passenger comfort, which he tried out off the Brighton Chain Pier, were then in progress. Certainly a sombre and dramatic account of a wild day together trying out the boat from that pier stems from a period when they were worried about their future, and reveals not only the attractive persistence of his amateurish scientific efforts but a momentary glimpse of the intimacy of their life together in turbulent times.

A great storm was blowing round the pier as he tried in vain to launch the floats, and as the huge waves hit the pier-head Parnell remarked, or so she says, that 'the old place could not last long', and for a moment he picked her up and held her over the sea, fantasizing about jumping in with her so that they could be free for ever. 'As you will, my only love,' she says she replied, 'but the children?'

The incident does not quite tally with the mood of confident optimism he so consistently expressed throughout this year but, if only perhaps as a somewhat contrived allegory for the future, it may have a place in the record, at a time when his colleagues periodically wondered what it was that was keeping him from politics. It is also the only passage in her two volumes of memoirs in which Katie makes even an implied reference to their two living daughters.

Only five days before the divorce action was due to begin, Morley had a long and wide-ranging talk with Parnell, who came to see him in the

Brighton hotel where he was staying. He found Parnell in such a genial, open mood that he invited him to stay for dinner, and Parnell accepted. When at the end of dinner, having discussed at length aspects of the future Home Rule Bill, Morley asked him if 'certain legal proceedings' were likely to lead to his disappearance from the leadership for a time, Parnell replied in similar terms to those with which he had reassured Davitt and O'Brien, only this time even more explicitly: 'Oh no. No chance of it. Nothing in the least leading to disappearance . . . The other side don't know what a broken-kneed horse they are riding.'

It was a metaphor which Willie himself would have found particularly offensive, but it was aptly taken by Morley, who had heard disturbing stories of the sort of evidence the ex-Hussar's counsel had collected. He wrote to Gladstone to tell him the good news.

What had made it possible for Parnell to be so completely confident so shortly before the case broke, bringing with it disaster not only for him but for the prospects of nationalism in Ireland?

There can be no doubt whatever that, as in his reassurances to Davitt, O'Brien and others, he was being totally sincere. But a caveat needs to be entered at once about what Parnell's sincerity, in this instance, meant. As always, he was taking it for granted that the way in which he looked at things was the way in which others on his side would look at them too. He sincerely saw himself as having done nothing dishonourable in living adulterously for ten years with a woman who wanted to live with him and whose husband's feelings were apparently confined to his financial concern for his family's future. Moreover, that husband had for at least the first four years of the adulterous liaison sought to benefit from the political influence of the Irish leader it brought with it. It was true that such scorn as, in this analysis, could be directed at the husband for not being prepared to surrender the marriage for financial reasons could equally well be directed at the wife – and, indeed, at Parnell himself for going along with her wishes. But perhaps concern for the family's future could be presented as more morally acceptable in her case. What of course was not quite acceptable in this analysis, as Parnell might have presented it, was the assumption that Willie's feelings were not at some level affected. The 'My Dick'/'Your Boysie' relationship which had at least persisted between 1882 and 1886 was real enough. But then it seems possible that Parnell attached no significance at all to these pet names or the attitudes expressed in them. If so, he could with a clear conscience – at least as he saw it – say that the adulterous liaison broke no moral code.

However, as other people saw it, particularly in Catholic Ireland and in

Nonconformist Britain, adultery itself was the only moral issue, and all other considerations attending it were irrelevant. It is hard to see that even Parnell could have expected people in either country to accept as valid the concept of a justifiable – even moral – adultery, however explained. Certainly in reassuring Morley he meant something more practical than this.

What, in short, he meant was that Willie could be bribed into dropping the case and would thereafter agree to be divorced himself, thus permitting the present respondent and co-respondent to marry. This would by no means look irreproachable in Catholic Ireland, confirming as it would what the Church regarded as an adulterous liaison. But, in the circumstances, it could be tolerated in a Protestant – particularly in a Protestant with such calls on Irish public loyalty as Parnell. What steps, then, had been taken to get Willie to comply? Why, only five days after the meeting with Morley, was the most disastrous possible tactical course pursued?

Chapter 42

Parnell and Katie had had almost a year in which to decide how to deal with Willie's action in the divorce court. It is still difficult to find a sound rationale in what they allowed to happen.

There was an initial problem: they had at one time taken different views about what they wanted to happen. Parnell, so Katie told Henry Harrison in 1891 and recorded in her memoirs, wished above all for there to be a divorce so that he could marry her – if necessary allowing Willie to win his case. He seems partly to have thought he could let this happen, appearing himself as co-respondent, without incurring political disaster. But it was the other possibility, of persuading Willie to drop his case by offering him money, which presumably had lain behind Parnell's assurances to Morley. The earlier assurances to Davitt seem based primarily on Parnell's own moral interpretation of the case, namely that he was a truer husband to Katie than Willie – always an improbable starting-point for Catholic Ireland.

If for some reason it were to prove impossible to buy Willie off, the next best solution would be for Katie to bring a counter-claim for divorce against Willie. She told Harrison that she had had seventeen cases of Willie's infidelity. But she also told him and wrote in her memoirs that she did not want a divorce, because she feared it would injure Parnell. To bring a counter-action without first buying Willie off could certainly have been injurious. So for a time their tactics were concentrated on trying to bribe Willie.

Katie told Harrison that if she could have got £20,000 (some £900,000 today) to give to Willie, 'his charges against me would have failed and my counter-charges against him would have succeeded'. Presumably he would then have agreed to be divorced without bringing any counter-charges of his own. Willie himself told his own counsel, Sir Edward Clarke, that £20,000 was the sum he had been offered to drop the suit. Clarke said in his memoirs that he thought up to the very last moment that Willie would not appear in court. This would have made his case fail and the whole business seem indeed like a plot in the style of the Pigott affair, foundering in face of Parnell's stern moral probity. After the case, Willie told Chamberlain about the efforts that had been made to dissuade him from bringing it. 'Nobody except myself', he wrote, 'knows what a fight it was or the influences, religious, social and pecuniary, that were brought to bear in the hope of "squaring" me. The last offer was made to me through my son the evening before the trial and was equivalent to over £60,000.' Of course such 'a fight' showed at least that he must have been seriously considering taking the money.

The trouble for both Parnell and Katie was that neither of them could raise £20,000, let alone £60,000. Though Katie had indeed inherited a fortune from her aunt, the probate case being brought against her by the rest of her family froze the money and made it impossible for her to get at it. For Willie it was a risky business to agree to accept a bribe that was only a promissory note; the probate case would not be heard for some time, and if Katie were to lose it her credit would prove worthless. It was safer for Willie to join the rest of the family's suit against Katie and perhaps improve their chances of winning by allowing the divorce case to go ahead. The embarrassing details could certainly make it seem that Aunt Ben had been much deceived in the circumstances in which she had been led to bequeath Katie her fortune.

Why Parnell should have been able to be so confident so late that Willie could be bought off when the money was not available cannot be explained, unless there were some now unknown other possibility of borrowing the sum or otherwise getting hold of it. The problem caused by the probate suit cannot have occurred to them only at the last moment. Whatever the truth about this, the fact remains that until the very last moment – which means the moment of the opening of the court on Saturday 15 November 1890 – all concerned had been expecting Parnell and Katie to appear to contest the case.

The grounds for contesting it filed by Katie less than a fortnight before were, one might have thought, the very worst on which to try to do so. Adultery was denied and at the same time it was said that Willie had 'constantly connived at and was accessory to the said alleged adultery from the Autumn of 1880 to the Spring of 1886, by inducing, directing, and requiring the respondent to form the acquaintance of the co-respondent and to see him alone in the interest and for the advantage of the petitioner'. Cruelty by neglect was also alleged. The plea of connivance – an admission automatically of the 'alleged' adultery, if successfully presented – would in no circumstances have been allowable as grounds for her to divorce him. It would simply have preserved the marriage which Parnell himself was determined should end.

Their position thus seemed dangerously muddled. The muddle was compounded by the fact that Katie had added to her counter-plea one single charge of adultery, and that was against her sister, Anna Steele, who was of course a party to the family probate case against her. This looks merely like spite, and relations between the two sisters were certainly strained because of the probate case, as Harrison was able afterwards to see for himself. But if she were going to enter a counter-plea about Willie's adultery, why not the sixteen other infidelities of which she told Harrison she had cognizance? If brought at all, Willie's action was going acutely to embarrass Parnell politically, but in what actually happened he had the worst of all possible worlds.

They had both seen Katie's counsel, Sir Frank Lockwood, the day before the court opened, and before leaving they had promised that they would telegraph him by eight o'clock the following morning if he were to enter an appearance for them – the court opening at ten o'clock. That evening they went back to Brighton in a crowded Pullman. Katie, suffering from a splitting headache, found that the furtive glances of others looking at them from behind their newspapers had an uncanny effect on her, making her feel her fellow passengers were animals watching from their lairs. When they got home, Parnell sent her to bed, first giving her a glass of sparkling moselle to sip for her headache. After his own dinner he came up and smoked beside her bed while she tried to persuade him to go up to the court in the morning. 'What's the use?' he said. 'We want the divorce, and, divorce or not, I shall always come where you are.' He read her to sleep.

Next morning, she woke up after a long sleep to find him sitting beside her with her letters and tea and toast. She asked him what they were to do. He replied with a quiet laugh, 'I've done you this time, Queenie; I sent the telegram long ago, and they must be enjoying themselves in Court by now!'

Just as she had noticed that in the Pullman the day before he had seemed quite unconscious of the eyes darting at him from behind newspapers, so now, she said, he faced what was likely to come out of the hearing with total calm – even relief. Many years later she summarized what he had been saying to her that night. Although obviously not word for word, her account has an authentic ring. He told her to have no regrets for whatever might come out of the divorce for his public life:

I have given, and will give, Ireland what is in me to give. That I have vowed to her, but my private life shall never belong to any country, but to one woman.

There will be a howl, but it will be the howling of hypocrites; not altogether, for some of these Irish fools are genuine in their belief that forms and creeds can govern life and men; perhaps they are right so far as they can experience life. But I am not as they, for they are among the world's children. I am a man, and I have told these children what they want, and they clamour for it. If they will let me, I will get it for them. But if they turn from me, my Queen, it matters not at all in the end. What the ultimate government of Ireland will be is settled, and it will be so, and what my share in the work has been and is to be, also. I do wish you would stop fretting about me.

The court met next morning, Saturday 15 November. One of Willie's lawyers opened the proceedings by stating the plea and the earlier responses of both Katie and Parnell in which they denied adultery and to which Katie had added the charges of connivance, of Willie's own adultery (with Anna Steele) and of 'cruelty'. He was followed by Katie's counsel, Lockwood. He announced that he appeared for her, 'and I desire to take this opportunity of stating on her behalf that I do not intend to cross-examine any witnesses, to call in witnesses, nor to take any part in these proceedings'.

Sir Edward Clarke, representing Willie, said that this was as much news to him as it was to the court itself. Mr Justice Butt said it was news to him too. He asked if anyone was appearing for Parnell. No answer came from the court. Parnell was not represented. Whereupon, since Katie's solicitor was not going to intervene either, Willie's counsel was free to make the very most of the case. This he proceeded very successfully to do over that Saturday and the following Monday.

This disastrous course of action on Parnell and Katie's part had the sole advantage for them – all-important to Parnell – that they would be able to marry within six months of the decree. There was also an advantage for historical truth. Willie and the witnesses his counsel was about to call had all expected to be cross-examined in court. What they had come to say was already conditioned by anticipation of this. Willie, for instance, had put his diaries into court, expecting to be able to use them to substantiate his evidence. He was not in fact called upon to produce them; but it is unlikely that he would have put them into court, expecting cross-examination, if they had not in fact substantiated what he had to say in evidence. What is now of principal interest is the extent to which they might have confirmed what appears from many of the letters between him and Katie now read in court, namely that their relations continued at least until 1886 to be at times more affectionate than Parnell might have been happy to know about. Except, of course, that he could now read them in the newspaper reports of the case and it did not seem to worry him in the least.

Divorce cases in those days were heard before juries. Towards the end of the case, on 17 November, all evidence had apparently been called and Mr Justice Butt was preparing to send the jury out to consider their verdict when one of the jurors got up and addressed him. He said he could not see how all doubts about some of the counter-charges could be dispelled if there were no cross-examination of some of the witnesses. He would like Captain O'Shea himself to be cross-examined on this point. 'We are asked', he said, 'to decide on the question of the petitioner's neglect of his wife, my Lord, and I should like particularly to ask some questions as to that charge of neglect.'

The Judge allowed Willie to be recalled. His counsel, Sir Edward Clarke, agreed that any member of the jury could ask him questions. But he himself first further put to him the point about neglect and the separate living arrangements at Albert Mansions and Wonersh Lodge.

'During the whole time until the actual discovery of your wife's unfaithfulness, had you been living on perfectly friendly and affectionate terms with her?'

'Certainly.'

Willie said he had put some seven hundred letters between himself and his wife into court and had been in constant communication with her. 'Among these letters are a number of telegrams from Mrs O'Shea about her coming up to visit me and dine with me and all the rest of it. In none of those letters did Mrs O'Shea ever complain of the arrangement made between us.'

He said he used to go down to Eltham on Sundays 'and often besides, and Mrs O'Shea and my daughters constantly came up to Albert Mansions'.

The juryman who had first spoken then got up again and pressed him on the point. Willie said he did not mean that he had returned to his family every night from Albert Mansions. He had been constantly at Wonersh Lodge until he got into Parliament in 1880, and since then, he said, 'No one has ever made the slightest pretence that there was a want of attention on my part. In fact my diaries show clearly that I was a kind husband and a kind father. The diaries are put in and would be enough to satisfy anybody.'

This juryman seemed to have some doubt of Willie's integrity. Only once, however – and then without apparently realizing it – did he extract from him a certain shiftiness. The juryman asked how it was that, having challenged Parnell to a duel in 1881, Willie then invited him to dinner again. To which Willie replied that he did not. 'The dinner you refer to', he said, 'was before that.'

'But then', persisted the juryman, 'your evidence shows that you had him to dinner after that.'

'Certainly,' replied Willie: 'I did so because it appeared to me at the time that there was no foundation for my suspicions.'

'Did you often meet Mr Parnell at other times in London? Did he say to you, "I was dining at your house last night"?'

'Never, never,' replied Willie.

The evidence at the Special Commission of the letter Parnell had written from Kilmainham about his failure to find Willie at Albert Mansions on his way back from Eltham implied that this was less than the truth. But the point was not taken up. Earlier, questioned by his own counsel, Willie had denied that Parnell had gone straight to Eltham from Kilmainham when released on parole, whereas in his evidence to the Special Commission he had said that Parnell had.

'I suppose', the juryman now went on, 'there are hundreds of other letters that passed between you and your wife but have not been produced in court?'

'No, they are all in court even if they haven't been read.'

Another juror rose.

'Would you kindly give us the last date at which you lived with your wife? It appears that you stayed at the Queen's Hotel, Eastbourne, in June 1886. I should like to know on what later date you were with your wife?'

'I was with her at Brighton in the Autumn of that year at the Bristol, I think.'

'Would you kindly say whether that was the last occasion on which you lived with your wife?'

'Yes, that was the last occasion, but I have constantly seen her since.'

It is at this moment above all in the proceedings that the absence of professional cross-examination must be regretted. Letters between Willie and Katie earlier quoted in court had shown them to be writing to each other that autumn, in both September and October 1886, in much less affectionate terms than they had been using up till then; it was now 'Dear Kate' and 'Dear Willie', and they were signing themselves 'Yours, W. H. O'Shea' and 'Yours, K. O'Shea' while they disputed over whether she should formally renounce seeing Parnell. Had this then been followed by some last attempt at reconciliation at Brighton that autumn? If so, was it at least an attempt on her part to show Willie that, if the affair with Parnell continued, he need not feel wholly excluded? Evidence from his diary might have clarified the matter. It must now remain part of that opaqueness in which the triangular relationship is fixed for posterity.

As for the body of the evidence, the story of the way in which Parnell and Katie had had to conduct their lives for the past nine years was now specifically detailed for the first time. It became possible for the public to assess the strange mixture of prevarication and assurance that had attended their long domesticity. Few of the seven hundred letters in court were read out; more than six hundred which might have filled in the truth about much in the history of their intimacy are lost, apparently for ever. Many of the details which then emerged for the public were a surprise even to those in the world of politics and journalism who had at least been aware of the outline of the situation for a long time. The incident of the duel was recounted; the sleeping arrangements at Wonersh Lodge were detailed; it was established that Katie sometimes left Wonersh Lodge and was away all night when Parnell was not there either. The dates of birth of the three children of the first part of the marriage were listed, and Sir Edward Clarke, in a way he did not elaborate, thought it important to note that no child was born after Carmen in 1874 until another, who died, in February 1882. 'My daughter Clare', said Willie, was born in March 1883, and 'the youngest child' was born in November 1884. The various addresses at which Parnell and Katie had been together were listed – Brighton, Eastbourne, Brockley, Regent's Park – and the necessary witnesses were called to confirm their presence there, with Parnell figuring under the various simple aliases he had adopted from time to time – 'Smith', 'Stewart', 'Preston'.

Servants were called to relate how Parnell had stayed in the house at night with Katie when Willie had not been there. One related how Parnell, whom she recognized from a photograph produced, came to the house in Bedford Square, Brighton, every day she had been there. Another, from a house at Medina Terrace, Brighton, said that Mr Parnell 'never slept in the house when Captain O'Shea was at home, but he did so frequently when Captain O'Shea was away'.

Such phrases were no more than predictable accounts of everyday living for two people locked into a love affair which for many reasons needed to be kept private. But such stories inevitably acquired colour in the telling, elicited as they were by experienced counsel from witnesses drawn from the ordinary world into a lurid limelight, and not subject to cross-examination.

What was to become the most notorious incident of all was that of the servant Caroline Pethers, a widow then living at Cheltenham who had been the cook at Medina Terrace, Brighton, between November 1883 and February 1884. Her husband, then living, had been the manservant.

Two or three days after Captain and Mrs O'Shea had taken the house, she said, a gentleman appeared. She too recognized him from his photograph. 'He went then by the name of Mr Charles Stewart. Sometimes, he called when Captain O'Shea was at home, nearly always when he was away and always came to the house the beach way.'

This incidentally seems to suggest that, inasmuch as the Captain would almost certainly have known that the servant knew Parnell only as 'Mr Stewart', he was privy at least to deceit about his true identity.

'Mr Stewart' wore a light cloth cap over his eyes. He drove out at night with Mrs O'Shea, but never in the daytime.

It was Caroline Pethers who then provided the detail which epitomized the devastating humiliation for Parnell in all this evidence. She told the story of how the Captain had come one day and rung the front doorbell when Parnell and Katie were locked in the drawing-room together in the dark. Pethers's husband let the Captain in, and he went upstairs. Ten minutes later, she said, Parnell himself rang the front doorbell and asked to see Captain O'Shea. The only way he could have managed to be there, according to her, was by the use of two rope fire-escapes on the balcony outside the drawing-room. She said this had happened three or four times. It has been generally discounted as an invention, though it may only have been an elaboration of the truth. Willie himself later told the actor Beerbohm Tree, 'and the best of it was there was no fire-escape'. His son Gerard, on the other hand, while saying that the rooms in that house did have fire-escapes, and mentioning this at the time of the divorce to his father's solicitor as a possible explanation of Parnell's magical reappearance in the cook's story, thought it more likely that he would simply have slipped down the stairs to the basement, from where he could make his way on to the beach and back again. Certainly the fire-escape improved the story, delighted the music-hall and completed the destructive impact of the divorce.

There were other curious details. The various deceits practised seemed sometimes to have confused Parnell himself. In January 1887 an auctioneer in business at Deptford named George Porter, who acted as an agent for a landlord in Brockley, Kent, was told by his servant that a Mr Fox had called to see him one day while he was out. He said he would come back another day. When Mr Fox did return, he was the man Porter now knew to be Mr Charles Stewart Parnell. Porter took his prospective client to a house at 112 Tressillian Road, Brockley, and said he thought it might suit him. 'It belongs to a Mr Preston,' he added.

'That is my name.'

'I understood your name was Fox.'

'No. Fox is the name of the person with whom I was staying, but my name is Clement Preston.'

Preston/Fox/Parnell decided to take the house. But he refused to give any references, saying that a man with horses ought not to be called upon for references, and he had never given references before. He eventually agreed to pay fifty pounds down and took 112 Tressillian Road for twelve months.

This strangely inconsequential surface of his and Katie's rock-like liaison is further illustrated by some evidence from the housekeeper Katie employed there for at least five months, together with her husband who acted as coachman. This woman, Susan Honey, said that 'Mr Preston' came there from time to time, as did the lady who employed her, who was said to be 'Mr Preston's sister'. This 'sister' never slept there. She was the woman who had interviewed her for the job in a first-class waiting-room at Cannon Street station.

The element of farce in much of the case made the moral obloquy resting upon the formerly dignified figure of Parnell all the heavier. His failure to appear in court at all was something Sir Edward Clarke made the most of. Parnell 'had not even thought fit to appear . . . allowed judgement to go by default'. Implying that Parnell would have had to perjure himself, he commented, 'For some persons the criminal law has terrors which the moral law has not, and it is perhaps not to be wondered at that Mr Parnell does not venture to add a criminal offence to that course of faithlessness and falsehood by which during those years he has betrayed the wife of the friend who trusted him.'

There was a brief appearance by Katie's sister, Anna Steele, to rebut totally the unpursued counter-charge of adultery with her brother-in-law. The Judge summed up in the only way logical in the light of the uncontradicted evidence. The jury came to its conclusion almost at once: adultery and no connivance.

The political effect of these two days in the divorce court was to be understandably so devastating that Henry Harrison later strenuously sought to prove that behind Willie's decision to take action there lay a political conspiracy to which Chamberlain had been a conscious party.

While a divorce action with Parnell as co-respondent was clearly a prospect to be watched with some optimism by Liberal-Unionists, and at least one journalist in the summer of 1889 was asked what he thought the political effect of Captain O'Shea taking proceedings might be, Parnell's biographer, F. S. L. Lyons, insists convincingly that 'no solid evidence . . . has ever emerged to demonstrate the existence of such a conspiracy'.

That the action, as things turned out, did indeed destroy not only the rest of Parnell's political career but the chances of success for Irish nationalism for more than two decades was due to nothing so complex as a political conspiracy. It was due primarily to the simple human fact that Katie and Parnell had fallen in love in a way that was irrevocable, and Willie would have preferred them not to have done so.

And how on 17 November did the two of them react when they heard that the case was over? That morning's *Times* had contained seven full columns of the most lurid details of the uncontested evidence against them. The *decree nisi* was brought to Walsingham Terrace by her local solicitor that evening. 'We were very happy that evening,' Katie wrote, 'and Parnell declared he would have the "decree" framed.'

She teased him by saying that now she had been 'set completely free' he might want to marry someone else, but he did not think that funny.

Chapter 43

The sense of shock and confusion with which all sections of Irish nationalist opinion reacted to the shattering revelations in the divorce court was such that almost everyone's immediate instinct was to cover it up and present an outer picture of unity while inwardly trying to deal with their dismay. The only public figure who seemed effortlessly convinced that no serious political damage had been done was, typically, Parnell himself, who on the very day on which the first humiliating details became available in the newspapers, Monday 17 November, issued a flat statement saying nothing about the case but simply summoning members of the party to the usual eve-of-session meeting in London on 25 November. The nationalist newspapers themselves, verbally reeling, pledged continuing loyalty to Parnell as leader. The leader himself spent 'a happy evening' with Katharine in Brighton.

An impromptu party meeting in Dublin presided over by the party Vice-Chairman, Justin McCarthy, passed a unanimous resolution declaring that 'in all political matters [Parnell had] the confidence of the Irish nation'. Behind the scenes, though, McCarthy was anxious. It was a situation in which tensions in the party long present since the Galway election and active behind the front of Parnell's later magisterial remoteness were all too likely to spring dangerously to the surface.

Tim Healy was ill in Dublin with typhoid. A group of nationalists called on him to sound out his views in order to save him from having to leave his home for a big public meeting called at Leinster Hall for 20 November. They found him indignant at the highly critical moral tone of much of the English press – Liberal as well as Conservative – with its call for Parnell's resignation from the leadership. He said he was determined to teach 'these damned Non-conformists to mind their own business'. He not only came to the meeting and drafted the resolution in favour of Parnell which was to be carried unanimously; he also made a powerfully emotional speech in support of it, rousing the audience to a great demonstration of enthusiastic patriotic loyalty to their leader, and setting the tone for Irish public opinion for some days to come. This was soon to seem ironical.

'If', Healy asked, 'the Irish people and the Irish Party who have been ten years under the leadership of this man and who have been accused of harbouring all kinds of sinister ambitions, of greedy desires to pull him down, if we joined with this howling pack, would that be a noble spectacle before the nations?'

He ended by telling the audience, to great cheering, 'not to speak to the man at the wheel'. Earlier in his speech, however, he had at least dropped a word in the man at the wheel's ear about what he thought it might be appropriate for him to do in return for such support. 'Were Mr Parnell', he said, 'to resign his seat for Cork, he would be instantly re-elected and, if he were re-elected for Cork, would not his re-election to his former position to his colleagues follow as a matter of course?' A cable expressing confidence in Parnell from five of the six MPs then fund-raising in the United States, which had been read out to the meeting, helped complete a premature sense of triumph. But Healy's idea that some temporary resignation on the part of Parnell in due atonement for what the *Nation*, while backing him, called 'the heinousness of the offence', gained ground behind the scenes. Even Davitt – the one prominent nationalist who had come out openly and strongly against Parnell – only demanded his resignation for a few months.

That Parnell should resign, and not just temporarily, was the view of the Catholic Church, in which feelings among the hierarchy understandably ran high. On the day after the Leinster Hall meeting, Dr Croke, the nationalist Archbishop of Cashel, threw a bust of Parnell out of his hall where it had had a prominent place. He told Dr Walsh, the Archbishop of Dublin, that he had 'flung him away from me for ever'. Dr Walsh himself, while wary of making a public political intervention which could compromise the Church's own popularity, thought that the initial display of support at the nationalist meeting had been quite enough and that it was time for Parnell to 'do the right thing and resign'. At local meetings in support of Parnell, priests were often well represented, but the general feeling among bishops was, as the Bishop of Ardagh put it, 'A man false to God and to friendship cannot be expected to be true to his country – and especially that country being Catholic Ireland.'

What chance was there that Parnell would in fact agree to withdraw from the scene, at least for a time? With the knowledge of his character available to posterity, it is easy to see that there was none. Twice before the party meeting summoned at Westminster for 25 November the *Freeman's Journal* stated that, despite rumours, there was no question of him doing so. The second time was on the morning of the meeting itself.

An English journalist watched him walk through the Lobby of the House that day 'looking better than is his wont, seeming perfectly at ease, and reciprocating with all his old coolness the friendly greetings accorded to him by some of his political friends'.

At this meeting, after only one ineffectual attempt from an undistinguished member of the party to get him to resign for the time being, Parnell was unanimously confirmed as Chairman. When he rose to great cheering to thank them for their loyalty, he had them, as one present described it, 'hypnotized'. He managed somehow virtually to repeat the confidence trick with which he had reassured Davitt, O'Brien and others many months earlier, saying that when the time came (i.e. when the decree nisi became absolute in six months' time) he would make the case look very different from how it seemed at the moment and be able 'to hold my head as high, and aye, even higher, than ever before in the face of the world'. He said that there was no question of him having destroyed the O'Sheas' domestic bliss, which was more or less true, and that O'Shea had never been his friend, which was more or less not. Indeed he said that, since they first met O'Shea had been 'my bitter relentless enemy', which was patently false.

Despite what the *Freeman's Journal* had reiterated only that morning, many at the meeting seem to have thought that he would end by saying he was going to resign. One wrote that same day, 'Up to a minute before Parnell finished his address I thought he would conclude by announcing his resignation. We all expected it. I was led to believe it by his most devoted follower [his secretary, Henry Campbell].' This belief among a considerable number of those present helps explain the relative ease with which they had re-elected him; it also explains some of the bitterness in later stages of the crisis. 'We were being cajoled and humbugged and led to our doom with Machiavellian ingenuity,' wrote one Member later.

Parnell sat down having said nothing about resigning. It is easy in the light of what was to happen next and of the disaster that was to be the ten months left of his life to see his decision as a literally fatal mistake. Two conflicting considerations in this respect may be kept in mind when following his story to its tragic end – tragic not only for himself but for Ireland and for the next generation. The first is that it is by no means clear that, having once resigned, it would have been possible for him to return to leadership of a party which already contained so much independent ambition even when under his control, and against the inevitable hostility of the Catholic Church. Second, it was his stubbornness now which was to remove him from the scene altogether within ten months. The subsequent failure of the party without his leadership in the next twenty-five years to exploit effectively that tactical influence he had won for it within the British political system suggests that only he in charge of that party might have been able to exploit it.

In any case, he now determined to keep control of the party as if his determination alone, as so often in the past, were sufficient power. Within weeks he had engulfed himself in a spiral of self-destruction. Given his personality, it is difficult to see how he could have done anything else.

No one had been waiting for news of his resignation from the party leadership more eagerly than his English political ally Gladstone. He had been prepared to admit that in the very nature and character of the alliance it had to be the Irish themselves who were seen to take the decision. He had no doubt in his mind about what was the right one.

He had early been made aware of the difficulties likely within his own Liberal Party if the alliance were to be continued with a proven adulterer. The journalist W. T. Stead, once Editor of the *Pall Mall Gazette*, had written to him on the day of the Leinster Hall meeting of 20 November, 'I know my Non-conformists well and no power on earth will induce them to follow that man to the poll, or you either, if you are arm-in-arm with him.'

There was plenty of evidence in the press and in Gladstone's mailbag that Stead was right. That same day the *Methodist Times* carried an article which said that if the Irish race deliberately selected 'an adulterer of Mr Parnell's type' they were incapable of self-government. 'So obscene a race', it continued, 'as in these circumstances they would prove themselves to be would obviously be unfit for anything but a military despotism.'

Through John Morley, soundings had been taken from Justin McCarthy ahead of the meeting on 25 November. Morley had learned that the party was not going to throw Parnell over; voluntary withdrawal by Parnell himself would be something different. Gladstone himself had then met McCarthy the day before the meeting and conveyed that he thought the Liberals would lose the election if Parnell remained. This, he said, would put Home Rule beyond his own reach at his age. Apparently he said no more than that, although he had already written to his former Home Secretary, Harcourt, to say that Parnell's deciding to continue as leader of the Irish party would render his own continuance as leader of the Liberal Party 'little better than a nullity'.

McCarthy had left to give the message to Parnell, but Parnell had made sure that at Brighton he should be difficult to find by anyone. Gladstone decided that neither Parnell nor the Irish party should be left in any doubt at all about his attitude and wrote a letter to Morley which he was to show to Parnell. In this he said virtually the same thing as he had said to Harcourt: namely, that if Parnell continued in the leadership it would render his own [Gladstone's] leadership of the Liberal Party 'almost a nullity'. In other words, not only would the Liberals lose the next election but the alliance between the Liberals and the Irish party would have to break up, and with that would go any hope of Home Rule.

It would appear essential for Morley to catch up with Parnell in time to show him the letter before the party meeting, which was not until the afternoon of the next day, 25 November. But it turned out that he seemed unable to do so. This was odd. He certainly made an appointment with Parnell for the 25th. But Parnell, notoriously elusive anyway, could be expected in this situation to be hard to find. However, if a journalist could watch him chatting with people as he made his way through the lobbies on the way to the meeting, why could Morley not have been there looking for him? He was in fact, with the letter on him all the time, by then back with Gladstone at Carlton Gardens, where Gladstone was staying.

The explanation is possibly that Morley, hoping that Parnell would decide to retire anyway after hearing of the conversation between Gladstone and McCarthy the day before, thought that the veiled threat in the letter would thus not be necessary and might possibly antagonize him, and so felt little sense of urgency about making contact. As it was, the decision to confirm Parnell as Chairman took place without any awareness within the party of the threat.

Even if the communication had been delivered in time, it is extremely unlikely that it would have made any serious difference. Whatever exactly McCarthy may have told Parnell about his talk with Gladstone the day before – and Gladstone's friendly remarks in the course of this may have diminished its implications in the telling – Parnell's demeanour both at the meeting (where the Members were told nothing of Gladstone's latest position) and in his encounter with Morley that was to follow soon afterwards makes it clear that his instinct for independence of action was in charge, that his mind was made up and that nothing would have altered it. A disclosure of the letter at the meeting would simply have brought forward slightly that internal party crisis which in any case began to take shape a little later that evening as news of the content of the Gladstone letter spread. The letter was officially published the next day. This was equally of no special consequence, for it did nothing to change the way things were by then already going.

Morley did eventually get hold of Parnell as he came away from the meeting. Parnell apologized for not having been able to see him before but said he had got a message from him only as he came into the House, 'by which time it was too late'. Then, as they walked together down the corridor to Gladstone's room, he casually told Morley that he had just been re-elected Chairman of the party. Morley, writing an account of the interview the same day, said that as he read Gladstone's letter out to him he knew from the look on his face that he was 'obdurate'.

Parnell then gave a first glimpse of the strategy with which he intended to fight out the present crisis – very typically removing the main subject under discussion from the agenda altogether as of no real importance. As if his mind, under the impact of these events, were reverting automatically to the last time events outside the parliamentary scene had brought about a major crisis, he spoke in the sort of terms with which he had given life to the national scene ten years before, in the days of the Land League. He said that he had made up his mind to stick to the House of Commons, and to his present position in the party, until he was convinced – and he would not soon be convinced – that it was impossible to obtain Home Rule from a British parliament. And he made clear his reasons for not, even temporarily, resigning. He said, Morley recorded that day, that 'if he gave up the leadership for a time, he should never return to it; that if he once let go it was all over'. Morley added that 'his manner throughout was perfectly cool and quiet, and his unresonant voice was unshaken. He was paler than usual, and now and then a wintry smile passed over his face.'

As news of what was in Gladstone's letter began to circulate round Westminster, consternation seized members of the party who had only voted for Parnell's re-election hoping that he would afterwards temporarily resign. He was twice approached and asked to call a new meeting. He refused to do so. But a party rule made it possible for an immediate meeting to be summoned by 'requisition' if enough signatures were collected. Thirty-one members now signed such a requisition for a meeting next day, 26 November, in the afternoon. This was almost exactly half those who had been present to vote his re-election. The meeting would be held against his will. What was to alter the course of Irish history and become known as 'the Parnell split' had already begun.

When the party met on the afternoon of Wednesday 26 November, the one-time Fenian who had in the early days been one of Parnell's most faithful supporters, John Barry, moved that another formal meeting of the party be held on Friday 'to give Mr Parnell an opportunity of reconsidering his position'. Parnell simply said that he could not and would not reconsider his position, because he had been unanimously elected by the party the day before. 'It is useless to ask me. Upon the party should rest the responsibility of its vote.'

He managed to get the current meeting adjourned to Monday 1 December, by which time, he was to see to it, an entirely new situation had arisen. Sexton said that if an intelligent foreigner had entered the room while the meeting was going on he would have imagined that the entire party was being tried for adultery with Parnell as the Judge.

That night in Brighton, according to Katie, he warned her that the future was going to be 'tough' and began to work on a preliminary draft of a manifesto to the Irish people. 'The smoulder in his eyes', she said, 'grew deeper as he wrote.'

The next day, Thursday 27 November, when he went into the House of Commons he found Healy sitting there. Healy had arrived from Ireland that morning, still looking ill; but he had been getting better and presumably had stayed away from the re-election meeting of the 25th to see what adjustments were necessary to his tactical position since his Leinster Hall speech. Having read the newspapers on the 26th, he sent a telegram to that afternoon's meeting to say that Gladstone's continuance as leader of the Liberal Party was all-important.

Parnell now sat down on the benches near him but did not speak to him. The same day Healy signed a cable with Sexton to the delegation in America telling them that a large majority of the party was now going to vote for Parnell's resignation and asking for their support in the interests of 'practical unanimity'. He had already accurately gauged not only the mood of the leading men in the party, whom he found 'unanimous', but also that of Parnell himself, whom he described, when writing to his wife in Dublin that evening, as 'holding on like grim death'. Parnell would, he thought, 'cut up nastily at the finish'. Healy said he would not be surprised if Parnell took National League funds in Paris for his own purposes, or, in the case of those Members who were paid, cut off the salaries of those who opposed him.

On Friday 28 November Parnell spent the greater part of the day finalizing his manifesto at the house of one of his MPs at 31 Eccleston Street, Chester Square. Early in the day, Justin McCarthy went to see him there and found him 'very quiet outwardly', though he could see he was 'greatly excited'. Parnell talked for a time of the situation which had led up to the divorce case itself, saying that when the decree was absolute he would make a statement 'which would put him straight except for the actual crime'. If these words, which McCarthy later noted, were in fact the ones Parnell used, they reveal very clearly his failure to accept what a weak position he was in at least as far as public opinion in Catholic Ireland and Nonconformist England was concerned. There it was the actual 'crime' of adultery that mattered most; condonation, connivance or even neglect on the part of the husband were not central issues.

Talking now to a friendly and civilized colleague like McCarthy, however, these last were the only considerations he saw as relevant. He would show, he said, that in twenty-three years of married life, O'Shea had spent – in days – only a total of one year with his wife; that he had carried on with 'fast women' and had been 'quite willing to sell her to keep his seat in Parliament'. Parnell did not seem to realize that this last statement might imply that there had been a buyer. If he had 'defended' the case, he said, he would have sacrificed the one person whose interests he was bound beyond everything in the world to protect. Thus he was still seeing an impressive defence for himself in what would have been no 'defence' in law to O'Shea's suit and would, indeed, have maintained the legal marriage until Katie herself sued for divorce. Such a concerned approach might be capable of arousing moral sympathy for him in some quarters, but there was a large majority of politically minded people in both countries to point out that there was no mention of the importance of such concern in the Ten Commandments. When the decree was made absolute six months later, he no longer bothered with such a defence – it was by then far too late. His immediate subsequent marriage to her, which in his own mind made defence unnecessary, in some respects made things even worse.

His simplistic approach to the divorce indicated the alarming overconfidence with which he was now prepared to raise the crisis to a level above the divorce altogether. It was not surprising that the kindly and gentle McCarthy hearing all this in Eccleston Street felt perturbed. What he had also heard from Parnell's solicitor seemed to confirm his apprehension that Parnell was now isolating himself in a dimension with Mrs O'Shea where the normal laws of human reason and political common sense might not apply. The solicitor, George Lewis, reported, 'They are absolutely happy and devoted, and all day together – he smoking cigarettes, she by him, never wearying of each other.' 'Mrs O'Shea', Parnell had told him, 'has not one friend in the world except myself, and we neither of us care what anyone thinks.'

When McCarthy came back later that day with J. J. O'Kelly and John and William Redmond to see what Parnell had written, his worst fears were confirmed. They spread to other members of the party. Healy, writing to his wife again just before six o'clock that evening, had heard by then of this manifesto, designed 'to crush both ourselves and the Gladstonians'. Parnell, he said, was 'fighting like a tiger', but his doom was sealed. 'It is a dreadful spectacle,' he wrote, 'with a lunatic trying to smash the great fabric that has been completed under his authority.'

But if madness, there was method in it.

The manifesto which Parnell had prepared was in one sense perfectly calculated to appeal to those emotions on which he had risen to fame and authority with the Irish people long ago. There was a tone in it reminiscent of his approach of ten years before, when he had regularly and so successfully combined the detail of practical politics with a limitless vision of national aspiration so familiar in traditional populist lore. Then the practical politics had revolved around the land agitation, now around Home Rule.

But the situation was very different from the winter of 1880–1. November 1890 was a world away from the time when a turbulent popular agitation in Ireland, semi-organized for action, looked to him for a political lead at the head of a few fiery young supporters at Westminster. A mature political Irish party at Westminster, under the banner of his authority, seemed now on the brink of achieving Home Rule through an alliance which he had himself engineered with one of the two great English parties of the day. The Irish party which he had created to help him do this now had an authority in its own right. Now in his manifesto he implied that the alliance was a trap and that those in the party who continued to consider it of primary importance were betraying the national cause.

It was a bewildering document. It turned recklessly aside from the party, whose members, except for the chance given to McCarthy and the other three to express their dismay, were not consulted. At the same time it was a clarion call which for anyone steeped in the emotional tradition of Irish national feeling carried a familiar ring of sense. It was also a clear indication that, whether sensibly or not, Parnell was already quite indifferent to the fact that the split in the party which was now there might widen irreconcilably.

The manifesto was headed 'To the People of Ireland' and began by saying that, since the independence and integrity of the party seemed to have been 'sapped and destroyed by the wirepullers of the English Liberal Party', it had become necessary 'to take counsel with you, and, having given you the knowledge which is in my possession, to ask your judgment upon a matter which solely devolves upon you to decide'. *Solely*. Defeat for him within the party itself could thus be discounted. And, although he was to make a characteristic fight of it in the coming week, he was clearly already taking defeat there for granted.

Gladstone's letter to Morley, Parnell said, claimed 'the right of veto' on the party's choice of leadership. (Gladstone, of course, had taken the utmost pains with his 'almost a nullity' phrase not to put it like this, but it was not unreasonable politician's licence so to render it.) This claim, Parnell went on, undermined the party's independence, which was, for Ireland, her only safeguard under the Constitution, and threatened indefinite postponement of Home Rule.

There followed information about his visit to Gladstone at Hawarden in the previous year which, strangely, he admitted he had never communicated to any of his English colleagues for the whole of the past twelve months. Nor, incidentally, though he did not say this, had he given any sign in that time of the information worrying him. This information, he now said, would show them, the Irish people, just what would happen if 'you consent to throw me to the English wolves now howling for my destruction'.

In the first place, said Parnell, Gladstone had made it clear that the Irish representation in the imperial parliament would have to be reduced from the present figure of 103 to 32. This in itself was of no consequence to a nationalist, but Gladstone had also said – or so Parnell related – that the settlement of the land question was not to be given to the Irish parliament under Home Rule but was to be referred to Westminster. And while Gladstone did say that he intended to reintroduce there his own Land Purchase Bill of 1886, he also said – again according to Parnell – that he would put no pressure on his own party to back it. The severe reduction of the number of Irish seats would therefore be a serious threat to further Irish agrarian reform. The Irish party would have been deprived of its effective power of manœuvre, and, as Parnell now put it, 'the Irish Legislature was not to be given the power of solving the agrarian difficulty and . . . the Imperial Government would not'.

On a separate point about the way future Home Rule would work, Gladstone had apparently said that 'having regard to the necessity for conciliating English opinion', the police in Ireland would have to be left under the control of the Westminster Government for an indefinite period – say ten to twelve years – within which period Westminster would also retain the appointment of judges and resident magistrates.

Parnell also maintained that Gladstone had said he could do nothing for the tenants involved in the Plan of Campaign, who would also be outside the jurisdiction of the new Irish parliament.

The further extent to which Gladstone's thinking on Home Rule would place a future Irish parliament in the pocket of Westminster was indicated by an alleged suggestion from Gladstone that Parnell himself should become Chief Secretary for Ireland in the next Liberal Government and that 'a legal member' of the Irish party should fill 'one of the law offices of the Crown'. (An ingenious incidental gibe at the self-seeking nature of Healy's ambition was intended here.) Parnell said he had indignantly rejected any such proposal for thwarting the independence of the party.

His manifesto moved towards its conclusion with the words:

Sixteen years ago I conceived the idea of an Irish Parliamentary Party independent of all English parties. Ten years ago I was elected the leader of an independent Irish parliamentary party. During these ten years that party has remained independent and because of its independence has forced upon the English people the necessity of granting Home Rule to Ireland. I believe that party will obtain Home Rule only provided it remains independent of any English party.

There was a characteristic sleight of hand in the argument here. For it was precisely not on the English people that Parnell had forced acceptance of Home Rule; it was on Gladstone himself, who had lost his ministry for the sake of it and was still prepared to stand by it in principle but whom Parnell was now reviling.

The manifesto was full of such logical holes, the greatest of which revolved round the question, Why, if the Hawarden meeting of a year before had yielded such a highly unsatisfactory outlook for the nature of Gladstone's next Home Rule Bill, had Parnell spent a whole year saying nothing to anybody about this? The pledge to silence over the conversation which Parnell said had been taken there could not possibly have bound any skilled political leader in such tactical circumstances, let alone someone of the character of Parnell. Above all, why had he, immediately after leaving Hawarden, actually gone out of his way to praise Gladstone and suggest that the meeting had been so satisfactory?

The document was reliable only in two respects. First, in its final words, which rejected for the Irish people 'a compromise of our national rights by the acceptance of a measure which would not realize the aspirations of our race', it proclaimed the authentic tone of Irish nationalism as he, above all, had from the outset sought to sustain it. This was the tone of his speech at Wexford as far back as 1875 and at Ballinasloe in 1878, his speech at Cincinnati and other places in the United States in 1880, and countless other speeches throughout the days of the Land League, camouflaged as all such speeches often were from time to time by characteristically ambivalent circumlocutions. But again that was in another age. Parnell had made no public speech in Ireland at all for the past five years.

Second, the manifesto could be relied on as a clear indication that Parnell was already determined to fight in the bitterest fashion, recklessly and independently, come what may. In this respect, the battle that was to be fought out the following week in Committee Room 15 of the House of Commons was not really the epoch-making event it can be made to seem, for all its conspicuous drama and even moments of high if bitter entertainment. The epoch had begun the weekend before. It was not to end until thirty years later, in times as different from 1890 as 1890 was from the days of the Land League, though closer in spirit to the latter, thus giving a certain retrospective validity to the final words of Parnell's sad and defiant manifesto.

Chapter 44

The manifesto was in the newspapers on the morning of Saturday 29 November.

The London correspondent of the *New York Times* cabled that it 'came with the detonating force of a dynamite explosion . . . It is a terrible thing to have to record the public suicide of a great public man.'

He went on to say what others were saying, namely that there were reasons for thinking that Parnell's mental balance had completely broken down. This *New York Times* man was an old enemy of Parnell's but the thought was echoed by Labouchere, the radical MP, who wrote in his journal *Truth*, 'I have always perceived in Mr Parnell a certain weirdness which under great stress might develop.' Five of the six party delegates travelling in the United States sent London a cable saying that they had originally suspended judgment until reading the manifesto but that they had now read it 'with the deepest pain. It fully convinces us that Mr Parnell's continued leadership is impossible.' Timothy Harrington, the one dissentient of the group, had heard Dillon and O'Brien come to this conclusion 'with intense pain . . . We are, with our eyes fully open, again wrecking the only hope which Ireland had probably in the present century . . . I find it quite impossible to control myself, the tears rush to my eyes.'

The cable reached the National Liberal Club in London at eleven o'clock that evening. Healy, who was staying there, was in the smoking-room when it came and heard it greeted with a cheer by a group of members. He refrained from cheering too, solely out of respect for one of Parnell's supporters, Edmund Leamy, who was also in the room. Healy had just written his daily letter to his wife in Dublin. 'Parnell's Manifesto', he said, 'is a black production, and instead of weakening his opponents has made them more solid.' He went on to describe how Parnell had spent part of that day in the Library of the House of Commons, where the Irish Members often went on Saturdays. He had been canvassing them for support, trying at times 'to influence by entreaty', but without apparent success.

Also that Saturday Parnell had called a meeting at the Westminster Palace Hotel consisting mainly of those party members likely to support him, but including Justin McCarthy. McCarthy asked Parnell what he would do if he were voted out of the leadership at the meeting due to begin in Committee Room 15 on the following Monday. 'I will fight you everywhere,' Parnell replied. 'I will go to Cork and be re-elected. I will oppose you wherever you put up.'

It had not yet quite come to that; Parnell was about to produce an ingenious fighting tactic which he may or may not have had in mind when he wrote his manifesto.

At lunch-time this Saturday Gladstone had delivered an unhesitating and explicit refutation of the manifesto account of the Hawarden conversations. A journalist who saw him at Carlton Gardens described him as looking 'very brisk and overflowing with a kind of battle glee'.

But Parnell now went for Gladstone's flank. If, he told McCarthy at the Westminster Palace Hotel meeting, he could get acceptable assurances from Gladstone about the nature of the next Home Rule Bill – particularly on those areas of land reform and the police singled out by the manifesto – then he would resign. This was shrewd. If Gladstone could be brought to commit himself, with guarantees on such matters for future Home Rule, then the whole operation could be seen as having skilfully advanced the nationalist cause. Parnell could then safely make the gesture of temporary resignation without any fear of not soon being welcomed back to advance and safeguard the cause still further. If Gladstone were not to give such guarantees, then a certain shiftiness could be seen to attach to the Liberal leader which could make the allegations in the manifesto plausible.

It was interesting that McCarthy, in the note of this Parnell proposal which he wrote next day, said that up to this point Parnell had been 'shuffling and evasive' but that then 'his manner became sweet and bland'. On the whole, though, McCarthy too was inclining to the view that Parnell was out of his mind.

Gladstone of course was too skilful a politician to be so easily cornered when McCarthy went to try to get such reassurances from him the next day. But his reply that he could no longer deal with Parnell himself but only with that party whose authority Parnell had renounced by appealing to the Irish people did itself have an evasive air, and in any case left him open to similar approaches by the party itself. For Parnell, the manœuvre did much to encourage confidence among those members of the party who wanted to support him. As one of these later wrote, 'it cleared the way. It showed that Parnell was fighting for principle and not for self.' In Parnell's eyes the two were in any case virtually indistinguishable.

All weekend he concentrated on rallying what support he could. The *New York Times* man watched him in the House of Commons that Saturday appealing to those who were moving against him. There was much agonizing among members. Healy, who was not agonizing, told his wife of one member who had decided to support Parnell and said that he was 'very wretched and wishes he was dead'. He wrote too of another who had had a sleepless night because he could not make up his mind. According to Healy, John Redmond, who was definitely for Parnell, estimated their support at fifteen; he himself put it at twenty.

On Sunday 30 November the Archbishop of Dublin finally came off the fence on which, for fear of looking politically intrusive, he had pretended to be sitting. Bringing the issue back to the point from which Parnell, with his manifesto, was quite successfully diverting it, he declared categorically, 'If the Irish leader would not, or could not, give a public assurance that his honour was unsullied, the Party that takes him or retains him as leader can no longer count on the support of the bishops of Ireland.' If there were any waverers who had not yet made up their minds for or against Parnell when the party met at noon on 1 December in Committee Room 15 of the House of Commons, the Archbishop's timely intervention would have helped them to do so. The likelihood that any would actually change their minds as a result of what they were to hear in the debate seemed remote.

The whole party attended except for the six members in America, one who was in prison for Plan of Campaign activities and five who were ill, including Willie O'Shea's old running mate for Co. Clare, the O'Gorman Mahon. One seat was vacant, at Kilkenny, waiting as it were to formalize in a by-election whatever was now to be decided in Committee Room 15. Writing to his wife the night before, Healy had thought he would not be taking much part but would leave most of the necessary statement to Sexton. His assumption was that the debate could not go on for long. It was to last six days.

The course of the debate was fully documented at the time by *Freeman's Journal* reporters who were present throughout. The style of the antagonists on each side is what is chiefly interesting now that the excitement of a result, which can be seen as inevitable, has itself evaporated. It was a style which was to characterize the next ten months of Irish politics, during which Irish constitutional nationalism would begin to fossilize.

A curious scene was enacted at the Westminster Palace Hotel on the morning before the meeting took place. This revealed something of the tension with which Parnell awaited it. Justin McCarthy came in with his son, Huntley – the Member for Newry – to tell of his interview with Gladstone the day before. 'And what answer', asked Parnell with uncharacteristic personal abruptness, 'have you brought from your shuffling friend? I will hear it with no shuffling.'

McCarthy replied that he would tell him, but expected to be heard without interruption and 'with good breeding'.

The sweetness of Parnell's personal manner on which so many people had often commented had quite deserted him, even with McCarthy, who was an old personal friend. 'I have more good breeding than you,' he snapped.

Huntley McCarthy burst out, 'That's a lie,' and Parnell rushed at him. Others present held him back. Huntley responded to calls for him to withdraw the remark by saying, 'I will not withdraw. He insulted my father and I say he is a liar.' Whereupon his father asked him to withdraw it, and he did so and left. Curiously the son was to make a speech in favour of Parnell in the course of the Committee Room 15 debate, though he was to secede with his father at the end of it.

All emotion was now unduly volatile. Justin McCarthy came away from this preliminary encounter on the first day saying that Parnell was 'quite mad'.

In Committee Room 15 itself the anti-Parnellites, though undoubtedly in a majority, had one major disadvantage: namely, that Parnell himself was in the chair and very characteristically had no qualms at all about turning the procedural mechanism to his advantage. His opponents had hoped to table an immediate resolution terminating Parnell's leadership. But Parnell, as Chairman, insisted with technical correctness that the motion before them was still that of the previous Wednesday, which proposed that a full meeting to enable him to reconsider the position be held 'on Friday next'. 'Friday next' had then meant 28 November, but now on 1 December Parnell ruled that the motion was still valid: Friday next – now 5 December – was what it said, and that had to be debated. This ruling, redolent of his admiration for *Alice in Wonderland*, was of small consequence, because he did say he was prepared to accept amendments; but it shows Parnell's important sense of his own mastery even in a situation as precarious as this – a sense of mastery quite free from any care that it might be leading him astray. He went on to reject an amendment which called for his chairmanship to be terminated, but accepted one from a supporter, Colonel Nolan, which said that the whole question of the chairmanship should be postponed until Members had been able to consult their constituents and meet in Dublin. What he was calling for, said Nolan, was an Irish plebiscite. It was on this amendment, which encapsulated the Parnellite position and which, even if rejected, would not determine the question of the chairmanship, that the debate began, and continued all that day and into the next.

The real question they were discussing was whether, particularly in the light of Gladstone's 'nullity' letter and the countering manifesto, Parnell should continue to be leader.

Some sharp things were said from the first. Sexton took a dig at Parnell's long and frequent absences from the political scene, which on this first day was about as close as they got to Mrs O'Shea. He defined what he saw as the main issue in view of Gladstone's letter: 'If the leader is to be retained, in my judgment the cause is lost.'

Healy, who decided not to leave it all to Sexton, took on the weak points in the manifesto. The 1886 Home Rule Bill, which Parnell had accepted, had also reserved the police and the judiciary to the Westminster parliament, without giving the Irish any representation in the Westminster parliament at all, and Parnell had accepted that. And if the outlook for Home Rule in the Hawarden talks had been as dismal as Parnell was suddenly saying in the manifesto, why immediately after those talks had he said in a speech at Liverpool that 'the forces of liberalism . . . will rally at the next General Election to the assistance of our grand old leader' – meaning Gladstone. Either, Healy said, Parnell's speech at Liverpool had been false or his manifesto was false.

He told his wife later that day that he 'faced him from five or six feet' as he said this, 'and he seemed to feel the arguments'. Indeed it was one of the few moments that day when Parnell lost his composure: 'I will not stand an accusation of falsehood from Timothy Healy.' Healy withdrew the remark 'out of respect for the chair'; but the point he had made remained.

Anyway, he went on, why had Parnell at least not told the party about the allegedly unsatisfactory Hawarden talks? Were they bankrupt in his confidence?

As for his own original support of Parnell at the Leinster Hall meeting ten days ago, 'Aye, we stood up for Mr Parnell against the bulls of the Pope of Rome; it was not likely we would allow ourselves to be influenced by the declamation of a single Wesleyan pulpit.' But he had changed his view and now thought Parnell ought to go because the

Liberals were antagonistic and it was Parnell himself who had led the party to see that the only hope for Home Rule was with the Liberals and Gladstone. Without that alliance and the support of the party he had taught to join it, Parnell's power had gone. 'We cannot found our position upon sentiment, upon the claims of friendship, upon anything except the awful necessities that surround us in the presence of a trembling Irish cause.'

'My speech broke Parnell,' Healy wrote to his wife; but Healy was a man whose gifts were matched by his conceit, and his wish to feel that he had broken Parnell was sharpened often by a recurrent sense of frustration at finding him partly out of reach. Certainly Parnell's response does not read particularly effectively today, but an awe still attached to his presence in that room which probably made it seem more impressive than it now sounds. That awe was not yet destroyed among his opponents. Even Sexton when making his attack had concluded by saying that he had a love and regard for Parnell such as he could never feel for any other leader.

But there was a petulance in Parnell as he rounded on Healy: 'Who trained him? Who saw his genius? Who telegraphed to him from America to come to him and gave him his first opportunity and chance? Who afterwards got his first seat in Parliament for him? . . . That Mr Healy is here to-day to destroy me is due to myself.'

All the more reason, it might be argued, to respect the judgement of a man with such a reference when he gave his view on the leadership of the party.

Even Parnell's awkward question for the party – about why it had unanimously voted for his re-election on 25 November – had a rather feeble ring. 'Why', he asked, 'did you encourage me to come forward and maintain my leadership in the face of the world, if you were not going to stand by me?'

This ignored the whole point of his opponents' position, which was that Gladstone's attitude and the consequent danger to the Liberal alliance had not then been disclosed to them.

His reply to his critics about the Hawarden talks was not convincing either. He said he had not said anything about them both because they were confidential and because Gladstone's views on Home Rule were in fact not then set, but still evolving. But these two objections, if sound, applied equally well to the morning on which Parnell published his manifesto. The prospective lines of Gladstone's evolutionary thinking on Home Rule had neither troubled him at Liverpool immediately afterwards nor apparently at any time until a few days ago when Gladstone's 'nullity' letter had appeared. That letter had said nothing about Gladstone's views on what might or might not be in a new Home Rule Bill. And yet Parnell's responding manifesto claimed to know how they had 'evolved'. The excuse was weak.

But it was in this area of the argument that Parnell had already seen his tactical opening. He was now to exploit it with all his old deft, opportunist skill.

Earlier in the day, in the first pro-Parnell speech after Sexton's attack, John Redmond had said, 'Where we are asked to sell our own leader to preserve an alliance, it seems to me that we are bound to enquire into what we are getting for the price we are paying.' Parnell had then interrupted him with the words 'Don't sell me for nothing. If you get my value you may change me to-morrow.' This now became the platform on which the whole issue was to be argued. He knew from his morning conversation with McCarthy that Gladstone was not prepared to give any assurances on Home Rule to him personally; but, if such assurances could be obtained for the party on terms no less favourable than 1886, then Parnell could indeed afford temporarily to retire as leader, for he would be able to reappear as someone who, having engineered acceptable Liberal commitments on the details of Home Rule, had really acted as leader all along. If, on the other hand, the party could obtain no reassuring commitments from the Liberals, then the manifesto could be seen as justified and there was no need for the party to sacrifice its leader to the Liberal alliance. It depended, of course, on how a satisfactory commitment was to be defined.

To establish this position now became Parnell's principal tactic. Significantly when McCarthy, who followed him on this first day, reproached him for not having confided the detail of the Hawarden talks to the party and called it a vital error of judgement, Parnell himself spoke up and agreed with him. 'I am glad', he said disingenuously, 'I have told it all now, before the mischief was done.'

Healy, who had shown himself easily Parnell's most effective antagonist, gave a vivid and surprisingly sympathetic picture of Parnell's demeanour in his evening letter to his wife. He showed once again how difficult it was to escape from the combination of Parnell's charm and his established mystique, however shiftily he might behave.

Parnell had, he said:

borne himself wonderfully during the meeting, except for one or two interruptions or gestures. He was dignified in the conduct of the proceedings, just as if he had no personal concern in them, and laughed at each point as good-humouredly as anybody else, when there was occasion . . . I cannot conceive any other man going through such an ordeal with so much dignity. I feel sorry for him . . . He is however perfectly unscrupulous and would invent any lie or statement to help himself.

On the second day, 2 December, the subject of the divorce itself came up more often, being given by a number of speakers as in itself a sufficient reason for Parnell's retirement from the leadership. The weakness of this argument was, of course, that the party had, before Gladstone's letter, already voted unanimously for Parnell's leadership to continue in spite of it. The only justification for urging it anew could be that put forward by the ex-Fenian J. F. X. O'Brien, who said he had so voted only on the widely held assumption that day that Parnell would retire voluntarily once the vote re-electing him had been taken. The divorce, he now reminded the room, was 'intolerable and a disgrace'.

The one direct mention of the divorce the day before had come from a Protestant who spoke of Parnell wronging 'the purest of existing nations'. On this second day, curiously, the least shocked or inhibited speech about the divorce came, in favour of Parnell, from an ardent Catholic who said that as a Catholic he was 'ignorant of the existence of the divorce court and, as a nationalist, refused to believe the evidence of British witnesses'.

But understandably the weight of the political argument on this second day was concentrated on the familiar question of the day before: how independent could the party afford to be if Home Rule could come about only through an alliance with the Liberals, who themselves had to confront the veto of the House of Lords? Only one speaker raised the possibility of again trying to play one English party off against the other in the cause of Home Rule. This, in the circumstances of late 1890, hardly appeared within the realms of possibility. But, whichever way the Irish party might try to get Home Rule through a hostile parliamentary system, it was going to need a leader of consummate political skill such as only Parnell of all possible leaders had ever seemed capable of showing. It was he, after all, who had first placed Home Rule on the real political agenda.

This was an awkward consideration that must have troubled many anti-Parnellite minds prepared to think beyond the constricted rivalry of Committee Room 15. Among some of them, as well as among the Parnellites, feelings about the mythical quality that could still attach to the name of their leader in Ireland must have stirred alongside the rational arguments. It was a quality that might somehow enable the constitutional dilemma of Home Rule to be resolved on a different plane from the House of Commons alone. And that after all was related to the question they had been technically debating for two days: Nolan's amendment that the whole issue of the leadership should be postponed prior to consultation with the Irish people and a meeting in Dublin.

A whiff of excitement reminiscent of the Land League days ten years before may have been in the air for some supporters of the amendment. If so, reality was quick to intervene. A vote was finally taken at the end of the second day. There were forty-four against and twenty-nine including Parnell, for. A split between Parnellites and anti-Parnellites was now formally established. More important, the mirror in which Parnell had been able to hold himself up to the Irish people had publicly cracked.

Healy wrote that evening:

It is now evident that we shall have a big fight in the country afterwards . . . Clearly while we are fighting them here on the basis that they will be bound by the decision of the meeting, they have no intention whatever of being so bound, and will embarrass us in Ireland by elections . . . Our men are solid, and he is certain to be defeated, but he is fighting every point with tenacity . . . His rulings in the Chair have been shameless, but I believe he is unconscious of this, and that he feels exactly as you might expect a god to feel – that he could not be wrong.

Parnell spent that night at the Westminster Palace Hotel. He slept for twelve hours and was late arriving at Committee Room 15, where the first stage of his tactic for ultimate survival was put into effect by a new amendment to the resolution for adjournment until 'Friday next', which was still standing. The new amendment, in the name of one of his supporters, J. J. Clancy, proposed that in view of the differences of opinion between Gladstone and Parnell as to what was said at Hawarden about the police and about the settlement of the land question the party whips should, before any further debate, find out from Gladstone, Morley and Harcourt (the likely next leader of the party) 'what their views are on these two vital points'. Clancy added that, should acceptable assurances be given by the Liberal leaders on these points, then Parnell would retire.

A new air of hope was suddenly in Committee Room 15, though Sexton, welcoming it, called the hope 'faint'. He asked the all-important question, Who was to judge whether the Liberals' replies were satisfactory or not? The majority of the party, or Parnell himself? Having been forced to accept to fight on ground of Parnell's choosing, he had manœuvred him into the one awkward corner there.

Healy said directly to Parnell, who had by then arrived in the room, that if he could meet Sexton's point that it should be for the majority of the party to decide whether Liberal thinking on the new Home Rule Bill was satisfactory or not, then 'my voice will be the first, at the earliest possible moment, consonant with the liberties of my country, to call you back to your proper place as leader of the Irish race'. This was greeted with loud and prolonged applause.

Parnell eventually said he needed time to consider his answer, and the meeting was adjourned until the next day.

Healy in his letter that evening wrote, 'There is some chance of a settlement, and we have agreed to a truce until to-morrow.' He said he could not tell his wife what the new proposals were, as he was bound to secrecy, but the tone of the rest of his letter showed that the bitterness which might have grown still sharper had the debate continued that day still remained a force in his mind. He talked of Parnell preferring 'Kitty to his country', and went into a certain amount of detail about the personal side of the O'Shea affair. What precisely was the source of Healy's information is not clear, but he wrote of Parnell:

His main subject of anxiety before the divorce was the custody of the child Clare. He consulted lawyers in the City some months ago as to whether, if he bolted out of the country with her, he could, under foreign law, be brought back and compelled to give her up. He, therefore, was prepared to bolt then, and leave us all 'in the lurch', if he could safely have done so.

It is unlikely that Healy could have heard this much without knowing of the existence of the daughter born in the year after Clare, Katie, about whom Parnell might have been equally concerned. The fact that Healy here makes no mention of her may be explained by his further instalment of gossip in the next paragraph:

It seems O'Shea maintains that Clare is his own child, and he told Labouchere that whenever Kitty came up to his flat in Victoria Street she insisted on renewing their old relations, and he swears he will keep Clare on this account.

The inference seems to be that O'Shea did not feel that Katie was his child, though it is clear that husband and wife continued to be on affectionate terms at least in correspondence during the period of her conception. It is clear too that, at least on the level of gossip, Healy had heard a lot. Reporting that Parnell, in his statement to the party when it had re-elected him on 25 November, had said there was some other man in the case, he wrote, 'This is of course Weguelin, so she must have been in relation with both.' The 'of course' indicates some familiarity with the details of Parnell's situation. It was a situation with which, and perhaps for psychological as well as political reasons, Healy seems to have been at times almost personally obsessed.

The Irish Catholic hierarchy's understandable obsession with it was given its first full public airing the next day, when Parnell was due to deliver his considered reply to Sexton and Healy. The bishops' pronounce-ment asked if Catholic Ireland 'so eminently conspicuous for its virtue and the purity of its social life', could 'accept as its leader a man thus dishonoured, and wholly unworthy of Christian confidence'. The pronouncement may well have had some effect in hardening attitudes in Committee Room 15.

While the truce was on, the atmosphere between the two sides was apparently as friendly and cordial 'as if', wrote Healy that day, with a number of them sitting amicably together round a table, 'nothing had occurred. Parnell is as bland as ever with us, just as if we had said nothing to ruffle him.' The day before, some Healy supporters had thought that Parnell might have a revolver on him and be on the point of drawing it against Healy. One had actually stepped forward to prevent this. Now, however, as Harcourt wrote in something like a panic in a note to Gladstone, 'Healy, Sexton and Parnell are at this moment hob-nobbing over their whisky downstairs. They are not waiting for you to make peace for them. They have signed it already and at your expense ... There is no reality, no sincerity in their professed antagonism to Parnell's leadership. They have tried their strength, been beaten and surrendered at discretion.'

But Harcourt had got it wrong, reckoning without the true severity of the antagonisms already aroused, the ambition that went with them, and the ability, above all, of Parnell's devious overconfidence to provoke them further. Even within the calm of this twenty-four-hour Irish truce there was anxiety and distrust. Healy, while taking comfort that Parnell was obviously under pressure from his own followers to agree to retire in principle, and seeing at least a chance of keeping the party together, was also writing, 'I don't know whether the thing is a trick or if Parnell means to act honestly and retire.' McCarthy described this day after the storm of the previous day as one of 'sudden and, I fear, treacherous quietude'. He thought that Parnell's offer to resign if satisfactory reassurances were obtained from Gladstone had been made 'only to gain time and in the hope that Gladstone may refuse and thus give him ground for saying that Gladstone is betraying us'. If, McCarthy added, Gladstone would tell the deputation in detail what he had told him privately the previous Sunday, namely that Parnell's account of Hawarden talks in his manifesto was incorrect, 'we are safe, and Parnell must go out: but if he declines and is too reticent Parnell will be immensely strengthened'.

Like Harcourt, McCarthy was being too pessimistic. He too was reckoning without the quality in Parnell to which Healy had referred when he had written, 'he feels exactly as you might expect a god to feel – that he could not be wrong'. There was more than a touch of this quality about Parnell's approach to many aspects of life, but in politics it had been best defined by himself when in relation to the British Government he had said, 'They will do what we can make them do.' But he was now applying the principle in a more immediately delicate situation to former colleagues who had learned their political skills from him and were in a majority against him.

When he rose to speak after the twenty-four-hour adjournment, on Thursday 4 December, it was to respond to Sexton's and Healy's queries about who was to be the judge of the Liberals' reply and whether he would resign if the party agreed that it was satisfactory. It is easy to think now that from his point of view the manner, at least, of his response was a mistake. But his energies were then concentrated not on careful calculations but on the grand, audacious sweep of that self-possession which had always been the mainspring of his political drive.

He could not, he said, surrender his responsibility to the party. And he said it in just the way to excite the maximum hostility in those who already opposed him in that room – summarizing, not incorrectly, in a single sentence one truth about his whole career to date. 'My responsibility', he told them, 'is derived from you to some extent, but it is also derived from a long train of circumstances and events in which many of you, and I speak to you with great respect, have had no share. My position has been granted me, not because I am the mere leader of a parliamentary party, but because I am the leader of the Irish nation . . .'

However it was five years since he had spoken to the Irish nation on Irish soil in the spirit that had given him that position. He was taking a gamble. The years 1879–81 had given him unquestionably a position as political leader of the Irish nation such as no one except O'Connell had ever held before. The evolving nature of British democracy in his time gave him considerably more power in that position than had been O'Connell's. In the years after Kilmainham he had maintained this position in a less revolutionary climate but had achieved historic success by inducing the Liberals to adopt Home Rule – a revolutionary step within the Constitution. The successful aspect of that achievement in fact rather overshadowed the basic failure involved: namely, that a Liberal Government could not even get Home Rule through the House of Commons, let alone the House of Lords. But a sort of self-satisfaction with the achievement so far, resting on future hope and fortified by social progress under land-purchase provisions, had made the political climate in Ireland very different from what it had been ten years before. Parnell, by immolating himself in domestic happiness in England, and even in his attitude to the Plan of Campaign actually separating himself from disruptive events in Ireland, confirmed in person the qualitative change that had come over the climate of nationalist politics since ten years before. He was talking now as if he had the option of reverting to those earlier days at will.

A small hint that his political mind might be wandering under the influence of vanity appeared in a further sentence of this speech. He continued, 'And you, gentlemen, know, and I know, that there is no man living, if I am gone, who could succeed in reconciling the feelings of the Irish people to the provisions of the Hawarden proposals.'

This was true, certainly, but it was a total irrelevance. The whole point of his case was that the so-called Hawarden proposals could not be reconciled with the feelings of the Irish people, so how could there ever be any question of him doing that?

He said, referring to Gladstone, 'You are dealing with a man who is an unrivalled sophist.' 'Which?' rejoined John Barry, the one-time Fenian who had done much to bring extremist support behind Parnell in the early days.

What Parnell now proposed in addition to the Clancy amendment was that the party should adopt another resolution as well, by which it agreed that no Home Rule Bill could be acceptable to the Irish people which did not give Ireland both immediate control of the police and power to deal with the land question. Then if the party were to decide that the views expressed by the Liberal leaders conformed with this resolution he would retire. It was a neat manœuvre by which he maintained his claim to be responsible for what the party should decide while theoretically giving it the freedom to make the decision itself. If, of course, Gladstone were to be unable to respond along the lines of the resolution, then, if that resolution were accepted, he could remain leader because the Liberal alliance would have disintegrated. What he overlooked, or at least calculatingly disregarded, was the likelihood that the majority against him could say with some reason that the Liberal alliance on any terms was the only hope for Home Rule in the British parliament and therefore must be stuck to at all costs. They had already made clear by their vote on the Nolan amendment that they did not want an appeal to the Irish people through the constituencies in an 'Irish plebiscite'. He knew, therefore, that were his resolution not to be accepted he was on his own.

Healy, in opposing the idea of his resolution, was quick to unmask the suave trick behind it. He attacked him for in effect refusing to submit the matter to the judgement of the party. 'Do you think we are children?' he asked.

Parnell said he had given his answer and would stand or fall by it before Ireland.

'Then you will fall, Mr Parnell; and now that both sides have made up their minds what is the use of further debate?'

Healy became angry and let the true cause of the whole crisis come nearer the surface again. 'Now that a speech appealing to what a certain gentleman known to us all called in the Special Commission the "hillside men" has been delivered,' he told the room, 'our position is plain.' This was a direct reference to Willie who had used the phrase at the Special Commission.

'Hear! Hear!' said Parnell, unabashed.

'Let us come then to the issue,' said Healy. 'You declare the country is for you – go to it. Go to it.'

There was cheering.

'So we will,' said Parnell.

There were counter-cheers.

When Healy asked what it was that had broken off the Liberal alliance to which Parnell had given his support as late as last June, Parnell's supporters replied, 'Gladstone's letter'. Healy gave his own answer: 'The stench of the divorce court'. And he accused Parnell, in a slightly muddled allusion, of being 'a Frankenstein who having created this Party is able and determined to destroy it'.

Parnell, if he were to go it alone in Ireland, needed above all to get something on the record about the present positions of Gladstone and the party on the future Home Rule settlement. Rightly judging with Healy that the two sides were deadlocked, he now backed away from his resolution. He said he was not actually moving it but placing it on the record. He proposed that the party, when it had Gladstone's answer, should in fact express its opinion on it by resolution – adding disingenuously, 'I want to have an expression from the party, first or last, so that the responsibility should be thrown off my shoulders.'

His manœuvring at this point has been categorized as a failure, but it prevented the break-up of the party for a couple of days during which he could obtain that clearer definition of respective positions which might be useful for the future. The principal thing he was to get was an eventual clear refusal from the Liberals to commit themselves publicly on details of the next Home Rule Bill.

But first the Clancy amendment had to be passed, which sought to resolve the differences of recollection about the Hawarden talks. This cleared the way for a bipartisan delegation to call on Gladstone at 12.30 on Friday 5 December. Healy, who formed part of the delegation, wanted the break with Parnell, but like Parnell he wanted it to be a clean one for the future. Behind the scenes he had been urging the Liberals to give some assurances, at least to the extent of saying that the Westminster parliament would definitely deal with the land settlement and that the time for the disbandment of the Royal Irish Constabulary would be specified in the next Home Rule Bill rather than left open. He believed that, however untrustworthy Parnell himself might be, his followers were sincere and would leave him if Gladstone gave any real pledge.

Gladstone himself was inclined to consider giving assurances of some sort, but Harcourt and Morley had dissuaded him from doing so. He sent the delegation away again, saying that there was no recollection problem about the Hawarden talks as far as he was concerned and that if they wanted to see him they must come with another mandate. A new amendment now had to be passed in Room 15 asking Gladstone for a conference for 'an intimation of the intentions of himself and his colleagues with respect to . . . the settlement of the Irish land question and the control of the Irish Constabulary in the event of an Irish legislature'. But the attitude of the Liberals had hardened in the course of the day. Gladstone replied that he would not be in a position to discuss future Home Rule legislation with the party until it had settled the problem of its leadership.

There might at some point earlier in the week have been a chance of such a dismissive reply acting in Parnell's favour, but after all the bitter words that had already been heard in Committee Room 15 it merely signalled the end at last of that long, traumatic scene and what Healy, writing that evening, called its 'racking suspense'. 'I don't suppose I shall ever be the same man after this week,' he added. 'None of us will perhaps.'

But there were bitter words yet to come, the most famous of all from him.

Chapter 45

The debate came to its inevitable conclusion the next day, Saturday 6 December. The evening before, Healy and Sexton had again asked Parnell to agree to retire and he had replied that he would think about it overnight. On the Saturday morning they called on him at the Westminster Palace Hotel. He repeated his now familiar position: he owed a responsibility to Ireland; he would not retire. They told him that no matter what happened they would walk out of Committee Room 15 at six o'clock that evening.

As Healy and Sexton were leaving the hotel, Parnell took Healy aside by one of the pillars in the hall and asked him to shake hands with him, saying there was no truth in the story then circulating that he had had a revolver in his pocket in Committee Room 15; he had not carried one for the past two years. They shook hands. It was a bizarre scene in the light of their encounter a few hours later.

The final drama in Committee Room 15 on the afternoon of Saturday 6 December 1890 was vividly recorded by eyewitnesses at the time. That record is packed with intense visual imagery.

First the undercurrent of excitement as, calmly enough, the report on the dealings with Gladstone was read through, while Parnell, still technically Chairman, a shade paler than usual, sat smiling grimly to himself and stared at the desk in front of him; Healy sat back in his chair with arms folded. Then the sudden outbreak of chaos as a Parnell supporter, John O'Connor, called by Parnell, rose to put a motion censuring Gladstone, while at the same time an opponent of Parnell, William Abraham, rose holding a paper on which was written the motion that Parnell's leadership of the party should be terminated. He shouted its words a few feet from Parnell, who rose too and, as the paper was thrown on to the table, seized it from McCarthy to whom it had been passed and looked for a moment as though he were about to strike him; but then he crumpled the paper up into his pocket, shouting against the uproar that he was the Chairman until the party deposed him, and that as such he had called John O'Connor. There were cries of 'You are not our

Chairman' and 'Dirty trickster', as Parnell stood there looking straight ahead of him and, continuing to call on O'Connor, cried, 'Order! Order!' with his face deadly pale and his eyes burning fiercely. He was Chairman, he said, until he was deposed.

'Allow us to depose you,' cried Healy.

The tension momentarily relaxed as an anti-Parnellite asked the meeting to respect Parnell so long as he was in the chair and to let O'Connor be heard. While O'Connor was speaking, Parnell took the paper on which Abraham's motion was written from his pocket, smoothed it out, and gave it back to McCarthy, to whom he apologized. He then turned away and opened a newspaper, the *Freeman's Journal*.

Shortly afterwards came the appalling climax. O'Connor was talking about Gladstone when a Parnell supporter, John Redmond, called out that Gladstone was now 'master of the Party'. 'Who', sneered Healy, rising to put his hands on the table, and jerking his long neck forward, 'is to be mistress of the Party?'

Parnell threw his newspaper away and, with his face contorted with pain, made two desperate efforts to get up from his chair. When he did manage to rise, it looked so clearly that he was about to strike Healy that a number of Healy's friends clustered round to protect him. One of them called out, 'I appeal to my friend the Chairman.'

'Better appeal . . .' cried Parnell, his right arm and clenched fist close to Healy's face, his voice shaking with emotion, 'Better appeal to that cowardly little scoundrel there who dares in an assembly of Irishmen to insult a woman.'

Had they so appealed, it could have had little effect. Healy was to use uglier terms for Katie in the months to come. But the moment faded. Parnell fell back into his chair, breathing heavily. The confrontation foreshadowed, in miniature, the course of events over the next ten months.

On this Saturday afternoon in Committee Room 15 there could be only one end to all this, and the gentle McCarthy led the way. He and forty-three other opponents of Parnell left the room, to convene elsewhere and constitute themselves the Irish party under his chairmanship. Twenty-six members remained behind in support of Parnell. After the weekend the seceders took over the traditional Irish party seats below the gangway in the House of Commons, although Parnell, with a certain historic symbolism, retained his own individual place among them. Curiously, Alfred Robbins of the *Birmingham Post* noted all sections of the party 'chatting together with each other in their old familiar friendly way'. This air of studied unreality was the only comfort to be found. The true reality, of course, was not going to be found in the Palace of Westminster at all but in Ireland.

Parnell, when left alone with his own supporters the previous Saturday, had said of his opponents, to become known as the 'anti-Parnellites', that they 'dreaded the lightning of public opinion in Ireland . . . It was this Irish opinion they wished to stifle, that they have recoiled from; and it was this Irish opinion they fled from.'

On the evening of Tuesday 9 December the House rose for the Christmas recess. Parnell told Robbins that he 'had not the slightest fear of carrying with him the Irish people'. A journalist who met him at Euston asked him obligingly what message he had for the Irish people. 'Tell them', he said, 'that I will fight to the end.' That at least was to prove true.

Travelling on the same train to Holyhead that Tuesday, though in a carriage at the opposite end, was Healy. A by-election happened to be pending conveniently in North Kilkenny. Over it, battle could now be joined at once.

At this most critical moment in the whole of Parnell's political career, we are lucky to have a series of graphic eyewitness pictures of his appearance and personal demeanour to augment the dramatic story of how that battle began. Just before leaving London he had asked the man who was to be his first biographer, R. Barry O'Brien, to stand by as a possible candidate for him in the coming by-election. Leaning back on his seat in the smoking-room of the House of Commons, Parnell had looked 'tired, ill, distressed . . . seemed absolutely without energy . . . quite absent-minded', and spoke 'in a very low voice and as if suffering from physical pain'.

But Parnell had always been a man of mercurial vitality, and Robbins of the *Birmingham Post*, who saw him on the evening he left, described him as being 'in the highest spirits'.

On arrival in Dublin he could indeed be seen transformed. Dublin had always been his stronghold, and he was received there once again as that 'Uncrowned King' that Healy of all people had once dubbed him. Healy himself, on arrival, was assaulted in the street by an indignant Parnellite supporter. Parnell, on his first evening in the city, had a rapturous welcome from a vast audience assembled to greet him in the Rotunda Rooms. A young woman who had been waiting expectantly for him in the crowd there, craned her neck as the cheering began:

... and there was the tall, slender, distinguished figure of the Irish leader making its way across the platform ... the house rose at him; everywhere around there was a sea of passionate faces, loving, admiring, almost worshipping that silent, pale man. The cheering broke out again and again; there was no quelling it. Parnell bowed from side to side, sweeping the assemblage with his eagle glance.

His black frock coat, she said, was buttoned tightly across his chest, giving him a 'look of attenuation'.

A journalist who had not seen him for five years found him

less studied in his attire than formerly. His face was paler, his hair more meagre and it was unkempt and long at the back, curling slightly over his collar. He was thin. His features were those of a man who had been recently sick ... But he still gave evidence of that unconquerable self-command which was so marked a feature of his personality. His eyes glistened with fire and feeling ... his voice sounded with thrilling clearness.

What he said also took people back to the Parnell of earlier days. Passionately he declaimed in a style very different from his studied House of Commons manner the underlying principle of what was to be his campaign during the next ten months. Suddenly it was clear that the terms of reference of Irish politics were to be moved back something like ten years:

'I have never said that this constitutional movement must succeed ...' he said. 'We stand at the parting of the ways ... It is an issue which means the life or death of the constitutional movement ... If Ireland cannot win upon this line within the constitution, she can win upon no other line within the constitution, and if our constitutional movement of today is broken, sundered, separated, discredited and forgotten, England will be face to face with that imperishable force which tonight gives me vitality and power, and without which we are broken reeds ... And if Ireland leaves this path upon which I have led her ... I will not for my part say that I will not accompany her further.'

The message was clear and enthusiastically received by that Dublin audience. But Dublin was not Ireland, and 1890 was not 1880 or 1881, and the immediate task was to carry North Kilkenny with him.

The next morning saw the quasi-revolutionary Parnell in action after breakfast in Dublin. The first skirmish in the campaign had already been won by his opponents, who had taken control of his paper, *United Ireland*. A man walking down O'Connell Street that morning saw a crowd suddenly rush towards *United Ireland*'s offices, and he followed them to its doors to find them firmly barred against any onslaught. Sticks and revolvers were being circulated in the crowd when suddenly a carriage drove up at speed, stopping so abruptly that the horse collapsed on the road. Out sprang Parnell himself, 'his face pale with passion, his dark eyes flaming . . .'

A pickaxe and a crowbar appeared and, while some of his supporters forced their way in through the basement, Parnell smashed in the main door with the crowbar and led the crowd inside. The besieged anti-Parnellite staff had prudently got out the back, and Parnell was once again in charge of *United Ireland*.

The eyewitness had by now secured a vantage point in a house opposite and eventually watched Parnell emerge at an upper window of the *United Ireland* building:

His face was ghastly pale save only that on either cheek a hectic crimson spot was glowing. His hat was now off, his hair dishevelled, the dust of conflict begrimed his well-brushed coat. The people were spell-bound, almost terrified, as they gazed on him. For myself I felt a thrill of dread, as if I looked at a tiger in the frenzy of its rage, and then he spoke, and the tone of his voice was even more terrible than his looks. He was brief, rapid, decisive, and the closing words of his speech still ring in my ear: 'I rely on Dublin. Dublin is true. What Dublin says today Ireland will say tomorrow.'

But the immediate question was, what would North Kilkenny say? On his train journey down to his own constituency in Cork, he experienced the first rumbling indications of the sort of hostility he could be facing. At some of the stations at which the train stopped he received a cheering welcome; at others the reception was divided. At Mallow, the home of William O'Brien, who, now in the delegation in America, had come out against him, a hostile address was thrust into his hand when he opened the window and a man on the platform abused him. He slammed the window shut and pulled the curtains down while a crowd crying 'Bring him out' battered at the carriage door and a priest paced up and down the platform denouncing Parnell as a blackguard and a libertine. He arrived in Cork to find a traditional welcome waiting for him from his constituents and emphasized energetically enough the theme of the campaign, which had indeed attracted his candidate, a wealthy Tipperary landlord: namely, 'no dictation from the Liberal Party, or any English Party; Ireland to stand up for herself alone rather than that'.

But the Cork friend with whom Parnell stayed that night was worried by his appearance. He looked, he said, 'like a hunted hind, his hair was dishevelled, his beard unkempt, his eyes restless'. For supper he swallowed two raw eggs, one after the other, in a glass, and then went off to bed. The next day he started campaigning at full stretch in exactly the same sort of way as he had so often expended his energies in by-elections in days gone by. It was the sort of constituency in which, in the days of the Land League, he would have triumphed. The machinery of the Irish National League was still technically at his disposal, but it was much weakened by the inevitable dissensions within itself over the split. In the circumstances, which included the unconstitutional nuances he had expressed in Dublin, he was to attract, and needed to attract, the support of those Fenians and neo-Fenians often known as 'the hillside men' – those men thought of as dreaming of the day when they could fight the British army on the hillside. His appeal to such men became a routine basis for attack by his opponents – in particular by Michael Davitt, a hillside man of another generation.

Davitt was managing the technical side of the anti-Parnellites' campaign behind Sir John Pope-Hennessy, the sometime Tory Home Ruler who was their candidate. But, it was Healy who gave that campaign its venomous force. In response to Parnell's relatively sophisticated political argument about Gladstone's dictation and the possible need to look to a new approach in order to escape from him, he launched a straight-forward assault on Parnell's sexual conduct which could hardly fail to be effective in a Catholic country where sexual repression was as venerated as in Ireland. In the old Land League days Parnell would have had the priests (if not always the bishops) and the average tenant farmers with him. Now on the whole he had neither. His support, as an observant local police sergeant noted, tended to be among the larger farmers and employ-ers, the professional classes and those adult males too poor to qualify for the household vote. But the sergeant noted at first that the odds among those prepared to bet seemed to be on Parnell.

They were odds which were to lengthen remarkably sharply as Healy got under way with the serpent tongue which was to be the hallmark of his campaign. As he arrived at his hotel in Kilkenny he had begun as he intended to go on – calling back at a jeering crowd, 'Three cheers for Mrs O'Shea!' Elsewhere he said that they had been 'within a kick of the goal of Home Rule' when Parnell had 'disgusted every woman and child in England, neglecting his business at the House of Commons and being always down with Mrs O'Shea'. He described her as 'a bad woman who hates Ireland, who cares nothing for Ireland, who has been spending the money of the Irish people and ruined Parnell'.

There were now quite uninhibited references to the Galway election of 1886. He and Biggar had known then, he said, that Parnell was 'prostituting a seat in Parliament to the interests of his own private intrigues'. O'Shea had the Galway seat for 'the price of his wife'.

It is just possible that Parnell might have been able to moderate somewhat the Catholic Church's judgement on his adultery had he been able to explain openly what he had always seen as Willie's unashamed connivance. There is some correspondence between himself and Dr Walsh, the Archbishop of Dublin, to suggest that negotiation to this effect may have been on the cards. But at all costs he wished to avoid, during the *nisi* period of the divorce, any introduction of evidence which might prevent him from marrying Katie at the end of it. And connivance accepted by the court would have annulled the divorce. In any case, even with the Archbishop of Dublin's understanding, it is difficult to see how, after so much moral condemnation of the adultery by the Church, he could have won more than a marginal adjustment of the reproach which Healy exploited so crudely.

The North Kilkenny campaign was unlike anything he had experienced before. It was unlike anything Ireland itself had experienced for many years. The intense hostility was between Irishmen; British rule was only incidentally the enemy. For the Parnellites the real villain was not so much even Gladstone – who was out of office anyway – as any man prepared to surrender Ireland's chance of independence to him by letting him dictate leadership of the Irish party. For the anti-Parnellites the villain was the convicted adulterer Parnell. The nearest analogy from the near-past to the prevailing election atmosphere was to be found in those constituency battles of 1880 when Fenians had intervened actively against parliamentary nationalists and Parnell had on one occasion, at Enniscorthy, been spattered with bits of egg and orange and had his trousers torn so that a waiter had to mend them as he ate his dinner. Now, at a meeting at Castlecomer, where the men working in the local mines had been effectively organized by Davitt, lime was thrown in Parnell's eyes and he appeared for a time with a white bandage across his face – at which the anti-Parnellites jeered because they said that what had hit him was chalk.

His demeanour at Castlecomer was noted by an observer to be such as he could ill afford to have observed: his dignity, and with it the almost mythical status that had long been the basis of his political strength in Ireland, was showing signs of damage. He had been claiming to be the same man as he had been ten years before. But even before the stuff was thrown into Parnell's eye this English journalist had found him:

not the same man as he had been ten years before. The change in the Uncrowned King's mien and manner was positively startling. It was no longer the dignified, self-possessed Charles Stewart Parnell of old . . . Mr Parnell's face was thinner than I had ever seen it. The lustre of the eyes was gone. They seemed tired and dazed. He smoked, or rather half-smoked a number of cigarettes, throwing one away and lighting another . . . the 'Uncrowned King' is breaking down.

Finally, in keeping with this new lowered image, he and his entourage had fled from the hostile meeting in something like panic, galloping away down the main street in their carriages in full flight, cursed by a crowd pursuing them with mud and gravel.

This same journalist described Parnell's bizarre appearance at an eve-of-poll meeting: a huge bandage covered one half of his face, and he wore a strange hunting-cap, peaked back and front, with flaps on either side of his face tied under his chin. The speech he made there, the journalist said, sounded 'like the knell of a lost cause', though it was better than some of the other speeches he had made in the previous ten days.

He had never been one for easy, traditional rhetoric. Purposeful coherence and the deliberate pursuit of meaning had always been his strength, capable of rising to an effective climax. Now at times he rambled in a slovenly, unkempt manner that matched his deteriorating physical appearance. At that first meeting at the Rotunda Rooms in Dublin, in dealing with Healy's accusations of neglect of duty over the years since the defeat of the Home Rule Bill, he had bizarrely likened himself at Eltham to Wellington retiring behind the lines of Torres Vedras to winter quarters in the Peninsular campaign, but at the same time putting his own withdrawal down to illness. 'God knows,' he said, 'it was not a [good] time when I was crippled in strength, when it was doubtful that I might ever come again before you, to confront me with a movement of mutiny . . .' He stamped his feet and wrung his hands, there were tears in his eyes uncomfortably like self-pity. 'Ah yes, they bided their time and they thought I was dead, and that they might play round my corpse and divert the Irish nation from the true issues involved . . .' He was to conjure up an image of his own death several times in the coming months.

This was not the old Parnell. But that Dublin audience loved him because they loved the old Parnell and could still see him as such, even when he said things like 'I am too unworthy to walk with you within the sight of the promised land, which, please God I will enter with you.'

His trouble was that, while claiming to be on the offensive – taking the battle to Ireland for the people of Ireland to decide – he was really on the defensive, and he had never let himself seem on the defensive before, even when on weak ground. The most sweeping way he could seem offensive now was by suggesting, if necessary, a change of ground altogether.

There was of course nothing new for him in pointing the Irish people, if necessary and however vaguely, in an alternative direction to Westminster. Ambivalence about the value to Irish national aspirations of the English Constitution had been implicit in his patriotic attitude for years, though only periodically asserted. It was just that for many years now, since he had succeeded in apparently turning that Constitution to Ireland's advantage by making the Liberal Party adopt Home Rule, it had not been necessary to think of any other direction in which to go. Above all, the assumption that Liberal Home Rule was the road to whatever 'independence' might eventually mean fitted comfortably, even complacently, into the circumstances of his personal domestic life. But now – though he would not have seen it this way – new developments in his personal domestic life had most uncomfortably disrupted that assumption.

Imprecision had always prevailed in his mind above what any alternative might actually be. The orthodox Fenian doctrine of armed rebellion had, in the light of reality, always been to him a practical irrelevance, though in theory in no way repugnant. Traditionally, too, there had been since the days of O'Connell that other step which might be taken to change reality: withdrawal from Westminster altogether to demonstrate from Ireland the will of the Irish people – with whatever effect that might have on English government. Although the years 1880 and 1881 had produced conditions which might theoretically have been advantageously turned towards such a course, there had not been then, as he had had to recognize, the political strength in the Irish parliamentary party to make anything of them. It was a different world now. Ireland itself was much less unsettled than it had been ten years before. The parliamentary party was potentially infinitely stronger than ten years before, but was split about whether anything needed to be done at all. He was in the anomalous position of having to say that the future must now be seen as wide open.

Hindsight over the next ten months makes it difficult now to see how open that future might have been. As the industrious police sergeant had noted, the odds at first were thought to be on Parnell's candidate, Vincent Scully, winning the North Kilkenny by-election. Had he done so, the future pattern of those ten months, with their sudden and tragic personal climax and all it was to mean for the future, might well have been very different.

The Kilkenny campaign identified clearly the two main factors which could determine the final issue: on the one hand the unequivocal condemnation of Parnell by the Irish Catholic Church, as a moral outcast and unacceptable leader; on the other, his hitherto almost mythically formidable political stature. The local Bishop in the constituency, the Bishop of Ossory, while happy to note that every parish priest but one was an anti-Parnellite, commented, 'No doubt but the first choice of the people would be Parnell. We had to dislodge him from their prejudices, which with weak, ignorant and unreflecting people is no easy task.'

Parnell himself was doing something to help in this respect among the sophisticated. There was his unwonted disorganized manner, his new uncharacteristic invective against former colleagues – calling a man who had publicly slighted Katie 'a gutter-sparrow', Davitt 'a hound', and McCarthy, the new Chairman of the party, 'a nice old gent, for a tea-party' – and his hint of recklessness towards that more open future which won the support of traditional old Fenians like John O'Leary and the founder of the Irish Republican Brotherhood himself, James Stephens. All this combined to let many English commentators take refuge in the thought that he was going mad. They remembered that there was said to be a convenient history of mental unbalance in his family. Even Edward Hamilton, Gladstone's former secretary, was inclined to this view, but could not help admiring Parnell's 'great bounce and swagger' and his 'splendid audacity' and thought there might be method in his madness.

To those who saw him behind the scenes, Parnell was in fact still very much himself. He could unburden himself daily by letter and telegram to Katie. On the night of the poll, R. Barry O'Brien found him calm and relaxed, even though realizing that his man had been well beaten. 'But it is only the first battle of the campaign,' Parnell told him. 'I will contest every election in the country. I will fight while I live.'

Next morning, as the votes were being counted, no man in the room seemed in better humour or less anxious. Davitt was walking nervously up and down. 'What will he do now?' Davitt asked O'Brien. 'He is beaten by at least a thousand votes.' O'Brien told him, 'One defeat, twenty defeats, won't affect him.'

He went back to Parnell. 'He looks very uncomfortable,' said Parnell. 'What is the matter with him?'

But, as Parnell well knew, Davitt had been right: Scully was beaten by more than eleven hundred votes.

Parnell repeated in public what he had said to O'Brien: he would fight in every constituency. When it seemed that the British constitution was not going to get Ireland anywhere, he and his colleagues would 'shake the dust off our feet of the Palace of Westminster'. And, fully aware of the charge that he was appealing to the hillside men, he took it head on, saying he would renew to the men of Kilkenny the pledge he had made to the citizens of Cork in 1880: 'I will never allow my name and my authority to be used to tempt the people of Ireland into any hopeless struggle – either constitutional or otherwise – and when constitutional struggle, if it ever does (I don't say it ever will), becomes useless and unavailing, at that moment I will declare my belief to you and will take your advice and be guided by your judgement.'

The ability to detach himself from events when necessary had always been one of his strengths. He spent the afternoon shopping in Kilkenny. That evening he returned to Dublin where, as Lyons has written, 'the ever-faithful Dubliners greeted him as warmly as if he had won a great victory'. Passing the old Irish Parliament House on College Green, which was now the Bank of Ireland, he rose in his carriage, as he had done shortly before being taken off to Kilmainham, and he again now pointed to the building significantly, which the crowd applauded. Only the large bandage across his eye gave him a rather unnerving look.

The Dublin faithful would turn out more faithfully than ever ten months later, when his carriage would again pass that way, but his gesture by then would be only a sad and desperate memory. It is difficult not to see him on this December evening in 1890 already isolated, already lost.

There would be two more by-elections in the six-month period after Kilkenny. He would lose them both. His own sudden death the following autumn can be seen as a sort of foregone conclusion. But history does not see things that way.

He was not particularly thrown by losing at North Kilkenny, because there were still uncertain factors on the political horizon. There were possible regional differences in the nature of the Church's involvement at parish level. In spite of the Church, with really intensive campaigning he might soon be able to revive the full legendary stature of that name and of the authority with which he spoke. As in the days of the Land League, some of his Fenian supporters made up in effective quality for their relative smallness in numbers. There was also still the partially unknown quantity of the party delegation headed by Dillon and William O'Brien in America.

Certainly the majority of this delegation had committed themselves by cable to the majority in Committee Room 15, but they had done so from afar, free from the trauma that had fixed those present in the room into attitudes from which it would take them years to escape. Of the five who had condemned Parnell, two – Dillon and O'Brien – were central to any future thought about the distribution of power within the party. And for all their commitment to opposition to Parnell they retained unresolved feelings of respect and affection for him. 'You have torn our souls asunder,' O'Brien was to write of him in March 1891, when attempts at reconciliation had finally failed.

Dillon had wanted Parnell beaten at Kilkenny, but in the hope that it would make him amenable to negotiation. While condemning Parnell as unfit to be leader, he equally condemned the violent attacks on him by Healy and others. 'It infuriates me to read of Parnell being hounded down by priests,' he told O'Brien. He and O'Brien were in any case doubly distanced from the infighting. They had escaped abroad from English jurisdiction when on bail for Plan of Campaign offences and were due for imprisonment at once on return. They could view the future with particular detachment.

Negotiations between Dillon, O'Brien and Parnell did eventually take place, in France – in Boulogne mainly, but also in Calais and Paris – in January and February. In the course of these a number of proposals were put to Parnell not on the whole dissimilar from some of the projects devised in Committee Room 15. They therefore seemed inevitably doomed. Neither Parnell's pride nor Healy's sense of tactics was likely to agree to anything resembling what they had found unacceptable before. The greatest care was taken by O'Brien in such proposals to make it easy for Parnell to accept retirement from the leadership by keeping a special place for him in the Irish National League, but this was just what Healy did not want. In any case, Parnell did not want to give up the leadership. Tempers might have cooled after the end of the Kilkenny by-election, but the hostility between the two was all the colder for that.

Healy was appalled at the prospect of any negotiation. Aware of the purpose for which O'Brien was about to arrive in Boulogne from New York, he said categorically of Parnell in a public speech in Dublin, 'I say we will have no dealings with him. We will have no compromise with him. We will have nothing with him except combat and we will give him nothing but defeat ... We have beaten him and will hunt him wherever he shows his head.'

When he went to Paris to see O'Brien, he sent a message to Gladstone to say there was no chance of the party ever coming to terms with

Parnell. Writing to his wife from Paris, he found his mistrust of O'Brien's adventure totally justified: '. . . all his reproaches were for us. He had no phrase against the other side.'

It is not easy to assess how seriously Parnell entered into these so-called 'Boulogne' negotiations. He certainly spent a great deal of time discussing O'Brien's and Dillon's various proposals, and devoted to them the care and thought that he had always put into his work whenever he set pen to paper. He suspended his campaigning in Ireland for a time while the various talks were in progress. It had never been easy to assess his exact objectives when at work on an issue – in terms of Irish nationalism, always one of his strengths – but Healy's own unremitting antagonism to negotiations at all is probably the key to Parnell's interest in at least examining what they might lead to. If they could be a way of preventing Dillon and O'Brien from making common front with Healy, obviously they could be to his advantage.

There was also a third party to the negotiations, though not actually present at them. As in the Committee Room 15 proposals, acceptable guarantees from Gladstone about the future terms of the next Home Rule Bill were an essential part of anything that Parnell could be brought to agree to. Yet anything like a concession to Parnell was unlikely to be forthcoming from a Liberal Party which had already rejected any dealings with him in order not to offend the Nonconformist conscience on which much of its vote depended.

R. Barry O'Brien was close to Parnell at the time of the Boulogne negotiations, though not necessarily someone to whom he fully opened his mind. O'Brien told him in the House of Commons one evening that people did not really believe in the negotiations and thought he was talking of peace but meaning war all the time. Parnell answered with a smile, 'Well you know, if you want peace you must be ready for war.' But on another occasion he did say to him, 'Some good may come out of these negotiations. We may pin the Liberals to something definite yet.'

Alfred Robbins, the shrewd political commentator of the *Birmingham Post*, wrote at the time about the negotiations:

The question of real importance is whether Mr Parnell means upon any condition to withdraw from an active participation in Irish political life, and that question I have very little doubt in answering in the negative . . . It is true that he has offered to lay down such share of the leadership as he retains if certain concessions are obtained from Mr Gladstone; but it is equally true that he has never said he would permanently withdraw, while the concessions he seeks have a striking faculty of growth.

In the middle of February, Parnell told Robbins that the rupture over the negotiations was complete. Very typically he 'emphatically disowned responsibility for this', but said at the same time, 'I stand on precisely the same platform as I did in Committee Room 15.' That alone was a succinct explanation of why the negotiations had broken down. William O'Brien and Dillon gave the whole thing up, returned to Ireland, and immediately went to prison.

Parnell had already started campaigning again. There was another by-election pending, in North Sligo. He drove himself hard, just as in the days of the Land League, giving himself little rest.

It is not easy to say how reliable are some of the reports of his exhausted appearance in these months – they were often written down after his death, when people were happy to record their prescience of the tragedy to come – but certainly he was travelling almost continuously. Every weekend he would leave Brighton, where he was living with Katie, for London, Holyhead and Dublin. He would address a meeting or meetings on the Sunday, return to Dublin on Monday to direct operations from his committee room, and then return to London, and appear from time to time in the House of Commons while living at Brighton. During the negotiations with Dillon and O'Brien he would also be travelling to France, and returning for occasional meetings in England, before going back to Brighton to start all over again the following Saturday to Ireland. R. Barry O'Brien, seeing him one night looking tired and harassed, told him he was overdoing things. 'Yes,' Parnell replied, 'I am doing the work of ten men. I feel quite well, it does me good.'

Katie says she 'begged him' to spare himself the fatigue of this constant journeying, but he was unable to rest without it. The strain was often apparent, and, though he did not know it, was slowly killing him. Many explanations had been given at times for his periodic bouts of ill-health – kidney disease and cancer among them. Modern medical opinion, after studying the extensive reports of his symptoms, has concluded convincingly that he was suffering from coronary heart disease. Both his father and his grandfather had died in their forties. Someone watching him speak at Navan at the beginning of March described him as looking 'like a sick eagle'.

He still had advantages in Ireland. The *Freeman's Journal*, the most widely read newspaper of the Catholic voting classes, remained at this stage loyal to him, and he technically held control of the Irish National League. The latter, however, had inevitably been weakened by the divisions within it parallel to those within the party, and now, in March, a Convention was held in Dublin under Healy's aegis to found a new, specifically anti-Parnellite political organization, the National Federation. The four Archbishops of the Catholic Church attended the Convention, and the London *Times* correctly described it as 'essentially the organization of the Church for political purposes'. There, lest anyone should think that negotiations with Parnell might ever be in the air again, Healy made clear 'I would never consent for one hour to remain in the party of which Mr Parnell was the leader. I will never tolerate him. I will never consent to him in any shape or form.'

Three days earlier, such balance in favour of Parnell as still existed had been further redressed by the foundation of a new national newspaper, the *National Press*. Under Healy's editorial direction it sounded at once the battle-note which had won the North Kilkenny by-election, totally approved by those long rows of clerical black coats present at the National Federation Convention. For a predominantly Catholic electorate there could be no equally effective counterblast to his definition of 'the real political issue at stake' as 'the shameful revelation of the divorce court'. Parnell was, he said, 'the real, sole, manifest author of the evil', who must not complain if home truths were told which would go to the very roots of the controversy.

Healy himself had something more direct than home truths to complain about from Parnellite supporters, though, being a man of courageous spirit as well as venom, he did not complain. He had already been assaulted on the street on the day he arrived in Dublin for the North Kilkenny by-election, and had had the windows of his house in Mountjoy Square broken. Now, on an evening in March, a Parnellite supporter came up to him in his hotel in Cork, accused him of betraying his country, and hit him repeatedly in the face, smashing his glasses, splinters from which went into his eye. He was unable to play any direct part in the North Sligo election campaign, which took place at the end of March, with polling-day on 3 April.

This by-election, too, Parnell lost by a good margin – though a smaller one than at North Kilkenny. The improvement in the Parnellite vote may have had something to do with the fact that the territory, remote in places, had a genuine rebel tradition from 1798 when, for a short time under the French, it had housed a first Irish Republic. Some of the priests here responded less readily to the bishops' and archbishops' call to arms. There was, all the same, much Parnellite complaint about clerical influence, and reciprocally the anti-Parnellites complained of bullying and intimidation. Sexton in the *National Press* said that Parnell had brought in hooligans, 'the spade-handle brigade from Mayo'. Here Parnell went out of his way to make a special point of appealing to the small tenants of the area. With crude demagogy he pointed out that if police recruiting were stopped in the area for the next six years so much money would be saved that a quarter of a million tenants could live rent-free for ever and others would have their rents considerably reduced. Otherwise he stuck to the steady theme that no decent Irish party was going to take its orders from the English Liberals. As to the question of himself and leadership, he said he would gladly give way to any acceptable leader who appeared, but: 'Can you make any of them a leader? Can you select the foul-mouthed Tim Healy? Can you trust the uncertain and wobbling Tom Sexton? And can you follow hysterical Davitt? You cannot.'

Haggard and tired he might be looking, but no one could say that he had lost confidence in himself. And the results, after North Kilkenny, could almost be said to be encouraging: 3,261 to the anti-Parnellites, 2,493 for Parnell. Healy himself was quite worried: 'Who knows what pitfalls we may walk into in other districts if an election arises? . . . The whole affair has given our men an awful shake and has enormously encouraged Parnell.'

But Parnell had still lost the only two by-elections since the split. His prospects for the next general election, in his mind throughout, were looking increasingly questionable. Theoretically he still had twenty-six Members of Parliament to support him, but how many of those would win at a general election in the prevailing climate of clerical condemnation?

His greatest asset – greater than any arguments he could muster about the need for an Irish party's independence if it were to win an independence worth having, and the need to look beyond England's constitution altogether if necessary – was the established authority of his own name. But the split itself, by definition, had shown part of that authority disestablished. The events of 1891 had further emphasized the point. Just before the North Sligo election, an incident had occurred out of which he came badly in a way he would never have done before. His ability to seem different from other men was fast deserting him.

He had rashly at one point offered to resign his seat in Cork and fight for it all over again on his new status if Tim Healy's brother, Maurice, a fellow Member for Cork City, would do the same. But when Maurice Healy had agreed, placing his resignation in the hands of the anti-Parnellite whip to be delivered to Parliament as soon as the Parnellite whip should deliver Parnell's, Parnell evasively backed down, saying he would wait for that resignation to go in before his did. Tim Healy said that this showed Parnell 'not merely a libertine, but a coward and a sneak'.

In the aftermath of this, in the House of Commons a fortnight later, Parnell suffered a humiliation of a sort which in the past he would always have been able to rise above. This time he failed to do so. When Maurice Healy rose during the discussion of an Irish Sunday Closing Bill to say that 'neither on this nor any other public question' did Parnell represent the city of Cork, he added that if Parnell wished to test this he could easily keep the promise he had made to his constituency. Parnell simply sat there staring straight ahead of him, saying nothing.

There was a change in the political atmosphere too, a lowering of the ideological temperature at least, to match the apparent reduction in his status. He was appealing to Ireland as a man who embodied, as in the past, the national aspirations of Ireland in all their emotional vagueness. But he was doing so at a time when he himself, by keeping Gladstone and the Liberal Party to Home Rule over nearly five years, had appeared to make Ireland's aspirations more precisely detailed than ever before. The arguments in the Boulogne negotiation proposals, as in Committee Room 15, had been all about specific legislative details: the handling of the constabulary, the land question, the retention of Irish Members in an imperial parliament. He himself had brought the emotional ideology of nationalism down to these everyday matters, and until the divorce-court proceedings, with their impact on the Liberal Party, had been satisfied to keep them there. Even in the days of the Land League it had been uphill work to link an abstract cause of nationality to the more urgent practical everyday questions of land tenure and rent. He himself had had to admit in 1880 in his interview with the *Wiener Allgemeine Zeitung* that the cause of nationality by itself did not come first in the average Irishman's mind. Now that he himself had managed to bring the Irish mind to see nationality as a coherent everyday matter in the form of Home Rule, his special appeal was rarefied indeed, concealed in ambiguities about constitutional action and some alternative.

The emotional depth of his personal appeal was one for headier days like those of the Land League. The politics of these days of 1891 were bitter, but heady only for those temperamentally inclined to find them so. There might be talk of Parnell's welcoming 'the hillside men', but the process was also the reverse: the hillside men were welcoming him, just as men like Brennan, Boyton and Sheridan had done ten years before. The everyday interests of the average voter were no longer drawing them so easily to wider national thoughts. And the Church, very much one of the voter's everyday interests, turned him away from them. Parnell's real achievement in these times was to build a legacy of expectation for another generation, self-educated as they were soon to be with new thoughts about Irish identity.

It was a legacy to be taken up in words by poets like Yeats and Joyce, who, in the way of poets, made something other of it, loftier and haunting. And it was to be taken up by men of action like Patrick Pearse, himself a poet, and James Connolly and Michael Collins, who made their own thing of it too. Others in our own day have taken it up, and made something cruel and pointless of it, which would have horrified Parnell.

As has often been pointed out, here, as so often in Irish history, myth and reality intertwine. The Parnell myth had a life of its own. Here we are concerned only with the reality of what was Parnell's life, of which perhaps the most important fact to remember at this time is what he said to R. Barry O'Brien when discussing, in one of their conversations in 1891, the possibility of 'a real Parliament for Ireland in times to come'. 'I am a young man,' he said, 'and can wait.'

He was still only forty-five. He would have been only forty-seven when the House of Lords rejected the second Home Rule Bill passed by the Commons in 1893. It is difficult to see that he would have just waited another eighteen years until another Liberal Government passed a Home Rule Bill it could not implement. But the circumstances were by then so different that such historical speculation is more than usually irrelevant.

In June 1891 he still felt young. The future stretched far ahead. On 25 June he married Katie legally at last at a register office in Steyning, Sussex, with two of her maids as witnesses. He was in high spirits. Waiting for the maids to arrive, he looked at himself in a mirror on the wall and, adjusting the white rose in his frock coat, said – or so she tells us – 'It isn't every woman who makes so good a marriage as you are making, Queenie, is it? And to such a handsome fellow too!' He blew a kiss to her in the glass.

He had already told her how he thought she looked 'lovely in that lace stuff and the beautiful hat with the roses! I am so proud of you!' he said.

Back at 10 Walsingham Terrace, their house at the extreme western end of the front, they gave interviews to various reporters and then went for a walk, passing through brickfields, in which, typically, Parnell stopped to talk to the men at work, and then going down to the sea. There, she says, they talked of the summer visits they were going to make to Avondale and 'of the glorious days when he need never go away from me'.

But there could be no question of taking her to Avondale yet. He had to get back on to the campaign trail. A third by-election was pending, in Carlow. In his letters from Ireland he continued of course to address her as he had done over the past ten years as 'My own Wifie' and to sign himself 'Your own Husband'.

In Ireland the marriage had made things even worse, compounding in the eyes of the Catholic Church the original sin of adultery. On the wedding day itself the hierarchy, speaking, it said, 'as pastors of the Irish people', had announced that 'Mr Parnell, by his public misconduct, has utterly disqualified himself to be their leader.'

The by-election in Carlow, in which A. J. Kettle, his old colleague of the Land League days, stood as his candidate, was the most crushing defeat of all. This could be seen as an omen for the general election in which he still hoped to triumph. But, perhaps because he was so happy to have been able to marry Katie properly at last, he seemed not at all dejected. A cousin of the then Chief Secretary for Ireland, Arthur Balfour, saw him on the boat coming back from Ireland after the by-election and found him 'in the highest possible good humour and good spirits'.

To many people it was beginning to look like an increasingly depressing political end-game. But most accounts of meetings with him in these months of 1891, while they often stress his pale and haggard appearance, generally portray him not as depressed but rather as affable, even humorous, and above all sweet-natured. Justin McCarthy, nominally his most formal opponent, having displaced him as Chairman of the party, was quite disconcerted by the cordiality Parnell continued to show him. Spotting McCarthy in the House one evening only a few weeks after the split, Parnell had left a friend he was with and come across 'with beaming eyes' to shake his hand affectionately and ask how he was. 'Of course,' McCarthy wrote a few days afterwards, 'I replied in as friendly a fashion as I could . . .' And one afternoon three months later, as they found themselves sitting next to each other in the House, 'He began', wrote McCarthy that same day, 'a long and most friendly talk about things in general – not politics – as if nothing had ever happened between us. He is inexplicable.'

The reason he could remain so well-balanced in private was obviously just because, however physically exhausting the continual journeying might be, he could return happily every week to the pleasure of Katie's loving company. However inaccurate, even misleading, parts of her memoirs may be, there can be no doubt whatever of the genuineness with which they convey the strength of their love. Since long before the register office at Steyning it had indeed been a true marriage. Every morning and every evening when he was away during these months of 1891 he sent her a telegram; he would write too when he could, giving details of the way the campaign was going. He ended a letter from the heart of the North Sligo by-election by asking her to wire him every day.

The viciousness of Healy's attacks in the *National Press* and in public speeches mounted in intensity. In June a series of articles in the *National Press* beginning with one entitled 'Stop Thief' had accused Parnell of misappropriating money contributed to the party, in the days before the split, passing it not only to his present Parnellite section but also to his own private pocket. Nothing could have illustrated more dramatically the extent to which the public perception of Parnell had deteriorated than that not only should it have been possible for such articles to be published but that it should not have seemed worthwhile for him to bring a libel action.

On the other hand such a level of insults did in one way do him a service: the concentration of personal attack against him forced him to emphasize less the issue of leadership of the party, which had become an increasingly unrealistic one, and enabled him to try to appeal to higher things.

Speaking at Thurles, Co. Tipperary, at the beginning of August he said what he had said before but now with plainer emphasis. 'It is no longer a question of leadership. It is a question of whether our country is worthy of being a nation.'

But this too, like the authority of his own name, now had something of a hollow ring.

The trend of events left him more and more isolated – a fact which the great weight of support for him only in Dublin itself and, to an extent, in adjacent Midland counties, made clearer. Not only had three by-elections gone against him: the *Freeman's Journal* was wavering and would desert him before the end; the *National Press* and Healy stepped up increasingly salacious attacks on him and Katie; and Dillon and O'Brien when they came out of prison at the end of July both declared firmly against him.

He hardly even bothered to argue back against Dillon and O'Brien but expressed chiefly personal sorrow and even affection for his former acolyte O'Brien, who had now gone his own way.

The Catholic Church continued to express, in terms which must today seem repugnant and even unchristian to all but the most dogmatically

correct, its additional horror at the solemnization by marriage of his
enduring love for Katie, acceptable as it was according to the teaching of
his own Church. The Bishop of Raphoe said it 'only caps a climax of
brazen horrors' and the Archbishop of Dublin, Dr Walsh, described it as
'a public compact for the continuance of their shameful career'.

Even some of his supporters, good Catholics, now abandoned him for
what he had done. Healy had not hesitated to encourage them at the
Carlow by-election in mockery of the Steyning ceremony: 'He says he is
going to bring her over to Ireland. I don't like talking about Mrs O'Shea
[*A voice: "Kitty and Parnell"*] because it is a nasty subject, but I did not
invent Mrs O'Shea. I did not . . . run down the fire escape for her . . . A
man in the crowd said a while ago, "Why can't you let her alone?" Why
could not Mr Parnell let her alone? [*Cheers and laughter.*]' He was to
wait until after Parnell was dead to call her in public, twice, 'a convicted
British prostitute'.

The death, when it came, was totally unexpected, except possibly at some
level of consciousness by himself. Campaigning on, at Listowel, Co.
Kerry, three weeks before it happened, he told the crowd, 'If I were dead
and gone tomorrow, the men who are fighting against English influence
in Irish public life would fight on still; they would still be independent
nationalists; they would still believe in the future of Ireland a Nation.'

In the political vacuum of sorts that was to be left in Ireland for
years after his death, such words were to have resonance. In terms of
Irish nationalism as it was in September 1891, when there seemed no
question of him being anything but very much alive for years to come,
they may be seen in conjunction with what he had said at Westport
only a week before. Speaking of what had happened in the period
since he had come to lead the party so long ago, he had said, 'The
slow progress has been disappointing, but at least it was sure; it cannot
be re-called. No step that the Irish nation has taken can be retraced.
No gain once won can be taken from you. They all constitute a stronger
basis from which to advance for further progress and fresh conclusions,
and although the progress of these twelve years may have been slow it has
been sure.' And he had gone on to remind the crowd of the terrible
lessons of the rebellion of 1798 and its shedding of blood without hope of
victory.

When, in part of his speech the following week, he praised the Fenians
of 1865 (whose rebellion in 1867 had been equally without hope of
victory, though relatively bloodless), there was no contradiction in

anything he was saying. Those Fenians had, he said, kept alive the spirit of nationality in the heart of the Irish people. And it was this 'spirit of nationality' with which he had always identified himself since his earliest days in the House of Commons.

By what precise stages such spirit might eventually achieve for Ireland Emmet's goal of becoming one of the 'nations of the earth' he had always been realistic enough to leave vague. He ruled out armed rebellion not because it was wrong but because it had no apparent chance of success. He was a constitutionalist because constitutionalism was the only mechanism available. Whether that constitutional approach meant accepting the Constitution itself as the final identity for Ireland was something he had always been careful to leave in an ambivalence bordering on duplicity. He had accepted Home Rule in 1886 as a final settlement. He had not said that he would do so for ever. Now in September 1891 he was in one sense in a luxurious position after so many years of responsibility. If the general election were to go the same way as the by-elections, he would at least be a free agent. R. Barry O'Brien had told him he thought he might possibly get five seats but would not be surprised if he were returned absolutely alone, to which Parnell replied impassively, 'Well then, I shall represent a Party whose independence will not be sapped.'

He could afford now to stand back a little and survey the future from a certain Olympian viewpoint. This could help suggest an almost god-like presence at the election.

His speech at Listowel was on Sunday 13 September. His energy was indeed Olympian, greater than ever before. It was small wonder that he was looking tired, as many people noticed, but he was happy and seemed well. He had been at Avondale in the middle of August hoping to get some shooting but had been too busy, spending much of his time in Dublin on arrangements to set up a new paper, the *Irish Daily Independent*, ready to back him now that the *Freeman's Journal* was deserting him. He had been looking too to the affairs of his Wicklow iron-mine and stone quarries. Then for the next six weeks he travelled continuously, back in the middle of the week to Brighton to see Katie, then back again at weekends via Holyhead to Dublin for meetings, to return soon afterwards via Holyhead to Brighton, and then back again.

'What is the man at?' jeered the *National Press*. 'Cannot he stay in Ireland for two days running, without bouncing back to England to bask in the light of the Saxon smile?'

It was of course her smile and the great sense of security she gave him that made it possible for him to bear the meetings which he had always disliked, even in the days of the Land League, and the continual virulent personal abuse from Healy and the *National Press*. 'Mrs O'Shea's registered husband', 'a repulsive personality', Healy was calling him.

After Westport on 6 September and Listowel on 13 September he was at Cabinteetly on the 20th, where his sister Emily went with him. She said he was 'in capital spirits', though his superstitious nature was upset by the crowd pressing so hard against the windows of the carriage that they broke the glass. But though it was raining all the time, during which he spoke with his head uncovered, he thought it had been a good meeting. He took his sister and her daughter to dinner at a hotel in Bray, where he reminisced about their childhood together at Avondale and, as the sky had now cleared, talked to his niece about the stars.

His line of argument at the meeting had indeed been a spirited one, to the effect that the measure of Home Rule they were likely to get now would be all the better just because of the existence of one Irish party quite independent of Gladstone to keep him up to the mark. To which the *National Press* responded the next day venomously but to some point with the comment, 'This means, if it has any meaning at all, that Mr Parnell committed adultery with Mrs O'Shea in the interests of Home Rule, and that the revelations of the Divorce Court ... [were] his crowning benefaction to his country.'

The day this appeared, Parnell, back in Dublin on his way back to Brighton again, was reported as saying that in the sixteen years of his public life his mind had never been so free from care nor his heart so confident of the future as during the past ten months. Years before, he himself had once described Gladstone, who had been expressing optimism in discomforting times, as like a schoolboy walking through a graveyard in the dark, whistling to keep up his spirits. But the likelihood is that in his own present case his relatively carefree look at his predicament was genuine enough. It was North Kilkenny that had been the shock and had sent him into disarray; he had adjusted in a fashion now to a new situation. He was after all, as he had pointed out to R. Barry O'Brien, only forty-five and could wait. He went happily off on his weekly visit to Brighton again.

Katie thought he looked ill and exhausted when he arrived at Walsingham Terrace, but he was very cheerful and happy, and she could not get him to lie down and rest as she wanted. She even tried to get him to go to see a specialist he had once been to see with her in London when he was exhausted from overwork and who had diagnosed bad circulation. But he laughed off her suggestion, saying he was only a little tired. 'You do not *really* think I am ill, do you?'

She said she thought he was *too* tired and begged him to give himself a real, long rest from the struggle in Ireland. But, or so she relates, he said he would rather die than do that and went off again 'bright and happy' to Dublin for a meeting in Creggs in Co. Galway on Sunday 27 September.

When he got to Morrison's Hotel he sent a note round to the doctor friend and supporter who had looked after him when they had been together in Kilmainham, Joseph Kenny. There was a slightly disoriented tone about it: 'I shall be very much obliged if you can call over to see me this afternoon, as I am not feeling very well and oblige yours very truly Chas. S. Parnell.' He added a postscript asking him not to tell anybody he was unwell lest it get into the newspapers.

Kenny came round. It was a particularly wet autumn in Ireland, and he found Parnell suffering from acute rheumatic pains as well as general debility. He advised him not to go to the meeting planned next day at Creggs, but Parnell said he had given his word and must go. One of his party organizers who went with him to catch the night mail-train to the West also found him complaining of rheumatism in his wrist and shoulder. At the station for the West, a small crowd of supporters was waiting for him. A young man among them shook his hand and found, he was to write years later, that it no longer had the firm grip he had felt previously, though Parnell's eyes were keen and his mouth firm. The young man's name was Arthur Griffith. Just under thirty years later he became first Prime Minister of the Irish Free State. The train stopped at Athlone in the way to Creggs, and Parnell made a short speech about his new paper, the *Irish Daily Independent*. It was arranged that no one should shake his hand because of the pain.

As the train left Athlone, one of the crowd fell on to the rails under it and was killed. The accident upset Parnell very much; he looked for omens in many things, from the falling of a picture from the wall to crossing someone on the stairs. He walked agitatedly up and down the carriage for a time.

When they arrived at Roscommon, from which they were to travel the few miles to Creggs next day, he went to a chemist for some medicine and his arm was put in a sling. He was wearing the sling when he spoke at the meeting next day. He had sent his usual morning telegram to Katie before leaving, saying that they were having 'terrible weather'. But, though it was raining as he spoke, he refused an umbrella someone offered him. The discomfort seems to have got into his speech, for a reporter who was there found he could take down all the first part in longhand.

He spoke quite a bit about his health, saying he was not in good physical condition that day, but, though he had been ordered by his doctor to stay in bed in Dublin, he had not wanted to disappoint them. 'However,' he said jokingly, 'do not think that any very material damage will come to me from this meeting. If I was to allow the suggestion of such a thought we should have our enemies throwing up their hats and announcing that I was buried before I was dead . . . I hope when I see you again at the next General Election, to ask for your votes, that you will find a very considerable improvement physically.'

But on the way to Dublin in the train next day he was feeling a lot of pain, though he talked to the reporter all the way back. He stayed on in Dublin for three days, meaning to return to England each day but held up by the need to discuss arrangements for the new paper, and suffering all the time from what he thought of as his 'rheumatic pain'. Once someone made him drink some brandy because he thought he looked so weak.

Finally he was off. He telegraphed Katie as usual from Holyhead, and when he got to London he first took a Turkish bath, in the general healing properties of which he much believed, before going down to her at Walsingham Terrace.

He was glad to be back. Indeed, she relates that he said, 'You may keep me a bit now.' He ate a good dinner and laughed off the suggestion that he ought to have the specialist, Sir Henry Thompson, down from London to see him. But there was a disturbing moment that evening when he suddenly threw away his half-smoked cigar, of which he was normally so fond, and found he could not walk to the bedroom, even with his stick, without her assistance. She said she would telegraph to Thompson in Wimpole Street to come down the next day, but he rejected the idea, appalled by the thought of the fee the man would charge to come all that way.

Next day, Saturday 3 October, he felt better, enjoyed the cigar he smoked after breakfast, and waved it with pleasure at an engraving of the muscular young couple in Lord Leighton's picture *Wedded* which she had bought while he was away. They discussed the agreement for a country house they were going to rent for a time, and where he said they would spend part of their 'real "honeymoon"'. He even wrote a letter about his symptoms to Wimpole Street.

But on the Sunday he was worse again; and on her own initiative she sent for a local doctor he liked, who kept him in bed and presumably gave him some form of sedative or painkiller. He could not sleep that night.

Next morning he had a high temperature and was in great pain. He began to be delirious, trying to get out of bed, though he was unable to stand, and said to Katie, 'Hold me tight then, yourself, till I can fight those others.' Then he talked of the sunny land where they would go when he was better and where they would be happier than in politics. But suddenly that evening, when he seemed to be dozing, she heard him mutter, 'the Conservative Party'. They were almost the last words she heard him say. The very last according to her, came late on the evening of Tuesday 6 October, when he suddenly opened his eyes and said to her straightforwardly, 'Kiss me, sweet Wifie, and I will try to sleep a little.'

It seems very likely he would have said something like that.

The coronary thrombosis struck during the night.

Epilogue

Katie lived on until 5 February 1921, when she died of heart disease at Littlehampton in Sussex, aged seventy-six. She is buried there.

Willie died at Hove in 1905, aged sixty-five.

The law suit over Aunt Ben's fortune (some £7 million today) was settled out of court. It was divided in a complex way between Katie and her five children on the one hand, and Willie and the Woods on the other. On Katie's side, Gerard, Norah and Carmen were allotted a larger proportion of the capital sum than Clare and little Katie. Willie and Katie were left with comfortable life incomes. But a dishonest solicitor and bad investments had reduced Katie's income considerably by the time her book was published in 1914.

Parnell's will, which left Avondale to Katie and the children, proved invalid because he had not remade it since his marriage. The house was therefore inherited by his next of kin, his brother John Parnell, who, unable to deal with the enormous debts with which the house was encumbered (some £2,000,000 today), sold it eventually to a Dublin butcher. The house later became the property of the Irish Forestry Commission and has been enthusiastically redecorated and refurbished in the style of Parnell's day.

Gerard O'Shea served in the First World War and survived to become a consultant on a Hollywood film about Parnell starring Clark Gable and Myrna Loy. He married a cousin, Christabel Barrett-Leonard, and went with his family to Canada at the beginning of the Second World War, where he disappeared from history.

Norah looked after her mother lovingly to the end. She told Henry Harrison that Katie never stopped mourning Parnell, who, she believed, in times of great depression came to her in the night to draw her out of the black waves. Norah also wrote in a letter to Henry Harrison dated 1921 that her mother had taken to 'the follies of so many human ways of forgetting for a little while'. Norah herself became a nurse at Queen Charlotte's Hospital in London but contracted a painful disease, lupus, of which she died in 1923.

Carmen married a Dr Arthur Buck who lived in Brighton. But she used to come up to London to go racing at Kempton Park and other courses with an Edward Lucas who inherited a baronetcy and whom she married after Dr Buck had divorced her in 1914. Her stepson, later Sir Jocelyn Lucas, who first saw her in 1910, remembered her as 'beautiful and kind'. He wrote to this author many years later: 'My youthful heart went out to her.' But as the *Times* obituary of his father was to say, Sir Edward was 'a noted judge of wine', and Carmen developed a taste for it too. This second marriage failed and she died in the same year as her mother, 1921.

Parnell's first surviving daughter, Clare, married a Dr Bertram Maunsell but died giving birth in 1909 to a son, Parnell's grandson, Assheton Clare Bowyer-Lane Maunsell, who died in the British Army in India of enteric fever in 1934.

His second surviving daughter, Katie, married in 1907 a Lieutenant Moule of the East Lancashire Regiment who was posted to West Africa, from which they did not return to England until after her mother's death in 1921. She seems to have been living for a time in some poverty in Camden Town in the 1930s but died in Dublin in an asylum in 1947.

Parnell's sister Anna campaigned for the first Sinn Fein candidate in a by-election in County Leitrim in 1907, but afterwards went to live in England, where she called herself 'Cerisa Palmer'. She was drowned in the sea at Ilfracombe in 1911.

His sister Emily's marriage to Captain Dickinson broke up; she married another army captain younger than herself but that marriage collapsed too, soon after a honeymoon spent at Monte Carlo. Her sister-in-law, John Parnell's wife, describes Emily's mind as 'somewhat deranged' in later years, and, though she had adequate capital, she died in the South Dublin poorhouse in 1918.

His sister Delia's marriage to the millionaire Livingston Thomson was not a success; she made at least one attempt at suicide. She died soon after her mother in the 1890s.

His much-loved sister Fanny had died in 1882, and his sister Sophia, who married the solicitor Alfred McDermott, had died in 1877. The latter's son, Tudor, Parnell's nephew, was one day to attack Healy with a horsewhip in the Dublin Four Courts after Parnell's death, when Healy had been referring to Katie as 'a proved British prostitute'.

Parnell's favourite sister after Fanny was Theodosia, who in 1880 had married a Commander Paget of the Royal Navy. He had been in charge of a coastguard station off the coast of Clare in the 1890s, but they had moved to Surrey by the time of the third Home Rule Bill in 1912. Paget died in 1917; Theodosia died in 1920 in London. Her son, Cyril, married in 1928 and it is through their children that the last line from Parnell survives. On the centenary of his death in 1991 the name Paget appeared in the Avondale visitors' book below that of the then Taoiseach of the Irish Republic, Charles Haughey, who had visited the house on the same day.

Parnell's elder brother, John Howard, who inherited Avondale, was an Irish Nationalist MP for Meath from 1900 to 1905; he published his memoirs in 1916 and died in 1923. Parnell's younger brother, Henry, died in 1915.

Parnell's mother, Delia, died in March 1898 at Avondale, after apparently falling into an open fire and setting light to her dress a few days before.

At the General Election of 1892 which brought the Liberals to office under Gladstone with the help of Irish Nationalists, Parnell's old supporters from the split won nine seats against seventy anti-Parnellites. The party was not to be reunited until February 1900 under John Redmond.

In 1893 Gladstone's second Home Rule Bill was passed by the House of Commons by a small majority but was rejected by the House of Lords.

Gladstone died in 1898.

It was not until after two General Elections in 1910 that the Liberals, dependent on Irish votes in the House, introduced in 1912 a third Home Rule Bill. This time, since the passing of the Parliament Act in 1911, the

House of Lords could only delay the Bill but could not prevent it from becoming law. Though it received the Royal Assent on 18 September 1914, it was immediately suspended until the end of the war which had broken out on 4 August and until some amending legislation could be introduced to make special provision for six counties of Ulster.

By the end of the war national feeling in Ireland had grown significantly, partly due to failure to implement the Home Rule Act after so many nationalist Irishmen had volunteered for and died in the British Army, and partly due to the emotional impact of a small minority rising of Easter 1916 under Patrick Pearse and James Connolly, and the executions of them and fourteen other men which followed.

At the General Election of 1918 an overwhelming number of Irish constituencies (seventy-three) voted for an Irish Republic and a party, Sinn Fein, whose members were pledged not to take their seats at Westminster but to sit in Dublin as an Irish parliament of an Irish Republic. A secretly organized campaign of assassination of police and other British representatives began, and in September 1919 the so-called Irish parliament (the Dáil) was suppressed. Violence against British rule increased, carried out in the name of the 'Irish Republican Army'. With the introduction to Ireland of counter-insurgency reinforcements for the Royal Irish Constabulary, to be known as the Black and Tans, the character of the violence developed into guerrilla warfare in which the majority of the Irish people, though originally opposed to violence, supported the IRA. The eventual enactment on 23 November 1920 of a Home Rule Act, but with a separate parliament for six counties of Ulster, was by then too late. On 11 July 1921 a truce between the IRA and British forces came into effect.

The British Government invited the chief organizer of the IRA, Michael Collins, and other Irish leaders to London for negotiations. These led in December 1921 to the creation of an Irish Free State for all Ireland with constitutional status as a Dominion, its own armed forces and a parliament on whose powers the only restriction was the oath of allegiance which its members had to take to the Crown. The six counties of Ulster had the option to secede and did so at once on ratification of the so-called 'treaty'. A civil war in Ireland between that section of the IRA which accepted this treaty (now the Irish Army), and that which did not, ended with victory for the former in 1923.

The first representative of the Crown in the Free State, as Governor-

General, was Tim Healy. He died in 1931. The oath of allegiance was dropped from the Free State constitution in 1933.

In 1937 the Free State formulated a new constitution which changed the name of the state to Eire. That constitution claimed that the national territory of Ireland 'consists of the whole island of Ireland' but that, without prejudice to that claim, in the prevailing circumstances the Irish parliament recognized that its laws would not apply to the area of the six counties given the right to secede by the treaty. In 1949, with the same constitution, the state became the Republic of Ireland.

Sources

To look for sources from which to extend and deepen perception of Parnell is to find oneself restricted to what has long been readily accessible. This does not mean that the access has always been fully exploited. The Irish, British, American and French newspapers of the day are still capable of yielding material which has not been previously publicized, which occasionally can even be used to revise the traditionally received account of events. Fresh insights are similarly to be found from old volumes of Hansard, and from those other official volumes which contain full division lists of every debate in the House of Commons. I have taken advantage of manuscript material in the British Library, the National Library of Ireland and the New York Public Library. A survey of specific sources used chapter by chapter appears below.

In an attempt to order the narrative of Parnell's life in its political context, certain books of our own time are indispensable: F. S. L. Lyons, *Charles Stewart Parnell* (London, 1977); Conor Cruise O'Brien, *Parnell and His Party, 1880–90* (Oxford, 1957); F. S. L. Lyons, *The Fall of Parnell* (Toronto and London, 1960); and Frank Callanan, *The Parnell Splits 1890–91* (Cork, 1992). I have made general use of these four.

For historical insight into Parnell's County Wicklow and family background, R. F. Foster, *Charles Stewart Parnell: The Man and His Family* (Harvester, 1976), is essential. Jane McL. Côté, *Fanny and Anna Parnell: Ireland's Patriot Sisters* (London, 1991), is also of a high standard on a lesser scale.

Paul Bew's *C. S. Parnell* (Dublin, 1980) is the best short work – 145 pages with an original touch. T. W. Moody's *Michael Davitt and the Irish Revolution 1846–1882* (Oxford, 1981) is of great value for the period it covers. J. L. Hammond's *Gladstone and the Irish Nation* (London, 1938), updated by M. R. D. Foot in 1964, still holds its place as a useful political framework.

Of older works, R. Barry O'Brien's *Charles Stewart Parnell 1846–1891* (2 vols., London, 1898) is still worth while, partly because O'Brien, a good journalist, knew Parnell well, and partly because he was writing within a few years of Parnell's death though without that detail of his personal life which was later to become available. Other biographies written before F. S. L. Lyons's major work are now only of secondary interest: M. M. O'Hara, *Chief and Tribune: Parnell and Davitt* (Dublin, 1919); St John G. Ervine, *Parnell* (London, 1925); Joan Haslip, *Parnell: A Biography* (London, 1936); Jules Abels, *The Parnell Tragedy* (London, 1966).

The primary works available consist of memoirs. Of these, Katharine O'Shea's *Charles Stewart Parnell: His Love Story and Political Life* (2 vols., London, 1914) is of course in a class of importance by itself. The book's defects and its virtues are discussed in the text. The many letters published there from both her husbands, together with the *Times* report on 17 and 18 November 1890 of the Divorce Court proceedings in the case of *O'Shea* v. *O'Shea*, provide the principal source for the study of Parnell's private life. An additional source of great value in this area is to be found in Henry Harrison, *Parnell Vindicated: The Lifting of the Veil* (London, 1931), a closely argued analysis of the love affair based on conversations he had with Katharine O'Shea/Parnell in Brighton in 1891 very shortly after Parnell's death. He did not, however, record these conversations until many years later and long after the publication of her own book. He was devoted to Parnell's memory and his argument does not always bear the weight he puts upon it.

The value of the memoirs of Parnell's political colleagues varies, though all obviously are of interest. All are affected by the sometimes considerable interval between the events they describe and the period in which they came to write about them. The passionate feelings aroused by the split in the party in the last year of his life inevitably give some emotional distortion to their hindsight. In this respect, an otherwise fairly humdrum first book by T. P. O'Connor, *The Parnell Movement* (London, 1886), is refreshing for having been written even before the introduction of the first Home Rule Bill, but his *Charles Stewart Parnell: A Memory* (London, 1891) is more rewarding. Michael Davitt, *The Fall of Feudalism in Ireland: The Story of the Land League Revolution* (London, 1904), is essential by reason of the important participation of its author in the events described, though inevitably self-centred. Its detailed dating is not always accurate. T. M. Healy, *Letters and Leaders of My Day* (2 vols., London, 1928), is inaccurate in more than that, but contains invaluable first-hand evidence from contemporary letters. Frank Hugh O'Donnell, *A History of the Irish Parliamentary Party* (2 vols., London, 1910), though egocentric and more than tinged with disrespect for Parnell's character, has a certain honesty in its assessment of his personality and contains at least one letter of which the implications seem to have been insufficiently explored. William O'Brien's *Recollections* (London, 1905), *An Olive Branch in Ireland and Its History* (London, 1910), *Evening Memories* (Dublin, 1924) and *The Parnell of Real Life* (London, 1926) inevitably suffered to a certain extent from the working of his imagination as a novelist across the lapse of time but reveal much of the attractive side of Parnell's character, particularly in passages included from his contemporary diaries. T. P. O'Connor, *Memoirs of an Old Parliamentarian* (2 vols., London, 1929), employs an old journalist's ability to summarize events and attitudes of forty years before in which he played a not unprominent part. In some ways the most useful memoir-text from Parnell's old colleagues is to be found in Justin McCarthy and Mrs Campbell Praed, *Our Book of Memories* (London, 1912), because it contains a number of impressions and descriptions transcribed by Mrs Praed within days of their contemporary utterance by McCarthy. His *Reminiscences* (2 vols., London, 1899), *Story of an Irishman* (London, 1904) and *Irish Recollections* (London, 1911) are of some use but in inverse proportion to their length. Some vivid glimpses of Parnell, and to a lesser extent of the O'Sheas, are to be found within Wilfrid Scawen Blunt, *The Land War in Ireland* (London, 1912), which contains passages from his contemporary diary, in L. J. Kettle (ed.), *Material for Victory: The Memoirs of Andrew J. Kettle* (Dublin, 1958), being memoirs compiled before 1916, and in J. J. Horgan, *Parnell to Pearse* (Dublin, 1948).

Family memoirs are represented by those of his brother, John Howard Parnell, *Parnell* (London, 1916), plodding but necessary, and of his sister Emily Dickinson, *A Patriot's Mistake* (Dublin, 1905), often unreliably fanciful.

To commemorate the centenary of Parnell's death in 1991, two excellent paperback volumes containing academic essays were published. *Parnell in Perspective*, edited by D. George Boyce and Alan O'Day (London, 1991), and *Parnell: The Politics of Power*, edited by Donal McCartney (Dublin, 1991). Three first-class essays on aspects of Parnell appear in R. F. Foster, *Paddy and Mr Punch: Connections in Irish and English History* (London, 1993).

Other works of use, some essential, are specified under individual chapter headings below together with other references, which are not exhaustive. The principal Irish newspaper consulted has been the *Freeman's Journal* (hereafter referred to as *FJ*; other works mentioned above are subsequently referred to by a short-title system).

Chapter 1

Parnell's funeral and its preliminaries: *Brighton Times*, 9, 16 October; *Brighton Herald*, 10, 17 October; *Irish Times*, 10, 12, 14, 17 October; *FJ*, 8, 12 October; *Wicklow Newsletter*, 17 October.

'The old revolutionary': J. J. O'Kelly; William O'Brien and Desmond Ryan (eds.), *Devoy's Post Bag* (2 vols., Dublin, 1953), I, p. 267.

'one English Member of Parliament': R. B. Cunningham-Graham, first President of the Scottish Labour Party.

Parnell's death from a heart attack is diagnosed by Professor J. B. Lyons in McCartney, *Parnell*, p. 179.

Dunsink Observatory: Margery Brady, *The Love Story of Parnell and Katharine O'Shea* (Dublin, 1991), pp. 7, 27.

Chapter 2

Dislike of pronunciation of Parnell: O'Shea, *Charles Stewart Parnell*, ii, p. 110.

The Famine: R. F. Foster, *Modern Ireland 1600–1972* (London, 1989), an unsurpassed encyclopaedic analysis of that whole period, writes that the traditional view of the Famine as a 'watershed in Irish history . . . does not stand up to examination' (p. 318). Dealing in economic terms, he correctly points out that it was the agricultural disruption at the end of the Napoleonic Wars which precipitated the socio-economic crisis of the next thirty years. But that crisis did reach a climax in human terms in the years 1845–9 and that experience left an indelible imprint on Irish popular memory, itself a major determinant in the course of Irish history.

'nearly one-eighth of the entire Irish population': *Select Committee on Poor Laws (Ireland)*, Parliamentary papers 1849, XVII, p. 467.

'Government Commission': the Devon Report, named after its Chairman, the Earl of Devon, Parliamentary Papers 1845, XIX-XXII.

'A landlord': W. J. O'Neill Daunt, *A Life Spent for Ireland*, (London, 1896), p. 76.

'thinning . . . getting straight': Nassau W. Senior, *Ireland: Journals and Conversations* (2 vols., London, 1868), i, p. 35.

Carlisle Tower, Lismore: the inscription was still just legible in 1992.

Wicklow in the Famine: *Select Committee on Poor Laws (Ireland)*, Parliamentary Papers 1849, XVII, pp. 454, 463–5, 467.

Dinner parties in the Famine: Dickinson, *Patriot's Mistake*, pp. 1–5. The date is identifiable through internal evidence as 1849. Mrs Parnell's poem: Robert McWade, *The Uncrowned King* (Edgwood, USA, 1891), pp. 63–4.

Stewart family: Côté, *Fanny and Anna*. Avondale: John Parnell, *Parnell*, pp. 9, 14–16; R. B. O'Brien, *Charles Stewart Parnell*, i, pp. 33–4; Côté, op. cit., pp. 41–3; Cassell's *Illustrated Handbook for Ireland* (London, 1853), p. 52.

Mrs Parnell's social life: *Dublin Evening Mail*, 15 February 1861, 20 March, 9, 16, 23 June 1862, 5, 18 March, 12 May, 15, 29 June, 31 July, 4 August 1863. For daughter Emily's fashionable London life, see Dickinson, op. cit., pp. 13–32.

Fanny's comment on Tory atmosphere: Fanny Parnell, *The Hovels of Ireland* (65-page pamphlet; New York, 1880), p. 55.

Parnell's father's will: *Notes and Queries*, 6th series, vol. x, 2 February 1884, p. 98.

Wicklow evangelicalism: Côté, op cit., pp. 32–3.

Parnell's childhood: John Parnell, op. cit.; Dickinson, op. cit.; McWade, op. cit.; Thomas Sherlock, *The Life of Charles Stewart Parnell* (Dublin, 1882); and R. B. O'Brien, op. cit., I, pp. 32–9. I tend to doubt the 'Englishness' of the nurse as suggested by John Parnell, who says her name was pronounced 'Tupny'. 'Mrs Twopenny' is accepted as English by Lyons. Charles Parnell later spoke of a nurse so named, but I believe this may have been a child's-play corruption of Mrs Gaffney, the wife of the gardener on the estate. Katharine Tynan (Hinkson) rightly emphasizes the importance of Irish peasant emotional influence on Parnell's early upbringing. See K. Tynan, *Memoirs* (London, 1924), p. 5.

Parnell's father's death: He was not actually playing cricket although most writers, following John Parnell and Emily Dickinson, say that he was. His name does not appear in the lists of the Wicklow team in any of the newspapers (*Wicklow Newsletter*, 2 July 1859; *Saunders Newsletter*, 4, 8 July 1859). His death was announced in the *Wicklow Newsletter* of 9 July simply as being in the Shelbourne Hotel, Dublin, 'after a short illness'.

Parnell and the stumping: see scores in *Wicklow Newsletter*, 25 June 1864. The story itself is found in R. B. O'Brien, op. cit., I, p. 52. 'Daisy-clipper': *Wicklow Newsletter*, 9 July 1864. Militia: *Wicklow Newsletter*, 4 March, 20 May 1865. September cricket: *Dublin Evening Mail* 9, 11, 13, 14, 15, 18 September 1869.

Chapter 3

General: D. G. Boyce, *Nationalism in Ireland* (London, 1982); W. E. Vaughan, *Landlords and Tenants in Ireland 1848–1904* (Dundalk, 1984); Barbara Solow, *The Land Question and the Irish Economy 1870–1903* (Cambridge, Mass., 1971); Tom Garvin, *The Evolution of Irish Nationalist Politics* (Dublin, 1981).

'the prostrate condition': *Kilkenny Journal*, 19 August 1848.

Agrarian outrages: Parliamentary Papers 1881, LXXVIII, p. 887.

'regeneration of Irish agriculture': William O'Connor Morris, 'The Land System of Ireland', in *Oxford Essays* (London, 1856), p. 199.

'Time unhappily': William O'Connor Morris, *Letters on the Land Question of Ireland* (London, 1870), p. ix.

Viceregal Lodge: Extracts from *Diaries of George Howard, Seventh Earl of Carlisle* by his sister, Caroline Lascelles (privately printed), p. 396. *Dublin Evening Mail*, 29 June 1863.

'Aleria': *Irish People*, 21 May, 18 June, 16 July, 1 October 1864. Fanny's identity revealed by John O'Leary, *Recollections of Fenians and Fenianism* (2 vols., London, 1896), I, p. 1.

Parnell's invitations to Viceregal Lodge: *FJ*, 31 January, 3, 14 February 1866.

Mrs Parnell 'aiding Fenian conspirators': *Saunders Newsletter*, 4 December 1866; *Irish Times*, 20 February 1867.

Arrest and trial of chemist (Power) and consequences for Mrs Parnell: State Paper Office (Dublin Castle, 1866), letters 23311, 23550; State Paper Office (Dublin Castle, 1868), 1619, 1721; State Paper Office (Dublin Castle, 1866), VIII, c 7, 11; *FJ*, 6 February 1868.

Mrs Parnell back at the ball: *FJ*, 8 March 1867.

Parnell's reaction: McCarthy, *Reminiscences*, II, pp. 109–10. He wrongly remembered the search as taking place at Avondale. See also O'Connor, *Parnell: A Memory*, p. 25; John Parnell, *Parnell*, pp. 70. 72.

Chapter 4

Parnell at Magdalene, Cambridge: O'Connor, *Parnell: A Memory*, p. 21. I am grateful to Mr G. W. Martin, sometime Research Fellow of Magdalene College, Cambridge, for private information; also for his article 'A Parnell Centenary' in the *Magdalene College Magazine and Record*, new series, no. 14, 1969–70, p. 12. See also *Irish Historical Studies*, vol. XIX, No. 73 (March 1974). Sleepwalking: R. B. O'Brien, *Charles Stewart Parnell*, I, pp. 40–41. Examinations: *Cambridge Chronicle and University Journal*, 9 June 1866; *Cambridge Independent Press*, 22 December 1866. Drowning incident: Dickinson, *Patriot's Mistake*, pp. 50–59; Harrison, *Parnell Vindicated*, pp. 430–36; *Cambridge Independent Press*, 5 January 1867. Magdalene has since made amends to Parnell by erecting a memorial plaque to him.

Parnell's land: In Parliamentary Papers 1876, LXXX, pp. 50, 211, he is shown as the thirteenth largest landowner in Co. Wicklow with 4,962 acres, while his brother John had 1,641 acres in Co. Armagh.

Twenty-first birthday: *Wicklow Newsletter*, 29 June 1867; *FJ*, 19 July 1867: Dickinson, op. cit., pp. 63–78.

FitzWilliam election and address: *FJ*, 9 November 1868; *Wicklow Newsletter*, 28 November 1868.

Station Road row: *Cambridge Independent Press*, 22 May 1869; *Cambridge Chronicle and University Journal*, 22 May 1869. The account given by R. B. O'Brien in op. cit., I, pp. 42–3, is a paraphrase of the report in the *Cambridge Chronicle and University Journal*, which is less detailed than that in the *Cambridge Independent Press*. See also Davitt, *Fall of Feudalism*, p. 107; *Magdalene College Magazine*, 1869–70, p. 10.

Cricket: *Cambridge Chronicle and University Journal*, 8 May 1869.

Glendalough row: *Wicklow Newsletter*, 4 September 1869. Captain Dickinson's fondness for drink is recorded in Dickinson, op. cit. This is a good example of evidence about Parnell long readily available from newspapers but ignored by writers about him. Roy Foster was first to publish it in *Parnell: The Man and His Family*, pp. 120–21.

Cricket, and other Wicklow information: *Wicklow Newsletter*, 6 March, 14 August, 18 September, 27 November 1869, 1 January, 30 July, 13 August 1870; *The Irish Sportsman and Farmer*, 16, 23 April, 7, 21 May 1870 (this paper only began publication in 1870).

Miss Woods: John Parnell, *Parnell*, pp. 62–3, 74–8, 80–81, 88–9. Parnell in the USA: John Parnell, op. cit., pp. 90–91, 100–103; R. B. O'Brien, op. cit., I, pp. 54–6; O'Connor, op. cit., pp. 29–31. Parnell's appearance and speech: O'Connor, op. cit., pp. 40, 213.

Chapter 5

'hung, drawn and quartered': J. F. X. O'Brien (later MP), who led an attack on Ballyknockane Barracks, Co. Cork.

Home Government Association: David Thornley, *Isaac Butt and Home Rule* (London, 1964), p. 92 and *passim*.

Blennerhassett: A. M. Sullivan, *New Ireland* (2 vols., London, 1877), p. 321ff.

1798: O'Connor, *The Parnell Movement*, pp. 258–9; R. B. O'Brien, *Charles Stewart Parnell*, I, p. 53.

Parnell's reading: R. B. O'Brien, op. cit., I, p. 53; Robert F. Walsh, *Memorial Volume to Charles Stewart Parnell* (New York, 1892), p. 8; *The Special Commission* (*Times* reprint), part XX, p. 5. This is part of the *Times* pocket reprint of proceedings before the Special Commissioners appointed under the Special Commission Act 1888. The full official documentation is to be found in eleven substantial volumes, with a further index volume, published by HMSO (London, 1890). Parnell's evidence appears in VII, pp. 1–369.

Church and Home Rule: Thornley, op. cit., pp. 151, 154.

At Avondale: John Parnell, *Parnell*, pp. 111–17, 125, 130–31; R. B. O'Brien, op. cit., I, p. 51.

Wicklow election: R. B. O'Brien, op. cit., I, pp. 56–7 (account from an interview with John Parnell); *FJ*, 5 March 1874 (letter from Richard T. C. Johnson); *Nation*, 7 February 1874; Dublin *Evening Mail*, 4, 10 February 1874.

Dublin election: R. B. O'Brien, op. cit., I, pp. 73–5, 76; *FJ*, 3, 9, 11, 12, 13, 17, 20, 21 March 1874; *Dublin Evening Mail*, 9, 19 March 1874; Kettle, *Material for Victory*, p. 18; O'Donnell, *Irish Parliamentary Party*, pp. 106–7; National Library of Ireland, MS 26,742 (letter from Parnell dated 1 April 1874).

Chapter 6

Home Rule: David Thornley, *Isaac Butt and Home Rule* (London, 1964), pp. 99–102, 160–68, 196, 230. *Daily Telegraph*: *FJ*, 4 July 1874. Parnell active: *FJ*, 13 July, 8 August, 10 October 1874. R. B. O'Brien dismisses Parnell's twelve months after the Dublin by-election in a sentence as having been spent quietly on his estates at Avondale (*Charles Stewart Parnell*, I, p. 76). Egan: *Special Commission* (*Times* reprint, 1890), xx, p. 8. Parnell's winter activity: *FJ*, 12, 13 October 1874, 22, 23 January, 24 February 1875. Theodosia concert: *Wicklow Newsletter*, 19 September 1874. Racing: *Wicklow Newsletter*, 13 March 1875. Mitchel: *FJ*, 27 July, 30 December 1874, 6 March 1875.

Meath election: R. B. O'Brien, op. cit., I, pp. 77–8; *Meath Herald and Cavan Advertiser*, 3 April 1875; *FJ*, 2, 10, 13, 20 April 1875; *Nation* 17, 24 April 1875; *Wicklow Newsletter*, 24 April 1875.

Chapter 7

(Newspaper references are to the year 1875.)

Parnell in the House: *Nation*, 1 May; Hansard, 3, CCXXIII-VI; R. B. O'Brien, *Charles Stewart Parnell*, I, pp. 85–6, 96, where he states particularly misleadingly, '. . . up to the end of 1876 he continued undistinguished, and almost unnoticed. He had not yet, so to say, drawn out of the ruck.' This has been universally followed by subsequent writers. Parnell's own suggestion occurs in his evidence before the Parnell Commission in 1889.

Parliamentary background: David Thornley, *Isaac Butt and Home Rule* (London, 1964), pp. 167, 235–7. Obstruction: *The Times*, 23 April; *Nation*, 1 May, Parnell's maiden speech: Hansard, 3, CCXXIII, 1643–5; *Nation*, 1 May; R. B. O'Brien, op. cit., I, p. 85. Later speeches: Hansard, 3 CCXXIII, 1915, CCXXIV, 42, 185; *Nation*, 29 May. Reception at Avondale: *FJ*, 18 May. Keppel Street: McCarthy, *Reminiscences*, II, pp. 89–91, 93. Questions: R. B. O'Brien, op. cit., I, p. 85; McCarthy, op. cit., II, p. 104; Hansard, 3, CCXXIV, 1625, CCXXV, 158, 1201–2, 1204 (Butt). Other interventions: Hansard, 3, CCXXVI, 96, 335, 370–71; *FJ*, 28 July, 2, 3, 4, 12 August; *Nation*, 31 July. Henry Lucy: *World*, 21 July, 27 October, 25 November.

Chapter 8

(Newspaper references are to the year 1875.)

Hyde Park speech: *Nation*, 7 August; *FJ*, 30 August (letter of James W. Cavanagh).

O'Connell Centenary celebrations: *FJ*, 4, 7, 9, 11 August, 17 November; *Nation*, 14 August, 27 November.

Home Rule League: *FJ*, 15 September.

Wexford: *FJ*, 4 October; *Wexford Independent*, 5 October; *Enniscorthy News*, 9 October; *Nation*, 9, 23 October.

Navan: *FJ*, 7, 8 October.

Chapter 9

(Newspaper references are to the year 1875 except where otherwise stated.)

Tenant farmers: *FJ*, 19 October. Galway: *Nation*, 30 October. Grattan: *FJ*, 9 November.

Centenary committee row: *FJ*, 13, 15, 17, 22, 24 November; *Nation*, 20, 27 November.

Parnell's Dublin speech: *FJ*, 29 November, 1 December.

Return from France and Home Rule: *FJ*, 1, 5, 15 January 1876; *Nation*, 8 January 1876.

Chapter 10

(Newspaper references are to the year 1876.)

Home Rule: *FJ*, 6, 7, 19 January: *Pall Mall Gazette*, 8 January. IRB: Letter from Charles Kickham to John Devoy dated 29 April, in William O'Brien and Desmond Ryan (eds.), *Devoy's Post Bag* (2 vols., Dublin, 1953), I, p. 164. *Daily Telegraph*: *Pall Mall Gazette*, 8 February.

Gladstone: *World*, 6 September.

Fenian prisoners: Hansard, 3, CCXXVII, 113–14; *FJ*, 9 February.

Obstructing: *Nation*, 19 February.

Parliamentary questions: Hansard, 3, CCXXVII, 263, 561, 682, 1025–6; *FJ*, 29 February; *World*, 8 March; David Thornley, *Isaac Butt and Home Rule* (London, 1964), pp. 275–6.

Home Ruler attendance: *FJ*, 4, 8 March; *Nation*, 19 February.

Obstruction: *FJ*, 4, 7, 8, 10, 11, March: *Nation*, 11, 18 March.

Chapter 11

(Newspaper references are to the year 1876.)

Gratitude from Forster: Hansard, 3, CCXXVIII, 424, 426–7; *World*, 29 March, 'Under the Clock by One of the hands' (Henry Lucy).

Avondale: *Wicklow Newsletter*, 25 March, 22 April. Dublin: *FJ*, 24 April.

Fenians: *FJ*, 19 April. However, Charles Kickham, President of the IRB, was still prepared to continue to give the party the IRB's support on the grounds that 'it might effect *some* good' (William O'Brien and Desmond Ryan (eds.), *Devoy's Post Bag* (2 vols., Dublin, 1953), I, p. 164).

Rathdrum races: *FJ*, 1 May; *Wicklow Newsletter*, 6 May.

Plimsoll: Hansard, 3, CCXXIX, 78–9.

Cattle diseases: Hansard, 3, CCXXIX, 183.

Disraeli: Hansard, 3, CCXXIX, 1045–6.

'a fortnight's obstruction': *FJ*, 26, 30, 31 May; Hansard, 3, CCXXIX, 1397–1400, 1495ff; *World*, 7 June. *FJ*'s reservations: 12 June. Constabulary: Hansard, 3, CCXXX, 572.

Home Rule motion, Butt, Smyth: Hansard, 3, CCXXX, 738, 743, 752.

Hicks Beach, Parnell and Repeal: Hansard, 3, CCXXX, 803. 'No murder at Manchester': Hansard, 3, CCXXX, 808. Twice '. . . murder': Hansard, 3, CCXXIX, 1046–8. This speech may have been overlooked by historians because it is not listed under Parnell in the index to this volume of Hansard.

Chapter 12

(Newspaper references are to the year 1876.)

Home Rule debate lost: Hansard, 3, CCXXX, 819ff. *FJ, Irishman, Nation*: *FJ*, 8 July.

Harold's Cross: *FJ*, 5 July.

Dublin Convention: *FJ*, 22, 23 August.

Avondale: *Wicklow Newsletter*, 19, 26 August.

O'Connor Power: *FJ*, 18 July.

IRB: R. V. Comerford, *The Fenians in Context: Irish Politics and Society 1848–82* (Dublin, 1985), particularly pp. 203–7, 211–14, 225–8.

Mission to USA and return: William O'Brien and Desmond Ryan (eds.), *Devoy's Post Bag* (2 vols., Dublin, 1953), 1, p. 208; *New York Herald*, 13, 29 October; *Irish World*, 14, 28 October; *Nation*, 11, 18, 25 October; *United Irishman* (Liverpool), 18 November; R. B. O'Brien, *Charles Stewart Parnell*, 1, pp. 100–102; John Parnell, *Parnell*, pp. 146–8.

Chapter 13

(*Newspaper references are to the year 1877.*)

General: John Parnell, *Parnell*; O'Donnell, *Irish Parliamentary Party*; McCarthy, *Reminiscences*; R. B. O'Brien, *Charles Stewart Parnell*, 1, pp. 138–9.

Parnell in House of Commons. Land: Hansard, 3, CCXXXII, 346, 465. Obstruction: Hansard, 3, CCXXXII, 1069, 1070, 1073, 1247–8, 1439, 1442, 1642, CCXXXIII, 366, 523–8, 532–4, 543–5, 616–22, 639–42 (Butt, 642), 680–82 (Butt, 680); *FJ*, 24 February, 6, 9, 16, 20, 27, 28 March, 6 April. King-Harman: *FJ*, 21 March. Mitchell Henry: *FJ*, 25 January. Prisons Bill: Hansard, 3, CCXXXIII, 616–38; *FJ*, 27, 28, 29 March, 6 April. Henry Lucy: *World*, 11 April. Mutiny Bill: Hansard, 3, CCXXXIII, 1045–50 (Butt, 1049); *FJ*, 13, 14, 16, 17, 20 April. Parnell's hunters: *FJ*, 6 April.

Chapter 14

(*Newspaper references are to the year 1877.*)

'wantonness and folly': *FJ*, 14 April. Parnell's reply: *FJ*, 17 April. Marine Mutiny Bill: *FJ*, 17 April; Hansard, 3, CCXXXII, 1223, 1226–30, 1235–6.

Parnell's lecture and reply to Butt: *FJ*, 23 April, 26 May.

Marine Mutiny Bill: Hansard, 3, CCXXXIII, 122–6, 1455–65.

Home Rule motion: *FJ*, 25, 26, 27 April; Hansard, 3, CCXXXII, 1746–1846 (Parnell, 1761).

Army Estimates: Hansard 3, CCXXXV, 651–62.

South Africa Bill: *FJ*, 25, 26 July, 1, 2, 3 August; Hansard, 3, CCXXXV, 1768–9, 1805–44, CCXXXVI, 177–205, 227–303.

Chapter 15

'New departure': *FJ*, 14 August 1877.

Letter to *The Times*: *FJ*, 31 July 1877.

Rotunda Rooms and Sackville Street: *FJ*, 22 August 1877.

Home Rule Confederation of Great Britain: R. B. O'Brien, *Charles Stewart Parnell*, I, pp. 144–6 (there is an inaccuracy in this passage: Butt was not present when Parnell was elected).

'*ne plus ultra*': *FJ*, 10 December 1877; *Nation*, 15 December 1877.

Fenians. In 1873: William O'Brien and Desmond Ryan (eds.), *Devoy's Post Bag* (2 vols., Dublin, 1953), I, p. 299. 'I find myself in prison' (Michael Davitt), *Irishman*, 14 December 1878, cited in Moody, *Davitt*, p. 183.

Parnell. In Paris: O'Brien and Ryan, op. cit., I, pp. 267–8. With O'Kelly in London: O'Brien and Ryan, op cit., I, p. 269. Carroll's view: O'Brien and Ryan, op. cit., I, p. 280; Davitt's view: Davitt, *Fall of Feudalism*, pp. 110–11. With Carroll at reception for Davitt in Dublin: *FJ*, 14 January 1878. Carroll: O'Brien and Ryan, op. cit., I, p. 298. In House: Hansard, 3, CCXXXVIII, 194; *FJ*, 19 January 1878. Surrey Hotel meeting: O'Brien and Ryan, op. cit., I, pp. 298, 323–4; O'Donnell, *Irish Parliamentary Party*, 271–6.

Capital punishment: *FJ*, 15 March 1878; Hansard, 3, CCXXXVIII, 1274.

Ferguson and 'new departure': *FJ*, 29 May 1877.

Factory and Workshops Bill: Hansard, 3, CCXXXVIII, 303–57 (frequently), 456–614, 879–93.

Chapter 16

(*Newspaper references are to the year 1878.*)

General: *FJ*; Davitt, *Fall of Feudalism*; Moody, *Davitt*, pp. 186–220; John Devoy, *The Land of Eire* (New York, 1882); Paul Bew, *Land and the National Question in Ireland 1858–82* (Dublin, 1978); William O'Brien and Desmond Ryan, *Devoy's Post Bag* (2 vols., London, 1953), I; Hansard, 3, CCXXXVIII, CCXXXIX.

St James's Hall meeting: *FJ*, 11 March (contains a long account of prison conditions for Davitt); Moody, op. cit., p. 196.

St Helens meeting: Davitt, op. cit., pp. 111–13; Moody, op. cit., pp. 206–8, 210; Fenian meeting: Moody, op. cit., pp. 205–6.

Butt: *FJ*, 9, 10, 12, 13, 20, 24 April, 6, 11, 14, 17, 27 May.

Parnell. Islington: *FJ*, 27 May, 1, 3, June. 'Childish' resolution: *FJ*, 31 May, 5 June. On Committee of House: *FJ*, 8 July. 'Forbearance of House': Hansard, 3, CCXXXVIII, 1662.

Home Rule Confederation of Great Britain: *FJ*, 22, 23, October; *The Times*, 16 October.

Chapter 17

'New departure': Moody, *Davitt*, p. 251ff.

Home Rule Confederation: *FJ*, 22, 23, October 1878.

O'Connor Power in Co. Mayo: *FJ*, 28 October, 2 November 1878.

Parnell. At Ballinasloe: *FJ*, 3 November 1878. In Kerry: *FJ*, 18 November 1878, 5 February 1879. At Avondale: *FJ*, 3 December 1878. In Belfast with Biggar: *FJ*, 11 February 1879. At Kilnaleck: *FJ*, 15 April 1879.

Dillon: *FJ*, 1 December 1878. 'Sinking ship': *FJ*, 5 February 1879.

Cattle trade: *FJ*, 2 January 1879.

Agricultural crisis: W. E. Vaughan, *Landlords and Tenants in Ireland 1848–1904* (Duldalk, 1984); J. Donnelly Jr, *The Land and the People of Nineteenth-century Cork* (Cork, 1985); Paul Bew, *Land and the National Question in Ireland 1858–82* (Dublin, 1978); Barbara Solow, *The Land Question and the Irish Economy 1870–1903* (Cambridge, Mass., 1971).

Chapter 18

(Newspaper references are to the year 1879.)

General: Davitt, *Fall of Feudalism*; Moody, *Davitt*; W. E. Vaughan, *Landlords and Tenants in Ireland 1848–1904* (Duldalk, 1984); J. Donnelly Jr, *The Land and the People of Ninteenth-century Cork* (Cork, 1985); Paul Bew, *Land and The National Question in Ireland 1858–82* (Dublin, 1978); *FJ*; Hansard, 3, CCXLIII, CCXLVI-VIII.

Civil Service Estimates: Hansard, 3, CCXLVI, 1276–9, 1287–9, 1298, 1302, 1321.

Army Discipline and Regulation Bill: Hansard, 3, CCXLVI, 1578–80, 1582–3, 1591–3, CCXLVII, 194–6.

Tenants' Defence Association: *FJ*, 17, 18, 24 April.

Naas Poor Law Guardians: *FJ*, 29 May.

Irishtown meeting: Moody, op. cit., pp. 284–6, 288–92.

Parnell in House: *FJ*, 28 May. Butt's death: 6, 7, 12, 14 May. Gabbett: *FJ*, 14, 17 May. Voters in England: *FJ*, 27 May. Army discipline: *FJ*, 21 May, 11, 18, 20, 28 June, 1, 4, 7, 15, 19 July. Zulu War: *FJ*, 28 May, 13, 17 June; Hansard, 3, CCXLIII, 1886. 'Holocaust': Hansard, 3, CCXLIV, 1091. Prison warders: *FJ*, 10 June. 'Constructive murder' and Criminal Appeal: Hansard, 3, CCXLV, 336–8.

Devoy: Moody, op. cit., pp. 296–303.

Meetings. Westport: Moody, op. cit., pp. 303–6; *FJ*, 9, 12 June. Milltown: *FJ*, 16 June. Claremorris: *FJ*, 16 June. Archbishop of Tuam and Davitt: *FJ*, 10 July.

Chapter 19

(*Newspaper references are to the year 1879.*)

Ennis by-election: Healy, *Letters and Leaders*, 1, 68–72; *Clare Examiner and Limerick Advertiser*, 23 July; *FJ*, 28 July. Limerick Junction: *FJ*, 28 July, 9 August; *Clare Examiner and Limerick Advertiser*, 9 August (Edmund Dwyer Gray). *Pall Mall Gazette*: *FJ*, 5 September.

Meetings. Limerick: *Clare Examiner and Limerick Advertiser*, 6 September. Tipperary: *FJ*, 22 September. Davitt at Tuam: *FJ*, 22 September. Newry: *FJ*, 17 October. Navan: *FJ*, 15 October; *Clare Examiner and Limerick Advertiser*, 18 October. Belfast: *FJ*, 15 October. Enniscorthy: *FJ*, 27 October. Davitt at Killaloe: *FJ*, 27 October. Galway: *FJ*, 2 November. Roscommon: *FJ*, 17 November. Brennan and Parnell at Balla: *FJ*, 24 November. Parnell in Dublin: *FJ*, 22 November. Castlerea: *FJ*, 8 December.

Rejected Convention: *FJ*, 15, 17 November. Land League: *FJ*, 22 October; Davitt, *Fall of Feudalism*, pp. 168–80.

Wicklow priest: *Wicklow Newsletter*, 27 September.

Parnell at Dublin Home Rule meeting: *FJ*, 22 August.

Reductions of rent: *FJ*, 30 October, 1, 3 November.

Mitchell Henry: *FJ*, 1 November. King-Harman: *FJ*, 12 November.

'Republican garrison': *FJ*, 19 November.

Dillon: *Nation*, 11 October, cited by F. S. L. Lyons, *John Dillon* (London, 1968), p. 32.

Wicklow workhouse: *Wicklow Newsletter*, 22 November.

Skibbereen and Galway (Mitchell Henry letter): *FJ*, 15, 20 December.

Balla eviction sequel: *FJ*, 13 December.

Parnell's depature for USA: *FJ*, 22 December.

Chapter 20

Parnell in USA: R. B. O'Brien, *Charles Stewart Parnell*, I, p. 198; *New York Times*, 31 December 1879, 1, 2, 3, 5, 9, 10, 11, 14, 26, 27 January, 5, 19, February 1880; *Irish World*, 17, 24 January 1880 ('John Brown's Body'); Healy, *Letters and Leaders*, I, pp. 80–88.

Fanny Parnell: William O'Brien and Desmond Ryan (eds.), *Devoy's Post Bag* (2 vols., Dublin, 1953), I, p. 487.

Cincinnatti speech: Lyons, *Charles Stewart Parnell*, pp. 111–12.

Parnell in Iowa: Article by Kenneth E. Colton in *Annals of Iowa*, April 1940, vol 22, no. 4; *Iowa State Register*, 24 January, 11, 18 February 1880, and other local papers; Elbert Hubbard, *Little Journeys to the Houses of Great Lovers* (New York, 1906), vol. XVIII, no. 5; 'Virgilius', *Parnell, or Ireland and America* (New York, 1880).

Chapter 21

Letters: O'Shea, *Charles Stewart Parnell*.

Arrival at Queenstown: Healy, *Letters and Leaders*, I, p. 89.

Parnell, egg on face at Enniscorthy: Andrew Dunlop, *Fifty Years of Journalism* (Dublin, 1911), pp. 153–4.

O'Shea candidacy for Co. Clare: *Clare Freeman and Ennis Gazette*, 27, 31 March 1880. Election address and canvassing: *Clare Freeman and Ennis Gazette*, 3 April 1880; Denis Gwynn, *The O'Gorman Mahon* (London, 1934), pp. 246–8.

O'Shea on day of Parnell's election: O'Connor, *Parnell: A Memory*, p. 82; O'Connor *Memoirs*, I, pp. 46–7; O'Shea, op. cit., I, p. 134.

Chapter 22

From this point onwards substantial reference to Katharine O'Shea's book becomes essential for consideration of Parnell's private life. References to page numbers in that work are not always given in these notes, but most of the close personal details about him and almost all his personal letters stem from that source. Other letters are from *The Times* of 17 and 18 November 1890.

Her son Gerard O'Shea participated in the editing of the book, but the extent to which he may have distorted the essential truth to favour his father has been exaggerated, particularly by Henry Harrison in *Parnell Vindicated*. Harrison infers that at the time of the publication of the book Katie was in her dotage, but at a press conference for the book on 22 April 1914, at which Gerard O'Shea sat beside her, 'all interviewers described her charm, humour and intellectual alertness', according to R. F. Foster (*Paddy and Mr Punch*, chapter 7). It is difficult to think that the book contains matter she had not wished to include.

Joyce Marlow, *The Uncrowned Queen of Ireland* (London, 1975), is helpful in filling out the background of the Wood family and the early years of the O'Shea marriage. See also Margaret Leamy, *Parnell's Faithful Few* (New York, 1936).

Parnell and Forster: Hansard, 3, CCLII, 167.

'a bit of a bully': Blunt, *Land War*, p. 29.

'old friend and business associate': Chrisopher Weguelin, elected in 1868 Liberal MP for Youghal but unseated on petition. He is sympathetically mentioned in O'Shea, *Charles Stewart Parnell*, I, p. 120. Tim Healy, in a letter to his wife (3 December 1890), has information to suggest that Katie had had an affair with Weguelin (*Letters and Leaders*, I, p. 333). Part of a copy of a letter between her and Willie in the National Library of Ireland seems to confirm this.

O'Shea's maiden speech: *Clare Freeman and Ennis Gazette*, 3 July 1880; Hansard, 3, CCLIII, 1146–9.

'a lady in the case': Healy, op. cit., I, p. 98.

Autumn public meetings: all details are from the *FJ* (call of 'O'Shea!': 20 September).

Chapter 23

The action in this chapter takes place between Tuesday 21 September and Monday 18 October 1880. It is covered in O'Shea, *Charles Stewart Parnell*, I, pp. 144–6, 152–3. The letter on p. 152, headed simply 'Dublin Tuesday', is placed out of sequence. Parnell wrote 'on my return from Ennis', where he had been on Sunday 19 September. Tuesday was 21 September. The letter should be read before the letter dated 22 September on p. 144.

The public events are covered in *FJ*. New Ross: 27 September. Kilkenny and Cork events, with accounts of other meetings: 4, 5, October. Dillon in Cork: 11 October. Longford: 18 October.

Chapter 24

General: O'Shea, *Charles Stewart Parnell*, I, pp. 154, 156–8.

Agrarian outrages: *FJ*, almost daily through the autumn and winter of 1880.

Meetings (references to *FJ*). Longford: 18 October 1880. Galway: 25 October 1880 ('legislative independence': Lyons, *Charles Stewart Parnell*, p. 138). Brennan at Westport: quoted in 6 January 1881. Sheridan at Clonmacnoise: quoted in 6 January 1881. Boyton at Cahir: quoted in 5 January 1881. Brennan, 'self-reliance', Carrick-on-Suir: quoted in 4 January 1881. Brennan at Clonmacnoise: quoted in 6 January 1881.

Parnell and *Wiener Allgemeine Zeitung* interview: *FJ*, 17 January 1881.

Davitt: William O'Brien and Desmond Ryan (eds.), *Devoy's Post Bag* (2 vols., Dublin, 1953), II, p. 24. Cork land-agent: J. Donnelly Jr, *The Land and the People of Nineteenth-century Cork* (Cork, 1985), p. 271.

Outrages: Fifty men with blackened faces: *FJ*, 11 November 1880. Man's ears: *FJ*, 1 December 1880. Donkey's ears: *FJ*, 3 December 1880. Carded widows: *FJ*, 2 December 1880. Loughrea threat: *FJ*, 2 December 1880. Rough times for bailiffs: *FJ*, 2 December 1880. Countryside: *FJ*, 2 November 1880. Matt Harris: *FJ*, 25 October 1880.

Parnell. Threatening letter: *FJ*, 16 December 1880. Shooting landlords: *FJ*, 2 November 1880. At Limerick: *FJ*, 2 November 1880. At Athlone: *FJ*, 8 November 1880. Rebuke to Tipperary: *FJ*, 2 November 1880. Rejection of three Fs: *FJ*, 2 November 1880.

O'Shea at Milltown Malbay: *Clare Freeman and Ennis Gazette*, 8 September 1880.

Chapter 25

(*Newspaper references are to the year 1880 unless otherwise stated.*)

General: O'Shea, *Charles Stewart Parnell*; Harrison, *Parnell Vindicated*; *The Times*, 17 November 1890; *FJ*.

'nothing . . . for special reprobation': Blunt, *Land War*, p. 452.

'My own love': O'Shea, op. cit., I, p. 153.

F. H. O'Donnell meeting: O'Donnell, *Irish Parliamentary Party*, II, pp. 286–7.

Henry Harrison. Katie's story: *Parnell Vindicated*, pp. 118–29, 167–80. Conclusion: op. cit., pp. 239–66.

Athlone meeting, and collapsing platform: *FJ*, 8 November.

Parnell. At Limerick: *FJ*, 3 November. At Belleek: *FJ*, 10 November. At Ballyshannon and Enniskillen: 11 November.

Boyton on Parnell: *FJ*, 8 November.

Divorce Court evidence: *The Times*, 17 November 1890.

Evictions: Figures from Parliamentary Papers, given in tables by Moody, *Davitt*, pp. 562–3, 567.

Chapter 26

(*Newspaper references are to the year 1880.*)

General: O'Shea, *Charles Stewart Parnell*, I, pp. 163–5.

Parnell at Kilkenny: *FJ*, 6, 7, December; *Waterford Daily Mail*, 7, 9 December (hunting).

Dillon and Boyton at Fethard: *FJ*, 7 December.

Healy's trial: *Cork Examiner*, 15, 16 December.

Chapter 27

O'Shea. Apology to party meeting: *FJ*, 28 December 1880. Sitting and voting with Parnell party: *FJ*, 19, 21, 27 January, 2, 3, 4 February 1881; His 'Honourable Friend': Hansard, 3, CCLVII, 393.

State trial: *FJ*, 28, 29, 31 December 1880, 3, 4, 5, 6 January 1881; O'Shea, *Charles Stewart Parnell*, I, pp. 169–72.

Davitt: William O'Brien and Desmond Ryan (eds.), *Devoy's Post Bag* (2 vols., Dublin, 1953), II, p. 23.

Parnell: Hansard, 3, CCLVII, 192–203 (shooting Parnell, 195; 'unwritten law', 200; landlord intimidation, 202); *FJ*, 7 January 1881.

O'Donnell: *Irish Parliamentary Party*, II, p. 15.

'What a revelation': Henry Lucy, *A Diary of Two Parliaments* (London, 1886), pp. 108–9.

Chapter 28

Parnell in the House: Hansard, 3 CCLVII, 902–14 (abolishing landlordism, 'shedding blood' for Ireland, 906–7).

Lyons: *Charles Stewart Parnell*, p. 146. Professor Moody also suggests that Parnell was saying that the initiative would be his (*Davitt*, p. 458). But see Hansard, 3, CCLVIII, 912.

Parnell. And House of Commons Library: R. B. O'Brien, *Charles Stewart Parnell*, I, pp. 268–76. With Davitt and Kettle: Moody, *Davitt*, pp. 460–62; Kettle, *Material for Victory*, pp. 39–42; Davitt, *Fall of Feudalism*, pp. 301–2. Cable to US: Davitt, op. cit., pp. 297–8.

Anna and Ladies' Land League: Côté, *Fanny and Anna*, pp. 154–60.

Arrest of Davitt: Moody, op. cit., pp. 464–5.

Chapter 29

(Newspaper references are to the year 1881.)

'Turning point': C. C. O'Brien, *Parnell and His Party*, p. 59.

Suspensions: Hansard, 3, CCLVIII, 68–88.

Outrages: According to Constabulary Returns, they increased from 2,590 in 1880 to 4,439 in 1881 (Moody, *Davitt*, pp. 567–8).

'State next to rebellion': J. Donnelly Jr, *The Land and the People of Nineteenth-century Cork* (Cork, 1985), p. 278; Paul Bew, *Land and the National Question in Ireland 1858–82* (Dublin, 1978), pp. 167–8.

Healy's story: Healy, *Letters and Leaders*, I, pp. 107–110. Land League executive movements: *FJ*, 4–15 February. Dillon: *FJ*, 4, 9, 10, 11, 12 February. Biggar, Brennan, Harris and Louden: *FJ*, 11, 12 February. Lyons's statement following Healy that 'the executive assembled in Paris within a couple of days of Davitt's arrest [3 February]' is plainly incorrect. Healy himself may well have gone to Paris immediately, since his name does not figure in any of these reports. Parnell's movements may be less confidently traced in *FJ*, 4, 8, 9, 12, 14, 15, 18, 19, 21 February; *Le Figaro*, 14, 16, 17, 19 February. Lomasney's letter: William O'Brien and Desmond Ryan (eds.), *Devoy's Post Bag* (2 vols., Dublin, 1953), II, p. 36.

Parnell in Paris also: *L'Intransigeant*, 16, 19, 26, 27 February, 2 March. Davitt's *Fall of Feudalism*, pp. 305–6, suggests that Healy's version of the story was in circulation before that book was published in 1904. Davitt himself was in prison at the time of the Paris executive meeting. O'Shea, *Charles Stewart Parnell*, covers the event but in very confused fashion (I, pp. 165–6), but Parnell's letters on pp. 178–80 clearly relate to this period.

Meeting with le Caron: *Twenty-five Years in the Secret Service* (London, 1892), pp. 171, 175, 177.

Chapter 30

(Newspaper references are to the year 1881.)

O'Shea. Davitt's treatment: Hansard, 3, CCLVIII, 260; House of Commons Division Lists 1880, Cappagh: Hansard, 3, CCLX, 1535.

Parnell back in House: 3, CCLVIII, 1247–9.

Clara meeting: *FJ*, 21 February.

Parnell. In Paris again: *FJ*, 24, 25, 26, 28 February, 3 March. Coercion Bill: Hansard, 3, CCLIX, 336 ('respect for Fenians', 339). At Birmingham, Cork, Dublin, Manchester, Newcastle, Rotunda Rooms Convention, Hilltown: *FJ*, 9, 11, 13, 14, 18, 24, 25 April.

Other meetings. Boyton at Tralee: *FJ*, 3 March. Boyton in Kilmainham: *FJ*, 10 March. Brennan at Claremorris: *FJ*, 2 May. Dillon at Grangemockler: *FJ*, 6 May.

Land Law (Ireland), Bill, Parnell: Hansard, 3, CCLX, 933; Parliamentary Papers 1881, pp. 18, 21.

Chapter 31

(Newspaper references are to the year 1881.)

O'Shea. Active: Hansard, 3, CCLIX, 324, 332, 499, 1334. Sir George O'Donnell's petition: BM Add. MSS 44269 (5 April). Walks out: *FJ*, 7 May. Voting for Land Bill: House of Commons Division Lists 1881 – all other Division information in this chapter from the same source. Gladstone: BM Add. MSS 44265 (10 June).

Parnell. And Dr Croke: *FJ*, 7, 9, 11, 12 May. Land Bill: Hansard, 3, CCLXI, 883–97. 'Looking pale': *FJ*, 27 May. O'Brien and *United Ireland*: W. O'Brien, *Recollections*, pp. 297–308.

Duel incident: O'Shea, *Charles Stewart Parnell*, I, pp. 187–91; *The Times*, 17 November 1890. The month of January given in O'Shea was clearly a misprint or other error. The correct July dating of the letter and other details of the incident are revealed in the Divorce Court (*The Times*, 17 November 1890).

Chapter 32

(Newspaper references are to the year 1881.)

Parnell. Commons order of business and suspension: Hansard, 3, CCLXIV, 385–90. O'Shea, *Charles Stewart Parnell*, I, pp. 199–200. Lucy comment: Henry Lucy, *A Diary of Two Parliaments* (London, 1886), pp. 163–4. Freudian slip: Hansard, 3, CCLXV, 511. And his sister Anna: Hansard, 3, CCLXV, 556–7. At Ulster by-election: *FJ*, 29, 30, 31 August, 1, 2, 3, 5, 6, 7, 9 September (putting an end to landlords north and south, Cookstown, 5 September). At Dublin convention: *FJ*, 16 September. Hero's welcome in Dublin: *FJ*, 26 September. Maryborough convention: *FJ*, 27 September. At Cork: *FJ*, 3 October. At Mallow: *FJ*, 4 October. At Waterford: *FJ*, 6 October. Land League, Dublin: *FJ*, 8 October. In Wexford: *FJ*, 10, 11 October.

Hicks Beach: *FJ*, 22 September. Maynooth manifesto: *FJ*, 29 September.

Convention: *United Ireland*, 24 September. Fanny Parnell's poem: *United Ireland*, 30 September.

Chapter 33

(Newspaper references are to the year 1881.)

Egan: *FJ*, 8 October.

Parnell. At Enniscorthy: *FJ*, 10 October. Letters: O'Shea, *Charles Stewart Parnell*, I, pp. 200–201, 207 ('the movement is breaking fast'). At Wexford: *FJ*, 10, 11 October; R. B. O'Brien, *Charles Stewart Parnell*, I, pp. 311–12. Arrested: *FJ*, 13, 14 October. Letter to Dillon: F. S. L. Lyons, *John Dillon* (London, 1968), pp. 58–9.

Harrington letter: National Library of Ireland, Harrington Papers 8578.

Henry George: Letters to Patrick Ford, Henry George Papers, New York Public Library.

Captain Moonlight: *United Ireland,* 5 November.

Chapter 34

Parnell in Kilmainham: O'Shea, *Charles Stewart Parnell,* I, pp. 207–44; W. O'Brien, *Recollections,* pp. 365–7, 384–402; Kettle, *Material for Victory,* pp. 57–8.

Harrison: *Parnell Vindicated,* pp. 218–38 (particularly pp. 223, 224 and 238).

Herbert Gladstone's diary: A. B. Cooke and J. R. Vincent, 'Herbert Gladstone, Forster and Ireland 1881–2', I and II, in *Irish Historical Studies,* September 1971 and March 1972.

Chapter 35

General: O'Shea, *Charles Stewart Parnell,* I, pp. 243–61; Tom Garvin, *The Evolution of Irish Nationalist Politics* (Dublin, 1981), pp. 352–66; Lyons, *Charles Stewart Parnell,* pp. 189–207; Letter to Ford, 22 April 1882, Henry George Papers, New York Public Library.

O'Shea to Gladstone: BM Add. MSS 44269, letters dated 8, 13, 18 April, 3, 4, 7, 10 May 1882. Gladstone to O'Shea: BM Add. MSS 62114A, letter dated 11 April, Add. MSS 44269, letters dated 15, 18 April, 7 May 1882.

O'Shea to Chamberlain: J. L. Garvin, *The Life of Joseph Chamberlain* (2 vols., London, 1932), I, p. 350. Chamberlain to O'Shea: J. L. Garvin, op. cit., I, p. 351. Chamberlain to Gladstone: J. L. Garvin, op. cit., I, p. 352.

Chapter 36

General: Tom Corfe, *The Phoenix Park Murders* (London, 1966), *passim*; Davitt, *Fall of Feudalism,* pp. 355–64; P. J. Tynan, *The Irish National Invincibles and Their Times* (London, 1894) – self-important but an insider's account – pp. 427–91; O'Shea, *Charles Stewart Parnell,* I, pp. 262–74; McCarthy and Praed, *Book of Memories,* pp. 95–8; Joseph Chamberlain, *A Political Memoir* (London, 1953); O'Donnell, *Irish Parliamentary Party,* II, pp. 121–2; *Special Commission* (HMSO, 1890), V, pp. 522–79, evidence of Patrick Delaney (Delaney, serving life imprisonment for involvement in the Phoenix Park murders, may be suspected of giving the sort of evidence to the Commission which he may have thought they wanted to hear).

Egan: Corfe, op. cit., pp. 137–40, 214, 231, 248, 250. McCafferty: Corfe, op. cit., p. 141.

Chamberlain: J. L. Garvin, op. cit., I, pp. 360–68.

Spencer: R. B. O'Brien, *Charles Stewart Parnell*, I, pp. 354–5, but see also A. B. Cooke and J. R. Vincent, 'Lord Spencer on the Phoenix Park Murders', in *Irish Historical Studies*, vol. XVIII, no. 72 (September 1973).

Lord Frederick Cavendish: Hansard, 3, CCLXIX, 1602. Trevelyan, then Chief Secretary, revealed that while Forster had had police protection which was withdrawn when he left Ireland, 'with regard to my lamented predecessor, no precautions were taken at all'. Cavendish's arrival had not been notified to the police who were unaware that he was coming until he appeared in the procession entering Dublin with Spencer. He was then looked upon as part of Spencer's party and no special steps were taken to protect him.

Chapter 37

Land Court cases: *Irish Land Commission*, 'Accounts and papers', 1882, LV, p. 379.

Parnell: Hansard, 3, CCLXIX, 323, 672–4; A. L. Thorold, *Henry Labouchere* (London, 1923), pp. 161–70.

O'Shea in House: Hansard, 3, CCLXIX, 140–41, 672–4.

Remarks about Gladstone in Hamilton diary: D. W. R. Bahlman, *The Diary of Sir E. W. Hamilton 1880–1885* (2 vols., Oxford, 1972), I, pp. 272–3, 247, 253, 269 (night walks), 290, 327–8, 409 (bomb damage).

Chamberlain: J. L. Garvin, *The Life of Joseph Chamberlain* (2 vols., London, 1932), I, pp. 369–74.

Katie O'Shea: O'Shea, *Charles Stewart Parnell*, II, pp. 1–17 (the term 'envoy' should be treated with reserve). 'P for pig' letter: O'Shea, op. cit., II, p. 197.

Forster attack on Parnell: Hansard, 3, CCLXXVI, 607–34. Parnell: Hansard, 3, CCLXXVI, 628, 716–25. O'Shea: Hansard, 3, CCLXXVI, 725; Henry Lucy, *A Diary of Two Parliaments* (London, 1886), pp. 236, 238, 246.

W. & K. O'Shea letters to Gladstone: BM Add. MSS 44269.

Parnell's 1889 statement: 13 December 1889, quoted by C. C. O'Brien, *Parnell and His Party*, p. 280.

Parnell, personal details: O'Shea, *Charles Stewart Parnell*, II, pp. 46–57 (revolver practice, p. 48; cobweb cure, p. 50), 71–3 (beliefs), 108–20 (poem, p. 113), and *passim*; Harrison, *Parnell Vindicated*, p. 123.

National tribute: *FJ*, 12 December 1883; Lyons, *Charles Stewart Parnell*, p. 246.

Chapter 38

General: J. Chamberlain, *A Political Memoir* (London, 1953); C. H. D. Howard, 'Documents relating to the Irish "Central Board" Scheme 1884–5; in *Irish Historical Studies*, March 1953, and 'Joseph Chamberlain, Parnell and the Irish "Central Board" Scheme 1884–5', in *Irish Historical Studies*, September 1953; J. L. Garvin *The Life of Joseph Chamberlain* (2 vols., London, 1932), II, pp. 575–605; A. B. Cooke and John Vincent, *The Governing Passion: Cabinet Government and Party Politics in Britain 1885–86* (Harvester, 1974); C. C. O'Brien, *Parnell and His Party*, pp. 90–108; BM Add. MSS 4316 ff.14, 18, 20, 56446, 44269; A. L. Thorold, *Henry Labouchere* (London, 1923); R. F. Foster, *Lord Randolph Churchill: A Political Life* (Oxford, 1981); James Loughlin, *Gladstone, Home Rule and the Ulster Question 1882–93* (Dublin, 1986); Hammond, *Gladstone*, pp. 348–454; Lyons, *Charles Stewart Parnell*, pp. 268–92.

Chapter 39

General: Lyons, *Charles Stewart Parnell*, pp. 312–40; C. C. O'Brien, *Parnell and His Party*, pp. 166–84; T. W. Moody, 'Parnell and the Galway Election', in *Irish Historical Studies*, March 1955.

'Dick and Boysie': For example, 22 December 1885, O'Shea, *Charles Stewart Parnell*, II, p. 214.

Letter to Gladstone: BM Add. MSS 44269.

O'Shea voting: Annual House of Commons Division Lists 1881–5 (British Library shelf-mark no. BS91/3); O'Connor, *The Parnell Movement*, p. 531. O'Shea in the House: Hansard, 3, CCLXVI, 435, 488, 1209, 1572, CCLXVII, 958. He is absent from Hansard, CCLXXXVII and CCLXXXVIII, and appears only once in CCLXXXIX at the end of June. As 'Dervish Pasha': *Independent and Munster Advertiser*, 17 June 1882. Rejected by Clare: *Nation*, 20 June 1884, cited by Lyons, *Charles Stewart Parnell*, p. 321. And Fenian support: O'Shea, op. cit., II, pp. 200–201, 214–15. Katie and 'the chicks': O'Shea, op. cit., II, pp. 205–6. Parnell unsatisfactory: O'Shea, op. cit., II, pp. 89, 92, 212. Packing his shell with dynamite: O'Shea, op. cit., II, p. 90. An oblique reference to this letter appears during Willie's cross-examination by Sir Charles Russell in the Special Commission hearing (*Special Commission: Evidence of Mr O'Shea* (*Times* reprint), II, p. 86). Scene with Parnell in Shelbourne: Letter to Chamberlain, cited in Lyons, op. cit., p. 318. Fenian testimonial to O'Shea in Wardour Street pub: *Special Commission* (*Times* reprint), II, pp. 78–80; Sent to IRB: O'Shea, op. cit., II, p. 215. I am assuming this is 'the document' referred to in this letter.

Callan: Lyons, *Parnell*, pp. 306–7.

Parnell and O'Connor: O'Connor, *Memoirs*, II, pp. 94, 99; O'Shea, op. cit., II, p. 107.

'Parnell's mistress': Blunt, *Land War*, p. 28.

Healy: A. L. Thorold, *Henry Labouchere* (London, 1923), p. 251; Moody, op. cit., pp. 325–6.

Biggar, letter to O'Donnell: O'Donnell, *Irish Parliamentary Party*, II, p. 289. George Mulqueeny: *Special Commission* (HMSO), VI, p. 381. O'Shea evidence: *Special Commission* (*Times* reprint), II, pp. 75–86.

O'Shea voting with Parnell: House of Common Divisions Lists 1884.

Letters of August 1884: *The Times*, 17 May 1890.

Katie's correspondence with Gladstone: BM Add. MSS 44269 ('A Proposed Constitution for Ireland', 30 October 1885). The text is to be found in O'Shea, op. cit., II, pp. 18–20, but is misdated there to early 1884. Other letters: BM Add. MSS 44269; Hammond, *Gladstone*, pp. 451–4. Correspondence a secret: Wilfrid Scawen Blunt heard only just before the vote on the Home Rule Bill on 7 June 1886 that Willie had been boasting that Gladstone had been in correspondence with Parnell through his, O'Shea's, wife, 'which, strange as it sounds, is perhaps not impossible' (*Land War*, p. 142).

Hamilton diary: BM Add. MSS 48642.

'Hawarden kite': Hamilton diary entry for 17 December, cited in Lyons, op. cit., p. 309,

Chapter 40

General: Lyons, *Charles Stewart Parnell*, pp. 341–56; C. C. O'Brien, *Parnell and His Party*, pp. 159–66, 184–92; J. L. Garvin, *The Life of Joseph Chamberlain* (2 vols., London, 1932), II, p. 159ff. (particularly communication with Parnell, pp. 166–7, 168–9; and letter to Gladstone, p. 172); A. B. Cooke and John Vincent, *Governing Passion: Cabinet Government and Party Politics in Britain 1885–86* (Harvester, 1974), pp. 312–433 – a valuable diary-style analysis of events from the end of 1885 to 10 January 1886. Hamilton diary: BM Add. MSS 48642, 25, 27, 29, 31 May, 2, 4, 6, 8 June 1886; Hansard, 3, CCCIV–VI.

Parnell. Second Reading speech: Hansard, 3, CCCVI, 1168–84. Refuses to name Carnarvon to Hicks Beach: Hansard, 3, CCCVI, 1199–1200.

Gladstone. Second Reading debate conclusion: Hansard, 3, CCCVI, 1215–40; Hansard Division Lists 1240–45. Note Healy's encouragement to Gladstone on defeat, quoting a Negro orator: 'God and one make a majority' (1245).

Belfast riots: The official death toll was thirty-one, but the actual number was probably around fifty (Jonathan Bardon, *A History of Ulster* (Belfast, 1992), p. 382).

Pall Mall Gazette and exchange of letters: *The Times*, 17 November 1890. The editor, W. T. Stead, told Reginal Brett (later Lord Esher) in 1890 that O'Shea had assured him after this incident that he had no complaint to make of his wife's relations with Parnell but that a subsequent line in the *Pall Mall Gazette* of 18 December 1886 to the effect that Parnell was at Eltham, when O'Shea did not know this, had 'first opened his eyes'. And though he had then denied the accuracy of that report, 'suspicion for the first time entered my mind' (diary entry for 16 January 1890 in Reginald Brett, *Viscount Esher: Journals* (London, 1914), p. 208).

Karlsbad incident: *The Times*, 17 November 1890. Katie's 20 August letter: Part of this is in the National Library of Ireland. Plan of campaign: Lyons, op. cit., pp. 360–68 (including William O'Brien's account of meeting, in *Evening Memories*); C. C. O'Brien, op. cit., pp. 201–13; Blunt, *Land War*, pp. 430–35.

Special Commission: Articles of 7, 10, 14, 18, 24, 26 March, 12, 18, 19, 20 April, 13, 20 May, and 1, 7 June 1887 were reprinted by *The Times* in one of their series of pocket books in 1888 and 1889. Part XIII, the evidence of Soames and McDonald, includes copies of seven 'fascimile' letters allegedly written by Parnell.

Very useful too is John McDonald, *The Daily News Diary of the Parnell Commission* (London, 1889), especially for Pigott (pp. 156–64, 349). See also Alfred Robbins, *Parnell: The Last Five Years* (London, 1926), pp. 64–129.

O'Shea in Madrid: J. L. Garvin, op. cit., II, p. 395.

Morley letter to E. Russell: 3 May 1888, BM Add. MSS 62993 f.145.

Mary Gladstone on Parnell: Mary Gladstone, *Letters and Diaries*, p. 411, cited by Lyons, op. cit., p. 450. Gladstone's comment: Cited by Lyons, op. cit., p. 450 and by Hammond, *Gladstone*, p. 604. Gladstone continues, 'He is certainly one of the very best people to deal with that I have ever known' (Hammond, op. cit., p. 605).

Chapter 41

Hawarden meeting: Hammond, *Gladstone*, pp. 603–4; *The Times*, 20 December 1890. Liverpool: *The Times*, 20 December 1890.

O'Shea and Chamberlain: J. L. Garvin, *The Life of Joseph Chamberlain* (2 vols., London, 1932), II, pp. 397–401. Willie here calculates (p. 399n) that he had had an annual income since 1880 of about £120,000 (in today's terms) apart from any presents from Aunt Ben, and that Katie had had an annual income from Aunt Ben of about £200,000 a year in today's terms.

Cardinal Manning: O'Shea, *Charles Stewart Parnell*, II, pp. 221–7.

'Dreadful scene': J. L. Garvin, op. cit., II, pp. 400–401: Reginald Brett, *Viscount Esher: Journals* (London, 1914), pp. 210–11.

Interview with O'Shea: *FJ*, 28 December 1889.

Irish reaction: *FJ*, 4, 6, 16 January 1890.

Hamilton diary: BM Add. MSS 48642, 1 January 1890.

Dr Kenny: F. S. L. Lyons, *John Dillon* (London, 1968), p. 114.

Archbishop Walsh: Lyons, *Charles Stewart Parnell*, p. 466.

The party in 1890, and the divorce: C. C. O'Brien, *Parnell and His Party*, pp. 240–83.

Morley: John Morley, *Recollections* (London, 1917), pp. 251, 253–4.

Parnell with Katie: O'Shea, op. cit., II, pp. 144–54.

Chapter 42

The divorce proceedings are extensively covered in many columns of *The Times* of Monday 17 and Tuesday 18 November 1890; but see also O'Shea, *Charles Stewart Parnell*, II, pp. 158–61. For other background reading, see Alfred Robbins, *Parnell: The Last Five Years* (London, 1926), pp. 132, 146; McCarthy and Praed, *Book of Memories*, pp. 255–6; Sir Edward Clarke, *The Story of My Life* (London, 1918), pp. 273, 285–6, 289; Harrison, *Parnell Vindicated, passim* but particularly pp. 136–66.

O'Shea to Chamberlain: Chamberlain Papers, cited by Lyons, *Charles Stewart Parnell*, p. 463.

Fire escape: O'Connor, *Memoirs*, II, pp. 276–7.

Chapters 43, 44 and 45

The principal sources used for this account of the split and its consequences have been: Lyons, *The Fall of Parnell*, and Callanan, *The Parnell Split*. These two books provide their own extensive encyclopaedia of references from contemporary newspapers and eyewitness reports of the events in Committee Room 15 of the

House of Commons and their consequences. The extensive references in Callanan's pioneering work are listed usefully at the end of each chapter. Further details of this time can be found in Alfred Robbins, *Parnell: The Last Five Years* (London, 1926); R. B. O'Brien, op. cit., II, pp. 289, 291–2; and M. M. O'Hara, *Chief and Tribune: Parnell and Davitt* (Dublin, 1919), pp. 316–17.

For Parnell's illness and death see O'Shea, *Charles Stewart Parnell*, II, pp. 250–76, and J. B. Lyons, 'Charles Stewart Parnell and His Doctors', in McCartney, *Parnell*.

Index

Abraham, William, 584–5
Administrative Central Board for Ireland, 471–5
agrarian outrages, 29, 191, 211, 253, 255, 272, 276, 316–17, 333–4, 390, 396, 406, 409, 456, 525–6; *see also* Ribbonism and Ribbon Societies
agriculture (Ireland): economic crises in, 132–3, 176–7, 180, 181–3, 185, 525
Allen (Fenian, hanged 1867), 186
American Civil War, 23
American Independence: centenary (1876), 118
American Ladies' Land League, 329
American League, 461
Amnesty Association, 52, 61, 83, 87–90
Annesley, Hugh Annesley, 5th Earl, 273
anti-Parnellites, 586, 590
Armagh, 490–91
Army Discipline and Regulation Bill 1879, 185–6, 193
Arrears Bill 1882, 456, 460
Athenry, 266
Athlone: 1880 election, 230–31; CSP speaks in, 277, 287–9; platform collapses at, 289; supporter killed in, 607
Aughavannah, 54, 251–4, 386, 484, 543
Avondale: CSP's home and life at, 15, 17–18, 70, 80, 90, 120, 250–51, 270, 295, 387, 484; CSP inherits and manages, 22–3, 40–41 46, 53; cricket at, 23–4, 41; CSP keeps open to family, 466; mortgaged, 466–8; sold and refurbished, 610

Balfour, Arthur James, 446, 525, 528–9, 541
Balla, 212
Ballinasloe Tenants' Association, 163, 174, 177, 181, 567
Ballygawly, 376–7
Ballylanders, 334
Ballyshannon, 290
Barntown, 262
Barrett-Leonard, Christabel (*later* O'Shea), 610
Barry, John, 90, 129, 160, 229–30, 262, 453, 561, 580
beef: imports to Ireland, 132, 182
Belclare, 250
Belfast, 100, 205

Belleek, 290
Ben, Aunt, *see* Wood, Mrs Benjamin
Bentley, Robert, 42–3
Berliner Tageblatt, 5
Bessborough, Frederick George Brabazon Ponsonby, 6th Earl of, 352–3
Biggar, Joseph Gillis: elected MP, 65; parliamentary tactics (obstructionism), 78–9, 86, 103, 105, 110, 118, 132–4, 136, 149, 155, 326–7; attacks Disraeli over Fenian prisoners, 111; in Home Rule Confederation, 121; at Power's Manchester lecture, 122; nationalist views, 122; on Prisons Bill, 139; and South Africa Bill, 146, 151; and CSP's withdrawal from Commons, 147; at 1877 rally for obstructionism, 153; meets O'Leary, 156; and death of McCarthy, 158; and leadership of Home Rule party, 166; at Ulster Home Government Association meeting, 176; and National Land League, 202; recalls CSP from North America, 223; welcomes CSP on return, 226; charged with conspiracy, 280; and 1881 Paris meeting of Land League executive, 335–6; returns to Commons, 341; and Invincibles, 435; and CSP's relationship with Katie, 497–9; and O'Shea's election for Galway, 497–9, 590; voting in Commons, 499
Black and Tans, 613
Blennerhassett, Rowland Ponsonby, 53, 106
Blunt, Wilfrid Scawen, 284, 497, 518
Boers, 147, 348, 358
Boucicault, Dion: *The Shaughran*, 158
Boulogne, 180; 1891 negotiations, 595–7, 600
Bourke, Canon, 193
Bowyer, Sir George, 91
boycotting, 211, 254, 276, 280, 530
Boyle, 250, 262
Boyton, Michael: and Land League, 250, 252, 255–6, 262, 268–9, 271, 302, 376, 395; charged with conspiracy, 280, 316; and CSP's reputation and power, 289, 600; hostility to eviction, 351; arrest and imprisonment, 351; release, 395; in Kilmainham, 400; criticizes Home Rule Members, 433
Brady, Joe, 158, 458
Brennan, Thomas: at Home Rule League meet-